Acceptance and Commitment Therapy

The Clinician's Guide for Supporting Parents

Koa Whittingham
Queensland Cerebral Palsy and Rehabilitation Research Centre (QCPRRC), UQ Child Health Research Centre, The University of Queensland, Brisbane, Australia

Lisa W. Coyne
Department of Psychiatry, Harvard Medical School, Boston, MA, United States

The McLean Obsessive Compulsive Disorder Institute for Children and Adolescents (OCDI Jr.), McLean Hospital, Belmont, MA, United States

New England Center for OCD and Anxiety (NECOA), Boston, MA, United States

AF795314

ELSEVIER

ACADEMIC PRESS
An imprint of Elsevier

Academic Press is an imprint of Elsevier
125 London Wall, London EC2Y 5AS, United Kingdom
525 B Street, Suite 1650, San Diego, CA 92101, United States
50 Hampshire Street, 5th Floor, Cambridge, MA 02139, United States
The Boulevard, Langford Lane, Kidlington, Oxford OX5 1GB, United Kingdom

Copyright © 2019 Elsevier Inc. All rights reserved.

No part of this publication may be reproduced or transmitted in any form or by any means, electronic or mechanical, including photocopying, recording, or any information storage and retrieval system, without permission in writing from the publisher. Details on how to seek permission, further information about the Publisher's permissions policies and our arrangements with organizations such as the Copyright Clearance Center and the Copyright Licensing Agency, can be found at our website: www.elsevier.com/permissions.

This book and the individual contributions contained in it are protected under copyright by the Publisher (other than as may be noted herein).

Notices
Knowledge and best practice in this field are constantly changing. As new research and experience broaden our understanding, changes in research methods, professional practices, or medical treatment may become necessary.

Practitioners and researchers must always rely on their own experience and knowledge in evaluating and using any information, methods, compounds, or experiments described herein. In using such information or methods they should be mindful of their own safety and the safety of others, including parties for whom they have a professional responsibility.

To the fullest extent of the law, neither the Publisher nor the authors, contributors, or editors, assume any liability for any injury and/or damage to persons or property as a matter of products liability, negligence or otherwise, or from any use or operation of any methods, products, instructions, or ideas contained in the material herein.

British Library Cataloguing-in-Publication Data
A catalogue record for this book is available from the British Library

Library of Congress Cataloging-in-Publication Data
A catalog record for this book is available from the Library of Congress

ISBN: 978-0-12-814669-9

For Information on all Academic Press publications
visit our website at https://www.elsevier.com/books-and-journals

Publisher: Nikki Levy
Acquisition Editor: Nikki Levy
Editorial Project Manager: Ali Afzal-Khan
Production Project Manager: Bharatwaj Varatharajan
Cover Designer: Miles Hitchen

Typeset by MPS Limited, Chennai, India

Working together to grow libraries in developing countries
www.elsevier.com • www.bookaid.org

Acceptance and Commitment Therapy

Contents

1. Introduction 1

References 5

Section 1
Theoretical and scientific background 7

2. Parenting 9

Parenting (and child development) in an evolutionary context 9
The four streams of evolution 10
The evolution of parental care 13
The evolution of human parental care 16
Unique features of contemporary parenting 20
What is good parenting? 25
The theoretical frames 27
Acceptance and commitment therapy 29
Compassion-focused ACT 33
DNA-V 34
Chapter summary 35
References 36

3. Connect: the parent–child relationship 39

Attachment theory 41
Attachment across cultures 44
How does parenting influence attachment? 45
A dyadic perspective 48
Emotional development and the parent–child relationship 51
Relationship and emotion-focused parenting intervention 53
A contextual behavioral perspective on attachment and emotional connection 54
Applying attachment, emotional availability, and meta-emotion theory to parenting 57
Chapter summary 58
References 58

4. Shape: building a flexible repertoire 63

Parent–child interaction: Rosa and Gabriela 66
Direct conditioning: respondent and operant conditioning 66
Respondent conditioning 66
Operant conditioning 67
Indirect conditioning: modeling, derived relational responding, and rule-governed behavior 72
Functional analysis of behavior 76
Problematic behavior patterns in families: coercive cycles 76
Supporting behavior change 79
Respondent conditioning strategies 79
Operant conditioning strategies: antecedent and consequent manipulation strategies 79
Antecedent strategies 79
Consequence strategies 81
Behavioral parenting intervention 86
Research on acceptance and commitment therapy/relational frame theory and parenting 87
Acceptance and commitment therapy for parent psychological well-being 87
Acceptance and commitment therapy for augmentation for behavioral parenting interventions 88
Acceptance and commitment therapy for parenting/child behaviors 89
Three key behavior principles in shaping adaptive child behavior 90
Connect and shape 90
Chapter summary 95
References 95

Section 2
The bedrock of clinical practice 101

5. Case conceptualization 103

Assessment 104
Intake interview 105
Questionnaires 108
Monitoring 109
Observation of parent–child interaction 111
Functional analysis of child and parent behavior 112
Fan's noncompliance 115
Leo's avoidance of social/performance situations 117
Using clinical relational frame theory and acceptance and commitment therapy models 119
Mei Lin, Tao, and Fan 119

Andrea, Lucia, and Leo 120
Fan 122
Mei Lin and Tao 123
Leo 124
Lucia and Andrea 124
Functional analytic psychotherapy and the parent–child relationship 125
Quick and easy tips 128
Sharing your case conceptualization with the parent 129
Chapter summary 130
References 130

6. Therapeutic relationship 131

Acceptance and commitment therapy and the therapeutic relationship 131
Two mountains metaphor 133
Setting the stage/dialogue 133
Therapist as a secure base 134
Complexities of therapeutic relationship/s in parenting intervention 136
Functional analytic psychotherapy and the therapeutic relationship 141
Evoke, reinforce, repeat 143
Building and maintaining a common understanding 144
Client resistance 145
Resistance to specific techniques 146
Supporting home practice 148
Chapter summary 149
References 149

Section 3
ACT processes 151

7. Values and proto-values 153

What are values? 154
Proto-values 159
DNA-V model 160
How do values apply to parent–child interaction? 160
Intrinsic reinforcement and persistence 160
Parental sensitivity and attachment 162
Flexible parenting 162
Rule-governed Behavior 163
Importance of values in other domains of living 164
Values and history 164
Supporting proto-values development 165

Brooke and Kai 166
Parent–child interaction 166
What's happening for Brooke and Kai? 167
Working with values clinically 168
Setting the stage for values work 168
Simple questioning 169
Sweet moments 169
Sweet moments exercises 169
Prompts 170
Values as the other side of pain 170
Metaphors 170
Going West metaphor 170
Guiding stars metaphor 171
Experiential exercises 171
Time travel and take a new perspective 171
A magical place 172
Values meditation 172
Values meditation script 172
Tuning in to values 175
Developing a rich and flexible repertoire of valued acts 176
Encouraging home practice 177
Working with Brooke and Kai 177
Troubleshooting 179
How do I make sure I'm getting values not pliance? 179
What if the client tells me goals instead of values? 179
What if the client is so disconnected from their values that they doesn't know what their values are? 179
Overabundance of values 179
When valued action has another function 180
When children misbehave (or when parenting is hard) 181
Four key developmental periods and values 181
Infancy and values 181
Early childhood and values 182
Middle childhood and values 182
Adolescence and values 183
Using values with specific issues 183
Parental mental health problems and values 183
Parental grief and values 183
Childhood externalizing problems and values 184
Childhood internalizing problems and values 184
Childhood neurodevelopmental disabilities and values 184
Peer problems and bullying and values 185
Marital conflict and values 185
Expressed emotion including critical and intrusive parenting and values 185
Emotion dismissiveness and values 185
Inconsistent, harsh, or punitive parenting and values 186
References 186

8. Experiential acceptance of parent, child, and relationship 187

What is acceptance? 188
A behavioral account of acceptance and experiential control 189
DNA-V model 193
How does acceptance apply to parent–child interaction? 194
The parenting control agenda 194
Experiential avoidance and dysfunctional parenting 195
Parental experiential acceptance and child emotional development 196
Experiential acceptance and compassionate parenting 197
Acceptance and development 197
When history shows up 198
Experiential acceptance and emotions 199
Moira and Raven 200
Parent–child interaction 200
What's going on for Moira and Raven? 201
How to work with acceptance clinically 202
Simple questioning 202
Noticing acceptance within the parent–child interaction 202
Metaphors 203
Controlling the ocean 203
The swamp 204
Experiential exercises 204
Tantrums and control 204
Sleep and control 205
Getting rid of thoughts experiment 206
Getting rid of thoughts experiment script 206
Meditation 207
Mindfulness of emotions script 207
Accepting space for parent and child 208
Accepting space for parent and child script 208
Pause and breathe script 210
Working with Moira and Raven 211
Troubleshooting 213
Confusion with acceptance and compassion 213
More than just emotions 213
Accept, so we can ignore? 213
Acceptance and trauma history 214
Four key developmental periods and acceptance 214
Infancy and acceptance 214
Early childhood and acceptance 215
Middle childhood and acceptance 215
Adolescence and acceptance 216
Using acceptance with specific populations 216
Parental mental health problems and acceptance 216
Parental grief and acceptance 216
Childhood externalizing problems and acceptance 217

Childhood internalizing problems and acceptance 217
Childhood neurodevelopmental disabilities and acceptance 217
Peer problems and bullying and acceptance 217
Marital conflict and acceptance 218
Expressed emotionincluding critical and intrusive parenting and acceptance 218
Emotion dismissiveness and acceptance 218
Inconsistent, or harsh and punitive parenting and acceptance 218
References 218

9. Contact with the present moment including shared psychological presence 221

What is contact with the present moment? 222
The history of mindfulness 224
Mindfulness and acceptance 225
Benefits of mindfulness 226
DNA-V model 227
How does contact with the present moment apply to parent–child interaction? 227
What is mindful parenting? 227
Shared psychological contact and relationship 228
Shared psychological presence and effective parenting 228
Psychological contact and mental health and well-being 229
Maya, Michael and Reo 229
Parent–child interaction 230
What's happening for Maya, Michael, and Reo? 231
How to work with mindfulness clinically 233
Assessing parental mindfulness 233
Simple questioning or prompts 233
Metaphors 233
The metaphor of the six animals 233
Meditation 234
A taste of mindfulness meditation 234
A taste of mindfulness meditation script 234
Mindfulness of breathing meditation 235
Mindfulness of breathing meditation script 235
Mindful walking meditation 236
Antenatal mindfulness meditation 237
Antenatal mindfulness meditation script 237
Mindfulness of baby meditation 238
Mindfulness of baby meditation script 238
Parenting: a mindfulness meditation 239
Parenting: a mindfulness meditation script 239
Wake up! A quick mindfulness meditation 241
Wake up! A quick mindfulness meditation script 241
Mindfulness within daily life 241

Mindfulness within daily life for children and adolescents 242
Encouraging home practice 243
Working with Maya, Michael, and Reo 243
Troubleshooting 244
Do we have to do mindfulness meditations? 244
What if they don't have the time? 245
Is mindfulness and relaxation the same thing? 245
What if parents experience paradoxical reactions to mindfulness or have a history of trauma? 245
Mindfulness with a purpose 246
Four key developmental periods and contact with the present moment 246
Infancy and contact with the present moment 246
Early childhood and contact with the present moment 247
Middle childhood and contact with the present moment 247
Adolescence and contact with the present moment 247
Using mindfulness with specific populations 248
Parental mental health problems and contact with the present moment 248
Parental grief and contact with the present moment 248
Childhood externalizing problems and contact with the present moment 248
Childhood internalizing problems and contact with the present moment 248
Childhood neurodevelopmental disabilities and contact with the present moment 249
Peer relations and bullying and contact with the present moment 249
Marital conflict and contact with the present moment 249
Expressed emotion including critical or intrusive parenting and contact with the present moment 249
Emotion dismissiveness and contact with the present moment 249
Inconsistent, or harsh and punitive parenting and contact with the present moment 250
References 250

10. Flexible languaging 253

What is flexible languaging? 254
How we learn language: the development of our symbolic system 254
Flexible languaging, rule-governed behavior, and fusion 257
DNA-V model 259
How does flexible languaging apply to parent–child interaction? 260
Flexible languaging and workable parenting 260
Parenting rules 260
Supporting flexible languaging 263
Supporting the development of helpful tracking and proto-values 263
Aoife, Ciara and Niamh 265
Parent–child interaction 265

What's happening for Aoife, Ciara, and Niamh? 267
Working with flexible languaging clinically 268
Signs of parental inflexible languaging 268
Metaphors 269
Passengers on the bus metaphor 269
Superhero's dilemma 269
Playing the game 270
Experiential exercises 271
Meditations 272
Mindfulness of thoughts meditation script 273
Mindfulness awareness, parent, and child 273
Flexible languaging games for parent and child 274
Taking parents from pliance to tracking 275
Taking children from pliance to tracking 276
Encouraging home practice 277
Working with Aoife, Ciara and Niamh 277
Troubleshooting 280
Defusion is not about whether the thoughts are true or false 280
What if defusion doesn't work or feels invalidating? 280
Four key developmental periods and flexible languaging 280
Infancy and flexible languaging 280
Early childhood and flexible languaging 281
Middle childhood and flexible languaging 281
Adolescence and flexible languaging 282
Using flexible languaging with specific populations 282
Parental mental health problems and flexible languaging 282
Parental grief and flexible languaging 282
Childhood externalizing problems and flexible languaging 283
Childhood internalizing problems and flexible languaging 283
Childhood neurodevelopmental disabilities and flexible languaging 283
Peer relations and bullying and flexible languaging 283
Marital conflict and flexible languaging 284
Expressed emotion including critical and intrusive parenting and flexible languaging 284
Emotion dismissiveness and flexible languaging 284
Inconsistent, or harsh and punitive parenting and flexible languaging 284
References 284

11. Flexible perspective taking 287

What is flexible perspective taking? 288
DNA–V model 295
How does flexible perspective taking apply to parent–child interaction? 295
Parental flexible perspective taking and sensitivity 295
Parental flexible perspective taking and mental health 296
Developing child's flexible perspective taking 296
Flexible perspective taking and growth mindset 297

Gretchen and Sebastian 297
Parent–child interaction 298
What's happening for Gretchen and Sebastian? 298
Working with flexible perspective taking clinically 299
Use of mindfulness 301
Use of defusion 302
Simple questioning 303
Metaphors 303
The battlefield metaphor 303
Your relationship with your child: a film 304
Experiential exercises 304
An experiment in perspective 305
A second experiment on perspective: an experiment for two 305
A third experiment in perspective: time traveling 306
Meditations 307
Parenting: a context for parent and child script 307
Seeing as-content and as-process from as-context script 308
Work with Gretchen and Sebastian 310
Troubleshooting 312
Defense of self-as-content 312
Deficits in self-as-process 313
Four key developmental periods and flexible perspective taking 313
Infancy and flexible perspective taking 313
Early childhood and flexible perspective taking 314
Middle childhood and flexible perspective taking 315
Adolescence and flexible perspective taking 315
Using flexible perspective taking with specific populations 315
Parental mental health problems and flexible perspective taking 315
Parental grief and flexible perspective taking 316
Childhood externalizing problems and flexible perspective taking 316
Childhood internalizing problems and flexible perspective taking 316
Childhood neurodevelopmental disabilities and flexible perspective taking 317
Peer problems and bullying and flexible perspective taking 317
Marital conflict and flexible perspective taking 317
Expressed emotion including critical and intrusive parenting and flexible perspective taking 317
Emotion dismissiveness and flexible perspective taking 318
Inconsistent, or harsh and punitive parenting and flexible perspective taking 318
References 318

12. Compassionate context 321

What is compassion? 322
DNA-V model 326
How does compassion apply to parent–child interaction? 327
Self-compassion and parental well-being 327
Compassion and parenting 327

Parental compassion for the child 328
Compassion and history 328
Shame-based parenting 329
Parenting to shape compassion in children 329
Yasmin and Amir 329
Parent–child interaction 330
What's happening for Yasmin and Amir? 332
Working with compassion clinically 332
Noticing compassion, shame, and criticism within the parent–child relationship 332
Noticing parental evolved defenses and compassion capacities 333
Reality check: not your fault 333
Reality check: not your fault script 334
Soothing rhythm breathing exercise 335
Compassionate figure 336
Compassionate figure script 336
Accessing the compassionate self 336
Tuning into the compassionate self 337
Compassionate letter writing 337
Empty chair technique 338
Safe place imagery 339
Safe place imagery script 339
Self-compassion meditation 340
Self-compassion meditation script 340
Compassion for your child 341
Compassion for your child script 341
Supporting the development of compassion in children and adolescents 342
Encouraging home practice 343
Working with Yasmin and Amir 343
Troubleshooting 346
Fear of compassion 346
Four key developmental periods and compassion 346
Infancy and compassion 346
Early childhood and compassion 347
Middle childhood and compassion 348
Adolescence and compassion 348
Using compassion with specific populations 349
Parental mental health problems and compassion 349
Parental grief and compassion 349
Childhood externalizing problems and compassion 349
Childhood internalizing problems and compassion 349
Childhood neurodevelopmental disabilities and compassion 350
Peer relations and bullying and compassion 350
Marital conflict and compassion 350
Expressed emotion including critical and intrusive parenting and compassion 350

Emotion dismissiveness and compassion 351
Inconsistent, or harsh and punitive parenting and compassion 351
References 351

13. **Committed action and exploration** 353

What is committed action and exploration? 354
DNA-V model 356
How does committed action apply to parent–child interaction? 356
Parenting for a flexible, broad behavioral repertoire for the child 356
Parenting control agenda 357
Exploration and development 358
Scott, Harry, and Ava 359
Parent–child interaction 359
What's happening for Scott, Harry, and Ava? 360
Working with committed action clinically 361
Setting goals and practice opportunities 361
Building resilience through debriefing 362
Working with willingness 363
Acting from the whole hexaflex 363
Getting off the hook 364
Metaphors 366
Jump metaphor 366
Parent supporting child exploration 366
Encouraging home practice 367
Working with Scott, Harry, and Ava 367
Troubleshooting 370
Refining parenting strategies in practice 370
It is tough work 370
Four key developmental periods and committed action and exploration 371
Infancy and committed action and exploration 371
Early childhood and committed action and exploration 371
Middle childhood and committed action and exploration 371
Adolescence and committed action and exploration 372
Using committed action with specific populations 372
Parental mental health problems and committed action and exploration 372
Parental grief and committed action and exploration 372
Childhood externalizing problems and committed action and exploration 372
Childhood internalizing problems and committed action and exploration 372
Childhood neurodevelopmental disabilities and committed action and exploration 373
Peer relations and bullying and committed action and exploration 373
Marital conflict and committed action and exploration 373

Expressed emotion including critical and intrusive parenting and committed action and exploration 374
Emotion dismissiveness and committed action and exploration 374
Inconsistent, or harsh and punitive parenting and committed action and exploration 374
References 374

14. Integrating Acceptance and Commitment Therapy with other interventions 377

Parenting intervention 378
Behavioral activation 380
Exposure therapy 381
Postnatal care 383
Infant crying and sleep: a case illustration 384
Infant sleep 386
Aurora, Christopher, and Amelia 392
Parent–child interaction 393
What's happening for Aurora, Chris, and Millie? 395
Working with Aurora, Chris, and Millie 396
Chapter summary 399
References 399

15. Conclusion 403

References 405

Index 407

Chapter 1

Introduction

Chapter Outline

References 5

Parental care is intimately associated with the complex and intricate coevolutionary relationships that exist among the core features of humanity: a large brain, flexible social cooperation, language, symbolic thought, and intersubjectivity (Hrdy, 2011). Humans are *flexible cooperative breeders*. That is, our children are not raised just by their biological mother; rather, fathers, grandparents, aunts and uncles, older siblings, and nonfamilial caregivers all may be involved in raising a child. Systems of care organize around children in a *flexible and opportunistic* way, sensitive to context, and we too, as clinicians supporting parents and children, are part of this flexible and cooperative network in its modern form.

Acceptance and commitment therapy (ACT), the wider literature of relational frame theory (RFT), and the complimentary approach of compassion-focused therapy (CFT), are approaches emblematic of contextual behavioral science. These approaches have clear implications for parenting and the parent–child relationship, from finding meaning in parenting, to supporting the child's emergence into the symbolic world, to responsive and attuned parenting, to supporting the child's burgeoning perspective-taking abilities, to compassionate parenting. ACT, RFT, and CFT can be used to support parents in their enjoyment of and persistence in parenting well - in a flexible, workable, and compassionate way - even when psychologically difficult. Further, it can be used to understand and predict what kinds of parenting behavior might contribute to the development of psychologically flexible and prosocial children with broad and flexible behavioral repertoires. The research supporting these links is still in its infancy—there is much work still to be done—but the theoretical links are clear and consistent with existing research in areas such as attachment theory, metaemotion theory, theory of mind, and parental mind-mindedness.

When ACT, RFT, and CFT are integrated with existing literature across the relational–emotional, behavioral, and developmental areas a model begins to emerge: a model of how parental psychological flexibility can

Acceptance and Commitment Therapy. DOI: https://doi.org/10.1016/B978-0-12-814669-9.00001-1
© 2019 Elsevier Inc. All rights reserved.

Contact with the present moment including shared psychological presence
- Supports parental sensitivity and models contact with the present moment
- Parent is aware of changes in the parent-child relationship over time
- Supports parent responding proactively instead of reactively

Experiential acceptance of parent, child and relationship
- Supports adaptive and workable parenting
- Parent models acceptance and responds with acceptance to child emotion
- Parent is accepting of changes in the parent-child relationship
- Parent responds to emotions as opportunities for closeness and learning

Flexible languaging
- Parent and child play flexibly with language, e.g. pretend play, fiction and language games
- Relational framing abilities are supported in everyday interactions
- Parent develops flexible and workable parenting rules (tracks)
- Parent supports child in developing flexible and workable rules (tracks)

Flexible perspective taking
- Parent is aware of the child's ongoing psychological experience (other-as-process) and responds to the child as having a perspective of their own (other-as-context) and this supports sensitive, responsive parenting
- Parent can shift moment to moment from the dynamic, changing relationship (us-as-process) to the enduring relationship in time (us-as-context) and see challenges as part of development
- Parent models perspective taking and discusses perspective taking in everyday life

Values and supporting child proto-values
- Parenting is grounded within parenting values, supporting sensitive, responsive parenting and adaptive parenting behavior
- Parent lives values in other life domains at the same time as parenting, supporting parental wellbeing, exposing the child to a range of experiences and modelling valued living
- Parent supports developmentally appropriate experimentation
- Parent describes the child's enjoyment and prosocial behavior verbally, supporting the development of proto-values

Compassion for parent and child
- Parent models self-compassion, compassion for others and receiving compassion
- Parent shows compassion for the child; sensitively responding to the child's expressions of distress and suffering

Committed action and exploration
- Parent adopts a flexible, experiential parenting stance discovering what works
- Parent adopts a sensitive and responsive parenting style
- Parent provides positive reinforcement for a variety of adaptive behaviors; including shaping behaviors
- Parent reinforces effort, flexible experimentation and exploration
- Parent refrains from reinforcing dysfunctional child behaviors including coercion
- Parent refrains from hostile, intrusive or coercive parenting behavior
- Parent can persist, when functional, even in the presence of difficult private events in self and child

Nurturing psychological flexibility.

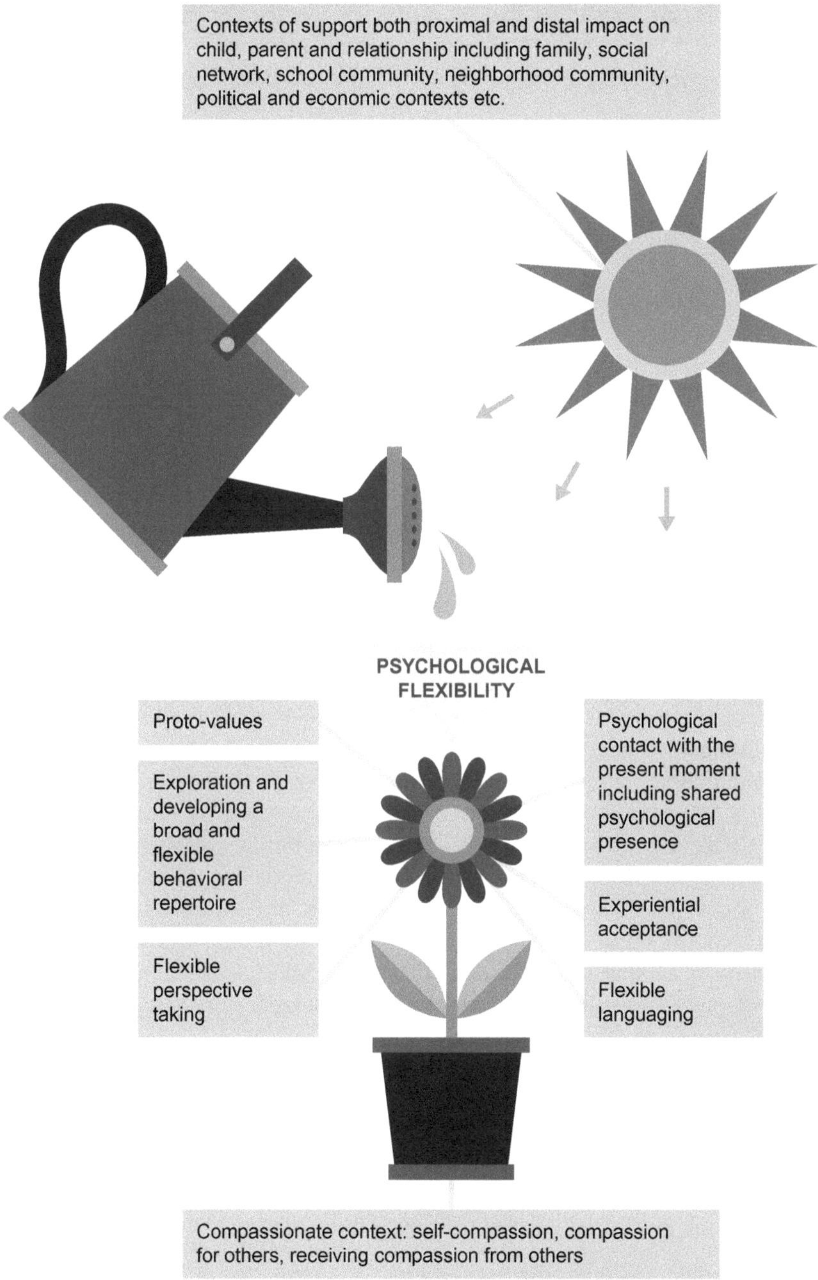
Contexts of support both proximal and distal impact on child, parent and relationship including family, social network, school community, neighborhood community, political and economic contexts etc.
PSYCHOLOGICAL FLEXIBILITY
Proto-values
Exploration and developing a broad and flexible behavioral repertoire
Flexible perspective taking
Psychological contact with the present moment including shared psychological presence
Experiential acceptance
Flexible languaging
Compassionate context: self-compassion, compassion for others, receiving compassion from others

(Continued)

support parental interaction that, in turn, supports the development of a psychologically flexible child. If the therapy of ACT is a way of *intervening*—a kind of medicine when psychological health has been compromised—then flexible parenting is a way of growing psychologically flexible people *organically*, through ordinary day-to-day interactions. This relationship between parental psychological flexibility, parental behavior, and the growth of a psychologically flexible child is illustrated in the following diagram:

Applying the ACT/RFT lens to parenting leads us to emphasize the resilience of a flexible experiential approach to parenting with the parent discovering workable parenting solutions. This flexible, workable parenting style can be understood as an evolutionary approach (Hayes & Sanford, 2015; Hayes, Sanford, & Chin, 2017). It is parenting using the principles of evolution: variation, selection, and the retention of adaptive traits. Parents flexibly vary their behavior, experimenting with different approaches (variation), since some behaviors work and some do not (selection). The behaviors that work are selected and retained, that is, the parent uses them again (retention). If selected behaviors stop working parents again experiment, reintroducing variation into their parenting. Thus, parenting evolves over time, and evolves with the development of the child.

One key potential contribution of ACT, RFT, and CFT to parenting research and intervention is the ability to integrate an at times fractured scientific literature and scientific and clinical community. The field of parenting science and intervention is often split into two worldviews: the relational–emotional (including attachment theory) and the behavioral. However, an evolutionary, contextual paradigm is wide enough to contain both. Within this book we have done the best we can to move toward a united parenting science and intervention approach grounded within an evolutionary, contextual paradigm. The ACT, RFT, and CFT communities are uniquely posed to bring about this change, with an emphasis on an evolutionary approach, strong background in basic behavioral science, grounding within attachment literature (CFT), and basic concepts that easily relate to core components of the relational–emotional literature including shared psychological contact, perspective taking, and compassion.

In this book you will find theory, research, practical hands-on knowledge, experiential exercises, metaphors, and clinical case studies. You will find information for beginners—for novices in acceptance and commitment therapy as well as for novices in parenting intervention—and you will also find in-depth discussion for seasoned ACT therapists and academics.

This book is divided into the following three sections:

1. Theoretical and scientific background.
2. The bedrock of clinical practice.
3. ACT processes.

The first section is the theoretical and scientific background. The first chapter briefly introduces all of the key theoretical frames used in this book through considering the evolution of parental care and parenting in the modern world. It also includes our *parent–child hexaflex*. All of the usual ACT components (as well as compassion) are present, but each in a more expansive and developmentally attuned way. The other two theoretical and scientific chapters are *Connect: The Parent–Child Relationship* and *Shape: Building a Flexible Repertoire*. They cover the emotional–relational and the contextual behavioral literature on parenting, respectively.

The second section, The Bedrock of Clincial Practice, covers the therapeutic relationship and case conceptualization, especially how to conduct a functional analysis and a formulation from an ACT perspective. This includes the application of functional analytic psychotherapy to the therapeutic relationship and the parent–child relationship.

The third section covers the ACT processes, with a chapter for each process within our parent–child hexaflex, and a final chapter on integrating ACT with other interventions. This is where we get practical, with experiential exercises and metaphors (including original exercises and metaphors) as well as case studies.

This book also covers the full spectrum of child development: from infancy through adolescence, along with a diversity of clinical presentations from anxiety to neurodevelopmental disorders, to conduct problems, and to postnatal depression and perinatal loss.

Navigate this book to suit your needs.

References

Hayes, S. C., & Sanford, B. T. (2015). Modern psychotherapy as a multidimensional multilevel evolutionary process. *Current Opinion in Psychology*, *2*, 16–20.

Hayes, S. C., Sanford, B. T., & Chin, F. T. (2017). Carrying the baton: Evolution science and a contextual behavioral analysis of language and cognition. *Journal of Contextual Behavioral Science*, *6*(3), 314–328.

Hrdy, S. B. (2011). *Mothers and Others*. Cambridge: Harvand University Press.

Section 1

Theoretical and scientific background

Chapter 2

Parenting

Chapter Outline

Parenting (and child development) in an evolutionary context 9
The four streams of evolution 10
The evolution of parental care 13
The evolution of human parental care 16
Unique features of contemporary parenting 20
What is good parenting? 25
The theoretical frames 27
Acceptance and commitment therapy 29
Compassion-focused ACT 33
DNA-V 34
Chapter summary 35
References 36

I cried two times when my daughter was born. First for joy, when after 27 hours of labor the little feral being we'd made came yowling into the world, and the second for sorrow, holding the earth's newest human and looking out the window with her at the rows of cars in the hospital parking lot, the strip mall across the street, the box stores and drive-throughs and drainage ditches and asphalt and waste fields that had once been oak groves. A world of extinction and catastrophe, a world in which harmony with nature had long been foreclosed.

Roy Scranton, "Raising My Child in a Doomed World,"
New York Times, July 16, 2018

Walking, I can almost hear the redwoods beating. . . .It is a world of elemental attention, of all things working together, listening to what speaks in the blood. Whichever road I follow, I walk in the land of many gods, and they love and eat one another. Walking, I am listening to a deeper way. Suddenly all my ancestors are behind me. Be still, they say. Watch and listen. You are the result of the love of thousands.

Linda Hogan, Dwellings: A Spiritual History of the Living World

Parenting (and child development) in an evolutionary context

The raising of children is a core and essential part of human life. And yet, we are at risk of underestimating just how critically important it truly is. But what exactly do we mean by "raising children"? The notion of "parenting"

Acceptance and Commitment Therapy. DOI: https://doi.org/10.1016/B978-0-12-814669-9.00002-3

© 2019 Elsevier Inc. All rights reserved.

as we usually understand it in contemporary contexts is said by some to be a recent Western cultural construct (Lancy, 2015, 2017). However, taking a broader view of being a parent, the successful nurture and launch of offspring is a central pursuit of many organisms, including humans. But what do we mean by "successful"?

From an evolutionary perspective, raising offspring "successfully" might be said to involve facilitating children's development such that they fit the context in which they live and hence are more likely to survive and produce their own offspring. Throughout history, parents have raised their children to fit the context and culture in which they live: ancient Spartan parents raised militant children who would thrive in the culture of ancient Sparta, Australian Aboriginal parents raised children skilled in social belonging in a kinship-based forager society, and contemporary American parents raise children to navigate contemporary American culture with its flickering, moment-to-moment e-culture, its ocean of boundless knowledge at one's fingertips, its digital social realms, its swiftness of technological innovation. Needless to say, 20th century Western children would no more excel at war games in Sparta than would Spartan children understand Twitter. Thus parenting must be sensitive to one's context—both within the family and in the world at large. Yet, at its most basic, the goal of raising children also involves the *continuation of the species*. Raising a child who fits a cultural context, where that particular culture is in and of itself not sustainable, is also an evolutionary dead end. From this perspective, parenting is not just raising one's own children to survive but also ensuring that society itself survives. Parents might then parent for a future *beyond* our current social and ecological context—that is, they might parent toward a better world.

Within all the variation in human parenting, are there aspects of parenting that have been shown to be beneficial and healthful to children across the arc of their lives? Are there aspects of parental care that are quintessentially human? And how does parental care nurture our very humanity, such that our children become the best versions of themselves? To fully address this, we must consider how behaviors evolve over time and within and across species.

The four streams of evolution

Life first evolved on Earth over 3.5 billion years ago (Altermann & Kazmierczak, 2003). Approximately 545–520 million years ago, the Cambrian explosion took place: the rapid appearance of a diverse array of lifeforms, possibly triggered in part by the development of associative learning (Ginsburg & Jablonka, 2010). For evolution to occur, a characteristic must *vary*, the context must *select* specific variants, and the selected variants must be *retained* (Hayes, Sanford, & Chin, 2017). Although we usually think of genetic evolution, the story of evolution is written across four dynamic and interacting dimensions, occurring in genetic, epigenetic, behavioral, and symbolic streams (Jablonka & Lamb, 2005), as illustrated in the diagram below. For all four dimensions context defines evolution—it drives adaptation.

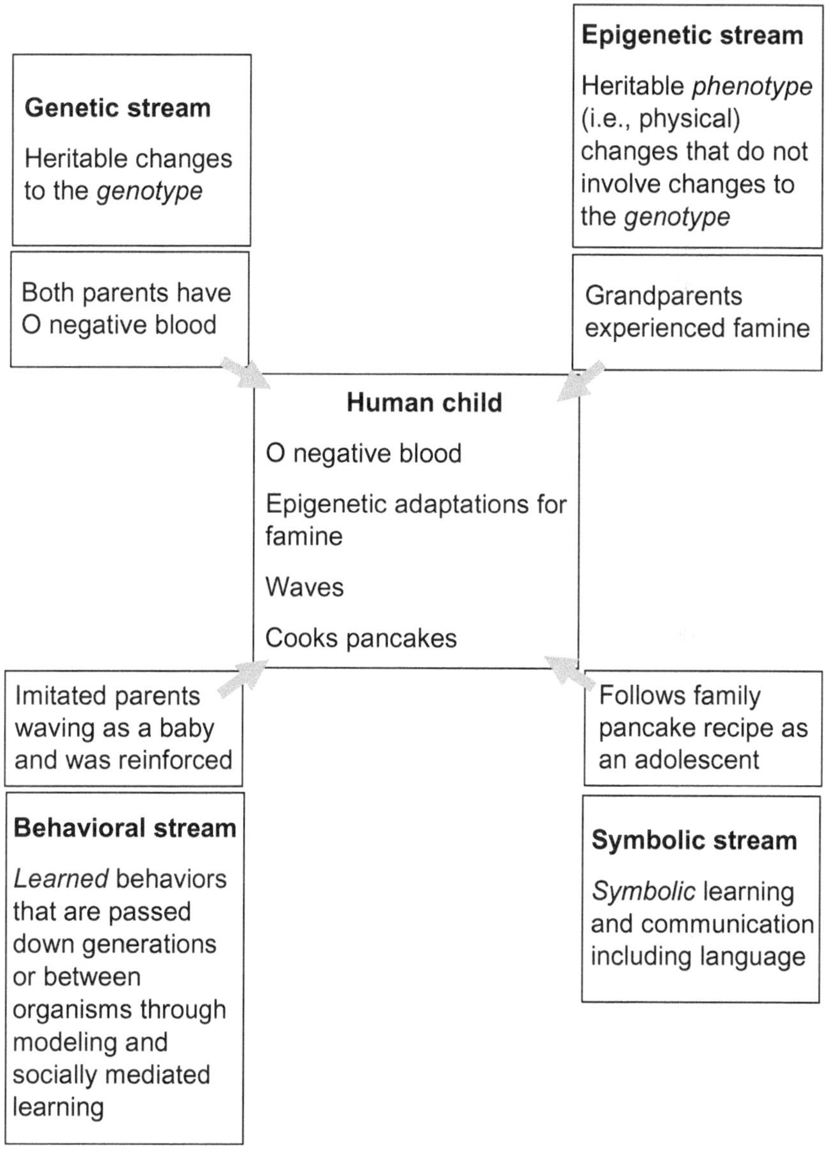

The four streams of evolution.

The *genetic* dimension of evolution is perhaps the most widely studied and certainly what we usually think of when we think of evolution. Genetic variation, coupled with the selection of traits that are best fit for the environment and the passing on of genes to offspring, results in evolution of the *genotype* over time. Recent work suggests that the transmission of genes is not merely vertical—or parent to offspring—but can also occur *horizontally*, or across organisms (Soucy, Huang, & Gogarten, 2015). This accounts for gene transfer across bacteria and archaea, and is implicated, for example, in antibiotic resistance (von Wintersdorff et al., 2016).

Epigenetics refers to the study of heritable *phenotype* changes—the observable characteristics of an organism— that do not involve changes to the *genotype* (Jablonka & Lamb, 2005; Waddington, 1942). For example, epigenetic development includes cellular transmission and body-to-body transmission between mother and developing embryo. Epigenetics can impact upon the expression of specific genes.

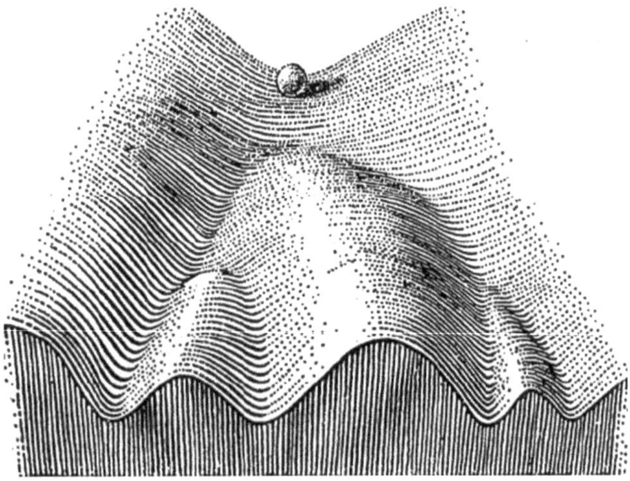

The epigenetic landscape (Baedke, 2013).

Epigenetics gave rise to the notion of plasticity in the development of an organism; this concept was taken up in developmental psychology as representative of phenotypic variability as children experienced different environments (Gottlieb, 1991). As illustrated by Waddington's "epigenetic landscape" metaphor (above), child development occurs through the mutual, bidirectional influence of genes and the environment.

Evolution not only occurs at the level of physical differences across organisms; so too does it occur across the expressions of behavior. Within an individual organism, behaviors can vary, be selected by the context, and retained. Hence, respondent and operant conditioning can be understood as evolutionary processes. Learned behaviors can also be passed down from parent to offspring, and this is the *behavioral* stream of evolution: socially mediated learning, including imitation and learning through social interaction. Behavioral evolution may influence the phenotype of an organism. For example, compared with rats in impoverished environments, rats interacting with enriched environments demonstrate more robust neurogenesis and synaptic density; they also demonstrate greater reductions in the release of dopamine and acetylcholine, that is, biological resilience to stress (Segovia, del Arco, & Mora, 2009).

The fourth dimension of evolution is the symbolic stream. *Symbolic* evolution incorporates all symbolic thought and communication, including language (Deacon, 2018; Jablonka & Lamb, 2005). Within the behavioral and the symbolic streams horizontal transmission (organism to organism; rather than just parent to offspring) is common. Further, the epigenetic, behavioral and symbolic streams all significantly influence the context driving further selection, and with the symbolic stream, this degree of influence over selection is extensive. The human ability to process information symbolically was essential to the rise of our ability to learn *indirectly*, rather than through direct experience alone. For example, a human can learn where the best berries can be found *indirectly* by being told by another human without any direct contact with the berries. This ability is key to collaboration in social groups, to the transmittance of information over time and distance, and to imagining multiple realities as a problem-solving strategy. This capacity is also central to the human transmission of complex symbolic culture, either by individuals, within dyads, or within much larger societal groups. If you are going to receive an enormous cultural inheritance from the behavioral and the symbolic streams, then you want to ensure that you are receiving it from the right people—from people who are invested in your welfare. For humans, one of the functions of the attachment system is that it orients children as to who are the best people to learn from.

The evolution of parental care

In order to understand the development of what is uniquely human in parental care via the four streams of evolution, it is helpful to consider the evolution of parental care across species. The first examples of parental care were rudimentary. Initially, organisms evolved in their ability to recognize and protect (or, simply, not eat) their offspring. Over millions of years, some species began to invest in their young, to build nests to incubate eggs, and to protect them from predators. Later, organisms began to care for their hatchlings. From these beginnings, for some species, parental care became more sophisticated, and the mechanisms by which it was transmitted grew more diverse. For example, birds likely learn how to nurture young from their parents, in the same way that they learn birdsong (i.e. through the behavioral stream) (Jablonka & Lamb, 2005). Parental care supports vertical transmission within the behavioral stream, with parents passing learned behaviors down to their offspring.

Extensive early parental care in mammals provided an engine for complex and extensive behavioral evolution. Early parental care is definitional to mammals: mammals are named after the mammillary gland that produces milk for our offspring. This extensive early parental care favored the evolution of affective signaling systems. For example, mothers who were attuned to the subtle cues and signs of their babies were more likely to have offspring who survived, and babies who could effectively and safely signal were more likely to survive (Hrdy, 2011). Thus mammals evolved socio-emotional signaling systems. These capacities, once evolved, could be coopted and extended to other kin and affiliative relationships (Gilbert, 2015). That is, mammals could form complex social groups, maintained through affective signaling.

Evolution operates not just at the level of individuals, but also at the level of groups (Hayes et al., 2017). Hence, characteristics that support successful groups may also be selected by evolution. Affective signaling supports successful social groups. Many mammalian species live in groups, or form complex and negotiated alliances. Mammals adapted to give and receive complex social signals beyond the parent–child bond, including signals communicating affiliation and safety, as well as social rank and social competition. Social threat—the threat of exclusion from the group or the threat of aggression from a member of the same species and group—is responded to differently than threat from a predator (Sloman, Gilbert, & Hasey, 2003). In particular, submissive displays evolved to communicate the termination of aggression by the dominant animal without injury. In short, mammals evolved complex social motivational systems, motivational systems covering parental care, kinship, affiliative relationships, seeking sexual partners, forming groups, securing support for parenting, and social rank within groups.

This evolution of complex affective signaling involved anatomical changes. The ventral vagal complex facilitates our mammalian ability to socially soothe and to seek comfort in the presence of other mammals, and includes affective communication such as facial expressions, vocalizations, and gestures. The vagus is an important component of the autonomic nervous system and comprises three components in humans: (1) the oldest is the dorsal vagal complex associated with immobilization, dissociation, or shutdown responses; (2) the sympathetic nervous system or mobilization system associated with fight or flight behaviors; and (3) the youngest *mammalian* component: the ventral vagal complex associated with the affective signaling system (Porges, 1997). Importantly, the ventral vagal complex can downregulate the sympathetic nervous system. Thus affective signaling and affiliation are connected to safety in mammals: we seek safety and comfort in each other.

This evolutionary adaptation set the stage for a rich stream of behavioral transmission and cultural evolution seen throughout the mammalian world, especially in mammals with family and social groups, like whales. For example, whales have been observed to transmit culture to their young through teaching their songs (Garland et al., 2011). They have also been observed to grieve the loss of family members, and this capacity is predicted by encephalization (Bearzi et al., 2018). Parental care does not merely support the behavioral dimension of evolution through the passing down of behavior vertically from parent to child. Rather, childhood is a period of flexible experimentation, characterized by play. Parental care, the careful watchful gaze of the parent, makes this period of playful experimentation and behavioral flexibility possible. Behavioral or cultural traits are also transmitted *horizontally*, or within social groups outside the parent–child dyad. For example, the songs of humpback whales show a distinct pattern of horizontal transmission through pods, with song types extending through populations like cultural ripples (Garland et al., 2011). This in-built flexibility, with each generation having the opportunity to innovate and discover the world anew, gives the behavioral dimension of evolution a key advantage over the genetic and the epigenetic streams—that is, rapid adaptation to sudden environmental change is possible.

Affective signaling, seen across mammals, is a core aspect of the parent–child relationship in humans too (and indeed, all human social interactions). The parent–child dance is a responsive dance; it is a dance of emotional exchange. Safety is a key aspect of this parent–child dance. The attachment system of the child orients toward the attachment figure, prompting the child to seek proximity to and nurturance from the parent (Bowlby, 1988). The child learns to use the parent as a secure base for flexible experimentation and exploration as well as a safe haven to withdraw to when under threat. The manner in which a particular child achieves this proximity is learned, it is honed to fit the parental care that the child has received since birth. The insecure attachment patterns of anxious avoidance and anxious ambivalent attachment are often adaptive behavioral patterns for the child to show in the parent–child relationship itself. That is, these patterns, in the relationships for which they were developed, do succeed in maximizing proximity and nurturance. However, these learned patterns have consequences for the child's long-term ability to seek soothing from others and to self-soothe. The quality of parental sensitivity and responsiveness is related to the child's attachment style as well as to the full breadth of child development from emotional and behavioral development, to cognitive development, to social and relational development (Eshel, Daelmans, Cabral de Mello, & Martines, 2006; Sroufe, 2005). Grounded with mammalian affective signaling and social motivational systems, human parental care evolved to be more complex still.

The evolution of human parental care

Complex and intricate coevolutionary relationships exist between human parental care and the core features of humanity: a large brain, flexible social cooperation, language, symbolic thought, and intersubjectivity (Hrdy, 2011).

Human infants are born immature and highly dependent and remain so for a particularly extended period of time in comparison to other mammals. This is not so our large heads can fit through the birth canal, as is sometimes erroneously suggested—efficient upright locomotion with wide, womanly hips is possible—but, rather, it is likely due to the metabolic demands of a large and growing brain and the adaptive benefits of stimulation outside of the womb to brain development (Dunsworth, Warrener, Deacon, Eillison, & Pontzer, 2012). The immature and highly dependent nature of human infants is sometimes expressed by saying that they are secondarily altricial (Ball, 2009). Our infants show signs that we developed from precocial ancestors—mammals born highly mature (think: horses). Like precocial mammals, singleton birth is typical and our milk has a low-fat and high-lactose content, necessitating frequent feeds. However, unlike precocial mammals, our newborn babies can neither follow nor cling to us. Unlike other altricial mammals—mammals born highly dependent and immature (think: cats)—we cannot nest. Our babies typically do not have siblings to nest with and our low-fat milk necessitates frequent feedings. Beginning with a highly dependent infancy, humans have an extended childhood. Human children progress though four key developmental phases over many years: infancy; flexible experimentation and language acquisition in early childhood; stable acquisition of skills and abilities through modeling and play in middle childhood; and flexible experimentation and risk-taking in adolescence, before we finally take up the mantel of adulthood (Gopnik, 2017). From birth to adulthood a human child is a lengthy investment.

How have we adapted to care for such dependent offspring? And how is this adaptation related to our unique capacities as a species? Comparing human parental care to that of our closest living relatives, the Great Apes, the startling difference is that humans are *cooperative breeders* (Hrdy, 2011). That is, parental care is not the domain of the biological mother alone; it also involves the father and *alloparents* (caregivers other than the parents). Great Ape mothers remain in continuous physical contact with their babies, and do not allow others to handle them (in spite of interest). In contrast, human parenting is a cooperative activity. Systems of care organize around the child in a *flexible and opportunistic* way: the father, grandparents, aunts and uncles, older siblings, and nonkin affiliative bonds may all be part of the care system of an individual child.

Flexible cooperative breeding is an important part of the complex coevolution of our unique human features (Hrdy, 2011). It favored the evolution of human infants capable of eliciting committed care from their mother and alloparents. Without continuous physical contact between mother and child, *psychological contact* became important. Traits that allowed for psychological connection, in the absence of physical contact, were selected (e.g., babbling). Apart from humans, the only other primates who show babbling during infancy are also cooperative breeders. Hence, it is likely that babbling first evolved as a way of maintaining psychological contact at a physical distance, and later became important for the development of language. Human babies are also skilled at eliciting *attuned* interactions—responsive interaction patterns in which the baby's own mental states are reflected back to them by the parent or alloparent. This attunement extends upon mammalian affective signaling to provide rich psychological connection.

Attuned, responsive interactions are crucial to human emotional and social development and shape the child's attachment behavior. The attachment system orients the child toward the attachment figure, prompting the child to seek proximity to and nurturance from the parent (Bowlby, 1988). Human children, like all primates, need physical proximity with their caregivers. However, the human attachment system also prompts children to seek *psychological* proximity within attuned interactions (Hrdy, 2011). Psychological contact between parents, alloparents, and offspring, in the form of attuned interaction, made possible the evolution of flexible cooperative behavior, language, and perspective taking. It also makes possible the learning of cooperative behavior, language, and perspective taking by each new generation of humans. Human infants are born seeking attuned interactions, seeking contingent interactions with their caregivers. This makes human infants particularly primed to learn from their caregivers.

Communication between parent and child begins with joint attention, stimulus orienting, and generalized imitation, which are directly trained in infancy, and then enters the symbolic stream to develop into increasingly sophisticated language. According to relational frame theory (RFT) our capacity to *arbitrarily* relate stimuli—to relate stimuli in a manner not dependent on physical characteristics—is the capacity underlying human language and complex cognition. This capacity allows us to be part of the *symbolic* stream of inheritance, learning language and complex cognition from our parents and alloparents (other caregivers), and innovating with these abilities within our generation. It also underlies our capacity for self-awareness, perspective taking, and flexible cooperation.

A pattern of parental care that includes complex attuned interactions with multiple caregivers over an extended childhood makes the learning of language, complex cognition, self-awareness, and perspective taking possible. Further, our capacities of language, complex cognition, self-awareness, and perspective taking, supercharge our parenting. Human parents routinely take their child's perspective, track their child's unfolding experience of the world, use their child's past behavior to predict future behavior, develop a verbal understanding of their child, and seek verbal advice from others on parenting. The sensitive and responsive parenting—parenting that involves not just physical proximity but also psychological—that human children need to flourish requires a parent with the ability to flexibly change perspectives and use language.

Thus from an evolutionary perspective, our species extended childhood and parental care is connected in intricate ways to our very humanity. We are the result of an evolutionary bargain: extended parental care, for the capacity to language and flexibly cooperate. The remarkable success of this evolutionarily bargain is evident all around us. Uniquely among the species of Earth we are *flexibly* cooperative on a *massive* scale (Harari, 2011). Like other mammalian species, we continue to show the capacity for cooperation based on kinship and affiliative bonds grounded in trust and reciprocity. But this mammalian cooperative system has a maximum capacity: there are only so many people that you can personally know well enough to either love or trust. For humans, the capacity is approximately 150. Our ability to relationally frame gives us the capacity to build large-scale and flexible cooperative networks using language and symbols, networks extending into the millions.

For humans, cooperation can be built and maintained not merely through interactions, kinship, love, trust, and reciprocity within the physical world, but also through the symbolic world. Using language we can and do build cooperative networks around fictions, social constructs, imagined orders or myths—or from an RFT perspective, shared meaning. As verbal beings, heirs of the symbolic inheritance stream, we live not just in a physical world, but also in an intersubjective symbolic world. Shared fictions, or social constructs, have functions for us. But unlike the functions of the physical world (e.g., the ability of water to relieve thirst), the functions of our shared fictions are dependent upon a jointly constructed verbal world. One salient example is money. One hundred American dollars has designated functions within our current economic system. These functions rely upon a wide cooperative network in which money and a 100-dollar American bill, in particular, have socially agreed upon meanings. Outside of this intersubjective reality, a 100-dollar bill is merely its physical properties: a small piece of paper with patterns and drawings on it. Yet, within this intersubjective verbal world 100 American dollars has a clear value.

This intersubjective verbal world and the cooperative networks it allows us to build are a major part of human life. We (the authors) may never know you (the reader). We may never physically meet. But we are already jointly participating in multiple extensive cooperative networks. We can write this book, it can be published and sold, and you can purchase it, all because we, the publishers, and you live within multiple intersubjective worlds, from the world views within acceptance and commitment therapy, to the global economic system. We all live within an intersubjective verbal web. Within this verbal web we have built cooperative networks consisting of millions of people.

Our cooperative networks themselves, in turn, facilitate and supercharge our ability to derive relations, to develop language, complex cognition, and flexible perspective taking. Through extensive cooperative networks, we are not merely verbal but many humans are now literate and participating in formal education to a greater degree than at any point in our previous history. Many of us have instant access to much of our species' cumulative behavioral and symbolic inheritance. Further, through globalization, increased travel and trade, and the internet, we are connected and routinely exposed to a variety of perspectives and cultural inheritance streams. We have exponentially increased our capacity for horizontal transmission within behavioral and symbolic evolution.

Our capacity for flexible cooperation can be used for a prosocial goal, or for an antisocial goal. It can be harnessed toward the flourishing of our species and other life on Earth or used for our ultimate destruction. Beyond cooperation, the verbal context, our shared relational frames, shape the nature of our cooperation. What kind of cooperative networks do we want to build? And toward what ends?

Compared to all other life on Earth, this is what makes the human species unique: our capacity to build extensive, even limitless, networks of flexible cooperation. No other species on Earth can do it. Human history is a progression toward larger flexible cooperative networks, and this capacity is intricately tied with our extended childhoods and parental care.

Given this evolutionary context to the development of human parental care, we might pause and ask: What features of parental care and child development are quintessentially human?

- As mammals, human infants are born with the instinct to suckle for comfort and nutrition.
- As mammals, humans form complex bonds involving affective signaling. As humans, we build on this capacity with a need for psychological connection and attuned, responsive interactions.
- Human infants are born highly dependent and we have an extended childhood.
- Humans are flexible cooperative breeders. Our familial and caregiving systems are flexible and opportunistic.
- Human children develop attachment bonds with their caregivers, learned patterns of interacting, which maximize proximity to and nurturance from caregivers. This includes using the caregiver as a secure base for exploration and a safe haven for refuge.
- Human children are capable of forming multiple attachment bonds; they come into the world prepared to receive care from multiple caregivers.
- Humans, both children and parents, are soothed within an affiliative social context of safety and care. The activation of our affiliative system, and the actions of the ventral vagas, downregulate our threat system and

the sympathetic nervous system, restoring balance. The caregiving that children receive in childhood, in particular, has consequences for their long-term ability to seek soothing from others and to self-soothe.
- Human children play and experiment flexibly. Parental care, by keeping children safe, and functioning as a secure base, allows for this important developmental period of flexible experimentation.
- Human parenting, from birth and across the lifetime, is characterized by parental responsiveness and psychological connection. Sensitive responsiveness to child cues and attuned interaction is the template for intersubjectivity and human sociality.
- Human parents pass an extensive behavioral and symbolic inheritance onto their children, and each generation innovates, building on this behavioral and symbolic inheritance through experimentation and horizontal transmission.
- Our strength, as a species, is our capacity for flexible experimentation. Our parenting is diverse, flexible, and cooperative.

Unique features of contemporary parenting

The contemporary world in which humans live is unlike anything seen before in human history or prehistory (Harari, 2011). We have built and sustained larger cooperative networks than ever before. We participate in networks that, quite literally, span the globe. Regional cultural variations, of course, still exist. But increasingly, humans from different parts of the world are able to participate in global cooperative networks involving trade, travel, common economic and political concepts, and cooperative endeavor. Technology allows for instant face-to-face communication between two people living in different regions of the world, and it allows for strangers of completely different backgrounds and living in different countries to meet. Children may be raised far away from grandparents, or their parents may travel overseas for a time during their childhood, but it is also easy for children to have regular face-to-face communication across such physical distance thanks to modern technology. Many nations and cities have embraced multiculturalism, with many people within the modern world living in an increasingly complex cultural melting pot. As the dominant cooperative networks become larger and more extensive, our world becomes smaller and closer to home.

Science and technology is a dominant cultural force within the cooperative networks of our day (Harari, 2011). The scientific and technological endeavor, coupled with capitalism, fuels a rapidly changing world. The current generation of parents have experienced, within their own lifetime, sweeping and unpredicted global technological changes (with the internet being the prime example). As a result, many parents today are consciously raising their children for an unpredictable technological future. Since technology is developing so rapidly, parents are unable to assess the risks and the benefits. The research is often too far behind for us to know the risk and benefits of today's technology let alone to predict the technological skills our children may need in the future. The potential benefits and costs (e.g., of screens, gaming, and computer use) in terms of mental health, attention, and social skills are complex. Behavior may be shaped in positive or negative ways. A different set of skills may be reinforced and strengthened in a technological environment (a set of skills that will be necessary in the future?), and screens may be used as avoidance or to create connection or even to level the playing field, allowing children with disabilities to participate on equal footing, or for children to socialize without prejudice. These are not simple questions for parents to untangle. Further technological dilemmas, for parents and societies are fast approaching including gene-editing technology and expanding automation (Harari, 2015). At the same time, environmental crises such as climate change and mass extinction require urgent solutions. Our current way of life is unsustainable; this leaves future generations to address unprecedented global problems for which no comprehensive solutions currently exist. This will require cooperation and prosocial behavior across groups on a global scale. Flexibility is our species' strength and the current generation of children will need to be more flexible than ever before.

Science has also been applied to parenting itself, to child development itself, and, indeed, to the human condition. Without such scientific endeavor, this book, of course, couldn't be written. Modern parents, more than ever before, have access to scientifically based knowledge on parenting itself. However, we are also living in an age where opinions can be easily shared and spread, whether they are evidence-based or not. Further, many key parenting topics, such as infant sleep, remain controversial even among scientists. Even professionals within the parenting area may remain closely tied to a specific "camp" without a broader understanding of all of the relevant scientific theories and evidence. As a result, the current generation of parents is bombarded with parenting advice: from health professionals, other parents, the community, and social media. Much of it is contradictory. In addition, social media greatly extends the scope of social comparison, allowing parents to constantly compare their children to others and themselves as parents to others.

Although famine, natural disasters, war, and infectious disease remain the experience of many of the humans living on this planet, now, for the first time in human history, human communities exist where people experience an unprecedented degree of protection from such calamities (Harari, 2011). For the first time in human history, it is possible for a mother to believe, based upon a rational evaluation of probabilities in her community, that she will never lose a child. More than that, many of us in industrialized nations believe that a mother *should not* ever lose a child. For the first time, humanity has the knowledge necessary to dramatically reduce child mortality, and if we have not successfully done so in every region of the world and with every community, most of us attribute this not to fate, but to a failing of humanity. Child mortality, for the first time in our species' history, is understood not a natural and unavoidable part of parenting, but rather as a solvable problem. In our evolutionary past, there was a shift to an extended childhood and an increased parental investment in fewer offspring. In recent times, those of us living with access to modern medicine and political stability have taken this bargain further still. Within communities that are sheltered from the calamities of famine, natural disasters, war, and infectious disease, we have fewer children, we expect all of our children to survive until adulthood, and we invest all the more into the success of each individual child.

Current trends toward "hot house" parenting and "helicopter" parenting should be understood in this context. Contemporary parents in Western countries spend a greater amount of time with their children than at any previous point from 1960s onward (Dotti Sani & Treas, 2016). Many parents engage in efforts to deliberately optimize their child's cognitive development—from playing classical music to their fetus in the womb, to teaching literacy or numeracy before the child has enrolled in school, to scheduling numerous extracurricular activities chosen by the parent for their enriching potential. Seen within a historical context, including reductions in child mortality and the number of children, increases in formal education, rapidly moving technological advancement, and supercharged behavioral and symbolic evolution, this overall trend is an understandable adaptation to the realities of contemporary life.

Yet, depending upon exactly how parents "hot house" or "helicopter" parent, there are potential costs. Some parents may prioritize the optimization of their child's cognitive development *at the expense of* the parent–child relationship and wider social and emotional development. The reduction in unstructured play time is problematic. The flexible experimentation of play is a core advantage of the developmental period of childhood, and it is beneficial in numerous ways. Through play children learn how to be curious and discover their skills within the world, how to be resourceful and innovative, how to generalize skills into unplanned and unpredictable environments, and how to engage in mindful risk-taking. Boredom, and unstructured play time, is important for the development of innovation, creativity, and self-directed behavior. Contemporary parents may find themselves unsure of how to balance between providing the caring, nurturing environment of free play and exploration and adequately preparing their children for an unpredictable technological future requiring greater formal education than at any point in our past history.

Parents negotiate this balancing act, as they also negotiate a balancing act of their own, between work and home life. In forager and agricultural societies, home life and work life are not separate spheres (Hrdy, 2011). The caring of children is performed by parents and alloparents along with the other tasks of life. The societal shift triggered by industrialization led to what we now think of as the "traditional" family model (although it is actually quite recent): a breadwinner father who *leaves home* to go into the world of work and a stay-at-home mother who *stays at home* to care for the children. In this "traditional" vision, home and work life are separated into two separate spheres: the public and the private sphere. Men inhabit the public sphere of work and women and children the private sphere of the home. In many ways, this division between the public and the private spheres of work and home life continues today, but with women rejoining the workforce in greater numbers. While the mother works, children spend time with their fathers, extended family, or paid caregivers such as nannies or childcare centers. Humans are flexible and opportunistic cooperative breeders. In many families, this is a modern variation of alloparenting behavior that would, in many ways, be familiar to our forager ancestors. But what is arguably quite different is the continued division of human life into two separate spheres, with parents, particularly primary caregivers and mothers, finding themselves in the difficult position of juggling the two. As all working parents can attest, this juggling act can be a significant source of stress, and many parents feel pressured to juggle these competing spheres in ways that they are simply not happy with.

Any discussion of contemporary parenting and childhood would be incomplete without mentioning school. While schools existed in ancient times, *mass* education is a distinguishing feature of contemporary life. Mass education has become a worldwide phenomenon, particularly in the developed world (Meyer, 1992). From the late 1800s to the present day it has expanded throughout the world and expanded in scope with an increasing number of years of schooling. A primary school level of education is enshrined as a basic human right in the UN's Declaration of Human Rights, and improving the education of children within developing nations remains a major aspect of charitable endeavors. We are, collectively, better educated than any previous generation and our children will be better educated still.

Formal schooling and its importance for later success in life have conferred adaptive value upon specific traits: selective attention, the ability to sit still, the capacity to work quietly. The variance that children may show in these traits now has clear valence—these traits are now being selected. Formal schooling also results in the majority of children spending significant amounts of time with same-age peers rather than playing within multiage groups of children as was the norm in societies before formal schooling. Further, in many countries formal schooling has features that are at odds with child development. Formal schooling varies from country to country in terms of starting age, time spent at school, time spent doing homework, available resources, degree of autonomy and respect given to teachers, the use of high-stakes standardized testing, and the emphasis on educational equity. All of these factors may affect the developmental appropriateness of schooling. An early starting age for formal schooling may been cutting short the time of free play and flexible experimentation that characterizes early childhood. Lengthy school hours and homework cut into developmentally important unstructured play time. Further, the degree of autonomy given to teachers as well as the use of high-stakes standardized testing—testing with consequences to the students, staff, and school—and the general cultural emphasis on educational equity and inclusiveness relate to the ability of teachers to teach flexibly and inclusively, in a manner that takes into full account the developmental readiness of each child. The educational success of the Finnish model, a model with a later school starting age of 7, lower school and homework hours, a high degree of autonomy and respect for teachers, a lack of high-stakes standardized testing, and a strong emphasis on educational equity, highlights the benefits of a school system that aligns with the developmental needs of children (Sahlberg, 2015).

Finally, in much of the developed world, parenting is delayed. Compared to our forager ancestors, many parents today begin their parenting career with extremely limited experience in caring for children. Today, it is not unusual, in terms of childcare experience, for someone to jump from being a 3-year-old playing with a doll straight to being a 30-year-old holding one's own newborn. Yet, human parenting, like any other aspect of human life is learned. This learning gap has been filled by professionals—midwives, nurses, doctors, psychologists, lactation consultants, teachers, and others—as well as by self-designated "experts." Googling for parenting advice, or searching for books on parenting, will bring you both excellent evidence-based information and poor-quality advice without an evidence base. It is not always easy for parents to separate the two.

In sum, what are the key features of contemporary parenting?

- We are living in a rapidly changing technological world. Many parents are consciously preparing their children for an unpredictable technological future.
- At least in the most privileged communities of the developed world, we are having fewer children, expecting each child to survive until adulthood and investing even more into each individual child.
- This increased investment can be seen in so-called "hot house" parenting and "helicopter" parenting. Instead of being a "good enough" parent, parents may aspire to actively optimize their child's development particularly cognitive development and educational success. Although this strategy is understandable from an historical perspective, it may have potential costs in terms of the parent–child relationship, social and emotional development and the loss of unstructured play time.
- Children today are expected to be better educated than ever before.
- Children today will need to be more flexible than ever before.

- Parents are likely to begin parenting with limited hands-on experience with children. Yet, parenting is learned. This learning gap is filled by professionals and self-designated "experts."
- Although the modern world includes travel and migration, technology allows for children to maintain connections to parents and alloparents from great distances.
- Work life and home life are two separate spheres (the public and the private sphere) and parents must juggle the two.
- Science is a dominant cultural force of our time, and it has been applied to childhood and parenting. Parents today have better access than ever before to scientific understandings of parenting. However, it is not always easy for parents to separate evidence-based advice from advice that lacks an evidence base.
- School is a key feature of contemporary childhood in the developed world and much of the developing world. Supporting your child to success in school is then a key feature of contemporary parenting. Yet, there are features of formal schooling that are at odds with child development. This can be significantly challenging for some families.

What is good parenting?

We've already discussed the quintessential features of human parenting; these are also core features of *good* parenting. At the heart of how humans parent is a pattern of parental responsiveness, a pattern of attuned and psychologically present interaction. A style of responding sensitively to the child's cues is related to multiple child developmental outcomes, from secure attachment, relational outcomes, and social and emotional development, to cognitive development and educational success (Eshel et al., 2006; Sroufe, 2005). With sensitive and responsive caregiving, children can use the parent as a secure base for exploration. This allows children to capitalize on the free experimentation and play of childhood. Human children experience a lengthy childhood and a highly dependent infancy. Good parenting is grounded in understanding this fact. Further, good parenting is supported by a cooperative network of alloparents.

Our strength, as a species, is our flexibility. Good parenting, too, is flexible. It is flexible to the needs of the child, the needs of the parent, and the wider physical and cultural realities of both. As a result, we should expect diversity within what we consider to be good parenting. With increasing globalization, and the fact that much of the scientific endeavor occurs with WEIRD (White Educated Industrialised Rich Democratic) samples, our scientific understanding of "good parenting" can be biased toward the norms in WEIRD populations. It is also natural, as a clinician or a researcher, to have a personal bias toward families similar to your own. In working with parents it is important that we recognize, instead, the tremendous variability within good parenting and, indeed, within human flourishing. Unusual parenting strategies are sometimes adaptations to particular circumstances, even healthy adaptations.

Beyond looking to our evolutionary story and what is quintessential about humanity, what more can we say about good parenting? What does it mean to *successfully* raise a child? Throughout human history, parents may have answered this question in different ways, depending upon their cultural context. Ancient Spartan parents, for example, aimed to raise warriors and the mothers of warriors: warriors who were either victorious in battle or who died trying. In a sense, this was good parenting for ancient Sparta. They were raising their children to best fit the context and the culture in which they lived. We too have been influenced by the cultures in which we live in what we regard as good parenting. For example, throughout most of human history and within the majority of cultures it is considered normal, natural, and healthy for young children to cosleep (i.e., share a sleeping space) with their mother. Even with flexible cooperative breeding including in some cultures highly involved fathers and alloparents the norm for human children has been to sleep with their mothers (Hrdy, 2011). Yet, in contemporary Western cultures where independence is highly prized, many parents attempt to avoid bedsharing between mother and child from birth, and for some, bedsharing is a cultural taboo and a source of shame.

Thus with awareness of cultural biases, and with acknowledgment of the diversity and flexibility within good parenting, let's consciously name our values and endpoints *as clinicians*, so that good parenting can be discussed in further depth and without unnamed assumptions. Within this book, good parenting is understood to be parenting that is consistent with the long-term health and wellbeing of children, parents, and society. It is parenting that is most likely to support the child's development of *psychological flexibility*. *Psychological flexibility* is the ability to persist or change in your behavior with full awareness of context and in the service of valued ends. Psychological flexibility is related to psychological health and wellbeing (Kashdan & Rotteberg, 2012), and it is the key outcome of acceptance and commitment therapy (ACT). Good parenting then, from an ACT perspective, supports children in developing all of the elements of psychological flexibility: experiential acceptance, psychological contact with the present moment, a rich understanding of personal values, flexible languaging, flexible perspective taking and a broad and flexible behavioral repertoire, including a repertoire rich in prosocial skills (note: psychological flexibility will be discussed further). Taking on a compassion-focused therapy (CFT) perspective, good parenting also supports children in developing the capacity to be compassionate to themselves and others and to receive compassion (note: CFT will be discussed further). For good parenting, the contingencies operating between the parent and the child, the cycles of reinforcement, support ongoing child development towards the cultivation of a psychologically flexible and compassionate adult.

Within this book, we emphasize the importance of a flexible, workable parenting style grounded in an evolutionary and contextual behavioral reading of the science related to parenting. Flexible parenting is about approaching parenting with an open mind and creativity. It is about taking a flexible, experimental approach to parenting—an approach of discovering what works for you and for your child. A flexible, workable approach to parenting is resilient and enduring. This approach enables parents and children to discover creative solutions for the challenges they face. It is also flexible in terms of the child's ongoing development, allowing parents to track developmental changes in their child and to shift and change in their parenting to fit their child's current developmental needs. Flexible, workable parenting is grounded within the parent's own psychological flexibility, including the parent's own values, psychological presence in the present moment, experiential acceptance, flexible perspective taking, flexible languaging, and flexible and committed action.

This flexible, experiential approach to parenting can, itself, be understood as an evolutionary approach. It is parenting using the principles of evolution: variation, selection, and the retention of adaptive traits. The parent flexibly varies their behavior, experimenting with different approaches (variation), since some behaviors work and some don't (selection). The behaviors that work are selected and retained, that is, the parent uses them again (retention). If selected behaviors stop working the parent again experiments, reintroducing variation into their parenting.

Finally, good parenting is consistent with self-care and with the parent's own long-term psychological wellbeing. It is well understood that parental adjustment is related to the parent–child relationship and to child outcomes. Parenting a human child into adulthood is a task taking at least two decades. Thus good parenting, in the long-term, must include self-care.

The theoretical frames

Some of the key theoretical frames of this book have already been briefly introduced: evolution, attachment theory, and RFT. The attachment and wider emotional–relational literature is explored fully in Chapter 3, Connect: the parent–child relationship, and the behavioral literature is explored fully in Chapter 4, Shape: building a flexible repertoire. All of the key theoretical frames within this book are nested within the overarching paradigm of evolutionary science. See the following diagram.

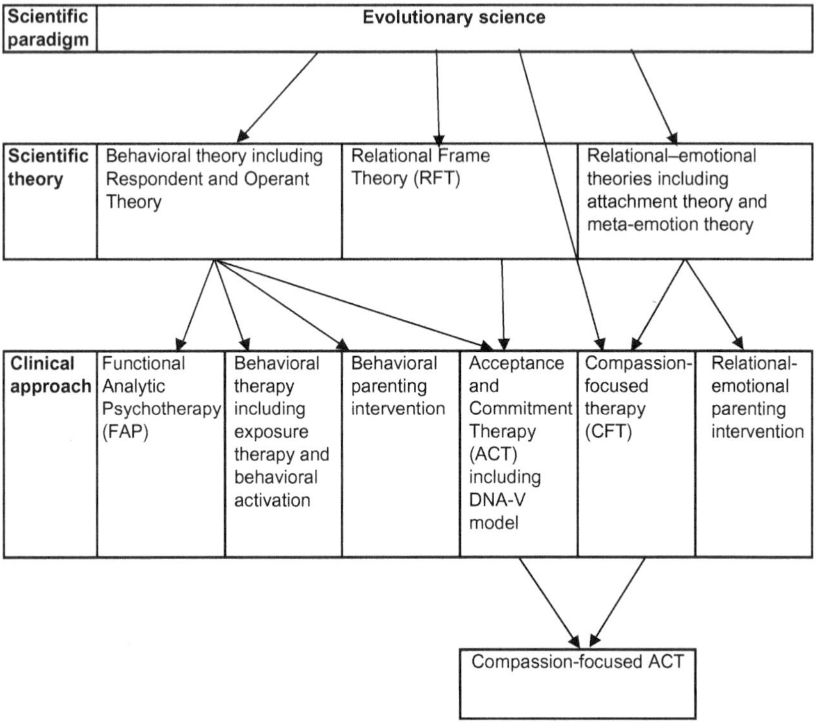

Theoretical frames.

Within contemporary culture, even within clinical approaches to working with parents and the scientific literature on parenting, there is sometimes an apparent tension between attachment theory and the related emotional–relational approaches to parenting and behavioral theory and the related behavioral approaches to parenting (Whittingham, 2015). This apparent tension is sometimes even construed as a difference in scientific paradigm. We contend that this false and unhelpful. It undermines scientific progress and the better provisioning of support to families. We maintain that attachment theory and behavioral theory are *not* conflicting scientific paradigms. In fact, attachment behavior can be understood in behavioral terms as a behavioral class shaped by the operant function of obtaining proximity to and nurturance from caregivers (Mansfield & Cordova, 2007). In turn, parental responsiveness can be explained in behavioral terms as when parental caregiving is under the appropriate and appetitive contextual control of the child's signals (Whittingham, 2015).

Both the relational–emotional and the behavioral theoretical frameworks are, we suggest, best understood as nested within the wider paradigm of evolutionary science. Understood from a wider evolutionary science paradigm, it is clear that any conflict is not truly at the paradigmatic level in a scientific sense. Rather, we suggest that there are misunderstandings between academic lineages, differences in philosophical assumptions, as well as normal and healthy scientific debate around specific issues. From within a wider evolutionary paradigm, it becomes possible to resolve misunderstandings, to debate philosophical assumptions, and to resolve scientific debate with empirical data and open discussion, and hence, to push the field forward.

Within this book you will find an approach to working with parents that integrates the attachment and wider emotional–relational literature with the behavioral literature within an evolutionary paradigm. ACT brings, we think, a powerful new way of understanding these theoretical debates, and in carving a path forward for the field. ACT has explicitly positioned itself within evolutionary science. ACT is grounded within the behavioral therapeutic tradition, with respondent and operant theory already core theoretical underpinnings. Further, many of the core concepts within ACT such as psychological presence in the present moment, experiential acceptance, or flexible perspective taking clearly relate to core theoretical components within the emotional–relational theoretical framework. This remarkable synergy will be explored in depth throughout this book.

Acceptance and commitment therapy

Core to this book is acceptance and commitment theory ("ACT"). ACT (said as the word "act") is a psychological intervention that incorporates both *acceptance* strategies and *commitment* or behavioral change strategies with the purpose of increasing psychological flexibility. Psychological flexibility is the ability to engage in effective, flexible behavior—whether that is changing or persisting in behavioral patterns—with full psychological contact with the present moment in the service of chosen values.

ACT is grounded within a behavioral theory of language and complex cognition called RFT. RFT is explained fully in Chapter 4, Shape: building a flexible repertoire. In brief, according to RFT our capacity to *arbitrarily* relate stimuli—to relate stimuli in a manner not dependent on physical characteristics—is the capacity underlying human language and complex cognition. It allows us to participate in the symbolic inheritance stream. It means that we live not just in a physical world, but also in an intersubjective symbolic world. Money is a salient example. A human child can learn that a 10-dollar bill is *worth more* than a 5-dollar bill even though that relation is *arbitrary*—not a relation of physical property—and will, furthermore, *derive*—without further learning—that a 5-dollar bill is *worth less* than a 10-dollar note. RFT is a powerful account of intersubjectivity, language, complex cognition, and meaning. As such, RFT can add to our understanding of parenting, through a rich perspective on the symbolic behavior of parent and child, the meaning of child behavior for the parent and the meaning of parent behavior for the child.

As humans live in both the physical world and an intersubjective symbolic world; our behavior at times may be the result of symbolic relations or the derived properties of stimuli. In other words, sometimes we do what we do because we are following *verbal rules*. In ACT, this is referred to as *cognitive fusion* (Hayes, Strosahl, & Wilson, 2003). With *cognitive fusion*, behavior may become inflexible and insensitive to context. Thoughts may also be experienced as literal truths. The opposite of cognitive fusion is *cognitive defusion*, and promoting defusion is a core component of ACT. As we tend to relate to the verbal, symbolic world as if it were the real physical world, we naturally attempt to *control* psychological stimuli (e.g., we try to avoid particular thoughts, feelings, memories, sensations, and behavioral impulses). This *experiential control* is rule-based and includes *experiential avoidance*, or attempts to avoid particular experiences, and *experiential attachment*, or attempts to increase or prolong private experiences.

Experiential avoidance, in particular, has been implicated in parenting stress and psychological functioning (Blackledge, 2005; Cheron, Ehrenreich, & Pincus, 2009; Coyne & Thompson, 2011; Evans, Whittingham, & Boyd, 2012; Whittingham, Wee, Sanders, & Boyd, 2013); parenting behaviors (Murrell, Wilson, LaBorde, Drake, & Rogers, 2009; Shea & Coyne, 2011); the quality of parent–child relationships (Shea & Coyne, 2011); parental bonding (Evans et al., 2012); parental grief (Whittingham et al., 2013); and child emotional and behavioral functioning across developmental periods from birth (Greco et al., 2005) to early adulthood (Coyne, McHugh, & Martinez, 2011). Studies targeting experiential avoidance in parents have demonstrated decreases in parent distress (Blackledge, 2005; Brown, Whittingham, Boyd, McKinlay, & Sofronoff, 2015; Whittingham, Sanders, McKinlay, & Boyd, 2014, 2016) as well as improvements in parenting (Brown, Whittingham, Boyd, McKinlay, & Sofronoff, 2014; Whittingham et al., 2014) and decreases in child behavioral problems (Brown et al., 2014; Whittingham et al., 2014). The opposite of experiential control is experiential acceptance, and again, promoting experiential acceptance is a core component of ACT.

Within ACT, psychological flexibility is often understood as comprised of six interrelated and overlapping components: (1) contact with the present moment or mindfulness, (2) experiential acceptance, (3) cognitive defusion, (4) values, (5) self-as-context, and (6) committed action. Within these six components both acceptance (acceptance and defusion) and behavior change (values and committed action) components are included with mindfulness and self-as-context overlapping in each group. These six elements are sometimes presented diagrammatically as a "hexaflex."

Within this book, the six interrelated components will be understood and examined in a more expansive way. Our adapted version of the hexaflex, the parent–child hexaflex (see the following) is an expanded and developmentally applicable hexaflex, in part inspired by the innovations of the DNA-V model (which we will discuss soon). The parent–child hexaflex represents the psychological flexibility of the parent in interaction with the child as well as the developing psychological flexibility of the child and the dynamic interaction between parent and child.

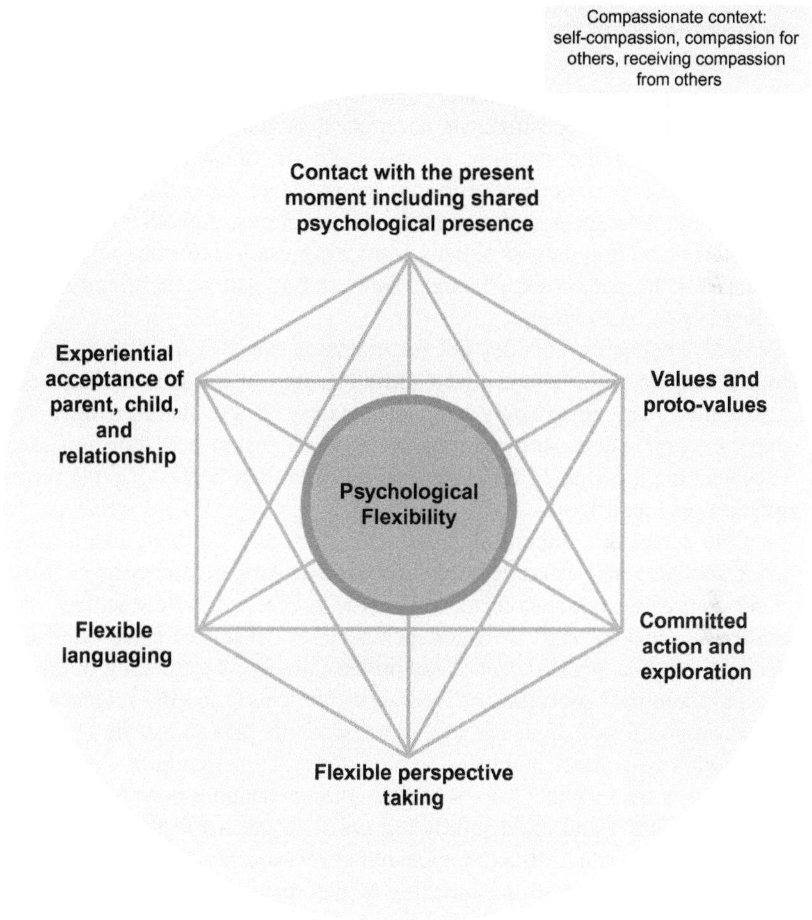

The parent–child hexaflex.

Within the parent–child hexaflex, the six interrelated processes expand upon the original processes as follows:

- Valuing also includes protovalues: the developing values of children and adolescents. In young children, protovalues may be as simple as the recognition that the child enjoys a particular activity or has engaged in prosocial behavior scaffolded verbally by the parent.

- Contact with the present moment includes shared psychological presence. It also includes present moment bodily awareness; for example, awareness of mobilization flight or fight or immobilization shutdown reactions. In addition, it includes an understanding of emotions, embodied reactions, and behavioral impulses as signals containing useful information, both as signals for the person experiencing them and as part of an affective signaling system with others.
- Experiential acceptance is distinguished from experiential control including both experiential avoidance and experiential attachment. Parental experiential acceptance includes acceptance of the child's psychological experiences and the ongoing parent–child relationship. This includes shifts in the experienced relationship across development. In addition, it includes an awareness and acceptance of emotions, embodied reactions, and behavioral impulses as signals containing useful information, both as signals for the person experiencing them and as part of an affective signaling system with others.
- Flexible languaging includes not just defusion but also the child's learning of language, the parent and child's learning to track, and the parent and child's learning to apply language flexibly. It also includes willingly experiencing fusion, shifting flexibly between fusion and defusion, and experiencing the kind of fusion-within-defusion that is part of pretense in pretend play and fiction.
- Flexible perspective taking includes self, child, and the relationship. That is, it includes self-as-context but also self-as-process, other-as-context, other-as-process, us-as-context, and us-as-process. It also includes the ability to flexibly shift between perspectives with awareness. Self-as-process, other-as-process, and us-as-process involve the tracking of ongoing psychological processes of the parent, the child, and the relationship. Us-as-process is the dynamic and developmental aspects of the relationship. Other-as-context includes the recognition of the child as a perspective in their own right. Us-as-context is the unchanging perspective from which the parent and child jointly engage with the world through shared psychological contact. It is the unchanging relationship.
- Compassion is added to the hexaflex as the context for the development of psychological flexibility, drawing on CFT. A reciprocal relationship exists between compassion and psychological flexibility, with compassion supporting psychological flexibility and psychological flexibility in turn supporting compassion. As the hexaflex is depicting psychological flexibility, we are depicting compassion as part of the context supporting flexibility.
- Committed action and exploration includes, for the parent, acting on their parenting values with willingness for what is present psychologically in the moment. It also includes parental ability to persist, when functional, even in the presence of difficult private events for self or child. This is

where ACT intersects with other evidence-based interventions including parenting interventions, postnatal care, exposure therapy, and behavioral activation. For the child, this is about exploration and about the parent supporting the child's development of a flexible and broad behavioral repertoire through shaping and reinforcement of a wide variety of adaptive behaviors.

Within this book there is a specific chapter for all of the six processes where each will be examined in depth.

Compassion-focused ACT

CFT developed independently of ACT; however, due to a high degree of synergy between the two therapies, both in theoretical grounding within the evolutionary paradigm, and in clinical strategy and focus, there is currently strong collaboration and cross-fertilization between the two communities. In particular, Tirch, Schoendorff, and Silberstein (2014) developed an integrated CFT and ACT approach. This book grounds itself within this integrated approach as well as draws on wider CFT literature, in particular the work of Paul Gilbert and colleagues.

CFT is grounded in an evolutionary account of social motivational systems—parental care, kinship, forming groups, seeking sexual partners, forming reciprocal alliances—and functional emotional systems—response to threat, seeking resources, seeking safety, and downregulation. Gilbert (2009) breaks the complexity of evolved emotional motivational systems into three systems for ease of understanding: the incentive/resource-focused system, the threat system, and the affiliative system. The incentive/resource-focused system is about desiring, consuming, wanting, joy, and excitement. It is the system involved in ensuring that we seek out needed resources. It is likely associated with the dopaminergic (reward) system. The threat-focused system is associated with fear, anxiety, anger, and disgust. It involves the amygdala and the limbic system as well as the serotonergic system and the sympathetic system. It is associated with the mobilization fight or flight response as well as the older immobilization or shutdown response. The affiliative system, evolved from the capacities for parental care, is associated with contentment and connection, a sense of social safety and peacefulness. Importantly, the affiliative system can provide balance and downregulation to the other two systems.

Within CFT it is said that evolution has given us a "tricky" brain. Some of our evolved motivational systems can be problematic for us, fueling social competitiveness and us versus them thinking. In addition, many aspects of dysfunctional behavior and mental health can be understood through an evolutionary lens as evolutionarily adaptive defenses turned maladaptive. For example, submissive behavioral displays, a defense against social threat, can be seen within depression and social anxiety, and defenses to cope with defeat and entrapment, including a reduction in exploration, can be seen within depression. Further, due the ways in which the human brain has evolved through a gradual tinkering of existing systems, the newest human capacities of language and complex cognition can create glitches with our older mammalian motivational system. For example, through rumination or self-criticism, we can constantly evoke our own threat motivational system.

The solution of CFT is to leverage our affiliative system and the capacity of this system to downregulate our other social motivational systems, provide balance, and enhance social cooperation. Hence, a focus on compassion. Gilbert (2009) defines compassion as sensitivity to suffering coupled with the motivation to prevent or alleviate suffering. Unpacking this definition, the deep clinical synergy between ACT and CFT becomes clear (Tirch et al., 2014). Sensitivity to suffering involves mindfulness, acceptance, and flexible perspective taking. Motivation to prevent or alleviate suffering is connected to flexible perspective taking as well as values and committed action. CFT and related techniques will be explored more thoroughly in later chapters.

DNA-V

The DNA-V model is a developmentally sensitive model of ACT developed by Hayes and Ciarrochi (2015). It stresses three fundamental perspectives that can be used to consider human behaviors as they develop in children and adolescents, but that also are pertinent to parents. These are described as perspectives we all have, in the same way that we all have DNA. The D refers to the Discoverer, or the behavior class that tries new things, takes risks, and "discovers" how one's behavior interacts with the world around us. A good way to recall the discoverer is to consider a child learning to walk—stand up, fall down, and stand up again. The N refers to the Noticer, or our behavior of noticing the world around us, and taking in data to connect with others, informing via our senses and physiology. The noticer is about taking in the world and learning either to respond or react with awareness. The A stands for the Advisor, and it represents our ability to predict and navigate our lives with the verbal behavior more commonly known as self-talk (it should be noted D, N, A, and V can all have verbal behavior). We use our advisor for judgments, evaluation, problem solving, and rule making. The V is for valuing and vitality. We begin with vitality and as humans develop we learn to use a verbal construction of the things most important to us as a compass for behavior. Surrounding DNA-V are two very important perspectives—self-view and social-view. In self-view, young people are taught to take a bigger perspective to see that their self comprises all of their D, N, A, and V, and that this can change and become more flexible. They are not fixed. For social-view, attachment and connection with others is seen to have a reciprocal influence on the development of our D, N, A, and V behaviors—in other words, our social context changes how our DNA-V behaviors develop. In the DNA-V model of ACT, adolescents are taught, experientially, how to access each of these classes of behavior, to discriminate among them, and to pay attention to what skill—D, N, or A—they choose in considering their behavior, the behavior of others, and their context. They learn that all three classes of behavior are important to develop and that bigger perspectives on their self- and social-view are important, and a nuanced understanding of which ones to use in what situations underpins flexible and adaptive risk taking. The DNA-V model is illustrated in the following.

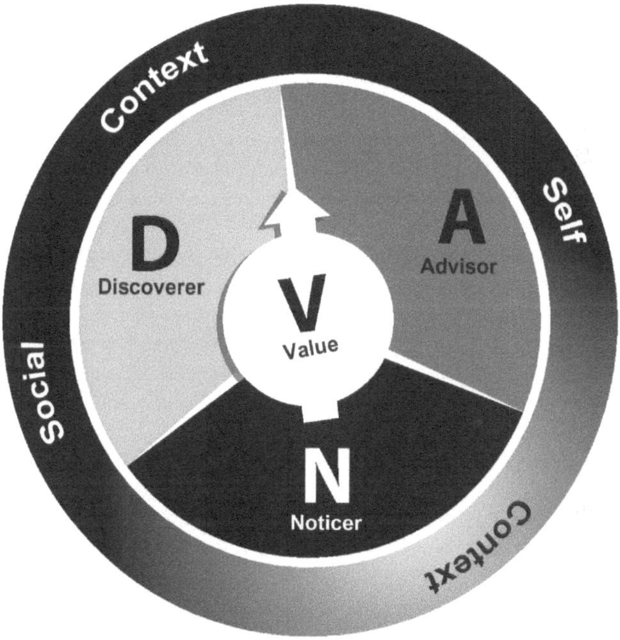

The DNA-V model.

Although in this book the elements of ACT are organized by our parent–child hexaflex, the basic approach of this book can be fully integrated into a DNA-V approach. Throughout this book, we will give some guidance as to how our expanded hexaflex components relate to the components of the DNA-V model.

Chapter summary

Parental care evolved hand in hand with our very humanity: flexible cooperation, language, perspective taking, and compassion. Looking at parental care from an evolutionary perspective, the key features of parenting for humans are flexible, cooperative caregiving systems including alloparents, a responsive pattern of care including attuned interactions, and flexibility in parental care. From an ACT perspective, good parenting is parenting that supports the child's development as a psychologically flexible human being, with a rich set of values, the skills of mindfulness and experiential acceptance, the capacity to flexibly language and flexibly perspective take and a board and flexible repertoire of behavior. This book is grounded in the evolutionary paradigm and understanding the science, theories, and approaches related to parenting from within an evolutionary, contextual perspective.

References

Altermann, W., & Kazmierczak, J. (2003). Archean microfossils: A reappraisal of early life on Earth. *Research in Microbiology*, *154*(9), 611–617. Available from https://doi.org/10.1016/j.resmic.2003.08.006.

Baedke. (2013). The epigenetic landscape in the course of time: Conrad Hal Waddington's methodological impact on the life sciences. *Studies in History and Philosophy of Science Part C: in History and Philosophy of Biological and Biomedical Sciences*, *44*(4B), 756–773.

Ball, H. (2009). Bed-sharing and co-sleeping: Research overview. *NCT New Digest*, *48*, 22–27.

Bearzi, G., Kerem, D., Furey, N. B., Pitman, R. L., Rendell, L., & Reeves, R. R. (2018). Whale and dolphin behavioural responses to dead conspecifics. *Zoology*, *128*, 1–15.

Blackledge, J. T. (2005). *Using Acceptance and Commitment Therapy in the support of parents of children diagnosed with autism.* (66), ProQuest Information & Learning, US.

Bowlby, J. (1988). *A secure base: Parent–child attachment and healthy human development.* New York: Basic Books.

Brown, F. L., Whittingham, K., Boyd, R. N., McKinlay, L., & Sofronoff, K. (2014). Improving child and parenting outcomes following paediatric acquired brain injury: A randomised controlled trial of Stepping Stones Triple P plus acceptance and commitment therapy. *Journal of Child Psychology and Psychiatry*, *55*(10), 1172–1183. Available from https://doi.org/10.1111/jcpp.12227.

Brown, F. L., Whittingham, K., Boyd, R. N., McKinlay, L., & Sofronoff, K. (2015). Does Stepping Stones Triple P plus Acceptance and Commitment Therapy improve parent, couple, and family adjustment following paediatric acquired brain injury? A randomised controlled trial. *Behaviour Research and Therapy*, *73*, 58–66. Available from https://doi.org/10.1016/j.brat.2015.07.001.

Cheron, D., Ehrenreich, J., & Pincus, D. (2009). Assessment of parental experiential avoidance in a clinical sample of children with anxiety disorders. *Child Psychiatry Human Development*, *40*(3), 383–403.

Coyne, L. W., McHugh, L., & Martinez, E. R. (2011). Acceptance and commitment therapy (ACT): Advances and applications with children, adolescents, and families. *Child and Adolescent Psychiatric Clinics of North America*, *20*(2), 379–399. Available from https://doi.org/10.1016/j.chc.2011.01.010.

Coyne, L. W., & Thompson, A. D. (2011). Maternal depression, locus of control, and emotion regulatory strategy as predictors of preschoolers' internalizing problems. *Journal of Child and Family Studies*, *20*(6), 873–883. Available from https://doi.org/10.1007/s10826-011-9455-2.

Deacon, T. W. (2018). Beneath symbols: Convention as a semiotic phenomenon. In D. S. Wilson, & S. C. Hayes (Eds.), *Evolution and contextual behavioral science* (pp. 67–84). Oakland: Context Press.

Dotti Sani, G. M., & Treas, J. (2016). Educational gradients in parents' child-care time across countries, 1965–2012. *Journal of Marriage and Family*, *78*(4), 1083–1096. Available from https://doi.org/10.1111/jomf.12305.

Dunsworth, H. M., Warrener, A. G., Deacon, T., Eillison, P. T., & Pontzer, H. (2012). Metabolic hypothesis for human altriciality. *Proceedings in the National Academy of Sciences*, *109* (38), 15212–15216.

Eshel, N., Daelmans, B., Cabral de Mello, M., & Martines, J. (2006). Responsive parenting: Interventions and outcomes. *Bulletin of the World Health Organisation*, *84*(12), 991–998.

Evans, T., Whittingham, K., & Boyd, R. (2012). What helps the mother of a preterm infant become securely attached, responsive and well-adjusted? *Infant Behavior and Development*, *35*(1), 1–11.

Garland, E. C., Goldizen, A. W., Rekdahl, M. L., Constantine, R., Garrigue, C., Hauser, N. D., ... Noad, M. J. (2011). Dynamic horizontal cultural transmission of humpback whale song at the ocean basin scale. *Current Biology*, *21*(8), 687–691. Available from https://doi.org/10.1016/j.cub.2011.03.019.

Gilbert, P. (2009). *The compassionate mind*. London: Little, Brown Book Group.

Gilbert, P. (2015). An evolutionary approach to emotion in mental health with a focus on affiliative emotions. *Emotion Review*, *7*(3), 230–237. Available from https://doi.org/10.1177/1754073915576552.

Ginsburg, S., & Jablonka, E. (2010). The evolution of associative learning: A factor in the Cambrian explosion. *Journal of Theoretical Biology*, *266*(1), 11–20. Available from https://doi.org/10.1016/j.jtbi.2010.06.017.

Gopnik, A. (2017). *The gardener and the carpenter*. London: Vintage publishing.

Gottlieb, G. (1991). Experiential canalization of behavioral development: Theory. *Developmental Psychology*, *27*(1), 4–13.

Greco, L., Heffner, M., Poe, S., Ritchie, S., Polak, M., & Lynch, S. (2005). Maternal adjustment following preterm birth: Contributions of experiential avoidance. *Behaviour Therapy*, *36*, 177–184.

Harari, Y. N. (2011). *Sapiens a brief history of humankind*. London: Vintage.

Harari, Y. N. (2015). *Homo deus a brief history of tomorrow*. London: Vintage.

Hayes, L. L., & Ciarrochi, J. (2015). *The thriving adolescent*. Oakland: New Harbinger Publications.

Hayes, S. C., Sanford, B. T., & Chin, F. T. (2017). Carrying the baton: Evolution science and a contextual behavioral analysis of language and cognition. *Journal of Contextual Behavioral Science*, *6*(3), 314–328. Available from https://doi.org/10.1016/j.jcbs.2017.01.002.

Hayes, S. C., Strosahl, K. D., & Wilson, K. G. (2003). *Acceptance and commitment therapy: An experiential approach to behavior change*. New York: Guilford Press.

Hrdy, S. B. (2011). *Mothers and others*. Cambridge: Harvand University Press.

Jablonka, E., & Lamb, M. J. (2005). *Evolution in four dimensions*. Cambridge: MIT Press.

Kashdan, T. B., & Rotteberg, J. (2012). Psychological flexbility as a fundemental aspect of health. *Clinical Psychology Review*, *30*, 865–878.

Lancy, D. F. (2015). *The anthropology of childhood: Cherubs, chattel, changelings*. New York: Cambridge University Press.

Lancy, D. F. (2017). *Raising children surprising insights from other cultures*. New York: Cambridge University Press.

Mansfield, A. K., & Cordova, J. V. (2007). A behavioral perspective on adult attachment style, intimacy, and relationship health. In D. W. Woods, & J. W. Kanter (Eds.), *Understanding behavior disorders: A contemporary behavioral perspective*. Reno: Context Press.

Meyer, J. W. (1992). World expansion of mass education 1870-1980. *Sociology of Education, 65* (2), 128–149.

Murrell, A., Wilson, K., LaBorde, C., Drake, C. E., & Rogers, L. (2009). Relational responding in parents. *Behavior Analyst Today, 9*, 196–214.

Porges, S. W. (1997). Evolution: an evolutionary by-product of the neural regulation of the autonomic nervous system. In C. S. Carter, I. Lederhendler, & B. Kirkpatrick (Eds.), *The integrative neurobiology of affliation* (pp. 62–77). New York: New York Academy of Sciences.

Sahlberg. (2015). *Finnish Lessons 2.0 What can the world learn from the educational change in Finland?* New York and London: Teachers College Press.

Segovia, G., del Arco, A., & Mora, F. (2009). Environmental enrichment, prefrontal cortex, stress, and the aging of the brain. *Jounral of Neural Transmission, 116*(8), 1007–1016.

Shea, S. E., & Coyne, L. W. (2011). Maternal dysphoric mood, stress, and parenting practices in mothers of Head Start preschoolers: The role of experiential avoidance. *Child & Family Behavior Therapy, 33*(3), 231–247. Available from https://doi.org/10.1080/07317107.2011.596004.

Sloman, L., Gilbert, P., & Hasey, G. (2003). Evolved mechanisms in depression: The role and interaction of attachment and social rank in depression. *Journal of Affective Disorders, 74*, 107–121.

Soucy, S. M., Huang, J., & Gogarten, J. P. (2015). Horizontal gene transfer: Building the web of life. *Nature Review Genetics, 16*(8), 472–482. Available from https://doi.org/10.1038/nrg3962.

Sroufe, A. L. (2005). Attachment and development: a prospective, longitudinal study from birth to adulthood. *Attachment & Human Development, 7*(4), 349–367. Available from https://doi.org/10.1080/14616730500365928.

Tirch, D., Schoendorff, B., & Silberstein, L. R. (2014). *The ACT practitioner's guide to the science of compassion*. Oakland: New Harbinger Publications.

von Wintersdorff, C. J., Penders, J., van Niekerk, J. M., Mills, N. D., Majumder, S., van Alphen, L. B., … Wolffs, P. F. (2016). Dissemination of antimicrobial resistance in microbial ecosystems through horizontal gene transfer. *Frontiers in Microbiology, 7*, 173. Available from https://doi.org/10.3389/fmicb.2016.00173.

Waddington, C. H. (1942). The epigenotype. *Endeavour, 1*, 18–20.

Whittingham, K. (2015). Connect and shape: A parenting meta-strategy. *Journal of Contextual Behavioral Science, 4*(2), 103–106. Available from https://doi.org/10.1016/j.jcbs.2015.03.002.

Whittingham, K., Sanders, M. R., McKinlay, L., & Boyd, R. N. (2014). Interventions to reduce behavioral problems in children with cerebral palsy: An RCT. *Pediatrics, 133*(5), e1249–e1257. Available from https://doi.org/10.1542/peds.2013-3620.

Whittingham, K., Sanders, M. R., McKinlay, L., & Boyd, R. N. (2016). Parenting intervention combined with acceptance and commitment therapy: A trial with families of children with cerebral palsy. *Journal of Pediatric Psychology, 41*(5), 531–542. Available from https://doi.org/10.1093/jpepsy/jsv118.

Whittingham, K., Wee, D., Sanders, M., & Boyd, R. (2013). Predictors of psychological adjustment, experienced parenting burden and chronic sorrow symptoms in parents of children with Cerebral Palsy. *Child: Care, Health and Development, 39*(3), 366–373.

Chapter 3

Connect: the parent–child relationship

Chapter Outline

Attachment theory 41
Attachment across cultures 44
How does parenting influence attachment? 45
A dyadic perspective 48
Emotional development and the parent–child relationship 51
Relationship and emotion-focused parenting intervention 53
A contextual behavioral perspective on attachment and emotional connection 54
Applying attachment, emotional availability, and meta-emotion theory to parenting 57
Chapter summary 58
References 58

When the first stars of evening appeared in the sky, Koala Lou crept home through the dark and up into the gum-tree. Her mother was waiting for her. Before she could say a word her mother flung her arms around her neck and said, "Koala Lou, I DO love you! I always have and I always will."

And she hugged her for a very long time.

-Mem Fox, *Koala Lou*

Life is best organized as a series of daring ventures from a secure base.

-John Bowlby

Piglet sidled up to Pooh from behind.

"Pooh!" he whispered.

"Yes, Piglet?"

"Nothing," said Piglet, taking Pooh's paw. "I just wanted to be sure of you."

-A.A. Milne, *The House at Pooh Corner*

Parenting is, first and foremost, a *relationship*—an emotional connection. Children *love* their parents. Parents *love* their children. Children need parents who love them, who are capable of forming an emotional connection with them. Children need to develop in the context of emotional

Acceptance and Commitment Therapy. DOI: https://doi.org/10.1016/B978-0-12-814669-9.00003-5
© 2019 Elsevier Inc. All rights reserved.

connections—psychological presence including affective signaling and attuned interactions—with others. The parent–child relationship is a loving relationship that is supported by parenting behaviors that both influence and are influenced by the child. It is important to remember that while attachment is often discussed as an entity, it is actually a dynamic, transactional exchange of behaviors between parent and child that can signal safety and security, or inconsistency and incoherence.

For children, the parent–child relationship is the first relationship. The child's most basic understandings of how relationships work will develop in the context of their relationship with their parents. Unsurprisingly, the transactional process that we know as attachment and emotional availability is implicated in the development of social competence and psychological well-being. The experiences of downregulation of the threat system via the stimulation of the affiliative system through the affective signaling within the parent and child relationship become the template for how children learn to downregulate their own threat system as well as how to signal need and receive love and care in other relationships across their lifetime (Gilbert, 2009).

Attachment has a number of functions including:

- maintaining physical proximity between parent and child (and hence maintaining the child's safety);
- maintaining psychological proximity between parent and child through attuned interactions—contingent interactions in which the parent mirrors the child's psychological state (and hence providing the learning needed for the development of intersubjectivity and, later, language);
- a "validity check" that the child is learning from a trusted source;
- affective signaling with the child's threat system downregulated through the stimulation of the child's affiliative system;
- supporting the facilitation of optimal child development thorough exploration of the world and learning from others including play;
- supporting children's developing ability to track their experiences and developing a template for adaptive social behavior;
- supporting entry into the symbolic world including learning language; and
- supporting the child's psychological well-being.

Within the parent–child attachment relationship the parent acts as both a *safe haven* for the child when under threat and as a *secure base* for the child's exploration (Bowlby, 1958, 1982, 1988). That is, the parent responds to the child's bids for nurturance; comforting and soothing the child, answering the child's affective signals with signals of safety and care. The parent's sensitive and attuned response to the child stimulates the child's affiliative system, downregulating the child's threat system and restoring parasympathetic balance (Gilbert, 2009). The parent also acts as a *secure base* for the child's exploration. Through predictable and consistent parenting, and parental proximity as a watchful gaze, the child's safety is optimized and the child *feels* safe and is able to explore their world. Further, as part of being a *secure base*, the parent nurtures child exploration and play. The parent shows interest in the child's exploration and inner world, reinforcing child exploration and play through attuned interaction and expressions of enjoyment and delight. The parent also encourages exploration, at times even *scaffolding* exploration and play. That is, the parent through encouragement, prompts, and joint play, supports the child so that the child is able to perform a task that he or she is incapable of doing alone—a task within the *zone of proximal development*, to use the Vygotskian term (Karimi-Aghdam, 2017). This supports the child's ongoing learning and development. For example, a parent and a child may do a puzzle together, a puzzle that the child could not complete alone. The parent lets the child lead and provides the needed *scaffolding* so that the child is able to complete the puzzle. "Do you think it'd be easier if we found the corner pieces first?" the parent might say. By supporting play and exploration, the parent supports a child's robust exploration of the world including the development of a broad, flexible repertoire of behavior, trial-and-error learning directly from the environment, and the development of tracking or developing verbal rules for understanding the natural consequences of actions. The "world" that the child explores is not just the physical world experienced through the five senses, but also, since humans are "languaging" creatures, the *symbolic* world, derived through verbal behavior.

As extraordinary as it may sound today and as bizarre as it might seem to many parents, the fact that children need an emotionally available and loving parent was previously unrecognized by scientists and professionals (Karen, 1998). The lack of a loving parent was not recognized, for example, as a factor in the failure of institutionalized children to thrive. In fact, some organizations using foster care deliberately moved children from home to home in order to prevent the formation of a bond, oblivious to the damage they were doing to children. Children's hospitals refused parental visitation or had strict visitation policies, sometimes allowing visits as infrequently as once a week. Institutions and hospitals feared infection and often had strict no-contact policies for staff to prevent infection spreading. Across the world, there were multiple researchers and clinicians attempting to draw attention to this issue, but extraordinarily, this was reacted to with skepticism by the majority of clinicians working with children (it is possible that the sheer scale of the suffering caused avoidance in staff so extreme they were unable to acknowledge the suffering at all). It was into this world that John Bowlby stepped in, with ideas that were radical and controversial and would be the seeds of attachment theory.

Attachment theory

Unlike his psychoanalytic contemporaries, and in common with contextualists, Bowlby was interested in how the *environment* of the child, in particular the emotional quality of the mother–child relationship, affected the child's psychological health and later adjustment (Bowlby, 1958, 1982, 1988; Karen, 1998). Working in a time when prolonged separations between mother and child were part of routine medical care, Bowlby became interested in the effects of this objective, measureable aspect of the environment on the child. Bowlby collected and synthesized the observations of professionals across the world who were calling for attention to maternal deprivation and the effects of parent–child separation, specifically the three stages he and others observed in children: protest, despair, and finally, detachment.

With time, Bowlby was also influenced by Konrad Lorenz's work on imprinting in birds, and Harry Harlow's research demonstrating that infant monkeys became attached, not to a wire "mother" with a nipple for feeding as was predicted by both psychodynamic and behavioral theories at the time, but to the soft, cloth "mother" who provided comfort but no milk (Harlow, 1958). In other words, attachment does not develop because the parent meets the baby's needs for nourishment. Instead, it is an affective exchange centering on *emotional* needs, particularly the providing of a *safe haven* through contact–comfort when under threat. The imprinting behavior of birds and the behaviors of infant monkeys toward the soft, cloth "mother" provided animal models for human attachment behavior. The infant's attachment system orients the child toward the attachment figure, prompting the child to seek proximity to and nurturance from the parent (Bowlby, 1958, 1982, 1988). From a contextual behavioral perspective, attachment behavior is any behavior with the *function* of obtaining proximity to and nurturance from the caregiver (Mansfield & Cordova, 2007).

The collaboration between Bowlby and Mary Ainsworth was key to shaping attachment theory into what we know today (Karen, 1998). Ainsworth's major contribution to attachment theory was the development of the Strange Situation procedure and the documentation of different attachment styles. The development of the Strange Situation procedure was grounded in detailed observations of mothers and infants first in Uganda and then in America. From these in-depth observations of mother–baby pairs, Ainsworth developed a detailed picture of attachment formation across infancy, including documenting the infant's use of the mother as a *secure base*. From this understanding, she developed the Strange Situation procedure as a standardized procedure to see attachment behavior in a laboratory setting and used it for the first time with American mothers and babies.

The Strange Situation procedure begins with the mother and the baby both present in a room with toys (Ainsworth, Bell, & Stayton, 1971; Ainsworth, Blehar, Waters, & Wall, 1978; Karen, 1998). A stranger enters and the mother leaves. The mother then returns and the stranger leaves. Then, the mother leaves the baby alone in the room. The stranger returns and attempts to comfort the baby. Finally, the mother returns. The Strange Situation is performed between the ages of 12 and 18 months and allows the infant's reactions to separation and reunion to be expressed and observed. Ainsworth originally observed three attachment styles. The secure attachment style, the most common attachment style in middle class American samples, is where the baby becomes distressed and protests separation, seeks comfort from the mother when the mother returns, and is comforted and calmed in her presence. A child with a *secure attachment* is balanced between exploration on the one hand, and maintaining connection to the attachment figure on the other.

Ainsworth also documented two anxious attachment styles (Ainsworth et al., 1971, 1978; Karen, 1998). The *anxious–ambivalent* attachment style is where the infant, during the Strange Situation, shows extreme distress upon separation and when reunited both seeks the mother and expresses anger and resistance. Children with anxious–ambivalent styles are hyperviligent to signs of rejection or abandonment, which distracts them from flexible exploration. The *avoidant attachment* style is where the infant, in the Strange Situation, appears nonchalant during separation and does not seek comfort from the mother in reunion, or may approach but then look away and not signal a desire to be picked up. Although avoidant children may appear independent, in Ainsworth's home observations the avoidant children were indistinguishable from the ambivalent children: they were both anxious and clingy at home. All three of the attachment styles documented by Ainsworth are effective in maximizing proximity and nurturance within the relationship between the child and the caregiver. That is, for anxious–ambivalent children, that behavioral pattern keeps their parents closer, and for anxious–avoidant children, that behavioral pattern keeps their parents closer. In other words, all of these forms of attachment lead to *predictable* interactions between parent and child.

To these three attachment styles a fourth was later added by Mary Main: *disorganized attachment* (Main & Soloman, 1986). Main proposed that disorganized attachment is likely to arise when the parent is behaving in a frightened, threatening, or disassociating manner, particularly when the cause is not comprehensible to the child because it isn't triggered by an external stimulus (Hesse & Main, 2006). Under such conditions children are caught in a bind: their attachment system tells them to seek refuge in their attachment figure, yet their attachment figure's behavior is triggering their threat system. Seek refuge or flee? Upon reunion in the Strange Situation infants with disorganized attachment may display fear, disorientation, or conflicted behavior (Grangvist et al., 2017). Disorganized attachment is common in children experiencing maltreatment, but it is not universal to children experiencing maltreatment, and there are pathways to disorganized attachment other than maltreatment, such as a parent's unresolved trauma or loss (e.g., a previous stillbirth). In fact, many parents of children displaying disorganized attachment may be sensitive and responsive outside their episodes of frightened, threatening, or disassociating behavior. At the age of six, children with disorganized attachment typically demonstrate a pattern of controlling their parent; for example, through coercive behavior or through role-reversal caretaking (Main & Cassidy, 1988).

Bowlby and Ainsworth argued that attachment behavior in humans has clear evolutionary advantages. Attachment maintains physical proximity to the parent, so that the parent can keep the child safe (Bowlby, 1958, 1982, 1988). Importantly, the fact that we are flexible cooperative breeders (i.e., people other than the biological mother are highly involved in childcare), meant that human children began seeking not just physical proximity but also *psychological* proximity or shared psychological contact with their caregivers (Hrdy, 2011). Affective signaling, and its association with feelings of safety and parasympathetic balance is something we have in common with other mammals. But humans take this further. We also have *attuned* interactions: contingent interactions in which the parent mirrors the child's psychological state. This attunement is exactly the right environment for an infant to learn intersubjectivity and later language.

In a 30-year longitudinal study on the long-term developmental sequelae of attachment, attachment security was shown to be associated with emotional regulation and social competence in middle childhood and adolescence, as well as with emotional quality of adult relationships and mental health in adulthood (Sroufe, 2005; Sroufe, Egeland, Carlson, & Collins, 2005). Consistent with attachment theory, children with ambivalent attachment were particularly challenged by contexts requiring flexibility and exploration; for example, they showed less flexibility on a problem-solving task during the preschool years. Children with avoidant attachment found interpersonal closeness challenging. Both anxious–ambivalent and anxious–avoidant attachment styles were associated with less teacher-rated independence in middle childhood however, they showed dependence in different ways. Ambivalent children openly elicited nurturance, while avoidant children approached in a roundabout way and often elicited controlling behavior from the teacher. A history of secure attachment in infancy buffered children against stress later in life, reducing the impact and enabling greater recovery. Although both ambivalent and avoidant attachment both predicted psychological disorders later in life, the majority of those children did not go on to develop a psychological disorder. Disorganized attachment was, however, a strong predictor of later psychological disorders, particularly dissociation. The parental care received at later time points was also important. For example, parental ability to support emerging autonomy was important during adolescence. Attachment security and care across the early childhood years predicts outcomes better than attachment security alone.

Attachment across cultures

Attachment theory is a universal theory. It is suggested that attachment phenomena is an evolved and hence universal aspect of human behavior, although it may present differently across cultures. There has been some controversy about how differing patterns of attachment styles in different cultural samples should be understood. Within the original middle-class American sample, the pattern of attachment styles was: 70% secure, 20% anxious–avoidant, and 10% anxious–ambivalent (Ainsworth et al., 1971; van IJzendoorn, 1990). Avoidant classifications have been found to be more common in western European samples, and ambivalent classfications more common in Israeli and Japanese samples (Van Ijzendoorn & Kroonenberg, 1998). However, a meta-analysis found that intracultural variation was *15 times greater* than intercultural variation. That is, aggregated samples from within particular countries were more similar to samples in *other* countries than other samples in the same country (i.e., there was more within-group variability than between-group variability).

That there is cross-cultural similarity in attachment styles is consistent with an investigation into beliefs about maternal sensitivity across cultures by Mesman and colleagues (Mesman et al., 2016). Although culture does, of course, influence parenting practices, there was remarkable convergence across cultures (26 cultural groups in 15 countries) regarding beliefs about maternal sensitivity (Mesman et al., 2016). In particular, the importance of maternal warmth and the ability of the mother to read the cues of her infant was stable across cultures. Effects of cultural group on sensitivity beliefs were largely—but not entirely—explained by sociodemographic variables such as whether families lived in a rural or an urban setting. Diversity in the spread of attachment styles across samples was likely underpinned by a number of factors, including culture, but also experiences of disadvantage and poverty, intergenerational transmission of trauma, rural or urban lifestyles, and the availability of specific provisions such as maternity leave. This complexity should not be simplified into "cultural values" as some cultural practices have developed to support survival in harsh environments and may quickly change if the environment changes.

How does parenting influence attachment?

The reciprocal system to the infant's attachment system is the parent's caregiving system. The caregiving system is our affiliative system—the site of affective signaling, social safety, and compassion (Gilbert, 2014). This system responds to the infant's attachment bids. In Ainsworth's original research, the mother and baby's behavior during home observations was also rated (Ainsworth et al., 1971, 1978; Karen, 1998). She found that the mothers of the insecure babies could be warm, loving, and competent in many ways. However, the mothers of the insecure babies were rated as poorer on four dimensions. The four key parenting dimensions that differentiated the mothers of secure and insecure babies were:

- *sensitivity* or responding to the baby's cues;
- *acceptance* of the baby;

- *cooperation* with the baby's rhythms and needs; and
- psychological *availability* to the baby.

All four of these parenting dimensions relate to psychological flexibility in various aspects, including shared psychological presence, experiential acceptance, flexible languaging, and flexible perspective taking (see relevant chapters). Parental sensitivity, in particular, has been demonstrated to be associated with child outcomes (Eshel, Daelmans, Cabral de Mello, & Martines, 2006), including the development of internalizing behavior (Kok et al., 2013). Although it is not the only factor, maternal sensitivity plays a significant role in the development of secure attachment (De Wolff & van IJzendoorn, 1997; van IJzendoorn, Goldberg, Kroonenberg, & Frenkel, 1992), and it is an important way attachment styles are transmitted across generations (Verhage et al., 2016). The soothing that children receive (or not) in response to their attachment behavior develops their affiliative system, consolidating their capacity to receive soothing from others, as well as their ability to soothe themselves (Gilbert, 2014).

From a contextual perspective, parental sensitivity can be understood as when the parent's caregiving behavior is under the contextual control of the infant's behavior or cues (Whittingham, 2014). That is, a sensitive, responsive parenting style is not merely warm, it is also *sensitive to the affective signaling of the child*. Sensitivity requires flexible perspective taking. It is easy to recognize when parenting is failing to be sensitive due to a lack of warmth. However, it can be challenging to recognize *warm* insensitive parenting in practice. Thinking through examples of warm insensitive responses in a romantic relationship can be helpful. Imagine that you are stressed and overloaded with tasks and you signal that to your romantic partner, appealing for help. A warm, sensitive response would be to assist with the tasks. That is, after all, what you are asking for. Responding to that bid for nurturance by purchasing a bunch of flowers would be warm but not sensitive because, as nice as flowers are as a romantic gesture, it just does not answer the need expressed in the bid. To be sensitive, the parent's caregiving must be more than warm and more than "nice." It must also *be sensitive to the moment-to-moment psychological state of the child*, it must take into account the child's perspective, it must respond to the child's needs, and it must be appropriately and flexibly timed to the child's ongoing psychological experiences.

Attunement occurs when the parent and child are sharing an experience, when they are emotionally in sync. During an *attuned* interaction the parent "mirrors" the child's psychological state. All parent and child dyads have moments of misattunement; the important thing is that misattunement is not the dominant theme of the relationship and that moments of misattunement are repaired. The *still-face paradigm* is a classic illustration of misattunement in infancy (Mesman, van Ijzendoorn, & Bakermans-Kranenburg, 2009). It also illustrates the importance of shared experience through affective signaling. In the still-face paradigm, the mother and baby initially interact normally, allowing for a baseline. Then the mother stops reacting to the infant and instead gives a blank, still face. Finally, the mother reacts normally again. A review and meta-analysis of the still-face paradigm confirmed the still-face effect: in response to the still face infants show a reduction in expressions of positive affect and gaze, as well as an increase in expressions of negative affect (Mesman et al., 2009). Infants who show a smaller still-face effect at 5 months are more likely to be securely attached at 1 year. Further, maternal sensitivity predicted infants' physiological response to the still-face paradigm at 5 months of age in an at-risk (poverty) sample (Conradt & Ablow, 2010). Literature examining the still-face effect in infants of depressed mothers is not clear (Mesman et al., 2009).

Empathic attunement, or a parent's awareness and acceptance of their child's thoughts and emotions-in-context, as linked with sensitive and responsive parenting in a sample of 128 30-month-old children (Coyne, Low, Miller, Seifer, & Dickstein, 2007). Empathic attunement includes the ability of parents to take the child's perspective flexibly, across situations and development, and to accurately track child behaviors-in-context so that parents are aware of, attuned to, and respond effectively to their children's thoughts and feelings. These processes map onto flexible perspective taking and shared psychological presence within the parent–child hexaflex (see the relevant chapters). It also includes an openness to and acceptance of inconsistent or novel information about one's child. Parents are able to track and incorporate different or unexpected behavior in their children so that their parenting behaviors develop and change in concordance with their child's growth and development of new skills. Parents are also open to and willing to receive, reflect, and empathize with a wide variety and valence of emotions, and shifts of emotion in different contexts, such that parents do not view their child in a rigid way; for example, as "angry all the time," or "always too emotional." These aspects of empathic attunement relate to the acceptance and flexible languaging aspects of the parent–child hexaflex (see the relevant chapters). Interestingly, mothers more attuned to their own emotions were also more attuned to their children, suggesting that a greater capacity for self-awareness and acceptance is related to a greater capacity for other awareness and acceptance. Additionally, maternal empathic attunement was negatively related to maternal depression (Coyne et al., 2007).

A parent's own history and attachment style impacts on the attachment style of their children both via parental sensitivity and through other pathways (known as the "transmission gap," the part of the transmission of attachment style that is unexplained by sensitivity; Verhage et al., 2016). The birth of a child and the continued parenting of a child naturally generate feelings in parents that are related to their own experiences in early attachment relationships. These learned responses within relationships are called *internal working models* (Bowlby, 1958, 1982, 1988), and include our emotive, cognitive, and behavioral action tendencies in response to relationships. Parents may respond to these experiences by trying to avoid them, or by being aware and accepting of them, understanding their origins. For parents with histories of insecure attachment themselves, whether or not they are aware and accepting of their own emotional reactions will impact on their ability to be sensitive and responsive parents, meeting their own children's attachment needs. Hence, experiential acceptance is relevant to understanding the transmission of attachment across generations. Even for parents who, overall, have a secure attachment style, elements of insecure attachment are likely to still be present, and hence awareness and acceptance are still important.

In addition to the parent's own attachment history, other parental risk factors may also impact on the development of the attachment relationship, including the parental mental health. Maternal risk factors have been shown to contribute more to the attachment classification than child risk factors (van IJzendoorn et al., 1992). Parenting practices, especially practices supporting proximity and physical contact, may also impact on the development of the attachment relationship by giving opportunities to repair maternal sensitivity. In an experimental study 49 low-income mothers were randomly assigned to receive either a soft baby carrier that enables baby wearing and close physical contact or a style of baby carrier that enables carrying the baby in a baby seat without physical contact. The mothers receiving the baby-wearing style of carrier showed greater contingent responsiveness at 3.5 months and their babies were more likely to be securely attached at 13 months (Ainsfeld, Capser, Nozyce, & Cunningham, 1990).

A dyadic perspective

Although parental factors are important in explaining the developing relationship between parent and child, child factors also matter, with attachment patterns developing in concert with the child's behaviors and characteristics (Groh et al., 2017). For example, there is an interplay between maternal sensitivity and infant irritability in response to the still-face paradigm. Maternal insensitivity and infant irritability both predict more extreme still-face effects, and there is an interactive effect with irritable infants with insensitive mothers doing worse still (Gunning, Halligan, & Murray, 2013). There is, therefore, a kind of mutual adaptation that must take place between parent and child. For some parents and children the differences may be wider, and greater adaptation needed. Not every parent and child is best suited to each other in terms of temperament and needs; for some, greater accommodation is necessary to bridge the gap.

The concept of "goodness of fit," developed by Thomas and Chess (1977), suggests that children have different temperaments—for example, inhibited and disinhibited—and thus demonstrate different patterns of behavior that then trigger different parental responses. For example, a particular child might be born with an inhibited temperament and a tendency to avoid novel situations. This temperament will bring out different responses in different parents: some parents might respond in a warm and sensitive way that nevertheless gently encourages approach, others in an emotionally dismissive or even harsh way, and others still in a warm, soothing manner that inadvertently reinforces avoidance. The first parent, who is warm, sensitive, and encouraging of approach is a "good fit," and with that parental response an inhibited child is likely to thrive. In contrast, an inhibited child with an emotionally dismissive parent or even a parent who is warm and soothing but inadvertently encourages reinforcement is a "bad fit." Nevertheless, a disinhibited child may thrive in such an environment. Sensitive and responsive parents are able to track their children's needs, given their particular patterns of strength and vulnerabilities, and even a sensitive parent may find this easier with some children than others. Goodness of fit between parent and child is relevant across different periods of development—that is, a particular parent and child might be a good fit in some developmental stages and not in others—and this is a potent predictor of outcome (Hipson & Seguin, 2016; Lerner, Lerner, & Zabski, 1985; Talwar, Nitz, & Lerner, 1990).

In addition, there is evidence to suggest that some individuals have a heightened sensitivity to the environment, for better or for worse, a kind of developmental receptivity to environmental effects (Ellis, Boyce, Belsky, Bakermans-Kranenburg, & van Ijzendoorn, 2011). That is, some children may be "dandelions"—hardier and less likely to suffer ill effects in less than optimal conditions, whereas others may be "orchids"—more sensitive to the environment, including more likely to suffer ill effects in less than optimal conditions but also more likely to thrive in optimal conditions. Within the population it is suggested that about 80%–85% of children are "dandelions," likely to thrive even in suboptimal conditions. However, the remaining 15%–20% are "orchids," and may not be as resilient if parental sensitivity and caregiving are less than optimal or in the presence of other stressors. The existence of "orchids" can be important for parents to understand: it may be exactly the challenging child who is benefiting the most from a parent's sensitive and responsive care in the sense that "orchids" are more sensitive to the environment including parenting. This has empirical support, with research showing that maternal parenting in infancy had a greater influence on first-grade adjustment for children who had difficult temperaments compared to children with less difficult temperaments (Stright, Gallagher, & Kelley, 2008).

Emotional availability theory is a fully dyadic viewpoint and an expansion upon attachment theory. Emotional availability refers to the emotional quality of a relationship, including the affect and behavior of both participants in the relationship (Biringen, 2009; Biringen, Derscheid, Vliegen,

Closson, & Easterbrooks, 2014). It is a multidimensional construct with four parent (or caregiver) dimensions: sensitivity, structuring, nonintrusiveness, and nonhostility; and two child dimensions: responsiveness and involvement. The concept and the associated observational scale can be applied across developmental stages, from infancy to adolescence (although there is less research to date on adolescents), and it offers a broader way to assess the emotional quality of a relationship beyond attachment–salient experiences of separation and distress. A fully dyadic understanding is taken of each of the dimensions. For example, parental sensitivity is not understood as a quality of the parent, but rather a pattern of interaction that shows up in the context of a particular relationship. The responsiveness of the child is needed for a parent to demonstrate optimal sensitivity.

Optimal sensitivity involves creating an overall positive and authentic affective climate within the relationship including accurate parental perception of the child's emotional expressions and behaviors and appropriate response to these (Biringen, 2009; Biringen et al., 2014). Structuring is the ability of the parent to guide, *scaffold*, and mentor the child. Nonintrusiveness is lack of interference, overdirection, or overprotection. It is dependent on the child's level of development and the feedback of the child. Nonhostility is the absence hostile responses including covert hostility such as nonverbal expressions of stress or frustration or boredom. Child responsiveness is the child's emotional and social responsiveness to the parent. Child involvement is the child's ability to appropriately (without reliance on negative behaviors) involve the parent in activity and play, to include the parent in interaction.

Emotional availability is related to attachment security (Ziv, Aviezer, Gini, Sagi, & Koren-Karie, 2000). In 687 Israeli parent–child dyads, dyads who were rated higher on the emotional availability observational assessment were more likely to have secure attachment as measured by the Strange Situation procedure. In particular, the mothers of secure infants were more sensitive and structuring and their infants were more responsive and involving. Emotional availability did not clearly distinguish between different types of attachment insecurity, but it is possible that this was because the study focused on observations of a play context, and attachment–salient observations may be necessary to make those distinctions. Emotional availability also distinguishes between depressed and nondepressed mothers (Vliegen, Luyten, & Biringen, 2009), with mother–infant dyads with depressed mothers showing poorer scores on all aspects of emotional availability except hostility. A quarter of the depressed mothers had sensitivity and structuring scores in the clinical risk zone. Further, more than half of the depressed mothers stopped the play interaction before 30 minutes, demonstrating the challenge for depressed mothers of interacting with their children (none of the nondepressed mothers stopped the interaction early). Emotional availability between parents and children has been shown to be associated with diverse child outcomes including child internalizing and externalizing behaviors, kindergarten readiness, and child empathy (Biringen, 2009; Biringen et al., 2014).

Emotional development and the parent–child relationship

How parents respond to their child's emotion and emotional expression impacts upon child development throughout childhood and adolescence, including emotional and social development, emotional regulation, and externalizing behavioral problems (Eisenberg, Cumberland, & Spinrad, 1998; Gottman, Katz, & Hoover, 1996, 1997; Johnson, Hawes, Eisenberg, Kohlhoff, & Dudeney, 2017). From infancy, sensitive caregiving moderates the infant's arousal and affective state. In early childhood, parental response to child emotion is crucial to a child's ongoing emotional development. Parenting that is dismissive, disapproving, or punishing of child emotional expression is associated with poorer child outcomes. Parenting that is *accepting*, that includes the verbal labeling of the child's emotions and includes *scaffolding* of appropriate behavior around emotions, is associated with better child emotional and social outcomes (Gottman et al., 1996, 1997; Katz, Wilson, & Gottman, 1999)

Gottman et al. (1997) dubbed parent's emotions and thoughts about their own and their child's emotion *meta-emotion*, and a parent's general approach to emotion *meta-emotion philosophy*. Optimal parental responses to a child's emotion have been called emotion coaching. In early to middle childhood, emotion coaching has five key components:

- *awareness of emotions* in themselves and their children including lower intensity emotions;
- viewing emotions, including negative emotions, as *opportunities for learning and intimacy*;
- *validating* children's emotions;
- *verbally labeling* or encouraging children to verbally label their emotions; and
- *problem solving* the situation with the child or *setting limits* on behavior.

Parents who do not use emotion coaching with their child are more likely to see negative emotions as harmful and to understand the expression of negative emotion itself, particularly anger, as a misbehavior and a reason for discipline.

Early childhood is a crucial time for emotional development. Anyone who has ever met a toddler knows that early childhood is a time marked by intense, powerful emotions and flamboyant emotional expression. In particular, early childhood is marked by frustration and anger. Anger, and other associated negative emotions, often go hand in hand with problematic behaviors, particularly temper tantrums (Giesbrecht, Miller, & Muller, 2010).

It is not surprising that this is the case. Young children are at once active and exploring the world, busy at attaining mastery, and also, paradoxically, quite dependent—even helpless—to control their environment. Further, they are still developing their perspective-taking and reasoning abilities. Without perspective taking, many of their parent's instructions must seem like the irrational demands of a dictator who is awesomely powerful, and repeatedly and deliberately inflicts the worst-possible state of affairs on everyone in the family for no good reason. Emotional development takes time. The complexities of emotion cannot be learned all at once and parents must be patient through the early childhood years.

Into late-middle childhood and adolescence, parental emotion coaching and emotional availability is likely to continue to be important. However, some adaptations are made with the increasing autonomy of the child (Greenberg, 2002). For example, in early childhood it is important that the parent *verbally label* or encourage the child to *verbally label their emotions*. The parent's *labeling of emotions* is crucial to the child developing the language to describe their emotional life. However, by late-middle childhood and certainly by adolescence, children can be expected to have developed a vocabulary for emotional expression. A parental labeling of the child's emotion may no longer be appropriate. Instead, it is the adolescent who leads in putting the emotional experience into words with the parent reflecting that, as a therapist does with an adult client. In problem-solving too, the parent should let their adolescent child lead in finding solutions, being a supportive presence as needed. As children age parents also need to be more careful about waiting for their child's invitation to engage in emotional discussion. For younger children, the display of emotion in front of the parent may be considered enough of an invitation. But into late-middle childhood and adolescence, parents need to be more watchful of opportunities for emotional discussions, waiting for clear invitations in order to show respect for their child's increasing autonomy and right to privacy.

It is often useful to distinguish between primary, secondary, and instrumental emotions (Greenberg, 2002). Primary emotions are our core and initial emotional reactions, and may be adaptive or maladaptive (e.g., reflecting earlier traumatic learning). Secondary emotions are our emotional reactions in reaction to our primary emotional reaction. This distinction can be important, because in interpersonal interactions, it is not unusual for our primary emotion to be masked by a secondary emotion. For example, a common scenario is for a primary emotional reaction of hurt to be quickly masked by anger. In such a situation, acknowledgment and *validation* of the hurt is most likely to shift the interaction in a positive direction. Instrumental emotions refer to learned emotional expressions, ways of affective signaling that have been reinforced in the past. For example, children who have learned that whining or crying increases the chances that they will get their own way. If an emotional expression is instrumental then the expression can be quickly turned off if required. Instrumental emotions should be validated not by validating the feigned emotion, but by recognizing and acknowledging the desire. For example, if the parent believes the child is putting on a sad display to push the parent into being allowed to stay longer at the park, instead of saying, "you are feeling sad," the parent can say, "you want to stay longer at the park." In such a situation, the parent might also *scaffold* and *shape* more adaptive behaviors by adding, "try asking in a normal, friendly voice and we'll see what we can do."

Optimal responsiveness is likely to be different for each emotion, because each emotion motivates us toward different actions (Greenberg, 2002). As a primary and adaptive emotion, sadness grieves, anger empowers, and fear supports escape from danger. Thus, optimal emotion coaching involves understanding the message in the emotion. An emotion-coaching parent recognizes, for example, that anger is saying "I'm offended" and asks what has offended the child. This is explored with acceptance and validation, even if the parent's own actions have offended the child. For fear, it is important that the parent does not humiliate or shame the child for feeling afraid. For sadness, it is important that the parent responds with tenderness, allowing grieving to take place.

Relationship and emotion-focused parenting intervention

Interventions grounded within attachment theory, emotional availability theory, and meta-emotion theory have been found to be effective (Biringen et al., 2014; Cassidy et al., 2017; Cohen et al., 1999; Duncombe et al., 2016; Havighurst, Wilson, Harley, & Prior, 2009; Kim, Woodhouse, & Dai, 2018; Muir, 1992; Wilson, Havighurst, & Harley, 2012). Attachment and emotional availability-based interventions may be focused on directly changing parental sensitivity or on changing the parent's internal working models of attachment, that is, the symbolic representations of the relationship for the parent (Cohen et al., 1999). The intervention often includes either video-based guidance or parent–child interactions in session, with the therapist exploring and supporting the parent's thoughts and feelings as they come up as well as guiding the parent in exploring the feelings and responses of the child. In a meta-analysis of interventions targeting parental sensitivity and infant attachment security with 70 included studies positive effects were confirmed for both parental sensitivity and infant attachment security, with interventions that improved parental sensitivity also improving infant attachment security (Bakermans-Kranenburg, van Ijzendoorn, & Juffer, 2003). The most successful interventions were moderate in length and focused on shifting the behavior of the parent.

Parenting intervention grounded in meta-emotion theory has also been shown to be effective in improving the emotion coaching of parents and improving child behavior (Havighurst et al., 2009; Wilson et al., 2012).

In one RCT, an meta-emotion-based parenting intervention was found to be equally effective as a behavioral parenting intervention for reducing child externalizing behavior (Duncombe et al., 2016). There was a moderating effect of age, with older children particularly benefiting from the meta-emotion-based parenting intervention according to teacher ratings.

A contextual behavioral perspective on attachment and emotional connection

From a contextual behavioral perspective, both direct and indirect conditioning influence the development of attachment styles and emotional–relational development (for a complete explanation of direct and indirect conditioning see the next chapter, Chapter 4, Shape: building a flexible repertoire). Looking at direct conditioning firstly, attachment behavior is shaped into attachment repertoires or attachment styles by the response of the parent (Mansfield & Cordova, 2007) in concert with the child's behaviors and characteristics (Groh et al., 2017). That is, the child learns, through direct conditioning, how to behave in order to maximize proximity to and nurturance from the parent. Attachment bids may be reinforced, ignored, or even punished by the parent, and this may occur in a predictable or an unpredictable way (for explanations of the terms "reinforce" and "punish" see Chapter 4, Shape: building a flexible repertoire). From a behavioral perspective, children with learning histories in which attachment bids were consistently reinforced more often than ignored or punished would be expected to develop patterns of behavior that we recognize as a secure attachment style. If responses of ignoring or punishment are probable than a form of insecure attachment may result. If there is a high probability of punishment then disorganized attachment is likely. Parents may also be very warm and nurturing, but their behaviors may be unpredictable, or not contingent on child responses. Predictability in parent–child responding itself appears to be an important reinforcer for children. When children's needs are met with swift and contingent parent responses consistently, they feel safe and protected. A lack of predictability may also lead to a disorganized attachment style in children, as they are unable to predict which behavior is likely to be effective.

Respondent conditioning, in which a biologically potent stimulus is paired with a neutral stimulus repeatedly, over time and comes to imbue the neutral stimulus with similar psychological properties (see the next chapter for a full explanation), also plays a role in parent–child relationship quality and emotional availability. For example, a parent who is punitive toward a child's emotions may come to be a conditioned cue for that child, leading to a child's *conditioned emotional response* of fear to the parent themselves. On the other hand, a child who expresses intense negative emotions and tantrums frequently may become aversive to parents, who then may either increase their efforts to overprotect or become avoidant when the child is expressing negative emotions.

Both child and parent emotional distress may also influence conditioning processes in parent-child dyads. Some parents may consistently respond to expressions of distress, but not to nondistressed bids, or vice versa. For example, in families of anxious children, anxious parents are more likely to be dismissive or critical of negative emotions, or intrusive and controlling in the presence of anxiety (McLeod & Weisz, 2005) and, as a result, anxious children may learn to show a different pattern of attachment behavior when anxious than when sad or content. Depressed parents are more likely to model more negative emotion and to be less responsive to positive emotion (Shaw et al., 2006). If depressed parents consistently respond to their child's negative emotions but not their positive emotions, the attachment interaction between parent and child may be different depending on whether the child is experiencing positive or negative emotion. This may be one mechanism explaining the greater vulnerability of children of depressed parents to depression (Silk, Shaw, Forbes, Lane, & Kovacs, 2006; Silk, Shaw, Skuban, Oland, & Kovacs, 2006). It is important to note that these relationships are likely bidirectional and transactional, with child behaviors leading to particular emotion socialization practices, as in depressed mothers (Forbes et al., 2008). Thus, children may develop behavioral patterns where they adaptively express and regulate certain emotions, but not others.

The development of attachment style is further complicated over the course of child development. Although this transactional pattern becomes solidified in early childhood, it plays out in continuing behavioral interactions in later childhood and adolescence. Attachment styles are not set in stone during infancy; rather we continue to learn throughout our lives. For instance, Wahler and Dumas (1986) suggest that child-initiated coercion in later childhood may be a bid to repair an unpredictable family environment. They based this thinking on the finding that mothers of conduct-disordered children were more consistent when their children were coercive vs. when they were not. This, Wahler reasoned, reduced children's sense of uncertainty (Wahler, 1994, 1997; Wahler & Dumas, 1986). Thus, a particular parent and child may, overall, fit one pattern of attachment and emotional availability in early childhood and a different pattern in middle childhood or adolescence. In addition, children have multiple attachment figures, even from infancy. Into middle childhood and adolescence, children's relationships with teachers, other non-kin caregivers, and peers may come to form part of the complexity of the child's attachment style and emotional learning. Hence, although we can understand attachment style as categorical, such that people can be classified as having overall a specific attachment style, the reality is more complex (Mansfield & Cordova, 2007). In reality, we demonstrate specific attachment behavioral patterns in the context of specific relationships, and we all have insecure attachment elements to our learning histories in one form or another.

Indirect or symbolic conditioning models are also relevant to the development of attachment styles and emotional learning. Indirect conditioning involves verbal behavior; i.e., learning in the absence of direct training. A key type of indirect conditioning is derived relational responding. Derived relational responding and relational frame theory (RFT) is a behavioral account of language, and is described in detail in the next chapter (Chapter 4, Shape: building a flexible repertoire). However, we will include a short explanation here. Humans can derive meaning from symbols based on context—if I know what "too hot" means, and I know what "fire" is, then I can derive that I should not touch a white-hot poker, even if I have no direct experience with it (Hayes, Barnes-Holmes, & Roche, 2001). Although I have never been burned by a white-hot poker, it has some of the psychological properties of "too hot" and "fire" for me—I might even experience a flush of fear if I feel I am too near the poker. Simply put, because we have language, we experience symbols as "the real thing." Derived relational responding gives our imaginations and abstract thinking their potency, and accounts for how we respond to our thoughts, in the absence of direct experience.

This type of learning is important to consider in attachment because it imbues the transactional pattern between parent and child with *meaning*. This can be seen, for example, in the importance of the *meaning* a parent ascribes to their child's behavior. A parent who reads an adolescent's irritable behavior as meaning the adolescent is distressed and acting that way as a bid for nurturance, is going to respond very differently to a parent who reads an adolescent's irritable behavior as meaning the adolescent is irrational and cranky. The symbolic representations of the parent are, thus, important to understanding parental sensitivity, emotional availability, and emotion-coaching behavior. From an RFT perspective, psychodynamic and cognitive constructs such as *internal working models* (Ammaniti, van, Speranza, & Tambelli, 2000; Bowlby, 1958, 1982, 1988), *mind-mindedness* (see Chapter 11, Flexible perspective taking) (Meins & Fernyhough, 2015; Meins, Fernyhough, Arnott, Leekam, & de Rosnay, 2013), and *empathic attunement* (Coyne et al., 2007) are *symbolic* representations. Such parental symbolic representations have been associated with children's adaptive behavior and psychological well-being (Walker, Wheatcroft, & Camic, 2012) over time (Meins, Centifanti, Fernyhough, & Fishburn, 2013). This too makes sense. From relationships, children learn not just a pattern of behavior through operant and respondent conditioning processes, but a rich set of symbolic representations of relationships, and this symbolic learning also influences their ongoing pattern of behavior. Some aspects of parenting intervention focus on shifting the meaning of the child's behavior for the parent (i.e., shifting the parent's symbolic representations) in order to bring about downstream change in the parent's behavior, and hence also, on the child's outcomes.

Perhaps more importantly, "derived relational responding" not only imbues attachment with meaning, but also underlies the development of a symbolic representation of the world—including the child's understanding of "self," and of how the child relates with and to others (McHugh, Stewart, & Almada, 2019). The attachment system orients the child not merely toward physical proximity but also toward *psychological* proximity (Hrdy, 2011). Human infants seek out shared psychological presence with their caregivers in the form of *attuned interaction*; and attuned, contingent interaction in which the parent mirrors the child's psychological state is a potent reinforcer. For example, this process of an attuned pattern of interaction facilitates joint gaze, which is "the practice of sharing attention (usually visual) by following the focus of another person's attention or by drawing their attention to one's own focus of attention" (Farrant & Zubrick, 2011; Williams, Whiten, Suddendorf, & Perrett, 2001). First, joint attention between parent and infant is an outcome in and of itself; next, it facilitates the development of emotional reciprocity, and "mutual regulation of emotions and interests", all of which are foundational to the development of language (Farrant & Zubrick, 2011). Facilitation of joint gaze or joint attention is crucial to the development of language insofar that it allows mothers to guide their infants' gaze toward an object that they find meaningful, such that they can then name the object (Baldwin, 1993a, b; Baldwin, Markman, Bill, Desjardins, & Irwin, 1996). Baldwin (1993a, b) and Baldwin et al. (1996) suggested that this joint-attention skill facilitates the vast vocabulary expansion that occurs at around 18–20 months when children learn that words or symbols refer to objects, and 24-month-olds' ability to learn word–object relations even when the object is temporarily out of sight of the child and/or adult when the novel word is spoken (Scofield & Behrend, 2011). Thus, symbolic learning including language rests on the bedrock of learned intersubjectivity, learned through attuned interaction.

Applying attachment, emotional availability, and meta-emotion theory to parenting

The attachment, emotional availability, and meta-emotion literature can be understood as resulting in the following *principles* for parenting:

1. Parents should cultivate a sensitive, responsive pattern of parenting. That is, a style of parenting that is warm and also *sensitive to the child's ongoing psychological experiences*, that answers their child's bids for nurturance, and takes into account their child's needs.
2. Parents should cultivate *awareness and acceptance* of their own and their child's emotions. This should include acknowledging, empathizing with, and validating their child's expressed emotions.
3. Parents should minimize as much as possible intrusive, emotion-dismissive, and punitive parenting behavior.

Chapter summary

The psychological availability of the parent to the child—and the emotional availability within the parent–child relationship—is a core bedrock for child development. Attachment and emotional availability can be understood from a contextual perspective. In the next chapter, *Shape*, we will explore the behavioral theories and research in depth.

References

Ainsfeld, E., Capser, V., Nozyce, M., & Cunningham, N. (1990). Does infant carrying promote attachment? An experimental study of the effects of increased physical contact on the development of attachment. *Child Development*, *61*(5), 1617–1627.

Ainsworth, M. D. S., Bell, S. M., & Stayton, D. J. (1971). Individual differences in Strange Situation behavior of one-year-olds. In H. R. Scaffer (Ed.), *The origins of human social relations*. London: Academic Press.

Ainsworth, M. D. S., Blehar, M. C., Waters, E., & Wall, S. (1978). *Patterns of attachment: A psychological study of the strange situation*. Hillsdale, NJ: Erlbaum.

Ammaniti, M., van, I. M. H., Speranza, A. M., & Tambelli, R. (2000). Internal working models of attachment during late childhood and early adolescence: An exploration of stability and change. *Attachment & Human Development*, *2*(3), 328–346.

Bakermans-Kranenburg, M. J., van Ijzendoorn, M. H., & Juffer, F. (2003). Less is more: Meta-analyses of sensitivity and attachment interventions in early childhood. *Psychological Bulletin*, *129*(2), 195–215.

Baldwin, D. A. (1993a). Early referential understanding: Infants' ability to recognise refential acts for what they are. *Developmental Psychology*, *29*(5), 832–843.

Baldwin, D. A. (1993b). Infants' ability to consult the speaker for clues to word reference. *Journal of Child Language*, *20*(2), 395–418.

Baldwin, D. A., Markman, E. M., Bill, B., Desjardins, R. N., & Irwin, J. M. (1996). Infants' reliance on a social criterion for establishing word-object relations. *Child Development*, *67*(6), 3135–3153.

Biringen, Z. (2009). *The universal language of love*. Boulder: EA Press.

Biringen, Z., Derscheid, D., Vliegen, N., Closson, L., & Easterbrooks, M. A. (2014). Emotional availability (EA): Theoretical background, empirical research using the EA Scales and clinical applications. *Developmental Review*, *34*(2), 114–167, epub ahead of print.

Bowlby, J. (1958). The nature of the child's ties to his mother. *International Journal of Psychoanalysis*, *39*, 350–373.

Bowlby, J. (1982). *Attachment and loss: Attachment* (Vol. 1). New York: Basic Books.

Bowlby, J. (1988). *A secure base: Parent–child attachment and healthy human development*. New York: Basic Books.

Cassidy, J., Brett, B. E., Gross, J. T., Stern, J. A., Martin, D. R., Mohr, J. J., & Woodhouse, S. S. (2017). Circle of Security-Parenting: A randomized controlled trial in Head Start. *Developement and Psychopathology*, *29*(2), 651–673.

Cohen, N. J., Muir, E., Lojkasek, M., Muir, R., Parker, C. J., Barwick, M., & Brown, M. (1999). Watch, wait and wonder: Testing the effectiveness of a new approach to mother-infant psychotherapy. *Infant Mental Health Journal*, *20*(4), 429–451.

Conradt, E., & Ablow, J. (2010). Infant physiological response to the still-face paradigm: Contributions of maternal sensitivity and infants' early regulatory behavior. *Infant Behavior and Development*, *33*(3), 251–265.

Coyne, L. W., Low, C. M., Miller, A. L., Seifer, R., & Dickstein, S. (2007). Mothers' empathic understanding of their toddlers: Associations with maternal depression and sensitivity. *Journal of Child and Family Studies*, *16*(4), 483–497.

De Wolff, M., & van IJzendoorn, M. H. (1997). Sensitivity and attachment: A meta-analysis on parental antecedents of infant attachment. *Child Development*, *68*(4), 571–591.

Duncombe, M. E., Havighurst, S. S., Kehoe, C. E., Holland, K. A., Frankling, E. J., & Stargatt, R. (2016). Comparing an emotion- and a behavior-focused parenting program as part of a multsystemic intervention for child conduct problems. *Journal of Clinical Child & Adolescent Psychology*, *45*(3), 320–334.

Eisenberg, N., Cumberland, A., & Spinrad, T. L. (1998). Parental socialization of emotion. *Psychological Inquiry*, *9*(4), 241–273.

Ellis, B. J., Boyce, W. T., Belsky, J., Bakermans-Kranenburg, M. J., & van Ijzendoorn, M. H. (2011). Differential susceptibility to the environment: An evolutionary–neurodevelopmental theory. *Development and Psychopathology*, *23*(1), 7–28.

Eshel, N., Daelmans, B., Cabral de Mello, M., & Martines, J. (2006). Responsive parenting: Interventions and outcomes. *Bulletin of the World Health Organisation*, *84*(12), 991–998.

Farrant, B. M., & Zubrick, S. R. (2011). Early vocabulary development: The importance of joint attention and parent–child book reading. *First Language*, *32*(3), 1–22.

Forbes, E. E., Shaw, D. S., Silk, J. S., Feng, X., Cohn, J. F., Fox, N. A., & Kovacs, M. (2008). Children's affect expression and frontal EEG asymmetry: Transactional associations with mothers' depressive symptoms. *Journal of Abnormal Child Psychology*, *36*(2), 207–221.

Giesbrecht, G. F., Miller, M. R., & Muller, U. (2010). The anger-distress model of temper tantrums: Associations with emotional reactivity and emotional competence. *Infant and Child Development*, *19*, 478–497.

Gilbert, P. (2009). *The compassionate mind*. London: Little, Brown Book Group.

Gilbert, P. (2014). The origins and nature of compassion focused therapy. *British Journal of Clinical Psychology*, *53*(1), 6–41.

Gottman, J. M., Katz, L. F., & Hoover, C. (1996). Parental meta-emotion philosophy and the emotional life of families: Theoretical models and preliminary data. *Journal of Family Psychology*, *16*(3), 243–268.

Gottman, J. M., Katz, L. F., & Hoover, C. (1997). *Meta-emotion: How families communicate emotionally*. Mahwah, NJ: Lawrence Erlbaum Associates.

Grangvist, P., Sroufe, A. L., Dozier, M., Hesse, E., Steele, M., Van Ijzendoorn, M. H., ... Duschinsky, R. (2017). Disorganized attachment in infancy: A review of the phenomemon and its implications for clinicians and policy-makers. *Attachment and Human Development*, *19*(6), 534–558.

Greenberg, L. S. (2002). *Emotion-focused therapy*. Washington DC: American Psychological Association.

Groh, A. M., Narayan, A. J., Bakermans-Kranenburg, M. J., Roisman, G. I., Vaughn, B. E., Pasco Fearon, R. M., & van Ijzendoorn, M. H. (2017). Attachment and temperament in the early life course: A meta-analytic review. *Child Development*, *88*(3), 770–795.

Gunning, M., Halligan, S. L., & Murray, L. (2013). Contributions of maternal and infant factors to infant responding to the still face paradigm: A longitudinal study. *Infant Behavior and Development*, *36*(3), 319–328.

Harlow, H. F. (1958). The nature of love. *American Psychologist*, *13*, 673–685.

Havighurst, S. S., Wilson, K. R., Harley, A. E., & Prior, M. R. (2009). Tuning in to kids: An emotion-focused parenting program—Initial findings from a community trial. *Journal of Community Psychology*, *37*(8), 1008–1023.

Hayes, S. C., Barnes-Holmes, D., & Roche, B. (2001). *Relational frame theory: A Post-Skinnerian account of human language and cognition*. New York: Plenum Press.

Hesse, E., & Main, M. (2006). Frightened, threatening, and dissociative parental behavior in low risk samples: Description, discussion and interpretations. *Development and Psychopathology, 18*(2), 309–346.

Hipson, W. E., & Seguin, D. G. (2016). Goodness of fit between daycare teacher–child relationships, temperament and prosocial behavior. *Early Child Development and Care, 186*(5), 785–798.

Hrdy, S. B. (2011). *Mothers and others*. Cambridge: Harvand University Press.

Johnson, A. M., Hawes, D. J., Eisenberg, N., Kohlhoff, J., & Dudeney, J. (2017). Emotion socialization and child conduct problems: A comprehensive review and meta-analysis. *Clinical Psychological Review, 54*, 65–80.

Karen, R. (1998). *Becoming attached*. Oxford: Oxford University Press.

Karimi-Aghdam, S. (2017). Zone of proximal development (ZPD) as an emergent system: A dynamic systems theory perspective. *Integrative Psychological and Behavioral Science, 51*, 76–93.

Katz, L. F., Wilson, B., & Gottman, J. M. (1999). *Meta-emotion philosophy and family adjustment: Making an emotional connection. Conflict and cohesion in families: Causes and consequences*. Mahwah, NJ: Lawrence Erlbaum Associates Publishers.

Kim, M., Woodhouse, S. S., & Dai, C. (2018). Learning to provide children with a secure base and a safe haven: The Circle of Security-Parenting (COS-P) group intervention. *Journal of Clinical Psychology, 74*(8), 1319–1332.

Kok, R., Linting, M., Bakermans-Kranenburg, M. J., van Ijzendoorn, M. H., Jaddoe, V. W., Hofman, A., … Tiemeier, H. (2013). Maternal sensitivity and internalizing problems: Evidence from two longitudinal studies in early childhood. *Child Psychiatry & Human Development, 44*(6), 751–765.

Lerner, J. V., Lerner, R. M., & Zabski, S. (1985). Temperament and elementary school children's actual and rated academic performance: A test of a 'goodness-of-fit' model. *Jounral of Child Psychology and Psychiatry, 26*(1), 125–136.

Main, M., & Cassidy, J. (1988). Categories of response to reunion with the parent at age 6: Predictable from infant attachment classifications and stable over a 1 month period. *Developmental Psychology, 24*(3), 415–426.

Main, M., & Soloman, J. (1986). Discovery of an insecure-disorganised/disoriented attachment pattern. In T. B. Brazelton, & M. W. Yogman (Eds.), *Affective development in infancy* (pp. 95–124). Westport: Ablex Publishing.

Mansfield, A. K., & Cordova, J. V. (2007). A behavioral perspective on adult attachment style, intimacy, and relationship health. In D. W. Woods, & J. W. Kanter (Eds.), *Understanding behavior disorders: A contemporary behavioral perspective*. Reno: Context Press.

McHugh, L., Stewart, I., & Almada, P. (2019). *A Contextual Behavioral Guide to the Self: Theory and Practice*. California: Context Press, 232 pages.

McLeod, B. D., & Weisz, J. R. (2005). The therapy process observational coding system-allilance scale: Measure characteristics and prediction of outcome in usual clinical practice. *Journal of Consulting and Clinical Psychology, 73*(2), 323–333.

Meins, E., Centifanti, L. C., Fernyhough, C., & Fishburn, S. (2013). Maternal mind-mindedness and children's behavioral difficulties: Mitigating the impact of low socioeconomic status. *Journal of Abnormal Child Psychology, 41*(4), 543–553.

Meins, E., & Fernyhough, C. (2015). *Mind-mindedness coding manual, version 2.2*. Unpublished manuscript, University of York, York.

Meins, E., Fernyhough, C., Arnott, B., Leekam, S. R., & de Rosnay, M. (2013). Mind-mindedness and theory of mind: Mediating roles of language and perspectival symbolic play. *Child Development, 84*, 1777–1790.

Mesman, J., van Ijzendoorn, M., Behrens, K., Carbonell, O. A., Cárcamo, R., Cohen-Paraira, I., ... Zreik, G. (2016). Is the ideal mother a sensitive mother? Beliefs about early childhood parenting in mothers across the globe. *International Journal of Behavioral Development, 40* (5), 385–397.

Mesman, J., van Ijzendoorn, M. H., & Bakermans-Kranenburg, M. J. (2009). The many faces of the Still-Face Paradigm: A review and meta-analysis. *Developmental Review, 29*(2), 120–162.

Muir, E. (1992). Watching, waiting, and wondering: Applying psychoanalytic principals to mother–infant intervention. *Infant Mental Health Journal, 13*(4), 319–328.

Scofield, J., & Behrend, D. A. (2011). Clarifying the role of joint attention in early word learning. *First Language, 31*(3), 326–341.

Shaw, D. S., Schonberg, M., Sherrill, J., Huffman, D., Lukon, J., Obrosky, D., & Kovacs, M. (2006). Responsivity to offspring's expression of emotion among childhood-onset depressed mothers. *Journal of Clinical and Child Adolescent Psychology, 35*(4), 490–503.

Silk, J. S., Shaw, D. S., Forbes, E. E., Lane, T. L., & Kovacs, M. (2006). Maternal depression and child internalizaing: The moderating role of child emotion regulation. *Journal of Clinical and Child Adolescent Psychology, 35*(1), 116–126.

Silk, J. S., Shaw, D. S., Skuban, E. M., Oland, A. A., & Kovacs, M. (2006). Emotion regulation strategies in offspring of childhood-onset depressed mothers. *Journal of Child Psychology and Psychiatry, 47*(1), 69–78.

Sroufe, A. L. (2005). Attachment and development: A prospective, longitudinal study from birth to adulthood. *Attachment & Human Development, 7*(4), 349–367.

Sroufe, A. L., Egeland, B., Carlson, E. A., & Collins, W. A. (2005). *The development of the person: The Minnesota study of risk and adaptation from birth to adulthood.* New York: Guilford Publications.

Stright, A. D., Gallagher, K. C., & Kelley, K. (2008). Infant temperament moderates relations between maternal parenting in early childhood and children's adjustment in first grade. *Child Development., 79*(1), 186–200.

Talwar, R., Nitz, K., & Lerner, R. M. (1990). Relations among early adolescent temperament, parent and peer demands, and adjustment: A test of the goodness of fit model. *Journal of Adolescence, 13*(3), 279–298.

Thomas, A., & Chess, S. (1977). *Temperament and development*. New York: Brunner/Mazel.

van IJzendoorn, M. H. (1990). Developments in cross-cultural research on attachment: Some methodological notes. *Human Development, 33*, 3–9.

van IJzendoorn, M. H., Goldberg, S., Kroonenberg, P. M., & Frenkel, O. J. (1992). The relative effects of maternal and child problems on the quality of attachment: A meta-analysis of attachment in clinical samples. *Child Development, 63*(4), 840-458.

Van Ijzendoorn, M. H., & Kroonenberg, P. M. (1998). Cross-cultural patterns of attachment: Aa meta-analysis of the strange situation. *Child Development, 59*, 147–156.

Verhage, M. L., Schuengel, C., Madigan, S., Fearon, R. M. P., Oosterman, M., Cassibba, R., ... van, I. M. H. (2016). Narrowing the transmission gap: A synthesis of three decades of research on intergenerational transmission of attachment. *Psychological Bulletin, 142*(4), 337–366.

Vliegen, N., Luyten, P., & Biringen, Z. (2009). A multimethod perspective on emotional availability in the postpartum period. *Parenting: Science and Practice, 9*(3-4), 228–243.

Wahler, R. G. (1994). Child conduct problems: Disorder in conduct or social continuity? *Journal of Child and Family Studies*, *3*(2), 143–156.

Wahler, R. G. (1997). On the origins of children's compliance and opposition: Family context, reinforcement, and rules. *Journal of Child and Family Studies*, *6*(2), 191–208.

Wahler, R. G., & Dumas, J. E. (1986). Maintenace factors in coercive mother–child interactions: The compliance and predicatability hypotheses. *Jounral of Applied Behavior Analysis*, *19*(1), 13–22.

Walker, T. M., Wheatcroft, R., & Camic, P. M. (2012). Mind-mindedness in parents of preschoolers: A comparison between clinical and community samples. *Clinical Child Psychology and Psychiatry*, *17*(3), 318–335.

Whittingham, K. (2014). Parenting in context. *Journal of Contextual Behavioral Science*, *3*(3), 212–215.

Williams, J. H. G., Whiten, A., Suddendorf, T., & Perrett, D. I. (2001). Imitation, mirror neurons and autism. *Neuroscience and Biobehavioral Reviews*, *25*(4), 298-295.

Wilson, K. R., Havighurst, S. S., & Harley, A. E. (2012). Tuning in to kids: An effectiveness trial of a parenting program targeting emotion socialization of preschoolers. *Journal of Family Psychology*, *26*(1), 56–65.

Ziv, Y., Aviezer, O., Gini, M., Sagi, A., & Koren-Karie, N. (2000). Emotional availability in the mother–infant dyad as related to the quality of infant–mother attachment relationship. *Attachmant & Human Development*, *2*(2), 149–169.

Chapter 4

Shape: building a flexible repertoire

Chapter Outline

Direct conditioning: respondent and operant conditioning 66
Respondent conditioning 66
Operant conditioning 67
Indirect conditioning: modeling, derived relational responding, and rule-governed behavior 72
Problematic behavior patterns in families: coercive cycles 76
Functional analysis of behavior 76
Supporting behavior change 79
Respondent conditioning strategies 79
Operant conditioning strategies: antecedent and consequent manipulation strategies 79
Antecedent strategies 79
Consequence strategies 81
Behavioral parenting intervention 86
Research on acceptance and commitment therapy/relational frame theory and parenting 87
Acceptance and commitment therapy for parent psychological well-being 87
Acceptance and commitment therapy for augmentation for behavioral parenting interventions 88
Acceptance and commitment therapy for parenting/child behaviors 89
Three key behavior principles in shaping adaptive child behavior 90
Connect and shape 90
Chapter summary 95
References 95

Through others we become ourselves.

—Lev S. Vygotsky

We are only just beginning to understand the power of love because we are just beginning to understand the weakness of force and aggression.

—B.F. Skinner

What goes around, comes around.

—Common saying

I've missed more than 9,000 shots in my career. I've lost almost 300 games. 26 times I've been trusted to take the game's winning shot and missed. I've failed over and over and over again in my life and that's why I succeed.

—Michael Jordan

Acceptance and Commitment Therapy. DOI: https://doi.org/10.1016/B978-0-12-814669-9.00004-7

© 2019 Elsevier Inc. All rights reserved.

A core aspect of parenting is raising flexible, connected children with broad and flexible behavioral repertoires capable of effective action within the contexts in which they live. *Shaping* is a process through which novel, complex behavior is developed through the reinforcement of a series of successive approximations. It is a powerful tool in behavior change, and is a key aspect of parenting children. In the previous chapter, we discussed the importance of connection; specifically, establishing the parent as a secure base for a child through shaping, or consistent reinforcement of an ongoing, transactional series of behaviors between the dyad. Shaping connection, as we saw, is not only important to children's emerging emotion regulation and social competence, but it is also the conduit for entry into the symbolic world, a template for future relationships, and key to nurturing a child's understanding of the self. For example, as discussed in the previous chapter, children learn language via parent responses: first, parents respond consistently and sensitively to infant burbles, coos, and gestures, reinforcing the infant's expression. Next, parents evoke and reinforce joint attention, which underpins the receptive and expressive language and thus supports the development of a symbolic understanding of the world and a sense of self. This sets the stage for communication of complex and abstract ideas. What begins as cooing turns to "ma! ma!" to "milk" to "I'm hungry" and, eventually, to "I'd like to have my friends over for dinner Saturday night. Do you think we could get pizza from that place on Main Street? Chloe says their pizza is awesome." It is worth noting that the shaping of these complex social behaviors and symbolic responding in children—whether or not this is done consciously—occurs through contextually sensitive parental reinforcement that continues throughout childhood and adolescence.

Our view of shaping is informed by evolutionary and contextual behavioral perspectives. From an evolutionary perspective, behaviors that are effective are selected and become more probable; those that do not work for a child are not, and become rare or extinguish. Behaviors are evoked by context, which supports flexibility in one's behavioral repertoire: for example, children may learn to behave respectfully to their teachers, but to be rowdy and silly at home with their siblings. Shaping is a developmental and, often a social process: an individual acts and another reinforces. Since situational and social demands on a child also change across development, it is necessary for the reinforcement of behaviors to be dynamic—sensitive and responsive to changing developmental needs. For example, parents of young children may shape safety behaviors when crossing a street: *Look both ways, always!* In adolescents, parents might shape mindful risk- taking to encourage thorough exploration of the world: *Why don't you give it a go?* Once a behavior is mastered, the next, more evolved and complex iteration is reinforced, and so on. While simple behaviors become increasingly complex, the repertoire of the child broadens and becomes increasingly flexible as necessary across various situations and environments.

In order to understand and fully support the process of shaping in parent–child interaction, it is important to comprehend the process of learning. Specifically, two behavioral theories explain the process of learning: direct and indirect conditioning. *Direct conditioning*, which encompasses Respondent and Operant conditioning, refers to learning processes in which an organism is learning through direct contact with the environment. Simply put, one learns that fire is hot by touching a flame. *Indirect conditioning*, on the other hand, encompasses the symbolic world, and refers to processes by which organisms learn *indirectly*, either through modeling, or through contact with *verbal rules* that describe actual contingencies. In other words, a child may learn *not* to touch a flame because she observes that her mother is very careful around fire, and tells her, "Don't touch—it's hot!" The contingency, or *"if–then"* relationship between behavior and consequences, embedded in this rule, is *if I touch the fire, I will get burned.*

Both classes of conditioning are implicated in child development and parent–child interaction. Both assume that behavior has a lawful relationship to the environment, and that we only understand the "why" of behavior in terms of its *function*, or its effect on the environment. As such, both approaches posit that behavior is predictable and malleable. Said another way, behavior always *makes sense:* we continue to engage in behavior because it has a predictable, *desirable* function. From an evolutionary perspective, behaviors continue because they are selected; behaviors cease because they are not successful. From this perspective, we can consider cultural shifts—for example, our current fascination with technology and screens and memes—as the evolution of social behavior mediated by belonging, a powerful social reward. We get the "in joke"; thus we are part of a whole, and this brings us coherence and comfort. Considered in this way, we can observe these processes operating from the level of a single parent–child dyad to whole societies.

It is critical to comprehend that we can't understand behavior in the absence of context. Moreover, in order to understand if our perception of why a behavior occurs is correct, we must take on a pragmatic viewpoint—in short, we need to understand how the behavior *works for an individual, given their learning history, in their present context* (Hayes, Strosahl, & Wilson, 2003). Behavioral models of learning, therefore, give us access to specific strategies that allow us to not only describe and explain behavior, but to influence it with precision, scope, and depth (Hayes, Barnes-Holmes, & Wilson, 2012; Hayes et al., 2003). Although a thorough overview of models of learning is beyond the scope of this chapter, we provide a basic summary that will help inform clinical perspectives on learning processes, and in the use of shaping, in parent–child interaction. In the service of illustrating how these processes work in a practical way, consider the following parent–child interaction.

Parent–child interaction: Rosa and Gabriela

Rosa and her daughter Gabriela, who is 12, are getting ready to go to dance class. Gabriela drags her feet, getting ready slowly, taking her time to put on her dance clothes. Rosa gets more and more frustrated. "Hurry UP," she yells upstairs. "You are making us LATE!!" She knows that Gabriela gets anxious about class, and when she arrives late and all the other students notice her coming in, her anxiety intensifies. But she takes her time every time they go to class. Rosa can't understand it! *She just makes it so much worse for herself.* There is no response from upstairs, so Rosa pounds up the steps and bursts into Gabriela's room. *"What are you doing? WILL YOU HURRY UP Gabriela!! I don't understand why you do this!"* Gabriela, who is sitting on her bed, jumps up and gets right in her mother's face. "Leave me ALONE!" she screams. "I DON'T WANT TO GO!" She raises a hand as if to hit her mother. Rosa, shrinks back, shocked. Gabriela's tears begin. Rosa says quietly, "I can see you are not ready. We might as well just not go." She backs out of the room, closes Gabriella's door, and heads back downstairs. She feels tense and anxious being near Gabriela in her room, and needs to take some space.

Direct conditioning: respondent and operant conditioning

Respondent conditioning

Respondent conditioning (or associative, Pavlovian, or classical conditioning) is the process by which previously neutral cues take on the psychological properties of potent stimuli and come to elicit conditioned reflexive behaviors (Dixon & Rehfeldt, 2018). We are born with unconditioned responses (UR) to stimuli that have potent evolutionary value—threat, sex, hunger, for example. UR are simple reflexive behaviors like eyeblinks or salivation that are mediated by the autonomic nervous system and do not have to be learned. A conditioned response (CR) develops when a neutral stimulus (NS) has been repeatedly paired with and consistently predicts an unconditioned stimulus (US). With multiple pairings in which the neutral cue predicts the US, the NS takes on the psychological properties of the US even in its absence, thus becoming a conditioned stimulus (CS) and eliciting the CR. For example, a newborn baby will show an UR of rooting (searching for the nipple) in response to hunger (US). Week old babies will show a CR of rooting (searching for the nipple) in response to various CS including their mother's smell or being held in positions that they have come to associate with feeding.

It is important to note that conditioned emotional responses (CER) can arise through respondent conditioning processes. For example, if a parent uses punitive discipline with a child, over time, that parent's presence alone will come to elicit fear or unease in a child. This aspect of respondent conditioning is implicated in many behavioral issues; for example, the development of anxiety disorders (Allen, 2016; Bouton, Mineka, & Barlow, 2001; Mineka & Zinbarg, 2006; Mowrer, 1939). Respondent conditioning is also important to understanding trauma (VanElzakker, Dahlgren, Davis, Dubois, & Shin, 2014; Wicking et al., 2016) and in general emotional responses to ambiguous stimuli (Bishop, 2007; Bouton, 1988; Donley & Rosen, 2017). Rapid emotional shifts in reaction to ambiguous stimuli (e.g., an exaggerated startle response to an unspecified loud noise) may be under respondent stimulus control.

In our vignette above, Rosa experiences tension and upset in the presence of Gabriela and in her room; this may be a CER that reflects repeated pairing of Gabriela/her room (NS) with Gabriela's yelling and posturing (US). For Gabriela, her mother's presence (NS) may have come to elicit her anxiety (CER) due to repeated pairings of mom yelling/getting ready for dance class (US). Such associations are often signaled by intense emotion, and can be difficult to change. Additionally, Rosa may respond in a "knee-jerk" way to Gabriela's yelling—perhaps because the initial physiological arousal and anxiety she experiences is a CER.

One way a clinician might work toward shifting this, over time, involves *extinction.* Extinction in respondent conditioning involves weakening the CR through multiple presentations of the CS without the US. Simply put, in Pavlov's classical example, ringing the bell without bringing the food over and over results in the bell losing its predictive power, and thus, its psychological properties. In aversive parent–child interaction, when parents make "empty threats" repeatedly, children learn that they do not mean what they say: in essence, parents' words no longer elicit their children's compliance. In families reliant on harsh or coercive discipline, parents can come to have aversive psychological properties for their children. In other words, parents' presence alone can elicit unease or a sense of uncertainty in children. Helping parents rebuild more nurturing interactions, and ceasing using punitive discipline, is critical in extinguishing a child's CER to his or her parent. It is important to note that although the CR may be weakened it is never unlearned. Rather, both learned responses to the CS remain, existing in parallel, and the CR may reappear (Craske, Treanor, Conway, Zbozinek, & Vervliet, 2014).

Operant conditioning

Operant conditioning models posit that behaviors are evoked by context and antecedents and regulated by consequences (Dixon & Rehfeldt, 2018). Antecedents, or discriminative stimuli (S^D), are stimuli that signal that a particular behavior will be reinforced. For example, Gabriela's mother coming to knock on her door on a Saturday morning to remind her to get ready for dance class is an S^D for Gabriela yelling. It signals to Gabriela that her yelling behavior is likely to work. S^D are important because they explain how we learn to act a certain way in one context (e.g., school) and another way in a different context (e.g., at home). Consequences that *strengthen* behavior, that is, that make the behavior more likely to occur again in a similar context, are referred to as "reinforcers." Consequences that *weaken* behavior, that is, that make the behavior less likely to occur again in a similar context, are referred to as "punishers." In our example above, Gabriela yells at her mother to avoid going to dance class. Rosa finds this aversive, and so she acquiesces to Gabriela's behavior, and leaves the situation. This escape from the situation makes Rosa feel better, and the absence of Gabriela's yelling functions as a *reinforcer*—that is, Rosa is more likely to allow her to escape from demands again if she tantrums in the future. Unfortunately, Gabriela's tantrum was also inadvertently reinforced, because Rosa gave her the reward she sought.

Importantly, reinforcers and punishers are defined solely by their observed *effects* on behavior, rather than by any inherent properties they may have. For example, chocolate is not inherently reinforcing. It is a reinforcer for me (Lisa), but it is unlikely to be so for someone who has a chocolate allergy. Parents often run into this issue when they find themselves scolding children over and over. The parents often feel that scolding is a punisher—after all, scolding is not pleasant; however, the evidence tells another tale—if the misbehavior continues, scolding may actually function as a reinforcer. Another important example is praise. Parents often think that praise must be a reinforcer; after all, they are saying something nice. However, praise has been shown to have paradoxical effects, decreasing motivation and persistence in individuals with low self-esteem (Brummelman, Crocker, & Bushman, 2016); in other words, praise can function as a punisher. This makes sense. In essence, "good try" can come to mean "you failed!" in some circumstances. The important point is to know if a stimulus is functioning as a reinforcer or a punisher one must look to its effect on behavior.

Both reinforcement and punishment can be referred to as "positive" and "negative," and we have added examples in Table 4.1. *Positive* indicates that something is added: a positive reinforcer is an added consequence that increases the probability of a behavior; a positive punisher is an added consequence that decreases the likelihood of a behavior. *Negative*, on the other hand, means that something is removed. Positive reinforcers are often social (e.g., attention) or instrumental (e.g., obtaining an instrumental reward), and negative reinforcers frequently involve escape or avoidance of something unpleasant. Related to this are the terms appetitive and aversive control. Patterns of behavior focused on obtaining desirable stimuli are described as being under *appetitive control*, and patterns of behavior that are focused on avoiding aversive stimuli are described as being under *aversive control*.

TABLE 4.1 Positive and negative reinforcement and punishment.

	Reinforcer	Punisher
Positive	Parent praises child's politeness, leading to more frequent politeness	Parent yells at child for disruptive behavior in public, leading to less disruptive behavior in public
Negative	Upon child's request for help, parent removes uncomfortable tag from child's sweatshirt, leading to more frequent requests for help	When child hits sister with toy, parent removes toy for a brief period, thus leading to less frequent sibling aggression

Consider the following examples:

Example 1. A child is whining for a treat and a parent acquiesces and gives the treat. The child stops whining. The parent's behavior (acquiescence) is negatively reinforced by the removal of the child's whining. The child's behavior (whining) is positively reinforced by the parent's delivery of the treat.

Example 2. An anxious child asks a parent to give him reassurance about whether or not a seat on the bus is contaminated. The parent is distressed at her child's anxiety, and responds by soothing the child, saying "Of course it's not. It's fine." The child feels better, and sits. The parent relaxes. The child's reassurance seeking is negatively reinforced by the parent soothing away her anxiety. The parent's giving reassurance is negatively reinforced by removing her own anxiety.

Extinction is relevant to operant behavior too (Dixon & Rehfeldt, 2018). If a behavior is maintained through reinforcement, then repeated experiences of performing that behavior without reinforcement are likely to result in *extinction*. As with the extinction of respondent conditioning, extinction does not mean that the behavior is unlearned. Rather, both patterns of learning exist in parallel, and if the context signals that the reinforcer may be available again, the old behavioral pattern may reappear. The vulnerability of operant behaviors to extinction depends on the pattern of reinforcement for that behavior. In particular, behaviors that have been reinforced in a manner that is variable and unpredictable are more resistant to extinction. This is why, for example, gambling behavior may persist through a lengthy period of losses. This has implications for parents: when supporting the development of a new or rare behavior, it is important to reinforce every instance of that behavior. Over time, it is appropriate to *fade* reinforcement, or to offer it intermittently. If reinforcement for a particular behavior is variable and unpredictable then that behavior is resistant to extinction and thus more likely to be maintained.

The extinction of an operant behavior is usually accompanied by an *extinction burst*—a temporary increase in the behavior that can also include novel, unexpected behaviors. For example, imagine that you pressed the button to turn on your computer and it didn't turn on. In that very next moment, what would you do? Wouldn't the first thing you do be to press the button again? In fact, wouldn't you press the button many times, maybe even pressing it quite forcefully or holding the button down for a while? Might you even yell "turn on" or swear? Or give the computer a whack? That is the *extinction burst.* Importantly, the *extinction burst* shows up in parent–child interactions whenever parents change their parenting so that they are no longer reinforcing behaviors that they previously reinforced. It is crucial to prepare parents for the extinction burst so that they know that it is actually a sign that the new parenting strategies are working. After all, after pushing the button multiple times, cursing your computer, and giving it a whack, then what do you do? You learn that pushing the button no longer works and, when parents change their parenting, children will learn that pushing particular "buttons" no longer works too.

There are a few key principles to consider when using operant principles to support behavior development and change. Firstly, it is important to be aware of the relative benefits of appetitive rather than aversive control (Wilson, 2008). Aversive control tends to create patterns of behavior that are rigid, inflexible, and insensitive to aspects of the context other than avoiding the aversive. Consider, for example, an adolescent with an English assignment due on Monday. If the adolescent's studying behavior is under aversive control—say, her parents punish her harshly for poor grades—then while she will study hard, her studying behavior is likely to be rigidly focused on the aim of escaping her parent's displeasure and punishment. She is less likely to notice, for example, that she actually enjoys some aspect of the assignment, or that the poem or novel she's studying relates to her own life in some unexpected way. Further, her studying behavior won't be experienced as freely chosen and the continued threat of punishment is likely to be necessary for the maintenance of studying behavior into the next academic year. That is, if the adolescent's parents stop punishing her, or can no longer do so because she's now living out of home and attending university, then her studious habits are likely to abruptly cease. Focusing on aversive control is, thus, incompatible with growing broad and flexible behavioral repertoires that will be sustained in the long term; for that a focus on appetitive control is needed.

Timing is also important. Reinforcers are more effective when delivered immediately after a desired behavior, especially when that behavior is very clearly labeled. For example, descriptive praise such as "Good job putting your shoes away in your closet!" is often more powerful than general praise such as "Good job." Small immediate reinforcers—like verbal labeled praise or tokens—are more powerful than large, more distal rewards.

The most effective interventions bring behavior under naturally occurring contextual control. That is, the behavior is ultimately maintained by reinforcers that arise naturally in a given context. For example, if a child regularly practices the piano and others hear him and tell him how much they enjoy his music, then he is more likely to enjoy playing and consequently, continue to practice. His behavior is under naturally occurring contextual control. In contrast, if the child's parents reward him with chocolate each time he practices piano, then they may increase the amount he practices. However, the chocolate will not reinforce his intrinsic motivation to practice, and once his parents stop giving him chocolate, the piano playing will likely cease. To give another example, many parents teach their children to be polite by using words such as "please" and "thank you". The naturally arising positive reaction of parents and other individuals to polite language reinforces the use of polite speech over less polite language.

The nature and degree to which a particular consequence functions as a reinforcer or punisher is contingent upon the context in which it occurs. For example, I (Lisa) like chocolate, and tend to engage in a variety of behaviors to acquire it (go to the store and purchase, sneakily consume in the kitchen at midnight, etc.). However, if I've just eaten a large piece of chocolate cake, I might *not* be reinforced by *more* chocolate because I'm sated. Similarly, if I haven't had chocolate in weeks, a piece of chocolate seems a particularly desirable, exquisite reward. This illustrates what is called a *motivating operation*; said in lay terms, this means that *context* matters: a small reinforcer in the absence of other reinforcers has great value, but a large reinforcer among many other reinforcers may be devalued. In fact, in conditions of deprivation, behavior under appetitive control may narrow becoming rigid and inflexible, for example, under conditions of starvation our behavior is likely to narrowly focus on obtaining food (Wilson, 2008). Given the survival value of parents to children it is thus unsurprising that when parental attention and nurturance is thin, children may develop behavioral patterns narrowly focused on maximizing attention and nurturance at the expense of competing opportunities such as exploration.

This is also relevant to coercive parent–child interactions. For example, Snyder and Patterson (1995) proposed that *matching law* would explain coercive parent–child interaction in families of aggressive children. Matching law posits that child behavior is a function of *relative* reinforcement (Hernstein, 1970; Strand, 2000; Synder, 2004). Consistent with this hypothesis, Snyder and Patterson (1995) found that in families of aggressive children, compared with coercive behavior, noncoercive behavior was unsuccessful in terminating conflict bouts with parents. The opposite was true for nonaggressive children. Said another way, aggressive children received relatively more reinforcement for coercion than for more appropriate behaviors; non-aggressive children received more reinforcement for non-aggressive behavior than for aggression. More importantly, the relative benefits for coercion significantly predicted sustained child coerciveness several weeks later, as well as child arrests over the following 2 years (Schrepferman & Snyder, 2002).

Another way in which context is important is in terms of whether and how well a behavior *generalizes*, or is performed across particular contexts. Behaviors learned in a context tend to be specific to that context. This is because features of the context—specifically, discriminative stimulus or S^D—signal that reinforcement will be delivered in this setting. Thus it's important to encourage practice of a behavior across contexts to ensure that each context comes to elicit it (if that is what is desired). However, it may be the case that a behavior is only effective or appropriate in a particular context; thus supporting a parent's *tracking*, or sensitivity, to the effects of their behavior on the environment, is critical to the development of sensitive and varied repertoires of parenting behavior. For example, whereas an adolescent might appreciate a parent's praise in private, that same behavior in public might lead to embarrassment. If the parent is aware of this, if that particular feature of the context—being in public or private—is a S^D then parenting will be more effective.

Indirect conditioning: modeling, derived relational responding, and rule-governed behavior

Responses to stimuli may be *directly* (as in the case of classical or operant conditioning) and/or *indirectly* acquired. Humans do not learn only via their direct experience; they also learn through modeling, derived relational responding, and rule-governed behavior. *Modeling* involves observing the behavior of another and coming to understand the contingencies through observation (if I do x, I get y). Depending on the contingencies observed you may then be more or less likely to try the same behavior for yourself. For example, children who see people use coercive behavior and be reinforced for it is more likely to try out coercive behavior for themselves (even when they were the victim of the coercion).

Relational frame theory (RFT) provides an account of verbal conditioning processes. Encountered stimuli may gain their psychological properties indirectly, through verbal or *symbolic* means without an individual having any direct contact with them. For instance, children may learn not to touch flames not through direct experience of being burned, but rather, through repeated phrases from a parent, "Don't touch. Hot. Ouch!" This verbal learning process is called *derived relational responding* or *relational framing* (Hayes, Barnes-Holmes, & Roche, 2001; Torneke, 2010). For example, a mother tells her child that a 5-dollar bill is "less than" a 10-dollar bill. When she asks the child which he would like to have he replies that wants the 10-dollar bill. When asked why he replies that it is "more." His reply is based not on physical properties of the two bills (color, size, etc.) but on the *arbitrary* (i.e., based on social convention) relation of less than/more than. He has previously learned to "relationally frame" stimuli in accordance with the relation of comparison less than/more than and in the presence of the contextual cue "less than" he frames the 5- and 10-dollar bills in this way and *derives* that the 10-dollar bill is worth more and hence is the one to want. Note, he was not directly taught that the 10-dollar bill was more, rather he *derived* this from being taught that the 5-dollar bill was less.

RFT argues that humans learn to derive relations based on exposure to contingencies of reinforcement in the socioverbal community. Children begin to learn this skill in early toddlerhood. The earliest evidence of derived relational responding in children occurs in toddlerhood (at around the age of 18 months) when children learn, for example, that the spoken word "tree" is the same as an actual tree (Lipkens, Hayes, & Hayes, 1993). This is called *mutual entailment,*and is foundational to language. Next, in the absence of any direct instruction from parents, children might derive relationships between different types of trees or pictures of trees to both actual trees and the word "trees." This independent derivation is called *combinatorial entailment,* and is thought to underpin the explosion of language that occurs during the preschool years.

Derived relational responding, like all behavior, is under contextual control. Consider how parents teach young children the names of objects—or more specifically, how to *relate* the names of objects with the actual objects. Parents may point toward a particular object, and name it, repeating this over and over again, every time they and their child come into the presence of that object. Parents may reinforce joint attention to the object with praise and smiling. Eventually, the child learns to point to the object when the mother names it, which is then reinforced by the parent. Similarly, the mother might hold up a ball and ask, "What is this?" Over time and repetitions, the child learns to say "ball" in the presence of the object. When this occurs, the mother provides immediate reinforcement, perhaps by saying "Yes, that's the ball!" or actually giving the child the ball. Yet what's happening here is more important than simply learning a word: *through reinforcing successive approximations, joint attention, pointing, and ultimately, naming objects, parents shape the behavior of relating itself.*

When elements come to be related in a individual's mind, they tend to share psychological properties—the technical term for this is transformation of function. A previously neutral experience can suddenly take on new attractive or aversive qualities when related to something else. For instance, if a parent perceives a child as angry, and anger is related to noncompliance, then the child's expression of anger alone may elicit the parent's annoyance, or in operant terms, evoke a parent's lax behavior (Backen Jones, Whittingham, Coyne, & Lightcap, 2016). In this way, elements in a "relational frame" come to have particular functions or meanings based on an individual's particular learning history or context (S.C. Hayes et al., 2003). In families coercive behavior of each individual may not be regulated by any observable trigger, but rather by symbolic processes dictated by a historical context made up of covert, private experiences. This effect can help explain the differing "potency" and meaning of particular stimuli in coercive processes. Moreover, it may also account for the inflexibility and intransigence of coercive cycles, which can arise from weak and ineffective contextual control over relational learning processes. Importantly, RFT describes how language processes enable individuals to experience painful or stressful stimuli psychologically, even when the stimuli are not physically present. For example, the parent of a child with a disability may experience significant distress thinking about their child's future, even though they are currently in tranquil and peaceful surroundings.

With continued exposure to the socioverbal environment children gradually learn to derive a variety of relations, such as bigger/smaller (comparison), different than (distinction), and "a type of" (hierarchical; e.g., a dachshund is a type of dog; Hayes et al., 2001). These derived relations are often arbitrary: for example, American children learn through social conventions that a dime is worth more than a nickel, even though it is physically smaller. Eventually children's framing generalizes so that the contextual cues alone control the response pattern (Barnes-Holmes, Barnes-Holmes, Smeets, Strand, & Friman, 2004; Hayes et al., 2001). Importantly, this also includes *deictic* relational frames, or relations establishing perspectives of person, place, and time: I−you, here−there, now−then. From deictic relational frames, children learn to verbally discriminate their own behavior, that is, they learn that they have a consistent perspective—I, here, now—that is distinct from the perspective of others—you, there, then—and distinct from psychological content and that contributes to their sense of self (McHugh, Stewart, and Almada, 2019) (this is covered in depth in the chapter ten *Flexible Perspective Taking*). RFT researchers have provided a robust body of empirical evidence showing the diversity of patterns of derived relational responding as well as demonstrating how relational frames can be established and influenced (Dymond & Barnes, 1996; Roche & Barnes, 1997; Steele & Hayes, 1991).

One of the key implications of RFT for human well-being is that, due to our ability to derive relations, our behavior can be under the contextual control of the *derived* properties of the stimuli, rather than direct contingencies. That is, we can follow verbal rules. This ability has great evolutionary value; for example, the ability of a child to learn not to touch fire by the parent repeatedly saying "Don't touch, it is hot!" It can also be problematic. Rule-governed behavior can be broken into three basic types: (1) pliance (or counterpliance); (2) tracking; and (3) augmenting (Torneke, 2010).

Pliance refers to when rule following is under the contextual control of socially mediated consequences, and socially mediated reinforcement is given when the behavior is coordinated with the rule. For example, a parent tells his child that if she plays quietly while the parent makes a phone call she will be given a sticker. The child is quiet during the phone call (her behavior is coordinated with the rule) and the parent gives her a sticker. The child's behavior is functioning as pliance. A parent's behavior may also function as pliance. For example, a health professional tells the mother of a young baby that she must not breastfeed her baby to sleep because it is "bad parenting." The mother stops feeding her baby to sleep in order to be understood as a "good mother" by the health professional and the wider community. She is praised by the health professional and her community. Pliance can lead to inflexible behavior that is focused on pleasing others and winning approval even when doing so is counter to the direct contingencies in the context and not workable in the long term. Counterpliance refers to when the opposite behavior to the rule is followed, with behavior still under the contextual control of the rule but with social disapproval rather than approval being sought. A verbal rule that is functioning as *pliance* may be called a *ply*.

Tracking refers to rules that track the consequences, that is, the natural reinforcers, of actions. There is a frame of coordination between the rule and the context. For example, a father might notice that his four-year-old daughter is more likely to be cranky, to whine, and to have temper tantrums in the evenings if the family has a late dinner. In noticing the consequence of a late dinner (i.e., a crankier child), he is tracking the effects of behavior in context. As a result, he might experiment with ensuring that his daughter has an earlier dinner and continue to track the effects in context: Does an earlier dinner result in less cranky behaivor? In this way, tracking may support the development of flexible and novel behaviors that are shaped by trial and error, rather than by simple adherence to a rule, as in pliance. Both pliance and tracking are useful; however, it is important to notice when one might be more helpful than the other. Thus supporting the parent in learning how to track their own behavior accurately and flexibly is a key element of parenting intervention. Parents supporting children in learning how to track their own behavior accurately and flexibly is also a key element of good parenting. A verbal rule that is functioning as tracking may be called a *track*.

Clinicians can support parents in shaping rules that are informative and educate the child about how the family system and the world at large works rather than simply voicing parental approval or disapproval. For example, if an oppositional child takes a long time to get ready to go to a playdate, the natural consequence of that behavior is to reduce the duration of the playdate. Thus a parent might say, "The quicker you get ready, the more time you have to play with your friends!" In doing so, the parent is supporting her child in learning a generalizable *track*. Note also that this *track* is not only functional, it directs the child's attention to the potential *appetitive* consequence of their behavior: more playtime. It would be just as easy to say, "If you take forever to get ready, you will lose playtime," thus highlighting the potential *cost* of getting ready slowly. The former works better, as it helps the child understand contingency via working for an appetitive, rather than through working to avoid an aversive. It is a simple technique, but one that can help parents shape more adaptive behavior through supporting *tracking*. Furthermore, it is also important that we as clinicians support our clients in learning to *track* rather than just to *ply*, that is, to change in ways that are workable for them in the long term rather than merely changing to win our approval.

Augmenting involves motivation through changing the value of a stimulus. For example, a child might not be interested in doing homework because he feels that it is a drudgery. However, if his mother reminds him that doing homework is a step towards being an exceptional student, and if being an exceptional student is important to him, then he may be more willing to endure the "drudgery" of completing his homework. Within acceptance and commitment therapy (ACT) values are a motivative augmental.

Functional analysis of behavior

The only way to understand how behavior works is to conduct a functional analysis; that is, to observe it as it occurs in the environment. Described simply, a *functional analysis of behavior* allows one to discern why a behavior is occurring through understanding its function on the environment. This is ideally conducted through direct observations, which may also include direct manipulation of environmental contingencies. That is, a functional analysis is an ongoing experiment in which hypotheses are tested out and refined. For example, if a clinician thinks that a child's behavior is being reinforced by parental attention, then that clinician might ask the parent to ignore that behavior. If the parent starts ignoring the behavior and it immediately escalates the clinician has some evidence that their hypothesis is correct because the behavior is showing an extinction burst. If the parent persists in ignoring the behavior, and the behavior decreases in frequency and/or duration over time, then the clinician has further evidence that their hypothesis is correct. Clear understanding of the function of behavior—that is, how a behavior "works"—is critical to any behavior change. Below, we discuss coercive family processes from a functional analytic perspective inclusive of operant, respondent, and symbolic learning principles.

Problematic behavior patterns in families: coercive cycles

Both direct and indirect conditioning processes are implicated in parent-child relationships and family functioning. Parent–child interaction can be organized in unhelpful ways through patterns of reinforcement and punishment provided by each partner. Operant conditioning models of family interaction posit that the behavior of both parent and child is a function of antecedents and consequences. That is, the behavior of both the parent and the child is understood through the relationship between behavior and interpersonal processes including antecedents, reinforcers, and punishers within the ongoing interaction (Patterson, 1982). The relationship between parent and child behavior is bidirectional, with the parent influencing the child and the child influencing the parent (Dishion, Patterson, & Kavanah, 1992).

Coercion is an interpersonal process in which one person uses aversive means to control another person in order to obtain his or her goals (Patterson, 1982). This has been found in families with aggressive children (Synder & Patterson, 1995), as well as anxious children (Lebowitz, Omer, & Leckman, 2011). Both parents and children can engage in coercion. Coercion between parent and child occurs within a family system, and as such, is largely regulated by that system. Because this behavior is under aversive control, it is highly rigid and difficult to change. Moreover, operant and respondent conditioning models may not fully describe how coercion works in families, without attending also to the influence of symbolic processes.

Coercion theory analyzes coercive interactions between parent and child (Patterson, 1982). From an operant conditioning perspective, a coercive interaction might begin with the issuance of a command or instruction by the parent. In turn, the child responds with coercion (i.e., aggression), in an effort to escape from the parental demand. Youngsters may also set off this cycle with oppositional behavior, as the process is bidirectional (Coyne & Cairns, 2016). Coercion is used because coercion is fast and effective in changing another person's behavior. When parents use punitive means to coerce a child, it often ends misbehavior quickly. When an oppositional child coerces a parent, the parent may "give in" by acquiescing or removing a demand. However, coercive practices don't work in the long term, can lead to antisocial behavior, and predict sustained negative developmental outcomes such as oppositional behavior (Smith et al., 2014), academic failure and peer rejection, which in turn set the stage for the development of adult antisocial behavior (Patterson, DeBaryshe, & Ramsey, 1989).

Respondent conditioning can also help us to understand coercive family processes. The two-factor theory of anxiety posits that escape from classically conditioned aversive stimuli is maintained via operant reinforcement (Mowrer, 1939; Rachman, 1977). Parents may "give in" or respond harshly to child coercion to avoid or terminate the unpleasant emotions that arise during such interactions. Therefore one aspect of dysfunctional parenting is a CER. For instance, a parent might feel a sense of dread seeing a child approach in a toy store and holding an expensive toy, based on past pairing with just this situation and an embarrassing public temper tantrum. Giving in, or allowing the child to have the toy, may help the parent avoid or escape the sense of dread (CER). More importantly, contextual features of the situation in which the coercion is played out may also be associated with unpleasant emotions that are unrelated to the interaction, but nonetheless influence it.

Derived relational responding can also help us understand coercive family processes. Unpleasant child behaviors such as tantrums or noncompliance may come to have particular meanings for parents. For example, in the presence of such behavior, parents might experience thoughts such as, "I'm an incompetent mother", or perhaps feel deep anxiety that may evoke unhelpful parenting behavior, such as acquiescence or harshness. Lax or harsh parent behavior may function to avoid or escape these negative private events (i.e., the unpleasant thoughts and feelings parents experience in the context of child behavior) and as such, may contribute to the maintenance and intensification of coercion. Thus, child behaviors and parental responses can have symbolic meanings for parents that are potent and covert. It is critically important to explore these meanings with parents in order to have a full and workable understanding of why coercive interactions persist.

Coercive interactions are also emblematic of families raising children with anxiety including obsessive-compulsive disorder (OCD). Parents may perceive child anxiety as punishing and therefore engage in accommodation behaviors to relieve it, as well as to relieve their own anxiety (Lebowitz et al., 2011). Parent accommodation behaviors involve participating in a child's rituals, or facilitating child avoidance behaviors. Youth with anxiety and OCD can coerce parents into accommodation; for example, giving excessive reassurance, or allowing a child to skip school, or avoid participating in group sports or activities. At times, youth with anxiety or OCD engage in verbal or physical aggression to enlist parents in facilitating their avoidance.

Both types of coercive cycles represent the aversive control of behavior, which leads to narrow and inflexible behavioral repertoires. Although coercive parenting promotes the long-term continuation of behaviors parents would like to stop, as well as narrows the behavioral repertoire of the child, small and immediate reinforcers in the short term are more powerful than large but distant ones. Thus many parents settle for *relief* rather than behavior change. This coercive pattern can become further ingrained because the parent of a child who is regularly coercive is less likely to respond with attention to the child's positive behaviors. Such moments of calm are likely to be used by the parent for competing tasks or self-care (Sanders & Dadds, 1993). This, in turn, creates a context of deprivation, where parental attention is not abundant, and where problematic and coercive behavior is the best way to gain it.

Supporting behavior change

Respondent conditioning strategies

In our discussion of coercive family processes above, we described how stimuli—even parents or children—can take on aversive properties because they predicted time and time again a potent aversive stimulus. Here, we will discuss a respondent conditioning technique commonly employed with parent or child fear and anxiety. *Exposure* is a core aspect of intervention for anxiety disorders. From a respondent conditioning perspective exposure involves repeated presentation of the CS in the absence of the US; or repeated *approach* toward aversive stimuli. Over time and repeated trials, the CS ceases to have its aversive psychological functions, and the individual no longer engages in the CR.

Operant conditioning strategies: antecedent and consequent manipulation strategies

Antecedent strategies

In operant conditioning models, one can support behavior change through altering antecedents or consequences. Simply put, the principles involve *evoking* behavior (via antecedents), *reinforcing* behavior (via consequences), and *repeating* (Sandoz & Boone, 2016) through providing continued opportunities to practice. Antecedent *control* strategies involve the *prevention* of undesired behavior, or the evocation of adaptive behavior. In terms of supporting adaptive behavior, it's always easier and faster to employ antecedent control strategies in a sensitive and responsive way. Antecedent control procedures, specifically, prompting, are also critical in the shaping of novel or complex behavior.

Two concepts from Vgotskyian psychology can be useful in putting antecedent control strategies into a developmental context and in supporting parents in finding natural opportunities within everyday life to shape behavior. These two concepts are the zone of proximal development and scaffolding. The *zone of proximal development* is the distance between a child's independent developmental level—what he can do by himself—and the child's developmental potential—what she can do with guidance from adults or collaboration with peers (Karimi-Aghdam, 2017).

The interaction with others, the interaction that allows a child to reach beyond their developmental level to their developmental potential, is called *scaffolding*. For example, if a parent is taking a young child on an airplane, he might prepare by playing games involving taking a trip on an airplane, talking through the rules immediately before getting onto the plane, and bringing plenty of toys and snacks. By doing so, the parent is *scaffolding* his child's ability to be cooperative on the airplane, providing the necessary support so that the child can do something that she cannot do alone. Or, in the case of an adolescent, if a parent would like to have a challenging conversation about spending or excessive screen use, she might choose an environment and time of day in which the teen is most comfortable, and with some privacy, to initiate the talk so that it is more likely to be heard. Scaffolding can also involve providing verbal contingency to help bolster motivation: "Honey, just one more store—and then we can go get your favorite snack. I know you can do it." This statement may serve as an S^D for reinforcement, if the child persists. After all, context matters, and so does the child's current emotional and motivational state.

Scaffolding may include prompts, simplifying a task, breaking a task into steps, or providing *just enough* assistance. It is important that the *scaffolding* given is just enough that it allows the child to perform the behavior but does not involve the parent taking over from the child. An example of this comes from family-based treatment of child anxiety and OCD. Often, parents of anxious children *accommodate* their avoidance-based behaviors, and allow escape from anxiety-evoking situations. Thus family-based approaches teach parents to shape more *approach-based* behavior in the context of fear-eliciting situations. Often, because this is a new behavior for a child, *scaffolding* is needed: parents are taught to model this approach in the face of anxiety, to prompt by using encouraging words, and to engage in verbal behavior that supports the child's self-efficacy, even when frightened (Freeman et al., 2008).

There are a number of ACT techniques that constitute antecedent strategies, especially with regard to employing augmentals. As mentioned previously, a *value*, a core component of ACT, is a type of motivative augmental. For example, if a parent has the goal of using verbal praise consistently, but is finding it difficult because she is feeling overwhelmed or exhausted, a clinician might encourage a parent to touch upon their values to support effective action. The clinician might frame giving consistent verbal praise in the context of the parent's values by saying "Praising Rex's sitting down to do his homework, and staying on task, is a step toward shaping better harmony in your family." In addition, the ACT skills of present moment awareness and flexible perspective taking may be used to bring into awareness particular antecedents that may be helpful as S^D for sensitive and responsive parenting behavior. That is, with psychological presence in the present moment and flexible perspective taking, parents can better track aspects of their child's behavior or the wider context, that signal which parenting behavior might be most effective in that moment (S^D). Parents may notice, for example, that as they are in public and their adolescent's friends are present, that now is not the best time to praise their child as their child will be likely to find that embarrassing and unpleasant.

In addition, the same ACT skills can support parents in noticing their own intentions in a particular moment, to reconnect with their parenting values before responding and to notice the thoughts, feelings and behavioral tendencies that arise due to their own learning history without immediately acting on them. For example, a parent with a history of pregnancy or infant loss might notice a rising feeling of anxiety as they watch their toddler boldly exploring the playground and confidently approaching the big slide. The parent may notice the rising feelings of anxiety, and the behavioral tendency to "protect" their child by curtailing their exploration, and, at the same time, make a rational risk assessment, and in the service of supporting the child's exploration, refrain from bringing the child's exploration of the big slide to an end. Instead, the parent might decide that standing close enough to catch in the event of a fall is protection enough, and choose to do so while actively expressing delight and pride in their toddler's achievements (and while also accepting the ongoing feeling of anxiety as it waxes and wanes).

Consequence strategies

The other way to support behavior change is to manipulate the consequences of behavior; in other words, to reinforce adaptive behavior and avoid reinforcing problematic behavior. Punishment, the use of a consequence to weaken behavior, is also useful, but should only be used as a last resort, and always in concert with reinforcement strategies due to the problems associated with aversive control (discussed above). Common consequent control strategies include reinforcement of behavior through *attention*, *praise*, and *instrumental rewards*, and *shaping* to support the development of complex behavior, and *response cost*, *selective attention*, *consequences*, and *time-out* to diminish problematic behavior.

One of the simplest ways for a parent to reinforce a child's behavior is simply to pay greater *attention* to it. Although this is often simple for a parent to do, there are a number of potentially reinforcing qualities present in parental attention and some parents may benefit from more specific direction to enhance these. Firstly, parental attending to the child, and hence engaging in a *shared psychological presence* or being *psychologically available* to the child, is likely to be reinforcing in and of itself. Shared psychological presence is also likely to result in *attuned interaction,* another likely reinforcer. Smiling, shared laughter, nods, winks, physical affection, and other *social reinforcers* are also likely to be present with parental attending. Further, through attuned interaction the parent is likely to verbalize statements that make *intrinsic reinforcers salient* for the child. For example, a parent attending to his child's attempts to bounce a ball off the house and catch it is likely to exclaim, "you caught it!," thus pointing to the naturally occurring reinforcement that is an intrinsic part of bouncing a ball against a wall. A parent listening attentively to her adolescent play the guitar might notice, "Wow you nailed those tricky parts. Your extra practice has really paid off," thus pointing to the naturally occurring reinforcement that is an intrinsic part of playing the guitar.

Praise is another important way parents can reinforce their children's behavior. As stated earlier, *praise* often works best when it is descriptive, that is, when it specifies the exact behavior being praised. In order to avoid learning patterns that will generate paradoxical effects, praise should be genuine and sincere. That is, parents should say "good effort" when the child actually has put in good effort. If "good effort" means "wow you failed big time" children will learn this and it will cease to be a reinforcer. Consistent with shaping, parents should praise effort, not results, that is, they should reinforce the child's best approximation of the behavior, not only the perfect behavior and certainly not the achievement of an outcome alone. Finally, at times extrinsic *rewards* can be helpful, particularly in supporting the development of a new or rare behavior this may include the use of tokens or behavior charts.

How do more complex patterns of behavior form? *Shaping* is a procedure through which successive approximations of a behavior are prompted (antecedent control) and then reinforced in a graduated way. Once an individual achieves mastery of a particular step, often defined as consistently and correctly engaging in the desired behavior, then *that* step is no longer reinforced; instead, reinforcement is given after the *next* more complex step approximations to the desired response, starting with a behavior that they be easily produced (Miltenberger, Miller, Zerger, & Novotony, 2018). Consider how one learns how to play a musical instrument: the desired response—which may simply be playing a particular bar—is evoked and reinforced, and this process is repeated until the entire piece is mastered. The same process may happen in the development of social skills: a preschooler may learn how to initiate interactions with peers; to use his words to ask for a toy, to play in parallel with another peer, and to engage in complex pretend play. From a symbolic perspective, an understanding of theory of mind is also something that is likely shaped: first, children notice that others have emotions; then they may recognize that those emotions and thoughts differ from their own; subsequently, perspective taking and empathy develop.

The ACT strategies of valuing and committed action—in concert with antecedent control (as described above, coaching parents to notice their intention, and whether their action is consistent with their values), augments the reinforcing properties of shaping behavior for the parent. In other words, because a parent recognizes that using a parent strategy is a step toward, say, a "more harmonious family," simply engaging in that behavior becomes more reinforcing. In addition, flexible perspective taking in the form of self-as-context, specifically, stepping back from and observing one's own behavior in an accepting, nonattached way can lead to more mindful and effective parenting behavior.

Four strategies that involve removing reinforcement for problematic behavior include, *selective attention*, *natural consequences (here, consequences that weaken the occurrence of a behavior), response cost,* and *time-out*. Broadly construed, these constitute *extinction* procedures, or procedures in which reinforcement is no longer given for a target behavior. All of these procedures seek to *reduce* problematic behavior, and should be used in concert with strategies to increase adaptive behavior. In particular, parents should ensure they are reinforcing *competing* behavior, behaviors that are *alternatives* to the problematic behaviors. For example, a child cannot *both* share and fight over a toy. Part of extinguishing snatching, aggression, and tantrum behavior is therefore ensuring that the *competing* behavior of sharing is reinforced. Considering competing or alternative behaviors is especially important when the child has a skills deficit. In that case, alternative behaviors may need to be shaped. For example, in nonverbal children it is often important to focus on teaching and reinforcing appropriate communicative behavior in order to effectively extinguish problematic behavior such as yelling or tantrums.

Selective attention, sometimes called "planned ignoring," involves a parent withholding attention from child behaviors that function as bids for attention. For example, behaviors such as whining for a desired toy may be inadvertently reinforced by parents responding to it. Similarly, interruptions while a parent is on the phone may be inadvertently reinforced if parents respond to them, either in a positive or negative way. Thus, if parents desire to see less of a particular attention-seeking behavior, they may be instructed to withhold their attention from that behavior and instead attend more fully to more desirable child behaviors (e.g., asking for things "nicely" or being patient). When using this technique, parents can expect to see an extinction burst, or a temporary intensification of child misbehavior. It is important for clinicians to reinforce parents' efforts to continue using planned ignoring until the extinction burst remits.

The use of natural consequences involves either allowing the natural consequences of the child's behavior to unfold—for example, a child refuses to wear their coat and, as a result, gets cold—or implementing a consequence that is "logical," that is, a consequence that is brief, directly relates to the problematic behavior, and that makes sense in terms of real-life consequences in later life. For example, a child who draws on the walls may need to clean the drawing off. "We don't draw on the walls. You'll need to clean that off." A child who refuses to wear her bicycle helmet is unable to ride her bike. "You can't ride your bike if you don't wear a helmet. I'll put your bike away and you can try again in 5 minutes."

Response cost involves removing a reward each time a child engages in misbehavior. For example, if a child hits his sister with a toy, then the parent might briefly take away that toy and explain to the child, "Toys are for playing, not hitting. If you hit your sister, your toy goes away." It is helpful to remember that while this technique is useful for reduction of unwanted behavior, it does not help shape more appropriate behaviors. In the example above, parents might shape appropriate play with and sharing of a toy using labeled praise.

Time-out involves requiring a child to go, or bringing a child to, an area in which access to social (or other) reinforcers is limited, following engagement in a problematic behavior. A boring room or space in the house can be designated the time-out zone. However, the time-out area may simply be on the edge of whatever the current activity is—the seat near the playground at the park or the end of the aisle in the supermarket. Thus time-out can be portable and flexible. Time-out is a short procedure—no more than 2–5 minutes, and is not meant to be a punitive method. Once a child's time in the "time-out" area has elapsed, that child should be welcomed back to his or her activities. Contingencies surrounding time-out should be clearly specified for the child *before* the undesirable behavior occurs and may be briefly reiterated after the child is finished with the time-out. When aggressive behavior is at the center of a problem the parent can implement a time-out procedure, by matter-of-factly removing the child from situation and to a boring place in the house for 2 minutes.

Time-out in particular is often misunderstood: of the vast majority of parents who use it, 84.9% do so incorrectly (Riley et al., 2017). Moreover, although parents are perhaps most likely to search for how to use time-out on the internet, it is concerning that the information found there is highly inaccurate and may lead to inappropriate and ineffective use of time-out (Drayton et al., 2014). Specifically, only 2 of 58 mothers described time-out correctly, as *removal from reinforcement*; 25 described it as a tool to help children "calm down" (Drayton et al., 2017). To complicate matters, a recent study found that those parents most needing training in time-out were least likely to engage in behavioral parent training: half of parents of kids who would most likely benefit from time-out training either didn't attend or dropped out (Chacko et al., 2016).

A primer on how to use time-out:

1. Only use time-out in the context of positive behavior support/access to reinforcers; ONLY use when function of behavior is to gain attention/access to reinforcers, NEVER when function is escape from demands.
2. Use immediately after the misbehavior occurs/do this consistently.
3. Location should be in a boring place with not a lot to do; useful if parents can observe out of the corner of their eye.
4. Keep it brief; use a timer that's out of reach of the child (2–4 minutes is typical).
5. Parent ends it (not the child) and welcomes child back into activities.
6. Ensure follow through—for example, if the child leaves, direct her to go back and be persistent.
7. Never implement in anger—be matter of fact
8. Minimize attention to child in time-out—save the explaining for either before, or right after, and keep it brief.

Note that none of these strategies should be delivered in a harsh, punitive, or angry way—they should be applied in a consistent, kind, and firm manner. To borrow a term coined by Dadds and Hawes (2006) the management of misbehavior should not be *attachment-rich*, it should be *attachment-neutral*. That is, how the parent responds to misbehavior should not be rich in emotional and relational information for the child (e.g., themes of rejection). Attachment-related information is likely to be, in and of itself, reinforcing (even if it is unpleasant). The ACT skills are highly relevant to parental success in applying parenting strategies in a consistent, kind, firm, and *attachment-neutral* manner. In order to do so, it is beneficial for parents to maintain a connection with their values and to frame their use of parenting strategies as part of valued action. It is also beneficial for parents to notice their own thoughts, feelings, and behavioral tendencies as they rise without immediately acting on them, through psychological presence in the present moment and flexible perspective taking. If particular thoughts about themselves as a parent or the child arise—for example, "he's just a little shit" or "she hates me"—then flexible languaging, specifically defusion, is important to ensure that the parent does not experience those thoughts as literal truths. It is also essential that parents be able to demonstrate experiential acceptance, both for their own experiences including thoughts, feelings, and behavioral tendencies as they arise in that moment, and for their child's. With experiential acceptance of the child's thoughts, feelings and behavioral tendencies, they can focus not on reacting to their child's experiences per se but on effectively shaping their child's behavior when those experiences are present. Finally, committed action and exploration is important, in the sense that the parent needs to persist under pressure and to parent in a manner that is flexible, taking an experimental approach of discovering what works. Thus all aspects of psychological flexibility are relevant.

Parents may harness the power of rule-governed behavior by creating verbal contingencies in the family that support the child's development of tracking and help shift coercive cycles. For example, parents can support a child to *track the consequences of their own behavior* through verbal contingencies, rather than parental disapproval. For example, a father who finds his 4-year-old drawing on the wall could support tracking by saying, "we don't draw on the walls. Now you'll need to clean it off," rather than by saying, "don't draw on the wall! That's very naughty! You naughty boy!" The verbal contingencies can be phrased in a positive way, breaking coercive cycles. For example, a mother who wants to ensure that homework gets done might focus on the appetitive, rather than the aversive, by saying, "After your homework, you can watch TV," rather than saying "If you don't do your homework, you will lose TV". The former constructs an appetitive consequence, ie, watching TV rather than an aversive consequence, or losing TV." However, *the actual contingency is exactly the same: no homework, no TV; homework done, TV time earned.* Nonetheless, parents may call upon principles of RFT to help children derive appetitive relations between doing homework and a desired reinforcer, TV watching, such that doing the work actually has some reinforcing qualities. The construction of verbal rules, then, specifies what contingencies function as coercion (child avoids an unpleasant outcome), or reinforcement (child anticipates a pleasant outcome). It may be helpful to "reframe" verbal contingencies such that children have something to *work for*, rather than an aversive to avoid (Coyne & Cairns, 2016).

Behavioral parenting intervention

Parenting interventions grounded in behavioral principles are effective, particularly with decreasing externalizing and antisocial behavior, as has been confirmed in multiple meta-anlyses (Buchanan-Pascall, Gray, Gordon, & Melvin, 2018; de Graaf, Speetjens, Smit, de Wolff, & Tavecchio, 2008a, 2008b; Nowak & Heinrichs, 2008; Piquero et al., 2016; Thomas & Zimmer-Gembeck, 2007). One recent meta-analysis found that behavioral parenting interventions prevent antisocial behavior and delinquency with 32 out of 100 children in the intervention group offending compared to 50 in the control group (Piquero et al., 2016). In another recent meta-analysis, the effects of behavioral parent training on internalizing symptoms were also statistically significant although modest (Buchanan-Pascall et al., 2018). This may be driven more specifically by childhood depression symptoms, as family-based treatments for anxiety disorders tend toward moderate to large effect sizes (Ginsburg, Drake, Tein, Teetsel, & Riddle, 2015; Higa-McMillan, Francis, Rith-Najarian, & Chorpita, 2016). This suggests a need for parenting intervention explicitly targeting childhood depressive symptoms.

A systematic review looking at parenting as a mediator of the effect of parenting interventions found some evidence particularly for discipline and for a composite measure of parenting including positive parenting behaviors such as praise as well as lack of negative behaviors, discipline, and monitoring/supervision. Greater support was found for parenting as a mediator with younger children (Forehand, Lafko, Parent, & Burt, 2014). Consistent with this, a meta-analytic component analysis showed that the components most strongly associated with larger effects are increasing positive interactions, improving emotional communication skills, teaching the parent time-out, teaching parenting consistency, and parental practice of the parenting skills in session (Kaminski, Valle, Filene, & Boyle, 2008). Additional research on mediation, component analysis, and the development of parenting interventions specifically targeting child depression is needed.

Parenting interventions tend to be effective when applied in countries that are culturally dissimilar to the cultures in which they were developed, and may be particularly effective in cultures that are survival focused (Gardner, Montgomery, & Knerr, 2016). Programs with cultural adaptations are more effective in improving parenting behavior, especially when this adaptation involved adding elements to influence the target group rather than just matching program material and messages to the target population (van Mourik, Crone, de Wolff, & Reis, 2017). An alternative to adaptations per se is to ensure programs have a built-in flexibility and can be adjusted by the practitioner and the parent to fit specific individual, familial and cultural values. This validity of parenting interventions across cultures makes sense. The basic principles upon which the programs are based—the operation of respondent and operant conditioning within the parent–child relationship—are likely to be universal. However, it is important that the specific parenting strategies and the examples given suit the cultural context or it will not be salient for the parent.

Behavioral parenting interventions have also been adapted for families of children with neurodevelopmental disabilities. Similar to cultural adaptations, the adaptation included ensuring that the program materials were appropriate for the population. It also involved adding chaining as a parenting strategy and adding content addressing contingencies that are more common within the disabilities population; for example, protocols for addressing self-stimulatory behaviors, including self-stimulatory behaviors that cause physical harm (Sanders, Mazzucchelli, & Studman, 2003). Behavioral parenting intervention has been found effective in targeting externalizing behavior in families of children with neurodevelopmental disabilities (Tellegen & Sanders, 2013) including autism spectrum disorders (Whittingham, Sofronoff, Sheffield, & Sanders, 2009a, 2009b), acquired brain injury (Brown, Whittingham, Boyd, & McKinlay, 2015; Brown, Whittingham, McKinlay, Boyd, & Sofronoff, 2013; Brown, Whittingham, Boyd, McKinlay, & Sofronoff, 2014), and cerebral palsy (Whittingham, Sanders, McKinlay, & Boyd, 2014; Whittingham, Sanders, McKinlay, & Boyd, 2016) among others.

Research on acceptance and commitment therapy/relational frame theory and parenting

Research on ACT for parents continues to grow. Although there are a variety of studies evaluating individual components of ACT in parents (Coyne, McHugh, & Martinez, 2011), we will not review these here since they will be covered in the chapters focused on each ACT process. ACT has been used in a three different ways with parents: (1) to address parent psychological well-being, (2) to augment existing behavioral parenting interventions, and (3) to directly address parent and/or child behaviors.

Acceptance and commitment therapy for parent psychological well-being

In a repeated measures, within-subjects design, Blackledge and Hayes (2005) assessed the effectiveness of a 2-day, 14-hour group experiential ACT workshop to improve psychological well-being for 20 parents of children with autism. Parents reported significantly less distress at 3-month follow-up, with those with reporting clinical levels of symptomatology experiencing greater gains. Experiential avoidance and cognitive fusion were similarly reduced from baseline to follow-up, and results suggested that fusion mediated the relationship between treatment and symptom reduction (Blackledge, 2005).

Acceptance and commitment therapy for augmentation for behavioral parenting interventions

In one of the first case studies on ACT for parents, Coyne and Wilson described ACT used in conjunction with parent–child interaction therapy (PCIT) (Eyberg, Boggs, & Algina, 1995) for a 6-year-old male with severe aggression and noncompliance that had resulted in an extended school suspension. ACT components were used with the boy's mother to reduce the psychological barriers that would restrict new skill acquisition. For example, mindfulness and defusion procedures were incorporated with the planned ignoring and other components of the PCIT. Treatment continued for approximately 3 months. At posttreatment and 1-year follow-up, the parent reported increased compliance and reduced aggression; she also reported more consistent and appropriate use of behavior management strategies, and an increase in her own pursuit of valued activities. The mother also reported better relationship quality and greater confidence in her parenting skills (Coyne & Wilson, 2004).

More recent and rigorous work included two randomized controlled trials (RCTs) have tested the combination of behavioral parenting intervention with a brief (4 hours) group ACT intervention. In one RCT, the combined intervention of Stepping Stones Triple P (a parenting intervention for families of children with neurodevelopmental disabilities) and ACT was compared to a wait-list control for 59 families of children with acquired brain injuries. The intervention group showed improvements in child behavior, parenting style, parental distress, family functioning, and the couple relationship (Brown et al., 2013, 2014, 2015). In another RCT, 67 families of children with cerebral palsy were assigned to three groups: a wait-list control group, a combined Stepping Stones Triple P and ACT intervention, and Stepping Stones Triple P alone. Thus the additive effects of ACT above and beyond established behavioral parenting intervention were tested for the first time. Families who received Stepping Stones Triple P alone showed improvements in child behavior and emotional symptoms compared to the wait-list controls. Families who received the combined Stepping Stones Triple P and ACT intervention showed improvements in child behavior, dysfunctional parenting, child hyperactivity, parental psychological symptoms, child functional performance, and parent-rated child quality of life compared to the wait-list controls (Whittingham et al., 2014, 2016). No differences were found between the two intervention groups; however, given the small sample size and the efficacy of Stepping Stones Triple P alone this is not surprising. Overall, this study suggests an additive benefit of ACT above and beyond behavioral parenting intervention.

Acceptance and commitment therapy for parenting/child behaviors

In a recent, nonconcurrent multiple baseline across subjects design, Gould, Tarbox, and Coyne (2018) demonstrated that an ACT parenting intervention delivered individually via home coaching resulted in an increase in valuing behaviors in parents raising children with autism. Increases in overt values-directed parent behavior were observed for all participants. Gains were maintained posttraining, with the greatest effects observed more than 6 months posttraining.

To date, one published study has examined the use of ACT for families of children with anxiety disorders (Raftery-Helmer, Moore, Coyne, & Reed, 2016). Hancock et al. (2018) conducted an RCT in a sample of 193 anxious youth and their parent(s). Parents were involved concurrently with the child groups in a "parent-as-coach" approach. Participants were randomly assigned to one of three conditions: ACT, cognitive behavior therapy (CBT), or wait-list control. Youngsters in both the ACT and CBT group showed reductions in clinical severity ratings and number of anxiety diagnoses compared to participants in the wait-list control group. Gains in both the ACT and CBT conditions were maintained at 3-month follow-up. However, the researchers did not evaluate changes in parenting behavior or parent–child interactions (Hancock et al., 2018).

Recent work tested ACT in a group intervention with a sample of 23 parents of children with anxiety disorders and OCD (Levitt, Hart, Raftery-Helmer, Graebner, & Moore, 2018). The intervention was expected to lead to greater psychological flexibility in parents and reduced anxiety and avoidance in youth. Results showed that parents reported decreased child's internalizing symptoms and OCD posttreatment. Children also reported improved OCD and generalized anxiety symptoms. Parents reported significantly reduced cognitive fusion following the intervention, indicating improved psychological flexibility.

The existing research is promising, but more research on the application of ACT to parenting intervention is needed, including research examining mediators of treatment change.

Three key behavior principles in shaping adaptive child behavior

Taken together, the behavioral principles and strategies described above can be distilled into three key principles that underlie effective strategies for shaping child behavior:

1. Parents should *reinforce* a broad array of adaptive child behaviors in context. This should include reinforcing behaviors that are alternatives to any problematic child behaviors, and addressing any relevant skills deficits through *shaping*. Parents should attend to and praise *effort* rather than outcome; that is, they should reinforce imperfect but best possible approximations of adaptive behaviors (*shaping*).
2. Parents should ensure they do not inadvertently reinforce problematic child behaviors.
3. Parents should use punishment sparingly and always in conjunction with positive parenting strategies.

All parents are capable of learning these principles and applying them in a flexible way. This, of course, does not mean that the parent is perfect; that the parent always reinforces adaptive behavior or that the parent never reinforces problem behavior. In fact, once a behavior has been consistently reinforced and is firmly established it can be helpful for maintenance if the parent reinforces adaptive behavior in an intermittent and unpredictable way. Rather than perfection, it just means that when a pattern begins to develop, where the parent has started to reinforce a problematic behavior, the parent notices this and shifts their parenting accordingly.

Connect and shape

It is especially important for parents to attend to the function of a child's behavior when the child is both signaling attachment needs or experiencing heightened emotion *and also* engaging in problematic behavior. In this circumstance, the emotional–relational and the behavioral principles are both relevant and can be *simultaneously* applied, as part of the very same interaction. I (Koa) have previously outlined how the emotional–relational and behavioral principles can be combined in a parenting meta-strategy called *Connect* and *Shape* (Whittingham, 2015). It is important that parents understand how they can combine the emotional–relational and the behavioral principles in the very same interaction because it is common for problematic behavior to occur in tandem with heightened emotion and the signaling of attachment needs, especially during early childhood. The classic emotionally dysregulated temper tantrum is a perfect example While children's emotions should be viewed as valid and thus evoke empathy, parents may inadvertently shape inappropriate behavior in the *context* of those emotions. In this way, we can help parents more effectively by giving them skills to address behavior in context; here, in the presence of strong expressed emotions.

In addressing behaviors in the context of strong emotions using relational–emotional and the behavioral parenting principles *simultaneously*, it is firstly important to make a clear distinction between emotion and behavior. The child's emotions are to be *accepted* and *validated*, and their affective signaling of needs responded to sensitively. The child's emotions should never be punished and the parent needs to allow for the adaptive (or as adaptive as developmentally possible) expression of emotion. This does not contradict, however, shaping the child's behavior. In fact, setting limits upon the child's behavior and shaping their emotional expression into more adaptive forms of expression is consistent with meta-emotion theory (Gottman, Katz, & Hoover, 1996). If the problematic behavior requires immediate response (e.g., in the case of physical aggression) then the problematic behavior should be appropriately managed before beginning Connect and Shape (Whittingham, 2015).

The *Connect* and *Shape* meta-strategy includes the following:

1. The parent gives no attention to the problematic behavior (if the problematic behavior requires response then this is dealt with first). Instead, the parent focuses on the emotion. The parent validates the emotion, *verbally labeling* it; for example, "It is tough. You are feeling sad." If the parent suspects that it is an instrumental emotion, an emotional display feigned to get a particular result, then the parent should instead focus on validating the child's desire. For example, "you'd like to keep playing. I get that." In validating the parent aims to be accepting and empathetic but also calm and matter of fact.
2. Next, the parent *scaffolds* a more adaptive behavior. This scaffold often takes the form of a simple prompt or a reminder that a particular form of reinforcement is available given a particular behavior. It often involves reminding the child of the availability of parental soothing or parental assistance or both. For example, "If you want help, just ask," or "I'm here with a cuddle if you want it."
3. If the child persists in problematic behavior then the parent implements an appropriate behavioral strategy for the behavior; for example, selective attention (planned ignoring), consequences, or time-out. Selective attention is usually sufficient. This ensures the parent is not reinforcing the problematic behavior. The parent remains within sensory distance, with open and calm body language, conveying acceptance for the child's emotional state.
4. The parent may scaffold adaptive behavior again. For example, the parent might say, "I am happy to help. Just say 'help' if you want me to help." The parent makes his emotional availability and support clear without making assistance or soothing contingent upon problematic behavior.

Instead, soothing and assistance is contingent upon adaptive behavior, such as asking for help, or approaching the parent for a cuddle. Importantly, the parent is also not being intrusive. An angry child does not necessarily want to be immediately hugged. Instead, the parent allows the child to lead the interaction.

5. The parent waits until the child shows an adaptive behavior or a behavior that is, for that particular child, an approximation of an adaptive behavior. This should include the child approaching the parent for soothing or asking for assistance. The shift may be subtle—for example, moving physically toward the parent. The parent is aiming to *shape* adaptive behavior. Importantly, it is the *behavior* that the parent is shaping, not the emotion.
6. The moment the parent observes an approximation of an adaptive behavior, the parent responds with the help or the comfort that the child is asking for. Hence, the child's adaptive behavior is naturally reinforced.

The procedure is illustrated in full in the following flow chart for parents:

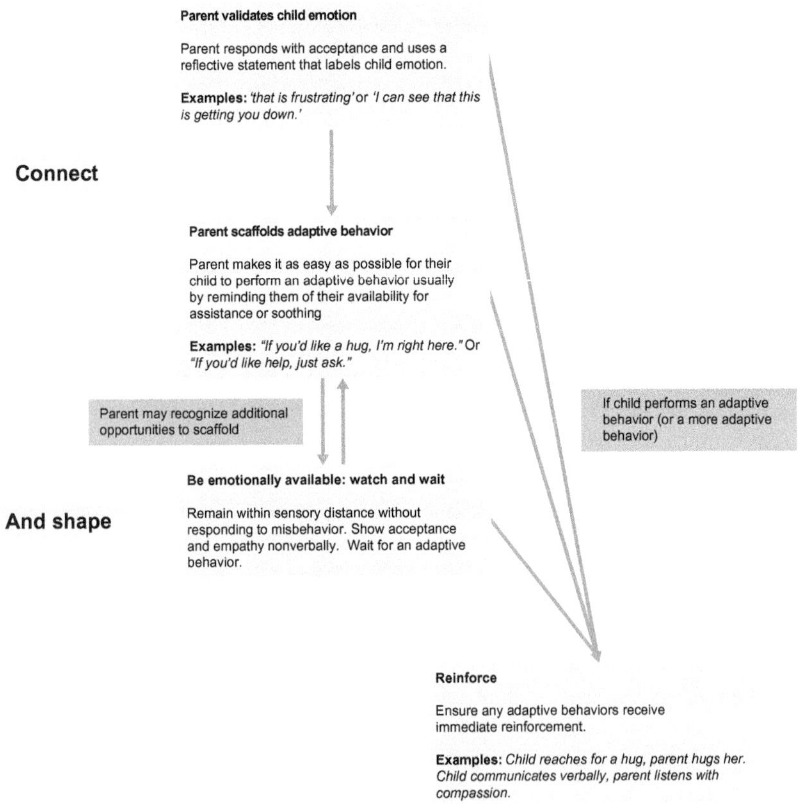

Connect and shape.

Here's an example:

Two-year-old Molly is trying to put a dress onto her dolly. She can't get the dress over her dolly's head. She screams and cries in frustration and begins to hit the dolly repeatedly against the floor.
Molly's mother, Sarah, hears her screams and steps into the room. She immediately names and validates Molly's emotion, "Oh Mol, wouldn't the dress go on dolly? That is frustrating."
Molly ignores Sarah and keeps smashing the dolly onto the floor and screaming.
Sarah moves into scaffolding an adaptive response, "I can help if you like. Just ask."
Molly tries to put the dress on dolly again. Again, it doesn't work and she starts hitting the dolly on the floor.
Sarah stands nearby. She consciously keeps her body language open. She draws upon mindfulness and experiential acceptance techniques to stay open to Molly's emotions, as well as the emotions that they trigger in her.
Molly throws the doll across the room with a scream.
Sarah continues to stand nearby. She is using *selective attention (or planned ignoring)* and hence while she remains calmly within sensory distance and emotionally available she does not give attention to Molly's throwing of the doll or her continued screaming behavior.
Molly continues to scream.
Sarah tries scaffolding again saying softly, "If a cuddle would help, I am right here."
Molly's screams turn to crying and she jumps up and runs to Sarah.
Sarah immediately wraps her arms around her and cuddles her tight, reinforcing Sarah's adaptive behavior of seeking comfort by approaching her for a hug. As Molly's crying begins to settle Sarah scaffolds help-seeking again, "If you want help I'd be happy to help."
Molly nods, drying her tears, "Yes, mama, help please."
Sarah smiles at Molly, "Alright, then. Let's look at this dolly together, huh?"
Sarah shows Molly how to put the dress onto the dolly, providing reinforcement for Molly's adaptive help-seeking behavior of asking for assistance verbally.

As we saw in the *Chapter Three Connect: the parent-child relationship*, attachment can be understood in behavioral terms: attachment behavior is any behavior shaped by the operant function of obtaining proximity to and nurturance from attachment figures (Mansfield & Cordova, 2007) Attachment styles are learned repertoires of attachment behavior, produced by the reinforcement, ignoring, and punishment the child has experienced for their previous attachment bids and whether or not this was predictable. Further, parental sensitivity can be understood as when the parent's caregiving behavior is under the contextual control of the child's cues (Whittingham, 2014).

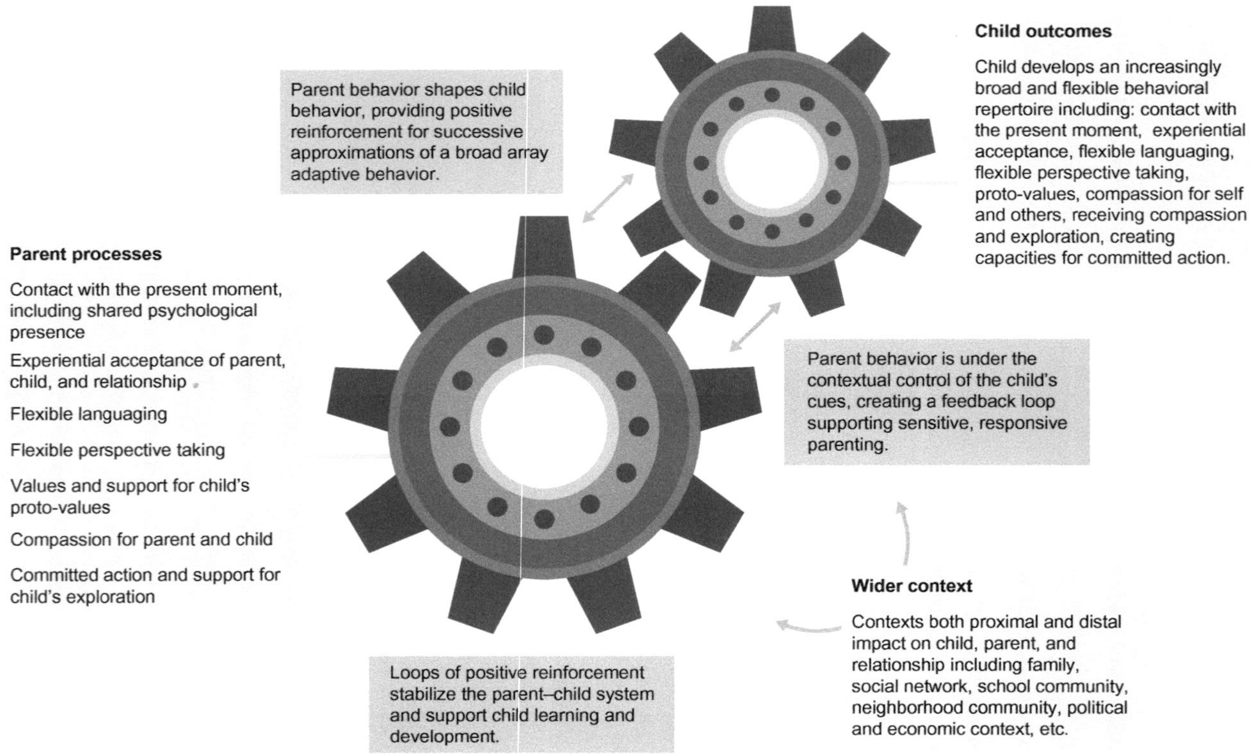

The engine of development.

In integrating the relational–emotional and the behavioral worldviews within the contextual approach, we can see how the parent–child relationship is stabilized through loops of positive reinforcement, and that this, in turn, drives child development and the acquisition of a broad and flexible behavioral repertoire. This complete picture of the parent–child relationship is illustrated in the following diagram:

The loops of positive reinforcement, from parent to child and child to parent, stabilize the parent–child system, and support the cultivation of an increasingly broad and flexible behavioral repertoire in the child.

Chapter summary

Behavioral theories describe how specific behaviors are acquired, strengthened, weakened, and shaped by context, and can be used to understand how parents can facilitate the cultivation of broad and flexible behavioral repertoires in their children. In the next chapter, we examine case conceptualization.

References

Allen, J. R. (2016). Effects of values development on parents' experiential avoidance in parent-child interaction therapy (Order No. 10110787). Available from ProQuest Dissertations & Theses Global: Health & Medicine; ProQuest Dissertations & Theses Global: Social Sciences.

Backen Jones, L., Whittingham, K., Coyne, L., & Lightcap, A. (2016). *A contextual behavioral science approach to parenting intervention and research. The Wiley handbook of contextual behavioral science* (pp. 398–421). Wiley-Blackwell.

Barnes-Holmes, Y., Barnes-Holmes, D., Smeets, P. M., Strand, P., & Friman, P. (2004). Establishing relational responding in accordance with more-than and less-than as generalized operant behavior in young children. *International Journal of Psychology and Psychological Therapy*, *4*, 531–558.

Bishop, S. (2007). Neurocognitive mechanism of anxiety: An integrative account. *Trends in Cognitive Sciences*, *11*(7), 307–316.

Blackledge, J. T. (2005). *Using Acceptance and Commitment Therapy in the support of parents of children diagnosed with autism.* (66), ProQuest Information & Learning, US.

Bouton, M. E. (1988). Context and ambiguity in the extinction of emotional learning: Implications for exposure therapy. *Behavior Research and Therapy*, *26*(2), 137–149.

Bouton, M. E., Mineka, S., & Barlow, D. H. (2001). A modern learning theory perspective on the etiology of panic disorder. *Psychological Review*, *108*(1), 4–32.

Brown, F. L., Whittingham, K., Boyd, R. N., & McKinlay, L. (2015). Does Stepping Stones Triple P plus Acceptance and Commitment Therapy improve parent, couple and family adjustment following paediatric acquired brain injury? A randomised controlled trial. *Behavior Research and Therapy*, *73*, 58–66.

Brown, F. L., Whittingham, K., Boyd, R. N., McKinlay, L., & Sofronoff, K. (2014). Improving child and parenting outcomes following paediatric acquired brain injury: A randomised controlled trial of Stepping Stones Triple P plus Acceptance and Commitment Therapy. *Journal of Child Psychology and Psychiatry*, *55*(10), 1172–1183.

Brown, F., Whittingham, K., McKinlay, L., Boyd, R. N., & Sofronoff, K. (2013). Efficacy of Stepping Stones Triple P plus a stress management adjunct for parents of children with acquired brain injury: The protocol of a randomised controlled trial. *Brain Impairment*, *14* (2), 253–269.

Brummelman, E., Crocker, J., & Bushman, B. J. (2016). The praise paradox: When and why praise backfires in children with low self-esteem. *Child Development Perspectives*, *10*(2), 111–115.

Buchanan-Pascall, S., Gray, K. M., Gordon, M., & Melvin, G. A. (2018). Systematic review and meta-analysis of parent group interventions for primary school children aged 4–12 years with externalizing and/or internalizing problems. *Child Psychiatry & Human Development*, *49*, 244–267.

Chacko, A., Jensen, S. A., Lowry, L. S., Cornwell, M., Chimklis, A., Chan, E., Lee, D., & Pulgarin, B. (2016). Engagement in behavioral parent training: review of the literature and implications for practice. *Clinical Child and Family Psychology Review*, *19*(3), 204–215.

Coyne, L. W., & Cairns, D. (2016). *A relational frame theory analysis of coercive family process. The Oxford handbook of coercive relationship dynamics* (pp. 86–100). New York, NY: Oxford University Press.

Coyne, L. W., McHugh, L., & Martinez, E. R. (2011). Acceptance and commitment therapy (ACT): Advances and applications with children, adolescents, and families. *Child and Adolescent Psychiatric Clinics of North America*, *20*(2), 379–399.

Coyne, L. W., & Wilson, K. G. (2004). The role of cognitive fusion in impaired parenting: An RFT analysis. *International Journal of Psychology and Psychological Therapy*, *4*(3), 469–486.

Craske, M. G., Treanor, M., Conway, C., Zbozinek, T., & Vervliet, B. (2014). Maximising exposure therapy: An inhibitory learning approach. *Behavioral Research and Therapy*, *58*, 10–23.

Dadds, M. R., & Hawes, D. (2006). *Integrated family intervention for child conduct problems*. Brisbane: Australian Academic Press.

de Graaf, I., Speetjens, P., Smit, F., de Wolff, M., & Tavecchio, L. (2008a). Effectiveness of the triple P positive parenting program on behavioral problems in children: A meta-analysis. *Behavior Modification*, *32*(5), 714–735.

de Graaf, I., Speetjens, P., Smit, F., de Wolff, M., & Tavecchio, L. (2008b). Effectiveness of the Triple P Positive Parenting Program on parenting: A meta-analysis. *Family Relations*, *57*(5), 553–566.

Dishion, T. J., Patterson, G. R., & Kavanah, K. A. (1992). An experimental test of the coercion model: Linking theory, measurement and intervention. In J. McCord, & R. E. Tremblay (Eds.), *Preventing antisocial behavior interventions from birth through adolescence*. New York: The Guilford Press.

Dixon, M. R., & Rehfeldt, R. A. (2018). Core behavioral processes. In S. C. Hayes, & S. G. Hofmann (Eds.), *Process-based CBT* (pp. 101–117). Oakland: Context Press.

Donley, M. P., & Rosen, J. B. (2017). Novelty and fear conditioning induced gene expression in high and low states of anxiety. *Learning and Memory*, *24*(9), 449–461.

Drayton, A. K., Andersen, M. N., Knight, R. M., Felt, B. T., Fredericks, E. M., & Dore-Stites, D. J. (2014). Internet guidance on time out: inaccuracies, omissions, and what to tell parents instead. *Journal of Developmental and Behavioral Pediatrics*, *35*, 239–246.

Drayton, A. K., Byrd, M. R., Albright, J. J., Nelson, E. M., Andersen, M. N., & Morris, N. K. (2017). Deconstructing the Time-Out: What Do Mothers Understand About a Common Disciplinary Procedure? *Child & Family Behavior Therapy*, *39*(2), 91–107.

Dymond, S., & Barnes, D. (1996). A transformation of self-discrimination response functions in accordance with the arbitrarily applicable relations of sameness and opposition. *Psychological Record*, *46*(2), 271–300.

Eyberg, S. M., Boggs, S. R., & Algina, J. (1995). Parent–child interaction therapy: A psychosocial model for the treatment of young children with conduct problem behavior and their families. *Psychopharmacology Bulletin*, *31*(1), 83–91.

Forehand, R., Lafko, N., Parent, J., & Burt, K. B. (2014). Is parenting the mediator of change in behavioral parent training for externalizing problems of youth? *Clinical Psychological Review*, *34*(8), 608–619.

Freeman, J. B., Garcia, A. M., Coyne, L., Ale, C., Przeworski, A., Himle, M., . . . Leonard, H. L. (2008). Early childhood OCD: Preliminary findings from a family-based cognitive-behavioral approach. *Journal of the American Academy of Child & Adolescent Psychiatry*, *47*(5), 593–602.

Gardner, F., Montgomery, P., & Knerr, W. (2016). Transporting evidence-based parenting programs for child problem behavior (age 3–10) between countries: Systematic review and meta-analysis. *Journal of Clinical Child & Adolescent Psychology*, *45*(6), 749–762.

Ginsburg, G. S., Drake, K. L., Tein, J.-Y., Teetsel, R., & Riddle, M. A. (2015). Preventing onset of anxiety disorders in offspring of anxious parents: A randomized controlled trial of a family-based intervention. *American Journal of Psychiatry*, *172*(12), 1207–1214.

Gottman, J. M., Katz, L. F., & Hoover, C. (1996). Parental meta-emotion philosophy and the emotional life of families: Theoretical models and preliminary data. *Journal of Family Psychology*, *16*(3), 243–268.

Gould, E. R., Tarbox, J., & Coyne, L. (2018). Evaluating the effects of Acceptance and Commitment Training on the overt behavior of parents of children with autism. *Journal of Contextual Behavioral Science*, *7*, 81–88.

Hancock, K., Swain, J., Hainsworth, C. J., Dixon, A., Koo, S., & Munro, K. (2018). Acceptance and commitment therapy versus cognitive behavior therapy for children with anxiety: Outcomes of a randomized controlled trial. *Journal of Clinical Child and Adolescent Psychology*, *47*(2), 296–311.

Hayes, S. C., Barnes-Holmes, D., & Roche, B. (2001). *Relational frame theory: A postSkinnerian account of human language and cognition*. New York: Plenum Press.

Hayes, S. C., Barnes-Holmes, D., & Wilson, K. G. (2012). Contextual behavioral science: Creating a science more adequate to the challenge of the human condition. *Journal of Contextual Behavioral Science*, *1*(1), 1–16.

Hayes, S. C., Strosahl, K. D., & Wilson, K. G. (2003). *Acceptance and Commitment Therapy: An experiential approach to behavior change*. New York: Guilford Press.

Hernstein, R. J. (1970). On the law of effect. *Journal of Experimental Analysis of Behavior*, *13* (2), 243–266.

Higa-McMillan, C. K., Francis, S. E., Rith-Najarian, L., & Chorpita, B. F. (2016). Evidence base update: 50 years of research on treatment for child and adolescent anxiety. *Journal of Clinical Child and Adolescent Psychology*, *45*(2), 91–113.

Kaminski, J. W., Valle, L. A., Filene, J. H., & Boyle, C. L. (2008). A meta-analytic review of components associated with parent training program effectiveness. *Journal of Abnormal Child Psychology*, *36*(4), 567–589. Available from https://doi.org/10.1007/s10802-007-9201-9.

Karimi-Aghdam, S. (2017). Zone of proximal development (ZPD) as an emergent system: A dynamic systems theory perspective. *Integrative Psychological and Behavioral Science, 51*, 76–93.

Lebowitz, E. R., Omer, H., & Leckman, J. F. (2011). Coercive and disruptive behaviors in pediatric obsessive-compulsive disorder. *Depress and Anxiety, 28*(10), 899–905.

Levitt, M., Hart, A., Raftery-Helmer, J. N., Graebner, E., & Moore, P. S. (2018). *Acceptance and commitment therapy for parents of anxious children: Pilot open trial*. Paper presented at the UMass Medical School Worcester.

Lipkens, G., Hayes, S. C., & Hayes, L. J. (1993). Longitudinal study of derived stimulus relations in an infant. *Journal of Experimental Child Psychology, 56*, 201–239.

Mansfield, A. K., & Cordova, J. V. (2007). A behavioral perspective on adult attachment style, intimacy, and relationship health. In D. W. Woods, & J. W. Kanter (Eds.), *Understanding behavior disorders: A contemporary behavioral perspective*. Reno: Context Press.

McHugh, L., Stewart, I., & Almada, P. (2019). *A contextual-behavioral guide to the self: Theory and practice*. Oakland: New Harbinger.

Miltenberger, R. G., Miller, B. G., Zerger, H. H., & Novotony, M. A. (2018). Shaping. In S. C. Hayes, & S. G. Hofmann (Eds.), *Process-based CBT* (pp. 223–232). Oakland: Context Press.

Mineka, S., & Zinbarg, R. (2006). A contemporary learning theory perspective on the etiology of anxiety disorders: It's not what you thought it was. *American Psychologist, 61*(1), 10–26.

Mowrer, O. H. (1939). A stimulus-response analysis of anxiety and its role as a reinforcing agent. *Psychological Review, 46*, 553–565.

Nowak, C., & Heinrichs, N. (2008). A comprehensive meta-analysis of Triple P-Positive Parenting Program using hierarchical linear modeling: Effectiveness and moderating variables. *Clinical Child and Family Psychology Review, 11*(3), 114–144.

Patterson, G. R. (1982). *Coercive family process* (Vol. 3). Oregon: Castalia Publishing Company.

Patterson, G. R., DeBaryshe, B. D., & Ramsey, E. (1989). A developmental perspective on antisocial behavior. *American Psychologist, 44*(2), 329–335.

Piquero, A. R., Jennings, W. G., Diamond, B., Farrington, D. P., Tremblay, R. E., Welsh, B. C., & Reingle Gonzalez, J. M. (2016). A meta-analysis update on the effects of early family/parent training programs on antisocial behavior and delinquency. *Journal of Experimental Criminology, 12*, 229–248.

Rachman, S. (1977). The conditioning theory of fear-acquisition: A critical examination. *Behavior Research and Therapy, 15*, 375–397.

Raftery-Helmer, J. N., Moore, P. S., Coyne, L., & Reed, K. P. (2016). Changing problematic parent–child interaction in child anxiety disorders: The promise of acceptance and commitment therapy (ACT). *Journal of Contextual Behavioral Science, 5*(1), 64–69. Available from https://doi.org/10.1016/j.jcbs.2015.08.002.

Riley, A. R., Wagner, D. V., Tudor, M. E., Zuckerman, K. E., & Freeman, K. A. (2017). A Survey of Parents' Perceptions and Use of Time-out Compared to Empirical Evidence. *Acad Pediatr, 17*(2), 168–175.

Roche, B., & Barnes, D. (1997). A transformation of respondently conditioned stimulus function in accordance with arbitarily applicable relations. *Journal of the Experimental Analysis of Behavior, 67*, 275–300.

Sanders, M. R., & Dadds, M. R. (1993). *Behavioral family intervention*. Boston, MA: Allyn and Bacon.

Sanders, M. R., Mazzucchelli, T., & Studman, L. (2003). *Practitioner's manual for standard Stepping Stones Triple P*. Brisbane: Triple P International.

Sandoz, E. K., & Boone, M. (2016). *Evoke, reinforce, repeat: Enhancing the creativity and sensitivity of your ACT work by incoporating a plain language behavioral perspective*. Paper presented at the ACBS World Conference, Seattle, WA.

Schrepferman, L., & Synder, J. J. (2002). Coercion: the link between treatment mechanism in behavioral parent training and risk reduction in child antisocial behavior. *Behavior Therapy*, *33*(3), 339–359.

Smith, J. D., Dishion, T. J., Shaw, D. S., Wilson, M. N., Winter, C. C., & Patterson, G. R. (2014). Coercive family process and early-onset conduct problems from age 2 to school entry. *Development and Psychopathology*, *26*(4), 917–932.

Steele, D. L., & Hayes, S. C. (1991). Stimulus equivalence and arbitrarily applicable relational responding. *Journal of Experimental Analysis of Behavior*, *56*, 519–555.

Strand, P. S. (2000). Responsive parenting and child socialization: Integrating two context of family life. *Journal of Child and Family Studies*, *9*(3), 269–281.

Synder, J. J. (2004). Child impulsiveness-inattention, early peer experiences and the development of early onset conduct problems. *Journal of Abnormal Child Psychology*, *32*(6), 579–594.

Synder, J. J., & Patterson, G. R. (1995). Individual differences in social aggression: A test of a reinforcement model of socialization in the natural environment. *Behavior Therapy*, *26*(2), 371–391.

Tellegen, C. ,L., & Sanders, M. ,R. (2013). Stepping Stones Triple P-Positive Parenting Program for children with disability: A systematic review and meta-analysis. *Research in Developmental Disabilities*, *34*, 1556–1571.

Thomas, R., & Zimmer-Gembeck, M. J. (2007). Behavioral outcomes of Parent–Child Interaction Therapy and Triple P-Positive Parenting Program: A review and meta-analysis. *Journal of Abnormal Child Psychology: An Official Publication of the International Society for Research in Child and Adolescent Psychopathology*, *35*(3), 475–495.

Torneke, N. (2010). *Learning RFT*. Oakland: New Harbinger Publications.

van Mourik, K., Crone, M. R., de Wolff, M. R., & Reis, R. (2017). Parent training programs for ethnic minorities: A meta-analysis of adaptations and effect. *Prevention Science*, *18*, 95–105.

VanElzakker, M. B., Dahlgren, M. K., Davis, F. C., Dubois, S., & Shin, L. M. (2014). From Pavlov to PTSD: The extinction of conditioned fear in rodents, humans, and anxiety disorders. *Neurobiology of Learning and Memory*, *113*, 3–18.

Whittingham, K. (2014). Parenting in context. *Journal of Contextual Behavioral Science*, *3*(3), 212–215.

Whittingham, K. (2015). Connect and shape: A parenting meta-strategy. *Journal of Contextual Behavioral Science*, *4*(2), 103–106.

Whittingham, K., Sanders, M., McKinlay, L., & Boyd, R. N. (2014). Interventions to reduce behavioral problems in children with cerebral palsy: An RCT. *Pediatrics*, *133*(5), e1249–e1257.

Whittingham, K., Sanders, M. R., McKinlay, L., & Boyd, R. N. (2016). Parenting intervention combined with acceptance and commitment therapy: A trial with families of children with cerebral palsy. *Journal of Pediatric Psychology*, *41*(5), 531–542.

Whittingham, K., Sofronoff, K., Sheffield, J., & Sanders, M. R. (2009a). Behavioral Family Intervention with parents of children with ASD:What do they find useful in the parenting program Stepping Stones Triple P? *Research in Autism Spectrum Disorders*, *3*, 702–713.

Whittingham, K., Sofronoff, K., Sheffield, J., & Sanders, M. R. (2009b). Stepping Stones Triple P: An RCT of a parenting program with parents of a child diagnosed with an autism spectrum disorder. *Journal of Abnormal Child Psychology: An Official Publication of the International Society for Research in Child and Adolescent Psychopathology*, *37*(4), 469–480.

Wicking, M., Steiger, F., Nees, F., Diener, S. J., Grimm, O., Ruttorf, M., ... Flor, H. (2016). Deficit fear extinction memeory in posttraumatic stress disorder. *Neurobiology of Learning and Memory*, *136*, 116–126.

Wilson, K. G. (2008). *Mindfulness for two*. Oakland: New Harbinger.

Section 2

The bedrock of clinical practice

Chapter 5

Case conceptualization

Chapter Outline

Assessment 104
Intake interview 105
Questionnaires 108
Monitoring 109
Observation of parent–child interaction 111
Functional analysis of child and parent behavior 112
Using clinical relational frame theory and acceptance and commitment therapy models 119
Mei Lin, Tao, and Fan 119
Andrea, Lucia, and Leo 120
Functional analytic psychotherapy and the parent–child relationship 125
Quick and easy tips 128
Sharing your case conceptualization with the parent 129
Chapter summary 130
References 130

If we value our children, we must cherish their parents.

John Bowlby

The way I see it, every life is a pile of good things and bad things. The good things don't always soften the bad things, but vice versa, the bad things don't always spoil the good things and make them unimportant.

The, Eleventh Doctor, *Doctor Who*

People aren't either wicked or noble. They're like chef's salads, with good things and bad things chopped and mixed together in a vinaigrette of confusion and conflict.

Lemony Snicket, *A Series of Unfortunate Events*

Every day of my grown-up life, I have wanted to do what my parents did. I have wanted to widen the province of love and weaken hate and bitterness in the hearts of my children. And I've done these things because of what I got from my family, all those lovely years when I was growing up, being loved and cherished and, unbeknown to me, and in the best way, honored, for myself.

Marian Wright Edelman, *Dream Me Home Safely: Writers on Growing Up in America*

Acceptance and Commitment Therapy. DOI: https://doi.org/10.1016/B978-0-12-814669-9.00005-9
© 2019 Elsevier Inc. All rights reserved.

One clear memory that I (Koa) have from my clinical training is being told the following joke by a professor during a lecture (the professor in question was Professor Tian Oei). A factory owner discovers that their factory is not working. Productivity is down. Everyone is miserable. Desperately, the factory owner seeks help from a renowned expert. The expert examines the factory from top to bottom. The expert speaks to every employee and observes performance over a number of days. Eventually, the expert takes a spanner out of her pocket and tightens a single screw on a single machine. Instantly the factory is transformed. Productivity is up. Employee morale is high. The owner is delighted. Until he gets the expert's bill, that is. He demands to know why he is being charged such an exorbitant price for tightening a single screw—something anyone could have done. "Oh," the expert replies, "I only charged you one dollar for tightening the screw. The rest of my fee is *for knowing that that is what had to be done*." In the same way, the most difficult and valuable aspects of a psychological intervention are not the intervention per se, but rather knowing what it is that needs to be done. That is, the formulation or the case conceptualization. Getting the formulation right is the first step of a successful intervention and the formulation is where you should return if the intervention is not going according to plan.

Assessment

Case conceptualization is always grounded within the integration of multiple forms of assessment that are organized around answering a particular question: typically, to define the nature of "the problem." This can mean gaining diagnostic clarity, or assessing problematic parent–child interaction. In the context of an evolutionary, developmental, and contextual behavioral perspective, the goal of this assessment would be to identify the most effective intervention, given the context of the parent–child relationship. For parenting interventions, the forms of assessment usually used include: an intake interview, norm-referenced parent- or child-report questionnaires, monitoring, and direct or indirect observation. Information may be collected from multiple sources including: one or both parents, other significant caregivers such as stepparents or grandparents, the child or adolescent themselves, and the school. The older the child is, the more likely it is that they will be included directly in the assessment process, with the clinician conducting an intake interview with the child and/or asking the child to fill out questionnaires, for example.

The involvement of the school in the assessment process is obviously only applicable for school-aged children and adolescents and is likely to be a greater focus if there are school-related issues. Where the challenges are solely between the parent and the child, with the child's school performance unaffected, the confirmation of this may be sufficient with no further information from the school needed. The complexity of building a relationship with multiple parents, parental figures, and significant caregivers in the child's life and conceptualizing the family system around the child and the parent–child relationship will be explored in depth in the following chapter on the therapeutic relationship. For now, keep in mind that depending on the family system, each form of assessment may involve multiple parents, parental figures, and/or significant caregivers. When help is sought from one parent in particular, the clinician may need to approach other caregivers for information in order to obtain a full picture, even if the other significant caregivers in the child's life do not become involved in the therapy per se.

Assessment is important for two reasons: (1) to give you the necessary data to develop an accurate case conceptualization that informs the basis for your intervention, and (2) to track client's progress throughout the intervention and to confirm whether or not gains have been made.

Let's explore each form of assessment.

Intake interview

The intake interview is similar to any other clinical intake interview, with the goal of collecting background information and history on the child, the parent/s, and the parent–child relationship/s, as well as an in-depth understanding of the current problems. This will help contextualize the delivery of the intervention. The intake interview may be with one or both parents, depending on who is seeking help, and in the case of an older child or adolescent the clinician may conduct an intake interview with the parents and a separate intake interview with the child in order to gain his or her perspective. Obviously, if the child is a baby or a young toddler, the intake interview may be conducted with the child in the room.

In terms of developing a full picture of the family's current situation, the following information should be obtained:

- Who are all of the significant caregivers in the child's life? What are the living arrangements? What are the caregiving arrangements?
- Of the caregivers who are the decision-makers? That is, who gets to vote on major decisions about how the child is raised? Is there conflict between the decision-makers? Is there conflict around who the decision-makers are?
- Of the caregivers, who is/are the primary caregiver/s? Who does the child spend the majority of their time with? Who tracks and manages the child's schedule and life; for example, communication with the school, ensuring homework is done, keeping up to date with medical, dental, and allied health appointments, making playdates with other children? Is there agreement on who the primary and secondary caregiver/s are and who

does what parenting tasks? Is this chosen and desired by all or a source of conflict?

- Does the child have any siblings? What are the relationships like between the child and sibling/s?
- What are the relationships between caregivers like? Do caregivers generally get along? Is there conflict over the child? Do caregivers support and respect each other or undermine and criticize each other?
- What are the important cultural considerations in the family? How do they impact decisions about caregiving?
- Is the family as a whole under any sources of stress; for example, financial difficulties or significant life events such as a death in the family?
- Apart from the concern causing the parent/s to seek help from you, are there any other health or psychological concerns within the family?

In terms of developing a full picture of the child's history, the following information should be obtained:

- Were there any challenges or concerns during the pregnancy, birth, or early infancy? What was/is the child like as a baby: easy or difficult? Inhibited or disinhibited? Were/are there concerns around feeding, sleeping or crying?
- Who did the child spend the bulk of their time with during infancy, that is, who was their primary caregiver? Were there any changes to this in the first three years of life? As a toddler, did the child go to someone if hurt or upset and if so who? Were there any lengthy separations (e.g., 5 days or more) between the child and the person/people responsible for the majority of their care in infancy during the first 3 years of life? How did the child react to ordinary, everyday separations from their primary caregiver? Did the child calm and accept nurturance from the primary caregiver when reunited? (Note: These questions are aimed at assessing likely attachment figures and patterns, as well as early separations.)
- If the child is in school, then how did they cope with beginning school? Are there challenges at school? How long have the challenges at school been a concern? Does the child have friends at school? Are there any concerns with bullying? Are there any concerns with academic performance? If the child isn't in school and is of school-age, why not?
- Has the child ever been diagnosed with a developmental disability? Or has their development ever been raised as a concern? When did the child first talk and walk?
- Does the child have any major health concerns? Any mental health concerns? Have they been in treatment before, and if so when, for what, and what was the nature of the treatment? How did treatment work?
- Has the child ever experienced trauma or adverse life events?
- Is there a family history of any mental illness?

In terms of developing a full picture of parental adaptation, the following information should be obtained:

- How would the parent/s describe their relationship with their child? Has that always been the case? How was the relationship in the early days?
- How would the parent/s describe their relationship to each other? What is the history of any relationship conflict?
- How would the parent/s describe their own adjustment and well-being at present? Is that a cause for concern or not?
- What is the families of origin of the parent/s like? If, as parents, they replicated the parenting that they themselves received would that be a good outcome or not? In what ways would it be good, and in what ways might it be bad? As a child, was there someone they could go to for help or comfort if they were distressed? If so, who? Why was that person special? These questions are assessing likely attachment figures and attachment patterns of the parent's themselves and can raise red flags for insecure attachment styles and potentially also a history of abuse/neglect. If the parent answers that there was no one that they could go to for help or comfort or if their answers lack any color, depth, or specifics even when prompted, for example, "Yeah, fine. Mum and dad worked hard for me," that's a sign of an insecure attachment style, specifically an avoidant attachment style that has not been reflected upon and processed. If the parent responds with a lot of unprocessed emotion—for example, anger, blame, and longing for their own parent—that's also a sign of an insecure attachment style, specifically ambivalent, that has not been reflected upon and processed. If the parent responds with depth and reflection, talking lucidly about the positive and negatives of the parenting they received that is a sign of a secure attachment style, either a secure attachment style formed during childhood or a secure attachment style "won" later in life with reflection, for example, "Well, overall, I suppose it would be a good outcome if I replicated my own parenting. I would say that my parents were good parents. But that doesn't mean I don't want to improve upon the parenting I received either! I think they did a good job given what they had to work with and I'm grateful to them, honestly, but I'd like to do better still. Mum and dad were affectionate and loving. I always knew I was loved, put it like that. So that was good. I want to keep that. But they really didn't have a clue about discipline. Sometimes they were too soft. I played them at times, I admit it. And other times they'd come down hard. My teenage years were a bit rough for us. Of course, they struggled financially in those years too. So, looking back, I get that they were doing their best. But I don't want to do that with my children."

During the intake interview, a significant amount of time should also be focused on assessing the presenting problem. Why have the parent/s sought help? What is the history of the presenting problem? In order to be able to gain rich information about the presenting problem, it is important to ask the parent/s to recall a specific example of the behavior in question. Prompt the parent/s to think of a recent and fairly typical example. Then ask them to walk you through what happened. Ask them to set the scene, telling you where and when. Ask for a full sense of what was happening immediately before the problem behavior. Then ask for a full description of the problem behavior itself. It may help to prompt the parents to describe it so that it is as if you can see it unfold, like watching from a camera in the room. How did they respond to the behavior? How did others respond? What happened next? When did the behavior end? What happened to bring the behavior to an end? What happened immediately after? All of this detail will be rich information for your formulation.

If conducting an intake interview with a child or teenager then you will be focused on gaining a sense of the problem from their point of view. What are their priorities or concerns?

When conducting an intake interview, it is often helpful to include the child with the parent for at least a portion of the session, for several reasons. First, there is a robust literature on informant discrepancies across parents and children, so inclusion of both is critical to obtaining all relevant perspectives. In addition, it will allow you, the clinician, an opportunity for direct behavioral observation of how the parent and child interact, and how they speak about "the problem" together.

Questionnaires

Questionnaires may be given to the parent/s, other significant caregivers, the teacher at school, and/or the child/adolescent themselves depending on the child's age, presenting problem, and the care situation.

There are multiple options for questionnaire assessment in parenting interventions including questionnaires that are in the public domain and are free to use. Domains you might want to consider assessing, depending on the presenting problem, include:

- Parental adjustment, including depressive, anxious and stress symptoms
- Parental psychological flexibility
- Parenting style
- Parent–child relationship
- Parent–child emotional availability
- Infant cry/fuss behavior
- Infant sleep behavior
- Child internalizing behavior
- Child externalizing behavior
- Child attention/hyperactivity

- Adolescent adjustment
- Adolescent attention/hyperactivity
- Adolescent psychological flexibility
- Family adjustment

In addition to assessing the presenting problem, you might also like to consider assessing constructs relevant to an Acceptance and Commitment Therapy (ACT) intervention including:

- Psychological flexibility
- Engagement in valued behavior
- Mindfulness
- Mindfulness in parenting
- Compassion
- Cognitive fusion
- Perspective taking
- Defusion

A complete examination of the available measures is outside the scope of this book. Along with monitoring, the questionnaires are an avenue of assessment that is important for keeping track of the success of the intervention. Therefore it is important to assess the presenting problem via questionnaires.

Monitoring

The parent may be monitoring a target behavior of the child or a target behavior of themselves or both. Monitoring should be informed by a thorough functional analysis (see later) of the contextual factors (antecedents and consequences) that maintain a behavior and, in turn, the information gained through monitoring will inform ongoing functional analysis. The target behavior may be a problem behavior or it could be a deficit, a behavior that the child or the parent needs to display more of; for example, for a child it could be independent play. In an adolescent, the adolescent too may be involved in the monitoring process, monitoring target behaviors in themselves. In this case, the target behaviors should reflect the adolescent's own goals.

Monitoring has three purposes: to gain information for conceptualization including functional analysis, to support the parent's development of insight, and to track the success of the intervention, that is, has the target behavior changed as desired through identification and manipulation of antecedents and consequences. Monitoring, in and of itself, can lead to behavior change and maintenance (Sanders & James, 1982).

In order to gain information for conceptualization and support the parent's development of insight, a diary-type format is used with the parent keeping track of specific episodes of the target behavior, including what happened immediately before the target behavior and what happened immediately after the target behavior. If the target behavior is quite frequent, as is often the case with when a parent has sought help for a problem child behavior, then the monitoring can also be done at the end of the day, so that the parent is not burdened with needing to write down details of the child's behavior at the high stress time when the child is actually engaged in that behavior, or when they themselves are midstream in a dysfunctional behavioral pattern. In addition to providing you, the clinician, with a rich source of information for conceptualization, monitoring the child or parent behavior often assists the parent themselves gain insight into the reasons their child or they themselves are behaving as they are. As monitoring often assists the parent in gaining insight into their and their child's behavioral patterns, monitoring itself often has an intervention effect. A parent may notice previously unnoticed patterns. For example, they may notice that their child's tantrum behavior usually occurs in a situation where the parent has asked their child to play independently for some time. They may notice that their own behavior of giving into their child's demands happens when they are overburdened with tasks. Or they might notice that their adolescent's whining behavior is often responded to by the adolescent getting what they want. Once the pattern is seen and understood, this insight provides the basis for behavioral change.

In order to keep track of the success of the intervention three possible monitoring methods are used, depending on the nature of the behavior: *frequency, duration*, or *time sampling*. Monitoring the *frequency* of a behavior simply means to keep a tally, so that the frequency of the behavior on any given day is known. It may, for example, be recorded that a particular 3-year child hit her sibling three times last Monday. Monitoring the *duration* of a behavior means timing a particular behavior when it occurs and make note of the duration. It may, for example, be recorded that a particular 6-year-old engaged in independent play for 15 minutes on Wednesday. *Time sampling* is a method of monitoring where the day, or a particular time period of the day, is divided up into specific blocks of time, for example, 15-minute intervals. For each interval, you record whether a behavior is present or absent. For example, a parent may record their own yelling behavior during the evening routine—from picking up children from childcare to putting their children to bed. Dividing up the 2-hour evening routine into 15-minute intervals they might record that yelling happened during three of the eight intervals on Thursday evening. All of these methods for monitoring give an accurate sense of the scale of the presenting problem, and can therefore be used to measure progress.

When asking parents or older children or teens to monitor their behavior, it's critical to "right-size" the task, to support consistent and accurate tracking of behavior. If monitoring is burdensome or inconvenient, or is not collaboratively planned between clinician and parent or child, it's unlikely that it will be done, especially in families experiencing multiple stressors. Thus how monitoring is assigned and consideration to make it feasible and sustainable given a particular family context is very important.

Observation of parent–child interaction

Conducting an observation of the parent–child interaction is an important part of the assessment process as it gives the clinician a direct window into the parent–child relationship and the patterns of interaction. Observations may be done in the clinic or in the family home. For younger children and infants the physical presence of the clinician themselves during the observation may not be problematic. However, for older children and adolescents, or depending on the nature of the presenting problem, it may be best if the clinician is not physically present as their presence could change the child's behavior. This can be accommodated by watching the parent and child through a camera, for example. In fact, with all the advantages of modern technology, it is possible for the clinician to conduct an observation of the parent and child in their home, while watching from their own home or clinic. Any video-conferencing software such as Skype or Zoom can be put to this use, provided the parent has a phone, tablet, or similar device, or the clinician is able to lend out a device for this purpose.

Depending on the presenting problem and the purposes of the observation, the observation may be tailored to capture specific challenging behavior itself, or it may simply be to gain a snapshot of parent–child interaction. If it is to gain a snapshot of parent–child interaction, then the clinician may simply instruct the parent to ensure they are interacting with their child during the observation as they normally would. Some aspects of the parent–child interaction—for example, how the parent responds to temper tantrums—are only observable if the child does engage in target behavior. However, other aspects of the parent–child relationship, such as parental sensitivity, are qualitatively present during all interactions and are always observable in some form. Alternatively, the parent–child interaction may be deliberately planned to maximize the chance that a problematic child behavior will occur. For example, if noncompliance is a concern, then the interaction may include the parent needing to elicit the child's compliance to clean up toys and start homework. Parent–child interactions should be a minimum of 20 minutes.

When watching a parent–child interaction consider the following questions:

- Does the parent have a sensitive and responsive pattern of interaction with the child? Remember, warmth is necessary for sensitivity but it is not sufficient. Does the parent seem to have an accurate sense of the child's perspective? Is parental affect positive and genuine? Is the parent accepting and flexible toward the child?

- Are there any expressions of parental hostility toward the child? For the observation, this includes noting very subtle covert expressions, such as statements that may be subtly mocking or nonverbal expressions of frustration or boredom. Remember, the parent is aware that that are being watched so any subtle signs of hostility probably reflect hostility that the parent is unable to hide.
- Is the parent intrusive? Does it feel like the parent is getting in the child's way? Or is the child able to lead the interaction? Does the interaction feel open and spacious or constrained and restricted?
- Is the parent able to scaffold the child's behavior? Is there evidence of the parent engaging in shaping—reinforcing progressive approximations toward adaptive behavior?
- Did you see any examples of the presenting problem in terms of the child's behavior? If so, take note of what happened immediately before and after the behavior. How did the parent respond?
- Did you see any examples of the presenting problem in terms of the parent's behavior? If so, take note of what happened immediately before and after the behavior. How did the child respond to the parent's behavior?
- Does the parent–child interaction contain plenty of positive reinforcement of the child for adaptive or approximations of adaptive behavior? Or is the parent neutral or negative when the child behaves adaptively?
- Does the parent–child interaction contain reinforcement of the child for any maladaptive behavior including but not limited to the presenting problem?

Functional analysis of child and parent behavior

A key aspect of observation of parent-child interaction, and thus, of the case conceptualization will be the functional analysis of the child and parent behavior. The primary goal of a functional analysis is to identify contextual factors - antecedents and consequences - that maintain child behavior. As discussed in previous chapters, behavioral parenting interventions involve two main strategies: reinforcing adaptive behaviors and minimizing reinforcement for unhelpful or inappropriate behaviors. In order to accomplish these goals, it's necessary to understand the contingencies that occasion and maintain behavior.

The simplest way to structure a functional analysis is the A–B–C method where A is the antecedent, B is the behavior, and C is the consequences. The behavior can be anything the person does. The behaviors that you focus on for your functional analysis are defined by the intervention goals. That is, you focus in on the problem behaviors of either the child or the parent. Remember, antecedents are stimuli occurring *before* the behavior that influence the occurrence of that behavior. Consequences are stimuli occurring *after* the behavior; in the case of operant behaviors, consequences affect the likelihood of the behavior occurring again in a similar context. Consequences that strengthen behavior are called *reinforcers* and consequences that weaken behavior are called *punishers*. Respondent and operant theory is covered in depth in Chapter 4, Shape: building a flexible repertoire. If you don't have a background in behavioral theory and practice, do not be alarmed by the technical jargon. You can begin to use the A–B–C method of functional analysis by simply thinking it through in these steps:

- What happens *before* the child engages in behavior (identify the antecedent)?
- What happens *after* the child's behavior (identify the consequence)?
- Based on what you have observed, what does the child's behavior *get* her (what is the function of behavior)?

Let's look at a simple example:

Fan is 3 years old. Her parents, Mei Lin and Tao, have sought out parenting support because they are concerned about Fan's frequent noncompliance. Following the assessment, including an intake interview with both Mei Lin and Tao, questionnaires, monitoring of noncompliance, and an observation of Mei Lin and Tao interacting with Fan in their own home (you observed the bedtime routine as it is a key time for noncompliance), you are ready to develop a case conceptualization. You begin by focusing on a functional analysis of the key child behavior that is of concern: noncompliance using the A–B–C method. You do this by examining the data that you have collected and asking: what happens *before*? You list that in the antecedent column. You then ask: what exactly does the behavior/s look like? You list that in the behavior column. Finally, you ask: what happens *after*? You list that in the consequence column.

Noncompliance

A Antecedent	B Behavior	C Consequence
Parent, Mei Lin or Tao, instructs Fan to do a nonpreferred activity, for example, having a bath or getting ready for bed, or leaving an activity she is enjoying for example leaving the park.	Ignores parent, says "no," shouts "no," cries, and screams, stamps foot, runs away.	Mei Lin and Tao try to convince Fan to comply verbally, repeating the instruction many times. The nonpreferred activity is often delayed or the preferred activity is prolonged. Sometimes the nonpreferred activity is skipped altogether; for example, sometimes Fan is allowed to not have a bath.

(*Continued*)

(Continued)

Now that you've put the behavior and stimuli into the appropriate columns you can begin to think about the contingencies. What is the likely function of the behavior? This is a behavior that is occurring frequently so it is likely that the behavior is being reinforced. Is there anything listed in the consequence column that could be functioning as a reinforcer? Yes, there is. Mei Lin and Tao's attempts to convince Fan to comply could be functioning as a positive reinforcer (parental attention). The delay or skipping of the nonpreferred activity such as bath time could be functioning as a negative reinforcer. And the continuation of a preferred activity such as playing at the park could be functioning as a positive reinforcer. You now have a hypothesis about the functions of Fan's noncompliant behavior. Based on this hypothesis you can make predictions about how Mei Lin and Tao need to change their parenting behavior in order to change Fan's behavior.

This functional analysis of the key presenting problem, Fan's noncompliance, can then be used as a starting point for a more expansive and in-depth conceptualization. To expand out from the functional analysis itself—to put Fan's behavior into a wider context—as well as to understand the behavior of Mei Lin and Tao more deeply, you can ask:

- Are there any historical antecedents that may be influencing Fan's noncompliant behavior? That is, is there anything that happened before Fan's behavior, but not immediately before, that also has influenced Fan's noncompliant behavior today?
- Does Fan have a skills deficit? That is, does she have, in her repertoire, an alternative behavior for the same context (i.e., a competing behavior)? And is that behavior reinforced? For Fan, this may involve considering whether or not she is, at times, compliant with her parent's instructions. Is her compliance reinforced? It also may include considering whether or not she ever expresses disappointment or frustration at task transitions in a more adaptive manner? And, if so, is that reinforced?
- Are there long-term consequences to this pattern of behavior? For example, the continuation of a skills deficit that further maintains the pattern in the long term?
- Finally, you can then turn your attention to Mei Lin and Tao themselves, by performing a functional analysis of the parenting behavior that is inadvertently reinforcing Fan's problematic behavior.

In particular, as you expand the functional analysis to take into account broader contextual variables and patterns, some of your ideas may be speculative. While you may have clear data on what happens immediately before Fan's noncompliant behavior, from the interview, monitoring and observation, your evidence for historical antecedents, and your hypothesises around their linkage to Fan's current behavior are likely to be speculative. It is perfectly acceptable to add events or stimuli with qualifiers such as "possible," "probable," or even question marks to remind yourself of the speculative nature of these aspects of your formulation. It is also acceptable to include questions, to prompt yourself to explore certain

(*Continued*)

(Continued)

possibilities within the intervention. Although an initial formulation is conducted at the beginning of an intervention, formulation is an ongoing exercise, and it is reviewed and revised throughout the intervention, the progress of the intervention itself informing its continued adaptation.

Let's expand the functional analysis to a more in-depth formulation as follows.

Fan's noncompliance

Historical antecedents: Possible ambivalent attachment style? In the observation, Fan was observed to cry and reach for Mei Lin and then to immediately pull back, then reach up crying again. Mei Lin's description of her own relationship to her mother was highly emotive and had themes of longing, consistent with an ambivalent attachment style. It is possible that there is a history of Mei Lin inconsistently responding to adaptive attachment behavior in Fan (i.e., adaptive behavior with the function of obtaining proximity to and nurturance from Mei Lin), while more consistently responding to problematic attachment behavior and emotional expression (i.e., seeking proximity and nurturance through misbehavior and tantrum behaviors). Fan's noncompliance and tantrum behaviors may hence have been reinforced and adaptive attachment behaviors (adaptive ways to see proximity and nurturance such as communicating needs verbally or physically approaching the parent for affection) may not.

Skills deficits: Noncompliance is specific to following instructions involving transition from a preferred activity to a nonpreferred activity. Possible skills deficits in emotional understanding, adaptive emotional expression, and maintaining adaptive behavior including approach behavior in a context of heightened emotions including frustration and disappointment. Are more adaptive behaviors for expressing frustration and disappointment being reinforced? Is approach behavior in a context of heightened emotion being reinforced (rather than trying to escape demands)?

A Antecedent	B Behavior	C Consequence
Parent, Mei Lin or Tao, instructs Fan to do a nonpreferred activity, for example, having a bath or getting ready for bed, or leaving an activity she is enjoying; for example, leaving the park.	Ignores parent, says "no," shouts "no," cries, and screams, stamps foot, runs away.	Mei Lin and Tao try to convince Fan to comply verbally, repeating the instruction many times. The nonpreferred activity is often delayed or the preferred activity is prolonged. Sometimes the nonpreferred activity is skipped altogether; for example, sometimes Fan is not allowed to have a bath.

(*Continued*)

(Continued)

Long-term consequences: If skills deficits in emotional understanding, adaptive emotional expression, and maintaining adaptive behavior including approach behavior in a context of heightened emotions including frustration and disappointment exist then the current behavioral pattern is maintaining the skills deficit. Fan has little opportunity to develop better emotional understanding, adaptive emotional expression, or to maintain adaptive behavior in a context of heightened emotion.

Likely contingencies: Mei Lin and Tao's repeated attempts to get Fan to comply could be functioning as a positive reinforcer. The delay or avoidance of a nonpreferred activity could be functioning as a negative reinforcer. The continuation of a preferred activity could be functioning as a positive reinforcer. This may be occurring in the context of skills deficits in emotional understanding, adaptive emotional expression, and maintaining adaptive behavior including approach behavior in a context of heightened emotions.

Mei Lin and Tao's response

A Antecedent	B Behavior	C Consequence
Fan ignores her parents, says "no," shouts "no," cries and screams, stamps foot, and runs away. Mei Lin and Tao report feeling "anxious and stressed" when Fan is noncompliant.	Mei Lin and Tao try to convince Fan to comply verbally, repeating the instruction many times. Mei Lin and Tao give in, delaying the transition to the nonpreferred activity, prolonging the preferred activity or avoiding the nonpreferred activity altogether.	Sometimes, after Mei Lin and Tao have repeated the instruction many times with increasing intensity, Fan eventually complies. When Mei Lin and Tao give in, Fan's aversive behavior of shouting "no," crying, screaming, stamping her foot and running away stops. There is likely a temporary reduction in stress/anxiety.

Likely contingencies: The fact that Fan sometimes eventually complies with Mei Lin and Tao's repeated instructions likely functions as a reinforcer for their continued and escalating attempts to verbally convince her to comply. The termination of Fan's aversive behavior is likely a negative reinforcer for Mei Lin and Tao's behavior of giving in. A temporary reduction in Mei Lin and Tao's stress/anxiety following giving in is also likely a negative reinforcer.

Let's explore another example with a different but also common problem.

Leo is 13 years old and his parents, Andrea and Lucia, have sought psychological and parenting support because they are concerned about Leo's social anxiety and how it is affecting his school performance. They are also aware that there are tensions within their relationship with Leo, and feel he has become withdrawn. They were prompted to seek help when Leo refused to give a presentation for assessment in English and consequently failed it. You do a full assessment with intake interviews, questionnaires, monitoring, and observation, collecting information from Andrea, Lucia, and Leo himself as well as Leo's school and are ready to develop a case conceptualization. You begin with the functional analysis of the key concern: Leo's refusal to take part in performative assessment at school and to engage in social activities. From there, you expand to a full in-depth assessment of Leo, Andrea, and Lucia. It might look like the following.

Leo's avoidance of social/performance situations

Historical antecedents: Possible long-term pattern of inhibition? Andrea and Lucia reported that Leo was "always shy." Leo reported that he was bullied in primary school and is still sometimes bullied now. Leo reports that he has two friends at school. If they are not present, he does not engage with others.

Skills deficits: Likely social and performance skills deficits.

A Antecedent	B Behavior	C Consequence
Leo needs to perform in front of the class, including assessment, being asked a question in class, being invited into a larger social group (apart from his two friends) or needing to engage with others at a family event.	Avoids social or performative situations, including refusing to do pieces of assessment. It may include refusal to speak, that is, ignoring the teacher's question, or withdrawing to a corner within a social event and looking at his phone.	Sometimes the demand for Leo to perform is withdrawn; for example, the teacher may ask another student, or Andrea and Lucia may leave Leo to look at his phone at a family event. It is likely that Leo experiences a temporary reduction in anxiety. Sometimes Andrea and Lucia or a teacher expresses frustration at Leo's behavior or uses coercive methods to try to force Leo to speak. This has included yelling at Leo, calling him names, or attempting to shame him.

Long-term consequences: Leo's skills deficit in social and performative skills is not addressed. His social skills are falling further behind his peers. Within the

(*Continued*)

(Continued)

extended family and Andrea and Lucia's social circle, others have ceased attempting to engage with Leo.

Likely contingencies: It is likely that the avoidance of social and performative situations is reinforcing Leo's behavior. It is also likely that the temporary reduction in anxiety reinforces Leo's avoidance behavior. This is occurring in the context of a skills deficit in social and performative skills. It is likely that Andrea and Lucia's coercive attempts to get Leo to speak in social situations have—instead of encouraging him to speak—actually taught him to persist in his refusal to speak, in order to avoid not just the social and performative situation but also the coercion. It is also likely that these attempts have damaged their relationship with Leo, contributing to the development of coercive patterns and Leo's withdrawal.

Andrea and Lucia's response

A Antecedent	B Behavior	C Consequence
Leo withdraws, looks at his phone, and refuses to speak including to direct questions. Andrea and Lucia report feeling "uncomfortable and embarrassed" and state that they "don't know what to do."	Andrea and Lucia withdraw their demand for Leo to perform or to engage socially. For example, they may allow him to spend a family social event looking at his phone and speaking to no one. Instead, they focus on the social event themselves. Andrea and Lucia also sometimes express their frustration with Leo at his behavior, including attempting to coercively push Leo into being social.	By withdrawing their demand for Leo to perform or engage socially and focusing on the social event themselves they experience all the richness of the social event and avoid an aversive interaction. It is likely that by focusing on the social event themselves, not on Leo's behavior they experience a temporary reduction in feelings of discomfort and embarrassment. It is likely that in expressing their frustration with Leo and attempting coercion they experience a temporary reduction in feelings of discomfort and anger.

Likely contingencies: It is likely that his parents' withdrawing their demands on Leo and focusing on the social event themselves is negatively reinforcing because it enables the avoidance of an aversive interaction and the engagement with the potential positive reinforcers present in a social event, as well as the temporary reduction in feelings of discomfort and embarrassment. It is also likely that his parents' expressing frustration with Leo and attempting coercive parenting is negatively reinforced by a temporary reduction in feelings of discomfort and anger.

Using clinical relational frame theory and acceptance and commitment therapy models

A contextual behavioral approach to functional analysis also considers the role of private events—thoughts, feelings, memories, sensations, and behavioral impulses—as antecedents and consequences of behavior. In addition, any of these may also be considered privately observable behavior, as behavior is anything that the organism *does*, that is, think*ing*, feel*ing*, etc. One aspect of this is to incorporate an Relational Frame Theory (RFT) analysis of the particular *meanings* of private events, such that clinicians may help parents or children to derive new or different meanings that serve them more effectively, given a particular context. Thus it is helpful to include an assessment of derived relational responding—or, the *meaning* of events for the parent, and if relevant, the child—in one's assessment. Consider the above examples of both Fan and Leo, and their parents.

Mei Lin, Tao, and Fan

Let's start by adding further information. During the intake interview with Mei Lin and Tao, they revealed that they both struggle with challenging thoughts about their parenting and Fan. Mei Lin reports that during challenging interactions with Fan she often has the thought "Fan hates me." She reports that this thought is particularly triggered when Fan engages in noncompliance or expresses negative emotions. Tao reports that he sometimes has the thought that Fan is "a little monster." During the intake interview both report puzzlement at Fan's behavior and state that they have "no idea" why she won't "be good." Both state that they want to be "good parents" and to "raise Fan well."

Understanding the meaning of Fan's behavior for Mei Lin and Tao sheds some light on their response to it. Both Mei Lin and Tao are inconsistent in enforcing compliance when they give directions. That is, they do not follow through, and hence inadvertently reinforce her tantrum behavior and behavioral avoidance of demands. For Mei Lin, Fan's tantrum and noncompliance means (i.e., has been coordinated with) "Fan hates me." This is likely to be highly aversive and associated with anxiety and distress. It is also likely to be related to other thoughts for Mei Lin, such as that she is being "mean" or that she's a "bad mother." Given the derived meaning, it makes sense that in the presence of Fan's tantrum and noncompliance Mei Lin engages in avoidance, backing down from the interaction, and letting Fan get what she wants to quickly terminate the tantrum behavior. For Tao, Fan's tantrum and noncompliance means (i.e., is coordinated with with) "Fan is a little monster." Again, this is likely to be highly aversive. Tao may, in turn, experience thoughts about the fact that he experiences this thought, for example, thinking that it makes him a bad father. This may be part of why he quickly seeks to terminate the tantrum behavior by giving in, to quickly re-establish "pleasant" interactions, ending such thoughts, and re-establishing himself as a good father. In addition, "Fan is a little monster" is a hopeless situation. It is likely to be related to thoughts that there is little that Tao can do to change Fan's behavior.

The clinician might then use this information to employ ACT mindfulness and acceptance processes in a more targeted way, to change the *function* Mei Lin and Tao's thoughts. For example, clinicians might discuss more selective use of direction-giving, and in this context, discuss enforcing compliance as equivalent with "good parenting," even if it elicits strong emotions from both parents and child. This might support more consistent and effective direction-giving, antecedent control strategies to use with Fan, or persistence in enforcing compliance through behavioral parenting strategies.

Andrea, Lucia, and Leo

Again, let's start by adding more information to the case. During the intake interview with Leo, he is not able to discuss his feelings about or immediately before social or performative situations in any depth beyond the fact that he doesn't want to do them. At one point in the interview he says that he is "just a reject." During the intake interview with Lucia and Andrea, Andrea admits that he is frequently "distracted by work" and finds it difficult to find the time and energy to focus on being a father and a husband. He also states that he finds himself struggling with a sense of shame about Leo's behavior, saying "what's wrong with him? Why can't he grow up?" Lucia admits that she sometimes blames herself, explaining "maybe I was too soft with him when he was younger?" Notably, Andrea and Lucia report feeling "embarrassed" and "uncomfortable" when Leo avoids social interactions.

Andrea and Lucia's feelings of embarrassment, discomfort, and shame around Leo's social behavior are likely related to how they respond to Leo. Firstly, when they allow him to escape social situations, this may relieve their sense of discomfort. But also, they may attribute particular meanings to their own intense feelings, perhaps that embarrassment/discomfort/shame is "intolerable," and if Leo also feels embarrassed in social situations, they may then derive that this is "intolerable" to him. Again, this may inadvertently reinforce his avoidance of social situations—as well as the experience of his own embarrassment and discomfort. A clear understanding of this may help Andrea and Lucia develop a different sort of relationship to their discomfort: clinicians might support them in modeling feeling embarrassed/uncomfortable and engaging in social situations anyway, such that Leo might observe, make similar attempts, and discover for himself how to engage in social approach. In addition, for Leo and Andrea, Leo's social difficulties mean that there is something fundamentally wrong with Leo: "just a reject" or "what's wrong with him?" This suggests that Leo's social difficulties cannot be changed. The clinician could ensure that, throughout the intervention, social skills are framed as a *skill*, as something that can be learned, practiced, and improved upon not as an innate ability.

Changing the relationship of parents to aversive private events is at the heart of ACT, and clinical RFT work can be addressed using particular ACT processes. Midlevel models of ACT processes including the hexaflex and DNA-V can also be used within a case formulation process, for both the parent and the child. These models focus on ACT processes for the parent and the child and can be used in conjunction with a functional analysis of specific target behaviors, as part of a full formulation. In fact, ideally a functional analysis is performed first, and then, from the functional analysis the clinician asks which ACT processes may or may not be involved. Does the parent or child have any particular strengths in terms of ACT processes? Does the parent or child have any particular weaknesses in terms of ACT processes? This can then form the basis of setting goals around the ACT processes focused on in intervention. Again, formulation is an ongoing process. It may be the case that initially you are unsure of the role of specific ACT processes within the parent–child interactions in questions or have tentative ideas only. Such thoughts can still form part of the initial formulation with their tentative nature noted.

Let's explore using the parent–child ACT hexaflex for the two cases earlier. Remember the parent–child ACT hexaflex looks like this:

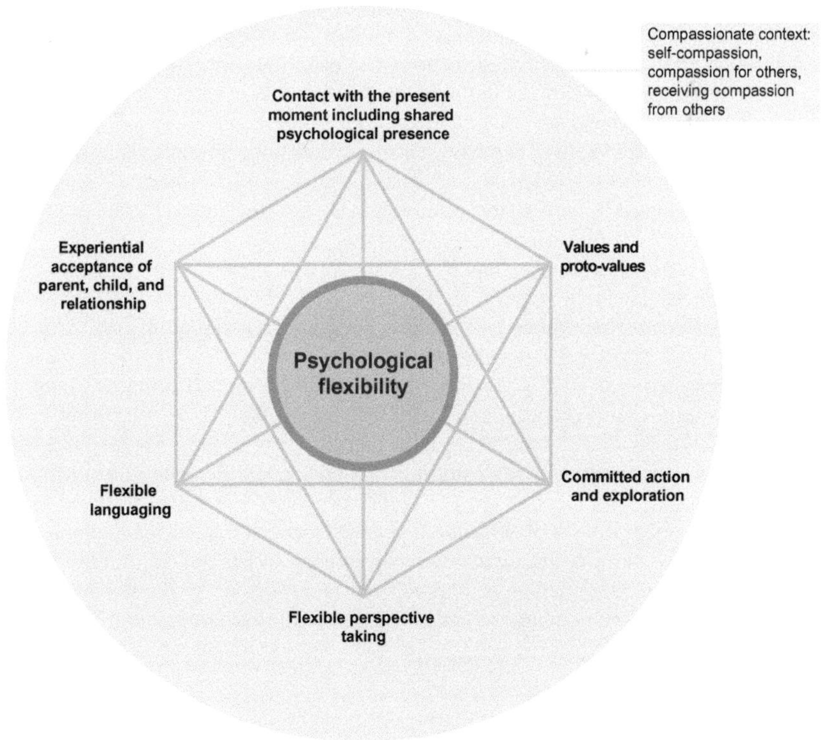

Let's explore each of the six processes on the hexaflex in turn for Fan and for her parents Mei Lin and Tao. You will notice that as Fan is 3 years old, her competencies in the six processes need to be understood developmentally and as emerging from within her social relationships. Considering the six ACT processes with children and adolescents is not so much about identifying deficits, but rather about considering the ways in which the child's context including the parent–child relationship is supporting the emergence of competencies within these areas in a developmentally appropriate way.

Fan

- *Contact with the present moment including shared psychological presence.* Fan's capacity to be mindful is developmentally appropriate. Are there attuned interactions with shared psychological presence?
- *Experiential acceptance of parent, child, and relationship.* Fan's capacity for experiential acceptance is emerging. Mei Lin and Tao focus solely on Fan's observable behavior—that is, they do not acknowledge or validate Fan's emotions of frustration and disappointment in transitioning to a new activity—and respond to Fan's expression of her frustration and disappointment by acting to quickly terminate that expression. In essence, they are not acting with acceptance of Fan's emotional life. The parent–child interaction is currently not supporting the development of experiential acceptance in Fan.
- *Flexible languaging.* Fan's languaging abilities are still developing. She may have a deficit in her ability to express her emotional experiences verbally. Her development of this ability may be supported by Mei Lin and Tao discussing Fan's emotions.
- *Values and proto-values.* Fan has a developmentally appropriate sense of her own preferences. Do Mei Lin and Tao reflect back to Fan her motivations and preferences in a manner consistent with her developing richer proto-values?
- *Flexible perspective taking.* Fan has a limited capacity for perspective taking as is developmentally appropriate for her age. Do Mei Lin and Tao support this as an emerging skill by talking about perspectives and sharing their tracking of Fan's ongoing self-as-process?
- *Committed action and exploration.* Some evidence for anxious-ambivalent attachment. Could preoccupation with attachment figure/s be interfering in exploration?
- *Compassionate context: self-compassion, compassion for others, receiving compassion from others.* When Fan is distressed she is engaging in coercive and disruptive patterns of behavior, and is not successful in eliciting compassionate and nurturing responses from her parents. At Fan's stage of development, her ability to receive compassion from others is key to developing her later ability of self-compassion and giving compassion to others.

(*Continued*)

(Continued)

Mei Lin and Tao

- *Contact with the present moment including shared psychological presence.* Mei Lin and Tao's capacity for mindfulness is unknown and needs to be explored. In particular, are they engaging in attuned interactions with shared psychological presence?
- *Experiential acceptance of parent, child, and relationship.* A deficit in experiential acceptance is likely as both Mei Lin and Tao appear to be avoiding their own experiences of anxiety and stress triggered by Fan's noncompliant behavior. They also demonstrate a deficit in acceptance of Fan's emotions.
- *Flexible languaging.* Mei Lin and Tao show evidence of rigidity in their parenting. They respond by either continuing to repeat verbal instructions or giving in to Fan's demands. In addition, there is likely fusion with unworkable thoughts, including for Mei Lin "Fan hates me" and for Tao, that Fan is "a little monster."
- *Values and proto-values.* It is likely that Mei Lin and Tao would benefit from a thorough exploration of their parenting values, as their expressions of potential values within the intake interview are vague and possibly mixed with verbal rules functioning as pliance (i.e., rule following with the function of receiving social approval). For example, they use the vague wording "good parent" and "raise her well." A richer sense of their values and how their values show up in challenging parenting situations may be useful.
- *Flexible perspective taking.* Mei Lin and Tao show poor ability to track other-as-process for Fan, that is, Fan's ongoing psychological experiences. This is evidenced in their puzzlement over why Fan is behaving as she is. Improving their ability to track Fan's ongoing psychological experiences will likely improve their parenting in many ways.
- *Committed action and exploration.* It is likely that the current parenting practices are not consistent with their parenting values, certainly, they are not working. A flexible, experimental approach to parenting, trying different parenting responses and discovering what works, is likely to be useful.
- *Compassionate context: self-compassion, compassion for others, receiving compassion from others.* There is some evidence that Mei Lin and Tao's capacity for compassion toward Fan is compromised. For example, calling her a "little monster."

Let's now turn to how this may apply for the other case that we have already introduced: Leo and his parents, Andrea and Lucia. As Leo is 13, the ACT processes are more directly relevant. Yet, they still need to be understood developmentally and as emerging from Leo's ongoing context and relationships to others.

Leo

- *Contact with the present moment including shared psychological presence.* Leo uses psychological avoidance, deliberately avoiding contact with the present moment. In the intake interview he is not able to discuss his feelings about or immediately before social or performative situations in any depth beyond the fact that he doesn't want to do them. It is possible that he has a deficit in mindfulness.
- *Experiential acceptance of parent, child, and relationship.* Leo shows a deficit in experiential acceptance as in avoids situations in which he may experience social anxiety. In addition, his developing capacity for experiential acceptance is not supported within his interactions with his parents. His parents do not demonstrate acceptance for his feelings; in fact, they have responded with coercion and shaming.
- *Flexible languaging.* It is likely that Leo is fused with certain self-stories; for example, that he is "just a reject."
- *Values and proto-values.* Leo was not able to give a sense of his emerging proto-values. This needs to be explored. It is likely that he is disconnected from his proto-values. Andrea and Lucia, also could not discuss Leo's interests in a rich way. Instead, they are focused on what they want him to do. It is likely that they are not supporting his emerging sense of his proto-values.
- *Flexible perspective taking.* Leo shows a deficit in his ability to track self-as-process, that is, his own unfolding psychological processes; for example, he is unable to discuss his feelings about and immediately before social or performative situations.
- *Committed action and exploration.* It is likely that Leo's pattern of behavior conflicts with his emerging proto-values. Certainly, it is not workable.
- *Compassionate context: self-compassion, compassion for others, receiving compassion from others.* Leo likely has a deficit in self-compassion.

Lucia and Andrea

- *Contact with the present moment including shared psychological presence.* Andrea likely has a deficit in mindfulness as he states that he is often distracted by work. For Lucia this is unknown and needs exploration.
- *Experiential acceptance parent, child, and relationship.* A deficit in experiential acceptance for both is likely, as both are highly conscious of their feelings of embarrassment and discomfort, and act to minimize these feelings rather than in Leo's long-term best interest. It is possible that Andrea's withdrawal from Leo, which he attributes to work, is also due to experiential avoidance of the feelings of shame Leo's behavior triggers in him. For both, their coercive behavior around Leo's behavior is likely partly due to experiential avoidance.
- *Flexible languaging.* There is likely fusion for both Andrea and Lucia—for Andrea with negative thoughts about Leo and for Lucia with self-blame. Rigid fusion to parenting rules or cognitions may be influencing their use of coercive parenting to try to change Leo's behavior.

(*Continued*)

(Continued)

- *Values and proto-values.* It is likely that a greater exploration of Andrea and Lucia's parenting values would be beneficial. Both have mentioned that Leo's withdrawal and the current lack of closeness in their relationship is troubling. Yet their own use of coercive parenting to try to change Leo's behavior was likely a key factor in the current distance in their relationship.
- *Flexible perspective taking.* Both Andrea and Lucia show a poor ability to track Leo's other-as-process, that is, Leo's ongoing psychological processes. This is shown in their use of coercive parenting without discussing at all the potential negative effects of this on Leo.
- *Committed action and exploration.* It is likely that the current parenting practices are not consistent with their parenting values (certainly, they are not working).
- *Compassionate context: self-compassion, compassion for others, receiving compassion from others.* Andrea and Lucia are both experiencing challenges in maintaining compassion for Leo.

The DNA-V model can be used in a similar way for parent and child, but this will not be explored in this book. For a full exploration of formulation using the DNA-V model we suggest you refer to *The Thriving Adolescent* by Louise Hayes and Joseph Ciarrochi (Hayes & Ciarrochi, 2015). The DNA-V model is outlined in Chapter 1, Introduction, of this book.

Functional analytic psychotherapy and the parent–child relationship

Another perspective that can be helpful for formulation in parenting intervention is the adaptation of functional analytic psychotherapy (FAP) principles to the parent–child relationship. FAP is a behavioral perspective on using the therapeutic relationship to spark therapeutic change (Kohlenberg & Tsai, 1991; Tsai, Kohlenberg, & Kanter, 2010). Within FAP, the therapist focuses on behaviors that are relevant to the client's presenting problems as they occur within the therapy room. The therapist uses operant principles to elicit behavior change, within the therapeutic relationship as the interaction unfolds within the therapy room. In FAP, this is done by focusing on three kinds of behaviors relevant to the client's presenting problems or clinically relevant behaviors (CRBs):

CRB1s: Problematic or maladaptive behaviors related to the client's presenting problems including avoidance. The aim is for CRB1s to decrease during the intervention.

CRB2s: Adaptive behaviors that are alternatives to the client's maladaptive behaviors and/or current behavioral deficits. The aim is for CRB2s to increase during the intervention. The therapist aims to recognize, evoke, shape, and reinforce CRB2s.

CRB3s: Client descriptions of their own behavior and the causes of their behavior. The aim is for CRB3s to become richer, more accurate, and functional. The therapist aims to recognize, evoke, shape, and reinforce CRB3s that are accurate and functionally focused.

The similarity of this way of thinking about therapeutic change within the therapist–client relationship to the unfolding of child development within the context of the parent–child relationship is readily apparent. The basic FAP framework can be adapted to the parent–child relationship and used as part of case conceptualization as well as in communication with parents (Whittingham, 2015). Adapting the FAP framework to the parent–child relationship involves viewing the parent as the agent of change within the unfolding development of the child. Instead of CRBs, the parent identifies *developmentally relevant behaviors*, both behaviors that are dysfunctional and need to decrease in frequency over time, and behaviors that are functional and that the parent needs to shape over time. Thus:

DRB1s: Problematic or maladaptive behaviors.

DRB2s: Adaptive behaviors that are alternatives to the client's maladaptive behaviors and/or current behavioral deficits. In particular, this should include any behaviors that represent improvements for that particular child, especially in the contexts in which the child engages in DRB1s. The parent should aim to recognize, evoke, shape, and reinforce DRB2s.

DRB3s: Parent and child descriptions of child behavior and the causes of child behavior. Firstly, the parent aims for their own DRB3s to become richer, more accurate, and functional (i.e., focused on the functions of the child's behavior). This is about the parent accurately tracking their child's behavior. It is also about the parent scaffolding and shaping the child's own DRB3s in a developmentally appropriate way. For a young child, this may simply mean sharing their own tracking of the child's behavior in a sensitive and appropriate manner. For an older child or adolescent, it may mean aiming to recognize, evoke, shape, and reinforce DRB3s in their child or adolescent that are accurate and functionally focused.

This way of thinking about the unfolding contingencies within the parent–child relationship offers a highly flexible way for parents to consider the unfolding contingencies within their relationship day to day—and year to year—while incorporating a wider developmental context. That is, instead of merely targeting a specific problematic behavior, it offers a way of seeing the parent–child interaction and child behavior in a longer-term view. In discussing this with parents, you can talk in simpler terms, such as speaking of DRB1s as behaviors to decrease or to stop feeding, DRB2s as behaviors to increase or to feed, and DRB3s as building understanding of behavior.

Let's see how this might apply to the two cases we introduced. First, to Fan, Mei Lin, and Tao:

DRB1s: stop feeding: Ignoring parent's instructions, saying "no" to parent's instructions, shouting "no," crying and screaming, stomping her feet, and running away when instructed to move to a nonpreferred activity. Mei Lin and Tao aim to stop reinforcing these behaviors.
DRB2s: behaviors to grow: Following through with parent's instructions, doing things that she doesn't want to do when needed, expressing disappointment and frustration in more appropriate ways, for example saying "I want to stay at the park," negotiating her needs and desires in more adaptive and appropriate ways for example saying, "Can I just finish this picture?" Mei Lin and Tao aim to notice, evoke, shape and reinforce these behaviors.
DRB3s: building understanding: Mei Lin and Tao come to see that Fan's noncompliance is reinforced by their response to it. They also come to see Fan's noncompliance in the wider context of her emotional development, in particular her need to develop adaptive ways to express disappointment and frustration as well as to negotiate her needs and desires. Mei Lin and Tao reflect this more accurate and functional track to Fan herself in small and developmentally appropriate ways, for example, reflecting back to Fan her feelings, such as "I understand you are sad that we have to leave the park. You were having fun."

Now let's see how this might apply to Leo, Andrea, and Lucia:

DRB1s: stop feeding: Avoidance of social or performative situations, including refusal to speak.
DRB2s: behaviors to grow: Any social engagement at school or at social events including any speech but also nonverbal responses and social actions such as helping to set the table or decorate, social engagement and interaction with his two friends, any social engagement and interaction with his parents, any more adaptive way of responding to anxiety including any approach behavior in an anxious context and sharing feelings of anxiety with others. Andrea and Lucia aim to notice, evoke, shape, and reinforce these behaviors.
DRB3s: building understanding: Andrea and Lucia come to see that Leo's avoidant behavior is reinforced by a temporary reduction in his anxiety. They also come to see that their coercive attempts to force Leo to speak in social situations have likely amplified his social anxiety and caused Leo to withdraw from them. As Leo begins to talk more with them again, sharing his inner life, they aim to recognize, evoke, shape, and reinforce CRB3s that are accurate and functionally focused; for example, Leo stating, "I guess I get freaked out at big parties. When I find a quiet spot and look at my phone I feel a bit better."

Quick and easy tips

Case conceptulization is a difficult skill to learn and develops over time, and with practice.! For beginners, here are some quick and easy tips to case conceptualization for when you get stuck. First, return to those basic principles in the Chapter 3, Connect: the parent–child relationship; Chapter 4, Shape: building a flexible repertoire.

So, from the Chapter 3, Connect: the parent–child relationship:

- Is the parent–child interaction consistent with sensitive and responsive parenting? Remember, sensitive parenting is not merely warm parenting. Is the parent's nurturance on cue? If not, that's something you'll want to focus on.
- Does the parent show *awareness and acceptance* of their child's experiences as well as their own?
- Is the parent hostile or intrusive? This includes criticism and covert signs of hostility such as frustration or boredom in interacting with their child. If so, that's something you'll want to reduce.

From the Chapter 4, Shape: building a flexible repertoire

- Is the parent providing the child with generous positive reinforcement for a broad array of behaviors? Does this include reinforcing behaviors that are *alternatives* to any problematic child behaviors? Does this include *shaping*, that is, reinforcing imperfect but best possible approximations of adaptive behaviors? If not, that's something you'll want to focus on.
- Are the parents reinforcing problematic child behaviors? If yes, that's something you'll want to reduce.
- Are the parents using a lot of punishment including coercion or punitive parenting practices? If so, that's something you'll want to reduce.

Other points to consider:

- Look for avoidance. What is the parent *avoiding* in behaving as they are? What are they avoiding in terms of child behavior or their relationship with their child? What might they be avoiding in terms of their own experience: thoughts, emotions, memories and sensations?
- Look for rigidity and inflexibility or narrowing of behavioral patterns. Is there a sense that the parent is stuck? That's a sign that the parent may be experiencing *fusion* with a verbal rule or thought.
- If you are seeing or hearing anxiety, look for avoidance.
- If you are seeing or hearing depressive symptoms, look for a deficit in positive reinforcement, a narrowing of behavior and/or a lack of psychological contact with the present moment.
- If a child keeps doing something, then it is likely that something that happens immediately after the behavior is reinforcing. Look for the reinforcer.
- Always consider: does the child have an alternative way to seek that reinforcer? If not, focus on building the child's repertoire.

Sharing your case conceptualization with the parent

Sharing your conceptualization of the problem with the parents, and in the case of an adolescent, with the adolescent as appropriate, is a key aspect of the intervention itself. It is crucial to the rest of the intervention that a truly shared sense of the reasons for and the purpose of the intervention is established. Further, the cultivation of insight into the reasons why certain patterns of interaction have happened and are continuing to happen is often a crucial aspect of any parenting intervention.

In sharing your conceptualization of the problem with a parent, it is best to avoid jargon unless specific jargon words are already familiar to the parent, or it the cases of an intelligent and well-educated parent, you make the judgement call that it would be most appropriate to give the parent a full explanation of the jargon. It is also best to ground your explanation of your formulation within the assessment itself. This makes it clear that you have listened to the parents, and that the perspective you share is merely an organization of the information that they have shared with you, not a judgement of them, or an outsider's viewpoint. It is also important to ask the parent for their opinion of your initial impressions and to ask for additional relevant information that you may have missed.

For example, in sharing your conceptualization with Mei Lin and Tao you might say, "During the intake interview, you said that you were concerned about noncompliance and tantrum behavior. Looking at the questionnaires that you completed and the monitoring that you did, yes, it does look like there is a significant amount of noncompliance and tantrum behavior happening. Noncompliance and tantrums are common in three year olds, but what you are experiencing with Fan is more than is typical. So you are quite right about that. And I did manage to see an example of Fan being noncompliant during the observation so I now have a really clear idea of what you are talking about. Looking at your monitoring, what I notice is that immediately after Fan refuses to do something you tend to either keep trying to convince her to do as you've asked or you give in, giving her a bit longer before the bath or bedtime or whatever. Is that right? Okay, that fits with what I saw in the observation too. So, given that, do you have any sense of what the pay-off is for Fan? Because often when children keep engaging in some kind of problem behavior we are accidentally rewarding them for it. It is very easy to do. That's right, I suspect that giving in to her, even if it is just delaying the bath or bedtime or whatever it is, is a pay-off for Fan. I'm also wondering about the fact that you keep trying to explain to Fan why she needs to do what you are asking her to do. It is really understandable why you are doing that. You are trying to reason with her which often works with adults, huh? The thing is children love parental attention. That's pretty much the most awesome thing there is to a child. And all of that explaining is a lot of attention. I'm wondering if that might be a bit of an accidental reward too. What do you think?"

Chapter summary

Case conceptualization, including functional analysis, is the key to ACT intervention. In the next chapter we look at the therapeutic relationship and how the therapeutic relationship supports intervention.

References

Hayes, L. L., & Ciarrochi, J. (2015). *The thriving adolescent*. Oakland: New Harbinger Publications.

Kohlenberg, R. J., & Tsai, M. (1991). *Functional analytic psychotherapy: Creating intense and curative therapeutic relationships*. New York: Plenum Press.

Sanders, M. R., & James, J. E. (1982). Enhancing generalization and maintenance effects in systematic parent training: The role of self-management skills. *Australian Psychologist*, *17*(2), 151–164.

Tsai, M., Kohlenberg, R. J., & Kanter, J. W. (2010). A functional analytic psychotherapy (FAP) approach to the therapeutic alliance. In C. J. Muran, & J. P. Barberm (Eds.), *The therapuetic alliance: An evidence-based guide to practice* (pp. 172–190). New York: Guilford Press.

Whittingham, K. (2015). Connect and shape: A parenting meta-strategy. *Journal of Contextual Behavioral Science*, *4*(2), 103–106.

Chapter 6

Therapeutic relationship

Chapter Outline

Acceptance and commitment therapy and the therapeutic relationship 131
Setting the stage/dialogue 133
Therapist as a secure base 134
Complexities of therapeutic relationship/s in parenting intervention 136
Functional analytic psychotherapy and the therapeutic relationship 141
Evoke, reinforce, repeat 143
Building and maintaining a common understanding 144
Client resistance 145
Resistance to specific techniques 146
Supporting home practice 148
Chapter summary 149
References 149

People are just as wonderful as sunsets if you let them be. When I look at a sunset, I don't find myself saying, 'Soften the orange a bit on the right hand corner.' I don't try to control a sunset. I watch with awe as it unfolds.

Carl R. Rogers, *A Way of Being*

It is not a question of starting. The start has been made. It's a question of what's to be done from now on.

B.F. Skinner

There is something of yourself that you leave at every meeting with another person.

Mr. Rogers

Acceptance and commitment therapy and the therapeutic relationship

The acceptance and commitment therapy (ACT) model, grounded in relational frame theory, is fundamentally a universal model of human suffering (Hayes, Strosahl, & Wilson, 2003). That is, within ACT, human suffering in all its forms, including forms that would meet clinical criteria for mental health diagnoses, in adults and children, are understood in terms of universal aspects human cognition and language. All of us, at

Acceptance and Commitment Therapy. DOI: https://doi.org/10.1016/B978-0-12-814669-9.00006-0
© 2019 Elsevier Inc. All rights reserved.

some point in our lives, will experience suffering: we are all, ACT expert and ACT novice, therapist and client, parent and child, swimming in the same sea.

The partnership between therapist and client, then, is fundamentally a partnership of equals. While the therapist brings to the team scientific knowledge of human suffering and parenting, the client brings their own expert understanding of their life, their child, and the context in which they live. Further, the scientific knowledge on human suffering and parenting is one step—applying this in everyday life is an ongoing journey that never ends. In this journey, the therapist and client are equals, both on their own paths, both experiencing their own challenges. There is no expert on life. There is no expert parent. There's also no expert therapist. For some parents, it may be useful to dispel the myth that you hold all the answers.

If you, the clinician, are a parent yourself, you may find that clients assume that you are a perfect parent, that you never struggle, lose your temper, forget your child's homework, miss a bid for attention, or accidentally intrude, and that your children are perfect children: always compliant, academically gifted, and socially stellar. It may be useful to explicitly address this. To share: as parents ourselves, we (Koa and Lisa) get this. Parenting is tough. All parents have their challenges, us included. All parents stuff up sometimes, us included. If you are not a parent yourself, you may find that clients assume that you then cannot understand what they are going through or perhaps you yourself are conscious of the fact that you don't have any children. As there is no expert parent, and you are not coming from a position of expertise, this lack of personal experience does not matter. Even if you were a parent, your experiences as a parent would be your own, and your experiences of your child would be of your child, not the client's. The client is the expert in their own life and their own child. In our experience of delivering parenting intervention before we became parents ourselves, once parents understood that we recognized their expertise in their own life and on their own children, that we didn't see ourselves as parenting experts, any concerns they might have had that we weren't parents ourselves disappeared.

Within ACT, both the therapist and the client are united in taking a flexible, collaborative, experimental stance, and discovering what works. As a therapist this means needing to "hold things lightly," and at times it may mean needing to practice defusion with preconceived ideas about what is happening for the parent and the child and what the parent needs to do to change things. Just as we ask clients to listen to their experience, so too, we need to let our experience be the ultimate guide.

The relationship between therapist and client is expressed well in the two mountains metaphor.

Two mountains metaphor

You are climbing your mountain. It is a big mountain and there are parts where the going is rough or even dangerous. My role is to be your spotter and your support. I might see that a particular spot is slippery and warn you of that, or I might see that if you to shuffle over to the left there's an easier way through, or I might notice a perfect spot for you to get a foothold on. I have a different perspective and that can be useful to you. But the important thing to realize is that I'm not at the top of your mountain looking down at you. That's not what my perspective is. I'm not some kind of mountain guru at the summit. In fact, I'm not the expert on your mountain at all. I'm climbing my own mountain, just over the valley. I don't need to fully know what it feels like to climb your mountain. You know what that feels like and I can trust you on that. But I can share what I can see, from over here on my mountain, and that different perspective can be useful to you.

Source: *Adapted from Twohig, M. (2004). ACT for OCD: Abbreviated Treatment Manual.*

Setting the stage/dialogue

There are a few components of setting the stage for a secure, collaborative relationship with a parent. This involves the concept of therapeutic alliance, which has been shown to have a robust relationship with treatment outcome (Karver, Handelsman, Fields, & Bickman, 2006). More specifically, two factors of critical importance are task agreement and bond (McLeod & Weisz, 2005). *Task agreement* refers to simply agreeing on what the "work" of psychotherapy is. *Bond* refers to the warm and empathic relationship developing between a client and therapist. To facilitate the development of these, it's important for the therapist to carve out a space to be authentic so that you can model emotion expression and regulation, as well as modeling exploration or, in other words, trial-and-error parent behavior. This will support the development of the parent "tracking" how their behavior works in their relationship with their child. The therapist might begin this by voicing their values (what their most deeply held wish is for their client) and vulnerabilities (their fears, concerns, potential weaknesses, and mistakes). Therapists might set the stage for this as follows:

Therapist: It sounds like you have been having a difficult time, and I am glad that you came in to see me. I am hoping that we can work together on how to best support your child—and also, on how to care for yourself in the inevitably challenging moments you will have with your child, as we move forward. It's my wish for you that you can find a way to help your child, and your relationship with him, thrive, even when it's hard.

Client: Thanks. I appreciate that. It has been quite a challenge, really, and I feel overwhelmed all the time.

Therapist:	The work that we do here might feel like an uphill battle sometimes, and that's ok—we will move through it together. Also, although it's my intention to be of service to you, and to collaborate with you, I will likely make mistakes. I might push too hard, or not understand something well, or say the wrong thing. I am sorry for that in advance—and I promise that if you tell me I've gone in a wrong direction, I will listen and hear you. I'm wondering if you might make a space for me to make mistakes as we work together? Would that be all right?
Client:	Yes, of course.
Therapist:	I very much want this work we do together to create a space where you can say—and show—whatever thoughts and emotions you are feeling. That will be important for me to begin to understand what it is like to be in your shoes—and the more I can do that, the more helpful I may be.
Client:	Sure, that makes sense.

Therapist as a secure base

Within any form of therapy it is important for the therapist to function as a secure base for the client's exploration. As therapists, we need to be warm, caring, sensitive, and compassionate. From a compassion-focused therapy (CFT) perspective, a warm, caring, sensitive, and compassionate therapist is activating the client's affiliative system, enabling the downregulation of the threat and the incentive/resource-focused systems, bringing balance and social cooperation (Tirch, Schoendorff, & Silberstein, 2014). Within any parenting intervention, we are asking the parents to explore, to experiment, to be flexible, trying new ways to see parenting and their relationships with their child, and trying new behaviors. We are also asking parents to explore themes and content that may be threatening in some way; for example, negative thoughts about themselves or their child, the ways in which their actions as parents have shaped their child's behavior today or the impact of their own experience being parented on their parenting. And finally, but importantly, we are asking the parent to be warm, caring, sensitive, and compassionate toward their child. Providing clear and unambiguous cues of social safety within the therapist–client relationship is crucial. Threat narrows behavior, social safety opens up the possibility of flexibility. Thus the provision of social safety, through a warm, caring, sensitive, and compassionate relationship is a core component of ACT. It's also important to provide a secure base for your client in which the therapist balances empathetic, understanding responses with exploratory responses that promote new discovery, the creation of new meanings, or trying something new (Greenberg, 2002).

In focusing on providing social safety or functioning as a secure base, it is helpful to remember that some parents may be particularly sensitized to threat, criticism, and shame due to their learning histories, and some parents may have insecure attachment styles. Consider also that parents come with a history of interactions with their children. Some children come with more challenging behaviors than others; some parents have better or worse "goodness of fit" with their children given their own temperaments, strengths, and vulnerabilities. For these parents, a gentle persistence with warmth, caring, sensitive, and compassionate responding will be an important aspect of the intervention. Even parents who have secure attachment styles and are not sensitized to threat and criticism, in general, may have become sensitized to criticism as a parent before seeking help from you. Many of us live in cultural contexts that are highly judgmental and shaming of parents. Any parent that is experiencing parenting challenges is likely to have heard a fair degree of criticism of their parenting!

Part of providing this social safety and secure base is normalizing what parents are thinking and feeling. This includes responding to their shared thoughts and feelings with acceptance as thoughts and feelings. That is, not taking the parent's thoughts and feelings as literal truths to be challenged to disputed, but taking them as thoughts and feelings and holding them in a gentle, defused manner. It may also include explicitly normalizing their reactions. For example, responding with, "I can certainly understand why you'd be feeling that way," or "I hear that a lot" so that the parent is explicitly made aware that their thoughts and feelings are normal and natural.

One area that this can be a challenge is when interactions between a parent and child have become particularly aversive, or coercive. Consider this example of a parent with an oppositional child:

Parent: You know, I have to say the same thing, over and over again. It's exhausting. And he just doesn't listen! It's like he is deliberately fucking with me. I know this is terrible to say, but there are times when... I don't even like him (looks down). It's a relief when he's off in his room, gaming. At least it's quiet. Sometimes...I just can't stand the sight of him.

Therapist: It sounds exhausting. I am imagining what it must be like in your shoes, when you come home after a long day, and have this experience (pause). And as you say those things, what shows up in you now?

Parent: (pause) It's really hard to say this...but sometimes I wish I never had him. That's terrible, isn't it?

Therapist: I can only imagine how hard it is to share this—thank you so much for telling me. Let's just stay here, in this space for a moment, and let whatever shows up be here now. I can hear your anger, and also your reluctance and sadness in sharing this. I want you to know that it's ok to feel what you are feeling, and that you are not alone. Many parents coping with these types of behaviors in their children feel the same way—only very few have the courage to speak about it. I appreciate you trusting me with this.

Much of the time, empathizing and reflecting parents' experience is probably an easy enough task. However, as in the example above, it can be very difficult at times *psychologically* because it requires psychological flexibility from us as therapists. Even if you find it relatively easy to be psychologically flexible with many of your clients, because you've gravitated toward working with clients who you are naturally compassionate toward (as we tend to do!), we all find it easier to maintain a flexible, compassionate stance with some people, and some people's thoughts and feelings than others.

Developing insight into the thoughts and feelings that you are more likely to become fused with and to the perspectives that you are less likely to be compassionate toward, will enable you to pause and deliberately focus on bringing acceptance, warmth, and compassion into the room at the right time. Within parenting interventions this is made more challenging because in actuality there are always multiple clients.

Complexities of therapeutic relationship/s in parenting intervention

So far, we have been exploring the therapist–client relationship as if there is only one. But in fact, in a parenting intervention there is always at least two clients: the parent and the child. Even with younger children where the therapist may not be working directly with the child at all, the purpose of the parenting intervention is often to ultimately improve outcomes for the child. With older children and adolescents, the therapist may have direct contact with the child as well as the parent. Of course, it is often more complicated still. There are often more than two clients as both parents may be participating in the intervention, and other caregivers such as stepparents and grandparents may also be involved, even if this involvement is indirect and through the parents themselves. For older children and adolescents the therapist may also have some contact with the school, and hence know and sympathize with the school's perspective. Siblings too may, to some extent, be present within the intervention context, even though they are not themselves the client. Shifting parenting is likely to impact upon the way the parent parents all of their children and many parents are conscious of this, deliberately trying out new parenting approaches with all of their children.

As therapists then we need to be able to take the perspectives of both the parent and the child, and to keep both of these perspectives in mind throughout the intervention. If both parents are part of the child's life—and it is appropriate— we need to do our best to build a warm, caring, sensitive, and compassionate relationship with both parents, maximally involving them both in the intervention. We may also need to build and maintain, to some extent, relationships with other caregivers such as stepparents, grandparents, or the school, depending on the intervention aims. From an evolutionary perspective, humans are cooperative breeders (Hrdy, 2011). Looking globally, and from an evolutionary lens, family units are flexible, opportunistic, and usually child-centered and kin-based. That is, there is no one blueprint for a family. Multiple caregiving systems are possible.

The first step in managing this complexity is in understanding the caregiving system around the child. Who are the child's caregivers? This includes the context (e.g., school or childcare) in which the child regularly spends time as well as all caregivers for the child. The caregiving system can be understood further by asking: who are the decision-makers? The decision-makers are the caregivers who get a vote on the major decisions of how the child is being raised; for example, deciding which school to send the child to. Within contemporary Western cultures the decision-makers are usually the child's parents but not always. One or both of the parents may have lost their decision-maker role through abuse, neglect, or partial or complete desertion of the child. This may include legally losing custody or the decision-maker role may simply have been abandoned by one or both of the parents within the family. Likewise, a stepparent or a grandparent may "win" the rights to the decision-maker role by taking on the full responsibilities of a parental figure. Their presence in the child's life as a decision-making caregiver may be of benefit to the child, and this may form part of a functioning caregiving system. Further, there is cultural variability in how caregiving tasks including decision-making are distributed within a family. Within some cultural contexts it is considered appropriate and normal for grandparents, aunts, and uncles to have a greater role in making some kinds of decisions than is usual in Western cultures. It is important not to push your own view of who the decision-makers should be, but rather, to ask who the decision-makers are and if that is part of a functioning caregiving system for the child. That said, in some families some caregivers, who the decision-makers do not believe have decision-making rights and who have not taken on the full responsibilities of a parental role, wish for the parents to follow their desires on how the child is raised. It may be appropriate to support the actual decision-makers in pushing back against this pressure.

Another way of understanding the caregiving system is to ask: who is/are the primary caregiver/s, and are there constraints on those individuals' time with their children? The primary caregiver/s are usually the person/s with whom the child spends the bulk of their time. They are often the same persons who track and manage the child's schedule and life; for example, managing the child's medical care. Who the primary caregiver/s is/are may shift over time. During infancy in particular there is likely to be a single primary caregiver, and it is most likely to be the child's mother both due to cultural norms and the biological realities of pregnancy, birth, and breastfeeding. During infancy and early childhood, the primary caregiver is likely to also be the child's primary attachment figure. That is, if the primary caregiver and other secondary caregivers are present, and the child is hurt or distressed, the child may be more likely to approach the primary caregiver for comfort. This can mean that primary caregivers end up doing the bulk of caregiving even when a secondary caregiver is present and available, simply because the child/ren come to them. In some families, the primary and secondary caregiver roles are consciously chosen and desired, that is, the primary caregiver wants to be the primary caregiver, and the secondary caregiver wants to be the secondary caregiver. In other families, the primary caregiver may, instead, find themselves forced into the role by sex/gender-related expectations, or the lack of readiness of any of the other caregivers to take on the bulk of the caregiving time and duties. Similarly, secondary caregivers may find themselves in that role due to sex/gender-related expectations or the financial needs of the family even though they may prefer to spend the majority of their time with their children. Secondary caregivers may include other family members such as grandparents. Grandparent care is a common form of regular childcare, and in many families it allows the primary caregiver within the family to combine their primary caregiver role with paid work. In some families, paid caregivers might also be involved such as childcare, family daycare, or nannies, and for older children and adolescents, school is usuallypart of a child's caregiving system.

It is important that parents and caregivers reflect on these roles, and remain open to renegotiating roles as children grow and develop, in line with what works best in their family. Within the caregiving system, it is also important that parents and caregivers recognize the qualitative differences within the primary and secondary caregiving roles and how that may influence their own perspectives and experiences. For example, one of the most challenging aspects about being the primary caregiver of an infant is the sheer unrelenting 24/7 nature of it, which is a challenge highly specific to the primary caregiver role. Another challenge that is a regular part of life as a primary caregiver is the challenge of needing to multitask parenting with other tasks. This challenge may be experienced by secondary caregivers at times as well, but it is a regular occurrence for most primary caregivers that they simply cannot escape from. Attempting to multitask homework supervision, cooking a healthy dinner, and being sensitive and responsive to a baby when you haven't had 1 minute to yourself for 24 hours and you haven't had sufficient sleep for a week is a challenge well beyond the sum of each of the individual tasks. Conversely, secondary caregivers may feel a desire to maximize the pleasure of the time that they spend with their child. They may feel a pressure to make their time count, to make it special. They may also feel more uncertain in their caregiving role or have less knowledge about the specifics of what is happening for the child right now. The primary caregiver/s need the secondary caregiver/s to understand and sympathize with the fact that, for them, parenting is often multitasked and unrelenting, to not judge their inability to juggle all of that on a particular day as incompetence. Conversely, the secondary caregiver/s need the primary caregiver/s to understand that they aren't going to be able to keep track of the tiny details of their child's experience to the same level, but they nevertheless can be fully competent at providing the child with care and to not judge their occasional knowledge gaps as incompetence. Similarly, they need sympathy for their desire to maximize the pleasure of their time with their child and some support in doing this, even though this may involve, for example, an extra treat for the child or a rough and exciting game a little too close to bedtime.

Understanding the different perspectives that primary and secondary caregivers might have due to differences in the primary and secondary roles related to simply understanding the different strengths, weaknesses, and perspectives of each caregiver as individuals. The parents and other caregivers need to be working in harmony, with basic agreement on the fundamentals of how the child is being raised and who has what role in doing that. However, that doesn't mean that they need to agree on everything, or that they each need to be doing exactly the same thing with the child. Rather, what is important is that the parents and caregivers respect each other and are not undermining each other. For example, it is not problematic for children to learn that at grandma's they are allowed to eat dinner picnic-style on the lounge room floor while watching a movie, but at home they need to eat dinner at the table. The parents' house rule of eating dinner at the table doesn't need to be enforced at grandma's for consistency's sake. Rather, what is important is that the parents and grandma are united in maintaining that the children need to sit at the dinner table at home, and can, as a treat, eat dinner picnic-style while watching a movie at grandma's house. From a behavioral perspective, being at grandma's house will come to function as a discriminant stimulus signaling the opportunity to eat dinner picnic-style. It is not inconsistent. It is simply more contextually complex than one blanket rule that all caregivers follow—complexity that children can be trusted to learn. In a nutshell, a harmonious and functioning caregiving system is *not* conflict-free in the sense that there is no tension between different perspectives because everyone agrees on everything all the time. Neither is it conflict-free in the sense that there is one true way for the child to be raised and this one true way is being rigidly adhered to by all whether they agree or not. Rather, a harmonious and functioning caregiving system is *flexible*, with differences in perspectives responded to with mutual acceptance. The strengths and weakness of each caregiver are understood, the strengths leveraged to the child's benefit, and the weaknesses covered by the other caregivers. Each caregiver values their child's relationships with the other caregivers for their child's sake, and values the needs of the other caregivers because meeting those needs is likely to lead to downstream benefits for the child.

There are a host of family factors that have been shown to influence child outcomes, whether across development or in the course of treatment. Although a thorough review of this literature is beyond the scope of our chapter, the following are areas that merit consideration across varying types of evidence-based child intervention. Moving from distal to proximal contextual factors:

- socioeconomic status (Lundahl, Risser, & Lovejoy, 2006);
- cultural differences; for example, the differences between collectivist and individualistic cultures (Gardner, Montgomery, & Knerr, 2016);
- minority status (van Mourik, Crone, De Wolff, & Reis, 2017);

- marital conflict and violence (Cummings & Davies, 2002; Vu, Jouriles, McDonald, & Rosenfield, 2016);
- parental psychopathology (Guild, Toth, Handley, Rogosch, & Cicchetti, 2017; Reyno & McGrath, 2006); and
- parenting styles and behaviors (McLoed, Weisz, & Wood, 2007; Yap, Pilkington, Ryan, & Jorm, 2014).

Once you have understood the caregiving system around the child, it is important to be aware that if the system isn't harmonious and functional, you are likely to feel greater sympathy with specific caregivers. In particular, you are more likely to feel sympathy for the parent/caregiver who is most like you. For example, if there is conflict between a mother and a father, female therapists often find it easier to sympathize with the mother than the father. If there is conflict around whether or not your intervention is necessary or helpful it is usually easier to sympathize with the parent who wants your help. After all, that's the parent who is being "nice" to you. If one of the parent/s is being openly critical of the other it is usually easier to sympathize with the parent who is being criticized than with the parent who is doing the criticizing. All of these reactions are natural and normal. However, it is important to be aware of this, and to specifically work to build your therapeutic relationship with the person for whom you do not feel natural sympathy. If one parent is reluctant to seek intervention or is critical of the other parent, that is all the more reason to build a strong therapeutic alliance and specifically engage that parent in the intervention. One simple way to ensure you are not gravitating toward giving greater warmth and attention to the parent with whom you most naturally sympathize is to consciously pull your attention back to the other parent, to consciously keep your questions balanced, by shifting between parents, continually asking for each parent's perspective. For example, if you know that as a female therapist you will naturally be drawn to sympathize with the mother, then during an intake interview you can consciously direct your attention back to the father, ensuring you keep eliciting his perspective and recollections as you proceed through the interview, giving both parents equal time and attention. With all of the decision-makers in particular involved in the intervention, the intervention itself can assist in resolving conflict around parenting and helping parents to learn how to parent as a team.

At times, the challenges within the parenting and caregiving system may be impacted upon by wider issues beyond parenting itself. For example, relationship issues between the parents, beyond merely parenting conflict, may be impacting on their ability to parent as a team. Familial problems within the extended family may also be impacting upon the caregiving system beyond conflict over the child. Mental health issues for parents or caregivers, or multigenerational caregiving needs (e.g., parents caring for aging grandparents) may also be impacting on the system. These issues may also need to be directly addressed rather than focusing solely on parenting per se. Throughout this book, the mental health of the parent and using ACT as a mental health intervention for parents will be explored. The use of ACT as a couple intervention is outside the scope of this book, but some guidance on supporting parents through marital conflict as part of a parenting intervention will be given.

Finally, in terms of the complexity of the therapeutic relationships within parenting intervention, it is not always the case that the parent's agenda is reasonable or benign for the child. This is especially the case for the agenda that the parent *initially has* when they first seek assistance. When conducting a parenting intervention it is always the case that both the parent and the child are clients, and as the therapist, we are working for the best interests of the parent, the child, and the relationship between them. At times, our role is *not* to simply give the parent advice or strategies to change their child's behavior in their desired way, but rather to (gently!) question their agenda, and to help shape their parenting in a manner that is more adaptive for them and their child. That is, it may be time to use the ACT skills, bringing acceptance, defusion, and values into the room to flexibly explore the parent's agenda rather than blindly accepting the parent's goals and giving the parent the means to achieve them.

Some questions that you may like to ask yourself before "buying into" a parent's agenda may be:

- Is this in the best interests of the child?
- What's the function of the parent's agenda for the parent?
- Is this developmentally appropriate?
- Are the parent's priorities in line with what is most important for the child at this point in the child's development?
- Are the parent's goals in line with their parenting values?

Functional analytic psychotherapy and the therapeutic relationship

We've already explored functional analytic psychotherapy (FAP) in Chapter 5, Case Conceptualization; in particular, how FAP can be applied to the parent–child relationship. To remind you, FAP is a behavioral perspective on using the therapeutic relationship to spark therapeutic change (Kohlenberg & Tsai, 1991). So while we can apply FAP to the parent–child relationship as we saw in Chapter 5, Case Conceptualization, we can also apply it as therapists to the therapeutic relationship itself.

Within FAP, the therapist focuses upon behaviors that are relevant to the client's presenting problems as they occur within the therapy room. The therapist uses operant principles to elicit behavior change, within the therapeutic relationship as the interaction unfolds within the therapy room. In FAP, this is done by focusing on three kinds of behaviors relevant to the client's presenting problems or clinically relevant behaviors (CRBs):

CRB1s: Problematic or maladaptive behaviors that are related to the client's presenting problems; they are often under aversive control, and represent avoidance (Tsai, Kohlenberg, & Kanter, 2010). The aim is for CRB1s to decrease during the intervention. Within a parenting intervention this is likely to include: reinforcing maladaptive child behavior, failing to reinforce adaptive child behavior (e.g., avoidance of feeling overwhelmed), ignoring or punishing a child's bids for nurturance, hostility or criticism of the child, intrusive parenting, inaccurate or unworkable tracks (e.g., "spare the rod and spoil the child"), pliance or following rules functioning as seeking social approval (e.g., "I know I'm not supposed to let my child sleep in bed with me, am I?"), and inaccurate tracking of the child's psychological experiences. Conceptually at least, it is important to consider in what ways these constitute avoidance-based responding on the part of the parent. For example, parents might grow either lax or harsh in their parenting responses to avoid or terminate an aversive child interaction. Similarly, a mother struggling with depression might seek to avoid her own overwhelming feelings, and thus fail to reinforce her child's positive emotion or bids for nurturance.

CRB2s: Adaptive behaviors that are alternatives to the client's maladaptive behaviors or and current behavioral deficits; these often constitute defused, approach-based behaviors (Tsai et al., 2010). The aim is for CRB2s to increase during the intervention. The therapist aims to recognize, shape, and reinforce CRB2s. Within a parenting intervention this is likely to include: refraining from reinforcing maladaptive child behavior, reinforcing adaptive child behavior, responding to a child's bids for nurturance, warm, and sensitive caregiving, accurate and workable tracks (e.g., "when I give him attention for that then I'm feeding that behavior"); parenting grounded in values (e.g., "I want to show her that I care about her interests so I'm going to go to her martial arts class with her"); and accurate tracking of the child's psychological experiences. Considering the role of parent private events, in order for a parent to use a selective attention or planned ignoring strategy to prevent inadvertent reinforcement of child misbehavior, he or she must be willing to allow themselves to experience frustration, embarrassment, thoughts of incompetence, or other uncomfortable feelings and cognitions. This awareness and acceptance of parent private events constitutes another mode of "approach."

CRB3s: Client descriptions of their own behavior and the causes of their behavior. The aim is for CRB3s to become richer, more diverse, accurate, and functional. The therapist aims to recognize, shape, and reinforce CRB3s that are accurate and functionally focused. Within a parenting intervention this includes both accurate tracking of the child's behavior and accurate tracking of the parent's own behavior. In order to facilitate this, as mentioned previously in this chapter, it is critical for therapists to create a space in which parents can discuss and experience trial-and-error learning.

Evoke, reinforce, repeat

FAP, used well, involves shaping in-session behavioral change (Kohlenberg & Tsai, 1991; Sandoz & Boone, 2016). This involves you, the therapist, thinking about how your relationship with your client may become a "context" in which you can evoke and reinforce your client's CRB2s such that they emerge in the therapy process, and will be generalized to the client's relationship with their child. Consider this example of dialogue between a therapist and the parent of an anxious school-aged child:

Therapist: Tell me a little bit about what happens in the morning when it's time for Sarah to get ready to go to school.

Parent: So it starts when I go to wake her up. Almost immediately she says her stomach hurts. I know she's lying, so I stay on her, but she just curls up in a ball, and either yells at me or simply doesn't answer. And the clock is ticking.

Therapist: Then what?

Parent: I did what you said, I kept going up there and telling her to get up, but I know it's just not going to happen, so I end up telling her she can have an extra hour or so in bed. But then sometimes she doesn't get to school at all. Last week she went only twice.

Therapist: So what is it like for you, being in this situation?

Parent: She just can't do it. It's just too hard for her.

Therapist: (noting the client has not responded to the question, and as such, that this may be a CRB1) Let me slow you down a bit, if you are willing. I'd really like to get a sense of what it's like to be in your shoes in that moment that seems to play over and over again in the morning. Close your eyes, see if you can walk back into that situation, and tell me what shows up. Take your time. (This illustrates an attempt to elicit the client's tracking of their emotional response to the situation, and as such, tries to evoke a CRB2).

Parent: (after a pause, quietly) It's just so hard for me to see her that way. What if her stomach really does hurt? What kind of parent would I be if I forced her to go to school?

Therapist: That is extremely helpful (reinforcing the CRB2 CB2 of "approaching" a painful private event). What else shows up—what feelings in your body? Thoughts? (a "repeat" attempt to evoke a CRB2)

Parent: My chest feels tight; my shoulders too—the back of my neck. And there's. . .a heaviness. A sadness. I don't like her feeling this way (CRB2).

Therapist: Thank you so much for sharing that with me—I can see how hard this is (reinforcing the CRB2).

This exchange, in which the parent is reinforced for her awareness—and approach to painful private events—has now made possible elaboration of how her *responses* to those private events might lead to the problematic behavior of allowing her daughter to avoid school. A reasonable next step for the therapist would be to help the parent to grow more flexible in her responses to her child's behavior (e.g., perhaps continuing to encourage her to get out of bed and go to school, even in the presence of anxiety) while also making space for her own difficult thoughts and feelings.

Within a parenting intervention, FAP can be applied by consciously looking for improvements in the parent's behavior, both parenting behavior per se, that is behavior directly toward the child, and the parents wider parenting behavior such as the parents tracking of their child's and their own behavior and their thinking about their parenting and their child. When improvements are found, reinforce them: acknowledge the parent's gains and point out the change that you have seen. As FAP operates within the therapy room this is made easier by bringing parenting into the room. This may include observations of the parent and child interacting or using roleplays to act out parenting challenges or new ways parents would like to respond to their child's behavior.

Building and maintaining a common understanding

One important aspect of building a strong therapeutic alliance is developing a common understanding or shared perspective of what is happening, what needs to be done, and how the intervention itself will address this. This common understanding is grounded within the assessment process, as well as an artful discussion of the formulation.

In discussing the formulation with the parent, which may or may not include a diagnosis:

- As much as possible use the parent's own words; for example, "You both said that you were concerned about Chloe's school attendance and you'd noticed that she seems more withdrawn at home."
- Avoid jargon as much as possible, instead building understanding using ordinary everyday words. One exception to this is if your client already knows some of the relevant jargon or is highly educated, and you judge that defining and using jargon will be experienced by the client as a show of respect and collegiality.
- If a diagnosis is to be introduced, first obtain a consensus and create a joint perspective on what is happening using the parent's own words and ordinary everyday language. When that consensus has been obtained then introduce the diagnostic label as the name for what is happening. For example, instead of saying to parents and their adolescent daughter, "after the assessment process I think Chloe has depression" say, "so during the assessment process you, Michael and Sandra, told me that you were concerned about Chloe's school attendance and you'd noticed that she seems more withdrawn at home. When I chatted with Chloe, Chloe said, and we agreed that we would talk about this together, that she's feeling quite down and tired a lot of the time and she's having a difficult time at school. Looking at the questionnaires, Michael and Sandra you answered

a lot of questions showing that you are seeing a lot of withdrawal and sadness in Chloe's behavior, is that right? And Chloe, in your questionnaires, you said that you were feeling quite down and like you aren't worth much. Have I got all of that right? So what you've all described to me is sounding like an experience that we call depression. Does that make sense?"

- Ask the parents (and child if relevant) if the formulation or the diagnosis (if given) makes sense to them. If they disagree, then take this as an opportunity to receive more information and to refine your formulation.
- For mental health diagnoses it often isn't helpful to make a big deal of the diagnostic label itself. For the intervention to proceed, it is usually more important that there is a common understanding on what is happening and hence what the intervention needs to focus on rather than on any labels per se.
- It is often helpful to frame the intervention in terms of what behaviors or skills to build, either in parent or child. This is not only useful to the parent, but also to you, as the therapist, to better conceptualize the "work" at hand, and to accurately track outcomes. The more specific, the better—for example, instead of discussing "helping Sam be better behaved," discuss perhaps "helping Sam learn how to accept set limits when he is feeling strong emotions."
- The assessment process itself, particularly monitoring, can be used to build the parent's understanding and to support the development of accurate tracking in the parent. The parent should then have an improved understanding of what is happening themselves, drawn from their own direct experience in doing the monitoring.
- Always, the ultimate arbiter is the client's experience and workability. As an ACT therapist there is no need to convince the client of any particular view or to defend your ideas or formulation. Instead, it is about supporting the client in experimenting and discovering what works.

Client resistance

When there is client resistance, the natural response of the therapist is to become fused with our way of seeing what is happening and to become defensive. Client resistance is a sign that we may need to pause and focus on our own psychological flexibility. Becoming defensive is rarely helpful to overcoming resistance. Where there is client resistance we might:

- Reflect on the therapeutic relationship. Is the therapeutic alliance strong? When both parents are involved in the intervention, and one parent only is resistant, has the therapeutic alliance with the resistant parent been neglected as you have naturally gravitated toward giving increased attention to the parent that is easier to work with? How can you ensure you

are providing a warm, sensitive, and compassionate relationship to the resistant parent?
- Is the resistance actually fresh information that needs to be fed back into the formulation? That is, is there something that you missed or misunderstood that you need to address and that is why the parent is resistant?
- Is there a previous learning history at play here? Has the parent been to see other providers and if so, how did that go?
- See the resistance through a FAP lens. Is the parent's reaction to you part of an ongoing pattern of behavior for this parent? Is it similar to how they react to the other parent and caregivers or to how they react to the child? If so, how can you use FAP principles to shape a more adaptive repertoire in the parent over time?

Resistance to specific techniques

It is common to come across clients who are not generally resistant, and with whom you have a strong therapeutic relationship, but where the client resists specific therapeutic techniques. This is different to a general problem of client resistance, and instead the client's challenges with the specific therapeutic techniques themselves need to be addressed. Here are some common examples:

- *Imagery*: It is not uncommon for clients to believe that they simply can't do imagery. As imagery is an aspect of some ACT and CFT exercises, a client's refusal to try imagery may rule out a large number of potentially beneficial exercises. In fact, it is likely that the client does have sufficient ability to do imagery. They simply have anxiety around generating the "right" kind of images or sufficiently detailed images or have a false expectation of what imagery is like for other people (after all no one knows what imagery is like for others!). Personally, I (Koa) wonder if these beliefs were so common before television. I suspect that the sequences common to children's television shows where a character's imagination plays out directly on the screen sets us up for unrealistic expectations of what imagery involves! You can correct the client's expectations, showing them that imagery is actually exactly what they are already doing, with a simple imagery exercise (Tirch et al., 2014). For example, you might ask your client to close their eyes and then ask them simple questions like: What did you have for breakfast this morning? What does your child's favorite toy look like? What do you think your child is doing right now? You can then discuss their experiences, emphasizing that what they just did *is imagery* and that if they answered the questions then they are already doing imagery well enough.
- *Metaphors*: Metaphors are a common ACT technique. Metaphors are so readily used in ACT because they undermine literal, rigid languaging,

promoting fresh insights and understandings. Unfortunately, you may come across challenges in using metaphors if you work with the autism spectrum disorders (ASD) population. When working with this population, don't automatically assume that metaphors will not work. But do be aware of the need to be more flexible. Consider using metaphors that are more concrete, or acting out the metaphors in a concrete way or creating metaphors that fit with the person's own experience and interests. Taking the time to craft a new metaphor that fits with the special interests of a person with ASD is likely to be more effective than using a metaphor out of the box. And remember, that when you are working with children with ASD, you will also be working with parents with undiagnosed ASD or the boarder autism phenotype (subclinical autistic traits) and these parents too, may benefit from more careful metaphor selection.

- *Roleplays*: Roleplays are an incredibly useful way to bring parenting into the therapy room (in fact, for any form of therapy roleplays are a useful way to bring the presenting problem into the therapy room and this includes using the empty chair technique. If it is in the room then it is much easier to target!). However, most clients are reluctant to participate in roleplays. It is uncomfortable! And, of course, we often find it so too! How many therapists feel comfortable with roleplays at professional workshops? It is such a useful technique that it is worth pushing past this resistance and encouraging the client to be willing to be uncomfortable in order to benefit from the roleplay. Normalizing their discomfort, while explaining the importance of bringing the parenting "live" into the therapy room and the benefits that they are likely to see, is usually sufficient.
- *Mindfulness*: Since ACT was first developed mindfulness has hit the big-time! Mindfulness is now "out there" in popular culture in a big way. This means that many of our clients will have had some contact with mindfulness before we introduce it to them. And their contact with mindfulness may not have been positive. They may have had a bad experience and now have a negative perception of mindfulness. Or alternatively, they may have a false (from an ACT perspective) understanding of what mindfulness is. For this reason, with some clients you might want to avoid the word mindfulness and instead talk about being psychologically present. For other clients you will need to discuss their past experiences with mindfulness upfront, exploring any bad experiences and correcting false understandings. For both mindfulness and acceptance it is crucial to ensure that clients understand *experientially* what we mean by mindfulness and acceptance in ACT. For some clients, negative experiences of mindfulness may be related to attempts to use mindfulness for experiential avoidance, or the use of mindfulness with a history of trauma, or other paradoxical reactions to mindfulness. For clients with a history of trauma or experiences of anxiety when practicing mindfulness, it may be useful to begin with an external point of focus (e.g., focusing on a visual

point), or a peripheral part of the body (e.g., feet or hands) rather than an internal and central part of the body (e.g., breathing). This often decreases the experience of paradoxical effects. It can also be important to encourage a gentle "dipping in" with the client anchoring themselves in a safe focus point and gradually dipping in to awareness of their full present moment experience.

Supporting home practice

Core to progression in any psychological intervention, including a parenting intervention, is generalization of behavior change outside the therapy room and into everyday life. Changes in the everyday parent and child interactions are key. In order to ensure that changes occur in everyday parent and child interactions, it is necessary to set and monitor home practice. In making home practice part of your parenting intervention it is important to:

- Set clear goals for home practice between sessions. Make sure the goals for home practice are specific and realistic. For example, "being nicer to my child" isn't a clear goal. How will the parent know if that is achieved or not? Instead, "noticing when my child is engaging in independent play and rewarding that with attention and praise" is more specific.
- Spend time discussing exactly when and how practice will happen and exploring any barriers, ensuring plans are realistic. If you and your client have already explored in session exactly when the parent can do the home practice and how any barriers can be overcome then the parent is more likely to be able to put that into practice.
- Sometimes parents jump straight to grandiose plans and goals. Instead, they may need to be brought back to more mundane and simple goals. Prompt parents to think of the little changes that they could make. For example, parents who are aware that they need to prioritize their couple relationship often leap straight to the goal of a date night. A date night may be nice, but for many families regular date nights might not be realistic. Instead, help the parent to focus on small but meaningful and sustainable changes that they could make. For example, regularly asking their partner how their day was and listening to the reply.
- Many parents are time poor. If this is an issue then explore how parents can solve this. Often clients see home practice as another task to be fit into a busy day. However, many aspects of home practice will actually be something to integrate into their existing lives not an additional task. That is, they are likely already spending time interacting with their children. They can choose a time that they already spend interacting with their children and turn it into a mindfulness of parenting exercise as well.
- It can be helpful in cultivating a new habit to tie the new behavior into a preexisting routine. For example, if a parent has the goal of forming the

habit of asking their adolescent child about their day more regularly, it might be useful to tie this into an existing routine that the parent and child have, say, when eating dinner together, or when the parent says goodnight.

- It may be beneficial to have parents state their goals for home practice aloud, based on self-regulation literature on making public commitments. That is, at the end of the session, after you set the goals for home practice together, ask the parent, "Okay. Just so we are both clear, what are your goals for this week?"
- Ensure the parent has the goals written down or a reminder of the goals in some form when they leave. There are multiple ways of doing this and you may do different things with different clients. You might write the goals down yourself as you talk them through and give that to the client, write the goals down yourself and send it to them as a text or email, ask the client to write the goals down themselves on to paper or their phone, or ask the client to enter the goals into their calendar.
- Always remember to check in on the home practice goals at the beginning of the next session. If you consistently begin each session asking about home practice you show that you value the home practice, which sets up the expectation that it will be explored. Ask how the home practice went and spend some time exploring the parent's experiences. If the home practice experiences are then drawn into the intervention itself—that is, used as part of the intervention—parents will see the value of them.
- If the parent did not do the home practice, then explore what went wrong, using this information to tailor the home practice goals for the next week.

Chapter summary

Within ACT the therapeutic relationship is fundamentally a warm and empathetic partnership of equals. The application of FAP can be used to leverage the therapeutic relationship for the intervention. Over the next seven chapters every aspect of the parent–child hexaflex will be explored in turn with specific intervention strategies and a case study for each.

References

Cummings, M. E., & Davies, P. T. (2002). Effects of marital conflict on children: Recent advances and emerging themes in process-oriented research. *Journal of Child Psychology and Psychiatry*, *43*(1), 31–63.

Gardner, F., Montgomery, P., & Knerr, W. (2016). Transporting evidence-based parenting programs for child problem behavior (age 3-10) between countries: Systematic review and meta-analysis. *Journal of Clinical Child and Adolescent Psychology*, *45*(6), 749–762.

Greenberg, L. S. (2002). *Emotion-focused therapy*. Washington, DC: American Psychological Association.

Guild, D. J., Toth, S. L., Handley, E. D., Rogosch, F. A., & Cicchetti, D. (2017). Attachment security mediates the longitudinal assocaition between child-parent psychtherapy and peer relations for toddlers of depressed mothers. *Development and Psychopathology*, *29*(2), 587–600.

Hayes, S. C., Strosahl, K. D., & Wilson, K. G. (2003). *Acceptance and commitment therapy: An experiential approach to behavior change*. New York: Guilford Press.

Hrdy, S. B. (2011). *Mothers and others*. Cambridge: Harvand University Press.

Karver, M. S., Handelsman, J. B., Fields, S., & Bickman, L. (2006). Meta-analysis of therapeutic relationship variables in youth and family therapy: The evidence for different relationship variables in the child and adolescent treatment outcome literature. *Clinical Psychology Review*, *26*(1), 50–65.

Kohlenberg, R. J., & Tsai, M. (1991). *Functional analytic psychotherapy creating intense and curative therapeutic relationships*. New York: Plenum Press.

Lundahl, B., Risser, H. J., & Lovejoy, C. M. (2006). A meta-analysis of parent training: Moderators and follow-up effects. *Clinical Psychology Review*, *26*(1), 86–104.

McLeod, B. D., & Weisz, J. R. (2005). The therapy process observational coding system-allilance scale: Measure characteristics and prediction of outcome in usual clinical practice. *Journal of Consulting and Clinical Psychology*, *73*(2), 323–333.

McLoed, B. D., Weisz, J. R., & Wood, J. J. (2007). Examining the association between parenting and childhood depression: A meta-analysis. *Clinical Psychology Review*, *27*(8), 986–1003.

Reyno, S. M., & McGrath, P. J. (2006). Predictors of parent training efficacy for child externalizing behavior problems a meta-analytic review. *Journal of Child Psychology and Psychiatry*, *47*, 99–111.

Sandoz, & Boone, M. (2016). Evoke, reinforce, repeat: Enhancing the creativity and sensitivity of your ACT work by incoporating a plain language behavioral perspective. In *Paper presented at the ACBS World Conference, Seattle*.

Tirch, D., Schoendorff, B., & Silberstein, L. R. (2014). *The ACT practitioner's guide to the science of compassion*. Oakland: New Harbinger Publications.

Tsai, M., Kohlenberg, R. J., & Kanter, J. W. (2010). A functional analytic psychotherapy (FAP) approach to the therapeutic alliance. In C. J. Muran, & J. P. Barberm (Eds.), *The therapuetic alliance: An evidence-based guide to practice* (pp. 172–190). New York: Guilford Press.

van Mourik, K., Crone, M. R., De Wolff, M. S., & Reis, R. (2017). Parent training programs for ethnic minorities: A meta-analysis of adaptations and effect. *Prevention Science*, *18*(1), 95–105.

Vu, N. L., Jouriles, E. N., McDonald, R., & Rosenfield, D. (2016). Children's exposure to intimate partner violence: A meta-analysis of longitudinal associations with child adjustment problems. *Clinical Psychology Review*, *46*, 25–33.

Yap, M. B. H., Pilkington, P. D., Ryan, S. M., & Jorm, A. F. (2014). Parental factors associated with depression and anxiety in young people: A systematic review and meta-analysis. *Journal of Affective Disorders*, *156*, 8–23.

Section 3

ACT processes

Chapter 7

Values and proto-values

Chapter Outline

What are values? **154**
Proto-values 159
DNA-V model 160
How do values apply to parent–child interaction? **160**
Intrinsic reinforcement and persistence 160
Parental sensitivity and attachment 162
Flexible parenting 162
Rule-governed Behavior 163
Importance of values in other domains of living 164
Values and history 164
Supporting proto-values development 165
Working with values clinically **168**
Setting the stage for values work 168
Prompts 170
Values as the other side of pain 170
Metaphors 170
Experiential exercises 171
Values meditation **172**
Tuning in to values 175
Developing a rich and flexible repertoire of valued acts 176
Encouraging home practice 177
Troubleshooting **179**
How do I make sure I'm getting values not pliance? 179
What if the client tells me goals instead of values? 179
What if the client is so disconnected from their values that they doesn't know what their values are? 179
Overabundance of values 179
When valued action has another function 180
When children misbehave (or when parenting is hard) 181
Four key developmental periods and values **181**
Infancy and values 181
Early childhood and values 182
Middle childhood and values 182
Adolescence and values 183
Using values with specific issues **183**
Parental mental health problems and values 183
Parental grief and values 183
Childhood externalizing problems and values 184
Childhood internalizing problems and values 184
Childhood neurodevelopmental disabilities and values 184
Peer problems and bullying and values 185
Marital conflict and values 185
Expressed emotion including critical and intrusive parenting and values 185
Emotion dismissiveness and values 185
Inconsistent, harsh, or punitive parenting and values 186
References **186**

Acceptance and Commitment Therapy. DOI: https://doi.org/10.1016/B978-0-12-814669-9.00007-2
© 2019 Elsevier Inc. All rights reserved.

He who has a why to live for can bear almost any how.

Friedrich Nietzsche

Happiness is not the reward of virtue, but virtue itself.

Baruch Spinoza

The values that we care about the deepest ... command our love. When those things that we care about so deeply become endangered, we become enraged. And what a healthy thing that is! Without it, we would never stand up and speak out for what we believe.

Fred Rogers

You have brains in your head. You have feet in your shoes. You can steer yourself in any direction you choose.

Dr Seuss

What are values?

Values are a key aspect of Acceptance and Commitment Therapy (ACT). In many ways, values are both the start and the end points of the therapeutic endeavor (in fact, in the 1999 book by Hayes, Strosahl and Wilson updated in 2003, values were presented at the end, just before committed action, whereas in more recent manuals, such as this one, they are often presented first) (Hayes, Strosahl, & Wilson, 2003). Values provide the reason for therapy itself, give dignity to the suffering that clients choose to face in the name of healing or their child's welfare, and provide the basis for choosing which actions to take. Other aspects of the ACT model have a lot to say about how a person may travel but it is values that provide the direction. In emphasizing the importance of chosen values, ACT is sharing common ground with philosophical traditions such as stoicism and existentialism, as well as contemplative traditions such as Buddhism where mindfulness is practiced in a larger context that includes choosing to follow specific ethical principles.

In Relational Frame Theory (RFT) terms, values are a type of motivative augmental (Hayes, Barnes-Holmes, & Roche, 2001; Hayes et al., 2003; Villatte, Villatte, & Hayes, 2016). Augmenting refers to a type of rule-governed behavior where the relational networks alter the degree to which particular stimuli function as reinforcers or punishers; and motivative augmentals do so by altering the degree to which previously established reinforcers or punishers function as reinforcers or punishers in the present moment (see Chapter 4: Shape: building a flexible repertoire). That is, values make previously established reinforcers or punishers salient in the current context through the transformation of stimulus functions. For example, the mother of a 5-month-old baby wakes up for the second time that night. The baby isn't easily settling and so the mother needs to get up and feed the baby, perhaps sing the baby a lullaby to help baby fall back asleep. As the mother picks up the baby, the mother is exhausted, the floor is cold, the baby is crying. The mother remembers their key parenting values—they want to "be there" for their child. Their child needs them. They can "be there" by fulfilling their child's needs and giving them comfort. Through the transformation of stimulus functions, the harsh, irritating noise of the baby's cry, a sound that woke the parent from much needed sleep, becomes an appeal for help. The task of feeding the baby, in the middle of the night, an exhausting and tiresome task becomes a tender act of care for a dearly loved child. The parent's touching upon a value in this situation doesn't make the floor less cold, or the crying less upsetting or the mother less exhausted; however, it does help that mother be more willing to experience them.

Defined as a midlevel term, which can be a useful heuristic, Wilson and Dufrene (2009) defined values within ACT as "freely chosen, verbally constructed consequences of ongoing, dynamic, evolving patterns of activity, which establish predominant reinforcers for that activity that are intrinsic in engagement in the valued behavioral pattern itself." To better understand values, let's break that definition down into its components.

The first aspect is "freely chosen." In this context, "freely chosen" means that valuing itself and associated valued patterns of behavior are not under predominant and ongoing aversive control. That is, the primary function of a valued pattern of behavior is not the avoidance of aversive stimuli or punishment. Parents don't *make* themselves behave consistently with their values; instead, they actively and willingly *choose* to do so. Thus the pattern primarily has an appetitive function and is driven by reinforcement. In fact, engaging in valued behavior has intrinsically reinforcing functions, even in the presence of aversive stimuli. Considering the example earlier, the parent awakened by her infant's cries experiences, and is reinforced by, her understanding that she is "being there" for her child, despite her tiredness and discomfort. This does not mean that aversive control is never involved in the pattern of the behavior. Ongoing patterns of behavior usually serve multiple functions with different functions dominating in subtly different contexts within our lives. It simply means that the predominant function is not the avoidance of aversive stimuli. For example, all parents of young babies would, at times, pick up their child, cuddle their child, talk to their child, or sing to their child in order to avoid the aversive stimuli of their baby's cries. Many parenting behaviors of parents of young babies are then, at times, under aversive control. However, for responsive and sensitive parents those same behaviors—physical affection, talking to their child, or singing to their child—are not *primarily* under aversive control. It is far more often the case that the parent's behavior is instead under appetitive control.

"Freely chosen" also means that valuing behavior needs to be distinguished from rule-following that is functioning as pliance, that is, acting a certain way in order to gain social approval. The primary function of values is not to gain social approval. Rather, their primary function is intrinsic to the individual who has chosen them. This particular aspect of values may be more difficult to distinguish in practice.

It is not unusual for clients to confidently answer values questions with verbal rules that are, in fact, followed for social approval, or for genuine values to have become rigidly entangled with pliance or avoidance or for the client to be attempting to gain the therapist's approval (Villatte et al., 2016). In the area of parenting in particular, there is a cultural saturation of parenting rules, and easily contactable expectations of what being a "good" parent means and what parenting is "supposed" to be like. Further, parents are often subject to approval and disapproval from others about their parenting, including being shamed. It happens in public from strangers, in family contexts from extended family, within friendship groups if methods of parenting differ, from health professionals, and within interactions with the school, even from our children themselves. Distinguishing values from pliance—rule-following to gain social approval—is thus going to be important. One key way to do this are to help the client to tune into the intrinsically reinforcing qualities, the "sweet spot" to borrow the language of Kelly Wilson. Valued action is not always pleasant. It may feel quite awful. But if there is no sweetness to it at all, then it may, indeed, not be a value. Another way of saying this is that when valued actions do occur, they tend to become a part of the person's behavioral repertoire because, by definition, they are naturally reinforced. A second key way to distinguish values and pliance is to, through an imaginary exercise or simply framing, prompt the client to consider what they would do if the opinion of others was irrelevant. This imaginal exercise assists in teasing out pliance and rigidity from values. Rigid and aversive "values" are no longer truly functioning as values.

The "freely chosen" aspect of values also means that values are dynamic and changing and influenced by context. They are not something that is fixed within a person for that person to discover. Rather it is up to the person to take a stance. Values may therefore shift and change with time and across different situations. For example, it is not unusual for parents to radically change in their parenting values once their anticipated child is born. It is also not unusual for parents to change in their values—in parenting and in other areas of living—in response to the ongoing experience of loving their child, a person who gradually unfolds into a valuing being in their own right. Values also don't exist in isolation, rather valuing is an act of balancing values in the unfolding moment-to-moment experience of living. There may be periods in a parent's life in which they are experiencing stress, and might weigh self-care as more important than taking their child to that extra school event; similarly, they might value teaching their child to be mindful of danger in the environment when he or she is a toddler, and then shift toward helping them to more fully and bravely explore the world as an adolescent.

Let's move on to the next part of the definition, "predominant reinforcers for that activity which are intrinsic in engagement in the valued behavioral pattern itself." Valuing and valued actions are primarily driven by intrinsic rather than extrinsic reinforcement. That is to say, the key reinforcers are fundamentally a naturally occurring aspect of performing the behavior. For example, acting on the value of being a loving parent, brings the parent into contact with the reinforcers of the pleasure of physical contact: the sweet smell of their child's hair, the warmth of their body, the softness of their skin, the pleasure of connecting with the child in that moment and the knowledge that this is meeting the child's needs. Even in challenging situations, intrinsic reinforcement may be available for a parent acting on such a value.

A parent who is currently in another country far away may derive a similar reinforcing sense of connection to their child by reaching out and touching the screen of the tablet together during a Skype call. A parent whose premature baby is still in the neonatal intensive care unit at hospital may derive a similar reinforcing sense of connection by putting their hands gently on their baby as their baby sleeps in the humidicrib. In fact, a parent who lost their baby to neonatal death may also derive a similar reinforcing sense of connection lovingly tending to their child's grave or memorial.

In all of these examples, extrinsic rewards including the approval of others is not necessary. The act in itself is rewarding. This intrinsic reinforcement is an important aspect of valued action because intrinsic reinforcement—reinforcement that is a naturally occurring aspect of the behavior is readily available in a ways that extrinsic reinforcement is not. It is less dependent on the external circumstances of someone's life.

Living a life that is rich in reinforcement is important for mental health, in particular for depression prevention and treatment. Having an easily contactable source of intrinsic reinforcement is obviously then supportive of mental health. Further, the intrinsic aspect is also important in terms of behavior maintenance. Put in simple terms, we teach exactly what we teach and so if we've taught a client to parent in a certain way for our social approval then they will parent in that way when our social approval is potentially available as a reinforcer. For positive parenting behaviors to persist and to generalize it is necessary that they come under the contextual control of intrinsic reinforcement. Arguably, that is exactly what sensitive, responsive parenting is—parenting that is under the contextual control of intrinsic positive reinforcement within the parent–child interaction.

This intrinsic quality is also related to another key aspect of values: they are flexible. The value of being a loving parent, for example, remains doable in some form even in the extreme situations of a premature baby in the neonatal intensive care unit, or a parent grieving a neonatal death. Even then, there are loving moves that one might make. Importantly for parents, the exact acts that a particular value might encompass shift and change as the child develops and grows. For example, being a loving parent changes across development; in infancy caring for basic needs, nurturing, being a consistent and loving presence, building attachment, at preschool age facilitating social competence, modeling emotion regulation, and social interactions and perspective-taking, then into adolescence it might include encouraging exploration and mindful risk taking, development of autonomy and individuation, again helping with emotion regulation. One particular aspect of being a loving parent—physical affection—may shift and develop from: physically holding your child for much of the day, stroking their skin and kissing them regularly; to receiving your child with open and loving arms when they come to you for a cuddle, at the same time as being mindful of not intrusively disturbing their play with your kisses; to being mindful that the ways you express affection need to shift to high fives and winks when peers are around during adolescence.

This flexible quality of values distinguishes values from goals (Hayes et al., 2003). Goals are inflexible. Goals are also something that can be fully achieved. You can write a list of goals and tick them off as they are complete. Not so with values—there is always more being a loving parent to do. This distinction between values and goals is made clear in the going West metaphor (given full later in this chapter). In the metaphor, values are the direction of travel, they are going West. Whereas goals might be the stopping points along with way: a valley, the top of a hill. You might climb to the top of the hill and be able to say that was achieved. But you'll never arrive at "West."

It is important to be mindful of the distinction between values and goals. It is not unusual for clients to list goals instead of values in values exercises . The flexibility of values enables greater behavioral flexibility and adaptation both to life challenges and to the change inherent in development. Values are like an everchanging smorgasbord. There isn't one way to live out a particular value. Rather, there are many options and choices, a smorgasbord of actions and goals to choose from in any moment. For example, the value "being there for my child" evokes multiple goals, actions, and concepts including physically being present, being psychologically present, being available, and in various ways at different times in the child's life. Goals may be part of the relational network, but they don't occupy the central place within the network that values do, the place that allows for flexibility.

Although valued action is connected to intrinsic reinforcement it is important for clients to realize that taking action based on values is not going to feel good all the time. Valued actions often involve turning toward not away from psychological pain. Further, living one's values may involve extrinsic punishment such as social disapproval. This appears to be a contradiction to the notion of distinguishing values from pliance by looking for the "sweet spot." In fact, it isn't a contradiction, but rather a subtle distinction. First, feelings of joy can be an effective signal that behaviors we are currently performing are valued acts. But this does not mean that valued acts are always associated with feelings of joy. Further, the "sweet spot" is not simply about uncomplicated joy. Rather, it is also about looking for that sweet satisfaction that may be present even in the midst of suffering. This kind of complex sweetness is often present at funerals. Even in the midst of unspeakable grief, when a poignant memory of the departed loved one is recalled there are often smiles, maybe even laughter, and certainly a warmth of feeling alongside the deep sorrow. Learning to understand this kind of complicated sweetness that can arise in the midst of pain as a pointer toward one's values can be useful. In fact, our pain itself can be a marker for our values. We do not hurt over things that do not matter to us.

Proto-values

As values are a complex form of verbal behavior, they develop throughout childhood and adolescence along with other forms of verbal behavior. We use the term "proto-values" to refer to a child or adolescent's developing values as well as to the evolutionary bedrock from which many proto-values and values emerge. The evolved motivational systems—present from the earliest days of infancy—are arguably the most basic groundwork for what, in adulthood, we can understand as values. Although not verbal, they are a kind of 'proto-values': the primeval soup from which values will slowly emerge. Many of the most common values cluster around key elements of our evolved motivational systems—values around being there for our children, being compassionate and caring, acting with integrity, a sense of justice or fairness, for example, relate to our evolved affiliative system in terms of kinship and affiliative bonds involving reciprocity (Gilbert, 2009). Values around exploration and learning relate to our evolved drive system. So, although an infant certainly cannot be said to *value* in the full ACT sense of the word, we can think of them as engaging in a kind of rudimentary *proto-valuing*. With language development, true proto-valuing, as in proto-valuing as a *verbal* behavior, emerges, is experimented with and becomes more complex. Gradually throughout childhood and adolescence proto-valuing approaches the full characteristics of valuing. Parents and other adults support children in the development and elaboration of proto-values by stating *verbally* a child's prosocial behavior, enjoyment, and exploration, for example, "that was great sharing" or "wow, you love running!" This form of shared proto-values, as a *verbal behavior of the parent*, may be present from birth. Thus, in its earliest form, proto-values are social. Like other forms of verbal behavior, proto-valuing and valuing are learned through social interaction and connection. Importantly, children and adolescents experiment with proto-values, before settling into the valuing of adulthood. Proto-values are *explored*. An important task of parenting is to support children in their development of proto-values and values, including to support children in experimenting with proto-values.

DNA-V model

If you are using the DNA-V model (Hayes & Ciarrochi, 2015), then the values work in this chapter falls neatly into the values component of the model. This includes the fact that in children and adolescents, values should be understood more broadly as *proto-values*, with normal developmental value experimentation and discovery. In other words, during childhood and adolescence, children are not only in the process of discovering what they value, but also learning how to track their own values-consistent behaviors in their rapidly expanding social worlds.

How do values apply to parent–child interaction?

Intrinsic reinforcement and persistence

The intrinsically reinforcing aspect of values is incredibly important to parenting. First, it is important because where parenting is concerned, long-term maintenance is absolutely crucial. Parenting is, by nature, a marathon not a sprint. Parents must maintain their positive parenting behavior over the course of many years in order to successfully raise their children to adulthood. And parenting does not stop there! Indeed, parents need to maintain positive parenting behaviors for the rest of their lives.

Not only is long-term maintenance absolutely essential, but also, positive parenting behaviors must generalize across a wide variety of contexts because parenting by nature happens across a wide variety of contexts. There are no sick days, no recreational leave, and no time when, once reached, you can "clock off." Although childcare may be organized in order to take a break, even while taking a break parents are necessarily always on call. Moreover, parenting values supporting flexibility in positive parenting must generalize across developmental periods. The demands of parenting, as well as what parenting behaviors are effective shift across development. For example, with younger children, parents may be more interested in supporting the development of a broad emotional lexicon in their children, to support the development of their social competence. However, in their youngster's adolescence, they may focus more on helping their teen navigate their first romantic relationships, or the increasing demands of school. The parenting value at the core functions as a compass; parenting behaviors will, and should, shift based on the parent's tracking of the effects of their behavior on their child. In this way, pursuing parenting values, coupled with tracking how these behaviors work in particular contexts, can support flexible, ongoing positive parenting behavior through child development.

Similarly, when parents are sick, stressed, or exhausted, it is critically important that they are able to contact reinforcement from engagement in valued positive parenting behavior. This is also essential when parents are alone and no one else but their child serves as a witness to their behavior, when they are in public and under the gaze of others, when they have a long list of other tasks to complete, as well as when they are feeling happy and relaxed. If positive parenting behaviors are not being maintained by intrinsic reinforcement, then there is no possibility of them continuing in a robust and consistent way. Consider the example of the parent of an anxious child who is skilled at encouraging their child to experience novel contexts—like initiating play with new children at the playground—they may be willing to push for "brave" social approach behavior, only to stop when their child begins to show fear. In that case, they might allow their child to leave the situation, potentially reinforcing social avoidance.

Parenting is also, upon examination, mostly comprised of small acts—a smile here, a cuddle there, persistence in selective attention, a book at bedtime, pausing in cooking dinner to respond, or a finding the time for conversation about peer group concerns. Each individual act may seem tiny and trivial but the sum total of the small acts repeated many times over that adds up to a significant impact in the long term.

Most of the time, these acts are not going to bring extrinsic reinforcement for the parent. A common complaint of primary caregivers of young babies is how terribly boring it all is. Positive parenting strategies to manage misbehavior often, due to the extinction burst, result in even more dramatic misbehavior in the immediate moment. All the loving cuddles and bedtime books often result in parents falling asleep exhausted without reading that book of their own. Parents do not often hear praise for their efforts. And, of course, there is no salary. In fact, the more time you spend parenting well, the more your career is likely to suffer in comparison to what it could have been had you never had children. This is not to create a dark and mournful picture of parenting—not at all! Most parents find parenting deeply rewarding. The point is this: it is the intrinsic reinforcement of parenting itself that makes it so.

Values—and the intrinsic reinforcement connected to valued acts—also provide purpose and meaning to difficult tasks of parenting. Many aspects of parenting are not easy. Being psychologically available when you are exhausted or stressed, multitasking parenting with household tasks or the realities of everyday living and, of course, managing misbehavior effectively (including on the days when you are also stressed, multitasking, and in public being judged!). There are many difficult moments in parenting: needing to forgive one's child, needing to say no. All of this is psychologically difficult. So why face it? Values give that why.

Parental sensitivity and attachment

As a clinician, you should never tell parents what their values *should* be. However, working with parents you will notice that many parents have parenting values that easily align with being a sensitive and responsive parent. Parents may speak of supporting their child's emotional development, or encouraging healthy and adaptive exploration of the world, or simply making sure that their children know that they are loved. The functions of parental sensitivity, of being a secure based and a safe haven, is in tune with all of these parenting values.

In addition, many parents value connection, meeting their child's emotional needs, in and of itself. Although values are freely chosen, they are freely chosen by human beings, with our evolved social motivational systems. It is no coincidence that many humans have values around social connection and emotional intimacy. Thus, for many parents, making values the compass for parenting behavior is in line with sensitive and responsive parenting behavior.

Parenting grounded within parenting values is also more likely to be, as Dadds and Hawes (2006) describe it as "attachment-rich." An attachment-rich parenting interaction is rich in emotional and relational signaling as well as shared psychological presence, that is parents are actually paying full attention to their children and saying or doing things that indicate their thoughts and feelings *about their children*, whether positive—"hello, my darling!"—or negative—"you drive me insane!" In families of children with behavioral problems, often the interactions around misbehavior are attachment-rich, while the interactions around more positive and neutral behaviors are often attachment-neutral. Attachment-rich interaction is in itself a powerful reinforcer of child behavior. Ideally, everyday interactions around positive and neutral behaviors should be attachment-rich—"thanks for helping me with that, my sweetie" with a warm smile—while interactions around misbehavior should be attachment-neutral—"you aren't sharing so the toy is going away for two minutes" in a neutral and calm tone. Parenting from values, rather than simply following a parenting rule functioning as pliance, is more likely to naturally produce the glint in the eyes, the genuine smile, the warmth of voice and the easily affection of a parent who is genuinely emotionally engaged with their child and hence support attachment-rich parenting responses to positive and neutral behaviors.

Of course, much of this is to do with that word we often avoid using in the parenting research and intervention world: love. Parents (by and large) love their children. This love and the way in which the love presents moment to moment in daily life, is what makes the challenging and long-term task of parenting worthwhile.

Flexible parenting

Values support the development of flexible behavior. Thus parenting from values is consistent with a flexible and experimental approach to parenting, in which parents relate to the task of parenting as an open and ongoing experiment, forming ideas about what might be happening for their child and experimenting with different approaches, discovering what is effective. Such a flexible and experimental approach to parenting fosters parental resilience in the long term. It allows for easy adaptation of parenting as children change with development and allows for adaptation to the specific needs of each individual child. Further, such a flexible, experimental parenting style is particularly adaptive if the parent experiences parenting challenges outside typical development, or beyond what they may have expected. If psychological contact with values is maintained, rather than simply with goals, it is possible to adapt and change when specific goals are thwarted or when life does not go according to plan.

Parents of children with disabilities or special needs in particular benefit from a flexible parenting style, because children with disabilities or special needs may particularly benefit from an individualized approach. Parental flexibility is also required as the children grow into conscious, valuing beings in their own right. From infancy, children have evolved motivational systems and simple preferences and even a baby may make known a preference that is different to the intentions of the parents. As children become verbal, proto-values also become verbalized, experimented with and increasingly elaborate. As children move into middle childhood, and especially into adolescence, they begin to act as valuing beings in their own right. Parents may find this period of value experimentation challenging. Perhaps the parents may feel that they can already tell what their child's value in an area of life will ultimately be (and they may even be right) but still, there is no short cut, they must be patient while their child experiments and be open to the fact that they could be wrong. To open your heart to your child, is to love a person without yet knowing exactly who that person is. This is what we mean when we say that the love of a parent for a child is unconditional. No other love is as without condition. A major task of parenting is to continue to remain open and unconditional in one's love. Or to be it another way, to be flexible.

Rule-governed Behavior

There are a number of dangers of parenting from rigid rules rather than accurate tracking of a child's behavior-within-context. First, if parenting behavior is under the control of a rule, such as *good mothers are always warm and kind*—then it is not under the contextual control of the child's cues. It may be warm, and even on cue (if that is what will gain the parent social approval from others in that moment), but if it is not under the contextual control of the child's cues, it isn't truly sensitive. Rule-governed behavior tends to be rigid and inflexible, and because it is less sensitive to environmental contingencies, may be harder to change.

When parenting based on rules, parents may also be disconnected from their own parental values and their own preferences and pleasures within the parent–child relationship.If parents adhere to the rule, *it's important to fit in with other parents,* then they may be disconnected from what actually works for them and for their child, pushing their child to compete with what other parents and children are doing, instead of seeing and understanding their child just as they are, and doing what works for their family.

Alice Gopnik (2017) talks about two parenting styles: the gardener and the carpenter. The gardener is patient and trusts in development as an inevitable unfolding process, seeking to understand and nurture the child they have. For the gardener parenting is about providing the nurturing environment that a child needs to thrive. The child can be trusted to grow into an adult in the same way that a seed will grow into a tree. The parents' role then is not to turn a seed into a tree but rather to nurture the seed as it grows and transforms. In essence, the parent accurately tracks the child's development, and uses that information to provide sensitive nurturance. The carpenter, instead, sees parenting as actively building a particular kind of child and actively, through parenting, sculpting a baby into a child, then into a teenager then into an adult. The carpenter has a particular final product in mind and sees their child as raw material to be shaped into the kind of person the carpenter wishes to produce. More than that, the carpenter sees their active construction as necessary and as driving their child's development. Carpenter parents, as Gopnik calls them, are often parenting based on rules they may have about how their children must develop building their children into particular into "final products."

Importance of values in other domains of living

When working with parents, parenting values are obviously incredibly important. However, what is equally important is the parent's values in other domains of living. It is not unusual to come across parents who can talk articulately about their parenting values, are clearly in psychological contact with their parenting values, and who live their parenting values well day-by-day in many ways big and small. And yet, once you ask about other domains of living you might find that the parents' values in those areas are being woefully neglected. In particular, parents of children with disabilities, chronic health, or mental health conditions are especially vulnerable to this. It may be that the focus of your values-related work is around assisting parents in better living their values in other domains of living, not just in the parenting domain.

Values and history

For parents with difficult histories in terms of how they themselves were parented—for example, parents who have a history of childhood abuse or neglect—the notion of values may be critically important. Such parents may fear that they themselves will play out the abuse or neglect that was inflicted on them. Understanding that their history is one thing, and their values another—they themselves can take a stance that is different to what they experienced. Even for parents without such challenging histories, reflecting deliberately on values rather than simply repeating their own childhood can be an important step toward more effective parenting.

Supporting proto-values development

By respecting, attuning to, and reflecting verbally on the preferences and expressed needs of children, parents can support children in becoming verbally aware of their own motivational systems as well as what is reinforcing to them. From these kinds of parent and child interactions, the most rudimentary of proto-values begin to evolve. For example, a parent notices that her baby kicks and squeals, looking toward the sky when she sees a bird. The parent responds with, "yes, a bird! You like birds, huh?" Having noticed her child's preferences for birds, the parent points birds out to their child, perhaps even deliberately taking their child to visit birds, like the seagulls at the beach. Through these experiences the child develops a rich learning history in relation to birds, and shows even greater enthusiasm for birds, which the parent continues to reflect verbally to the child. With time, and continued parent and child interaction, this initial preference may generalize to all animals. In middle childhood, the child themselves may state this as a proto-value, "I love animals!" With more time, and continued exposure to animals as well as general learning within the verbal community, this love of animals may become increasingly complex in numerous ways. It could become connected to aspirations around the environment, to values around helping and caring for animals or to a love of science. As the child, into adolescence, experiments with a complex array of proto-values, they may begin to settle into what may be, for them, core values in the full ACT sense of the world: values around protecting the environment, caring for all life or a love of the biological sciences. They may begin to experiment with valued action by volunteering for an environmental charity or an animal refuge or studying hard in biology with the intention of becoming a biologist or a veterinarian. Parents thus support the development of proto-values, and the elaboration of proto-values into values, by noticing the child's enjoyment, interests and prosocial behavior and reflecting that *verbally* for the child, as well as by being supportive and encouraging of exploration and proto-values experimentation.

Brooke and Kai

Brooke comes to her therapist's office with 3-month-old Kai on her hip. She smiles sadly as she puts Kai on the floor, on a bunny rug and places a rattle within reach. She's soon in tears, "I'm not coping. I'm not coping at all with this." She explains, "I am an absolute failure as a mum. I don't understand. I wanted this so badly. And I love him, don't get me wrong. I love Kai so much. But it is all so boring. I'm exhausted, miserable, lonely, and bored. I keep thinking: when do I get my life back? I'm so ashamed to even have those thoughts. I'm so selfish."

Brooke is a single mother working as an academic in media studies. She is currently on maternity leave and will be until Kai is 6 months old. However, she is considering returning to work early if she can organize childcare, as a desperate attempt to "get her life back." Sometimes it seems like returning to work is the solution, other times she thinks it'll only make things worse. On questionnaires, Brooke is in the severe range for depressive symptoms. Brooke is breastfeeding and reports no ongoing challenges in relation to the birth or breastfeeding.

Brooke says that she has joined a local mother's group. The mother's group meets weekly but Brooke only attends every second week or so. She says the women are "nice enough" but she "can't stand the judgement." She explains that she only attends if she can "put on a brave face" and look like she's got it "all together."

Imagine you could, unseen and unheard, observe a typical, ordinary interaction between Brooke and Kai. It might be something like this:

Parent–child interaction

Brooke places Kai down on a bunny rug in her lounge room with a rattle close by. She sits near to him on the couch.

Brooke sighs and her eyes drift to half-hooded slightly closed.

Kai cooes and babbles: "Ohhh ... cooo..."

Brooke remains as still as a statue, her eyes half-closed.

Kai continues to babble, "coo ... ga ..."

Brooke sighs and runs her hands over her face, "I'm so damn tired," she says to herself as she brings her legs up onto the couch, repositioning.

Kai babbles louder at this, "coo ... ah ..."

Brooke's eyes become half-hooded again. She yawns and her eyes open. She stares at the corner of the room.

Kai finds his rattle. He has managed to grasp it in his hand and begins to wave it around enthusiastically. The rhythmic sounds of his rattling adds to the music of his coos.

Brooke's face is still, unmoving, a slight frown playing about her lips. Her eyes are fixated on the corner of the room. She is lost within her own thoughts. If another adult were in the room, they'd instinctively say, "what's wrong, Brooke?" But no one else is present.

Kai plays with the rattle for several minutes, cooing as he does so. His movements with the rattle become bigger. He is sweeping his arm up and down in great waves now and his vocalizations are building to a crescendo.

(*Continued*)

(Continued)

"Ga! Ga!" Kai calls out.

Brooke remains still and staring. Lost in her thoughts.

Suddenly, there is a banging noise, a crack of plastic on bone. Kai has hit his own head with the rattle. He erupts into a storm of tears.

Brooke slowly turns to Kai, as someone waking up out of a daze. She frowns, "What happened, Kai?"

She walks over to him and she picks him up, "shh ... it is alright, you'll be okay."

What's happening for Brooke and Kai?

The most important task for the early months of parenthood has not successfully happened for Brooke and Kai: Brooke's parenting has not come under the contextual control of Kai's cues in a manner that is intrinsically reinforcing for Brooke. Although Brooke is ultimately responsive when Kai cries, she is not responsive to Kai's prosocial bids for attention and interaction. If this continues, Kai may come to fit an anxious-ambivalent pattern of attachment, as he learns that he must be hyperviligant to his mother's attention and use aversive behaviors such as crying to initiate interaction with her. This pattern of interaction between Brooke and Kai—diminished responsiveness on Brooke's part, coupled with reduced positive affect—is a common pattern of interaction between depressed mothers and their children.

Brooke is not in psychological contact with her values as a parent. This coupled with the sweeping life changes that being the primary caregiver to a young baby bring have left Brooke with a deficit in positive reinforcement. It is little wonder she feels bored and miserable and reports depressive symptoms.

From an RFT perspective, when Brooke is with Kai and is "lost in her thoughts," she may be entangled with derived relations about her competence as a mother including "I'm a failure as a mum" perhaps in an equivalence relation with "I'm selfish." She may be fused with beliefs such as "good mothers are selfless," or "good mothers never feel bored with their children." This may also be linked with fears of social censure. These may have significant aversive functions with her that hook her to such a degree that she is unaware of her surroundings, especially of Kai. Brooke reports concerns about the judgement of others, particularly the other mothers in her mother's group. She may be focused upon gaining social approval, that is, following rules functioning as pliance, rather than the consequences of her actions in context, that is, following rules functioning as tracking. Clinicians may help Brooke become more aware of the functions of these relations for her through acceptance-based experiential work; they may support the development of her tracking by helping her defuse from these thoughts and become more embodied in the present moment when with Kai, perhaps through facilitating a brief child-directed mindful appreciation each day. For example, clinician's might work with Brooke to choose a pleasant moment, perhaps a playful one, with Kai, and to practice present moment awareness, and

(Continued)

(Continued)

opening and allowing all thoughts and feelings to be explored with curiosity. Helping Brooke contact a sweet or meaningful experience of Kai in which they are connected, such that Brooke's mindful awareness is reinforced, might also become a touchstone for constructing a value (motivative augmental): perhaps that it is meaningful to Brooke to be fully present with Kai.

Working with values clinically

A key aspect of working with values is the ability to accurately assess a parent's values. Not merely so that you, as a clinician, can understand the client's values, but also to enable the parent themselves to psychologically access their own values. The assessment of values then is, in itself, also therapeutic. We will explore a number of ways to do this—from simple and easy questions, to metaphors and experiential exercises, to a values meditation. Different ways to assess values can assist in overcoming different potential obstacles.

Setting the stage for values work

It is important for values work to be experiential. This ensures the psychological functions of the values are fully present. It is often beneficial to begin the session with a brief mindfulness exercise, to ensure that parents are fully psychologically present and ready to engage in the values exercises in a mindful and curious way. The values exploration could be introduced to parents in the following way [adapted from ACT–PAC manual (Coyne & Moore, 2015)]:

How long has it been since you paused and considered what is truly important to you? Like most parents, you are probably too busy coping with the tasks of daily living, or perhaps, like many you've fallen into a pattern of jumping from crisis to crisis. You might feel exhausted and overwhelmed, numb, or checked out, or maybe you feel trapped.
Can you recall a time when you felt like this?
What happened to your parenting?
What feelings showed up for you? And did they color the whole interaction?
If you could describe those moments as "spaces," would they feel roomy and expansive, or rather, small and cramped areas in which you must fight to get out?

(Continued)

(Continued)

In crisis mode, it is hard to remember what's really important to us and it is hard to be creative in coming up with solutions. In crisis mode, we experience a kind of tunnel vision. The world may narrow to this one interaction, which, you may feel, is the barometer by which you must measure your entire success or failure as a parent. Is that how those moments have been for you?

Here's a different idea: what if you could step out of crisis mode? What if you could bring a bit of flexibility and creativity back and reconnect to what's important to you? What if you could choose how to respond to your child, and choose your direction, even when you are reacting to whatever is happening in the moment? Values are chosen directions or ways of being. You might think of your values as your chosen purpose. They are not destinations, but rather, points on a compass that guide us through our lives.

Simple questioning

Once a parent is centered through some brief experiential work, a simple question around values may be all that is necessary or all that is possible. Simple questioning around values may also be important in ongoing therapy, several sessions in. Values may have already been thoroughly explored, but a simple question may elicit the values relevant to a particular issue or interaction.

Simple questions to elicit values might include:

- What kind of a parent do you want to be?
- What matters most to you as a parent?
- What brings you joy as a parent?
- What do you want to do in your heart of hearts?
- What do you want this interaction with your child to be about?

Sweet moments

Parents can be prompted to look for the "sweet spot" in everyday life and recognizing this sweetness as a signal that they are acting on their values. This includes noticing moments of joy (without expecting that every valued action will feel good). It also includes noticing the sweetness that's possible even in the midst of pain. This way of tuning in to values is particularly useful in distinguishing values from pliance (rule-following for social approval). It can also be useful for increasing psychological contact with values in everyday life.

Sweet moments exercises

One way to get a better sense of your values is to look for moments of sweetness in your daily life and then ask: what am I doing? Why is this important? Valued acts don't always feel good. But moments of joy or contentment often happen when we are acting on our values. So noticing what we are doing when we feel that can be a good clue to working out our values. What can be particularly helpful to notice is those moments of complicated sweetness, sweetness in the midst of sorrow or stress. That is a big clue!

Prompts

Some clients benefit from using simple prompts. For example, ACT therapists can use values cards or lists of various qualities such as "kind" as starting points. Clients can be prompted to sort through the cards and to pick out what resonates best for them. From these starting points, clients can be encouraged to expand. This may be particularly useful for clients who are currently psychologically disconnected from their values.

Values as the other side of pain

As we don't hurt over what we don't care about our pain is itself a clue to our values. Sometimes clients find it easier to elucidate their areas of pain. From there, you can prompt clients to consider the flip-side: what value is attached to that pain? For example, a mother who experienced birth trauma and painful, difficult breastfeeding with early cessation, could be prompted to consider why her birth plan and plan to breastfeed mattered to her. She might list values of: being physically affectionate, promoting her baby's health, or parenting in a natural way. These values may then be the starting point of finding valued acts that can be done now.

Metaphors

Metaphors are widely used in ACT and may be used to explain the concept of values. The metaphor of values as a direction, seen in the going West metaphor, is useful for distinguishing between values and goals.

Going West metaphor

A value is a direction in which you want your life to go. A value is like say, going West. In contrast, a goal is a particular place you might walk to along the way. So you decide to head West, and along the way you might walk to the top of a hill, or to the end of a street. When you get to the top of the hill you can say "I'm here. I'm at the top of the hill. I've done it," but you never really get to say "I'm West" do you? You never actually arrive. In the same way, "being a loving parent" is never finished. There's always further to go.

The metaphor of values as guiding stars is useful for inspiring the courage and willingness necessary to make changes.

Guiding stars metaphor

It is like being from a sea-faring people, long before GPS, when sailors relied upon celestial navigation to cross the oceans. You are going on an adventure, beyond the known world, beyond all that you've known of life before. We don't know exactly where you'll end up along the way. You may encounter a sea monster or two, you may find yourself visiting beautiful tropical islands. Throughout the adventure your values are your guiding stars. Again and again, you'll look up from the inky black ocean, to the stars above, and finding your values, you'll know which way to go.

Experiential exercises

Experiential exercises can help the client to recontact aspects of their values that are currently obscured within their current context. Experiential exercises that involve flexible perspective taking, psychologically moving forward in time and looking back on now can be particularly beneficial in moving beyond the stickiness of current problems to the wider perspective.

Time travel and take a new perspective

Let's imagine moving far into the future. Maybe 20 or 30 years? The current challenges in your life, what you are struggling with now as a parent, are long since resolved.

Looking back on your life now, from that future perspective, what do you want these days, months and years with your child to have been about?

Now imagine your child 20 or 30 years in the future, all grown up. Imagine your child going about their daily life. What do you wish for your child? What characteristics do you hope to have fostered in your child? Now, again, look back on today, from that future perspective. What can you do today move toward that vision of the future?

Now imagine that your child, again 20 or 30 years in the future, is reflecting on their childhood. You might like to imagine that your child is talking to a friend or a partner. In reflecting on their childhood, your child begins discussing you, as a parent. What do you hope to hear your child say?

You probably want your child to say that you are a good parent, but push past that to the specifics. Don't dwell on what you think your child is likely to say. Instead, focus on what you hope to hear your child say.

Imagine your child completing these sentences:

I'll always be grateful to my parents for ...

I'm lucky I had the parents I had because ...

Something I value in my parents is ...

Experiential exercises can also be an effective means of teasing out values from pliance, by prompting the parent to imagine themselves in a context in which social approval is irrelevant.

A magical place

Imagine that you could spend time in a magical place with your child. In this magical place there is no one to judge you. There is no pressure. There is nothing to achieve. No one will ever know how you choose to spend this time with your child. Part of the magic of the place is that you are both completely protected. You can make every mistake in the book and your child will come to no harm at all. So, you don't have to concern yourself with getting anything right. Instead, in this magical place, you get to focus on one thing: enjoying parenting. If you could spend time in a magical place with your child, focused on nothing else but enjoying it, what would you do? And why?

Values meditation

Values across every domain of living can be touched upon in this values meditation.

Values meditation script

Get comfortable.
Breathe in and out.
Take a moment to tune into your breathing in and out.
Gently shut your eyes.
As your eyes close, you find yourself standing in front of a wooden gate within a high wooden fence.
You gently push the gate open and it creaks as it swings.
You step inside onto a winding path within a beautiful and overgrown garden.
Pause for a moment and take in your surroundings.
Noticing the trees, the plants.
Hearing the birdsong.
Step slowly and carefully down the path as it curves through the garden, knowing that the path leads to your heart.
As you come to the end of the path you find yourself looking at a small dwelling.
This dwelling is your heart.
What does it look like?
Don't force the visualization.
Let it come.

(*Continued*)

(Continued)

Do you see a cottage? Or a beachhouse? Or a tree house? Or that house you lived in as a child? Or some other kind of building?
There is no right or wrong. There is just what you find.
Step toward the door of your heart, slowly and carefully, noticing the scene.
Your heart contains all that matters most to you: the people you love, the activities that bring you joy, your principles, your dreams. It contains all that gives your life meaning and purpose.
In a moment, you are going to open the door and explore your heart.
Your heart doesn't have to look the same each time you open the door. In fact, it could change and shift during a visit. It contains all that matters to you, but different features may present themselves depending on what you've come here to learn today and what you'd like to ask.
We are going to explore your heart today step by step.
When you are ready, put your hand on the knob, and slowly open the door.
You open the door and step inside, finding yourself in the first room of your heart: the room of joy.
The room of joy is furnished with your own happiness.
But this room is not about escaping from sorrow or disappointment. It is not a trophy room representing your achievements. It is not a room for indulgence.
Rather, this room is devoted to those moments where you experienced joy in the midst of stress or sorrow.
Those activities you enjoy for their own sake.
Those moments of quiet and simple contentment.
Look around slowly and carefully.
What do you see?
How is this room furnished?
What might that represent?
What things are in this room?
And why are they there?
Are there pictures on the wall?
Are there people in this room?
If you wish, you can walk around the room.
You might like to pick something up to examine it more closely.
If there is a person in this room you might like to talk to them.
Take your time in exploring.
What does this room tell you about what matters most to you?
What does this room tell you about your values?
You might like to pause to write your insights down.
When you are ready to leave the room of joy, you notice another door.
You step up to this door and open it, stepping through into the room of purpose.
The room of purpose is devoted to your principles, the ethics by which you aim to live, and the promises and commitments you wish to uphold.

(Continued)

(Continued)

But this room is not a room of obligations. It is not a prison cell. It is not devoted to rules.
Rather, this room is devoted to the principles and commitments you have chosen for yourself.
We all make our mark on the world and this room contains the legacy that you wish to leave.
It is devoted to the principles you have in your deepest heart when you don't need to answer to anyone else and you are not ashamed of being who you are.
Look around slowly and carefully.
What do you see?
How is this room furnished?
What things are in this room?
What values do those things represent for you?
Are there pictures on the wall?
And what do the pictures mean to you?
Are there people in here?
Why are they here? What do they represent in your heart?
Again, feel free to explore the room fully.
What does this room tell you about what matters most to you?
What does this room tell you about your values?
You might like to pause to write your insights down.
When you are ready to leave the room of purpose, you notice another door.
You step up to this door and open it, stepping through into the room of connection.
The room of connection is devoted to connecting with others.
But it is not just about the easy falling in love moments or the times when other people fulfill your needs and expectations.
Rather, it is devoted to moments when you give love freely to those you care for.
When you are there for others even when that's difficult for you.
Moments when you listened, when you understood, when you laughed together.
Look around slowly and carefully.
What do you see?
How is this room furnished?
What things are in this room?
What values do those things represent for you?
Are there pictures on the wall?
And what do the pictures mean to you?
Are there any people in this room?
Again, feel free to explore the room fully.
What does this room tell you about what matters most to you?
What does this room tell you about your values?
You might like to pause to write your insights down.
When you are ready to leave, slowly walk through each door, closing it behind you.

(*Continued*)

(Continued)

Out of the room of connection, through the rooms of purpose and joy and back outside your heart.
Close the front door.
All of this is here, right here inside you, always.
Begin to step away from your heart onto the path.
Before you leave, take one last look.
Then, follow the curving path back through the overgrown garden to the wooden gate.
As you open the wooden gate and shut it behind you, you can open your eyes.
Stretch and reposition.
Allow yourself a moment to digest all that you've learnt.
Try to craft your insights into clear statements of your values.
I experience joy when I'm ...?
I want to be remembered for being ...?
I want to connect with others in a way that's ...?
How can you live these values more fully in your life?

Tuning in to values

Once values are understood by therapist and client then the therapist can prompt a tuning into values in the context of other aspects of the intervention. For example, a parent with depression can be prompted to tune into their values, finding the "sweet moments" thus increasing psychological contact with values in daily life. Parents can also be prompted to tune into values during interactions with their children including challenging interactions such as when they are needing to change how they manage misbehavior. There are a number of ways that therapists might prompt parents to tune into their values:

- Using everyday phrases that evoke a sense of values such as follow your heart, follow your gut, or listen to your inner wisdom, for example, "Don't parent to the problem, parent from your heart" or "Don't just parent by the book, listen to your inner wisdom too"
- Promoting the client to look for the complicated sweetness in their life
- Promoting the client to pause, breathe and ask: what do I want this interaction to be about in this moment?
- Using a simple discrimination task such as: is what I am doing about controlling my emotions or is it about being there for my children?

- Using flexible perspective taking with questions like: what would future me tell me to do? In ten years looking back on today, what will I have wanted this moments to have been about?

Developing a rich and flexible repertoire of valued acts

Parents should be supported to develop a rich and flexible repertoire of valued acts, both in the domain of parenting and in other domains of living.

Many people find it easy to list the big goals that they could achieve in the service of their values. What is often more challenging is considering the small acts that they could perform. Emphasizing the importance of the small can be helpful. It may also be helpful to directly address misconceptions around quality time with psychoeducation on children's developmental needs in terms of parental attention and time. Parents, in considering ways to live out their values, often think of big acts like a trip to the zoo or a family holiday. Help parents to understand that while huge bursts of time together in a lovely setting are fun, they are not necessary. What children need is the small pockets of time that arise day by day. Quality time is often only 30 seconds to 2 minutes in length. It is: pausing in cooking the dinner for a minute to look at a drawing, bending down to pick up your grizzly baby, and put them on your hip as you tidy the house, shooting a few hoops with your teenage child in the evening.

Parental values in other domains of living should also be considered. Significant numbers of parents will be living their parenting values well but neglecting their values in other domains of living. It is important to address this with a full understanding of the complexity of the lives that many parents may be living, and the enormity of the task of parenting itself. Even in best-case-scenarios parenting is an enormous time investment. If you are the parent of a child with a disability, chronic health or mental health condition, are a single parent, are parenting without supportive extended family, or are parenting under circumstances of financial difficulty then the burden of parenting may be significant. Being advised to "take a break" can be simplistic and unrealistic in any sustainable way. Even for parents who can regularly "take a break," if that is the only time they live out their values in every other domain of living, they are still at risk for experiencing and unrewarding life.

Thus, whether or not a parent is able to organize child-free time to perform a valued activity within another domain of living, it is important for parents to find ways to live out their values within other domains of living at the same time as parenting their child. It may not be possible to have a date night with your partner if you can't organize childcare. But you can still ask, "How was your day?" and listen to the reply. There are many simple ways parents can live out values in other areas of life while parenting at the same time: walking children to the park (living own values around exercise and outdoors), having music on in the background while playing with their children (living own values around music and artistic expression) or meeting up with friends in a child friendly environment (living own values around friendship and socializing) as a few examples.

Encouraging home practice

Home practice around values may include:

- practicing the values meditation,
- exploring values across different domains and writing down ideas to examine further in the next session, and
- setting a goal of a particular valued action, taking that action and noticing the effects.

Working with Brooke and Kai

This interaction occurs toward the end of the first session.

Therapist:	Brooke, there's something else I'd like to explore right now before beginning of our work together.
Brooke:	okay.
Therapist:	Motherhood can be damn tough and it can also be boring and miserable. It is easy and natural to zone in on the problems, the challenges, boredom or misery, and be very focused on them, to make parenting all about fixing the problem, whether that's boredom, or feeling miserable or a practical problem like baby not sleeping. Now, I don't want to suggest that all of that isn't important. It is and we are going to spend time on it all. But I don't want us to lose sight of the other side to this: what kind of mother do you want to be?
Brooke looks surprised:	Oh. Well, I want to be a good mother, of course.
Therapist nods:	oh yes I know that. Let me ask you to imagine something. Imagine that it is years in the future. All your current problems as a mother have been long solved: the boredom and the misery are long gone. You've well and truly gotten your life back. Little Kai is all grown up and you are so proud of him. He is talking to a friend or a partner about his childhood and you as a mother. Want would you want to have him say of you?
Brooke with tears in her eyes:	That I'm a good mother. He won't be saying that though ...
Therapist:	Push past the good mother bit. Get specific. He says, "The thing that is really special about my mother is ..."

(*Continued*)

(Continued)

Brooke:	She supported me ...
Therapist:	Nice, and?
Brooke:	She was fun. I want him to have fun.
Therapist:	Fun, alright. "I'm lucky my mother was so ..."
Brooke:	Patient. Kind.
Therapist:	Supportive. Fun. Patient. Kind. And, Brooke, let's imagine something slightly different now. Imagine you had a little piece of time with Kai with all the pressures removed. There was no one to judge you. Nothing you could do wrong. You are both completely safe and protected. You could just enjoy Kai. What might that look like?
Brooke (wiping away tears):	I'm not sure. But I'd want to have fun with him somehow.
Therapist:	Fun, again? Playful?
Brooke:	Yes, playful. I'd want to laugh with him.
Therapist:	Nice. So, what we are tapping into here, Brooke, is something that we call "values." Values are what we really care about in our heart of hearts, they are the direction we want to travel in. We will explore your values more, in other areas of your life as well. For now, I just want to say that I'd like the work that we do together to not just be about the challenges that you are facing but also about your values. Also about supporting you to be that patient, kind, supportive, and fun mother who has moments of playful laughter with Kai. Can we do that?
Brooke:	I'd like that, yes.

Brooke's therapist interwove ACT with behavioral activation (for Brooke's depression) and the promotion of sensitive, responsive mothering. Brooke's values, both as a parent and in other domains of her life, grounded the entire intervention, with Brooke and her therapist returning to her values again and again throughout therapy. At the end of therapy, Brooke is regularly engaging in fun and playful interactions with Kai and is enjoying those interactions. Her caregiving behavior has come under the contextual control of Kai's cues in a manner that is intrinsically reinforcing for Brooke. She has also built up a more richly rewarding life for herself across all domains of living, discovering ways to continue to live her values in other life domains while parenting Kai.

Troubleshooting

How do I make sure I'm getting values not pliance?

At times you may get the impression that the parent is recalling a list of parenting rules that they have learned will bring them social approval, or, at least, a reprieve from shame and social censure. One way to ensure that you are talking about freely chosen values, independent of social approval, is to use an experiential exercise that takes social approval out of the picture. For example, an experiential exercise in which the parent is asked to imagine what they would do if no one will ever know what they have done. Another way to tease social approval away from values is to look for the sweetness of the valued action. If the parent can tune in to reinforcement that is intrinsic to the behavioral pattern itself, independent of whether or not the behavior results in social approval, then it is truly a value.

What if the client tells me goals instead of values?

If the clients lists goals instead of values you can bring them back to the definitions of values and goals. Pointout that what they said is a goal, and ask them to consider why that goal matters to them. With such questioning you can get to the value behind the goal.

What if the client is so disconnected from their values that they doesn't know what their values are?

For clients who are quite disconnected from their values, prompts such as values cards can be a good way to start. For these clients in particular, a single session focusing on values is likely to yield only the beginnings of an accurate and rich sense of their values. Rather, values discovery should be seen as an ongoing process with continued experimentation and looking for the "sweet spot" in everyday life. Therapist and client can together build a richer understanding of the client's values over time.

Overabundance of values

An overabundance of values is not in and of itself a problem. In fact, it promotes resilience. Such a person can suffer many setbacks in life and still have a highly meaningful and rewarding life. However, sometimes people with an overabundance of values can become fused with perfectionistic ideas about achieving great things across every value in every domain. The enormous demands of parenthood can bring this to a head. Acceptance and defusion is relevant here but the core reality of human life is this: we have very little time on this Earth. Most of us do not get to do everything that matters to us or everything we enjoy.

Support parents with an overabundance of values to prioritize. Naming their core values can be helpful. It may also be helpful to talk about creating priorities for different times of life, and mapping out a plan for how values will be lived in different domains across their lifespan. They might even like to set themselves deadlines. For example, a parent with strong values around creativity especially creative writing may find that achieving their dream of writing a novel is just not realistic while their children are young, between parenting and working demands. They may decide that writing has a lower priority for now, and will be kept "ticking along" in small ways such as writing poetry or keeping a personal journal. At the same time, they might set themselves a deadline: if they haven't begun to write a novel by their 45th birthday they will do so then and will reprioritize other aspects of their life to make that possible.

When valued action has another function

Particular behaviors often serve multiple functions, with different functions dominating in different contexts. It is possible for a particular behavior to genuinely be connected to a key value, and yet, at the same time, for that behavior to serve another maladaptive function. For example, a parent may be using computer games, reading, or social media as avoidance. Yet, at the same time, that same parent may also have values around intellectual challenge, literature and connection with friends, making playing computer games, reading, or using social media potentially valued acts. To give another example, the specific choices a parent is making around potentially controversial topics such as breastfeeding, school choice, or sex education may be both consistent with their values and likely to gain them social approval in their social environment. It is not the form of the behavior, but the function that counts.

It is important, as therapists, that we don't make the mistake of simply classifying particular behavioral patterns *by form* into valued acts and maladaptive behavior. Instead, we need to be mindful of the moment by moment *function* of the behavior. Clients can be supported in identifying the function of a particular behavior in the moment with discrimination tasks. For example, a parent for whom social media use is both a valued act, in terms of connecting with friends, and an avoidance behavior can be prompted to pause and reflect before acting on the desire to engage with social media. The parent may be prompted to ask: what is engaging with social media for in this moment? Is it about connecting with my friends? Or is it about avoiding thoughts and feelings?

When children misbehave (or when parenting is hard)

Often it's hardest for parents to follow their values when it is most needed—at points when their children's behavior is challenging. It's important that parents are encouraged to be mindful of their inner experience in their interactions with their children so that they can begin to identify antecedents to avoidance-based, rather than values-based behavior. Here are some examples of typical points of departure for many parents:

- tantrum behavior when parents are trying to selectively attend to politeness or appropriate behavior and might instead give in to demands;
- fear and anxiety in children, when parents are attempting to encourage bold exploration and instead rush to soothe or comfort their child; and
- intense negative emotions, when it is important for parents to empathize with their child's behavior rather than attempt to shut it down.

Four key developmental periods and values

Infancy and values

Values are not fixed. They are not things sitting in a cupboard waiting to be discovered. Rather, they are dynamic and changing. They are stances that we choose. An ongoing act of creation. As a result, the earliest months of parenting can be a time of great change as parents choose their parenting values. For some parents, until their child is born there may have been lack of certainty about their values as well as an inability to fully envision how they will be lived out. Other parents find that their parenting values change, shift, or become richer in unpredictable ways once an actual child arrives. Further, in two-parent homes, parents need to find ways to parent together, including with slightly different values as well as different ideas about how values are best applied. In addition, the birth of a child has flow on effects on every other aspect of a parent's life. So parents will need to reassess how to best live out their values in other domains of living as well. Parents who are in psychological contact with their values in other domains of living, not merely goals, will be most resilient and flexible in doing this.

Arguably, the most important realization of the early months of parenting is for the parent to achieve a responsive, sensitive pattern of parenting behavior—for parenting behavior to come under the contextual control of the child's cues in a manner that is intrinsically reinforcing to the parent. That is, it is vital that the parent begins to take a stance, at least in core and common parenting values such as "being there for my child" and "being a loving parent." Additionally, the birth of a child is a seismic change, especially for the primary caregiver. Thus it is important to ensure parents recultivate a life rich in reinforcement as a parent, including living parenting values but also finding ways that other values can be lived as a parent.

Even from this earliest time, children have proto-values. In infancy, there is, of course, no verbal construction of proto-values at all. However, there are evolved motivative systems and preferences. All human infants can be said to value human connection in one sense of the word. This preverbal evolved motivative system, whereby humans seek connection, forms the basis for many elaborated verbally constructed values later on. Additionally, even from the earliest days an infant may show interest or enjoyment in certain kinds of activity and stimulation. This too is a proto-value in the earliest form.

Early childhood and values

Parenting values provide a kind of flexible consistency for parents and children as children change and grow. The exact ways in which parents live out their values may shift, but the values themselves provide a kind of flexible anchor.

In early childhood, parents are likely to be focused on managing common behavioral challenges, such as noncompliance, whinging, and temper tantrums. Hopefully, parents achieved a sensitive and responsive parenting style in infancy and have managed to extend that responsiveness into early childhood. But with early childhood, parents also need to find ways to prevent and manage misbehavior that are consistent with their parenting values. The management of common behavioral challenges is stressful for many parents. Due to the extinction burst, the implementation of positive, effective parenting strategies is likely to be initially met with worse behavior in that moment. A clear sense of parenting values is likely to help parents weather the storm and to be persistent in the face of resistance and challenging behavior.

It is important for parents to find ways to live out their values in other areas of life too, as well as parenting. In addition to benefiting parental mental health, doing so provides the child with rich exposure to facilitate the child in developing their own proto-values. As children have now entered the verbal community, proto-values begin to be partly verbally constructed. Parents may reflect back to children verbally, their own observations of the child's enjoyment and prosocial behavior. For example, a parent may say, "that was very kind of you" or "wow you love reading, don't you?"

Middle childhood and values

Within developed and developing nations, middle childhood is a time in which the focus is on schooling. Parents must assist their children in adapting to the new school environment, must negotiate with the school and advocate for their child, and must scaffold their child in understanding the new influences both good and bad on their behavior. Parental values in domains other than parenting may also inform how parents navigate the complex relationship between family and school.

At this age, children's own proto-values may begin, in a rudimentary way, to become more like the verbally constructed patterns of behavior that we see in adults. Children may experiment with behaviors, self-understandings and verbal rules. At this point proto-values may be quite simple such as "I like dinosaurs" or "I am kind." Children themselves may be increasingly developing proto-values for themselves and experimenting flexibly with them.

Adolescence and values

During adolescence, experimentation with valuing and self-identity becomes a key developmental focus. Parents may be challenged by conflict between their own values and the proto-values of their child. Parents may also find this time of experimentation a frustrating time, as they may feel that they already know what their child's values will ultimately be. However, they must remember that this time of experimentation is critical to their child's development and that they may, in fact, turn out to be wrong.

From an evolutionary perspective, the experimentation of adolescence, coupled with increased identification with peers rather than parents, plays a crucial role in generational innovation through horizontal transmission within both the behavioral and the symbolic evolutionary streams. Our flexibility as a species is grounded in this ability for each generation to build upon their cultural inheritance, innovating and imagining the world anew. Toward the end of adolescence, into emerging adulthood proto-values may increasingly come to resemble adult values in complexity and scope. They may also begin to stabilize.

Using values with specific issues

Parental mental health problems and values

Not living out your values or not being in psychological contact with valued living is a risk factor for mental health problems, particularly depression. For parents with mental health problems, ensuring they are both living out their values, across multiple domains of living, and in psychological contact with values day-to-day is an important part of the intervention and consistent with behavioral activation.

Parental grief and values

Values provide for flexibility when parenting beyond loss. When a child is lost, life is not how the parent expected. Goals are thwarted. However, key parenting values such as "I want to be there for my child" can still be lived, even if it is in unexpected ways, such as tending to a grave, lighting a candle, or writing their child a poem. Finding ways to live meaningfully with the loss as a major aspect of grief work (Murray, 2016).

Parents of children with disabilities or chronic health conditions can also experience a kind of grief, as life is not how they expected it to be. This grief may be cyclic, returning at key moments in the child's life. For these parents too, the flexibility of values can provide a helpful way forward.

Childhood externalizing problems and values

Implementing positive parenting strategies with children with externalizing behavior problems is challenging. Due to the extinction burst, the behavior is likely to get worse, not better, in the immediate moment and counterintuitively this worsening of behavior in that moment is actually a sign that the parenting changes are effective. Parents need to weather the storm of the extinction burst in order to see behavior change in their child. Psychological contact with values—remembering the purpose of undertaking something so difficult and unpleasant—can give meaning to weathering the storm and provide the courage and willingness necessary.

Further, parents of children with externalizing behavior problems often interact in attachment-rich (Dadds & Hawes, 2006) ways following misbehavior and attachment-neutral ways when their child is behaving well.For parents, t urning in to parenting values, when their child is behaving well, can increase the frequency of attachment-rich parenting interactions and hence positive reinforcement for adaptive child behavior.

Childhood internalizing problems and values

Values can provide the flexible bedrock of being the safe haven for the child to return to, as well as provide the courage and willingness necessary to be the secure base, for a child's exploration. In tuning in to parenting values, parents can find the courage that they themselves require to face their child's experiences of fear and anxiety, instead of engaging in overprotective parenting.

Childhood neurodevelopmental disabilities and values

Parents may be living parenting values well but there's a deficit in terms of values in other domains of living. In these circumstances, parents need to focus upon finding ways to live other values that are realistic small and possible to do while parenting.

In addition, parents of children with neurodevelopmental disabilities in particular need to be highly flexible in their parenting and attuned to the needs of their individual child. For parents of typically developing children, looking to the child's same-age peers to estimate what it is reasonable to expect of your own child will, for the most part, work well. However, for parents of children with disabilities or special needs, a more individualized and flexible approach is necessary for much of parenting. Further, even evidence-based parenting rules-of-thumb are more likely to fail. For example, regarding misbehavior, "they are probably doing it for attention, so ignore it," is a parenting rule-of-thumb that would serve the average parent of a typically developing child rather well. But it is more likely to be problematic for parents of children with disabilities or special needs, where the function of misbehavior is more likely to be complex.

Peer problems and bullying and values

Through reflecting back to children verbally their prosocial behavior, parents support their children in discovering prosocial proto-values. At first, these may be quite simple; for example, "it is important to share." Over time, these proto-values form the basis for developing more elaborative prosocial values as children get older.

Marital conflict and values

Finding ways to coparent can be challenging. Even at the level of values, there is no guarantee that the values of each parent will be exactly the same. However, at the level of values, rather than goals, or rules, or specific ideas about how to parent, there is, at least, flexibility and an enormous commonality of values between parents in general. If parents can identify areas in which they have the same values, or similar values, this can be a useful starting point to finding workable ways to parent together.

Expressed emotion including critical and intrusive parenting and values

Critical, hostile, and intrusive parenting behavior is likely to be contrary to parental values. A parent who is engaging in expressed emotion type of behavior is likely influenced by pliance or experiential avoidance. Parenting values can provide a useful starting point to developing an alternative parenting repertoire.

Emotion dismissiveness and values

Tuning in to parenting values often involves tuning in to the cues and emotional signals of one's child because almost all parents value something like "being there for my child," or "showing my child I love them,"

Inconsistent, harsh, or punitive parenting and values

The use of inconsistent, harsh, or punitive parenting is often connected to parenting behavior under the control of parenting rules or connected to experiential avoidance. Parenting values can provide a useful starting point to developing an alternative parenting repertoire.

References

Coyne, L. W., & Moore, P. S. (2015). *ACT for parents of anxious children manual.* New England ACT Institute/Early Childhood Research Clinic and University of Massachusetts Medical School.

Dadds, M. R., & Hawes, D. (2006). *Integrated family intervention for child conduct problems.* Brisbane: Australian Academic Press.

Gilbert, P. (2009). *The compassionate mind.* London: Little, Brown Book Group.

Gopnik, A. (2017). *The gardener and the carpenter.* London: Vintage publishing.

Hayes, L. L., & Ciarrochi, J. (2015). *The thriving adolescent.* Oakland: New Harbinger Publications.

Hayes, S. C., Barnes-Holmes, D., & Roche, B. (2001). *Relational frame theory: A post-Skinnerian account of human language and cognition.* New York: Plenum Press.

Hayes, S. C., Strosahl, K. D., & Wilson, K. G. (2003). *Acceptance and commitment therapy: An experiential approach to behavior change.* New York: Guilford Press.

Murray, J. (2016). *Understanding loss.* New York: Routledge.

Villatte, M., Villatte, J. L., & Hayes, S. C. (2016). *Mastering the clinical conversation.* New York: The Guilford Press.

Wilson, K. G., & Dufrene, T. (2009). *Mindfulness for two an acceptance and commitment therapy approach to mindfulness in psychotherapy.* Oakland: New Harbinger Publications, Inc.

Chapter 8

Experiential acceptance of parent, child, and relationship

Chapter Outline

What is acceptance? **188**
- A behavioral account of acceptance and experiential control 189
- DNA-V model 193

How does acceptance apply to parent–child interaction? **194**
- The parenting control agenda 194
- Experiential avoidance and dysfunctional parenting 195
- Parental experiential acceptance and child emotional development 196
- Experiential acceptance and compassionate parenting 197
- Acceptance and development 197
- When history shows up 198
- Experiential acceptance and emotions 199

How to work with acceptance clinically **202**
- Simple questioning 202
- Noticing acceptance within the parent–child interaction 202
- Metaphors 203
- Experiential exercises 204
- Getting rid of thoughts experiment 206
- Meditation 207
- Accepting space for parent and child 208
- Accepting space for parent and child script 22
- Pause and breathe 209
- Encouraging home practice 211

Troubleshooting **213**
- Confusion with acceptance and compassion 213
- More than just emotions 213
- Accept, so we can ignore? 213
- Acceptance and trauma history 214

Four key developmental periods and acceptance **214**
- Infancy and acceptance 214
- Early childhood and acceptance 215
- Middle childhood and acceptance 215
- Adolescence and acceptance 216

Using acceptance with specific populations **216**
- Parental mental health problems and acceptance 216
- Parental grief and acceptance 216
- Childhood externalizing problems and acceptance 217
- Childhood internalizing problems and acceptance 217
- Childhood neurodevelopmental disabilities and acceptance 217
- Peer problems and bullying and acceptance 217
- Marital conflict and acceptance 218
- Expressed emotionincluding critical and intrusive parenting and acceptance 218
- Emotion dismissiveness and acceptance 218
- Inconsistent, or harsh and punitive parenting and acceptance 218

References **218**

Acceptance and Commitment Therapy. DOI: https://doi.org/10.1016/B978-0-12-814669-9.00008-4
© 2019 Elsevier Inc. All rights reserved.

Life is not a problem to be solved, but a reality to be experienced.

Soren Kierkegaard

It was, he thought, the difference between being dragged into the arena to face a battle to the death and walking into the arena with your head held high. Some people, perhaps, would say that there was little to choose between the two ways, but Dumbledore knew—And so do I, thought Harry, with a rush of fierce pride, and so did my parents—that there was all the difference in the world.

J.K. Rowling, *Harry Potter and the Half-Blood Prince*

Love isn't a state of perfect caring. It is an active noun like "struggle." To love someone is to strive to accept that person exactly the way he or she is, right here and now.

Mr. Rogers

What is acceptance?

Within the acceptance and commitment therapy (ACT) model, experiential acceptance is defined as: psychological contact with internal stimuli—thoughts, feelings, memories, sensations, embodied reactions, and behavioral impulses, including mobilization states of fight or flight, and immobilization states of dissociation or shut down—without attempting to control them. That is, allowing our experiences to be as they are, without attempting to change the form or frequency of internal stimuli; instead, adopting an open, flexible and nonjudgmental stance to our internal experiences (Forsyth & Ritzert, 2018). This experiential acceptance may be closely related to a broader acceptance of not just our experiences themselves, but also the context in which certain thoughts, feelings, sensations, embodied reactions, and behavioral impulses are evoked. In order to understand why experiential acceptance might be helpful, it can be useful to contrast it with its opposite and to examine why we aren't always accepting of our own experience.

The opposite of experiential acceptance is experiential control, or the attempt to control our private events; for example, by avoiding, minimizing, or prolonging them. Experiential control is itself a universal aspect of human experience. It is not *always* problematic. At times, it can be helpful and it is certainly inevitably part of life with language. Yet, it can also get in the way of vital living. From an ACT perspective, it isn't the case that we need to eliminate experiential control in favor of experiential acceptance. Rather, we can benefit from building broader repertoires of experiential acceptance, learning to recognize when experiential control is unworkable in terms of living our values, and learning to deliberately switch from experiential control to experiential acceptance, in accordance with valued ends.

The two main forms of experiential control are experiential avoidance and experiential attachment. Experiential avoidance is when we attempt to avoid particular private experiences—thoughts, feelings, memories, sensations, and behavioral impulses. There is clear evidence that experiential avoidance is associated with multiple negative psychological outcomes including an increased risk of psychological disorders such as depression and anxiety, poorer relationships, and addiction (Blackledge & Hayes, 2006; Cheron, Ehrenreich, & Pincus, 2009; Coyne & Thompson, 2011). Experiential attachment refers to attempts to increase or prolong certain private experiences—thoughts, feelings, memories, sensations, and behavioral impulses. There isn't as much research on experiential attachment as for experiential avoidance, but it is clear that it too can be problematic (Gruber, 2011; Swails, Zettle, Burdsal, & Synder, 2016; Tamir & Ford, 2012).

It is important to recognize that experiential acceptance is not something that individuals either have or lack. Rather, each individual is more likely to control certain aspects of their experience, in particular contexts, depending on their learning history. Further, the context can support experiential acceptance or experiential control. In particular, a context of social safety and affiliation are more likely to support experiential acceptance, whereas contexts of threat are more likely to support experiential control.

A behavioral account of acceptance and experiential control

From an RFT perspective, experiential control arises predictably from verbal behavior. Through bidirectional relations words come to take on the stimulus functions of the things they represent. In other words, our brains experience words as "the real thing." For example, take a moment to call to mind your favorite food. Pause and say its name. Recall what it looks like. What it smells like. Remember the last time you ate it. Imagine lifting it to your mouth right now and taking a bite. Remember what it tastes like. How do you feel? Are you hungry? Do you feel desire for that particular food? Are you even salivating?

You responded to the word "food," even though there is no food physically present. Instead, words on a page took on the stimulus functions of food for you. In addition, of course, it is not just words on a page that have this power, but also the words we say internally to ourselves: our thoughts. And it isn't just words, but mental images, symbols, and memories.

If it makes sense to manipulate the physical world, to attempt to control it, then it is logical that we would also attempt to control our internal world as well. Harari (2011) argues that it was our languaging ability as a species that allowed us to effectively collaborate to obtain nourishment and avoid danger. Because we developed words to communicate possible events, to reflect upon the past and predict the future, we not only survived, but thrived, and spread. If you were an early human wandering the African savannah, you avoid lions and tell others to do so based on your past experiences. And what about angry warriors from a neighboring tribe? Avoid them! Or even meat that is somewhat old and smells a bit gross? Avoid it! Given the bidirectional nature of relational framing the next step simply falls out: avoid the thoughts of the lion, the angry warriors, and the gross-looking meat.

Derived relational responding—or, more simply put, our proneness to derive associations quickly, and influenced by our context—increases the reach of avoidance further still to cover all internal experiences. If you have had or witnessed bad experiences with lions, you might avoid thinking of lions. But you might also begin to avoid all stimuli associated with lions—being out in the savannah, the grass, perhaps even leaving the cave itself. As a matter of fact, it may be that the simple experience of anxiety in any context reminds you of lions. Thus, you might expand your efforts to avoid thinking of all of these things, or even feeling these emotions. And what about states of mobilization or fight or flight reactions? What if a certain shift in your bodily sensations—an accelerated heart beat or breathing—happens just before something awful? Again, you may learn to run away from the physical sensations you associate with threat. This state of affairs leads to a very limited behavioral repertoire indeed: the avoidance of danger, real or verbal.

This is complicated by the fact that we humans like to give reasons for our behavior—we get preoccupied with the why of our behavior. Reason giving expands the reach of experiential control further still. We learn, from our interactions with others in the languaging community, to give reasons for our behavior that attribute causality to our private experiences. Why didn't you come to the party? Because I was too down. Why did you yell at your child? Because I was so angry. Why did you have a good day with your child today? Because I was relaxed and calm. It makes sense, in the physical world, to control outcomes by controlling the causes of those outcomes. If reading to your child regularly is in a causal relationship with your child's later literacy then it makes sense to read to your child regularly. If giving your child sweet drinks daily causes dental decay and health problems later in life then it makes sense to avoid giving your child sweet drinks. By the same logic, if feeling sadness causes you to miss social events, then it makes sense to avoid feelings of sadness. If feeling angry causes you to yell at your child, it makes sense to avoid feelings of anger. If feeling relaxed and calm causes you to have a good day with your child, it makes sense to try to feel relaxed and calm.

Although experiential control is then a logical consequence of our languaging abilities and is not always problematic, it can lead to rigid and inflexible behavioral repertoires. First, in many circumstances it simply does not work. The research on thought suppression, for example, indicates that we are not actually particularly successful at suppressing thoughts

(Abramwoitz, Tolin, & Street, 2001). Unlike physical things, which we may have greater success at avoiding we are not adept at avoiding our own internal stimuli (Hayes, Strosahl, & Wilson, 2003), it is far easier to avoid an actual lion than thoughts of a lion. Thought suppression is particularly likely to backfire when we are attempting to suppress a particular thought for an extended period of time, such as over our entire parenting career. In fact, thought suppression attempts can actually increase the frequency of the thoughts we are intending to suppress.

Secondly, attempts at experiential control tend to lead to a narrowing of behavior. From an evolutionary lens, experiential control imposes unhealthy selection criteria onto the behavioral stream of an individual (Hayes & Sanford, 2015). That is, any behavior that temporarily controls the internal stimuli may be *selected*. Behavioral repertoires become more and more focused on experiential control and less focused on other competing potential selection criteria including values and the direct contingencies operating in the context. The insensitivity of behavior to direct contingencies in particular can mean that behavioral repertoires develop that are unworkable and yet the person may persist in the unworkable behavior. For example, if a parent attempts to avoid distressing internal experiences around parenting, say, memories of a traumatic birth, worries about the child's future, or memories of an abusive childhood, those internal stimuli are likely to be triggered by the child's themselves and by the act of parenting itself. If the parent makes experiential control the aim, then it is likely they will begin to parent in a narrow and rigid way, perhaps even avoiding the child (physically or psychologically) or certain parenting behaviors (such as physical affection or discipline). It is likely that experiential control will lead the parent away from their values. This phenomenon is encapsulated in the pithy ACT saying: control is not the solution—control is the problem. Returning to experiential acceptance, experiential acceptance reintroduces variation into the behavioral stream through contact with previously avoided stimuli and allowing healthier selection criteria such as values or direct contingencies to impact upon the behavioral evolution.

It is important to be clear on what experiential acceptance is and what it isn't. Experiential acceptance does not mean tolerance, endurance, succumbing to, or being defeated by, all of which include a sense of coercion, a sense of making oneself okay with something. There is no coercive element to experiential acceptance. Experiential acceptance is not forcefully grabbing oneself and forcing oneself to endure something. Rather, it is refraining from doing violence against oneself by attempting to cut out part of your own experience. Experiential acceptance has a compassionate and kind tone. It is also not purposeless. It is not an end unto itself. Rather, experiential acceptance is in the service of living chosen values. When experiential avoidance doesn't get in the way of valued living, it is not a problem. It is merely something that languaging minds do.

Experiential acceptance is about allowing, making room for, acknowledging, being willing—not about wanting, liking, or loving—but simply allowing thoughts and feelings to be as they are without attempting to manage them and being willing to experience the negative experiences that come as part and parcel of valued living. It also means broadening your attention so that it is inclusive of the difficult stuff—the unpleasant thoughts, feelings, memories, sensations, and behavioral impulses *and* all the other stuff that is also part of your unfolding experience.

The word "acceptance" is not compulsory. The word may, for many people, be linked in relational frames that make it closer to tolerance or endurance rather than experiential acceptance as is meant in the ACT model. For example, the word "acceptance" is often used in an experientially avoidant manner in Western cultures following a loss event. Parents of a child with a disability may have been told that they need to "accept" their child's diagnosis when they express their understandable distress (even though the parents have been acting consistently with accepting the diagnosis as a fact of the external world). The implication being that when the diagnosis is accepted the parent will no longer feel grief—sadness, anxiety, anger—around the diagnosis and that the parent needs to "get over" these feelings. This, of course, is not consistent with experiential acceptance as it is understood in ACT.

The word "willingness" or "allowing" may also be used for experiential acceptance and some ACT therapists and clients prefer these words. Regardless of the word that you choose to use as your default, it is important to recognize that it isn't about simply finding the right word. Natural language is messy and complex. The word "willingness" too can evoke elements of tolerance or endurance or pushing through something with brute strength such as willpower or, alternatively, a sense of wanting, desiring, or feeling prepared to experience something. The word "allowing" can also have a coercive feel, a sense of subjugation. So instead of focusing on finding exactly the right word, ensure the clients you work with truly understand what you mean using metaphors and experiential exercises, and be flexible, adapting your language to suit particular clients.

Another aspect of experiential acceptance that is important to distinguish, especially for parents, is that experiential acceptance is consistent with a compassionate response toward others. Just as experiential acceptance doesn't mean forcing oneself to endure particular experiences, it also doesn't mean, as a parent, forcing one's child to endure particular experiences. Instead, it involves accepting your own thoughts, feelings, memories, sensations, and behavioral impulses as well as your child's thoughts, feelings, memories, sensations, and behavioral impulses as well as your own internal experiences *in reaction to* your child's. It means allowing all of that to be as it is. Compassion, by definition, includes a desire to alleviate suffering. So within all of that mix of thoughts, feelings, memories, sensations, and behavioral impulses the parent is accepting there is a desire to alleviate the child's suffering. That too is accepted. Acceptance does not involve suppressing this desire, belittling your child's suffering or turning away from your child's suffering. Acceptance is a *being with* rather than a fixing.

When properly understood, acceptance and compassion actually go hand in hand. It is impossible to be experientially accepting in the ACT sense without taking a compassionate stance toward oneself. Further, without experiential acceptance, compassion breaks down. We cannot truly alleviate the suffering of ourselves and others without first opening ourselves up to understanding it. This will be explored further in the chapter on compassion.

It is also important to recognize that acceptance does not mean ignoring or dismissing your own feelings and behavioral impulses. Rather, it means tuning into and listening to your feelings, bodily reactions and behavioral impulses as potentially important sources of information. You may not choose to act on a particular behavioral impulse, but the fact that the impulse arose is not dismissed. Our moment to moment experiences are understood as arising from the evolved motivational systems of our species coupled with our unique learning history: they often contain information of important survival value.

The research to date suggests links between experiential acceptance, parental stress and mental health and bonding. For parents of infants born preterm, experiential acceptance predicts parental psychological adjustment (Evans, Whittingham, & Boyd, 2012; Greco et al., 2005). Experiential acceptance partially mediates the relationship between stress induced by early hospitalization within the Neonatal Intensive Care Unit and both parenting-related stress and parental posttraumatic stress (Greco et al., 2005). Experiential acceptance predicted parental adjustment, as well as the current intensity grief symptoms and the experienced burden of parenting in parents of children with cerebral palsy (Whittingham, Wee, Sanders, & Boyd, 2013). Parents with greater experiential acceptance reported that parenting was less burdensome and reported fewer current grief symptoms related to their child's diagnosis. In mothers of Head Start preschoolers experiential acceptance was found to mediate the relationship between maternal depressive symptoms and parenting-related stress, with lower levels of acceptance linked to higher parenting-related stress (Shea & Coyne, 2011). Experiential acceptance has been found to mediate the relationship between child behavior problems and maternal anxiety, stress, and depressive symptoms as well as the relationship between child behavior problems and paternal depressive symptoms in parents of children with autism (71 mothers, 39 fathers) (Jones, Hastings, Totsika, Keane, & Rhule, 2014).

DNA-V model

This relates to the noticer, discoverer, and social view within the DNA-V model (Hayes & Ciarrochi, 2015). The noticer expands upon traditional understandings of acceptance by including embodied awareness and noticing and listening to immobilization and mobilization and emotional reactions as signals and so does this component within the parent–child hexaflex. Discoverer overlaps with this in the sense of openness to experiential discovery in the moment; discovery of what is happening experientially for both the parent and the child. In addition, there is a *shared* element to this acceptance in that the parent accepts their own psychological experiences, the experiences of their child and the ongoing changes within the experienced parent–child relationship. This element relates to the social view in DNA-V.

How does acceptance apply to parent–child interaction?

The parenting control agenda

Most behavioral parenting models focus on how to change our behavior, and by extension, that of our children. In essence, then, they are about control. While this is an effective strategy for changing overt, observable behavior, it is problematic when control is applied to internal experiences. Control is not the solution, control is the problem. In addition to attempting to control our own internal content we can also attempt to control the internal content *of others*. If your child had a tantrum because they were angry then it makes sense to try to stop your child from feeling anger. If your child isn't playing with the other children at kindy because they are feeling shy then it makes sense to try to stop your child from feeling shy. If your child didn't study for their maths test because they have low self-esteem then it makes sense to fix your child's low self-esteem. And so, parents can focus on trying to change the internal experiences of their child in order to change their child's behavior instead of shaping behavior through contingencies.

The parenting control agenda can also come about because the internal experiences of the child and their expression triggers particular internal experiences for the parent. The parent may attempt to control their own internal experiences—by controlling the internal stimuli of their child. Parenting challenges themselves may be framed as needing to change how the child thinks or feels. Just as it may seem as if our own internal experiences need to change so that we can live the life we want to live it can seem as if our child's internal experiences must change so that our child can live the life we want them to have.

Attempting to control your child's thoughts, emotions, memories, sensations, or behavioral impulses is just as if not more unworkable as trying to control your own. With such a control agenda, parenting behavior may become quite aversive—the child may indeed end up eliciting the desired parent behavior, but the child's behavior may be functioning under aversive control. Or alternatively, the parent may jump to strategies that, indeed, elicit child compliance in that interaction, but lead to further problematic behavior in the future (such as offering bribes). The parent may, in fact, be moving away from, not toward, building a more effective and functional behavioral repertoire in their child. This stands in contrast to the effective shaping of behavior.

The parenting control agenda suggests that the parent must *win* in the interaction, forcing the child through willpower, aversion, or cleverness, to do *right now* as the parent wishes. Effective parenting, with an agenda of shaping behavior to grow a flexible and adaptive repertoire, in contrast, is already looking ahead, past the present interaction and asking: how can I influence my child, so that an adaptive behavior is more likely next time and the time after that? A parent with a shaping agenda measures success by how the child's behavior grows and develops with time. They can also recognize when they have miscalculated, and how to exit an interaction without escalation and without causing harm (i.e., without increasing the probability of aversive child behaviors in the future), to rethink and begin again tomorrow. To a parent with a shaping agenda, there is nothing lost in such a maneuvre, because the focus isn't on winning the interaction, or controlling their child's internal experiences, but on shaping behavior into the future.

Experiential avoidance and dysfunctional parenting

Dysfunctional parenting behavior, including harsh and punitive parenting as well as lax parenting, often has the psychological function, for the parent, of experiential avoidance. Often the goal is to stop, quickly in the moment a particular child behavior or emotional display, thus bringing to an end the internal experiences that the child's behavior is triggering in the parent. Thus, punitive and lax parenting behavior may be a different topology but have the same function. Harsh or punitive parenting may also be about punishing the child, as in making the child suffer.

Child misbehavior often includes triggers for difficult internal experiences for the parent including emotions such as anger, anxiety, sadness, and shame. Parents might experience thoughts like "I am a terrible parent" or "she's just doing it to annoy me" or "everyone is watching." It may also trigger a physical state of mobilization (fight or flight) or immobilization (dissociation, withdrawal). Further, misbehavior can often occur in contexts that are already psychologically meaningful for the parent. For example, when a child with a chronic health condition or disability refuses to cooperate with taking medication or doing physical therapy, it is not just the noncompliance per se but what that means psychologically for the parent: a worrisome and uncertain future. Attempting to manage misbehavior in a positive way therefore requires a high level of experiential acceptance. Due to the extinction burst, the duration and intensity of the misbehavior immediately after the parent has adopted behaviorally based parenting techniques for the first time is likely to be worse. Parents must persist through the extinction burst, even when they may be experiencing intense emotional and cognitive reactions to their child's behavior and the situation. Doing so requires experiential acceptance.

Lack of experiential acceptance is also at the root of parental dysfunctional accommodation to child anxiety. The parent unwillingness to allow child to experience fear, distress, or even a sense of emerging mastery because it is "too difficult" means that the child does not have the opportunity to learn adaptive behaviors when anxious. In fact, the child is actively taught to cope with anxiety through avoidance. The parent models avoidance, supplies the child with avoidant verbal rules, and reinforces avoidant child behavior. Reversing this dysfunctional pattern so that the parent is supporting the child in developing a repertoire of approach behavior requires that the parent develops experiential acceptance of the thoughts and feelings that their child's fear, distress, or challenges generate in them.

Parental experiential acceptance and child emotional development

Parental acceptance of the emotional life of their children—and the way that parent's respond to the emotions of their children—is linked to childhood emotional development and competence (Eisenberg, Cumberland, & Spinrad, 1998; Gottman, Katz, & Hoover, 1997). Gottman et al. (1997) and Gottman, Katz, and Hoover (1996) identified five parenting characteristics of emotion coaching: (1) parental awareness of emotions in themselves and their children including lower intensity emotions; (2) parent viewing emotions, including negative emotions, as opportunities for learning and intimacy; (3) parent validating children's emotions; (4) parent verbally labeling or encouraging children to verbally label their emotions; and (5) parent problem solving the situation with the child or setting limits on behavior (see Chapter 3: Connect: the parent–child relationship, for a more complete discussion). Parental experiential acceptance is integral to emotion coaching, as to perform any of these steps the parent must be aware and accepting of their own emotions as well as their child's.

Importantly, this awareness and acceptance should include low-intensity emotions and positive emotions. In some families, parents effectively emotion coach only particular kinds of emotions. For example, sadness may be accepted and handled well, but anxiety avoided. Emotion coaching continues to be relevant into middle childhood and adolescence, but with some adaptation for the increasing autonomy of the child (Greenberg, 2002). In particular, it is no longer appropriate for the parent to verbally label emotions; instead, the parent should allow the child to describe their own emotional experiences as well as to take the lead in problem solving. It is also important in late middle childhood and adolescence for parents to be more careful in waiting for a clear invitation from the child.

Experiential acceptance and compassionate parenting

Experiential acceptance is also fundamentally connected to the capacity for compassionate parenting. The definition of compassion includes sensitivity to suffering (explored fully in Chapter 12: Compassionate context). A requirement of compassion then is that you must, first, be aware of suffering, and maintain psychological contact with that suffering.

For parents, the suffering of their children almost always triggers an experience of distress for the parent as well. If the parent is experientially avoidant, they may dismiss the suffering of their child in order to avoid their own distress. Tears may be dismissed as crocodile tears. Playground fights may be dismissed as meaningless squabbles. Bullying may be dismissed as mere teasing. From such an experientially avoidant stance, parents miss opportunities to be compassionate toward their children.

We know that parents in general show a tendency to under-report internalizing symptoms in their children (instead, focusing on externalizing symptoms that get in the way of the parent's themselves). In spite of such close proximity and history, many parents are missing the distress of their children, and hence, missing opportunities for compassionate parenting. It is likely that many of these missed opportunities are related to experiential avoidance.

Acceptance and development

Flexible and developmentally appropriate parenting is grounded in a basic acceptance of development itself. That is, the parent needs to understand and accept the normal developmental stages that children progress through, the associated behaviors at each stage, and internal experiences that such behaviors may trigger in themselves. For example, it is necessary for parents to accept nightwaking during infancy, emotional tantrums during toddlerhood, and risk-taking during adolescence as normal and healthy aspects of each developmental stage.

This doesn't necessarily mean a parent won't be taking actions to shape behavior into the future. It just means the parent accepts their child as they are at this particular developmental stage. So, a parent of a toddler, for example, expects and accepts the emotional reactions of a toddler, while simultaneously parenting in a manner that bolsters emotional development in time and ensures tantrums are not reinforced. The parent of an infant expects and accepts nightwaking, while simultaneously ensuring their baby receives healthful circadian cues and has good sleep hygiene. The parent of a teenager understands that risk-taking is normal and a useful stage of life, while also supporting their child in having a face-saving way out of riskier experiences such as a code word to ask for help (e.g., phoning the parent and saying they feel sick).

This acceptance of development requires accurate understanding of child development. But it also requires experiential acceptance. It is one thing to know, as a fact, that most babies wake during the night, it is another to accept the nightwaking of your own baby as well as the thoughts and feelings that this might trigger in you at 2:00 a.m. in the morning. It is one thing to know, as most of us do, that adolescence is a time of experimentation and risk-taking. It is another to accept the experimentation and risk-taking of your own teenage child and the reactions you experience in response to their behavior. It is one thing to understand that temper tantrums are a normal part of toddlerhood. It is another to accept your own reactions to a vibrant tantrum in the middle of a shopping center, and instead of acting on your impulses to quickly shut the tantrum down, to both demonstrate acceptance of the emotions underlying the tantrum and to shape the behavior of your child, decreasing the likelihood of future tantrums. In order to fully accept child development, experiential acceptance is necessary.

This flexible and developmentally appropriate parenting style is linked to the gardener style of parenting (Gopnik, 2017). The gardener knows that a seed is a seed, a seedling a seedling, and a tree a tree. They do not expect a seed to act as a tree does.

When history shows up

The ongoing relationship between the parent and the child is not solely influenced by what is currently happening for the parent and the child. The parent's history often shows up—both the parent's history as a parent and the parent's history of being parented as a child.

The parent's history as a parent might include: memories of a traumatic birth, a difficult postnatal period, a challenging pregnancy, early hospitalization, preterm birth, diagnosis of disability, experiences parenting other children, and previous loss including child death, stillbirth, and miscarriage. It may also include circumstances leading up to the child's conception such as infertility on one hand, or an unplanned pregnancy on the other. Choices that the parent made in order to have or raise the child, and the consequences of that for the parent, may also be present. Thoughts, feelings, and memories relating to any aspect of this history may be psychologically present for the parent when interacting with their child and, in fact, may be triggered by the child themselves. Experiential acceptance is crucial to keeping parenting behavior calibrated to the ongoing interaction with their child not to historical events. Further, if the child themselves is triggering the internal stimuli, then attempts at experiential avoidance are likely to involve avoidance of the child themselves psychologically or even physically.

A parent's own history of being parented also shows up. Our own history of being parented is the single richest source of information we have in terms of what parenting might look like. It often provides a model, a blueprint in subtle and unspoken ways, even if it is in terms of what we don't want to do. For parents who were themselves abused or neglected as children this triggering of history may be especially problematic. Parents may experience flashbacks to their own childhood or find themselves feeling emotionally numb. They may also be deeply concerned about repeating with their own children any abuse that they experienced. Experiential acceptance of the thoughts internal stimuli as thoughts, feelings, memories, sensations, and behavioral impulses is an important part of maintaining choice in how to parent now with your own child. It is very important for parents to recognize that sometimes their own history shows up in the moment and colors their interactions with their child; to learn to discriminate when they are reacting to their child and when they are reacting to their history. To recognize this, and to catch moments of it happening, is to gain the freedom to choose our behavior and to act in accordance with values.

Experiential acceptance and emotions

Acceptance of emotions is one key aspect of experiential acceptance. For the parent, this includes acceptance of their own and their child's emotions. Distinguishing between primary, secondary, and instrumental emotions may be useful (Greenberg, 2002). The primary emotion is the initial emotional reaction to the situation. The secondary emotion is our emotional reaction to our emotional reaction. Secondary emotions can mask our primary emotions. For example, during interpersonal interactions it is not uncommon for a primary emotional reaction of hurt to be quickly masked by a secondary emotion of anger. Primary emotions may be adaptive or maladaptive. Adaptive primary emotions are functional reactions: adaptive sadness grieves, adaptive anger empowers, and adaptive fear helps us escape danger. Adaptive primary emotions tell us what we really care about. They point toward our values. Maladaptive primary emotions express deep wounds including traumatic learning. It can be helpful to ask: what is my primary emotional reaction here? And is that adaptive? What is the function of the emotion? And how it is best expressed? At times we may be stuck with the secondary emotions. In this situation, shifting attention to bringing awareness and acceptance to the other emotions including the primary emotion that we are also experiencing but not attending to can be useful. In parent and child interactions, it may be helpful for the parent to bear in mind that some of their child's angry responses may be secondary reactions to a primary emotion of hurt. Responding with tenderness to the child's hurt may be appropriate to shift the interaction in a more positive direction. Instrumental emotions are learned patterns of emotional expression, where certain affective signals have been reinforced in the past. For example, a child who has learned to whine or to cry in order to get their own way. If an emotional expression truly is instrumental then it can be quickly and easily turned off if the situation demands it. For instrumental emotions it is important not to validate the emotion per se (which isn't genuine) but the expressed desire (which is genuine). For example, in response to an emotional display to get an ice cream you might say, "you really want an ice cream, huh? Well, I don't blame you. I'd love an ice cream too."

Moira and Raven

Moira is a divorced mother of Raven, who is 15. Both mother and daughter struggle with anxiety. Moira has a long history of panic attacks and agoraphobia; Raven struggles with social anxiety and perfectionism, and school is painful for her. When Raven entered her first year of high school last year, it was a challenge—she was rejected by her friend group, who dispersed to seek new friendships—and she struggled in classes due to her difficulty speaking up and asking teachers for help; she also struggles with assignments that she can't do well, or "perfectly." Finally, she feels overly criticized by her mother, who dismisses her anxiety as "not a big deal," and views it as something that Raven should "just get over." Moira prides herself on "grinning and bearing it," which she views as mostly successful. The more Moira pushes, the more Raven retreats.

Imagine you could, unseen and unheard, observe a typical, ordinary interaction between Moira and Raven. It might be something like the following.

Parent–child interaction

Moira says, "How's the algebra homework coming, Raven?"

Raven is silent.

Moira sighs, "*Raven.* I asked you a question. How's the math homework?"

"Fine."

Moira looks over her shoulder, and notices that Raven has doodled all over her page, and there's no evidence of a math problem anywhere. *Oh, no, not this again. What the heck,* Moira thinks. *Why can't she just figure this out?*

Moira yells, "RAVEN. What is the deal? Have you done nothing? You've been sitting there for ages!"

Raven sits in silence for awhile before answering, "I don't get it."

"Did you talk to your teacher?" Moira asks.

"No," Raven answers with bite.

"Why not?" Moira demands

"She doesn't like me." Raven replies.

"It doesn't matter if she likes you," Moira replies, "She's your teacher and she's supposed to help you. Email her now."

"No, I'll just figure it out," Raven counters.

"NO, you will not," Moira says forcefully, "You will email her now, or I will do it for you. Show me the problem."

(*Continued*)

(Continued)

"MOM!" Raven replies angrily, trying to pull her book away, "Stop! I said no, and I'll figure it out!"

"What is wrong with you that you don't just ask for help when you need it? It's just silly! You're going to fail the next test if you keep this up!" Moira asks in frustration.

"Will you let me alone? I said I'd do it myself!" Raven yells.

What's going on for Moira and Raven?

Moira exhibits some behaviors common in parents of anxious children; namely, psychological control and dismissiveness toward Raven's emotions. It may be the case that seeing her daughter struggle in a way that resonates with her own anxiety is challenging for her. Raven, on the other hand, is engaged in avoidance—of her embarrassment and discomfort in talking to her teacher and asking for help, and perhaps of working on something that she's not good at. Moira uses coercion—or behavioral "if-then" contingencies to present an aversive outcome to force Raven into compliance with her direction to talk to her teacher. Theirs is an interaction emblematic of families raising anxious children, and is intensified due to Moira's own anxiety.

Both mother and daughter appear engaged in attempts to control their emotional experience. Raven avoids doing math and talking with her teacher in an effort to avoid feeling "not good enough," and her fear of negative evaluation by the teacher. Moira, on the other hand, is having difficulty experiencing her daughter struggling, as it elicits her own anxiety and overprotectiveness. In this context, she engages in coercion to push Moira as a strategy to deal with her own emotions instead of finding a way to help Moira figure the situation out on her own, which would be more developmentally appropriate, and perhaps, more effective.

From a clinical RFT perspective, what appears to be going on is that in the presence of Raven's anxiety, Moira may have derived relations between "being a good mother" and "fixes things," or "pushes." Moreover, Raven's anxiety may be in a frame of opposition with Moira's notion of "acceptance," as she clearly sees that it is something to "fix." Finally, there may be hierarchical relations across Raven's intensity of anxiety, with Moira experiencing each increase as less "acceptable," thus serving as an antecedent to increased directiveness and psychological control. Clinicians might work with Moira by deliberately pairing "anxiety" with "excellent learning opportunity" or "opportunity to develop skill" for Raven; they might introduce the notion of "struggle" as "acceptable" through modeling awareness and empathy, without soothing or "fixing," of Raven's expressed anxiety. Finally, clinicians might help Moira separate Raven's *behavior in the context of anxiety* with the *anxiety itself*, such that there's a little room for movement and choice to try something different, in a curious, defused way, rather than a rigid and inflexible way.

How to work with acceptance clinically

Simple questioning

A starting point for assessing experiential acceptance of the parent as well as supporting the parent in developing greater awareness of their own degree of acceptance in the moment (as opposed to avoidance or attachment) is simple questioning. Questions like:

- Is this something that you struggle with?
- Is this something that you cling to?
- Are you willing to have these thoughts and feelings, if that is what it takes?
- Is there an emotion or thought that shows up that triggers a "have to" or automatic response?
- Are there any other emotions here, beneath or next to this emotion, perhaps?
- Acceptance can also be rated on a likert scale from 1 to 10 where 1 is not at all and 10 is completely willing.

When assessing parental experiential acceptance through questioning it should be remembered that parental acceptance could be very different for different kinds of thoughts and feelings and in different contexts. Some parents may, for example, be highly accepting of sadness yet avoid anxiety and cling to a sense of achievement. It also must be remembered that none of us are going to be completely accepting all of the time. It is healthy and normal to have times when you might be avoidant or attached to certain experiences. Further, experiential acceptance is context dependent, with contexts of social safety supporting experiential acceptance and contexts of threat pushing toward experiential control. So the purpose isn't to eliminate experiential avoidance or attachment, rather it is to be able to discriminate between times when experiential avoidance or attachment is helpful and times when it is problematic and to be able to switch to experiential acceptance as a deliberate choice.

Noticing acceptance within the parent–child interaction

In addition to asking the parent directly about their level of experiential acceptance, you can also be mindful of experiential acceptance within the parent–child interaction and within how the parent talks to you about their child and their reasons for seeking help. Some clues that experiential avoidance or attachment may be part of what is happening for the parent are:

- If the parent does not succeed in using parenting skills that you know they have in a particular context or when the parent is under stress (note, some degree of this is, of course, universal! Everyone performs worse under stress and parenting is a task that it is often necessary to perform even when you are at your worst).

- If parenting varies between contexts, for example, a parent who uses positive parenting strategies skilfully at home yet fails to do so in public.
- If the parent does not readily describe their own or their child's emotions, even with prompting, or if the parent's description of their child's emotions is quite different from the child's own reports. Sometimes experiential avoidance is noticeable by what is absent, by the emotions that are not spoken of. This may also serve as a clue where a parent is accepting of some emotions, but avoidant of others.
- If the parent has a control agenda. Does the parent frame parenting challenges in terms of needing to change the internal experiences of the child?
- If the parent reports feeling physically numb or unaware of their body or a lack of bonding then this may indicate avoidance of physical sensations, states of mobilization and immobilization and related emotions. This may be particularly apparent in parents with a history of trauma.

Metaphors

This metaphor is inspired by a metaphor given by Harari (2011) in the book *Sapiens*, when comparing Western thought with Buddhism. Unlike some of the other metaphors it covers both forms of experiential control: acceptance and attachment.

Controlling the ocean

It is as if you are standing in an ocean. Waves are rolling in. Wave after wave rolling and crashing around you. And you are spending all of your energy trying to avoid the "bad" waves and keep the "good" waves. When a "bad" wave comes you fight it, try to push it away, try to stand your ground. When a "good" wave comes you open your arms to it, you want it to last forever, you try to keep it with you always. Yet, what does your experience tell you? The waves come and go, "good" and "bad." You can dive into them, bob on them, or surf them if you want. Whatever you do, the waves come and go. Instead of trying to fight some waves and keep others, you can simply allow the waves to come and go as they will.

The swamp metaphor is particularly useful in increasing willingness to experience certain experiences in order to live out values. This variation has been adapted particularly to fit parents and parenting.

The swamp

It is like everything you've been talking about—the nasty thoughts and painful feelings is a mucky, yucky swamp. And your child is on the other side. Now you don't want to step into the swamp. Who would? Who would choose to wade through a muddy, gross swamp? But your child is on the other side. And it isn't fair. I bet no one ever told you that in order to reach your child you would have to wade through swamps of pain, right? We could write essays on how unfair it is, right? And your child would still be on the other side. So, here's the thing, could you jump into the swamp, wading through all those nasty thoughts and awful feelings if that is what it takes to reach your child?

And you know what? There's another little twist to this story. Because your child is going to have a swamp of their own. And just like you, they are going to find that the only way to the people and things that matter to them is through the swamp. So jumping into your swamp is also about knowing that when the day comes when your child has a choice about jumping into their own swamp you'll be able to say "I've done this too. Let me show you how."

Experiential exercises

Is control the solution?

The struggle switch metaphor can be modified into an experiential exercise to illustrate the unworkability of the parent control agenda. It can be adapted to any specific issues in which the parent is hooked with a parenting control agenda, and is focused on attempting to control the internal experiences of their child either in order to change the child's behavior or to control their own internal experiences. This first script is focused on child behavior problems in the context of child emotion.

Tantrums and control

Let's do a little experiment.
Let's imagine you are feeling really angry right now. Furious. Outraged.
Could you just turn that feeling off?
Like is there a switch at the back of your head or something?
Anger isn't convenient right now so flick and it's gone?
Isn't really how we work, huh? That's the first thing to learn.
So, what might happen if you thought it was really important to get rid of the anger? What if you were hooked up to a machine and if you felt anything negative there would be horrible consequences?
What might happen then?
Might you feel anxious about feeling angry? Or angry about the machine or sad about the bad consequences?

(Continued)

(Continued)

So, that the next thing to learn. The more important it seems to be to not feel negative feelings, the more it seems that we have to get rid of them, the more it is our life is on the line, the more the negative feelings amplify.
So what if, you not feeling anything negative mattered to me? What if I hooked you up to a machine and I thought that if you felt angry or anxious or sad at all ever my life was on the line? What if I worked really hard to stop you ever feeling anything negative. Could I do that?
And if you became angry could I just get rid of that emotion?
Do you think you might pick up on my desperation to control your feelings? What might happen there?
Do you have a switch on the back of your head, by any chance?
No. Does your child?
Do you ever feel like you are trying to do that with your child's emotions? Maybe get rid of their anger to stop a temper tantrum?
Does it work?

This second script focuses on the parent control agenda around infant sleep. Although there is much that parents can do to support healthful sleep in their baby—good sleep hygiene grounded in an understanding of the healthy operation of the circadian clock and the sleep homeostat including ensuring that their baby receives appropriate circadian cues throughout the day, and that sleep is under the appropriate stimulus control of sleepiness—a parent cannot control when their baby falls asleep. This is a common issue for the parenting control agenda to make an appearance in infancy, and it is often quite unworkable, simply escalating parent stress, which makes sleep elusive even when the baby has finally fallen asleep. The dilemma is illustrated well in the following exercise.

Sleep and control

I want to do a little experiment with you. Is that okay? It is a simple experiment.
Stand up.
Wave your hands.
Stomp your feet.
Now, fall sleep.
What happened? Can you fall asleep the same way that you can move your body? Is there a switch and the back of your head, perhaps, that you can flick and just like that you fall asleep?
Alright, let's try that again. This time I want you to imagine that I'm not asking you. I'm commanding you. Somehow, your life is on the line here. If you can't do what I'm telling you to do there are going to be some big and nasty

(*Continued*)

(Continued)

consequences. It is really, really important that you do as I ask. Let's see what we notice.

Stand up.

Wave your hands.

Stomp your feet.

Now, fall sleep. Remember it is incredibly important. Your life is on the line.

What happened? What's it like to try to fall asleep when your very life depends on it?

Not only can we not choose to fall asleep whenever we want to, we cannot force ourselves asleep. Your mind will tell you to try harder. But if you experiment, like we just did, trying harder doesn't help, does it? In fact, it makes sleep less likely.

And what if getting you to go to sleep, here and now, really mattered to me? What if I thought I really absolutely had to get you to fall asleep here and now? What if I was working really hard to make that happen? What if I was pouring energy into it? Singing lullabies or fetching you anything I thought might help like a warm milk or a favorite blanket, while I watched the clock hoping you'd fall asleep quickly? Tick tock tick tock.

What might happen then?

If you just weren't ready for sleep, would a warm glass of milk and a lullaby send you to sleep?

Do you think you'd pick up on my stress or my desperation?

And isn't this situation just a bit familiar? Have you ever been in exactly this situation with your own baby? Has it felt like pressure cooker?

Do you think it's easy or difficult to sleep in a pressure cooker?

So, here's the thing. Although sleep is something we do we can't just choose to fall asleep when we want to and we certainly can't make our children fall asleep when we want them to. They don't come with sleep switches at the back of their necks. Believe me, I've looked.

Getting rid of thoughts experiment

This exercise focuses on the futility of attempting to eliminate specific thoughts.

Getting rid of thoughts experiment script

Let's say you had a photo of your child in your living room. One day you decide you don't actually like the photo. Maybe the lighting was poor or something. Could you solve that problem? What would you do? Sure, you'd take the photo down and get rid of it, right? And could you replace it with another photo? Sure, you could. Problem solved.

(*Continued*)

(Continued)

What if you had a memory of your child or a thought about your child that you didn't like. Could you solve that problem?
Notice that the problem solving part of your mind wants to get rid of the memory or the thought, just like you got rid of the photo.
What does your experience tell you? Does that work? Can you get rid of memories and thoughts that you don't like? Replace them with new ones, like replacing a photo on the wall?
It doesn't work so well, huh?

Meditation

Mindfulness of emotions

A mindfulness of emotions meditation can be an excellent way of learning greater experiential acceptance around emotions. Clients can practice focusing on particular emotions that they have a history of struggling with. Once learned, the visualizations can be recalled during everyday life. This meditation includes both visualizing the emotion as an object and as a creature. You can try both with clients, and they can continue with the imagery that is most effective for them. Some people find imagining the emotion as a creature particularly effective because it can elicit a sense of compassion for the emotion that makes allowing it to be easier.

Mindfulness of emotions script
Get into relaxed and comfortable posture.
Eyes may be closed or hooded.
Bring your attention to the present moment...
Noticing the sensations in your body...
And anchoring yourself in the rhythm of your breathing...
Bring to mind a particular emotion, an emotion you have a tendency to struggle with, to try to avoid. In order to do this you may need to recall a specific situation in which you experience that emotion.
Immerse yourself in the experience, and let the emotion grow in you.
Once the emotion is present, open yourself up your experiences in your body.
Gently scan your body...
Where is the emotion?
In your stomach? Your shoulders and neck? Your head?
Focus in on the most bothersome or intense sensation...
Imagine that the emotions were an object.
What color would it be?
What temperature would it be?

(*Continued*)

(Continued)

How would it feel to touch?
Would it be moving or stationary?
Would it be light or dense?
Try to bring a sense of curiosity or exploration to how you approach the emotion.
Breathe gently around the emotion...
With every in-breath, find yourself growing bigger and making room for the emotion...
Notice that you are bigger than the emotion.
You might like to continue exploring the emotion by imagining that the emotion is a creature.
If the emotion were an animal, what would it look like?
How would it feel to touch?
Would it be moving or stationary?
Would it be light or heavy?
What would it be doing?
Try to develop a sense of kindness toward the emotion-creature...
Consider that even though it may be ugly or aggressive, it has got nowhere else to go.
Try to make room for the emotion-creature...
This doesn't mean you have to like it or want it to be there...
It just means accepting it and allowing it to be there.
Spend some moments just sitting with the emotion....
When you are ready to end the exercise, do so gently, using your breathing as an anchor to bring your awareness back into the room...

Accepting space for parent and child

This meditation focuses on cultivating experiential acceptance for both parent and child. Again, once practiced the visualization can be used in everyday life. Parents may use prompts like "boundless as the sky" to bring the quality of acceptance to their experiences as they interact with their child.

Accepting space for parent and child script

Get into relaxed and comfortable posture.
Bring your attention to the present moment...
Noticing the sensations in your body...
And anchoring yourself in the rhythm of your breathing...
Bring your child to mind.
Bring to mind your child as they are right now at this stage in their life.

(Continued)

(Continued)

Recall all the little details: their facial expressions, their interests and passions, remember the last time you laughed together or what it feels like to hold their hand.

Your mind is probably very busy and that's okay.

Recall all of it: the stuff your mind says is good and the stuff your mind says is bad.

Let all of it come: all of the thoughts, the feelings, the memories, and the sensations. Bring it all to mind.

Recall a time when you felt disconnected.

Recall a time when you felt connected.

Remember what it was like the very first time you met.

Imagine meeting your child now, as they are at this point in their life, with that same sense of curiosity.

Who is this person you know so well?

Gently, as best you can, open yourself up to your child.

Open yourself up to your child, just as your child is, with all of your history, with all of the good stuff and all of the bad stuff, and with all the thoughts, feelings, memories and sensations that are triggered in you.

It is like flinging yourself wide open...

As if you are as boundless as the sky.

Notice that your heart is big enough to contain all of it.

You are big enough to contain all of it.

Your child.

Your history.

The good stuff.

The bad stuff.

Your thoughts, feelings, memories, and sensations.

Take a deep breath and find room for all of it.

You don't have to like it. You don't have to want it to be this way.

You just need to find room in your heart for your child as they are. And for you as you are.

When you are ready to end the exercise, do so gently, using your breathing as an anchor to return to the present moment....

Pause and breathe

This exercise is about catching behavioral impulses and physiological states, including states of mobilization or immobilization in the moment and accepting the experience as it is without acting on it. Mobilization may be apparent in an accelerated heart beat and breathing and an urge to fight back or flee. Immobilization might include a shutdown reflex, an urge to move away, or to dissociate or withdraw. This exercise is suitable for all parents but parents who have experienced trauma might find it particularly useful.

Pause and breathe script

As we go about our daily lives, our body scans our environment for signs of safety and signs of danger.
Even in situations when we know we are safe at a conscious level our body makes its own call.
Our body does its best to keep us safe.
By getting us ready to fight or flee.
Or by putting us in a shutdown mode, helping us tune out.
Our body does its best. But it doesn't understand the modern world.
It thinks history always repeats itself.
And its motto is "better safe than sorry".
Scan your body now gently and with compassion.
Is your body in a state of safety?
Relaxed and ready to play?
Or is it tense, on edge?
Or tuning out?
See if you can notice the shifts.
See if you can notice the difference.
Maybe you can feel it in your heart rate.
Or your breathing as it becomes faster and shallower.
Or in your expression as you frown or grimace.
Or in your shoulders as you tense ready for action?
Or maybe you feel it in an urge to zone out.
The need to look away.
A numbness, or a shutting down?
Notice your body shift.
Notice that your body is doing the best it can.
If you need to, shift your attention.
Focus on something external to you.
The ground under your feet.
The sun on your face.
Pick something you can see, and focus.
Or maybe focus on your fingers, wiggle them.
Or your toes, feel them.
Pause.
And when you are ready, gently dip back in.
Dip back in to experiencing your full experience in the moment.
Shifting as many times as you need.
Dipping in, opening yourself up.
Slowly and gently.
Let the ground under your feet support you.
The sky wide and boundless contain you.
Breathe.
Step toward what you value.
And right now maybe that's self-care.

Encouraging home practice

Home practice around values may include:

- Practicing acceptance exercises and meditations;
- Keeping a diary of emotions in parenting in order to bring greater awareness to emotional experience.

Working with Moira and Raven

This interaction occurs after Moira describes her conflict with Raven over homework.

Therapist:	So Moira, if you're willing, I'd like to see if we might go back to that fight with Raven. Can we do that?
Moira:	Sure, why not?
Therapist:	Close your eyes. Take a few moments to connect in with your breath. (pause). Notice the sensation of breathing...notice your body in the chair...and do a quick scan to see how you are feeling...take a few moments to simply make space for those thoughts and feelings. (pause). Now I'd like you to step back in time, into that moment where you and Raven were fighting over homework....see if you can imagine that scene as fully as you can...where were you...what time of day was it...what was going on for you in that moment...and step back into the skin of the person you were in that moment...notice Raven sitting at the counter with her schoolbooks...take a moment to notice her face...see if you can label the look on her face as she struggles...what do you see?
Moira:	She looks worried. Strained...her mouth is tight...she's tapping her pencil...
Therapist:	What feeling shows up in you as you watch her?
Moira:	Well, she should really have talked to her teacher...I don't know why she...
Therapist interrupts:	Slow down, Moira...I want you to go back to the look on her face...the strain...the worry. Take a moment to notice how you are feeling in your body as you see her. What do you notice?
Moira:	There's...a tightness. In my chest. Butterflies, too. My stomach.
Therapist:	Ok. Take a few moments to simply notice those sensations, and allow them to remain in your awareness... is there an emotion that goes with these?

(*Continued*)

(Continued)

Moira: becoming tearful	It's just. . .anxiety. . .I get so worried about her. . .I don't want her to be like me, to bear the burden of that anxiety. . ..
Therapist:	Slow down, and let yourself linger in this space for a bit. . .notice that when she feels anxious, your own anxiety is triggered. . .if you could go back to that moment, what might you do differently? What might you say to her, or want her to know?
Moira: pauses	I'm not sure. Perhaps. . .I wonder if I might be more understanding, or maybe tell her why I am worried. . .I'm not sure what the right thing to do would be. I don't think I'd yell at her though—that never seems to work. It just makes it worse.
Therapist:	Let's stay in this space of being uncertain, and curious about what might be the right next thing. If spending some time noticing your thoughts and feelings might help turn up the next right step for you, would you be willing to do that?
Moira:	I think so. I just feel so lost. . .I wish I had more to offer her to help.
Therapist:	Yes. This is a really difficult spot to be in. And what if it is the exact right place to be to discover what might work for Raven?
Moira:	Yes, that would be good. Hard. But good.

Moira's therapist led her through an experiential exercise to bring her into contact with avoided thoughts and feelings. This is a type of exposure to unwanted private events, and an opportunity to interact with them in a different, approach-based way, through a structured clinical interaction. When the therapist noticed that Moira was engaged in avoidance even in the current clinical exercise (e.g., reporting a thought, and engaging in problem solving and complaining about what Raven should have done), the therapist redirected her back to notice physiological sensations, as it might have been easier to notice and label those, as a way of shaping experiential acceptance. After Moira noticed and labeled those, she was able to report her emotions as well. Moreover, she was also able to voice uncertainty and some curiosity about next steps, which can be a sign that she is engaging in discovery and open to tracking, rather than pliance. This opens the door to shaping more authentic connection between Moira and Raven, and to Moira's greater openness to trial-and-error learning about what might be most helpful to Raven.

Troubleshooting

Confusion with acceptance and compassion

Acceptance and compassion actually go hand in hand. However, it is not uncommon for parents in the name of "acceptance" to become hardened or dismissive of the suffering of their child. This is not consistent with acceptance. The fact that such hardening or dismissive attitude is required, in fact, demonstrates that the parent is not accepting the child's emotions and the emotions that this generates in them. In the course of parenting, parents may need to make decisions in the child's long-term best interests that nevertheless cause suffering for the child now. It can be tempting, in such situations, for the parent to be experientially avoidant and dismissive of the child's emotions as well as their own. While this is understandable and certainly no one is going to be perfectly accepting all the time, an opportunity to model acceptance and demonstrate compassion is lost.

More than just emotions

A trap that therapists can fall into as well as clients is to focus narrowly on acceptance *of emotions*. Although that is an important component of experiential acceptance, experiential acceptance is also about making space for: thoughts, memories, sensations, and behavioral impulses. For people who have a history of trauma, acceptance of sensations including physiological states of mobilization and immobilization may be a greater focus than emotions. For many parents, acceptance of behavioral impulses may be the primary focus.

Accept, so we can ignore?

Another common trap we can fall into is to accept the experiences of thoughts, feelings, sensations, memories, and behavioral impulses while dismissing them as a source of information. That is to accept them yet then ignore them completely in choosing how to act. In fact, this is a slightly more aware form of dismissal and it is not consistent with experiential acceptance.

Experiential acceptance includes an understanding that our private experiences contain useful information: information we've inherited from millions of years of evolution in the form of evolved motivational systems, information about our context from our learning history and information about us. Instead of making room merely to dismiss, it is about making room so we can see our internal signaling systems up close, and decide when a particular signal is useful (and worth following) and when it is not.

This can be particularly relevant to parenting. As parents our internal signaling system for threat becomes highly active (Hahn-Holbrook,

Holbrook, & Haselton, 2011). Signaling to alert us to danger becomes all the more salient. New parents experience an increase in the frequency of anxious and intrusive thoughts. Our evolved signaling system protects us and our child from threats and what could be more threatening than a threat to our child? While we don't want to act on every signal from our threat system, the increased hyperviligence to threat in parenting is an evolved safety mechanism crucial to the successful raising of children. We also don't want to simply dismiss our concerns for the safety of our children.

In addition to our signaling system for threat, other emotional responses, physiological sensations and behavioral impulses are also useful. They form part of ongoing affective interpersonal communication, and as such, they contain vital information that assist us in bonding with and parenting our child. The reading of a baby's cues is at least partly based within our affliative motivational system (discussed in detail in Chapter 12: Compassionate context), and may be apparent to us in our physiological state, affective response and behavioral impulses toward our child, such as a sense of distress in hearing them cry or an impulse to hold them. With greater awareness and acceptance it is possible to recognize when our history or other contextual factors are getting in the way of connecting with our child as well as when our internal reactions are facilitating us in connecting with our child.

Acceptance and trauma history

For people with a history of trauma, jumping straight into experiential acceptance can be utterly overwhelming and unrealistic. Contexts of social safety promote experiential acceptance. It is difficult to be experientially accepting without a history of social safety. For people with a history of trauma, techniques drawn from compassion focussed therapy (discussed in Chapter 12: Compassionate context) may be particularly relevant, in order to build a repertoire of compassion, soothing, and social safeness, before working on experiential acceptance. In addition, experiential acceptance may be approached gently and gradually by "dipping in." It may be easiest to begin by focusing on an external stimulus, such as a picture, the sun on your face, or the ground under your feet, or to a part of the body that is an extremity, more removed from the vagal system, such as toes or fingers, and then to gently "dip in" to, and open yourself up to your full experiences in the moment.

Four key developmental periods and acceptance

Infancy and acceptance

From an attachment perspective, the parent is a safe, open holding space for the baby, functioning as both a secure base for exploration, and a safe haven for refuge and soothing (Bowlby, 1958, 1982, 1988). In order to function as such safe refuge and a secure base the parent must be able to maintain the open, flexible, and aware qualities of experiential acceptance. In a very real way, the parent's acceptance is acceptance for two. The parent's acceptance of the baby's internal experiences, the communication of these internal experiences to the parent and the reactions that this stirs up in the parent, provides the baby with an experience of acceptance. In a real sense, the parent, by being accepting, models acceptance for the child.

At the same time, the birth of a child massively increases our own emotional range (Greenberg, 2002). As parents we feel distress, anxiety, and grief at a whole new level as we feel not just for ourselves but also for our child. Intrusive, anxious thoughts are common in the perinatal period. Experiential acceptance is key to being able to listen to our bodily and emotional reactions as signals, taking the useful information that they contain, without simply becoming reactive.

Early childhood and acceptance

Within early childhood, experiential acceptance is a crucial aspect of emotion coaching (Gottman et al., 1997). Grounded in experiential acceptance, parents can label their child's emotions, respond to their children's emotions with acceptance (without dismissing them or immediately trying to change them), and offer to problem solve the situation together. Through such repeated experiences children become skilled in their own awareness and understanding of emotion.

Early childhood is also the time when noncompliance and temper tantrums are at their peak. Parental experiential acceptance is integral to being able to respond to misbehavior in a positive manner and to successfully using behavioral parenting strategies. Dysfunctional parenting may arise not due to a lack of skill but because the dysfunctional parenting behaviors have an avoidance function for the parent.

Middle childhood and acceptance

With middle childhood comes an increase in the experiences a child has outside the family environment. In particular it includes school. Parents may have their first experiences of watching, from a distance, as their child experiences social rejection, failure, or other challenges. This may be terribly painful for parents and parents may experience a strong behavioral predisposition to march up to the school and "fix" it. Parental experiential acceptance is key to knowing when communication with the school is needed, and when parents are better placed in scaffolding their child's ability to handle the situation themselves. It is also important to the parent capacity to support the child fully in their own emotional reaction, to see the situation clearly and to appropriately and effectively communicate with the school (if that is needed) or scaffold the child's ability to deal with the situation. There is a need to support the child through unpleasant experiences that are nevertheless, life lessons. To know that some suffering is fundamental to life and our children cannot be spared from it.

Adolescence and acceptance

Adolescence is a time of individuation, the need for belonging with peers, risk-taking, and experimentation. This may generate understandably uncomfortable reactions in parents. Yet, this developmental period of risk-taking, peer identification, and experimentation is crucial to healthy development. In order to continue to effectively parent, to continue to function as a secure base and a safe haven, it is crucial that parents maintain experiential acceptance of their own experiences, their child's experiences, and the reactions that their child's experiences generate in themselves.

Using acceptance with specific populations

Parental mental health problems and acceptance

It is well established that experiential acceptance is protective against mental health problems. Experiential avoidance, in particular, escalates and amplifies our emotional pain and is a key part of the cycle that can lead to and maintain mental health problems.

Parental grief and acceptance

Following a loss event grief is normal and grief isn't something that we quickly "get over." It is normal to continue to grieve years later—it is normal to continue to grieve for the rest of your life. Grief isn't healing a hole in your heart. It is learning with live with a hole in your heart.

Unfortunately many cultures including Western cultures are grief-avoidant. Further, particular kinds of grief can be disenfranchized, that is, the grief receives little social recognition or cultural support as a normal and healthy reaction (Murray, 2016). Perinatal loss remains a disenfranchised grief. The parents, often especially the mother, may feel that no one else recognizes who they lost or acknowledges their lost child's place within the family. The loss experienced by parents of children with disabilities or babies born preterm is also a disenfranchised grief. Grieving parents may receive multiple avoidant messages from family, friends, and wider society.

Childhood externalizing problems and acceptance

Using positive parenting strategies to manage externalizing behavior requires not just competence in the skills and strategies, but also a high degree of experiential acceptance. Experiential control is often pivotal to dysfunctional parenting behavior, whether that is the reinforcing of externalizing problems in order to directly control the child's behavior in the moment, with the loss of an opportunity to shape it into a more positive behavior in the long term, or in coercive parenting behavior, in which the parent avoids their own emotions by venting them in coercive or harsh parenting methods.

Childhood internalizing problems and acceptance

Parental experiential acceptance is necessary to effectively supporting children with depressive or anxious symptoms. If the parent takes a stance of avoidance toward the child's anxious or depressive symptoms, this models and reinforces avoidance for the child. Parental acceptance of their child's emotions and their own reactions to their child's emotions, is necessary to effectively support their child in building increasingly accepting repertoires.

Childhood neurodevelopmental disabilities and acceptance

In addition to experiential acceptance being important for parental grief, as already discussed, it is also important for parents to avoid the trap of focusing on "therapy" and "intervention" at the expense of the parent–child relationship. Parents of children with disabilities can become hooked into a pattern of intervention-orientated parenting in order to avoid thoughts about their child's future, and the accompanying distressing feelings. Although it is, of course, desirable for parents of children with disabilities to participate in maximizing their child's development through intervention, it is not desirable for this to interfere with the development of a sensitive and responsive parenting pattern.

Peer problems and bullying and acceptance

The aspect of experiential acceptance that involves noticing your own internal bodily and emotional reactions and listening to them as signals, as containing useful information, is relevant to peer problems. It is relevant for the child, in better navigating their social world, knowing when and how to handle a social challenge themselves and when to seek help. It is also relevant for the parent, in deciding when to step back and allow their child to attempt to solve a peer challenge for themselves, when to step in and scaffold, and when to step in fully, protecting their child from a social situation.

Marital conflict and acceptance

Lack of experiential acceptance can accelerate conflict and disconnection between partners, as partners may engage in efforts to control each other's internal stimuli in order to control their own and lack genuine emotional communication.

Expressed emotionincluding critical and intrusive parenting and acceptance

Critical and hostile behaviors on one hand, as well as emotionally overinvolved behaviors on the other, commonly have the function of experiential avoidance for the parent.

Emotion dismissiveness and acceptance

Experiential acceptance is a necessary component of parents being aware of and accepting of their children's emotions. Emotionally dismissive parenting behavior often has the function of experiential avoidance for the parent.

Inconsistent, or harsh and punitive parenting and acceptance

Inconsistent, harsh, and punitive parenting often has the function of experiential avoidance for the parent. Thus, increasing experiential acceptance in the parent, along with increasing the parent's skills at the same time, can be critical to decreasing the use of dysfunctional parenting practices.

References

Abramowitz, J. S., Tolin, D. F., & Street, G. P. (2001). Paradoxical effects of thought suppression: A meta-analysis of contolled studies. *Clinical Psychology Review*, *21*(5), 683–703.

Blackledge, J. T., & Hayes, S. C. (2006). Using acceptance and commitment training in the support of parents of children diagnosed with autism. *Child and Family Behavior Therapy*, *28* (1), 1–18.

Bowlby, J. (1958). The nature of the child's ties to his mother. *International Journal of Psychoanalysis*, *39*, 350–373.

Bowlby, J. (1982). *Attachment and loss: Attachment* (Vol. 1). New York: Basic Books.

Bowlby, J. (1988). *A secure base: Parent–child attachment and healthy human development.* New York: Basic Books.

Cheron, D., Ehrenreich, J., & Pincus, D. (2009). Assessment of parental experiential avoidance in a clinical sample of children with anxiety disorders. *Child Psychiatry Human Development*, *40*(3), 383–403.

Coyne, L. W., & Thompson, A. D. (2011). Maternal depression, locus of control, and emotion regulatory strategy as predictors of preschoolers' internalizing problems. *Journal of Child and Family Studies*, *20*(6), 873–883.

Eisenberg, N., Cumberland, A., & Spinrad, T. L. (1998). Parental socialization of emotion. *Psychological Inquiry*, *9*(4), 241–273.

Evans, T., Whittingham, K., & Boyd, R. (2012). What helps the mother of a preterm infant become securely attached, responsive and well-adjusted? *Infant Behavior and Development*, *35*(1), 1–11.

Forsyth, J. P., & Ritzert, T. R. (2018). Cultivating psychological acceptance. In S. C. Hayes, & S. G. Hofmann (Eds.), *Process-based CBT* (pp. 636–674). Oakland, CA: Context Press.

Gopnik, A. (2017). *The gardener and the carpenter*. London: Vintage Publishing.

Gottman, J. M., Katz, L. F., & Hoover, C. (1996). Parental meta-emotion philosophy and the emotional life of families: Theoretical models and preliminary data. *Journal of Family Psychology*, *16*(3), 243–268.

Gottman, J. M., Katz, L. F., & Hoover, C. (1997). *Meta-emotion: How families communicate emotionally*. Mahwah, NJ: Lawrence Erlbaum Associates.

Greco, L., Heffner, M., Poe, S., Ritchie, S., Polak, M., & Lynch, S. (2005). Maternal adjustment following preterm birth: Contributions of experiential avoidance. *Behavior Therapy*, *36*, 177–184.

Greenberg, L. S. (2002). *Emotion-focused therapy*. Washington, DC: American Psychological Association.

Gruber, J. (2011). When feeling good can be bad: positive emotion persistence (PEP) in bipolar disorder. *Current Directions in Psychological Science*, *20*, 217–221.

Hahn-Holbrook, J., Holbrook, C., & Haselton, M. G. (2011). Parental precaution: Neurobiological means and adaptive ends. *Neuroscience and Biobehavioral Reviews*, *35*, 1052–1066.

Harari, Y. N. (2011). *Sapiens: A brief history of humankind*. London: Vintage.

Hayes, L. L., & Ciarrochi, J. (2015). *The thriving adolescent*. Oakland, CA: New Harbinger Publications.

Hayes, S. C., & Sanford, B. T. (2015). Modern psychotherapy as a multidimensional multilevel evolutionary process. *Current Opinion in Psychology*, *2*, 16–20.

Hayes, S. C., Strosahl, K. D., & Wilson, K. G. (2003). *Acceptance and commitment therapy: An experiential approach to behavior change*. New York: Guilford Press.

Jones, L., Hastings, R. P., Totsika, V., Keane, L., & Rhule, N. (2014). Child behavior problems and parental well-being in famlies of children with autism: The mediating role of mindfulness and acceptance. *American Journal on Intellectual and Developmental Disabilities*, *119* (2), 171–185.

Murray, J. (2016). *Understanding loss*. New York: Routledge.

Shea, S. E., & Coyne, L. W. (2011). Maternal dysphoric mood, stress, and parenting practices in mothers of head start preschoolers: The role of experiential avoidance. *Child & Family Behavior Therapy*, *33*(3), 231–247.

Swails, J. A., Zettle, R. D., Burdsal, C. A., & Synder, J. J. (2016). The experiential approach scale: Development and prelimiary psychometric properties. *The Psychological Record*, *66* (4), 527–545.

Tamir, M., & Ford, B. Q. (2012). Should people pursue feelings that feel good or feelings that do good? Emotional preferences and well-being. *Emotion*, *12*(5), 1061–1070.

Whittingham, K., Wee, D., Sanders, M., & Boyd, R. N. (2013). Sorrow, coping and resiliency: Parents of children with cerebral palsy share their experiences. *Disability and Rehabilitation*, *35*(17), 1447–1452.

Chapter 9

Contact with the present moment including shared psychological presence

Chapter Outline

What is contact with the present moment? **222**
- The history of mindfulness 224
- Mindfulness and acceptance 225
- Benefits of mindfulness 226
- DNA-V model 227

How does contact with the present moment apply to parent–child interaction? **227**
- What is mindful parenting? 227
- Shared psychological contact and relationship 228
- Shared psychological presence and effective parenting 228
- Psychological contact and mental health and well-being 229

How to work with mindfulness clinically **233**
- Assessing parental mindfulness 233
- Simple questioning or prompts 233
- Metaphors 233
- Meditation 234
- A taste of mindfulness meditation 234
- Mindfulness of breathing meditation 235
- Mindful walking meditation 236
- Antenatal mindfulness meditation 237
- Mindfulness of baby meditation 238
- Parenting: a mindfulness meditation 239
- Wake up! A quick mindfulness meditation 241
- Mindfulness within daily life 241
- Mindfulness within daily life for children and adolescents 242
- Encouraging home practice 243

Troubleshooting **244**
- Do we have to do mindfulness meditations? 244
- What if they don't have the time? 245
- Is mindfulness and relaxation the same thing? 245
- What if parents experience paradoxical reactions to mindfulness or have a history of trauma? 245
- Mindfulness with a purpose 246

Four key developmental periods and contact with the present moment **246**
- Infancy and contact with the present moment 246
- Early childhood and contact with the present moment 247
- Middle childhood and contact with the present moment 247
- Adolescence and contact with the present moment 247

Acceptance and Commitment Therapy. DOI: https://doi.org/10.1016/B978-0-12-814669-9.00009-6

© 2019 Elsevier Inc. All rights reserved.

Using mindfulness with specific populations **248**
Parental mental health problems and contact with the present moment 248
Parental grief and contact with the present moment 248
Childhood externalizing problems and contact with the present moment 248
Childhood internalizing problems and contact with the present moment 248
Childhood neurodevelopmental disabilities and contact with the present moment 249
Peer relations and bullying and contact with the present moment 249
Marital conflict and contact with the present moment 249
Expressed emotion including critical or intrusive parenting and contact with the present moment 249
Emotion dismissiveness and contact with the present moment 249
Inconsistent, or harsh and punitive parenting and contact with the present moment 250
References **250**

The practice of meditation is not a method for the attainment of realization—it is enlightenment itself.

Dogen

All this he saw, for one moment breathless and intense, vivid on the morning sky; and still, as he looked, he lived; and still, as he lived, he wondered.

Kenneth Grahame, *The Wind in the Willows*

"Well," said Pooh, "what I like best," and then he had to stop and think. Because although Eating Honey was a very good thing to do, there was a moment just before you began to eat it which was better than when you were, but he didn't know what it was called.

A. A. Milne, *Winnie-the-Pooh*

What is contact with the present moment?

Contact with the present moment is also called mindfulness. Without contact with the present moment, we are living on autopilot. To be mindful, to be psychologically present, is often described as being awake. Mindfulness is about allowing the present moment to be just as it is and widening one's awareness to all that is in the present moment. Within acceptance and commitment therapy (ACT), the concept of contact with the present moment is interrelated with the concept of experiential acceptance. Whereas experiential acceptance is focused on maintaining contact with *internal* stimuli of thoughts, feelings, sensations, memories, and behavioral impulses, mindfulness also includes maintaining contact with *external* stimuli including with our *physical* context. Yet, there is necessarily an accepting quality to being psychologically present in your physical context, and, likewise, awareness within here and now is necessary to cultivating acceptance. The line between these two concepts then is not fixed, but rather one of emphasis.

Living without contact with the present moment, without contact with the external stimuli around us, is possible for us as a species because we are languaging beings. According to relational frame theory (RFT), humans live in two worlds: the physical and the symbolic (see Chapter 4: Shape: building a flexible repertoire, for further information on RFT). It is language that allows us to be physically somewhere, and psychologically somewhere else. Yet, our need for *shared* psychological presence is also highly characteristic of our species and, indeed, necessary for the development of language (Hrdy, 2011). Unlike the Great Apes, humans are flexible cooperative breeders, our children have multiple caregivers and are not raised in continuous physical contact with their mother. As such, shared psychological presence, *psychological connection*, is crucial, with human babies evolving to elicit shared psychological presence, or attuned interactions, from their caregivers. Contact with the present moment, in the form of shared psychological presence, is thus a necessary foundation to language (see Chapter 3: Connect: the parent–child relationship, for a more complete discussion), which, somewhat ironically, gives us the ability to be psychologically somewhere else.

Our symbolic abilities, including our ability to be psychologically somewhere else, have tremendous advantages. We can replay past events, imagine future scenarios, conduct thought experiments, and think up unique solutions to problems that haven't even happened yet. Our symbolic abilities are, indeed, a superpower. But every superpower has a cost and this is no exception. Our ability to psychologically disconnect from the physical world interacts poorly with our mammalian threat systems. When a nonverbal mammal such as a dog or a cat is threatened their bodies may mobilize in a fight or flight reaction and their attention may narrow to focus on the threat or, alternatively, their bodies may immobilize in a shutdown reaction which may include dissociation, fainting, or other shutdown responses. For the most part, these responses to physical threats are adaptive. When under physical threat, for example, from a predator, it is useful to not be distracted by other stimuli, such as food or a potential mate. In verbal humans, however, the capacity to be somewhere (and somewhen) else is limitless, and this gives our threat systems too, limitless potential. I can be physically in a park with my child on a sunny day, with birds chirping and children laughing. Yet although I am there physically I may be psychologically still arguing with my child about the importance of wearing shoes, or back in the birth suite giving birth, or in a possible future grieving my child's death.

We can get stuck in our symbolic world. We can be physically within a context that is nurturing and supportive, rich in positive reinforcement and deeply meaningful to us. Yet, we may be psychologically in our heads, responding to aversive stimuli within the symbolic world. Symbolic threats, too, can trigger our bodies to mobilize in a fight or flight reaction with narrowing attention or to immobilize in a shutdown reaction. This reaction, which is usually adaptive in response to physical threats, traps us within our own minds, entangled with threatening internal stimuli. And internal stimuli cannot be overcome by fighting, fleeing, or playing dead. It is like a bug in the human system, caused by two useful apps: the mammalian threat system and the human capacity for symbolic thinking interacting poorly. The way out of this trap is to be able to deliberately foster contact with the present moment, including shared psychological presence with others. The deliberate fostering of contact with the present moment has been called mindfulness.

The history of mindfulness

Mindfulness as an ancient concept with many nuances of definition. Mindfulness *as a deliberate practice* has been practized and elucidated within spiritual traditions of the Indian sub-continent for over 2500 years. It is a particularly rich tradition of how and why to practice mindfulness. Although ACT did not consciously draw upon Buddhism in its conception (Hayes, 2002), all of ACT's fellow travelers including mindfulness-based stress reduction (MBSR), mindfulness-based cognitive therapy (MBCT), compassion focussed therapy, and dialectical behavior therapy (DBT) did and so the concept of mindfulness within psychology broadly is deeply inspired by Buddhist traditions.

Within the Buddhist tradition, mindfulness is a multifaceted concept that includes: (1) a bare awareness of moment-to-moment experience; (2) metacognitive functions such as sustained attention, deliberate remembering, and a capacity for "gatekeeping," that is, for deliberately placing and sustaining attention in a wise manner; (3) an accepting quality; and (4) a subtle form of awareness free from all conceptual constructs (Kang & Whittingham, 2010; Tirch, Silberstein, & Kolts, 2016). This Buddhist definition is consistent with mindfulness as it is understood from an ACT/RFT perspective.

Within Buddhism mindfulness is one part of a path, the Noble Eightfold Path, and cannot be fully understood without the other elements. The Noble Eightfold Path includes three pillars: meditative awareness including right mindfulness and right concentration (the distinction between mindfulness and concentration isn't made in the psychological literature, mindfulness is often used to mean both); ethics including right speech, right action, right effort; and wisdom including right intention and right understanding (Tirch et al., 2016). In this, Buddhism and ACT are similar; within ACT too, mindfulness is one element of a whole; interrelated with concepts of experiential acceptance and defusion and grounded within values.

The Noble Eightfold Path as a whole must be situated within the Four Noble Truths. The Four Noble Truths, the very heart of Buddhism, state that:

1. Life is *dukkha*.
2. *Dukkha* is created by *tanha*.
3. We can be liberated from *dukkha*.
4. The Eightfold Noble Path is the way to liberation.

Dukkha is often translated into the English word "suffering" and while that translation is not incorrect as such, it misrepresents the full nuance of *dukkha* (Tirch et al., 2016). *Dukkha* does not just mean what English speakers would typically call suffering. Instead, it refers to a kind of fundamental dissatisfaction with life: the fact that positive states when attained do not last; that all states depend upon an interrelated web of causality and so nothing exists in its own right and by its own means; as well as the physical suffering that is bound up with life including age, sickness and death. The Buddha did not suggest that happiness doesn't exist or isn't attainable. Only that it is impermanent, inter-dependent and transitory.

Tanha is usually translated as craving or thirst, but Batchelor (2015) suggests that a better translation would be reactivity. Likewise, the liberation offered by the Eightfold Noble Path is traditionally understood as liberation from suffering through understanding the Four Noble Truths and walking the Eightfold Noble Path. Batchelor (2015), however, re-interprets the Four Noble Truths by reexamining the early texts from a secular perspective. He suggests that the Buddha is asking us, not to understand the truths but *to understand suffering itself* and to seek liberation not from suffering *but from reactivity*. This interpretation is remarkably consistent with ACT; *tanha* as Batchelor understands it is very similar to experiential control and psychological inflexibility.

For most of Buddhism's history the complete path, including meditation, has been restricted to the ordained sangha and the lineage of nuns, the female Sangha, was lost in many countries. As a result, Buddhist mindfulness practices have been passed down to us, over the 2500 years of Buddhist history, by celibate and childless men (Whittingham, 2016). Modern practitioners, however, are finding parenting rich in opportunities for personal development and mindful practice (Kabat-Zinn & Kabat-Zinn, 1997).

Mindfulness and acceptance

Experiential acceptance and mindfulness coexist. There is always an acceptance piece inherent in mindfulness too. To be fully in the present moment is to accept the present moment as it is. As Tara Brach says, suffering begins the moment we wish the present moment to be other than what it is

(Brach, 2003). The solution? A kind of radical acceptance of the present moment. The Stoics called this amor fati or the love of fate (Irvine, 2009). It is learning to embrace what is. Beyond experiential acceptance, this is a kind of acceptance of the physical world too, acceptance of your current circumstances. Like experiential acceptance, this does not mean actively liking or preferring your present circumstances and it does not mean refraining from taking any actions you can to improve your circumstances. It just means embracing the reality of now as what is, allowing what is to be, without wasting energy fighting reality.

Benefits of mindfulness

Mindfulness has been found to be linked with mental health and well-being (Baer, 2003; Blanck et al., 2018; Cooper, Yap, & Batalha, 2018; Perestelo-Perez, Barraca, Peñate, Rivero-Santana, & Alvarez-Perez, 2017; Shiyko, Hallinan, & Naito, 2017; Tomlinson, Yousaf, Vitterso, & Jones, 2018; Young et al., 2018). Within romantic relationships, mindfulness predicts decreased avoidant and anxious attachment patterns (Hertz, Laurent, & Laurent, 2014; Stevenson, Emerson, & Millings, 2017; Walsh, Balint, Smolira, Fredericksen, & Madsen, 2009). In parents, mindfulness is associated with decreased parenting stress, parental depressive symptoms, and child behavior problems (Beer, Ward, & Moar, 2013; Conner & White, 2014; Jones, Hastings, Totsika, Keane, & Rhule, 2014) as well as increased parent–child relationship quality and coparent relationship quality (Parent, McKee, Rough, & Forehand, 2016). Mindful parenting mediates the relationships between dispositional mindfulness and self-compassion and parenting stress and parenting styles (Gouveia, Carona, Canavarro, & Moreira, 2016). Maternal parenting-specific mindfulness was found to be related to maternal cortisol, a marker for HPA axis response, while performing the Still Face task with their 3–month-old infant. Further, maternal parenting-specific mindfulness at 3 months moderated the effect of life stress on mother and infant cortisol at 6 months, with mindful parenting predicting lower infant cortisol levels and more extended cortisol elevations in mothers in dyads experiencing high life stress (Laurent, Duncan, Lightcap, & Khan, 2017). Mindful parenting was found to be associated with less negative parental emotional expression during conflict, and this decrease in negative parental emotional expression mediated a relationship between mindful parenting and risk behaviors in adolescents (Turpyn & Chaplin, 2016).

Mindfulness programs have been developed and tested for pregnancy, birth and early parenting with promising results in maternal depressive and anxious symptoms (Bardacke, 2012; Dhillon, Sparkes, & Duarte, 2017; Dimidjian et al., 2014; Dunn, Hanieh, Roberts, & Powrie, 2012; Vieten & Astin, 2008). Mindfulness interventions have also been trialed with parents, showing benefits in parenting stress, depressive symptoms, anxiety, and well-being, as well as child adjustment (Bazzano et al., 2013; Benn, Akiva, Arel, & Roeser, 2012; Bogels & Restifo, 2014; Neece, 2014; Singh et al., 2006, 2007). In addition, mindfulness has been integrated into parenting interventions showing beneficial effects in parenting stress, parenting style and child adjustment (Coatsworth, Duncan, Greenberg, & Nix, 2010; Coatsworth et al., 2014; Dawe, Harnett, Rendalls, & Staiger, 2003; Harnett & Dawe, 2012; Whittingham, 2014).

DNA-V model

This relates to the noticer, discoverer and social view within the DNA-V model (Hayes & Ciarrochi, 2015). The noticer expands upon traditional understandings of mindfulness by including embodied awareness and noticing and listening to immobilization and mobilization and emotional reactions as signals and so does this component within the parent–child hexaflex. Discoverer overlaps with this in the sense of openness to experiential discovery in the moment; discovery of what is happening experientially for both the parent and the child. Our concept also includes a *shared* psychological presence which relates to the social view in DNA-V.

How does contact with the present moment apply to parent–child interaction?

What is mindful parenting?

Mindful parenting is about staying psychologically present with one's children, even in challenging moments. It challenges us to consider an interpersonal or a relational mindfulness; how might mindfulness be practiced mindfulness during interpersonal interactions (Falb & Pargament, 2012; Surrey & Jordan, 2012; Wilson & Dufrene, 2009). Relational mindfulness involves bringing mindful awareness to the moment-to-moment experiences including changes within yourself, changes in the behavior of another, and changes in the ebb and flow of an ongoing relationship. It includes listening fully without judgment and speaking from genuine awareness overlaps with the concepts of kindness and compassion.

Duncan, Coatsworth, and Greenberg (2009) proposed a conceptual model of mindful parenting as including: (1) listening with full attention, (2) nonjudgmental acceptance of parent and child, (3) emotional awareness of parent and child, (4) self-regulation in parenting, and (5) compassion for parent and child. This model, like other mindfulness models within psychology includes elements beyond mindfulness such as experiential acceptance and compassion.

Parental mindfulness has been found to be related to child internalizing and externalizing behavior via mindful parenting and reduced negative parenting practices across three developmental stages: young childhood, middle childhood and adolescence (Parent et al., 2016).

Shared psychological contact and relationship

Attachment is about proximity. That is, the evolutionary purpose of the attachment system is to maintain the child's proximity to the parent. It is easy to witness this in action: a child exploring further and further from their parent, the attachment bonds stretching physically to a point and then—*snap!*—the child is brought back to the parent, as if by a stretched too far rubber band. Any threat too makes the rubber band snap and contract, bringing the child safely back to the parent. Not only is the attachment system about proximity, but also physical proximity is key to developing an attachment bond in the first place. Children bond with the people they are in close physical proximity to. Physical proximity also supports the caregiving side of the attachment bond. Increased physical proximity (by wearing baby with a soft infant carrier) has been shown to increase the responsiveness of mothers to their babies at three and a half months of age in an experiential study with mothers randomly assigned to receiving either an infant carrier promoting the close physical proximity of baby wearing or an infant capsule style of carrier in which the baby is not worn close to the body (Ainsfeld, Capser, Nozyce, & Cunningham, 1990).

Parents, like all verbal humans, may be physically present, but psychologically somewhere else. And so attachment is also about *psychological* proximity. A parent who is emotionally available, sensitive and responsive to their child is, fundamentally, in psychological contact with their child. The parent and the child are living within a shared psychological space. Just as physical proximity is necessary for the parent to function as a safe haven and a secure base, as well as to notice the child's moment by moment cues and respondsensitively to them, so too is a psychological presence. A parent who is psychologically present, with the child, is more likely to notice cues and hence to be able to response sensitively to a child's needs sooner.

In addition, mindfulness can support parental ability to hold their own immediate reactions gently, so that instead of responding from experiential control or reactivity, they can respond from their own values, promoting responsive interactions.

Shared psychological presence and effective parenting

Present moment awareness is necessary for tracking— discovering what works—and being able to take a flexible and experimental approach to parenting. Effective parenting requires that parents perform a kind of lay person's functional analysis, 'seeing' the contingencies maintaining their children's behavior so that they can tweak the context accordingly.

Of course, most parents would not be able to explain their tracking of their child's behavior in precise behavioral jargon. But regardless of the exact language that they use noticing patterns in their child's behavior—how the context effects behavior, what happens before and what happens after, is the first step to the parent developing and testing out through experimentation with parenting strategies ideas about the contingencies underlying their child's behavior. Psychological presence with the child is necessary for this noticing to occur.

Mindfulness can support the parent in reacting in a conscious and chosen way to child behavior, rather than merely acting on autopilot. Unless the parents contacts the functions of the child's behavior and the affect their child's behavior has for them, in an open and accepting way then they may be reacting—or reactive— in unhelpful ways. Shared psychological presence between parent and child is then essential to implementing behavioral parenting strategies effectively because it is necessary to knowing which strategy to adopt when.

Psychological contact and mental health and well-being

Mindfulness has been found to be linked with mental health and well-being (Baer, 2003; Blanck et al., 2018; Cooper et al., 2018; Perestelo-Perez et al., 2017; Shiyko et al., 2017; Tomlinson et al., 2018; Young et al., 2018). This relationship is likely to be multifaceted. Mindfulness disrupts unhealthy psychological processes including rumination and worrying. Further, psychological contact with be present moment is necessary to be in contact with contingencies available within one's context. Contact with the present moment is important to deriving benefit from a richly reinforcing life—without psychological contact people may not benefit though reinforcement is present.

Maya, Michael and Reo

Maya and Michael seek parenting support with their only child, Reo. Reo is an eight year old diagnosed with high functioning Autism Spectrum Disorder (ASD). Michael and Maya both work full-time, Michael as an engineer and Maya as a nurse.

Maya and Michael seek parenting support due to concerns about Reo's behavior both at school and at home. They report that Reo shows frequent noncompliance at school and at home, and has 'meltdowns' consisting of yelling, screaming and sometimes aggression. They have previously sought assistance from an occupational therapist for sensory issues, emotional regulation and social skills. They have never sought parenting support before. Although there are significant behavioral challenges, Reo is doing well academically and has several friends at school.

(*Continued*)

(Continued)

Discussing the challenges with Maya and Michael, you notice that Maya attributes it all to Reo's ASD. Several times she says that she needs to 'find a way to help him understand.' Michael says that part of the problem is that Reo is a genius who 'won't tolerate stupidity'. He also says that Maya can be 'too soft' and that Reo needs to 'take responsibility for his actions'. It is possible that Michael may have an undiagnosed ASD himself, or at least the broader autism phenotype (autistic traits).

Imagine you could, unseen and unheard, observe a typical, ordinary interaction between Maya, Michael, and Reo. It might be something like this:

Parent–child interaction

Reo is playing with Lego in his bedroom. Michael and Maya are in the kitchen, a recipe book is sitting on the bench. Michael's parents are coming over tonight for dinner. Michael's phone pings and he looks at it, "Damn. Idiots. I've got to answer this."

Maya sighs, "Alright. I'll make a start."

Michael is already walking toward the study, "Thanks."

She gets the vegetables out of the fridge. She glances at the clock and swears under her breath. She runs to the bathroom and runs a bath. Maya calls out to Reo as she walks back to the kitchen.

Maya says in her native tongue, "Reo, honey, it is time for a bath."

"I just want to finish this, please, mum," Reo responds. He continues playing with his Lego.

Maya begins to chop vegetables for dinner. After two minutes she calls out again, "Reo, bath-time!"

"Nearly finished, mum!" Reo answers.

Reo continues playing with his Lego. Maya keeps chopping vegetables. Several minutes pass. Reo completes his project and begins to play with it running through the house swooping his creation up and down. When he gets to the kitchen he pauses and exclaims proudly, "Look what I made!"

Maya glances up from chopping the vegetables, "you are meant to be in the bath."

Reo sighs, "I just wanted to finish this. You didn't even look."

Maya shakes her head, "in the bath now. C'mon."

Reo runs away and Maya continues chopping the vegetables. Although it seems unlikely she chooses to believe for now that Reo has gone to have his bath. In fact, Reo has gone to the study.

Reo exclaims, "Look what I made, dad!"

Michael looks up from the screen: "the TARDIS"

Reo beams "Yep!"

Michael looks back at his email on the screen, "isn't quite right. I'll help you get it right after your bath. Go have a bath."

Reo frowns and zooms out of the room, playing with the Lego TARDIS and making loud noises. As he gets into the living area Maya looks up from chopping vegetables.

(Continued)

(Continued)

Maya shouts, "Reo! You are meant to be having your bath."
Reo turns to his mother and replies in a robot voice, "You will be assimilated."
Maya shakes her head, "Don't talk to me like that, Reo. And get in the bath. We don't have time for this tonight. Grandad and Grandma will be here soon."
"You are ruining my life!" Reo screams.
Maya pauses in chopping the vegetables, "I am not ruining your life. Do not say that, please"
Reo screams even louder, "You are ruining my life!"
Maya looks upset now, "Reo. That's a horrible thing to say. Apologize to me."
Reo yells, "No!" pointing to Bec he says in a perfect Dalek impression "Exterminate! Exterminate!"
"You are not going to exterminate me, Reo" Maya answers.
Reo laughs as he continues to point and say "Exterminate! Exterminate!"
"Stop that," Maya says, "Go and have a bath now please."
Reo screams loudly, "NO!!!"
"Reo, you have to have a bath. We need to get the dirt and germs off your body. Remember, the germs, Reo? You don't want Grandma and Grandad to think you stink do you?"
"NO NO NO!"
"That's it," Maya takes Reo's arm and tries to guide him to the bathroom.
Reo hits Maya while screaming, "I hate you!"
Maya's eyes well with tears and she steps away, "Reo, that's a horrible thing to say. You don't hate Mummy."
Michael stomps out, "Reo! Do not speak to your mother like that. You need to take some responsibility. If you aren't in that bath in the next five seconds you can stay in your bedroom all evening and I'll tell Grandma and Grandad that they can't see you because you've been too naughty."
Reo starts crying, hunched over, face downcast, "I wanna see Grandma and Grandad, Daddy. Please don't tell them I've been naughty. Please, Daddy."
Michael "Well?!"
Reo goes to the bathroom, gets undressed and steps into the bath, still softly crying. Michael follows, standing over him as he gets in.
"Wash yourself all over and get into your pajamas," Michael says firmly.
Michael leaves Reo to it, returning to the kitchen. Maya has dried her eyes and finished chopping the vegetables and meat. She still looks tender as she measures out the rice, putting it into the rice cooker. Michael begins to cook the meal. Reo comes in quietly a few minutes later in his pajamas. His eyes are still red from crying. The silence is deafening.

What's happening for Maya, Michael, and Reo?

Both Maya and Michael could benefit from being more mindful in their parenting. Reo is hungry for *shared* psychological presence, for attuned interaction. Both Maya and Michael missed opportunities to mindfully engage with Reo and

(*Continued*)

(Continued)

meet his needs for connection. Reo began by attempting to engage his parents in a positive and functional way by showing them his Lego TARDIS. But neither Maya nor Michael succeeded in being fully present for him, or in responding to his attempts to negotiate the timing of his bath in an appropriate way. Maya and Michael both gave Reo instructions in a mindless way, without taking into account Reo's perspective and without following through to ensure that the instruction was acted upon. Reo's noncompliance was hence inadvertently reinforced.

Both Maya and Michael show reactive parenting. Maya demonstrated signs of genuine hurt in reaction to Reo's comments. It is possible that her own history influenced the degree of her emotional reaction to what is, after all, the unknowing words of a child who is just trying to lash out in the moment. Greater awareness of her own low-level emotional reactions may have helped her to pause and choose how best to respond rather than to react. Michael's angry reaction to Reo's behavior quickly became harsh parenting behavior. In particular, Michael threatened a consequence (being in his room all evening and not seeing his grandparents) that was unnecessarily harsh and would not have given Reo the opportunity to recover. That is, if followed through, Reo would not have had the opportunity to behave well and be reinforced.

Both Maya and Michael escalated the interaction with Reo. Instead of parenting in a way that enabled Reo to downregulate his own negative emotional state, they escalated and amplified Reo's own emotional reactions and coercive behavior. There were also examples of coercion in Maya and Michael's parenting; specifically, using shaming to attempt to gain compliance. Maya suggests that if Reo doesn't have a bath then his grandparents might think that he stinks and Michael threatens to tell the grandparents that they can't see Reo because he has been too naughty. Context must be taken into account in judging whether or not a particular comment is shaming or an attempt to shame. Cultures and families vary in the extent to which playful mockery may be part of normal and loving interactions. However, Michael's comment certainly, from Reo's reaction, appears to hit home: Reo does react as if he is experiencing shame.

From a clinical RFT perspective, it appears worthwhile to explore what shows up for Maya as she continually gives directions to Reo in a disconnected, nonenforcing way. It may be, perhaps that she has derived relations among enforcing a rule and "too difficult," or "Reo will tantrum," as is often the case in families characterized by coercive interaction. Clearly, the two parents are on quite separate tracks, as there is little coordination across their behavior until it escalates. Supporting both Maya and Michael to, grounded in greater awareness, step back from their unworkable tracks, may help them to more effectively notice the consequences of their actions, and come up with a more helpful, coordinated response. This may require multiple tries, and heavy reinforcement from the clinician to develop over time. However, simple, undefended present moment awareness and curiosity about "what happens next?" is at the heart of it.

How to work with mindfulness clinically

Assessing parental mindfulness

Mindfulness can be assessed by observing the parent–child interaction as well as reflecting on the parent's account. Some signs that the parent is not mindful include:

- The parent fails to notice the child's cues.
- Parenting is reactive, or consequence based, rather than antecedent based. Instead of parenting according to an overarching plan or values, the parent is responding reactively from crisis to crisis.
- The parent responds to the child but there is a lack of full psychological presence or emotional availability to the parent's response.
- The parent is not engaging in adequate self-care, is not planning ahead and setting limits on what they can do broadly.
- There is a disconnect between the parent's reported experience of valued living and their life as understood by an independent observer. For example the parent may be reporting that they aren't living certain values well but when to get a full sense of their behavior day by day, there does seem to be many relevant valued acts.

Simple questioning or prompts

Awareness to the process of mindfulness can be brought through simple discrimination tasks or prompts. For example, you could say to the parent:

- Are you running on autopilot right now?
- Are you in your head or in the room?
- Are you with your child or somewhere else?
- Are you in the past, future or the present?
- Are you noticing your child like a sunset—like something to notice and appreciate—or like a math problem—like something to be solved?

Parents can also get into the habit of asking themselves these questions regularly throughout their day or at certain key times when they want to boost their mindfulness.

Metaphors

The metaphor of the six animals

This is a metaphor that the Buddha himself used to describe mindfulness. Image that six animals—a crocodile, a fox, a dog, a bird, a monkey and a snake—are

(*Continued*)

(Continued)

tired together with rope. Each animal is tied to the other five animals by their tail. If the animals were released like that, what would happen? Each animal would try to return to its habitat, pulling the others along. For a time the strongest would dominate until it falls asleep exhausted and then another animal would have its way. It would be chaos. The six animals represent the six senses (within Buddhist psychology the mental stream—imagining and thinking—is included as a sense). Practicing mindfulness, the Buddha suggested, is taking the knotted end of the ropes that bind that animals together and tying it to a post fixed into the ground. Each animal will still try to get to their habitat, but not even the strongest will succeed. Eventually the animals will become exhausted and give up, lying down on the ground still and quiet.

Meditation

Guided meditations are a key aspect of introducing and practicing mindfulness. For many people full mediations are not going to form part of their regular mindfulness practice, yet, doing a guided meditation in a therapeutic context where it can be debriefed and refined remains an ideal way to introduce mindfulness experientially to a client, ensuring that they fully understand the concept at an experiential level. Once this understanding is in place, it becomes possible to interweave mindfulness into daily living more effectively. It is thus important for ACT therapists to be skilled in facilitating a guided meditation. In order to guide a mindfulness meditation well, practicing the mindfulness yourself at the same time is beneficial. By doing each step yourself, fully and mindfully, as you speak, you naturally pace yourself well, and can learn to guide mindfulness with flexibility to the context.

A taste of mindfulness meditation

Mindfulness of eating or drinking is an excellent way to introduce the concept as well as to bring awareness to how mindful you typically are in your daily life. It is also a good way to practice mindfulness for children and adolescents.

A taste of mindfulness meditation script

Start by getting yourself a piece of food or a drink;
It can be anything you like;
Prepare your snack and find a quiet spot to eat or drink it;
Start by simply looking at it;
Look at it like you've never seen it before;

(Continued)

(Continued)

You might like to imagine you are an alien from another planet, a curious scientist or an adventurous explorer;
Now, explore the food or drink with your other senses;
You might like to touch it gently;
Or hold it in your hand;
Noticing the texture or the temperature;
You might like to smell it.
Now slowly bring the food or drink toward your mouth, noticing any changes in you;
Taste it;
Notice the flavor;
If it is food chew it slowly and carefully;
See if you can notice when you first feel ready to swallow;
Swallow slowly, noticing the sensations of swallowing;
Feel the food or drink moving down into your stomach.

Mindfulness of breathing meditation

Mindfulness of breathing is a classic popular way to practice mindfulness. Breathing is a physical and sensory experience that we are performing constantly. This means that, once we learn to be mindful of our breathing, we can use our breathing as an anchor to promote mindfulness in our daily life. This meditation should be performed in a comfortable but alert posture. For some people that might mean sitting crossed legged on a meditation cushion, or sitting on a chair, or even lying down. Eyes can be closed or open or hooded. If open eyes are preferred then you should rest your eyes on a comfortable focal point, a little below eye level. The advantage of keeping eyes open or hooded is that it allows some light in which helps to prevent sleepiness. The advantage of keeping eyes closed is that it minimizes distractions. It is best to do whichever works best at the time.

Mindfulness of breathing meditation script

Get yourself into a comfortable position.
Your position should feel comfortable, as well as promoting wakefulness at the same time.
Let yourself have a relaxed, comfortable posture.
Settle into it.
You can leave your eyes open, resting on a point of focus.
Or closed.
Or hooded, whichever you prefer.

(Continued)

(Continued)

Let your hands rest gently on your knees or in your lap or in some other comfortable posture.
Allow your mind to settle into the here and now.
Bring your attention to the sensations in your body...
Settle, gently, bring your attention to your breathing.
Notice its rhythm.
The pattern of in.
And out.
In.
And out.
Let your awareness drift to the sensations in your abdomen as you breathe.
Notice that you your abdomen inflates with every in-breath.
And deflates with every out-breath.
If you wish, you can even place a hand on your abdomen to help yourself focus on this sensation.
Inflation.
Deflation.
In.
Out.
Keep your attention on the sensation of breathing.
Try to bring a sense of curiosity or adventure to your awareness.
Explore what it feels like to breathe.
Stay with the sensations in your abdomen as long as you want to.
When you are ready, bring your awareness to the sensations at the tip of your nose.
The cool air rushing in.
The warm air rushing out.
In.
Out.
If you notice that your mind has wandered, that's okay.
It is just what minds do.
Gently bring your awareness back to your breathing.
Allow yourself to gently open to the breathing that is...
Let yourself rest in awareness of your breathing.
When you are ready to end the exercise, do so gently.
Bring your awareness with you back to the full present moment.

Mindful walking meditation

This is a guided meditation of walking and another classic and popular meditation. Walking meditation is a good way of breaking up a long meditation session. Meditating in a sitting posture for an extended time can be uncomfortable. It also has the advantage that, once you've learned to be mindful of walking, you can bring mindfulness to walks that you do in everyday life.

Mindful walking meditation

We want to walk with a comfortable and alert posture.
Start standing with your feet parallel, each foot comfortable under your hips.
Let your knees rest soft and unlocked.
Let your arms hang comfortably at your side or hold them gently, hands together, in front of your body.
Let your eyes rest on a point straight ahead.
Let your mind settle gently into the present moment.
Notice the floor or the ground under your feet.
Prepare to take a step.
Transfer the weight of the body into the one foot, noticing the changing pattern of physical sensations in the legs and the feet as the leg takes over the support of the rest of the body.
Allow the heel of the other leg to rise slowly from the floor, noticing the sensations in your calf muscle.
Allowing the whole of the foot to lift gently.
Staying aware of the physical sensations, slowly move your foot forward, placing it on the floor.
Transfer the weight of the body into this leg.
With the weight transferred allow the other foot to lift.
Move it slowly forward.
Continue to step slowly forward.
Step by step.
Staying aware of the patterns of sensations as you walk.
Aware of the ground beneath your feet.
Move slowly, allowing yourself time to notice each sensation.
If your mind wanders, gently bring your awareness back to the sensations of walking.
Use the ground as an anchor...
Let the ground reconnect you to the present moment.
When you are ready, you can gently walk a little faster, to an easy pace.
Keeping a mindful awareness of each step.
When you are ready to end this exercise do so gently, bringing your awareness to the full present moment.

Antenatal mindfulness meditation

This meditation is adapted from *Becoming Mum* (Whittingham, 2013). It is a mindfulness meditation for pregnancy, focusing on the developing baby.

Antenatal mindfulness meditation script

Get into a comfortable position.
Let your mind settle gently into the present moment.

(*Continued*)

(Continued)

Using your breathing as an anchor.
Bring your attention to your pregnant belly.
You may like to place your hands there.
Notice the weight of your baby inside you...
Notice the feeling of carrying another, of carrying your child.
Notice what your baby is doing.
Is your baby moving? If so, gently bring your attention to baby's movements, to the kicks and turns and rolls.
If your baby isn't moving, notice that baby is quiet at the moment.
You may find that thoughts arise, perhaps distracting thoughts about other things, or perhaps thoughts about your baby. Maybe you find that worried thoughts or guilty thoughts or sad thoughts arise about your pregnancy, your baby or birth. If so, gently let these thoughts go and bring your attention back to your baby as baby is in this moment.
You may find that feelings of love arise, or you may not. Either way, this is fine. See if you can simply be with your baby as baby is right now, without pressure on your baby or on yourself to be any particular way.
As you breathe each breath in, feel your breathing gently swirl around your baby like a caress.
Notice that your body is protecting and caring for your baby as best it can.
Gently bring your awareness back again and again to your baby.
When you are ready to end the exercise, do so gently, bringing your increased awareness of your baby with you into your everyday life.

Mindfulness of baby meditation

This meditation is adapted from *Becoming Mum* (Whittingham, 2013). It is a mindfulness meditation for parents with a baby and it involves focusing mindfully on the baby.

Mindfulness of baby meditation script

Let your mind settle gently into the present moment.
Using your breathing as an anchor.
Allow your attention to focus on your baby.
Perhaps your baby is in your arms or maybe you are watching your baby on the ground in front of you.
Slowly cast your eyes over your baby, noticing the details of baby's body...
Noticing toes, legs, arms and hands, little fingers...
Noticing baby's face.
Really pay attention to your baby, as if you are seeing your baby again for the very first time.

(*Continued*)

(Continued)

If your baby is in your arms, notice the weight of your baby and the feeling against your skin.
If your baby is in front of you, you might like to gently touch your baby, noticing how it feels to connect with touch.
You might like to smell your baby.
Notice your baby's breathing, the gentle rhythm of your baby's in and out breaths.
You might like to gently place your hands on your baby's chest or back to really focus on the breathing.
You may find that thoughts arise—perhaps distracting thoughts about other things, or perhaps thoughts about your baby. Maybe you find that worried thoughts, or guilty thoughts or sad thoughts arise about your baby...
If so, gently let these thoughts go and place your attention back to your baby as baby is in this moment...
You may find that feelings of love arise, or you may not. Either way, this is fine.
See if you can simply be with your baby as baby is right now, without pressure on your baby or on yourself to be any particular way.
If your baby is awake, notice your baby's reactions.
If your baby becomes unsettled or is fussy, it is okay to try to settle baby. As you do so, try to stay aware of your baby, try to be genuinely open to baby's fussiness.
Gently bring your awareness back again and again to your baby...
When you are ready to end the exercise, do so gently, bringing your increased awareness of your baby with you into your everyday life...

Parenting: a mindfulness meditation

This is a mindfulness meditation for being mindful during a parent–child interaction. It is suitable for parents of children of all ages. An ideal time to practice mindful awareness is during child-directed interactions. If you are coaching parenting skills in vivo, then you can also prompt mindfulness during those interactions too. It is helpful to have parents practice this at the beginning of an intervention, daily, for perhaps 5–10 minutes at a time, with the understanding that it is a practice that they should continue throughout their work. Parents can be asked to notice their children "like a sunset," with simple appreciation and tracking of their behavior and emotions, rather than a "math problem," or something to change or be solved.

Parenting: a mindfulness meditation script

As your interaction with your child begins.
Deliberately bring your awareness into the present moment.

(Continued)

(Continued)

You might like to use your breathing, that steady rhythm to anchor you.
Or the feeling of the ground under your feet.
Be here: in the unfolding moment.
Gently let your awareness focus on your child.
Let your child lead the interaction as much as possible.
If your child speaks then listen carefully with an open heart.
Take what your child says lightly and gently.
Let your child lead the conversation.
Let your child lead in any play.
Play within your child's world.
Exploring it with curiosity and openness.
If you become distracted then notice that and bring yourself back to the present moment with your child.
Perhaps re-anchoring yourself in your breathing or the ground under your feet.
Bring awareness to your interaction with your child.
Notice that although you see your child nearly every day.
Your child changes every day.
Recall how much your child has changed already.
The child that you are interacting with right now in this moment will soon be gone forever.
Here is an opportunity to fully appreciate your child as they are in this moment.
Take it.
Be open.
Be open to your child as they are and be open to yourself as you are.
Being open doesn't mean that you have to like everything that your child has done or is doing.
It doesn't mean that everything you think or feel must be positive.
It means holding all of that—your child as they are, and you as you are—gently and openly.
From this open sense of presence, you may find that a sense of connection emerges.
Perhaps you find joyous shared laughter, or spontaneous affection, or mutual understanding.
Or perhaps a playful ambition is realized together.
Connection can be carefree and fun.
It can also be quiet and tender.
Don't force it.
Let it come.
And when it does, notice how it feels to connect to your child.
Really notice how it feels.
As best you can, allow your interaction to come to a natural close.
Let your child lead that too.

(*Continued*)

(Continued)

If you need to bring the interaction to an end, then do so gently.
Bringing yourself back to the full present moment.
Keep the sense of connection with you.

Wake up! A quick mindfulness meditation

This is a quick mindfulness meditation for parents. It should take 2–5 minutes. Once it is learned it can be used in everyday life whenever some mindfulness is needed.

Wake up! A quick mindfulness meditation script

Ground yourself.
Notice the sensation of the ground under your feet.
Anchor yourself in your breathing.
Anchor yourself in its rhythm.
Notice any physical sensations.
Any thoughts.
Any emotions.
If it helps, then name them.
Then, gently, bring your awareness to your child.
Notice your child, just as they are, in this very moment.
Let your awareness rest in the full present moment.
And gently open yourself up to your experience and your child.

Mindfulness within daily life

While full guided meditations within therapy are often the ideal way to initially present mindfulness to a client, so that you can ensure that the client has a full and accurate experiential understanding of the concept, briefer mindfulness exercises are often ideal for practicing mindfulness regularly in daily life. Any activity at all can be an opportunity to practice mindfulness. For parents, practicing mindfulness during interactions with their children including high-risk parenting situations might prove particularly fruitful, for example:

- Mindfulness while feeding your baby.
- Mindfulness when comforting baby during the night or helping your baby fall to sleep.
- Mindfulness when bathing your baby or child.
- Mindfulness during story time.

- Mindfulness while playing with your child.
- Mindfulness for the first interaction after the school day.
- Mindfulness during the family meal.

Mindfulness within daily life for children and adolescents

The concept of mindfulness can also be introduced to children and adolescents and practiced together. When introducing mindfulness with young children parents should remember that the important thing is for children to have an experience of mindfulness, introducing the word or the concept at an intellectual level isn't necessary with young children. Instead, the parent can notice activities that support the child's developing attention and capacity for mindfulness and simply do more of these activities together. For children activities that include physical movement and/or a focus on specific sensations are often enjoyed and are easier focal points for mindfulness. Parents should also have realistic expectations. For young children spending a minute or two practicing mindfulness may be enough. Parents can practice mindfulness themselves of course during these mindful activities. There is no limit on what parents and children can do mindfully together. Parents should be inspired by their own child's interests. Whatever activity parent's choose, it should be introduced and performed in a playful manner. Mindfulness, for children and teenagers, is gentle, playful, and fun. It is not serious business. Some ideas for mindful activities are:

- I spy game—this can be adapted for younger children to be spying for objects of particular colors.
- Mindful listening to sounds, for example to bird calls at the park, waves at the beach, or the sound of a bell.
- Stargazing together, looking for the moon or particular constellations.
- Blowing bubbles together, chasing and popping the bubbles.
- Breathing with a pinwheel and watching it spin.
- Singing or dancing together—for younger children songs with physical actions that they can do with the parent at the same time might be particularly good (e.g., heads and shoulders or open shut them). For older children and teenagers dancing to their favorite music, with the parent supporting the child in noticing the music and noticing the way their body moves.
- Clapping games.
- Yoga poses or postures drawn from martial arts.
- Noticing the sensations of play doh or sand.
- Shadow puppets.
- Watching birds or fish.
- Drawing or coloring in together.
- Painting.

Encouraging home practice

It's important to support the development of a routine practice of mindfulness by addressing any logistical issues that might come up for parents; for example, parents being "too busy," or forgetting to do the practice. It's often helpful to choose a daily activity in which to practice mindfulness, so that it is integrated into routine activities, such as bathing, eating dinner, walking, tidying, etc. Moreover, it's also useful to help parents track antecedents that pull them out of mindful states—like irritation with a child, or feeling stressed. Home practice around mindfulness may include:

- Practicing mindfulness meditation.
- Practicing mindfulness during parent and child interactions.
- Practicing playful mindfulness activities, with parent and child together.
- Pausing, and anchoring in the present moment during everyday life.

Working with Maya, Michael, and Reo

The therapist introduces the concept of mindfulness early on, along with child-centered play. Maya and Michael are encouraged to bring mindfulness to their interactions with Reo, including deliberately practicing mindfulness during a child-centered and playful interaction. Maya and Michael practice this for during the week and are, in this session, discussing their experiences.

Therapist:	So, did you get the chance to practice mindfulness this week?
Michael:	Yeah, we both did.
Therapist:	And what were your experiences like?
Maya:	Well we both found it helpful. Don't you think, honey?
Michael nodding:	We did, yes.
Therapist:	Good. Shall we start with you maybe, Michael? How did you practice mindfulness and what did you find?
Michael:	Well, I go for a run a couple of times a week. So I tried doing that mindfully. I found it helped to clear my mind. I also practiced mindfulness while playing with Reo a couple of times too. I realized that I'm often playing with him but also distracted by other things, running through a problem at work in my head, trying to find a solution. When I just focused on Reo it was more enjoyable. And I think he liked it better too.
Maya:	I thought he was better behaved those days, actually.
Michael:	Yeah, I agree. Though I think we noticed his good behavior more too.
Maya:	Yeah, you are right.
Therapist:	That's really good. And yourself, Maya?

(*Continued*)

(Continued)

Maya:	I mainly focused on that anchoring thing that you showed us. Just pausing, slowing down and noticing my breathing, and then responding. And the mindful play too.
Therapist:	And what did you notice?
Maya:	How much I can just react sometimes. Like I'm all caught up and he just pushes my buttons and before I know it I'm saying and doing things I don't want to do.
Therapist:	Right, the automatic pilot thing?
Maya:	Oh yeah. I'm definitely on automatic pilot a lot. But the mindfulness helps.
Michael:	Manual override.
Maya laughing:	Exactly.
Therapist:	And were you able to use that manual override sometimes? To respond, not react?
Maya:	Yeah, I was. He really hurts me sometimes, you know?
Therapist:	The "I hate you" stuff?
Maya eyes with tears:	Yeah.
Michael:	He doesn't hate you.
Maya:	I know that. I do. But in that moment...
Therapist:	It feels like he does...
Maya:	Oh yes...
Therapist:	And that feeling makes you want to?
Maya:	Lash out right back. Or give him whatever he wants so he loves me again. Damn, that's not good parenting, huh?
Therapist:	The more awareness you have of your autopilot, the more you get to choose what you do.

The therapist continued with a full parenting intervention, integrating both relational and behavioral parenting strategies including emotion coaching, increasing reinforcement for functional behaviors and decreasing reinforcement for dysfunctional and coercive behavior. ACT was woven throughout the parenting intervention. The approach taken was informed by the literature on ASD. Reo has experienced a reduction in meltdowns, noncompliance and aggression, both at home and at school. Michael and Maya are currently focusing on building his emotional regulation and social skills. Michael has started taking Reo to a martial arts class and they are using this experience to introduce the concept of mindfulness to him.

Troubleshooting

Do we have to do mindfulness meditations?

Although scripts for mindfulness meditations and exercises are provided, mindfulness doesn't have to mean doing a specific mindfulness meditation on any regular basis. Doing a guided mindfulness exercise within therapy, and debriefing that exercise together, can be incredibly useful. People can bring preconceived ideas to the concept of mindfulness. As an experiential practice, the only way to truly understand the concept is to try it out, to experience it for yourself. Once your client grasps the concept of mindfulness, understands mindfulness experientially, when it is present and when it is not, they can then practice mindfulness within their daily life in a more relaxed and ad-hoc manner. Instead of doing mindfulness meditations and exercises per se, they might incorporate mindfulness into their daily life by performing particular daily tasks mindfully. For example, a regular walk home from the bus stop might be an opportunity to walk mindfully. For parents, an ideal opportunity to practice mindfulness is while they are interacting with their child.

What if they don't have the time?

Mindfulness does not have to be an additional task. Once the concept of mindfulness is fully grasped by experiencing mindfulness in the therapy context, and debriefing this to ensure that the parent has an accurate understanding, then mindfulness can be practiced by practicing mindfulness of daily activities. Any activity in fact can be done mindfully, and hence any activity can also serve the purpose of mindfulness practice. For parents, practicing mindfulness while interacting with their children may be a particularly fruitful time to practice mindfulness. Parents can also adopt the habit of asking themselves simple discrimination questions: Are you in the room or in your mind?

Is mindfulness and relaxation the same thing?

It is important to ensure that your client doesn't expect mindfulness to be relaxing necessarily. Some of the time, mindfulness exercises bring about a state of relaxation. When people find mindfulness relaxing this is not problematic and it is okay to enjoy that relaxing state. However, it is important to debrief this experience so that the client is not left with the expectation that mindfulness should be relaxing. Mindfulness is just about being mindful. Thoughts may not settle, emotions may not decrease. This is okay. When beginning mindfulness practice you may at first learn just how much you've been living on autopilot. This is okay too. It can be shocking to realize just how mindless you are.

What if parents experience paradoxical reactions to mindfulness or have a history of trauma?

A minority of people experience paradoxical reactions to any activity that may have a relaxing effect. That is, the state of relaxation itself triggers anxiety. This is more common in people with a history of trauma. Through respondent conditioning it is possible for a physiological state of calm or safety to come to function as a threat signal. Although the intention of mindfulness is not relaxation per se, mindfulness may still have the same paradoxical effect. Mindfulness may still be useful to people with trauma histories, including people who experience paradoxical reactions. It is often helpful to begin practicing mindfulness by being mindful of an external focus, as such a visual focus, or a peripheral part of the body such as hands or feet. An external or a peripheral body part focus is less likely to trigger an anxious response as it is removed from the vagal system. It is also possible to practice by initially narrowing attention to a specific focus, a focus that is associated with genuine calm, and then to slowly and gently ease into a more expansive mindful presence. It is like gently and gradually "dipping into" the full experience of the present moment.

Mindfulness with a purpose

Mindfulness is in the service of valued living. It isn't that we "should" be mindful and certainly not that we "should" be mindful all the time. It is about being psychologically present in our lives, to the extent that this helps us to live a life worth living. Mindfulness then is not prescriptive. Even in traditional Buddhist understandings mindfulness is a part of the Noble Eightfold Path, interrelated to and supported by other key elements. It is not an end unto itself.

Four key developmental periods and contact with the present moment

Infancy and contact with the present moment

The establishment of parental sensitivity and responsive parenting, with parenting behavior under the contextual control of child cues is an essential part of the earliest months of infant life. It is, arguably, the single most important parenting task of early infancy. And shared psychological presence is critical. It is necessary for parent and child to exist within the same psychological space in order for the parent to have awareness of child cues and emotional expression.

Ongoing sensitive and responsive parenting fuels child development, especially during infancy. While the child's ability to explore and to respond directly to their environment is contained by their own limited mobility, responsive parenting is like a dose-control system for stimulation, allowing the child's to obtain the right stimulation dose at the right time. Further, responsive parent and baby interactions are the engine of linguistic and social development (for further discussion see Chapter 3: Connect: the parent–child relationship). Shared psychological presence between parent and child is necessary to these interactions. A mindful parent notices their child's gaze and facial expressions and respond accordingly. For example, they might notice their baby looking at a cat and can respond with contextually relevant language, "oh look it's kitty! Hello kitty!" As well as by bringing the baby desired stimulation for example taking baby closer for a better look or helping baby to gently stroke the cat's fur.

Parental mindful awareness and acceptance of parental feelings including stress, frustration, and sadness is necessary to create a space to hold these gently without immediate reactivity, and to instead promote more responsive interactions. Formal mindfulness practice in a traditional sense is often not going to be realistic at this time. However, there are many rich opportunities to integrate mindfulness practice into daily tasks like feeding baby, cuddling baby, or interacting with baby.

Early childhood and contact with the present moment

The emergence of social competence, increased autonomy and mobility of these years can be stressful for parents. During the preschooler years non-compliance and tantrum behavior peak. Children shift from parallel play to more engaged interactive and pretend play in social environments. Parents can promote child mindfulness by scaffolding children's ability to read and effectively respond to social cues, initiate interactions, as well as recognize and regulate emotion. Parental mindful awareness of emotions and shared psychological presence with their child allows them to label and validated child's emotions as well as to use labeled praise to reinforce and shape prosocial behavior. This in turn supports the child's development of relational mindfulness as well as emotional and social development.

This age comes with much anxiety and hope for parents: will my child fit in, do they appear to act like other kids, are they learning, will they be accepted, are they fearful? The child's first experiences outside their initial home environment in kindy or school and the separation anxiety that children normally display can all be challenging emotionally for parents.

Parents may promote the development of attention and mindfulness in their child by jointly doing activities that are fun and require concentration, for example, coloring in together, or popping bubbles or singing songs while performing particular physical actions that go with the songs.

Middle childhood and contact with the present moment

This may be an ideal time for parents to introduce mindfulness to children in an explicit way. Embodied mindfulness practices like yoga or simply practicing mindfulness during physical movement—for example, sports, dance—or a sensationally rich experience may be more enjoyable to children. Mindfulness should be introduced in a playful and fun manner with realistic expectations about how long a child might practice mindfulness for. Just for a couple of minutes may be sufficient.

Adolescence and contact with the present moment

Parents may find ways they can practice mindfulness with their teenager or support their teenage child in cultivating mindfulness practices that suit them.

The teens own interests whether that be a particular sport or music or art can be used as the starting point to discuss and introduce mindfulness practices.

Parents may find it useful to identify a particular opportunity during the day where connection is most likely. Is there child most ready to connect in the first interaction after school? Over a family dinner? Just before bed? When a particular interaction is identified parents can focus on being mindful at that time.

Using mindfulness with specific populations

Parental mental health problems and contact with the present moment

Mindfulness plays an important role as an antidote to rumination and worrying. In addition, without psychological presence you may not benefit from reinforcement that is available within your life and context. For these reasons, mindfulness is an important addition to interventions for both depression and anxiety.

Parental grief and contact with the present moment

Following a loss event, it can be instinctive to want to escape from any reminders of the loss. However, this is often counterproductive, narrowing life and may even increase the risk of depression. With psychological presence in the here and now, the process of grieving can be given full priority. Psychological contact with the reinforcement available within your life as it is maintained, helping to prevent depression.

Childhood externalizing problems and contact with the present moment

Childhood externalizing problems are compounded when the parent acts on autopilot. Instead, they require conscious and deliberate parenting. This begins with accurately tracking the child's behavior, with noticing what happens before and after externalizing child behavior. This requires parental psychological presence. Then the parent needs to implement their planned parenting strategies without getting caught up in reactive parenting. Mindfulness is helpful for this too.

Childhood internalizing problems and contact with the present moment

Mindfulness can support the parent in managing child internalizing problems in a planned and supportive way instead of responding in a reactive way that may encourage child avoidance or other dysfunctional patterns.

Childhood neurodevelopmental disabilities and contact with the present moment

For parents of children with disabilities rules of thumb, even generally useful rules of thumb are more likely to become unworkable in practice. Therefore parents of children with disabilities particularly benefit from being able to accurately track their child's behavior, to notice what happens before and after their child's behavior so that parents can develop an accurate sense of the antecedents and the reinforcers, even if they are idiosyncratic. Mindfulness, a shared psychological presence with the child enables this.

Peer relations and bullying and contact with the present moment

Developing the capacity for shared psychological contact within peer interactions as well as the noticing of one's own internal bodily and emotional reactions and listening to these as signals is part of developing social understanding and social skills.

Marital conflict and contact with the present moment

Just as shared psychological presence with the child can enhance he parent and child relationship by supporting the parent in developing sensitive and responsive parenting, so too can shared psychological presence between partners support and enhance the spousal relationship. That is, with shared psychological presence, you are more likely to notice your partner's bids for care and nurturance, and hence are better posed to meet their needs, strengthening the relationship.

Expressed emotion including critical or intrusive parenting and contact with the present moment

Expressed emotion, critical, hostile, or overly involved parenting is often the result of reactive parenting. That is, parents may be reacting to automatic emotional and behavioral patterns, patterns that they may have learned as children being parented themselves. In developing a new pattern the first step is greater awareness of both internal and external stimuli, to be able to recognize the thoughts, feelings, and behavioral impulses arising and pushing toward reactive parenting, as well as to recognize and track the actual moment-to-moment interaction with the child.

Emotion dismissiveness and contact with the present moment

For a parent to tune in to the emotional needs of their child requires shared psychological presence, it requires that the parent is psychologically present to recognize the child's subtle affective signaling. Without mindfulness, the subtle affective signaling of children can go unrecognized and an emotionally dismissive parenting style may be the result.

Inconsistent, or harsh and punitive parenting and contact with the present moment

Inconsistent, harsh, or punitive parenting can be the result of parenting on autopilot, in a reactive manner. Key to overcoming reactive patterns of behavior is developing greater awareness of internal and external stimuli, recognizing the thoughts feelings and behavioral impulses arising, as well as being able to be psychologically present in the moment-to-moment interaction with the child. Mindfulness is also important to developing accurate tracks of self and child behavior. This tracking is important to recognizing when inconsistent or punitive parenting has developed as well as recognizing that it is not effective.

References

Ainsfeld, E., Capser, V., Nozyce, M., & Cunningham, N. (1990). Does infant carrying promote attachment? An experimental study of the effects of increased physical contact on the development of attachment. *Child Development*, *61*(5), 1617–1627.

Baer, R. A. (2003). Mindfulness training as a clinical intervention: A conceptual and empirical review. *Clinical Psychology: Science and Practice*, *10*(2), 125–143.

Bardacke, N. (2012). *Mindful birthing training the mind body and heart for childbirth and beyond*. New York: Harper One.

Batchelor, S. (2015). *After buddhism rethinking the dharma for a secular age*. Haven, KS: Yale University Press.

Bazzano, A., Wolfe, C., Zylowska, L., Wang, S., Shuster, E., Barrett, C., & Lehrer, D. (2013). Mindfulness Based Stress Reduction (MBSR) for parents and caregivers of individuals with developmental disabilities: A community-based approach. *Journal of Child and Family Studies*, Epub ahead of print.

Beer, M., Ward, L., & Moar, K. (2013). The relationship between mindful parenting and distress in parents of children with an autism spectrum disorder. *Mindfulness*, *4*, 102–112.

Benn, R., Akiva, T., Arel, S., & Roeser, R. W. (2012). Mindfulness training effects for parents and educators of children with special needs. *Developmental Psychology*, *48*(5), 1476–1487.

Blanck, P., Perleth, S., Heidenreich, T., Kroger, P., Ditzen, B., Bents, H., & Mander, J. (2018). Effects of mindfulness exercises as stand-alone intervention on symptoms of anxiety and depression: Systematic review and meta-analysis. *Behaviour Research and Therapy*, *102*, 25–35.

Bogels, S. M., & Restifo, K. (2014). *Mindful parenting: A guide for mental health practitioners*. New York: Springer.

Brach, T. (2003). *Radical acceptance embracing your life with the heart of a Buddha*. New York: Bantam Dell.

Coatsworth, J. D., Duncan, L. G., Greenberg, M. T., & Nix, R. L. (2010). Changing parent's mindfulness, child management skills and relationship quality with their youth: Results from a randomized pilot intervention trial. *Journal of Child and Family Studies*, *19*(2), 203–217.

Coatsworth, D. J., Duncan, L. G., Nix, R. L., Greenberg, M. T., Gayles, J. G., Bamberger, K. T., & Demi, M. A. (2014). Integrating mindfulness with parent training: Effects of the Mindfulness-Enhanced Strengthening Families Program. *Developmental Psychology*, Epub ahead of print.

Conner, C. M., & White, S. W. (2014). Stress in mothers of children with autism: Trait mindfulness as a protective factor. *Research in Autism Spectrum Disorders*, *8*, 617–624.

Cooper, D., Yap, K., & Batalha, L. (2018). Mindfulness-based interventions and their effects on emotional clarity: A systematic review and meta-analysis. *The Journal of Affective Disorders*, *235*, 265–276.

Dawe, S., Harnett, P. H., Rendalls, V., & Staiger, P. (2003). Improving family functioning and child outcome in methadone maintained families: The Parents Under Pressure programme. *Drug and Alcohol Review*, *22*, 299–307.

Dhillon, A., Sparkes, E., & Duarte, R. V. (2017). Mindfulness-based intervetnions during pregnancy: A systematic review and meta-analysis. *Mindfulness*, *8*, 1421–1437.

Dimidjian, S., Goodman, S. H., Felder, J. N., Gallop, R., Brown, A. P., & Beck, A. (2014). An open trial of mindfulness-based cognitive therapy for the prevention of perinatal depressive relapse/recurrence. *Archives of Women's Mental Health*, Epub ahead of print.

Duncan, L. G., Coatsworth, J. D., & Greenberg, M. T. (2009). A model of mindful parenting: Implications for parent–child relationships and prevention research. *Clinical Child and Family Psychology Review*, *12*(3), 255–270.

Dunn, C., Hanieh, E., Roberts, R., & Powrie, R. (2012). Mindful pregnancy and childbirth: Effects of a mindfulness-based intervention on women's psychological distress and well-being in the perinatal period. *Archives of Women's Mental Health*, *15*, 139–143.

Falb, M. D., & Pargament, K. I. (2012). Relational mindfulnes, spirituality, and the therapeutic bond. *Asian Journal of Psychiatry*, *2012*, 351–354.

Gouveia, M. J., Carona, C., Canavarro, M. C., & Moreira, H. (2016). Self-compassion and dispositional mindfulness are associated with parenting styles and parenting stress: The mediating role of mindful parenting. *Mindfulness*, *7*, 700–712.

Harnett, P. H., & Dawe, S. (2012). Review: The contribution of mindfulness-based therapies for children and families and proposed conceptual integration. *Child and Adolescent Mental Health*, *17*(4), 195–208.

Hayes, L. L., & Ciarrochi, J. (2015). *The thriving adolescent*. Oakland, CA: New Harbinger Publications.

Hayes, S. C. (2002). Buddhism and acceptance and commitment therapy. *Cognitive and Behavioral Practice*, *9*(1), 58–66.

Hertz, R. M., Laurent, H. K., & Laurent, S. M. (2014). Attachment mediates effects of trait mindfulness on stress responses to conflict. *Mindfulness*, Epub ahead of print.

Hrdy, S. B. (2011). *Mothers and others*. Cambridge, MA: Harvard University Press.

Irvine, W. B. (2009). *A guide to the good life*. Oxford: Oxford University Press.

Jones, L., Hastings, R. P., Totsika, V., Keane, L., & Rhule, N. (2014). Child behavior problems and parental well-being in famlies of children with autism: The mediating role of mindfulness and acceptance. *American Journal on Intellectual and Developmental Disabilities*, *119*(2), 171–185.

Kabat-Zinn, M., & Kabat-Zinn, J. (1997). *Everyday blessings the inner work of mindful parenting*. New York: Hyperion.

Kang, C., & Whittingham, K. (2010). Mindfulness: A dialogue between Buddism and clinical psychology. *Mindfulness*, *1*(3), 161–173.

Laurent, H. K., Duncan, L. G., Lightcap, A., & Khan, F. (2017). Mindful parenting predicts mothers' and infants' hypothalamic–pituitary–adrenal activity during a dyadic stressor. *Developmental Psychology*, *53*(3), 417–424.

Neece, C. L. (2014). Mindfulness-based stress reduction for parents of young children with developmental delays: Implications for parental mental health and child behavior problems. *Journal of Applied Research in Intellectual Disabilities*, *27*, 174–186.

Parent, J., McKee, L. G., Rough, J. ,N., & Forehand, R. (2016). The association of parent mindfulness with parenting and youth psychopathology across three developmental stages. *The Journal of Abnormal Child Psychology*, *44*(1), 191–202.

Perestelo-Perez, L., Barraca, J., Peñate, W., Rivero-Santana, A., & Alvarez-Perez, Y. (2017). Mindfulness-based interventions for the treatment of depressive rumination: Systematic review and meta-analysis. *International Journal of Clinical and Health Psychology*, *17*(3), 282–295.

Shiyko, M. P., Hallinan, S., & Naito, T. (2017). Effects of mindfulness training on posttraumatic growth: A systematic review and meta-analysis. *Mindfulness*, *8*, 848–858.

Singh, N. N., Lancioni, G. E., Winton, A. S. W., Fisher, B. C., Wahler, R. G., McAleaney, K. M., ... Sabaawi, M. (2006). Mindful parenting decreases aggression, noncompliance and self-injury in children with Autism. *Journal of Emotional and Behavioural Disorders*, *14*(3), 169–177.

Singh, N. N., Lancioni, G. E., Winton, A. S. W., Singh, J., Curtis, W. J., Wahler, R. G., & McAleaney, K. M. (2007). Mindful parenting decreases aggression and increase social behaviour in children with developmental disabilities. *Behaviour Modification*, *31*(6), 749–771.

Stevenson, J. C., Emerson, L. M., & Millings, A. (2017). The relationship between adult attachment orientation and mindfulness: A systematic review and meta-analysis. *Mindfulness*, *8*, 1438–1455.

Surrey, J., & Jordan, J. V. (2012). The wisdom of connection. In C. K. Germer, & R. D. Siegel (Eds.), *Wisdom and compassion in psychotherapy deepening mindfulness in clinical practice*. New York: The Guilford Press.

Tirch, D., Silberstein, L. R., & Kolts, R. L. (2016). *Buddhist psychology and cognitive-behavioral therapy a clinician's guide*. New York: The Guilford Press.

Tomlinson, E. R., Yousaf, O., Vitterso, A. D., & Jones, L. (2018). Dispositional mindfulness and psychological health: A systematic review. *Mindfulness*, *9*, 23–43.

Turpyn, C. C., & Chaplin, T. M. (2016). Mindful parenting and parents' emotion expression: Effects on adolescent risk behaviors. *Mindfulness*, *7*, 246–254.

Vieten, C., & Astin, J. (2008). Effects of a mindfulness-based intervention during pregnancy on prenatal stress and mood: Results of a pilot study. *Archives of Women's Mental Health*, *11*, 67–74.

Walsh, J. J., Balint, M. G., Smolira, S. J. D. R., Fredericksen, L. K., & Madsen, S. (2009). Preciting individual differences in mindfulness: The role of trait anxiety, attachment anxiety and attentional control. *Personality and Individual Differences*, *46*, 94–99.

Whittingham, K. (2013). *Becoming mum*. Brisbane: Pivotal Publishing.

Whittingham, K. (2014). Parents of children with disabilities, mindfulness and acceptance: A review and a call for research. *Mindfulness*, *5*(6), 704–709.

Whittingham, K. (2016). *Mindfulness and transformative parenting. Mindfulness and Buddhist-derived approaches in mental health and addiction* (pp. 363–390). Cham: Springer International Publishing.

Wilson, K. G., & Dufrene, T. (2009). *Mindfulness for two an acceptance and commitment therapy approach to mindfulness in psychotherapy*. Oakland, CA: New Harbinger Publications, Inc.

Young, K. S., van der Velden, A. M., Craske, M. G., Pallesen, K. J., Fjorback, L., Roepstorff, A., & Parsons, C. E. (2018). The impact of mindfulness-based interventions on brain activity: A systematic review of functional magnetic resonance imaging studies. *Neuroscience and Biobehavioral Reviews*, *84*, 424–433.

Chapter 10

Flexible languaging

Chapter Outline

What is flexible languaging? **254**
How we learn language: the development of our symbolic system 254
Flexible languaging, rule-governed behavior, and fusion 257
DNA-V model 259
How does flexible languaging apply to parent–child interaction? **260**
Flexible languaging and workable parenting 260
Parenting rules 260
Supporting flexible languaging 263
Supporting the development of helpful tracking and proto-values 263
Working with flexible languaging clinically **268**
Signs of parental inflexible languaging 268
Metaphors 269
Experiential exercises 271
Meditations 272
Mindfulness awareness, parent, and child 273
Flexible languaging games for parent and child 274
Taking parents from pliance to tracking 275
Taking children from pliance to tracking 276
Encouraging home practice 277
Troubleshooting **280**
Defusion is not about whether the thoughts are true or false 280
What if defusion doesn't work or feels invalidating? 280
Four key developmental periods and flexible languaging **280**
Infancy and flexible languaging 280
Early childhood and flexible languaging 281
Middle childhood and flexible languaging 281
Adolescence and flexible languaging 282
Using flexible languaging with specific populations **282**
Parental mental health problems and flexible languaging 282
Parental grief and flexible languaging 282
Childhood externalizing problems and flexible languaging 283
Childhood internalizing problems and flexible languaging 283
Childhood neurodevelopmental disabilities and flexible languaging 283
Peer relations and bullying and flexible languaging 283
Marital conflict and flexible languaging 284
Expressed emotion including critical and intrusive parenting and flexible languaging 284
Emotion dismissiveness and flexible languaging 284
Inconsistent, or harsh and punitive parenting and flexible languaging 284
References **284**

Acceptance and Commitment Therapy. DOI: https://doi.org/10.1016/B978-0-12-814669-9.00010-2

© 2019 Elsevier Inc. All rights reserved.

"When I use a word," Humpty Dumpty said in rather a scornful tone, "it means just what I choose it to mean—neither more nor less."

"The question is," said Alice, "whether you can make words mean so many different things."

"The question is," said Humpty Dumpty, "which is to be master—that's all."

Lewis Carroll, *Through the Looking Glass*

Words!
The way is beyond language,
For in it there is
No yesterday
No tomorrow
No today.

Seng-tsan, *Verses on the Faith Mind*

A little nonsense now and then is cherished by the wisest men.

Roald Dahl, *Charlie and the Chocolate Factory*

What is flexible languaging?

From an relational frame theory (RFT) perspective, language and symbolic thought, so characteristic of our species, is underpinned by *derived relational responding* (see Chapter 4, Shape: building a flexible repertoire, for a full discussion). Importantly, derived relational responding must be learned through multiple interactions with other languaging humans. For humans, language and social development go hand in hand.

How we learn language: the development of our symbolic system

The acquisition of language is a developmental process that begins in utero. Even before birth, the human fetus hears voices around them, and learns to recognize both particular voices and the phonemes within their language (Field, 1990). Human infants and their caregivers typically show *attuned* interactions—contingent interactions of psychological connection including protoconversations with conversational turn-taking between a speaking adult and a babbling infant (Field, 1990; Hrdy, 2011; Mesman, van Ijzendoorn, & Bakermans-Kranenburg, 2009). From these attuned interactions infants develop joint attention, or the ability to follow their parents' gaze, and are initiated into the symbolic world (Baldwin, 1993a, 1993b; Baldwin, Markman, Bill, Desjardins, & Irwin, 1996; Farrant & Zubrick, 2011; Williams, Whiten, Suddendorf, & Perrett, 2001). For example, a mother looks up at the night sky and points exclaiming, "Wow! The moon is beautiful and full tonight!" The infant looks up, following the mother's gaze, and is reinforced with rich stimulation and a joyful shared experience. "Yes!" the mother might add, reinforcing it further, "look at that *moon*!"

At around the age of 18 months, children learn to coordinate (or more simply put, to understand as "same" or "equivalent") the relation between words and their referents; for example, the spoken word "cat" is the same as an actual cat (Lipkens, Hayes, & Hayes, 1993). Across multiple interactions, such as the example of a mother and her baby looking at the moon above, parents both teach specific words, and *parents reinforce the behavior of deriving relations itself.* A recent systematic literature review confirmed that language-rich interactions with caregivers in the first 3 years of life predicts language and cognitive development (Zauche, Thul, Mahoney, & Stapel-Wax, 2016). Both the quantity and the quality of language exposure is key, including the quantity of words, lexical diversity, linguistic and syntactical complexity, intonation, and prosody. Further, an interactive context of caregiver responsiveness and positive regard supports the learning of language. Reading, singing, and storytelling all offer additional means of rich language exposure.

Derived relational responding explodes at about 27 months, when children learn increasingly complex patterns of derived relational responding, such as relating stimuli in terms of bigger/smaller (comparison), different than (distinction), and self-other (deictic) relations (Hayes, Barnes-Holmes, & Roche, 2001). Furthermore, once things come to be related, or joined in a *relational frame*, they tend to share psychological properties. If a preschooler likes Suzie because Suzie is nice, and Pat is Suzie's friend, that preschooler might also have positive feelings for Pat, even though they have never played together. The technical term for this phenomenon is *transformation of function*. An experience that has previously been neutral can suddenly take on new attractive or aversive qualities when related to something else. For instance, if a child perceives a parent as angry, and anger is related to the parent failing to attend to the child, the parent's expression of anger alone may elicit the child's annoyance, or in operant terms, evoke a child's oppositionality (Backen Jones, Whittingham, Coyne, & Lightcap, 2016). In this way, elements in a "relational frame" come to have particular psychological functions, or meanings, based on an individual's particular learning history, or context (Hayes, Strosahl, & Wilson, 2003).

It is no coincidence that the explosion of language within the preschool years coincides with the development of pretend play, as it also involves *symbolic* relations. Pretend play is engaged in with enthusiasm and delight by children the world over, provided there is sufficient opportunity (Lancy, 2015). During pretend play children act out adult roles, perform everyday activities and going beyond this, play out roles and activities from fictional depictions and from their own imagination. As symbolic thinking continues to develop, preschool children develop the capacity for joint play, playing with another within a pretend world of joint imagining. Doing so requires both the ability to respond to symbolic stimuli as if they were real phenomena, and the capacity to be flexible, adapting to the input of the play partner. Other forms of pretense also develop in the preschool years, such as fiction. At around age 4, children develop theory of mind, or the ability to imagine what others might be thinking and feeling as distinct from their own thoughts and feelings. Oral story-telling is probably as ancient as our species itself. And to the oral storytelling tradition we have added many variations of fiction: plays, novels, poetry, short stories, opera, television shows, movies, and role-player gaming. Through fictional worlds we learn, take other perspectives, explore new ideas, imagine possible futures, explore complex moral questions, and have fun. Fiction is not trivial: stories can cultivate perspective-taking and reduce prejudice, ultimately having real societal effect (Vezzali, Stathi, Giovannini, Capozza, & Trifiletti, 2015). Fiction plays an important part in our lives across the lifespan.

Into middle childhood, the mastery of specific relational frames is related to educational success in specific domains. Many derived relations including spatial (e.g., under), measurement (e.g., bigger), and ordinal (e.g., first) are foundational to mathematics (Rudd, Lambert, Satterwhite, & Zaier, 2008). Repeated exposure to spatial, measurement, ordinal, and other mathematics-relevant relational frames is considered to be a critical part of early education, and is called math-mediated language within the educational community. Further, language development and socioemotional competence are linked, that is, children navigate their social, emotional, and moral world through language and symbolic thinking (Eisenberg, Spinrad, & Sadovksy, 2006).

As children approach adolescence, derived relations become increasingly complex. Adolescents develop increasing autonomy in the midst of a developmentally driven emotional storm that includes a greater tendency toward risk-taking and sensation-seeking (Blakemore & Choudhury, 2006; Committee on the Science of Adolescence, 2011). The ability to derive relations among social (how am I doing in relation to others), spatial (does this behavior work at home vs at school vs at my job vs within my peer group), temporal (what does my past behavior teach me about how to behave in the future?), and deictic (how do I feel about me when I'm engaged in this behavior? Is this behavior consistent with the person I want to be?) contexts is critical to the development of mindful, effective exploration of the world, as well as a robust, flexible sense of self.

The research on *derived relational responding* to date supports this account of language and symbolic development. Derived relational responding strongly predicts intelligence (Belisle, Dixon, & Stanley, 2018; Cassidy, Roche, & Hayes, 2011; McLoughlin, Tyndall, & Pereira, 2018; Vizcaino-Torres et al., 2015). In addition, consistent with expectations, significant differences between the relational repertoires of typically developing children and children with autism have been confirmed (Kent, Galvin, Barnes-Holmes, Murphy, & Barnes-Holmes, 2017). Further, training in relational framing of hierarchy (A is a member of B or A is a type of B) and containment (A contains B or B is inside A) enhances classification abilities in young (5–7 year olds) children (Mulhern, Stewart, & McElwee, 2018). An online relational frame training program "SMART" was piloted with eight educationally challenged children aged between 8 and 12 years. After completing the program, the average IQ of the children shifted from 82 (Low Average range) to 96 (Average range); a gain of 14 IQ points (Cassidy, Roche, Colbert, Stewart, & Grey, 2016). Recently, a randomized controlled trial compared SMART to an active control of a computerized coding program in 28 children (10–11 years old). Significant effects of SMART were found in cognitive abilities and educational achievement as measured by intelligence and academic achievement tests the WISC and the WIAT, with an average rise in full-scale IQ of eight points (Hayes, & Stewart, 2016). This demonstrates that understanding language and symbolic development through an RFT lens may improve our ability to support symbolic development.

Flexible languaging, rule-governed behavior, and fusion

Our capacity for languaging leads to our ability to engage in rule-governed behavior, or behavior following verbal rules. Rule-governed behavior includes *tracks*—verbal rules that track the consequences of actions—and *pliance*—verbal rules-following under the control of socially-mediated consequences. Pliance can lead to rigid, inflexible behavior focused on winning approval that is insensitive to the direct contingencies and unworkable in the long-term. Tracking is generally more workable than pliance as it is focused on the context and direct contingencies. However, tracking too can be problematic if it is focused on the short term consequences only, if the tracks are incorrect or untestable or if the track doesn't fit with the person's current context (for a detailed explanation, see *Shape: Cultivating a Flexible Repertoire*). Parents need to be supported in learning how to track effectively, how to develop effective tracks, how to judge when a particular track is not workable, and how to judge when a particular track does not suit their context. That is, flexible languaging also includes problem-solving, judging, reasoning, and evaluating *effectively*, and being able to change your mind at a future date. Parents can support children in learning how to *track* rather than just *ply* by giving their child rules that educate the child about how the world works, rather than simply voicing parental approval and disapproval. For example, if a child makes a mess, and his mother responds by verbally voicing her disapproval of mess-making, this is likely to develop rule-following functioning as pliance ("don't make a mess otherwise people get angry"), whereas if the mother responds by calmly saying that the consequence of making a mess is that the mess needs to be tidied up and ensuring that the child does tidy up then this is likely to develop rule-following functioning as tracking ("if you make a mess then you have to tidy it up").

Cognitive fusion refers to when behavior is under the control of the derived properties of the stimuli (or verbal rules), rather than direct contingencies (Hayes et al., 2003). With fusion, we respond to words or thoughts as literal truths, as "the real thing." If I've had a frightening experience with a spider, then *thoughts* of spiders may have some of the same psychological functions for me, for example, they may evoke increased arousal, the emotion of fear or distaste, and the urge to avoid, or not think about, spiders. With cognitive fusion, behavior may become inflexible as the individual becomes insensitive to the context. For example, a parent may persist in efforts to "punish" a specific misbehavior, because "bad deeds must be punished" without noticing that the misbehavior is not decreasing in frequency over time, or that the misbehavior only occurs in specific contexts, suggesting that prevention is possible. Memories may also be experienced with all the psychological reality of the event happening in the here and now. For example, memories of a traumatic birth may be experienced as if they were literally happening in the present moment. Even thoughts about the future—"what if my child should die"—may have some of the psychological impact of the actual event.

As cognitive fusion can become problematic, *defusion*—the disruption of cognitive fusion— can promote psychological flexibility. Defusion involves decreasing the control of verbal rules and instead bringing behavior under the control of direct contingencies within the context (Hayes et al., 2003). With defusion, thoughts are experienced *as thoughts* not as literal truths. Importantly this is not about whether or not the thoughts are true. Even undisputedly true thoughts, as such "I am going to die" may be experienced from a fused (as a literal reality in the present moment) or a defused (as a thought) perspective. Defusion involves cultivating distance from thoughts by focusing on the *process* rather than the *content* of thinking. It also involves a broadening of attention to notice the physical world and cultivating sensitivity to the environment.

Flexible languaging is about becoming aware of the benefits and the costs of fusion, when it is workable and when it is problematic and being able to flexibly shift from fusion to defusion. This ability involves being aware of thoughts without feeling compelled by them. It also involves the ability to discriminate when to adhere to a rule (fusion) and when to hold that rule lightly (defusion) across particular contexts. For example, when you are absorbed in a good book you are responding psychologically to the words on the page as if they were real—you may see the glowing sunset in your mind's eye or feel the emotional twists and turns of the narrative, or flinch with the character during a fight scene, or even find yourself a changed person by the end of the story. However, you may, should the physical world require it of you, put the book down in order to attend to a pot that is boiling over, or siblings arguing. You may put it down with regret, certainly, but you don't *get stuck*. With flexible languaging, you can allow yourself to become fused with a verbal experience, or choose to step back from your thoughts and hold them lightly, depending on what will work best for you in a particular situation.

One way to support the development of flexible languaging is through play. For example, a 5-year-old child gets onto all fours and announces, "I am a cat! Meow!" His parent responds with playful fusion, "Oh, hello kitty" she says, scratching his ears and patting his head as he meows. She plays with kitty throwing a ball and gives kitty a saucer of milk. Eventually, she pushes the boundaries of fusion playfully, juxtaposing the symbolic and the physical world, by offering the "kitty" actual cat food (knowing that he will reject it in disgust). Parent and child laugh together, the child's symbolic world thoroughly explored, including its limits. Another playful way of exploring flexible languaging is linguistic nonsense. Children typically take great delight in linguistic nonsense and hence it is commonly found in children's literature, media, and songs. My grandfather (Koa) was highly skilled in the art of using linguistic nonsense to amuse children. One of his favorites was this koan-like phrase: if an egg and a half laid a chook and a half in a day and a half, what time would it be ("chook" is Australian slang for chicken)? Through linguistic nonsense children refine their relational framing skills and find the boundaries of language, where language breaks in down attempting to describe the physical world.

DNA-V model

In the DNA-V model (Hayes & Ciarrochi, 2015), flexible languaging is found in the advisor. Flexible languaging includes developing tracks (rather than simply pliance), and developing tracks that are true and workable, grounded in evidence and critical reasoning, as well as developing the capacity to flexibly update tracks with new information or experience. Crucially, flexible languaging requires that you can recognize when you are fused, when you are defused, and the workability of each in the moment. It requires that you can recognize when you've become stuck in fusion and shift. Within the DNA-V model, this means being able to notice when you've become stuck with the advisor, and being able to shift to discoverer or noticer, to engage with your thoughts or the world for the purpose of discovery with curiosity. Play and creative pretense are good examples of how we can flexibly shift from fusion to defusion and back again with awareness.

How does flexible languaging apply to parent–child interaction?

Flexible languaging and workable parenting

Being able to language flexibly is supportive of developing a flexible, workable parenting style including: recognizing unworkable fusion, being able to shift to defusion and developing workable tracks. Dysfunctional parenting styles, such as authoritarian or permissive parenting, are both rigid in different ways. Even inconsistent parenting ironically is underpinned by a rigidity of thought: the parent is often fused with the idea that nothing will work with their child.

Parents may become fused with many ideas, thoughts, or rules that may undermine workable parenting. For example: the child as aversive, that the child can't cope with anxiety, that the child's negative emotions are deserving of punishment, with attributions for the child's behavior or even with the child's expressed thoughts (Coyne & Cairns, 2016; Johnston & Freeman, 1997). For example, when children say things like "I hate you" a fused parent might take that literally—as their child literally hating them—whereas a defused parent might take that as "I'm hurting," "I'm angry," or even "please listen." Defusion also helps parents to hold attributions like "he is doing it to annoy me" or "she is just like her mother" or even "this is all my fault" lightly. In other words, such attributional thoughts may be present, but the parent can still take the most effective actions in the long term, without getting stuck in unworkable attributions.

The lack of sensitivity to context that fusion creates may mean that parents are unaware of mismatches between their child's development and their expectations of the child. For example, a parent who expects a young child to sit quietly for a lengthy period of time without toys or snacks or a parent who perceives their child's increasingly private manner in adolescence as sneaky, suspect, or a rejection of their parents. This can also be apparent if children develop ways of living or thinking that are different from their parents. For example, migrants can easily view their children's acculturation to the new country as oppositionality and a rejection of the parents.

Rigidity and fusion may even be present in parent's initial agenda when they seek help, as parents are often, in seeking help, asking for a new set of rules to follow. Of course, some parenting rules—"they are probably doing it for attention so ignore it" are better than others "spare the rod and spoil the child"—yet, if we simply give parents better rules without supporting the cultivating of a flexible, experimental approach to parenting, we may not have fully supported the parent's long-term resilience.

Parenting rules

Contemporary parents are saturated with parenting rules from a variety of sources: health professionals, school, family, friends, media, and cultural expectations. The problems with parenting rules that are false—for example, "spare the rod and spoil the child"—are obvious. But even an evidence-based parenting rule may lead to challenges if the parent fuses with the rule, if parental rule-following is functioning as pliance or if the parent does not recognize specific situations when that rule is unworkable. For example, the parenting rule "they are probably doing it for attention, so just ignore it" is, as parenting rules go, quite a good one. However, if a parent is fused with this parenting rule so that they are insensitive to context, they are at risk of missing the kinds of subtleties of contingency that no pithy rule can capture. For example, they might miss opportunities for prevention by failing to notice that their children engage in attention-seeking misbehavior in specific contexts: when they have little stimulation or attention; for example, when they are expected to wait quietly for a lengthy period of time. Without providing children with a stimulating context and rich in reinforcement for appropriate behaviors with developmentally appropriate expectations, ignoring of misbehavior may not be effective. In addition, child misbehavior is not always operating under the contingency of parental attention. Parents fused with the rule may fail to notice when their child's behavior has a different function. So, while evidence-based parenting rules may be helpful, their usefulness breaks down if parents are not also able to look to the context and see what works.

Many of the evidence-based parenting rules are worded in absolutist ways that may support pliance (rule-following for social approval) and build an insensitivity to context into the rule itself; for example "breast is best." While it is true that breastfeeding is the better alternative at a population level, this framing elicits pliance around winning social approval as a good mother and is insensitive to aspects of the context that may be relevant to individual decisions around infant feeding. Evidence-based parenting rules may also give a false understanding of the dose–response relationships. For example, eating guidelines, such as "eat two servings of vegetables and one serving for fruit per day" for 4–7 year olds, fail to give an accurate sense of the dose–response relationship between fruit and vegetable consumption and health. In fact, each additional serving of fruit or vegetable gives a health benefit with *greater* health gains per every additional serving at the lowest level of consumption, and diminishing gains for every additional serving (Wang et al., 2014). That is, if you are the parent of a 4-year-old fussy eater and you can shift your fussy eater from eating little to no fruit or vegetables to reliably eating one serve per day then that is a change worth making, even though you are still falling well short of the guidelines. Yet this may not be clear to a parent fused with the dietary guidelines who may instead feel that a fail is a fail and hence, give up alogether.

The parenting rules, taken together, are also contradictory. This is the case even when we focus on rules from "reliable" sources such as health professionals. Parents, for example, will hear contradictory advice from health professionals on infant sleep. Is cosleeping (bedsharing) safe or dangerous? Is night waking in babies normal or something to take action on? Is falling asleep on a feed normal or something to take action on? And when should action be taken, after 6 months or from birth?

Some contradictions, such as the controversy around infant sleep, are obvious but others are subtle and not necessarily apparent to parents. For example, many mothers in Western countries try to simultaneously follow the rules, "breast is best" and "never bedshare." In fact, these two rules are contradictory for many mothers in practice, together creating an unworkable situation such as an exhausted and sleep-deprived breastfeeding mother struggling to stay awake during yet another night feed, as the gentle calm of oxytocin laps at her brain and her own biology, both the sleep homeostat and her circadian rhythm, coax her to sleep. Unsurprisingly, the literature on sleeping and feeding behavior shows that bedsharing and breastfeeding are highly correlated (Kendall-Tackett, Cong, & Hale, 2011, 2012). For many women, breaking one of the two rules is a biological inevitably. Women who fight to keep to both rules perfectly often end up falling asleep with their baby on a chair or a lounge, exactly the situation in which cosleeping has been shown to be most dangerous. Many women live through this struggle and entirely blame themselves, feeling great shame in fact, never questioning the workability of the combination of rules they attempted to follow.

Parenting rules may also lure parents in with the false promise of certainty, a promise that a parent can "construct" a specific child, "build" the child to fit their plan. At times, parenting rules may function similarly to positive delusions, such as just world theory. Just world theory is the belief that good things happen to good people; bad things happen to bad people (Hafer & Begue, 2005). The simplistic rule hidden within parental fusion with rules is this: *good parents produce good children*. More than that, that parents can build not only a "good" child, but the child they want. Like other positive delusions it offers psychological protection of a sort, right up to the point when it doesn't, because the false promise is not fulfilled. Perhaps, this is why so many parents actively seek parenting rules, because the rules promise that if we follow them correctly, our children will be fine and we will remain in control, the diligent builder, constructing exactly the kind of child we want to have.

So, what's the alternative to fusion with parenting rules? The alternative is taking an experimental, *flexible* approach to parenting, discovering what works and holding ideas about parenting, self, and child lightly. Rules may still be followed at times, but they are held lightly and their workability in the specific contexts in which the parent and the child find themselves is questioned. This workable parenting approach involves giving up control—which is really terrifying for many parents. Of course, the control is, in fact, an illusion, but giving up that illusion is still frightening.

Supporting flexible languaging

Parents, through interaction, support their children both in the development of rich relational framing abilities and in the ability to language flexibly. It is clear that parent–child interactions rich in language predict later language development and intelligence (Hart & Risley, 1995; Zauche et al., 2016) and that specific types of language exposure predict child competence in specific domains; for example, mathematics or emotional understanding.

Parents can also support children in developing a flexible stance toward language. Parents can model defusion, in how they interact with their child's expressed thoughts. By responding to a child's shouted "I hate you!" by focusing on the needs and distress under the words, rather than taking the words literally, parents model a defused stance. The flexibility of language can also be modeled and practiced through play and playful interactions.

Play and fiction both involve flexibly shifting between fusion and defusion. There are rich opportunities for playful engagement with the limitations of language that naturally occur during playful interactions. We have suggested a number of games later in the chapter. However, the capacity is endless. General silliness and nonsense—exactly the kind of stuff that makes children laugh—is perfect. Putting a nappy in your head and insisting that it is a hat, pretending that you can't pronounce a common word until your child, giggling, shouts it at you, insisting that the cat going to be cooking dinner tonight, or getting down on the floor and saying that it is your turn to be the baby. Flexible languaging in the form of nonsense is also to be found in children's literature, media and songs.

Supporting the development of helpful tracking and proto-values

Life at school and home is guided by rules. Rules keep children safe from threats that they are not yet capable of understanding. "Brush your teeth morning and night," for example, protects children from tooth decay, a long-term consequence that a young child has no direct experience with and cannot fully understand the implications of. Rules also allow homes and schools to run smoothly. Without "put up your hand before speaking in class" or some similar rule, no classroom could function. Rules (from parents, school, and society) coupled with adult supervision also create a safe space for children in which developmentally appropriate risk-taking and experimentation may be freely engaged in without long-term repercussions. In other words, the boundaries of adult-given rules, which a child is probably following as pliance (in order to gain socially-mediated consequences specified in the rule) can create a safe space for experimentation and the discovery of tracks (rules about the world) and proto-values. This is particularly important during the preschooler years and during adolescence, two developmental periods when free experimentation and exploration is developmentally crucial.

During the preschool years this may involve giving children a physically safe space in which to play (i.e., removing unsafe objects from physical reach), with direct guidance about simple matters of safety and getting along socially (e.g., "wait your turn"), with adults always physically close and watching. Within that safe space, toddlers can then explore freely. The direct guidance and simple rules ("take your turn"), although likely functioning as pliance, create the boundaries of a safe space in which toddlers can explore and hence learn both tracks ("if you throw something it might break") and proto-values (enjoyment of animals reflected by parents saying "you love birds, don't you?").

During adolescence, it is important that adolescents have the ability to explore, with parents psychologically available with mentorship and guidance when needed. The laws and customs of wider society can be protective of adolescents or not. For example, how we manage issues of online safety and digital eternity, or the availability of adolescent friendly social events and activities, laws around licenses for driving cars, and the ability to purchase alcohol as well as how these laws are policed. In effect, society can provide adolescents with a similar safe space to what parents provide for toddlers—a space of open experimentation with the most potentially dangerous aspects removed or controlled. Where wider society doesn't sufficiently provide a safe space parents must delicately balance allowing for risk-taking with sufficient guidance and protection. Hopefully, adolescents have internalized some of the parent-given (or derived) rules and can take appropriate and mindful risks in order to learn their way in the world. As with toddlers, a safe space to explore, even if it involves following some rules as pliance, allows in the discovery of tracks and values.

Parents can also parent in a way that supports the development of tracking, rather than pliance or counterpliance. Harsh punitive discipline and lax discipline practices—discipline where the focus is on parental approval or disapproval—supports pliance or counterpliance (rule-following or breaking in order to gain social approval or disapproval). Managing problem behaviors with positive parenting strategies—discipline where the focus is in the real-world consequences of behavior—is more likely to support the development of tracking in children (following rules that specify the real-world consequences of behavior). Parents can also support tracking development by sharing their own observations of the consequences of specific behaviors. This needs to be done in an open, honest, and nonpunitive way. For example, if a parent says, "Never lie. Lying is bad" they are not supporting tracking as no consequences are apparent (apart from the parental disapproval). If the parent attempts to support tracking with, "If you lie, you'll just get caught and no one likes liars," then the parent's rule might be contradicted by direct experience. You don't *always* get caught in lies. And some liars are well liked. Instead, the parent could try to honestly track the real consequences by saying something like, "Lying isn't always bad. Sometimes we might lie to protect someone, or to spare someone's feelings. Sometimes that works out okay, or even for the best. Sometimes you might lie to get something for yourself and you might get away with it. But here's the problem with lying. If you are lying a lot, especially if you are lying to get things for yourself, then you will probably get caught at some point. And when that happens, people won't trust you anymore. For example, there are lots of things I let you do, without checking up on you, because I trust you. But if I couldn't trust you, I would check up on you a lot more, or just say no to certain things. I don't want our relationship to be like that. It is better if we can basically trust each other."

Aoife, Ciara and Niamh

Aoife and Ciara are mothers to Niamh, who is currently 2 and a half years old (or 2 years and 3 months corrected age). Niamh was conceived via sperm donation. There were some challenges in conceiving a viable pregnancy, with both Aoife and Ciara attempting to conceive in order to increase their chances and both initially experiencing a first trimester miscarriage several months apart. When Aoife conceived a viable pregnancy (Niamh) they decided to simply persist with that pregnancy, and for Ciara to carry their second child in several years' time. They are currently seeking fertility assistance to conceive their second child. Both Aoife and Ciara experienced significant grief following the miscarriages.

Niamh was born prematurely at 27 weeks gestational age. She spent the first 3 months of her life in hospital in the neonatal intensive care unit (NICU). Aoife describes this time as "harrowing." Niamh was diagnosed with cerebral palsy 6 months ago. She has hemiplegia, that is, she experiences motor impairment in one arm and leg only (her right). She is able to walk and her language development is within normal limits given her corrected age. She receives therapy from a physiotherapist and an occupational therapist.

Aoife scores high on anxiety but within the normal range for depression. Ciara scores in the mild range for both anxiety and depression. Ciara explains that since they began to talk about conceiving a second child, she is grieving deeply again for their previous losses. She is also feeling anxious about another loss or another premature birth. She reports that in the past month she has woken several times from a nightmare about experiencing another miscarriage. Aoife says that she is worried about Niamh. She explains it like this, "Every moment I'm not doing something with her to help her I'm thinking: should I be? I do a lot for Niamh. We both do. But how do we know when it is enough?"

Imagine you could, unseen and unheard, observe a typical, ordinary interaction between Aoife, Ciara, and Niamh. It might be something like the following.

Parent–child interaction

Aoife, Ciara, and Niamh are in the living room together on a weekend morning. Aoife and Ciara have ensured there are plenty of toys out for Niamh to play

(*Continued*)

(Continued)

with. Ciara is opening their mail and making a pile of bills to be paid, while Aoife sips at her morning cup of coffee and watches Niamh.
Niamh points at her dog toy, "doggie"
Aoife smiles at her, "Yes, doggie"
Ciara speaking to Aoife, "We have to pay the electrician too. Don't let me forget that."
Aoife nods, "I won't. It is on my email."
Niamh points to the dog toy again, "Look, doggie."
Aoife smiles, "Look, doggie."
Niamh speaks again, "Look, ma doggie"
Aoife smiles, "Yes your doggie. Woof woof"
Niamh giggles.
Aoife gets onto all fours on the floor and says playfully, "Woof woof woof woof."
Niamh laughs loudly. Niamh picks up the doggie with her left hand only, moving it on the ground like it is walking she starts to say, "Woof."
Aoife frowns and quickly moves to Niamh. She physically takes Niamh's right hand and places it on the dog toy so that Niamh is holding it in both hands, "No, Niamh, both hands remember."
Niamh grimaces slightly and visibly pulls back a little.
Aoife smiles, "Woof, woof."
Niamh drops the dog toy.
Aoife says "Oh aren't we going to play with doggie anymore?"
Niamh shakes her head. She walks toward a toy box filled with dolls. As she's looking in the toy box, Aoife moves up behind her and physically corrects her posture without saying anything. Niamh accepts this wordlessly.
Niamh opens the toy box and gets out a doll. She holds the doll using her left hand and with her right hand curled, "There, there, bebe."
Without speaking Aoife physically uncurls Niamh's right hand and positions it so that it is more involved in holding the doll, "Good girl, Niamh. Holding with both hands."
Niamh says "Feed, dolly" and, continuing to use both hands, puts the doll into a toy high chair. She begins to get toy plates, food, and cutlery out of another toy box using her left hand. Again, Aoife corrects how Niamh is manipulating the toys, encouraging her to use her right hand. Niamh frowns as she is corrected.
"Do you think she's getting better at using her right hand?" Aoife asks Ciara.
Ciara looks up and watches Niamh for a while, "I think so. We are doing everything the therapists said," Ciara pauses for a moment, "In fact, sometimes I wonder if we should back off for a while, just let her enjoy life. We are lucky she's here at all."
Aoife moves over to Ciara and puts an arm around her, "It was my body that let us down with Niamh. You'll be fine."
"I don't want another miscarriage," Ciara replies sadly, "I still miss them."

(Continued)

(Continued)

"It isn't likely," Aoife replies, "You've just got to keep reminding yourself of the odds and put all of that out of your mind."

Ciara sighs, "Alright."

Suddenly, their attention is drawn back to Niamh. Niamh is attempting to undress her doll with her left hand and is struggling to pull the outfit off. She is visibly frustrated. She starts screaming, "bad bebe! bad bebe!"

"Niamh," Ciara jumps in, "don't say that. Babies are never bad. You need to ask for help."

"Here," Aoife says, "Let me help you."

Niamh hands the dolly to Aoife with a grimace.

"Ah," says Aoife, "Look, the dress is just caught on her hands. Come here and we can do it together."

Aoife starts to help Niamh to hold the doll again in both hands, uncurling her right hand for her.

"No!" yells Niamh.

"It'll be easier with both hands," Aoife replies, "I'll help you, honey."

"No! No! No!" Niamh yells, "I hate you!"

"Niamh!" Ciara says, "Do not ever say that. Everyone in this family loves each other. Never, ever, say that."

Niamh starts crying.

Aoife sighs, "Look, sweetie, it is okay. Let me get dolly's dress off, okay?"

Aoife takes off the doll's dress and tries to give the doll to Niamh. At first Niamh keeps crying but eventually she takes it.

"Maybe dolly just needs a cuddle?" Aoife suggests, "There, there, baby."

Niamh cuddles the doll and says, "There, there, bebe."

What's happening for Aoife, Ciara, and Niamh?

Both Aoife and Ciara are capable of sensitive, responsive parenting, and this is apparent in the interaction. However, for both of them fusion is interfering with their ability to be sensitive.

Aoife appears to be fused with worries about Niamh's future and thoughts about doing everything possible for her. She is preoccupied with maximizing Niamh's bimanual coordination and motor development. As a result, she is correcting Niamh's posture and prompting her to use her right hand in an intrusive manner that is inconsistent with sensitive parenting. This included physically manipulating Niamh's body without permission or warning. Her preoccupation with motor development and bimanual coordination is also interfering her ability to follow Niamh's lead in child-led play. For example, it interfered with the dog game. She also missed an opportunity to follow Niamh's lead in feeding and caring for the baby doll. Both of these games were potentially developmentally rich. Aoife's preoccupation also interfered with her ability to focus on Niamh's developing emotional understanding and capacity to ask for help in an appropriate manner. Ironically, Aoife's preoccupation with Niamh's development is interfering with her ability to provide the kinds of sensitive, child-led interactions that enhance development.

Ciara demonstrated fusion with Niamh's expressed thought, "I hate you." Instead of responding to the distress and the function of such a statement, Ciara fused

(Continued)

(Continued)

with the content itself. In responding in that manner, Ciara has encouraged Niamh to take a fused stance to her own thoughts.

Several rules around miscarriage and grief are mentioned. In particular, Aoife directs Ciara to the rules, "remind yourself of the odds," and "put it out of your mind." Neither of these are likely to be effective ways for Ciara to cope with her grief. There are also hints at how Ciara and Aoife understand their experiences so far and it is possible that both are experiencing fusion with aspects of their stories. For example, Ciara says that they are lucky that Niamh is here at all, and Aoife says that it was her body that let them down last time. The meaning that Aoife and Ciara have given to their experiences so far, and the degree to which they are fused with certain aspects of their stories, will influence how they experience the next chapter in their parenting journey.

From a clinical RFT perspective, it may be that Aoife has derived relations between Naimh not using her right hand and "failure" as well as an imagined negative future for Niamh. She also appears to have "doing what the therapists tell us to do" in an equivalence relation to "good parenting," and perhaps, in opposition to the imagined negative future coming to pass. As described above, attachment to these "rules" renders her less sensitive to Naimh's behavioral response to her physical guidance: for Naimh, it is punishing, as she stops her play. Clinicians working with this family would do well to help fully elucidate the thoughts and feelings that are evoked in the presence of these derived relations, and then to practice stepping back from them into a state of defused awareness. Defusing from one's thoughts involves deriving a hierarchical relation between oneself as a thinker and one's thoughts; similarly, it may also foster a hierarchical relation between oneself as an actor, and one's actions. This would likely support a more mindful appreciation of Niamh's play as well as psychological contact with Niamh as a whole developing child including motor development but also cognitive, social, and emotional. It would also support the development of Aoife's tracking the effects of her behavior on Niamh, and allow her to try a different tack; for example, noticing and praising Niamh's attempts to use her right hand or timing prompts so that they don't interfere with Niamh's play and using gentle verbal rather than physical prompts.

Working with flexible languaging clinically

Signs of parental inflexible languaging

There are a number of signs that parents have become fused, or are otherwise unable to language flexibly. These may include:

- Rigidity of thinking about parenting or about their child's behavior. For example, "she's just got to do what she's told" or "nothing works, we've tried it all."

- A parent who is struck with particular thoughts about themselves or their child. For example, the parent may be stuck with "I am a bad parent" or "he is naughty" or "she is too sensitive."
- Rigidity about particular parenting rules. For example, if the parent is persisting in following a specific parenting rule, or parenting in a particular way even though it is clear from the direct contingencies that it isn't working.

Metaphors

The passengers on the bus metaphor is a popular metaphor for demonstrating the difference between fusion—struggling with thoughts—and defusion.

Passengers on the bus metaphor

It is like you are the driver of a bus and the bus is your life. You want to take your bus West, that's the direction you'd like to go. Your thoughts are like passengers on the bus. Sometimes the passengers are nice and polite. You probably don't mind taking those passengers along for the ride. But other times the passengers are nasty. The passengers might tell you to drive the bus in another direction, or criticize your driving, or say nasty things about the bus. So, what can we do? One thing you may be tempted to do is to start arguing with them, to turn around and yell at them, to tell them to sit down. But what's the problem with that? While you are busy arguing with the passengers your eyes are not on the road. Another thing you may be tempted to do at times is to strike a deal with them. Maybe you'll have a deal that you'll take the passengers where they want to go if they'll sit quietly. But what happens then to your plan of going West? What if you can, instead, acknowledge the passengers and take them along for the ride with your eyes on the road and your focus on driving the bus?

The next metaphor is useful for prompting awareness of when fusion is useful and when it isn't and being able to shift between the two states. Within the metaphor as presented here the character of Superman is used, but any figure with superhuman abilities can be used. You should choose a character that is culturally relevant in the contexts in which you work, and ideally, be flexible to client needs.

Superhero's dilemma

Our languaging minds, the bits of us that can talk, compare, imagine future scenarios, plan, problem-solve, allow us to experience an imaginary world—that is like a superpower. Compare us to the rest of the animals. We can cooperate with each other, pass knowledge down through the centuries, problem-solve

(*Continued*)

(Continued)

solutions to problems we've never experienced in real life, and imagine the future. It really is an incredible superpower! And superpowers are awesome, right? Sure. But superpowers aren't always the right tool for the job. Think about Clark Kent and Superman. Clark has some pretty incredible superpowers, right? And as Superman he can do some pretty amazing things. A runaway train, you want Superman. A torpedo heading for a major city? Superman. A burning building with people trapped inside? Superman. And Superman's superpowers aren't just great for fixing disasters or saving people either. If Clark feels like relaxing in Paris, what's he going to do? He's going to fly there as Superman. So here's the thing: why does Clark Kent exist at all? Why not just be Superman using superpowers constantly? He has a whole life as Clark Kent. What for? Well, he needs to be Clark Kent too. There's actually a lot that he can't do as Superman. Although his superpowers are pretty incredible, there's a lot of things that his superpowers can't do. What if there's a political crisis that needs news coverage? What if Clark Kent's parents miss their son and want to spend some time with him? What if Lois Lane needs some advice on a personal problem? Or Jimmy Olsen is putting on a photography exhibition and wants his friends to come along? Well, then you want Clark Kent. Some situations call for Superman, and some for Clark Kent. In the same way, some situations call for our superpower, or our languaging, comparing, problem-solving, fix it, imagining side, and other situations call for something different. For the bit of us that's a physical being in a physical world, the bit that experiences and learns from that direct experience, the bit that grows in wisdom, the bit that knows that not everything can be fixed, the bit that connects person to person, the bit that can hold our child and feel their warmth, the bit that acts in the world. It isn't about disliking our superpower. It is about knowing when to use it. And when to do something else.

This next metaphor explores recognizing when a rule is helpful and when it is not and how to flexibly shift between defusion and fusion, rule-following, and holding rules lightly.

Playing the game

One way of looking at rules is seeing them more like rules within a game. So think about sports or board games. Baseball, netball, chess, or monopoly. They all have rules, right? And if you are playing one of those games it is best if you stick to the rules, right? I mean some people might try to cheat and get away with it at times, but if we don't all for the most part stick to the rules the game just falls apart, huh? In order to play the game, and enjoy it, you need rules and you need to basically follow the rules while you play. But have you ever thought that the rules of games like baseball or monopoly were written into the fabric of the universe? Or, let me put it another way. Can you see that the rules of games

(Continued)

(Continued)

like chess or netball were created by people in order to play the game? They are arbitrary. They could be different. And have you ever made the rules different? Like when I play with children I often tweak the rules of board games or sports to make the game fair, so they'll have a good time too. Or you can tweak the rules so that the game goes faster too, right? And that's totally okay, because the point is to have fun, and the rules are there to support that. They can be changed at any time. And have you ever gotten stuck playing chess? Like you actually want to stop playing that game, because it isn't fun anymore but you just can't stop playing out the rules of the game? Like you are hungry and you want to cook dinner but you just have to keep moving pieces on the board. No, that doesn't tend to happen.

So, what if, a lot of our rules are like that. We just forget and get stuck in the game. What if there's a "succeeding in my career" game, a "supporting my child's academic abilities" game, and a "being seen as a good parent" game? All the games have rules and, for the most part, humans have created those rules in order to play the game. And each game has a point, right? Like, what if you could play along with the career success rules in order to obtain job security all the while knowing that the rules are no more meaningful or important than the rules of baseball? And what if you knew you could tweak the rules? So the point of the "supporting my child's academic abilities game" is for your child to be doing well academically without damaging their well-being. If the "standard" rules don't fit your child then maybe you can tweak them just like you can tweak the rules of monopoly so a younger child can play and have fun or so you can have a faster game? And what if you knew you could opt out of some games altogether at times? What if you could think—ah those are the "being seen as a good parent" rules. I'll play that game some of the time, to build a good working relationship with my child's school, for example. But apart from that, I'm opting out. I don't want that prize. Or even, right now, I'm hungry so I am just going to stop playing that game and go make some dinner.

Experiential exercises

There are many experiential exercises that can promote defusion. There are individual differences in how people respond to defusion exercises. Parents should be encouraged to experiment and continue to use what works for them. That is, continue to use techniques that create the distance from thoughts without feeling invalidating. Here are some examples:

- Singing the thought aloud to a well-known tune. For example, you could sing out loud, "I'm a rubbish dad" to the tune of "Happy Birthday."
- Saying the thought in a funny voice. For example, you could say the thought, "my children hate me" in the voice of Daffy Duck.

- Prefacing the thought with, "I'm noticing that I'm having the thought that...." For example, you might say, "I'm noticing that I'm having the thought that my child is going to get sick and die."
- Relating to your thought as a separate character and thanking it. For example, you might say, "Thanks, mind for providing the statistics on miscarriage."
- Taking a moment to picture the thought as a leaf flowing down the stream.
- Putting the scene onto a television or a movie screen and stepping back from the screen. You might like to experiment with pressing buttons like Pause or Rewind, or seeing yourself sitting on a couch watching. Maybe even eating popcorn. You could also imagine the scene on a computer screen. For example, if you get stuck in imagining your child experiencing an accident, see the scene of unfolding on a television screen.
- Freezing the scene right when the scenario is at its worst, and envisioning it as a painting. Imagine putting a frame around the painting and hanging it on your wall. For example, if you get stuck remembering past events, freeze them at their worst point and imagine them as a painting.
- Saying "I can't do this" and actually doing it at the sometime. For example, say "I can't lift my arm" while lifting your arm.
- Repeating a word over and over until it loses all meaning. For example, try repeating the word "milk" until it loses meaning and you are left with just the sounds. Then try it for a word that is psychologically meaningful.
- Stand and Say And...This is an exercise that involves considering the mind as a bully, and noticing thoughts as thoughts, and offering the response, "Ok. And?" said silently, to oneself.
- Repertoire of curiosity. Shaping a repertoire of curiosity in both parents and kids is very important—this is an effect of defusion too. One might think of this as instead of buying a thought entirely, reminding oneself to be curious about what would happen if one did things differently than dictated by a particular thought or rule. This supports defusion and tracking.

Meditations

Mindfulness of thoughts meditation

Mindfulness of thoughts meditations can be used to promote defusion. If the meditation itself is practiced then the imagery can be used to quickly prompt defusion in daily life. This version of mindfulness of thoughts uses the imagery of a leaf in a stream. Clients should experiment to find what imagery works best for them. Some people prefer the imagery of clouds in the sky, or a computer screen with scrolling words, or a parade matching past. Some people prefer to use no imagery at all. That is fine. The important point is to be watching thoughts arise.

Mindfulness of thoughts meditation script

Get yourself into a comfortable position.
Your position should feel comfortable, as well as promoting wakefulness at the same time.
Let yourself have a relaxed, comfortable posture.
Settle into it.
You can leave your eyes open, resting on a point of focus.
Or closed.
Or hooded, whichever you prefer.
Let your hands rest gently on your knees or in your lap or in some other comfortable posture.
Allow your mind to settle into the here and now.
Bring your attention to the sensations in your body...
Use your breath as an anchor to connect to the here and now.
Use the sensations of the floor beneath you to ground you in the present moment.
Bring your awareness to your thoughts.
As best you can, try to watch your thoughts.
Notice that your thoughts come and go.
You may like to imagine that you are sitting next to a stream.
The stream is your mind.
And your thoughts are leaves on the stream.
Thoughts arise, flow through your mind and then disappear again.
As each thought arises put it onto a leaf.
And float it down the stream.
Every so often you might notice that your thoughts pull you in.
As if you get pulled into the stream and carried down the current.
When that happens, pull yourself out of your thoughts and return to watching them.
Notice the thoughts arise then fade away...
Notice your thoughts, coming and going.
If you find yourself sucked into your thoughts, pulled into a remembered past or a hypothetical future then gently pull yourself back out.
Return to watching your thoughts.
When you are ready to end the exercise, do so gently.
Bring your awareness with you back to the full present moment.

Mindfulness awareness, parent, and child

Parental mindfulness practice, during parent–child interactions, can include focusing on noticing their own thoughts as they come up naturally during the interaction (see the chapter *Psychological Presence in the Present Moment* for a script for practicing mindfulness during a parent–child interaction). Parents may be prompted to focus on noticing their childlike as sunset—as something to appreciate and observe—rather than like a math problem—as something to be solved. Parents can focus on being aware of both their child, and their own ongoing thoughts.

Flexible languaging games for parent and child

Flexible languaging can be modeled and learned in a playful way. The kind of nonsense that children enjoy is naturally supportive of flexible languaging and there really is no limit to the kinds of fun silly games that parents and children can play. These are just some ideas:

- Rhubarb—take turns trying to get a point across when you can only say the word "rhubarb." For example, with gestures and pointing and saying the word "rhubarb" over and over you ask if your child wants a piece of toast.
- What is this?—take turns explaining what a common household object is with demonstrations. You can say it is anything except what it actually is. If you like you can pretend to be a salesperson trying to sell it. For example, your child tries to sell you a toothbrush as a multipurpose device good for brushing small animals and cleaning china.
- Opposites—say the opposite of what you mean. Try to have a whole conversation while saying the opposite of what you actually mean. For example, you are hungry so you say "I am not hungry."
- Don't say yes or no—one person asks yes or no questions that the other person needs to reply to truthfully without saying the words yes or no. For example, you ask your child "do you like sport?" and they answer "a lot."
- Saying silly things—each person takes turns at saying things that aren't true, the more outlandish the better. For example, you say, "the sky is bright red!" Once this is an established and fun game the parent might like to slip in an occasional potentially psychologically meaningful "silly thing." For example, the parent might say, "I don't like you" with an exaggerated expression to show it is another "silly thing." This should be done with care for the history of the parent and child relationship and responsiveness to the child's reaction.
- Say one thing, do another—say you are doing something while doing something else. For example, you could say you are sitting down while you are running on the spot. You can also play a variant of the game where you say that you don't want to do the very thing that you are doing or even you say you can't do the very thing that you are doing. Once this is established, this game can be extended into a defusion exercise to support approach behavior. For example, your child might say "I don't want to jump into the pool" while jumping into a pool.
- Word salad—create a story with a selection of random words. You can put random words into a hat and draw them out to start the game, or just take turns suggesting random words until you have a list. Once you have the list, try to quickly come up with a little story. Just say the story to yourselves

out aloud. Just a few sentences is fine. For older children you can try to get every word into just one sentence. For example, "The prince rode the motorbike he bought from the frog at the haunted house all the way to the village to get some ice-cream." Once established, you could add psychologically meaningful words to the list, for example, "bully" or "worry."

Taking parents from pliance to tracking

It is important that parenting behavior itself is under the control of tracks rather than pliance. It is important that the parent is able to flexibly tweak tracks, developing effective and workable tracks and that the parent takes a defused stance toward tracking. This can be supported by:

- Using defusion for parenting rules, especially rules functioning as pliance.
- Connecting parents to their values and choosing actions based in parenting values.
- Helping parents to think through child behavior in a manner that makes identifying the contingency, that is, tracking more likely. For example, identifying what happened before a particular behavior and identifying what happened immediately after a particular behavior. Language like "trigger" or "accidental rewards" can be helpful.
- Talking through a common interactional pattern—for example, the escalation trap—and asking parents to identify if that ever happens to them. For example, you might say, "sometimes we can get stuck in a trap where we escalate in our behavior with our child. And our children accidentally teach us to do this. Like maybe you start out saying politely that it is time for dinner. But they don't come to the table. So you say it again. And again. Louder and louder. And right when you are yelling, finally, they come. So you've learned to yell. Does anything like that happen to you? It happens the other way too. So maybe your child asks for a treat. You say no. They ask again and again getting louder and louder. Finally, you cave in because you are busy and you can't deal with all the nagging. And you've accidentally taught them to escalate to get what they want. Does that ever happen?"
- Monitoring of child behavior is a fantastic way to support the parent in developing workable tracks. In particular, monitoring what happens immediately before and immediately after the behavior as well as taking note of the wider context like the time of day the behavior tends to occur. The parent's discoveries can then be talked through at the next session. Many parents begin to develop better tracking with monitoring even before talking through with the therapist.

Taking children from pliance to tracking

Parents can support their child in shifting from pliance to tracking and in the discovery of proto-values. This may include:

- Accurately reflecting back to the child the real-world consequences of particular behaviors. This may take the form of observing the consequences of the child's own behavior; for example, "you did your music practice everyday this week. And you know what I've noticed? That piece has improved massively. You are playing those tricky bars really well now." It may also involve the parent sharing their understanding of the possible consequences of particular behaviors. It is important that the possible consequences are discussed accurately. It is tempting for parents to try to dissuade children from certain actions with exaggerated accounts. For example, "lying is always wrong so never lie" or "drugs destroy your brain." But an accurate account, supports tracking, and teaches children that parents are a reliable source of accurate tracks. For example, talking through accurate information on the potential side effects of specific drugs with an adolescent.
- Accurately reflecting back to the child the child's own interests and enjoyment can help the child to develop proto-values. Again, it is important that this is accurate. For it to be accurate it is necessary that the parent is tuned in to observing the child and takes a defused stance toward their own thoughts about what they want their child to be like. For example, with a young child it could be as simple as observing, "you really like animals, huh?" For older children and adolescents it might involve a conversation allowing the opportunity for self-reflection. For example, "you seem to be happier now that you are drawing in the evenings again. What do you like about drawing?"
- Accurately reflecting back to the child their own moral choices and behavior can help the child to develop proto-values. It is important that this accurately tracks the moral thinking of the child. For example, "I noticed that you shared your toy with Alice. That was a really kind thing to do. Alice seemed to really like that."
- Parents can, when safe, allow the child to experience the natural consequences of their actions. This may include allowing the child to experience the school-given consequences of behavior at school, or to experience the natural consequences of their behavior with their peers. A useful reflection for parents in knowing when to step in and when to allowing the natural consequences to play out may be best is: are the naturally occurring consequences safe? Are they going to teach them a useful track? Parents can then support tracking through reflection and discussion.
- It is often not safe to allow children to learn from the natural consequences of their actions. For example, the natural consequence of playing

on the road might be getting hit by a car. Parents can supplement natural consequences with "logical" consequences—consequences that mimic naturally occurring consequences or the kinds of societal consequences that certain actions have in adult life. As the consequence is created to match "real life" the child still learns a useful track. For example, if a child has flooded the bathroom and made a mess, the parent might instruct the child to clean up the mess. In most situations within adult life, the consequence of making a mess is that you have to clean it up. Hence, the child is learning a useful track.

Encouraging home practice

Home practice around flexible languaging may include:

- Trying out defusion techniques in everyday life.
- Parent and child playing with language and pretense together.
- Developing accurate tracks; for example, by monitoring child behavior.

Working with Aoife, Ciara and Niamh

The therapist, Aoife, and Ciara, are talking through the interaction above. The therapist videoed the interaction and they have watched it together.

Therapist:	Aoife, is it okay if we start with you?
Aoife: nods	sure.
Therapist:	What did you notice as you watched the interaction between yourself and Niamh?
Aoife: sighs	she just doesn't want to use both her hands....I mean I knew that, but it was so obvious from watching the video. Every time I reminded her it just spoilt her play, you know?
Therapist: nods	She did react like it was unwelcome, didn't she?
Ciara:	Well, maybe we should ease up on her? Just let her have a normal childhood for a bit?
Aoife: (tears in her eyes):	This is her future, Ciara. If she doesn't get better at using both hands then she has to live with that for the rest of her life. And we have to live with knowing that we didn't do our best for her... that we failed her....
Ciara:	But if she hates it...
Therapist:	I'm just going to pause you there, Ciara. We can definitely discuss and experiment with different approaches you might like to take to this. But I want to put that aside for a moment because I want to explore a little more what's happening for you right now, Aoife. "We have to live with knowing that we didn't do our best for her...that we failed her..."

(*Continued*)

(Continued)

Aoife crying:	Yes. My body failed her. I can't fail her now. I have to do everything I can.
Therapist:	You have to think about that bimanual coordination all the time, work really hard to ensure that Niamh's development is maximized...
Aoife crying:	Yes. That's it exactly. I've got to fix it. I mean, I know she'll always have cerebral palsy, but I've got to do my best, haven't I?
Therapist:	And is this there for you, when you see Niamh using one hand? Is this all there right before you prompt her to use two? Or move her hands for her?
Aoife:	Oh yes.
Therapist:	It is a real fix-it, problem-solving mindset.
Aoife:	It is.
Therapist:	You know, as humans, we have this incredible language-speaking, problem-solving, fix-it mind. We can learn from others, imagine future scenarios, and solve problems in our minds without having to test it out in the real-world. This part of us is responsible for all of this around us: human culture and civilization. I think of it as almost like a superpower. Your problem-solving fix-it superpower is helping you to identify what Niamh might want her body to be able to do 20 years from now, it has enabled you to learn from professionals who are up to date on the latest science on early intervention what you can do now to support that, and the moment the an opportunity to do that comes up bam! Your mind puts you on alert. Quick! It says! Two hands! That's incredible, huh?
Aoife: laughing	I never thought of it like that.
Therapist:	The thing is, sometimes superpowers are useful, and sometimes they aren't. Superman still spends a lot of time as Clark Kent. Wonder woman still spends time as Diana Price. Sure, you've got this superpower. But you are also a physical being in a physical world. Someone who learns from experience. What is your *experience* telling you?
Aoife: sighing	All my prompting isn't working. It is spoiling her play and she hates it. If she hates it she won't want to do it even more. It defeats the whole point then.
Therapist: nodding	So I'm wondering if you could hear that alarm going off in your head "Quick, two hands! Fix it! Do your best!" accept it as a useful signal from that problem-solving, fix-it part of you AND to experiment a little, to let your

(*Continued*)

(Continued)

	experience guide in learning exactly when and how to remind Niamh to use both hands…
Aoife:	So you are saying still remind her but in a different way?
Therapist:	I'm saying experiment and see what you learn. I'm thinking of towards the start of that interaction. Niamh got out a dog toy and you woofed, do you remember? She giggled. And you woofed again. You got on all fours. Do you remember that part of the interaction?
Aoife nods.	
Therapist:	That was a beautiful interaction. Niamh enjoyed it. You were in sync. But also: that was a developmentally enriching interaction. You were encouraging Niamh to explore her world through pretend play.
Aoife:	Oh. I hadn't thought of it like that.
Therapist:	Here's my question: how did you know to "woof"? How did you know to get on all fours? Did an alarm go off in your head "Quick, get on all fours and pretend to be a dog! Do your best! Maximize Niamh's development!"
Aoife: laughing	Of course not. I was just mucking around.
Therapist:	Absolutely, having fun, following Niamh's lead.
Aoife:	That's it.
Therapist:	Now that's the bit of you we need. It isn't that the superpower is bad. Listen to its alert. But we also need the bit of you that says "woof," hears a giggle, and "woofs" again. That bit of you is going to figure out how and when to support Niamh in learning to use both hands.
Aoife: laughing	Alright. I get you. I can experiment. Be a bit playful with it all.
Therapist:	Oh yes.

In the example, Aoife shifts from being fused with her thoughts around needing to "do her best" for Niamh, to defusion. She is able to relate to the thoughts as like an alarm: something potentially useful that she can listen to without necessarily needing to act on immediately. She tunes back into her ability to learn from direct experience, and leaves the session prepared to experiment and learn from direct experience when it is useful to act on the "alarm" and when it isn't, as well as experimenting with acting on the "alarm" in a more playful and flexible way. As the session continued, the therapist focused on Ciara's fusion around taking Niamh's statements "I hate you" and "Bad bebe" as literal content, supporting Ciara in instead focusing on the function behind these statements and responding to that. With more flexible languaging, Aoife and Ciara are able to stay sensitive, responsive, and flexible, even when they ensure sufficient bimanual practice is done. Acceptance and values processes are also important in grieving fully for their past losses, both the miscarriage and the challenge of Niamh's premature birth and disability.

Troubleshooting

Defusion is not about whether the thoughts are true or false

It is important to understand—and convey—that even true thoughts or rules can become unworkable with fusion, the classic example being "I am going to die." Many parents can become fused with thoughts attributing blame to themselves. These thoughts may have a degree of truth to them. It may really be the case, for example, that the parent passed on genes predisposing their child to develop an Autism Spectrum Disorder (ASD), or that the mother went into labor prematurely. Yet, fusion with such thoughts is unlikely to promote workable parenting. In fact, even rules that are often workable, or as workable as a pithy rule can be, (e.g., "they are doing it for attention, so just ignore it") may become unworkable in specific contexts if parents fuse with the rule.

What if defusion doesn't work or feels invalidating?

Specific defusion techniques need to be implemented flexibly. Any particular technique may, at times for specific people, fail to instigate defusion, or feel invalidating. Instead of relying on set techniques it is important to have experiential knowledge of fusion and defusion and how to flexibly shift between the two. Clients should be encouraged to experiment with defusion and to use whichever techniques work best for them.

Four key developmental periods and flexible languaging

Infancy and flexible languaging

Parents of babies are particularly vulnerable to fusion with parenting rules and to following parenting rules that function as pliance, as they are just developing an ongoing pattern of interaction with their child (once the pattern is in place, the reinforcement loops between parent and child stabilize the interactional pattern against external influences). Mothers, in particular, report a high amount of shame, social judgement, and criticism around their parenting in the postnatal period including how birth, feeding, and sleeping are navigated. Birth, feeding, and sleeping remain controversial topics. Not just controversial, but associated with shame (Thomson, Ebisch-Burton, & Flacking, 2014). Further, many of the parenting rules that parents hear in infancy are contradictory, sometimes in hidden ways; for example, the hidden contradiction between "breast is breast" and "never bedshare" discussed earlier. When the impossibility of the rules is revealed in practice women often blame themselves rather than questioning the workability of the rules.

Yet, it is never more important for parents to be sensitive to context. Arguably, the most important aspect of the early months of parenting is for parenting behavior to come under the contextual control of the baby's cues.

That is, for the parent to develop a pattern of sensitive caregiving. Ideally, the early months of parenting should be a time of discovery: discovering the unique features of your baby, discovering what brings you joy as a parent, discovering what works in your family. Rule-following should be minimized and any rule-following should be done flexibly.

In terms of the child's own developing flexible languaging it is important that the parents are able to provide rich language exposure, to speak beyond mere functional speech, in a way that is rich in relational frames and pleasurable to the parent. Voicing your own train of thought, as well as commenting on what the baby is doing as well as the baby's perspective is a good start. If the parent is able to live an active rewarding life with the baby this provides stimuli to prompt richer language too.

Early childhood and flexible languaging

It is important for parents to maintain a defused stance toward their own attributions about the child's behavior, as well as to their child's expressed thoughts (e.g., "I hate you!"). Instead of getting hooked into either of these, for the parent to maintain a workable parenting style, looking for the function behind particular behaviors and experimenting to discover what works.

Early childhood is a time of great experimentation. Many of the rules a parent sets for their preschooler are likely to initially function as pliance for the child (rule-following for social approval). Yet, by creating a safe space for the child with a few well-chosen rules functioning as pliance, children can be given open opportunities to flexibly experiment, learning tracks and proto-values from their own direct experience. If parents accurately reflect back for the child their observations of the child's enjoyment and the consequences of the child's actions, this supports this process.

Rich language exposure continues to be crucial in this time of life. It should include a rich variety of relational frames including deictic framing, and framing used in mathematics, for example. Parents should make the most of any naturally occurring situation where such frames can be used. For example, "look, the cat is under the table!" Symbolic thought is also vital to pretend play. Playing flexibly with shifting between fusion and defusion—as is essential in pretend play and fiction—as well as playing with language itself will build a child's flexible languaging capacities.

Middle childhood and flexible languaging

Parents can support flexible language in their child through pretend play, fiction, playing with language itself, and everyday nonsense. Child relational framing abilities are consolidated within school; for example, mathematics relational frames. Parents can continue to support the development of these relational frames too by using them within ordinary situations.

Reflecting to children the consequences of particular actions and doing so accurately is supportive in the development of workable tracks as is allowing children to experience the naturally occurring consequences of their actions where possible and using "logical" consequences that mimic naturally occurring consequences.

Adolescence and flexible languaging

Relational framing around self and social comparison are prominent. Parental support for flexibility in social comparison and identity formation is important. Adolescence is also a time of great experimentation. Parents must balance the creation of a safe haven for experimentation so that tracks and values can be discovered through direct experience.

In order for the parent to be able to support their child in flexible experimentation, parents need to be able to take a defused stance toward their own rules, attributions for their child's behavior, and their child's expressed thoughts.

Using flexible languaging with specific populations

Parental mental health problems and flexible languaging

Certain patterns of thinking are more common in depression and anxiety disorders. For example, depressed parents tend to be more negative about themselves, the future, and their ability to change things (Jacobs, Reinecke, Gollan, & Kane, 2008; Morris, Silk, Steinberg, Myers, & Robinson, 2007; Silk, Shaw, Skuban, Oland, & Kovacs, 2006). In families of anxious children, parent cognitions are often involved in overcontrol and lack of autonomy granting (Bogels & Brechman-Toussaint, 2006; Burstein & Ginsburg, 2010). Learning to hold these thoughts lightly, taking a defused stance toward such thoughts, can be helpful. In addition, bringing behavior under the control of values, rather than rules, and shifting from pliance to flexible tracking.

Parental grief and flexible languaging

Grief is a multidimensional and complex experience without exact steps and without a timeline. In spite of this, in many cultures, there are specific rules around grief. Grief is often thought to be time-limited, predominately about feeling sad, and something you need to "get over." These rules are not accurate and becoming fused with them is not likely to be helpful. Parents will also develop their own understanding or story about their loss experiences. Aspects of their story may include unworkable tracks, that is rules about how the world including loss works that are not workable in practice. For example, following miscarriage, a woman may become fused with thoughts like, "my body failed" or "I am not meant to be a mother."

Childhood externalizing problems and flexible languaging

In order for parents to manage misbehavior well it is important that they do not become fused to their attributions for child behavior (e.g., "he's just like his father") or to the child's expressed thoughts. It is also important for parents to develop workable tracks for their child's behavior and to take a flexible, experimental approach to parenting. Fusion with rules about negative emotions being toxic or dangerous, particularly anger, can also interfere.

Childhood internalizing problems and flexible languaging

Parental fusion with attributions for the child's internalizing symptoms, or thoughts about the child's ability to handle the intensity of emotion, their need to protect their child from emotion, or even rules about negative emotions being toxic or dangerous can all interfere in parental ability to manage internalizing problems.

Childhood neurodevelopmental disabilities and flexible languaging

Parents will develop their own understanding of what their child's disability means. This story may include attributions for the cause of the disability, the implications of the disability for the child's current life, and a particular vision of the future for their child. Aspects of the story may become problematic if fused with. For example, becoming fused with the thought, "my child's autism is my fault" is unlikely to be helpful, even if the parent can explain some "truth" of it, such as the heredity of ASDs. Likewise, fusion with particular expectations in terms of adaptations for their child can lead to unworkable parenting behavior in certain contexts; for example, leading the parent to expect unrealistic accommodations from other children. Fusion with specific expectations for the future can also be problematic, including expectations that are overly pessimistic or overly optimistic. For this group of parents, fusion with parenting rules is likely to become unworkable as the contingencies maintaining specific behaviors are more likely to be idiosyncratic and the assumptions inherent in the rule are less likely to apply.

Peer relations and bullying and flexible languaging

In being able to effectively support their child with peer problems, it is important that parents are defused with their own immediate thoughts and reactions, whether they are immediately defensive of their child, or immediately blaming of their child. This defused stance also enables the parent to hear and respond to social challenges their child is experiencing or even insults that have been said of their child, without taking the words as literal truths.

Marital conflict and flexible languaging

Finding ways to coparent can be challenging, and it is made all the more challenging if parents are fused with parenting rules, as any disagreement at the level of rules leads to conflict. If parents can, instead, take a defused stance toward parenting rules, including rules from their families of origin and discover what is workable within their own family through flexible experimentation, effective coparenting is more likely. It is also important to hold lightly stories about self, partner, and the relationship.

Expressed emotion including critical and intrusive parenting and flexible languaging

Critical, hostile, and intrusive parenting behavior is often a sign that the parent is fused to a parenting rule, to a thought, or to the child's expressed thoughts.

Emotion dismissiveness and flexible languaging

Fusion with thoughts around negative emotions being toxic or dangerous are likely to lead to parental emotion dismissiveness, as is parental fusion to particular interpretations of events that downplay the child's emotional world.

Inconsistent, or harsh and punitive parenting and flexible languaging

The use of inconsistent, harsh, or punitive parenting is often connected to parental fusion with parenting rules, attributions for child behavior, parental thoughts, or the child's expressed thoughts.

References

Backen Jones, L., Whittingham, K., Coyne, L., & Lightcap, A. (2016). *A contextual behavioral science approach to parenting intervention and research. The Wiley handbook of contextual behavioral science* (pp. 398–421). Wiley-Blackwell.

Baldwin, D. A. (1993a). Early referential understanding: Infants' ability to recognise refential acts for what they are. *Developmental Psychology*, *29*(5), 832–843.

Baldwin, D. A. (1993b). Infants' ability to consult the speaker for clues to word reference. *Journal of Child Language*, *20*(2), 395–418.

Baldwin, D. A., Markman, E. M., Bill, B., Desjardins, R. N., & Irwin, J. M. (1996). Infants' reliance on a social criterion for establishing word-object relations. *Child Development, 67*(6), 3135–3153.

Belisle, J., Dixon, M. R., & Stanley, C. R. (2018). The mediating effects of derived relational responding on the relationship between verbal operant development and IQ. *Behavior Analysis in Practice, 11*(4), 411–416.

Blakemore, S. J., & Choudhury, S. (2006). Development of the adolescent brain: Implications for executive function and social cognition. *Journal of Child Psychology and Psychiatry, 47* (3-4), 296–312.

Bogels, S. M., & Brechman-Toussaint, M. L. (2006). Family issues in child anxiety: Attachment, family functioning, parental rearing and beliefs. *Clinical Psychological Review, 26*(7), 834–856.

Burstein, M., & Ginsburg, G. S. (2010). The effect of parental modeling of anxious behaviors and cognitions in school-aged children: An experimental pilot study. *Behaviour Research and Therapy, 48*(6), 506–515.

Cassidy, S., Roche, B., Colbert, D., Stewart, I., & Grey, I. M. (2016). A relational frame skills training intervention to increase general intellligence and scholastic aptitude. *Learning and Individual Differences, 47*, 222–235.

Cassidy, S., Roche, B., & Hayes, S. C. (2011). A relational frame training intervention to raise intelligence quotients: A pilot study. *The Psychological Record, 61*, 173–198.

Committee on the Science of Adolescence, Board on Childeren, Youth and Families, Institute of Medicine and National Research Council of the National Academies. (2011). *The science of adolescent risk-taking: Workshop report 2011*. Washington, DC: National Academies Press.

Coyne, L. W., & Cairns, D. (2016). *A relational frame theory analysis of coercive family process. The Oxford handbook of coercive relationship dynamics* (pp. 86–100). New York: Oxford University Press.

Eisenberg, N., Spinrad, T. L., & Sadovksy, A. (2006). Emapthy-related responding in children. In M. Killen, & J. G. Smetana (Eds.), *Handbook of moral development*. Mahwah, NJ: Lawrence Erlbaum Associates.

Farrant, B. M., & Zubrick, S. R. (2011). Early vocabulary development: The importance of joint attention and parent–child book reading. *First Language, 32*(3), 1–22.

Field, T. (1990). *Infancy*. Cambridge, MA: Harvard University Press.

Hafer, C. L., & Begue, L. (2005). Experimental research on just-world theory: Problems, developments and future challenges. *Psychological Bulletin, 13*(1), 128–167.

Hart, B., & Risley, T. R. (1995). *Meaningful differences in the everyday experience of young Americian children*. Baltimore, MD: Paul H Brookes Publishing Co.

Hayes, J., & Stewart, I. (2016). Comparing the effects of derived relational training and computer coding on intellectual potential in school age children. *British Journal of Educational Psychology, 86*(3), 397–411.

Hayes, L. L., & Ciarrochi, J. (2015). *The thriving adolescent*. Oakland, CA: New Harbinger Publications.

Hayes, S. C., Barnes-Holmes, D., & Roche, B. (2001). *Relational frame theory: A post-Skinnerian account of human language and cognition*. New York: Plenum Press.

Hayes, S. C., Strosahl, K. D., & Wilson, K. G. (2003). *Acceptance and commitment therapy: An experiential approach to behavior change*. New York: Guilford Press.

Hrdy, S. B. (2011). *Mothers and others*. Cambridge, MA: Harvard University Press.

Jacobs, R. H., Reinecke, M. A., Gollan, J. K., & Kane, P. (2008). Empirical evidence of cognitive vulberability for depression among children and adolescents: A cognitive science adn developmental perspective. *Clinical Psychology Review, 28*, 759–782.

Johnston, C., & Freeman, W. (1997). Attributions for child behavior in parents of children without behavior disorders and children with attention deficit-hyperactivity disorder. *Journal of Consulting and Clinical Psychology*, *65*(4), 636–645.

Kendall-Tackett, K., Cong, Z., & Hale, T. W. (2011). The effect of feeding method on sleep duration, maternal well-being, and postpartum depression. *Clinical Lactation*, *2*(2), 22–26.

Kendall-Tackett, K., Cong, Z., & Hale, T. W. (2012). Mother-infant sleep locations and nighttime feeding behavior. *Clinical Lactation*, *1*, 27–31.

Kent, G., Galvin, E., Barnes-Holmes, Y., Murphy, C., & Barnes-Holmes, D. (2017). Relational responding: Testing, training, and sequencing effects among children with autism and typically developing children. *Behavioral Development Bulletin*, *22*(1), 94–110.

Lancy, D. F. (2015). *The anthropology of childhood: Cherubs, chattel, changelings*. New York: Cambridge University Press.

Lipkens, G., Hayes, S. C., & Hayes, L. J. (1993). Longitudinal study of derived stimulus relations in an infant. *Journal of Experimental Child Psychology*, *56*, 201–239.

McLoughlin, S., Tyndall, I., & Pereira, A. (2018). Piloting a brief relational operant training program: Analyses of response latencies and intelligence test performance. *European Journal of Behavior Analysis*, *19*(2), 228–246.

Mesman, J., van Ijzendoorn, M. H., & Bakermans-Kranenburg, M. J. (2009). The many faces of the Still-Face Paradigm: A review and meta-analysis. *Developmental Review*, *29*(2), 120–162.

Morris, A. S., Silk, J. S., Steinberg, L., Myers, S. S., & Robinson, L. R. (2007). The role of the family context in the development of emotion regulation. *Social Development*, *16*(2), 361–388.

Mulhern, T., Stewart, I., & McElwee, J. (2018). Facilitating relational framing of classification in young children. *Journal of Contextual Behavioral Science*, *8*, 55–68.

Rudd, L. C., Lambert, M. C., Satterwhite, M., & Zaier, A. (2008). Mathetical language in early childhood settings: What really counts? *Early Childhood Education Journal*, *36*(1), 75–80.

Silk, J. S., Shaw, D. S., Skuban, E. M., Oland, A. A., & Kovacs, M. (2006). Emotion regulation strategies in offspring of childhood-onset depressed mothers. *Journal of Child Psychology and Psychiatry*, *47*(1), 69–78.

Thomson, G., Ebisch-Burton, K., & Flacking, R. (2014). Shame if you do—Shame if you don't: Women's experiences of infant feeding. *Maternal and Child Nutrition*, *11*, 33–46.

Vezzali, L., Stathi, S., Giovannini, D., Capozza, D., & Trifiletti, E. (2015). The greatest magic of Harry Potter: Reducing prejudice. *Journal of Applied Social Psychology*, *45*, 105–121.

Vizcaino-Torres, R. M., Ruiz, F. J., Luciano, C., Lopez-Lopez, J. C., Barbero-Rubio, A., & Gil, E. (2015). The effect of relational training on intelligence quotient: A case study. *Psicothema*, *27*(2), 120–127.

Wang, X., Ouyang, Y., Liu, J., Zhu, M., Zhao, G., Bao, W., & Hu, F. B. (2014). Fruit and vegetable consumption and moratality from all causes, cardiovascular disease and cancer: Systematic review and dose-response meta-analysis of prospective cohort studies. *BMJ*, *349*, g4490.

Williams, J. H. G., Whiten, A., Suddendorf, T., & Perrett, D. I. (2001). Imitation, mirror neurons and autism. *Neuroscience and Biobehavioral Reviews*, *25*(4), 287–295.

Zauche, L. H., Thul, T. A., Mahoney, A. E. D., & Stapel-Wax, J. L. (2016). Influence of language nutrition on children's language and cognitive development: An integrated review. *Early Childhood Research Quarterly*, *36*, 318–333.

Chapter 11

Flexible perspective taking

Chapter Outline

What is flexible perspective taking? **288**
DNA–V model 295
How does flexible perspective taking apply to parent–child interaction? **295**
Parental flexible perspective taking and sensitivity 295
Parental flexible perspective taking and mental health 296
Developing child's flexible perspective taking 296
Flexible perspective taking and growth mindset 297
Working with flexible perspective taking clinically **299**
Use of mindfulness 301
Use of defusion 302
Simple questioning 303
Metaphors 303
Experiential exercises 304
A third experiment in perspective: time traveling 306
Meditations 307
Troubleshooting **312**
Defense of self-as-content 312
Deficits in self-as-process 313
Four key developmental periods and flexible perspective taking **313**
Infancy and flexible perspective taking 313
Early childhood and flexible perspective taking 314
Middle childhood and flexible perspective taking 315
Adolescence and flexible perspective taking 315
Using flexible perspective taking with specific populations **315**
Parental mental health problems and flexible perspective taking 315
Parental grief and flexible perspective taking 316
Childhood externalizing problems and flexible perspective taking 316
Childhood internalizing problems and flexible perspective taking 316
Childhood neurodevelopmental disabilities and flexible perspective taking 317
Peer problems and bullying and flexible perspective taking 317
Marital conflict and flexible perspective taking 317
Expressed emotion including critical and intrusive parenting and flexible perspective taking 317
Emotion dismissiveness and flexible perspective taking 318
Inconsistent, or harsh and punitive parenting and flexible perspective taking 318
References **318**

Acceptance and Commitment Therapy. DOI: https://doi.org/10.1016/B978-0-12-814669-9.00011-4
© 2019 Elsevier Inc. All rights reserved.

All beings are by nature Buddha,
as ice by nature is water.
Apart from water there is no ice;
Apart from beings, no Buddha

Gakuin Zenji, *Song of Zazen*

You have been my friend and that in itself is a tremendous thing.

E.B. White, *Charlotte's Web*

But the most important thing is, even if we're apart, I'll always be with you.

A.A. Milne, *Winnie The Pooh*

What is flexible perspective taking?

From an Relational Frame Theory (RFT) perspective, the sense of self is a learned behavioral repertoire. In particular, your "self" develops from the verbal discriminations of your own behavior (Hayes, Barnes-Holmes, & Roche, 2001). Perspective taking, then, is a complex pattern of relational responding in terms of deictic framing (Y. Barnes-Holmes, Barnes-Holmes, Roche, & Smeets, 2001; Montoya-Rodriguez, Molina, & McHugh, 2017), which establishes perspectives of person, place, and time. The three core deictic frames are: I–you, here–there, and now–then. Furthermore, more complex deictic framing extends these; for example: yesterday-today-tomorrow, near-far, us-them, or even expressions like "a long, long time ago." Deictic framing, like other forms of relational responding, is learned through multiple exemplar training within ordinary social interactions beginning in infancy (Montoya-Rodriguez et al., 2017). In other words, self-knowledge has social origins (Hayes, 1984). Simply put, our felt sense of who we are develops in the context of our social relationships, over time, and across different situations. Gradually, we learn that we have a consistent perspective—I, here, now—that is distinct from the perspective of others—you, there, then—as well as distinct from psychological content, from the particular psychological events of the moment. Our self-understanding is developmental, and becomes more complex over the course of our development (McHugh, Barnes-Holmes, & Barnes-Holmes, 2004).

The verbal community in which the developing child lives benefits from and hence reinforces speaking from a specific consistent perspective, "I" (Hayes, 1984). Thus two side effects of language are (1) that we gain *not only* a sense of self, *but also* a sense of others (e.g., "you"); and (2) a distinction between our ability to take perspective (e.g., you have a perspective different from my own) and the content of that perspective (e.g., you experience things differently than I do). In a sense, the human soul or spirit—the transcendent I–here–now perspective—is a by-product of language.

Verbal processes give us three senses of self, three corresponding senses of other, and three corresponding senses of relationship: self-as-content or the conceptualized self (other-as-content or the conceptualized other and us-as-content), self-as-process or the knowing self (other-as-process or the knowing other and us-as-process), and self-as-context or the transcendent self (other-as-context or the transcendent other and us-as-context). We define these below.

Self-as-content includes all conceptualizations about the self; for example, beliefs, evaluations, and thoughts (Montoya-Rodriguez et al., 2017). It can also be called the narrative self or the auto-biographical self. It is what you might tell someone about yourself if they asked, "Tell me a bit about you." For example, my (Lisa) idea that I am a mother who is scattered but intelligent is my "self-as-content," or my concrete story of who I am. Similarly, one's "other-as-content" is your idea of who someone else is. For example, my (Lisa) teenaged daughter takes after me, because she is bright, has a good sense of humor, and is also scattered. Likewise, us-as-content is your concrete story of a relationship. Many aspects of self-as-content, other-as-content and us-as-content are important for us to have psychological contact with in our day-to-day lives. For example, it is important to know if you have a peanut allergy, or if you are licenced to practice as a health professional, or how old your child is. However, self-as-content can also be problematic: for example, what if I (Lisa) considered my daughter's scattered nature or impulsivity "her fault," or something that is an unmalleable trait, rather than a behavior that might shift and change over time and various contexts? This might lead me to respond to her in similarly rigid and inflexible ways that don't foster her own flexibility or effective behavior.

Moreover, we naturally strive for a coherent and consistent self-as-content, other-as-content, and us-as-content, which can lead to oversimplification. For example, if you have the belief that you are a warm parent, then the times when you aren't warm might challenge the consistency of your conceptualized self, and you are likely to avoid or ignore moments when you are less than nurturing. This also applies to other-as-content and us-as-content; for example, once a parent has labeled their child as "shy," their child's ongoing behavior will be interpreted in terms of this label. This could lead to parent overprotectiveness or difficulty autonomy-granting (e.g., my child doesn't like large groups or parties, so I'll pick her up early/decline that invitation), which would fail to nurture the child's development of more flexible, approach-based behaviors.

Like all psychological content, we can contact self-as-content, other-as-content, and us-as-content from a stance of cognitive fusion or defusion. When fused (e.g., I am my conceptualized self), my idea of who I am and who others are is rigid, with defusion (e.g., I notice that this is how I think of myself, and of my child) it is flexible. This rigidity versus flexibility of the conceptualized self and other relates to the research on fixed versus growth mindsets (Dweck, 2006). Reinforcement of a conceptualized self that is rigid or trait-like leaves very little room for behavior change. However, supporting *behaviors* consistent with qualities one wants to nurture can shape a child's more fluid and growth-oriented view of themselves. From an ACT/RFT perspective, a fixed mindset can be understood as fusion with conceptualized self, and a growth mindset as a defused stance toward the conceptualized self.

Self-as-process is the experiencing self, the present-moment awareness of self-experience and flexible verbal self-knowledge as it unfolds moment to moment. Simply put, it refers to a defused awareness of one's way of being in a particular moment (e.g., I am tired, I am energized). It is highly related to mindfulness and can be described as mindfulness of the self. It includes a kind of self-monitoring; for example, knowing that you are hungry or feeling sad. Self-as-process directly informs our ongoing behavior. For example, if you recognize that you are beginning to feel hungry, then you begin planning when to have lunch. Other-as-process refers to the parent's ongoing awareness of the child's experiences moment-to-moment and us-as-process to the parent's ongoing awareness of the interactions between parent and child experiences, and both directly inform parenting behavior. In fact, both crucially underpin sensitive and responsive parenting. For example, a father that notices his baby flinches and looks away from his boisterous interaction, notices that his baby is reacting to his exuberance as intrusive and calms his interaction as a result. There are many workable verbal rules, both in terms of self-care and parenting that are impossible to implement without self-as-process, other-as-process and us-as-process. For example, "go to bed when you are feeling sleepy" or "feed baby as soon as she shows a feeding cue" are two rules that are impossible to implement without *as-process* awareness.

Self-as-context is the transcendent self. It is the perspective from which you can observe yourself; it is perspective as distinguished from psychological content. Self-as-context arises from deictic relations of I–here–now; it is the I–here–now perspective. Self-as-context is supported by mindfulness, defusion, and acceptance, and, in turn, can facilitate an accepting and compassionate stance toward the self. Self-as-context is associated with two types of relating—distinction and hierarchy. First, it can develop from distinguishing the observer self (I–here–now) from psychological content including thoughts, feelings, sensations, or memories (the conceptualized self; self-as-content). Second, it results from hierarchical framing between the observer self and psychological content including thoughts, feelings, sensations, or memories, with the observer self as a kind of host through which psychological content passes. Higher contact with self-as-context predicts lower depressive symptoms in adults (Atkins & Styles, 2016) and adolescents (Moran, Almada, & McHugh, 2018). Furthermore, establishing self-as-context through a hierarchical frame is more powerful than through a frame of distinction, with hierarchical relations associated with less distress

(Foody, Barnes-Holmes, Barnes-Holmes, & Luciano, 2013; Foody, Barnes-Holmes, Barnes-Holmes, Rai, & Luciano, 2015) and greater distress tolerance (Gil-Luciano, Ruiz, Valdivia-Salas, & Suarez-Falcon, 2017) and better cognitive performance in the presence of discomfort (Lopez-Lopez & Luciano, 2017).

Other-as-context is the recognition of the transcendent other (you–there–then), including the awareness that other people, too, contact the world from a transcendent perspective. It is the parent's awareness of their child as having a perspective and a mind of their own, as well as the ability to take that child's perspective beyond merely tracking the child's ongoing experience. For example, a parent might experience or understand their son as a person who remains the same individual, and yet who develops and changes over time, as they progress through childhood; this understanding differs from the conceptualized sense of a child (he is 3 years old today) or experience of one's child in the moment (he is being bratty). It also includes understanding that there is a distinction between another person and our own thoughts about and reactions to that other person. Whereas differentiating self and other at the level of content can generate judgment and distance, distinguishing between self-as-context and other-as-context allows compassion to emerge (Atkins, 2013). Empathy and compassion both involve the ability to take the perspective of the other (other-as-context) without losing awareness of one's observer self.

Us-as-context refers to understanding the parent–child relationship as an enduring *joint perspective* beginning at birth and extending throughout the child's development. *As-context* awareness can provide psychological space in which one can experience both *as-content* and *as-process* in a defused way, a space in which contact with *as-content* and *as-process* can be made flexibly (D. Barnes-Holmes, Hayes, & Dymond, 2001). For example, grounded within *as-context* awareness of self, other, and us, a parent might notice their beliefs that their son is stubborn (other-as-content) just like the parent themselves (self-as-content) and that two stubborn people leads to fights (us-as-content). Furthermore, the parent might notice that their son is, at this very moment, distressed and on the verge of throwing a tantrum (other-as-process), that they themselves are experiencing an urge to double down, to insist that their son comply (self-as-process), and that the potential for an escalation into a heated argument is present between them (us-as-process). The parent can notice all of this and hold it lightly, understanding that this moment will pass, seeing it from an enduring perspective that is larger than it all, seeing their self (self-as-context), their son (other-as-context), and their relationship (us-as-context), not as defined by these beliefs or present-moment experiences, but as a container large enough to hold it all.

Putting the RFT perspective in the context of the wider developmental literature, RFT is consistent with other theoretical approaches that see the development of self and other, and indeed cognitive development itself, as a socially mediated process. In fact, basic research has demonstrated that deictic framing is, in fact, a developmental process (McHugh et al., 2004). The earliest of social behaviors including early protoconversational interactions are likely an evolved preference for contingent reactions (Fonagy, Gergely, & Target, 2007). In other worlds, a human newborn comes into the world without social cognition per se, but with a preference for learning through social interactions. A human baby finds *attuned* interaction—interaction that is contingent and involves a mirroring of the baby's own psychological state—a salient reinforcer. With attuned social interactions, social cognition and intersubjectivity is developed. The attachment system may function as a kind of guarantee of knowledge legitimacy, by encouraging children to learn from attachment figures. Several bodies of literature, including on mentalization, theory of mind, parental mind-mindedness, and self-recognition are relevant (Coyne, Low, Miller, Seifer, & Dickstein, 2007).

Parental mentalizing involves interpreting behavior in terms of mental states and intention (Fonagy et al., 2007) and is thought to underlie sensitive and responsive parenting. The child is understood as constructing a subjective sense of self as one part of acquiring knowledge about the world through interactions with caregivers. In particular, interactions with a focus on the child's mental states. Consistent with an RFT perspective, our own minds are not understood as being transparent to us. Rather, just as we learn to interpret signals and signs of others as indicators of specific mental states so too do we learn to interpret our own cues as indicating our own mental states.

A related body of literature examines the concept of parental mind-mindedness. Mind-mindedness is the tendency of a parent to view their child as a psychological agent with a mind of their own (McMahon & Bernier, 2017). Mind-minded parents spontaneously use a greater number of mental-state words while interacting with their child. Parental mind-mindedness is thought to be one mechanism in the transmission of attachment and has been linked to the development of the child's theory of mind.

Importantly, the parent is thought to foster the child's development of perspective taking—not merely through frequent reference to mental states, but by *attuned or accurate* references to mental states (Fonagy et al., 2007; McMahon & Bernier, 2017). Coyne et al. (2007) found that in a sample of 128 mothers of 30-month-old children, parental empathic awareness was associated with observed measures of parenting sensitivity. Empathic awareness was conceptualized as the ability to take one's child's perspective and includes (1) understanding of and reflection on the child's motives, (2) the ability to hold a rich and detailed view of the child, and (3) willingness to accept and integrate new information into existing conceptualizations about one's child (Coyne et al., 2007; Oppenheim, Koren-Karie, & Sagi, 2001). Research on nonattunement in mind-mindedness has found that nonattuned comments are rare, but that is likely because the research is restricted to a free-play context. In attachment-rich interactions, or interactions in which the parent–child dyad is put under pressure, nonattunement is more likely.

One of the earliest signs of the development of the self is the passing of the mirror self-recognition test. The majority of children pass the mirror self-recognition test by 2 years of age (Courage, Edison, & Howe, 2004), that is, they take self-directed action to remove a mark that has been placed upon their head without their knowledge, if given a mirror. This shows that they recognize the image in the mirror as themselves. There are cultural differences in the development of self-awareness as measured by the mirror self-recognition test and by the alternative body-as-obstacle test, where the child must recognize that their body is an obstacle to achieving a goal (Ross et al., 2017). Children of individualistic cultures are more likely to achieve mirror self-recognition earlier, and children of collectivistic cultures more likely to achieve body-as-obstacle awareness earlier. This demonstrates the importance of learning in self-recognition development. Mirror self-recognition is restricted to humans and only a few other species, including chimpanzees (Hecht, Mahovetz, Preuss, & Hopkins, 2017). However, the ability is highly variable within chimpanzees, with some passing the test and some not. Chimpanzees who pass have more human-like whitematter tracts connecting frontal and parietal regions.

Theory of mind is the ability to understand mental states including thoughts, beliefs, desires, intentions, and emotions both those of others and our own. Theory of mind abilities in children are predicted by early joint attention and language development especially the early use of mental-state language (Derksen, Hunsche, Giroux, Connolly, & Bernstein, 2018). Theory of mind is also related to executive functioning. Early improvements in theory of mind are predicted by quality family interactions, particularly the parent's use of accurate mental state-rich language.

The classic theory of mind task is the false belief task. In this task, the child needs to recognize that a character will look for an object where they falsely believe it to be not where the object actually is. Babies and toddlers show some "implicit" theory of mind abilities such as spontaneous helping and anticipating an actor's behavior in the false belief task through eye gaze. However, children pass the false belief task verbally at about the age of three to four (Slaughter, 2015). By the age of 4 up to 10% of children's utterances refer to mental states with words like think, dream, know, and want.

Although the false belief task is the classic theory of mind task, theory of mind is broader than understanding false beliefs. Looking at theory of mind more broadly, children in Australia, America, and Europe acquire theory of mind concepts between the ages of 3 and 8 sequentially in the following order: diversity of desires, diversity of beliefs, differences in knowledge access, false beliefs, hidden emotions and, finally, sarcasm (Slaughter, 2015). In China and Iran a slightly different sequence is followed with children passing tasks related to understanding differences in knowledge access before understanding diversity of belief. This is likely related to cultural variations in parenting, again illustrating the importance of learning. The delay in theory of mind abilities within deaf children also illustrates the importance of language exposure (Jones, Gutierrez, & Ludlow, 2015). Children with Autism Spectrum Disorders (ASDs) show a deficit in theory of mind, passing theory of mind tasks at a later date than typical as well as passing hidden emotion tasks before false belief tasks, perhaps showing that false belief tasks are particularly something that people with ASDs find challenging (Slaughter, 2015).

There is some evidence that theory of mind abilities are related to deictic framing, with increases in theory of mind following deictic relational framing training (Weil, Hayes, & Capurro, 2011). Furthermore, deictic framing abilities show a similar developmental pattern of increasing competence (McHugh et al., 2004), including for false belief deictic framing protocols (McHugh, Barnes-Holmes, Barnes-Holmes, & Stewart, 2006) and for deception protocols (McHugh, Barnes-Holmes, Barnes-Holmes, Stewart, & Dymond, 2007). From an RFT perspective, false belief tasks involve a complex pattern of relational responding with deictic frames as well as understanding of the logical not (McHugh et al., 2006). Although this research is promising, to date, the research linking deictic relational responding and theory of mind is mixed (Montoya-Rodriguez et al., 2017). The deictic relational repertoire of children with autism can be improved with training, but this hasn't been shown to translate into changes in theory of mind, likely due to a failure of generalizability (Jackson, Mendoza, & Adams, 2014).

Deictic framing abilities continue to increase with age. Adolescents have been shown to be weaker on deictic tasks as compared to adults (McHugh et al., 2004). The now–then relation is more challenging than here–there and the reversed you-I ("if I was you and you were me") is easier than reversed now–then and here–there ("if here was there and there was here"). Diectic tasks may become increasingly complex in terms of the number of "jumps" of perspective; for example, from understanding that Sally has a false belief, to understanding that Andrew believes that Sally has a false belief, as well as including more subtly complex relational frames. For example, children begin using deictic time words as early as two. However, they don't show consistent adult like usage until between the ages of four and seven (Tillman, Marghetis, Barner, & Srinivasan, 2017). They initially may correctly understand that "yesterday," "last week," and "a long, long time ago" are in the past without being able to correctly order the concepts or to judge the relative distance of each from today or in relation to each other.

Theory of mind abilities predict social skills and prosocial behavior (Derksen et al., 2018), but the strength of the association between theory of mind abilities and prosocial behavior is surprisingly weak (Imuta, 2016).

Understanding another's perspective is not sufficient for prosocial behavior—there must also be a prosocial motivation. In fact, individuals with both high theory of mind abilities and a history of victimization may develop increased aggression (Derksen et al., 2018).

DNA–V model

This relates to the noticer, discoverer, self-view, and the social-view components of DNA–V (Hayes & Ciarrochi, 2015). The noticer and the discoverer are relevant in terms of self-as-process and other-as-process aspects, that is, the noticing and discovering of the moment-to-moment psychological process of the parent and the child. The self-as-context aspect relates to self-view in DNA–V. Other-as-context and the relationships between self-as-process and other-as-process relate to the social-view in DNA–V, that is, the tracking of the ongoing relationship between parent and child, as well as the parental recognition of the child as a perspective in their own right.

How does flexible perspective taking apply to parent–child interaction?

Parental flexible perspective taking and sensitivity

A parent's capacity and willingness to take the perspective of their child underlies parental sensitivity. In order to effectively respond to the child's cues, the parent must notice and track their child's cues. This involves other-as-process and us-as-process awareness. For example, an 11-month-old infant cries and tugs at her mother's top. The mother, tracking other-as-process, recognizes that she wants to have a breastfeed. This recognition is necessary to her being able to respond to the cue. The motivation for sensitivity is also linked to recognition of other-as-context and us-as-context. That is, recognizing that the child is an intentional being with a mind of his or her own. So, the mother doesn't just respond to the cue, but also attributes intentionality to the child's tugging at the top and treats the child's desire for a feed as something of importance.

The ability to be aware of and to track self-as-process and us-as-process is also useful. By tracking self-as-process, the parent can use their own reactions in a helpful way without becoming rigid or stuck in them. For example, a parent can recognize that the whining tone of their preschooler or the sarcastic remarks of their adolescent child are triggering a response of annoyance in themselves. They can both refrain from reacting to this feeling of annoyance, as well as to make use of this information by recognizing that their child's behavior is likely having a similar effect on others. Thus they can take effective steps to correct their child over time and not let a whining tone or sarcasm become a lifelong speech pattern.

Other-as-context means understanding children as having their own perspective, as well as understanding their child as someone who is constantly shifting and growing at the level of content and process. It means seeing the child as a conscious being, a "container" in which the conceptualized and the knowing child shifts, changes, and grows with time. With such an understanding, the parent does not expect the child to be static and unchanging at the level of content or process. Us-as-context means seeing the parent–child relationship as a "container" in which the conceptualized and experiential aspects of the relationship change and grow with time. Again, with this understanding, the parent does not expect the relationship to be static and unchanging either. Yet, they are anchored within an aspect of the relationship that is enduring.

Flexibly moving between all three types of self, other, and us awareness is important as is having a clear sense of differentiation between self and other. Without the clear differentiation of self and other, the parent could attribute to the child feelings and thoughts that are, in fact, their own. They could also become overwhelmed by the child's emotional reactions. Both undermine sensitivity.

Parental flexible perspective taking and mental health

Mental health is best supported by flexible self-as-content, as well as rich awareness of self-as-process, and self-as-context, particularly self-as-context supported by a hierarchical frame. If self-as-content is rigid then self-rules keep behavior inflexible and stuck in patterns that are not functional for parents or children. For example, depression in mothers of toddlers was related to lower empathic attunement and less-sensitive parenting (Coyne et al., 2007). High awareness of self-as-process is important for insight and for developing and acting on accurate and workable verbal rules including self-care. For example, with self-as-process, you can recognize that a particular event triggered an intense emotional response related to your history. You can then choose to engage in self-care. Without that initial recognition, self-care is not possible.

The research has linked self-as-context, particularly the hierarchical framing of self-as-context, to lower distress (Foody et al., 2013, 2015) and greater distress tolerance (Gil-Luciano et al., 2017).

Developing child's flexible perspective taking

There is a large literature base showing that parental interactions support in the development of perspective-taking abilities in children. In particular, parental mind-mindedness supports the development of child theory of mind abilities (Derksen et al., 2018; McMahon & Bernier, 2017). This means that the parent understands the child as an intentional being with a mind of their own, and uses attuned mental-state language spontaneously during interactions. Parental mind-mindedness, thus relies upon the parent's own flexible perspective-taking abilities.

Parental experiential avoidance, or rigidity in self-as-content or other-as-content, may undermine this process (Coyne et al., 2007). In order to respond to the child's mental states in a manner that promotes the child's development of flexible perspective taking, the parent must approach the child-as-process from a stance of acceptance. If the parent finds some mental states acceptable and others not then they will not accurately label mental states.

Flexible perspective taking and growth mindset

The literature on fixed versus growth mindsets can be related to the rigidity versus flexibility of the self-as-content. A rigid self-as-content can be understood as a fixed mindset, such as "I am bad at parenting." The conceptualized self is related to as a fixed and rigid entity, one that cannot be changed. Likewise, a fixed mindset involves relating to your qualities as if they were fixed and unchangeable (Dweck, 2006). In contrast, flexible self-as-content involves relating to aspects of the conceptualized self as a flexible, changeable, and growing entity. It can be understood as a growth mindset, in which personal qualities are understood as changeable through effort. For example, "I lack parenting skills. I am going to take a parenting course and learn how to parent better." The features of the conceptualized self may be the same—a deficit in parenting skill—but the features are related to as flexible, as something that is changeable. A growth mindset is related to persistence in the face of setbacks, motivation to put effort into learning, greater openness to criticism and, as a result, greater achievement over time (Dweck, 2006; Haimovitz & Dweck, 2017).

Process-focused parental praise, that is, praise for *effort and strategies*, is more likely to foster growth mindsets (Gunderson et al., 2018). Growth mindsets are also more likely to develop in the children of parents who see failure as a part of learning (Haimovitz & Dweck, 2016) and give process-focused criticism (Haimovitz & Dweck, 2017).

Gretchen and Sebastian

Sebastian is 13 and lives with his mother, Gretchen. Gretchen has become increasingly frustrated with their relationship and Sebastian's behavior and has decided to seek help. Gretchen explains that she is irritated with Sebastian because when he comes home from school, he avoids doing his homework and leaves his books and football gear all over the entryway to their house. He also is very short with her, and often gives single-word responses. Gretchen explains that the first thing he does is go upstairs and to play computer games. She has

(*Continued*)

(Continued)

become increasingly nagging, and he has become increasingly surly. She has tried speaking with him about starting a habit of homework first; of putting his football things away when he arrives at home, and of playing computer games *after* he has completed his homework. But his response to this is inconsistent, at best. She feels furious and exasperated. Sebastian seems to withdraw further when she is in this mood. After months of this, she finally decided that she will simply need to set limits and take away Sebastian's computer access until he does what she has asked him to do. But this didn't work either. Now Sebastian has become coming home later and later from school, and when she asks him where he has been, he says, simply, "out." Gretchen doesn't understand what's going on, and feels disconnected from him, and very concerned that he is so guarded and distant. She knows something is wrong, but she has no idea what—and that scares her.

Imagine you could, unseen and unheard, observe a typical, ordinary interaction between Sebastian and Gretchen. It might be something like this:

Parent–child interaction

Afternoon is turning to evening. Gretchen doesn't know where Sebastian is.

Finally, the front door opens, and Sebastian enters, immediately tossing his backpack on the table in the front hallway, and kicking off his shoes. He is quiet, and looks worn out.

Gretchen hears the door yells from the kitchen, "SEBASTIAN! What did I say about putting your stuff away? How many times do I have to tell you this? It's ONE SIMPLE THING. Why can't you just do it?"

Sebastian's shoulders stiffen, and he says, gruffly, "I'll do it in a minute."

Gretchen gets up from her chair and approaches as she talks, "NO, you will do it NOW."

Sebastian looks away, and darts quickly up the stairs to his room without answering.

"SEBASTIAN!" Gretchen yells, "Don't you walk away from me!"

Sebastian can hear her from behind the closed door of his bedroom. He leans up against it and sinks down onto the floor, putting his face in his hands. *She just doesn't get it,* he thinks. *I feel so alone. No one talks to me at school...and I have to come home to this.* He hears her yell again.

"Will you PLEASE LEAVE ME THE FUCK ALONE," he screams through the door, slamming his fist into it with each word.

"That's IT! I am TAKING YOU TO TALK TO SOMEONE!" Gretchen is fuming, feeling angry, and ashamed. *Where has that sweet boy gone,* she thinks.

What's happening for Gretchen and Sebastian?

This parent–child interaction shows an impoverishment in flexible perspective taking. Gretchen shows limited contact with as-process or as-context awareness for self, other and relationship. Instead, she appears fused to as-content about herself, Sebastian and their relationship, thoughts like "I just don't know how to reach him" or "I'm a terrible parent" and this is likely related to

(*Continued*)

(Continued)

uncomfortable feelings. Her parenting is rigid and inflexible. She shows little awareness of what the antecedents might be for Sebastian's "problematic" behaviors at home, or her contribution to the escalation of their interactions through rigid engagement in nagging (other-as-process and us-as-process). Her loss of contact with us-as-context, with the ability to understand her relationship with Sebastian as an enduring shared perspective, larger than her thoughts about that relationship or their moment-to-moment interaction, is painful and contributes to their disconnect.

From a clinical RFT perspective, Gretchen appears to have derived an oppositional relationship between "terrible parenting" and "knowing how to reach" her son. This may be driving her rigid and inflexible bids for his attention, which quickly become harsh, and authoritarian—and succeed in doing the opposite of what she hopes. She also appears to have derived an oppositional frame (a deictic now–then relation) between the surly teenager Sebastian is now and the "sweet boy" that has gone—which leaves her unable to access any "sweetness" in Sebastian in the present.

Clinicians might harness these derived relations through experiential work involving asking Gretchen to bring her "sweet boy" to the present, and to allow herself to visualize an interaction with him in as much detail as she can. Then, perhaps clinicians might ask her to imagine the outlines of that "sweet boy's" face in Sebastian's face now, to help transform some of the aversive functions that arise in his presence now. Finally, asking her to first notice the "sweet boy" before she addresses Sebastian with a question or demand may evoke a different emotional tone to her response to him—and perhaps offer her some new opportunities to track the effects of her behavior on his.

Working with flexible perspective taking clinically

The level of flexible perspective taking that a parent has will be apparent in how they talk about their child and their parenting challenges as well as in their interactions with their child. It also has to do with the breadth and complexity with which they describe their child and his or her behavior, as well as their ability to notice and assimilate inconsistent or surprising information about their child (Coyne et al., 2007), and it also will be apparent in their sensitivity to context. In particular:

- Some parents will be stuck on certain narrow pieces of self-as-content. This may be something that is negative "I am a bad father" or something that is neutral or even positive such as "I am a strict parent." Nevertheless this aspect of conceptualized self is held rigidly and gets in the way if flexible responding. You may even agree with the description as an overall description. It may be true enough. However, the parent loses contact with the moments in which this description doesn't hold, with the full complexity of who they are. This indicates as piece of rigid self-as-content. It may also indicate deficits in self-as-process and self-as-context. In sum, it is important to help parents shift from "I am" formulations about *who they are* to more accurately reflecting their thoughts and experiences; for example, "I am having the experience of..." or "In this situation, I feel..."or "I am learning..."

- Some parents may be stuck with certain conceptualizations about the child or their relationship. It may be something that is negative "she is naughty" or "we don't get along" or something that is neutral or even positive such as "he is a genius" or "we are like best friends." Nevertheless this aspect of as-content is held rigidly and intervenes with flexible and workable parenting. The description may even be true enough. But held rigidly the parent loses contact with the full complexity of the child and relationship moment by moment. Thus it is important to support parents shifting from rigid "he/she is" conceptualizations of stable, inflexible characteristics of their children to more a more fluid, lightly held perspective that attends to context; specifically, "He is learning," or "Given that he had a bad day, he may feel/need/think...."
- The parent may lack awareness of their own ongoing experiences. For example, the parent may be unable to tell you how they feel or may deny feelings that are noticeable in their affect and expression. This indicates a deficit in self-as-process. Consequently, clinicians may encourage parents to become more attuned to their emotional and physical state, such that they are able to make more mindful parenting choices. For example, a parent might shift from "I never know what to say to him" to "I'm feeling stressed about work, and anxious myself, and that seems to get in the way of me thinking clearly about how to speak to my son."
- The parent may lack awareness of their child's ongoing experiences within their context. For example, in a younger child or baby, the parent may persistently miss the child's cues. In an older child or teenager you might notice a parent downplaying their child's emotions, contradicting their child about the child's own experience, or attributing thoughts and feelings to the child that are implausible. This indicates a deficit in other-as-process and us-as-process (and a deficit that is interfering with parental sensitivity). Here, clinicians may help parents be curious and try to better track their child's experiences, and thus make better guesses about what their child might need, or how best to have their child hear them. For example, if an older child comes home from school and bullies her little brother, a parent might respond by sitting her down to see what her day has been like before immediately scolding her about the bullying. Doing so may allow the parent to find out important information, such as that the child did poorly on an important test at school.

- The parent may seem unable or unwilling to take the child's perspective at all. This may include persistent expectations that are not reasonable or are developmentally inappropriate, given the child's perspective or attributing a perspective to the child that is implausible or attributing no mental states to the child at all, seeing their behavior as random rather than intentional. It may also include seeing the child as a means to an end, relating to the child as a tool for achieving a dream of the parent, or like a toy or a doll. In short, the parent does not relate to the child as a person in their own right with a mind of their own. This indicates a deficit in other-as-context. There is likely a deficit in other-as-process as well. For these parents, clinicians can help parents contact what their children's behavior might mean to the child, ideally through experiential work.
- The parent may struggle to flexibly shift between the conceptualized, knowing, and transcendent aspects of self, other, and relationship. Such a parent may demonstrate contact with all aspects at times and yet persistently get stuck. The parent may have a deficit in the ability to contact *as-content* and *as-process* aspects from *as-context* awareness.
- The parent may struggle to differentiate between self and other. For example, the parent may attribute their own feelings to their child when this is implausible or the parent may become overwhelmed by the feelings of the child, as if the feelings were their own, interfering in their ability to respond sensitively. This may indicate deficits in both self-as-process and other-as-process. There may also be self-as-context or other-as-context deficits.
- The parent's account may have a scripted even emotionless feel. It may sound like an old story that has been told many times before. This indicates that the parent is in contact with as-content for self, other, and relationship.
- When fused with self-as-content, parents can get stuck in coercive interactions with their children such that they work to avoid or escape painful private events. For example, parenting behaviors geared toward making "I can't stand this kid right now" go away may grow punitive, or at the other end of the spectrum, lax, simply to get out of an uncomfortable situation. Such responses are not generally thoughtful or sensitive choices, and tend to intensify coercion and avoidance rather than shaping more meaningful interactions or responsive parenting.
- Loss of contact with us-as-context, especially when coupled with fusion with us-as-content, or painful us-as-process can be present in rigid, inflexible interaction as well as feelings of disconnection and loneliness.

Use of mindfulness

Mindfulness is a foundational step in building as-process awareness for self, other, and relationship. Any mindfulness exercise that uses self as a focus point—for example, mindfulness of breathing, body, thoughts, or feelings—is supporting self-as-process. Drawing your client's attention to the self in the moment—for example, with questions like "where do you feel that in your body?"—also supports self-as-process.

Likewise, any mindfulness exercise that uses the child as a focus point—for example, the mindfulness during a parent–child interaction exercises as given in this book—are supporting other-as-process and us-as-process awareness. Using questions and prompts to draw the parent's attention to the child, and the child's mental states in the moment, such as "what do you think she is wanting right now?" also supports other-as-process. Using questions and prompts to draw the parent's attention to the shifting, moment-to-moment ongoing interaction between parent and child supports us-as-process.

Mindfulness can also be used as a springboard into as-context awareness. Self-as-context can be facilitated by turning mindful attention onto the perspective taking itself. For example, weaving into a mindfulness of the breath exercise, "notice your breathing and then notice who's noticing it." Other-as-context experiences can be fostered in a similar way by, within a parenting mindfulness task, noticing the self as a noticer and then noticing that the child too is a perspective that is noticing. Us-as-context, by focusing mindfulness on the enduring joint perspective.

Use of defusion

Defusion is particularly useful for rigidity around as-content. Any defusion exercise can be applied to rigid aspects of conceptualized self, other, and relationship. Some defusion exercises that may be particularly useful are:

- Writing down words or phrases signifying the conceptualized self, child, or relationship on a piece of paper. Prompt the parent to hold the piece of 8 × 11 paper up to their face and to try to interact with their child. Then ask the parent to try interacting with their child with the piece of paper sitting in their lap or in their pocket. Emphasize that the parent is still in contact with the thought and have them notice the differences between interacting with the child with the thought blocking their line of sight, and with the thought present, but on their lap.
- Ask the parent to try carrying a number of words indicating "unwanted" stories of self, child, and their relationship on index cards during the day. Have the parent keep them in their pocket and look at them from time to time.
- Using a sticky label, put a particularly rigid piece of self-as-content onto a label and have the parent wear it on their clothes. Ask the parent to introduce themselves to you using the self-as-content. Model by following the parent's example, using an honest, but contextually appropriate bit of self-as-content from your own experience (e.g., "I am not enough").

Simple questioning

Simple questions and prompts built into therapy can support the development of as-process and as-context awareness by directing the parent's attention to particular aspects of their experience and context. These include:

- Questions and prompts supporting mindfulness in that moment. For example, "notice the tension in your body right now. How would you describe that tension?" or "notice your child's expression when you said that. What do you think he's feeling?"
- Questions and prompts supporting defusion, such as "notice the "I'm a bad mother" story is back" and "what do you notice happens in your body when you notice that thought arise?"
- Questions that are unexpected, that go beyond the expected narrative. Questions that are unexpected require the client to establish contact with as-process awareness in order to answer. This may be as simple as asking the client to describe the scene. For example, the parent leaps into a familiar narrative about a recent interaction with their child. The parent's description feels highly rigid and conceptualized. You could stop the parent and prompt contact with as-process awareness by getting the parent to describe the scene. You might say for example, "Wait a moment. Paint a picture for me. What was the time of day? Where were you? Were you standing or sitting? And where was your child?"

Metaphors

The following metaphor can be used to promote self-as-context. It uses the hierarchical relational frame of self as a context in which living is experienced. It can be used with any competitive activity that has two sides and in which there is also a wider context in which the competition happens. In this example, the battle and the battlefield is used, but you could also use a boardgame like chess (chess and the chessboard) or snakes and ladders (snakes and ladders and the snakes and ladders board) or a sport like football (football and the field).

The battlefield metaphor

It is as if you classify every bit of yourself, every thought, every feeling, every memory, and every fact as either being good or bad. And you line them all up. Here's all the good stuff—the positive thoughts about your child, the loving feelings toward them, the good memories, and a list of good facts. And here's all the bad stuff—the negative thoughts about your child, the angry feelings towards

(*Continued*)

(Continued)

them and the sad feelings about them, the bad memories and a list of bad facts. The good side. And the bad side. And it seems like the best thing to do is to eliminate the bad side. We don't want the bad side to win and so we become the general of the good army, trying to lead that side to victory. And the battle rages on and on. The bad stuff can't be vanquished. You can't kill a thought or a feeling or a memory. It all keeps coming back. And if you are the general of the good army that's a threat. Because you've got to win this war. But is that who you are, really? What if you aren't the general at all? What if you are the field on which they fight? And the wide-open sky they fight beneath? What if you are bigger than all of it? And you could contain it all?

The next metaphor is to promote greater flexibility toward as-content for self, other, and the relationship.

Your relationship with your child: a film

Imagine someone was going to make a movie about you and your child. Your whole life together to date condensed into about 90 minutes or so. Do you think 90 minutes could capture all the complexity of you, your child and your relationship or do you think you'd watch the movie and think that they'd left a lot out? Yeah, even if everything was accurate it'd be a simplified version, wouldn't it? It'd have to be. Some events would be left out, some important people in your lives would be left out, and some plot lines would be greatly simplified. Even if it was accurate it'd be a real simplification. And so much would depend on the director and the actors, right? They'd come with their own perspectives. Like imagine one director made the film and wanted it to be dark and gritty, and another director wanted it to be uplifting and family friendly, and yet another wanted to make a comedy. They'd be very different films, right? Yet they could all be accurate. And what about the differences between a big budget Hollywood version and a small budget indie version or even a Bollywood version. And then there's the actors. Imagine seeing yourself played by ten different actors. Like imagine the try outs. If they were talented you'd recognize yourself for sure. But they'd each have their own take on you. Imagine how many movies we could make! Each different, each accurate, and none coming close to capturing the full complexity of you, your child, and your relationship.

Experiential exercises

The following two experiments are inspired by the headlessness experiments of Harding (2012). The first is intended to promote self-as-context.

An experiment in perspective

This experiment involves noticing how things are from your own perspective. Of course, you are always seeing the world from your own perspective but often we don't really notice it. I'm going to ask you to put your knowledge of the world, even logic, aside and instead look at things as they are *in your experience.*

First of all point to an object in front of you. Focus on what you see and experience not on what you know or can deduce. In your experience, does what you are pointing to have a color? Does what you are pointing to have a shape? Does what you are pointing to have a size? Perhaps it is big or small? Is what you are pointing to a thing with definite boundaries? Can you see edges where it begins or ends?

Now turn your pointing finger around so you are pointing at your own face. Focus on what you see and experience not on what you know or can deduce. In your experience, does what you are pointing to have a color? Does what you are pointing to have a shape? Does what you are pointing to have a size? Perhaps it is big or small? Is what you are pointing to a thing with definite boundaries? Can you see edges where it begins or ends?

If you like, you can repeat the experiment in front of a mirror. Stand in front of a mirror. Point to yourself in the mirror. Focus on what you see and experience not on what you know or can deduce. In your experience, does what you are pointing to have a color? Does what you are pointing to have a shape? Does what you are pointing to have a size? Perhaps it is big or small? Is what you are pointing to a thing with definite boundaries? Can you see edges where it begins or ends?

Now step away from the mirror and turn your pointing finger around so you are pointing at your own face. Focus on what you see and experience not on what you know or can deduce. In your experience, does what you are pointing to have a color? Does what you are pointing to have a shape? Does what you are pointing to have a size? Perhaps it is big or small? Is what you are pointing to a thing with definite boundaries? Can you see edges where it begins or ends?

This second experiment builds on the first by incorporating other-as-context and us-as-context awareness.

A second experiment on perspective: an experiment for two

This experiment is about noticing how things are in your experience. It involves putting aside knowledge and logic, and instead, focusing on what you experience in your perspective.

If you have an older child then you might like to enlist your child in the experiment. Do it together, getting them to answer the same questions. If you and your child are doing the experiment together then find somewhere you can sit comfortably facing each other.

(*Continued*)

(Continued)

If you have a baby or a younger child then you can do the experiment yourself.
Sit comfortably so that you can watch your child.
Look at your child.
Notice the face in front of you. Take a moment to notice your child's expression.
Run your eyes over their face. Meet their eyes if you can.
Now, turn your attention back to notice who is noticing them.
Notice that enduring sense of perspective.
Notice it is the same you noticing your child now as the you who first saw your child maybe many years ago.
Notice that in front of you is your child's face.
In your experience, from your side, can you see your face?
Notice that your side is open and wide.
Notice that you are a space for your child to be.
Your openness, your lack of a face, provides the space for your child's face to show up for you.
Now imagine what it looks like from your child's point of view.
Your child too has their own enduring sense of perspective.
When did you first recognize that in them?
Your child's perspective is different to yours.
Yet, in a way it is the same.
Your child, too, is open and vast.
Your child's openness provides the space for your face to show up for your child.
From your perspective, you are openness, and your child's face shows up for you.
From your child's perspective your child is openness and your face shows up for them.
Yet always what is present is openness and a face.

A third experiment in perspective: time traveling

Engage the parent in an experiential exercise in which you have them call to mind a relevant developmental period in their past (i.e., to "time travel"). If they have an adolescent child, for example, have them go back to a specific event or situation during their own teen years when they might have been struggling. Have them step back into that space, and look out from their own, teenage eyes, and allow whatever thoughts and feelings might show up to arise. Have them notice what it felt like to be in that space, and ask them what it was the most needed back in that moment. Ask, "if teenage you could give you advice for what to say to your child now, what would she say?" Once the exercise is finished, you can use it as a touchstone for the parent to step back, and contact other-as-context and other-as-process in challenging conversations with their teen.

Meditations

Parenting: a context for parent and child

This meditation expands on the mindfulness meditation for a parent–child interaction given in previous chapters. It is suitable for parents of children of all ages.

Parenting: a context for parent and child script

As your interaction with your child begins.
Deliberately bring your awareness into the present moment.
You might like to use your breathing, that steady rhythm to anchor you.
Or the feeling of the ground under your feet.
Be here: in the unfolding moment.
Gently let your awareness focus on your child.
Let your child lead the interaction as much as possible.
If your child speaks then listen carefully with an open heart.
Take what your child says lightly and gently.
Let your child lead the conversation.
Let your child lead in any play.
Play within your child's world.
Exploring it with curiosity and openness.
If you become distracted then notice that and bring yourself back to the present moment with your child.
Perhaps reanchoring yourself in your breathing or the ground under your feet.
Bring awareness to your interaction with your child.
Notice your child as they are in this moment.
And then, notice who is noticing your child.
Notice there is your child.
There are your thoughts and feelings about your child.
And then there is you, noticing it all.
Notice that enduring perspective that's been present at every moment of your life.
From your childhood and throughout your life with your child.
Notice that you are open, that you can contain any thought, feeling, or experience.
Notice your child.
And then, notice who is noticing your child.
Recognize that your child, too, has their own perspective.
In your child's experience, your child notices you.
In your child's experience, your child is open.
Notice that your perspectives are different.
And yet, the same in their openness.
Notice too the moments when you share awareness.
When you notice something, together,

(*Continued*)

(Continued)

And notice who is noticing that,
Notice that you can be aware together.
As best you can, allow your interaction to come to a natural close.
Let your child lead that too.
If you need to bring the interaction to an end, then do so gently.
Bringing yourself back to the full present moment.
Keep the sense of connection with you.

Seeing as-content and as-process from as-context

This is a meditation on examining as-content and as-process grounded in as-context.

Seeing as-content and as-process from as-context script

Get yourself into a comfortable position.
Your position should feel comfortable, as well as promoting wakefulness at the same time.
Let yourself have a relaxed, comfortable posture.
Settle into it.
You can leave your eyes open, resting on a point of focus.
Or closed.
Or hooded, whichever you prefer.
Let your hands rest gently on your knees or in your lap or in some other comfortable posture.
Allow your mind to settle into the here and now.
Bring your attention to the sensations in your body...
Use your breath as an anchor to connect to the here and now.
Use the sensations of the floor beneath you to ground you in the present moment.
Notice your breathing.
And then, notice who is noticing it.
Notice the sensations of the floor beneath you.
And then, notice who is noticing it.
Notice the noticing self.
The enduring sense of perspective.
How long has that been with you?
Anchor yourself in it.
And, when you are ready,
Bring to mind a thought or a belief about yourself.
Examine the thought or belief with curiosity.
Like a child might look at a shell on the beach.
Or a colorful feather in a field.

(*Continued*)

(Continued)

Notice the thought, the belief and then, notice who is noticing it.
Notice the thought, and then gently scan your body.
Does the thought trigger any reactions in you?
Notice the reactions, and then, notice who is noticing it.
Notice that there are your thoughts and beliefs about yourself.
And then there's you, noticing them.
Notice that there are your reactions and experiences.
And then there's you, noticing them.
If you want to, you can repeat the exercise with a belief about your child.
Bring to mind a thought or a belief about your child.
Examine the thought or belief with curiosity.
Like a child might look at a shell on the beach.
Or a colorful feather in a field.
Notice the thought, the belief and then, notice who is noticing it.
Notice the thought, and then gently scan your body.
Does the thought trigger any reactions in you?
Notice the reactions, and then, notice who is noticing it.
Notice that there are your thoughts and beliefs about yourself.
And then there's you, noticing them.
Notice that there are your reactions and experiences.
And then there's you, noticing them.
When you are ready to end the exercise, do so gently.
Bring your awareness with you back to the full present moment.

Promoting flexible perspective taking in the child or adolescent

The child's development of flexible perspective taking can be supported by the parent through ordinary, everyday parenting interactions. For example:

- Through mind-mindedness, or empathic attunement to one's child. That is, seeing the child as an intentional being with a mind of their own from birth and providing, through interaction, exposure to rich mental-state language. The use of mental-state language should be frequent and also accurate. As children age, more subtle mental-state language can be used; for example, words such as "melancholy" or "elated." This may begin by parents helping children notice and label their own feelings, thoughts and physical sensations throughout the context of their day. Another way this occurs is through the parent modeling this noticing process with their own private events as well for example saying, "I'm feeling quite down today. I think it is because I've had a long week at work."
- Prompting perspective taking when reading stories or watching media through questions like, "how do you think she's feeling?" or "what do you think he is going to do next? "With older children, this can be expanded by deliberately seeking books and media that are subtextually complex, where perspective taking is required to fully understand the story at another level.

- Prompting perspective taking for other people and animals during everyday interactions with questions like, "do you think kitty likes that?" or "why is doggie barking? What does doggie want?" During middle childhood and adolescence this can include using perspective taking to understand and explore the child's social interactions with peers.
- Through mental state rich pretend play; for example, asking about the dolly's feelings or why doggie is dancing.
- By having "values and vulnerabilities" conversations with one's child; this is particularly impactful in middle childhood and adolescence. For example, a parent, after a fight with a teen, might say, "I am sorry to have yelled. It was wrong of me to speak to you like that, even though I was angry (vulnerability). It's just that I get so frightened at the thought of you not being safe when you come home late (vulnerability)—your safety and well-being are more important to me than anything (values), although I know this all comes out wrong sometimes (vulnerability)." This models for the child a willingness to accept and acknowledge unwanted or unhelpful behaviors in themselves, while demonstrating acting with intention, consistent with values.
- By giving both praise and criticism that is process-orientated, that is focused on effort and strategy, to support the development of flexible self-as-content.

Encouraging home practice

Home practice around flexible perspective taking may include:

- Practicing flexible perspective-taking exercises.
- Cultivating a habit of tracking as-process for self, child, and relationship. A journal or a diary may be useful.
- Being conscious of perspective taking, and talking about mental states in everyday life, using real-life social interactions, books, and media as opportunities.

Work with Gretchen and Sebastian

This interaction occurs early on in therapy.

Therapist:	Tell me a bit about your concerns for Sebastian.
Mom:	He's always sullen. I can't talk to him, and I'm worried that he may be drinking, or trying drugs with his friends. But I don't know any of his friends—he doesn't say much. He's like a ghost around the house—if it weren't for his messes everywhere, or the fights we have about those, I'd hardly know he's there. He just stays in his room, on the computer all the time. I am really tired of having to say

(*Continued*)

(Continued)

	things, like, 100 times to get him to do anything around the house.
Therapist:	Let's slow down here, and take a breath. (pause) This sounds really hard, and just listening to you, noticing the look on your face, how you are speaking, it seems like you feel really stuck. It seems like he feels like a stranger to you.
Mom: exasperated	YES! This is what I've been saying....
Therapist:	Yes. Let's slow down a little bit more—I know you are feeling urgency in trying to fix this situation, but let's just pause for a minute. I want to make sure I really get what it is like to be in your shoes when you feel this struggle. (pause) I notice you seem to look a little sad.
Mom: after a pause	...I guess I am just so worried about that sweet kid Sebastian once was...I miss him...I'm afraid I'm losing him.
Therapist:	Let's just stay with that for a moment, and allow for all those thoughts and feelings to be here. (pause) From this space, what do you feel is the most important thing you'd want him to know?
Mom: pausing	...I guess just...that I miss him, and I'm here...and I wish he would talk to me. And...
Therapist:	Yes? (pause) Whatever it is, let's try to make a space for it here.
Mom: quietly	It's just...I'm so scared that I'm doing something wrong. I don't know how to fix it.
Therapist:	I'd like you to step back for a moment, and see if you can imagine seeing things from his eyes. See if you can visualize yourself from his perspective, in, say, one of the fights you have with him.
Mom: pausing	Wow. I don't like how I look—so angry. If I were him, I wouldn't want to talk to me either.
Therapist: pausing	Just allow yourself to stay in this perspective for a moment. What would you say he most needs from you right now, in this fight, as he notices you yelling at him?
Mom:	I think just...to know that even if I am angry, I still love him, and I'm here, and wish he would talk with me. That he's more important than these fights, or his messiness.
Therapist:	What if we worked on that—on you reconnecting with him? Does that feel important, the right thing to do now?
Mom:	Yes, it does.

(Continued)

(Continued)

In the above example, Sebastian's mother moves from a rigid, inflexible, other-as-content perspective of Sebastian to contact both self-as-process (seeing herself yelling) other-as-process (noticing how he might feel in the moment), and other-as-context (that he is bigger and more important than his behaviors or choices in any given time). The therapist uses an experiential exercise in which he asks Sebastian's mother to shift through now–then, I–you, and here–there derived relations specifically to help shape her use of perspective taking in challenging parent–child interactions. In doing so, Gretchen is able to connect with her value of connection with Sebastian. Gretchen's therapist, through multiple such interactions, builds Gretchen's flexible perspective-taking abilities, along with her capacities for mindfulness, experiential acceptance, and contact with values. Gretchen begins to experiment flexibly with different parenting behavior and the interactions between her and Sebastian begin to shift.

Now when Sebastian comes home from school his mom notices that he seems quiet, preoccupied. Once again, he sets his football things down, haphazardly, in the hall, and quickly heads for the stairs. Sebastian's mom takes a breath, and notices that she is holding her body tightly. She was finishing up a project for work in the kitchen, and feels slightly irritated at the interruption in her flow of thought, and at the sight of the soccer gear everywhere. She also notices the tight, drawn look on his face, and thinks, *perhaps he had a bad day*. She notices this, breathes into it, and says, gently, "Sebastian?" At first, he does not appear to hear her, so she moves closer to him, noticing a bit of apprehension, "Sebastian?" He looks up. "Hi. I'm glad you're home." He grunts, looks down. "Just checking in with you, as I see you are in a hurry. Before you go upstairs, do you think we could sit down for a moment? I can make a quick snack, if you are hungry." She pauses, inwardly flinching, as she expects him to make a snotty comment and leave. Sebastian, to her surprise, slows his movements, glances at her briefly, and says, "Actually, yeah. I'm kind of hungry." He meets her eyes, and she smiles at the brief moment of connection. From these small shifts, change happens.

Troubleshooting

Defense of self-as-content

Most of us are deeply invested in defending our self-as-content, especially any aspects of self-as-content that have become rigid. There may be complex histories associated with those aspects of conceptualized self. Instead of attempting to change particular aspects of self-as-content directly, the focus needs to be on enhancing flexibility of self-as-content in general, as well as enhancing psychological contact with self-as-process and self-as-context. Aspects of self-as-content can then be contacted, as needed, from the perspective of self-as-context, with continued contact with self-as-process.

Deficits in self-as-process

An inability to describe how you are currently feeling emotionally or even physically is indicative of a lack of contact with self-as-process. It may be the case that a rich self-as-process repertoire never developed, most frequently due to a consistent pattern of experiential avoidance or lack of adult models. In this situation the parent themselves needs to learn to accurately track moment-to-moment psychological events in themselves as well as in their child. Mindfulness coupled with modeling as-process by accurately labeling the parent's psychological states can provide the opportunity for the parent to learn. A deficit in self-as-process may also be related to a history of trauma. It may be the case that rich self-as-process repertoires never developed due to childhood trauma or the case that a numbing to emotions or physical sensations has occurred as a part of a trauma response. If you suspect that trauma may be a factor, ensure mindfulness practices are done in a way that is sensitive to trauma. For example, if traditional focus points such as the breath are difficult, then use a focus point that feels safer for the client. Often a physical extremity, a part of the body more removed from the vasovagal system, such as the hands, can provide a safer focus point. If that feels unsafe, you might begin with mindful awareness of stimuli—like sound or color—outside of the body. Instead of the extremes of either supporting experiential avoidance, or demanding instant full willingness, allow the client to choose a safer focus point, and to "dip in" to the more difficult sensations and emotions, while anchored in the safe focus point.

Four key developmental periods and flexible perspective taking

Infancy and flexible perspective taking

With parenthood comes a shift in self-as-content, we discover who we are in this entirely new domain of "parenting" and the reality may be very different to our expectations. In addition, our new understandings of ourselves as a parent may conflict with our old and familiar understanding of ourselves in our other roles; for example, our understanding of ourselves as a partner, a worker, or a friend. This shift may be the seed of positive personal growth or it may simply be a challenge. Regardless, we instinctively strive for consistency within self-stories and so will attempt to smooth out and understand this new shift. Grounding of ourselves within self-as-context, tracking self-as-process, and examining pieces of self-as-content from this wider perspective is beneficial.

The most crucial aspect of parenting in the early months of infancy is for parenting to come under the contextual control of the baby's cues. That is, for the parent to develop a sensitive and responsive pattern of responding to their child. As-process and as-context awareness of the child and the parent--child relationship is crucial. That is, parents need to see their new baby as an intentional being with a perspective of their own and to be able and motivated to effectively and accurately track their child's ongoing psychological processes. Even before birth a conceptualized child is begins to develop in the mind of the parent. Small facts like a physical resemblance to one of the parents, the child's biological sex, or even aspects of the birth or early weeks may have rich psychological meaning in the mind of the parent. It is important for the parent to hold all of this lightly, from a larger us-as-context perspective.

Parental mind-mindedness in these early years—seeing the child as an intentional being and using mental state-rich language that accurately tracks the child's mental state—fosters the early development of prescriptive-taking abilities.

Early childhood and flexible perspective taking

The parent has likely developed a rich and detailed other-as-content for the child as well as an us-as-content for the relationship. Aspects of this conceptualized child may be particularly sticky and without a grounding in other-as-context and other-as-process may interfere with flexible and workable parenting. This is a time period when children become more mobile and autonomous, and take greater risks, further afield in the world. They also begin to develop social competence as they enter preschool and shift from parallel play to engaging with peers. It is also at this period that pretend play develops, in which children practice in rudimentary ways how to take on the perspectives of others: "I'll be the mommy, you be the daddy, and Cindy will be the baby." In a sense, this is a developmental phase in which children begin their own playful perspective taking, as their social worlds expand from home to daycare or preschool.

As children acquire the basic deictic frames they also acquire perspective-taking abilities, with most typically developing children passing the false belief task at 3–4 years of age. With emerging mastery of perspective taking comes greater emotional competence and social skill, as well as a reduction in behaviors such as temper tantrums and an increase in the ability to negotiate, reason and compromise. It should not be surprising that toddlers, with their rudimentary perspective-taking skills, engage in frequent temper tantrums and related behaviors. Without the ability to see the perspectives of others, other people must seem to be irrational tyrants, illogically inflicting undesirable events on everyone. Although greater perspective-taking abilities is related to better social skills, it is not necessarily the case that perspective-taking abilities will lead to prosociality. For example, with perspective taking also comes the ability to deceive and to manipulate others. Other ingredients too are needed, such as rich opportunities to practice prosocial behavior, as well as reinforcement for that behavior.

Middle childhood and flexible perspective taking

Perspective taking continues to develop to higher levels. For example, in the false belief task children acquire the ability to track that another person thinks that a third person thinks a particular false belief. Children also acquire the ability to understand hidden emotions and sarcasm as well as more complex deictic language, for example being able to order and understand the relation between "yesterday," "last week," and "a long, long time ago." They begin to experiment with reasoning from the perspectives of others, and respond to what they infer others might be thinking. Again, while perspective taking can be used in prosocial ways, it also may have a dark side. This is one of the developmental periods during which internalizing and externalizing problems can develop; when children start to feel self-aware, and self-conscious about peer evaluations, and their position in social hierarchies.

With improving perspective-taking abilities comes a more complex conceptualized self. Especially relevant at this age is the development of rigid self-as-content versus flexible self-as-content, particularly as it relates to academic pursuits. Children with more flexible self-as-content, which can be related to a growth mindset, are more likely to persist in learning.

Adolescence and flexible perspective taking

During adolescence, there is a normal developmental focus on the conceptualized self. Adolescents may experiment with different identities and be focused on finding a sense of self within the peer group, and more broadly, in the world. At this period, adolescents begin to imagine themselves as emerging adults and seek greater autonomy. This also occasions the process of noticing distinctions from their younger selves, as well as from their parents, as they begin to individuate. If adolescents do not feel at home in their social or school environments during this period, the development of visualizing their "future selves" and its concomitant independence may be constrained, as they may not feel a sense of belonging in the world, while they are still struggling with separating from parents. Some of these aspects of conceptualized self may be in conflict with the parent's conceptualized understandings of their child. The parent will need to be able to view all of that from a wider as-context perspective.

Using flexible perspective taking with specific populations

Parental mental health problems and flexible perspective taking

Mental health is best supported by self-as-context. In fact, higher contact with self-as-context predicts lower depressive symptoms in adults (Atkins & Styles, 2016) and adolescents (Moran et al., 2018). Contact with self-as-process is also important for self-care. In addition, rigidity in self-as-content can lead to self-rules and keep behavior inflexible and stuck in dysfunctional patterns.

Parental grief and flexible perspective taking

Experiences of loss may lead to specific aspects of conceptualized self. For example, a woman who has experienced repeated miscarriages may develop the self-concept of "I cannot protect my child." It is important to be able to take a defused stance toward such aspects of the conceptualized self; without doing so, behavior may become rigid and inflexible. For example, the woman may stop trying to fall pregnant, in spite of medical advice that with persistence she is likely to carry a child to term.

Childhood externalizing problems and flexible perspective taking

Parents of children with externalizing problems develop attributions for their child's behavior. Attributing the behavior to something stable and internal to the child is most likely to be problematic (Johnston & Freeman, 1997; Whittingham, Sofronoff, Sheffield, & Sanders, 2008, 2009). That is, when the parent's explanations of the child involve a rigid other-as-content, this is problematic. Flexible self-as-content and other-as-content, as well as contacting as-content with as-context awareness is necessary in order to work for change. Furthermore, contact with as-process awareness can bring valuable information.

Childhood internalizing problems and flexible perspective taking

The meaning that the parent gives to the child's internalizing symptoms impact upon the parent's ability to parent their child in a positive way. For example, rigid other-as-content around beliefs like, "she's sensitive" or "he's shy" may lead the parent to dismiss times when the child, in fact, acts counter to these simplified stories, times when the child is courageous or determined. This can, in turn, result in the parent limiting the child's opportunities to experience more varied situations in which being assertive or courageous would be practiced and potentially mastered (Apetroaia, Hill, & Creswell, 2015; Fisak & Grills-Taquechel, 2007; Kortlander, Kendall, & Panichelli-Mindel, 1997). These moments are exactly the moments that require parental attention to foster growth and change.

Childhood neurodevelopmental disabilities and flexible perspective taking

Parents of children with disabilities develop aspects of as-content around what it means to be the parent of a child with a disability, as well as what their child's disability means for them (Kurtz-Nelson & McIntyre, 2017; Whittingham et al., 2008). This may include developing rigid self-as-content, other-as-content, and us-as-content that does not allow for change. This can be part of the nurturance trap, where the parent of a child with a disability has expectations that are too low, and does not sufficiently challenge their child to reach their full developmental potential. Bringing flexibility to self-as-content and other-as-content, as well as enhancing as-context awareness can be beneficial.

Peer problems and bullying and flexible perspective taking

Flexible perspective taking underlies the ability to navigate peer interactions with skill. Strong flexible perspective-taking abilities increase the chances that a child will be able to successfully navigate bullying or coercive peer interactions as well as to harness the support of other peers. On the other hand, perspective-taking abilities alone are not a guarantee of protection from bullying or a guarantee of prosocial behavior. In fact, children who have experienced victimization themselves and have high perspective-taking abilities are at greater risk of developing a pattern of bullying behavior themselves (Derksen et al., 2018).

Marital conflict and flexible perspective taking

Marital conflict can spring from rigid self-as-content, other-as-content for the partner, us-as-content for the marital relationship, and other-as-content about the child (where the partners disagree). Differentiations at the level of self-as-content and other-as-content—you are like that and I am like this—are likely to lead to judgments and distance. Instead of emphasizing differences at a conceptual level, coparents need to emphasize their common humanity at a self-as-context and other-as-context level, as well as jointly (us-as-context) taking the perspective of their child (Narayan, Cicchetti, Rogosch, & Toth, 2015).

Expressed emotion including critical and intrusive parenting and flexible perspective taking

Critical, hostile, and intrusive parenting behavior may signal a deficit in perspective-taking abilities, particularly at the level of other-as-process, other-as-context, us-as-process, and us-as-context (Musser, Karalunas,

Dieckmann, Peris, & Nigg, 2016). That is, the parent may be unaware of the impact of their critical, hostile, or intrusive parenting on their child or lack an experience of their child as a perspective in their own right. Alternatively, the ability to perspective take may be intact, but the parent may lack motivation to care about the perspective of their child.

Emotion dismissiveness and flexible perspective taking

Emotion dismissiveness may indicate a deficit in other-as-process and other-as-context. The parent may be unable to successfully track their child's ongoing emotional experiences, or may be unable to sufficiently take the perspective of their child.

Inconsistent, or harsh and punitive parenting and flexible perspective taking

The use of inconsistent, harsh, or punitive parenting may be part of a deficit in perspective taking (Coyne & Cairns, 2016; Lunkenheimer, Ram, Skowron, & Yin, 2017; Roche, Ghazarian, Little, & Leventhal, 2011). The parent may have underdeveloped self-as-process, so that they do not recognize their own negative emotions at lower levels when self-care is a possibility. Instead of acting from insight into their own emotional reactions, emotions may be intermittently vented at the child. The parent may also be stuck with specific rigid aspects of conceptualized child, which result in the parent reading maliciousness into the child's everyday behavior.

References

Apetroaia, A., Hill, C., & Creswell, C. (2015). Parental responsibility beliefs: Associations with parental anxiety and behaviours in the context of childhood anxiety disorders. *Journal of Affective Disorders*, *188*, 127–133.

Atkins, P. W. B. (2013). Empathy, self-other differentiation and mindfulness. In K. Pavlovich, & K. Krahnke (Eds.), *Organizing through empathy* (pp. 49–70). New York: Routledge.

Atkins, P. W. B., & Styles, R. (2016). Measuring self and rules in what people say: Exploring whether self-discrimination predicts long-term wellbeing. *Journal of Contextual Behavioral Science*, *5*, 71–79.

Barnes-Holmes, D., Hayes, S. C., & Dymond, S. (2001). Self and self-directed rules. In S. C. Hayes, D. Barnes-Holmes, & B. Roche (Eds.), *Relational frame theory: A post-Skinnerian account of human language and cognition* (pp. 119–139). New York: Kulwer Academic.

Barnes-Holmes, Y., Barnes-Holmes, D., Roche, B., & Smeets, P. M. (2001). The development of self and perspective-taking. *Behavioral Development Bulletin*, *1*, 42–45.

Courage, M. L., Edison, S. C., & Howe, M. L. (2004). Variability in the early development of visual self-recognition. *Infant Behaivor and Development*, *27*, 509–532.

Coyne, L. W., & Cairns, D. (2016). *A relational frame theory analysis of coercive family process. The Oxford handbook of coercive relationship dynamics* (pp. 86–100). New York: Oxford University Press.

Coyne, L. W., Low, C. M., Miller, A. L., Seifer, R., & Dickstein, S. (2007). Mothers' empathic understanding of their toddlers: Associations with maternal depression and sensitivity. *Journal of Child and Family Studies*, *16*, 483–497.

Derksen, D. G., Hunsche, M. C., Giroux, M. E., Connolly, D. A., & Bernstein, D. M. (2018). A systematic review of theory of mind's precursors and functions. *Zeitschrift für Psychologie*, *226*(2), 87–97.

Dweck, C. S. (2006). *Mindset*. London: Robinson.

Fisak, B., & Grills-Taquechel, A. E. (2007). Parental modeling, reinforcement, and information transfer: Risk factors in the development of child anxiety? *Clinical Child and Family Psychology Review*, *10*(3), 213–231.

Fonagy, P., Gergely, G., & Target, M. (2007). The parent-infant dyad and the construction of the subjective self. *Journal of Child Psychology and Psychiatry*, *48*(3–4), 288–328.

Foody, M., Barnes-Holmes, Y., Barnes-Holmes, D., & Luciano, C. (2013). An empirical investigation of hierarchical versus distinction relations in a self-based ACT exercise. *International Journal of Psychology and Psychological Therapy*, *13*, 373–385.

Foody, M., Barnes-Holmes, Y., Barnes-Holmes, D., Rai, L., & Luciano, C. (2015). An empirical investigation of the role of self, heirachy, and distinction in a common act exercise. *The Psychological Record*, *64*, 231–243.

Gil-Luciano, B., Ruiz, F. J., Valdivia-Salas, S., & Suarez-Falcon, J. C. (2017). Promoting psychological flexibility on tolerance tasks: Framing behavior through deictic/hierarchical relations and specifying augmental functions. *The Psychological Record*, *67*, 1–9.

Gunderson, E. A., Sorhagen, N. S., Gripshover, S. J., Dweck, C. S., Goldin-Meadow, S., & Levine, S. C. (2018). Parent praise to toddlers predicts fourth grade academic achievement via children's incremental mindsets. *Developmental Psychology*, *54*(3), 397–409.

Imuta, K., Henry, J. D., Slaughter, V., Selcuk, B., & Ruffman, T. (2016). Theory of mind and prosocial behavior in childhood: a meta-analytic review. *Developmental Psychology*, *52*(8), 1192–1205.

Haimovitz, K., & Dweck, C. S. (2016). What predicts children's fixed and growth intelligence mind-sets? Not their parents' views of intelligence but their parents' views of failure. *Psychological Science*, *27*, 859–869.

Haimovitz, K., & Dweck, C. S. (2017). The origins of children's growth and fixed mindsets: New research and a new proposal. *Child Development*, *88*(6), 1849–1859.

Harding, D. (2012). *On having no head*. London: The Sholland Trust.

Hayes, L. L., & Ciarrochi, J. (2015). *The thriving adolescent*. Oakland: New Harbinger Publications.

Hayes, S. C. (1984). Making sense of spirituality. *Behaviorism*, *12*, 99–110.

Hayes, S. C., Barnes-Holmes, D., & Roche, B. (2001). *Relational frame theory: A post-Skinnerian account of human language and cognition*. New York: Plenum Press.

Hecht, E. E., Mahovetz, L. M., Preuss, T. M., & Hopkins, W. D. (2017). A neuroanatomical predictor of mirror self-recognition in chimpanzees. *Social Cognitive and Affective Neuroscience*, *12*(1), 37–48.

Jackson, M. L., Mendoza, D. R., & Adams, A. N. (2014). Teaching a deictic relational repertoire to children with autism. *Psychological Record*, *64*, 791–802.

Johnston, C., & Freeman, W. (1997). Attributions for child behavior in parents of children without behavior disorders and children with attention deficit-hyperactivity disorder. *Journal of Consulting and Clinical Psychology*, *65*(4), 636–645.

Jones, A. C., Gutierrez, R., & Ludlow, A. K. (2015). Confronting the language barrier: Theory of mind in deaf children. *Journal of Communication Disorders*, *56*, 47–58.

Kortlander, E., Kendall, P. C., & Panichelli-Mindel, S. M. (1997). Maternal expectations and attributions about coping in anxious children. *Journal of Anxiety Disorders*, *11*(3), 297–315.

Kurtz-Nelson, E., & McIntyre, L. L. (2017). Optimism and positive and negative feelings in parents of young children with developmental delay. *Journal of Intellectual Disability Research*, *61*(7), 719–725.

Lopez-Lopez, J. C., & Luciano, C. (2017). An experimental analysis of defusion interactions based on deictic and hierarchical framings and their impact on cognitive performance. *Psychological Research*, *67*, 485–497.

Lunkenheimer, E., Ram, N., Skowron, E. A., & Yin, P. (2017). Harsh parenting, child behavior problems, and the dynamic coupling of parents' and children's positive behaviors. *Journal of Family Psychology*, *31*(6), 689–698.

McHugh, L., Barnes-Holmes, Y., & Barnes-Holmes, D. (2004). Perspective-taking as relational responding: A developmental profile. *The Psychological Record*, *54*, 115–144.

McHugh, L., Barnes-Holmes, Y., Barnes-Holmes, D., & Stewart, I. (2006). Understanding false belief as generalised operant behavior. *The Psychological Record*, *56*, 341–364.

McHugh, L., Barnes-Holmes, Y., Barnes-Holmes, D., Stewart, I., & Dymond, S. (2007). Deictic relational complexity and the development of deception. *The Psychological Record*, *57*, 517–531.

McMahon, C. A., & Bernier, A. (2017). Twenty years of research on parental mind-mindedness: Empirical findings, theoretical and methodological challenges, and new directions. *Developmental Review*, *46*, 54–80.

Montoya-Rodriguez, M. M., Molina, F. J., & McHugh, L. (2017). A review of relational frame theroy research into deictic relational responding. *Psychological Record*, *67*, 569–579.

Moran, O., Almada, P., & McHugh, L. (2018). An investigation into the relationship between the three selves (Self-as-Content, Self-as-Process and Self-as-Context) and mental health in adolescents. *Journal of Contextual Behavioral Science*, *7*, 55–62.

Musser, E. D., Karalunas, S. L., Dieckmann, N., Peris, T. S., & Nigg, J. T. (2016). Attention-deficit/hyperactivity disorder developmental trajectories related to parnetal expressed emotion. *Journal of Abnormal Psychology*, *125*(2), 182–195.

Narayan, A., Cicchetti, D., Rogosch, F. A., & Toth, S. L. (2015). Interrelations of maternal expressed emotion, maltreatment, and separation/divorce and links to family conflict and children's externalizing behavior. *Journal of Abnormal Child Psychology*, *43*(2), 217–228.

Oppenheim, D., Koren-Karie, N., & Sagi, A. (2001). Mothers' empathic understanding of their preschoolers' internal experience: Relations with early attachment. *International Journal of Behavioral Development*, *25*(1), 16–26.

Roche, K. M., Ghazarian, S. R., Little, T. D., & Leventhal, T. (2011). Understanding links between punitive parenting and adolescent adjustment: The relevance of context and reciprocal associations. *Jounral of Research on Adolescence*, *21*(2), 448–460.

Ross, J., Yilmaz, M., Dale, R., Cassidy, R., Yildirim, I., & Suzanne Zeedyk, M. (2017). Cultural differences in self-recognition: The early development of autonomous and related selves? *Developmental Science*, *20*(3).

Slaughter, V. (2015). Theory of mind in infants and young children: A review. *Australian Psychologist*, *50*(3), 169–172.

Tillman, K. A., Marghetis, T., Barner, D., & Srinivasan, M. (2017). Today is tomorrow's yesterday: Children's acquisition of deictic time words. *Cognitive Psychology*, *92*, 87–100.

Weil, T. M., Hayes, S. C., & Capurro, P. (2011). Establishing a deictic relational repertiore in young children. *The Psychological Record*, *61*, 371–390.

Whittingham, K., Sofronoff, K., Sheffield, J., & Sanders, M. R. (2008). An exploration of parental attributions within the Autism Spectrum Disorders population. *Behaviour Change*, *25*(4), 201–214.

Whittingham, K., Sofronoff, K., Sheffield, J., & Sanders, M. R. (2009). Do parental attributions affect treatment outcome in a parenting program? An exploration of the effects of parental attributions in an RCT of Stepping Stones Triple P for the ASD population. *Research in Autism Spectrum Disorders*, *3*, 129–144.

Chapter 12

Compassionate context

Chapter Outline

What is compassion? **322**
DNA-V model 326
How does compassion apply to parent–child interaction? **327**
Self-compassion and parental well-being 327
Compassion and parenting 327
Parental compassion for the child 328
Compassion and history 328
Shame-based parenting 329
Parenting to shape compassion in children 329
Working with compassion clinically **332**
Noticing compassion, shame, and criticism within the parent–child relationship 332
Noticing parental evolved defenses and compassion capacities 333
Reality check: not your fault 333
Soothing rhythm breathing exercise 335
Compassionate figure 336
Accessing the compassionate self 336
Tuning into the compassionate self 337
Compassionate letter writing 337
Empty chair technique 338
Safe place imagery 339
Self-compassion meditation 340
Compassion for your child 341
Supporting the development of compassion in children and adolescents 342
Encouraging home practice 343
Troubleshooting **346**
Fear of compassion 346
Four key developmental periods and compassion **346**
Infancy and compassion 346
Early childhood and compassion 347
Middle childhood and compassion 348
Adolescence and compassion 348
Using compassion with specific populations **349**
Parental mental health problems and compassion 349
Parental grief and compassion 349
Childhood externalizing problems and compassion 349
Childhood internalizing problems and compassion 349
Childhood neurodevelopmental disabilities and compassion 350
Peer relations and bullying and compassion 350
Marital conflict and compassion 350
Expressed emotion including critical and intrusive parenting and compassion 350
Emotion dismissiveness and compassion 351
Inconsistent, or harsh and punitive parenting and compassion 351
References **351**

Acceptance and Commitment Therapy. DOI: https://doi.org/10.1016/B978-0-12-814669-9.00012-6
© 2019 Elsevier Inc. All rights reserved.

Making the decision to have a child—it is momentous. It is to decide forever to have your heart go walking around outside your body.

-Elizabeth Stone

Come and go with me, it's more fun to share.
We'll both be completely at home in midair.
We're flyin', not walkin', on featherless wings.
We can hold onto love like invisible strings.

-The Muppets, *I'm going to go back there someday*, The Muppet Movie

What is compassion?

Compassion focused therapy (CFT) has developed independently of acceptance and commitment therapy (ACT), yet recently, both communities have recognized synergy between the two approaches, with ACT interventions increasingly including elements of CFT. The synergy is so compelling that we couldn't write a book on how to apply ACT for parents without ensuring it included *compassion-focused* ACT. In this book, we are particularly grounding our exploration of CFT within the work of Tirch, Schoendorff, and Silberstein (2014) in building connections between the CFT and the ACT communities.

Within CFT compassion is understood as a motivational system, a social motive, and a social mentality that relies on competence in perspective taking, mindfulness, and experiential acceptance, and is fostered by certain kinds of social contexts (Gilbert, 2009, 2015b). Compassion is defined as sensitivity to suffering combined with the motivation to help alleviate and prevent it (Gilbert, Allan, Brough, Melley, & Miles, 2002). The CFT definition is thus two-pronged with two core aspects:

1. sensitivity to suffering and
2. motivation to help alleviate or prevent suffering (Tirch et al., 2014).

We can focus on:

1. the capacity to direct compassion to others,
2. the capacity to direct compassion to yourself and receive compassion from yourself, and
3. the capacity to receive compassion from others.

Some people are strong in one of these capacities—for example, directing compassion to others—and yet weak in others—for example, receiving compassion from themselves and others.

ACT processes and compassion are inter-related, with both supporting each other. The sensitivity aspect of compassion can be related to mindfulness, self-as-process, other-as-process, and experiential acceptance components of ACT. Without ongoing psychological presence, including mindfulness of the self and the other, suffering may go unnoticed. Without experiential acceptance, full sensitivity to suffering may not be experienced. Instead, the suffering may be immediately dismissed or avoided once it is noticed, unexplored, and unacknowledged. The motivation to alleviate and prevent suffering can be related to the values, committed action, self-as-context, and other-as-context aspects of the ACT. Many people have compassion-related values, and these values are related to the motivation to act to alleviate suffering. Where a person holds compassion-related values, committed action includes behaviors toward the alleviation and prevention of suffering. Self-as-context and other-as-context also relate to the motivation to alleviate suffering in terms of connection to a shared humanity and understanding both other people and yourself as conscious human beings with an ongoing perspective. On the other hand, a compassionate context, with self-compassion, compassion from others, and compassion for others, fosters and supports psychological flexibility. We find it easiest to be flexible in contexts of social safety and nurturance. Thus, psychological flexibility and compassion support each other.

CFT is grounded within an evolutionary model of functional emotional and social motivational systems, with compassion understood in this context (Gilbert, Gilbert, & Irons, 2004; Tirch et al., 2014). Certain patterns of behavior had important evolutionary implications for our ancestors, including being part of the group, finding sexual partners, forming pair bonds, attachment, parental care, securing alloparenting support, forming reciprocal alliances, gaining status within the group, response to threat, seeking resources, and seeking safety. What was, for our ancestors, associated with evolutionary success or failure has shaped our functional, emotional, and social motivational systems. Within CFT the complexity of emotion and motivational systems is broken down into a simplified three system model, simple enough to be of use clinically. The three systems are the affiliative system, the incentive/resource system, and the threat system.

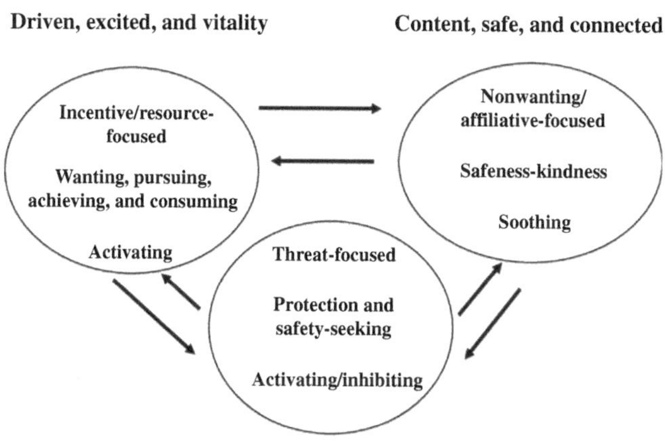

The affiliative, incentive/resource, and threat systems.

The incentive/resource-focused system (also called the drive system) is associated with drive, desire, consuming, achieving, joy, and excitement (Tirch et al., 2014). It is hypothesized to be associated with dopaminergic (reward) systems in particular. This is the system that regulates the seeking of resources. The threat-focused system is associated with anxiety, fear, angry, and disgust. It is thought to involve the amygdala and the limbic system as well as the activation of the serotonergic system. It is associated with defensive behaviors including both the mobilization of the fight or flight response and the immobilization of the shutdown response.

The affiliative system is an expansion of capacities that first evolved in the context of parental care; capacities that were co-opted by evolution and extended to other kin-based and non-kin affiliative relationships grounded in trust and reciprocity (Gilbert, 2015a,b). The affiliative system is associated with the giving and receiving of compassion. It is intricately linked with bonding, social affiliation, social safety, and nurturance. Mammals have evolved to experience a sense of safety and to soothe and downregulate the threat system, in the presence of stable, warm, and compassionate interactions with others. Thus, the affiliative system plays an important role in bringing parasympathetic balance to the three systems. Affiliative emotions impact how people perceive and react to threat (Gilbert, 2015a,b).

CFT is thus related to the work of Porges (1997). The threat system includes the dorsal vagal system shutdown response and the sympathetic nervous system mobilization or the fight or flight response. The affiliative system is the ventral vagal system, an emotional regulation and affective signaling system associated with a sense of safety and soothing, with the ability to downregulate the sympathetic nervous system. CFT also links with attachment theory (Tirch et al., 2014). The affiliative system is the site of attachment behavior, caregiving behavior, and the capacity to receive caregiving behavior.

The evolutionary model of CFT examines our evolved defenses in depth—evolved defense mechanisms to protect from harm and/or to minimize harms to the individual (Gilbert, 2001). Evolved defenses include vigilance to signals of threat or loss, mobilization behaviors of fight or flight, avoidance, hiding, immobilization shutdown behaviors, and withdrawal and submissive displays. Each strategy is functionally adaptive in a specific situation. For example, when attacked by a predator the immobilization or shutdown behavior may be effective in tricking the predator. When under attack, and escape is likely, flight may be the most effective strategy. When fighting back is likely to be victorious or to protect offspring, then attacking back may be adaptive. When under attack by a member of the same species, and escape or fighting back are not highly likely to work, then submissive behavior may be the best strategy. Submissive behavior terminates the attack of the aggressor, while conceding to the social hierarchy. This is complex, with the possibility that multiple strategies will be activated in one situation.

Importantly, for humans social rank is not merely maintained through aggression and submissive display. Rather, social rejection and loss of status register as social threats, and stimulate our evolved defenses including submissive displays and fight or flight. Submissive displays are intimately connected to the felt experience of shame. Social ranking is connected to competition over resources and is related to in-group versus out-group competition (Gilbert et al., 2004). Human social rank and competition is focused on creating positive emotions in the minds of others about us, that is, humans compete to be *socially attractive*, rather than compete through aggression (Gilbert, 2014). Although social threats are important, social rank per se is not the be-all and end-all of social competition. Not all people and not all mammals compete to be of the highest rank in the group. Rather, there are a number of salient social "prizes" to be won: belonging, affiliations, successful parenting, alloparenting support and sexual partners.

Evolved defenses for loss and social threat become dysfunctional when they are too easily aroused, prolonged, arrested, or ineffective (Gilbert, 2001). Like other evolved defenses—for example, vomiting or diarrhea—they have a range in which they are adaptive and a range in which they are not (Gilbert, 2015a,b). A defense is "arrested" when it is activated but the behavior cannot be fully expressed (Gilbert, 2001). For example, the instinct to escape is activated (flight) but escape is impossible and so it isn't attempted. A defense is "ineffective" if it is expressed but it does not succeed in minimizing harm. For example, when abuse triggers a submissive display, but the submissive display does not terminate the attacks of the abuser. Strategies that are arrested or ineffective may not be fully resolved, the person can remain in that defensive state. Due to the cognitive capacities of humans, we can also stimulate our own social motivational systems (Gilbert, 2001). This ability is harnessed in a positive manner in CFT, that is, self-compassion. However, the fact that we can stimulate our own evolved defenses is also part of the making of psychopathology. We have "tricky brains" —our newer human cognitive capabilities and our older mammalian social motivational systems do not interact smoothly, creating "bugs" (Gilbert, 2014). Another challenge that can develop is that the affiliative system may be associated with threat through respondent conditioning (Tirch et al., 2014). This may be particularly relevant for people with childhoods that included abuse.

Within CFT, a clear distinction is made between shame and guilt (Sloman, Gilbert, & Hasey, 2003). Although shame and guilt are frequently triggered by the same situation, shame is part of the submissive display, an evolved defense to social threats. In contrast, guilt evolved from caregiving and the need to avoid harming others. It is focused on minimization of harm and repair. Shame may be internalized, when memories of shame become crystallized into understanding of ourselves. We can also speak of external shame, or the experience of being shamed by another. Shame is not the key to moral behavior, guilt is. This has important implications for parents and parenting. It suggests that parental guilt, the recognition that your parenting behavior is causing harm to your child and the intention to repair, is an important and healthy part of parenting, but parental shame, a sense of shame and inferiority in a context of social competition with other parents, is harmful. It also suggests that parenting through shame is likely to have long-term harmful effects on children, but parenting in a manner that helps children to recognize the impact of their behaviors on others and make amends is supportive of developing morality.

There is evidence to support this model. Depression is associated with arrested flight (Gilbert, 2001), entrapment (Carvalho et al., 2013), defeat (Carvalho et al., 2013), shame (Cheung, Gilbert, & Irons, 2004), self-criticism (Irons, Gilbert, Baldwin, Baccus, & Palmer, 2006), and rumination (Cheung et al., 2004). Social withdrawal in depression and safety behaviors in social anxiety can be understood as submissive displays and harm limitation strategies in response to social threat and/or defeat (Gilbert, 2000). The evolved mechanism for defeat and entrapment may involve regulating positive affect and reducing exploration (Gilbert et al., 2002). Defeat then, may particularly play an important role in anhedonia. People experiencing depression commonly experience fantasies of escape, describe their life with themes of entrapment, and experience unexpressed anger, demonstrating arrested fight or flight responses (Gilbert et al., 2004).

The evolutionary framework behind CFT provides multiple rationales for focusing on increasing compassion including:

1. strengthening the affiliative system, through increasing self-compassion and the ability to receive compassion, can provide parasympathetic balance and is associated with well-being of the individual (Neff, Kirkpatrick, & Rude, 2007);
2. compassion can provide a balance for the more destructive elements of our evolved psyche such as social competition; and
3. when humans experience a sense of social safety and affiliation they are more likely to demonstrate caring and compassionate behavior for others (Gilbert, 2009, 2015a).

All three rationales are highly relevant to parenting. From an ACT perspective, a compassionate context supports psychological flexibility.

DNA-V model

Compassion relates to self-view and social-view within DNA-V (Hayes & Ciarrochi, 2015) in terms of self-compassion and to the social-view in terms of compassion for others and the ability to receive compassion. DNA-V supports the development of flexible perspective taking, which underpins the ability and practice of compassion for self and others. For example, a child might learn to notice self-critical thoughts originating with their "advisor," and choose to try a new strategy of more gentle self-talk (ie, from the "discoverer"), and observe how that works ("noticer").

How does compassion apply to parent–child interaction?

Self-compassion and parental well-being

The evolutionary framework behind CFT predicts that self-compassion is protective in terms of mental health and well-being, providing balance to the threat and drive systems. This has been confirmed in parents. Self-compassion is associated with fewer distressed reactions to children's emotions (Psychogiou et al., 2016) and predicts parental well-being over and above child symptom severity in mothers of children with Autism Spectrum Disorders (Neff & Faso, 2015). A brief online self-compassion resource was found to decrease birth-related trauma symptoms and improve breastfeeding satisfaction in mothers of infants in a prepost pilot study (Mitchell, Whittingham, Steindl, & Kirby, 2018). Given CFT theory, self-compassion should be considered particularly relevant where there are themes of shame, self-criticism, entrapment, defeat, or arrested fight or flight.

Compassion and parenting

When humans experience a sense of social safety and affiliation they are more likely to demonstrate caring and compassionate behavior for others (Gilbert, 2009, 2015a). This is obviously relevant to parenting. It suggests, firstly, that a repertoire of self-compassion is likely to be associated with more effective and caring parenting behavior. Indeed, parental self-compassion has been found to be associated with external attributions for child behavior and less parental criticism of the child (Psychogiou et al., 2016).

Importantly, this also means that a wider context of social safety and compassion is crucial to best supporting parents in their role of caring for their children. Social contexts of shame, judgment, criticism, and social competition contexts of social threat may undermine parental ability to best care for their children. This is important because many parents report experiencing shame, judgment, criticism, and social competition regarding their parenting: from birth, to infant feeding and sleeping, to milestone attainment, to child behavior, to academic success, to childcare arrangements, and working hours. The theoretical framework underlying CFT suggests that we have built a toxic social environment for parents, and that, instead, we should focus on providing parents with a context of social safety, *caring for* parents so that they can care for their children.

Even in a context of social safety, an individual must have competencies in the receiving of compassion. Some individuals struggle to receive compassion from themselves and others. This may be related to a learned fear of compassion, learned through respondent conditioning by the affiliative system activation being repeatedly paired with threat system activation. Parenting is an intensive and demanding task. Inability to receive compassion may interfere with the parental ability to receive appropriate support, including the involvement of alloparents (caregivers other than the parents, such as grandparents).

Parental compassion for the child

Parental compassion for their children is, really, the affiliate system doing what it originally evolved to do, as the other capabilities of the affiliative system evolved from parental caregiving capacity. Sensitive and responsive parenting involves being responsive to numerous mental and emotional states; not just suffering, but parental sensitivity and responsiveness to suffering is a poignant example where responsive parenting and compassionate parenting are one and the same.

Compassionate parenting requires sensitivity to the child's suffering—the ability to take the child's perspective, as well as the capacity for experiential acceptance—as well as *the motivation* to alleviate that suffering. It requires that the parent has the child's long-term best interests at heart. Children who are raised by sensitive and responsive parents, parents who function as a safe haven and a secure base, develop a strong affiliative system capacity (Tirch et al., 2014). They develop the capacity for self-compassion as well as the capacity of receiving compassion from others, both of which are associated with long-term mental health and well-being.

Compassion and history

Parenting can evoke difficult and traumatic aspects of the parent's own history, including their history as a parent (e.g., traumatic birth or previous loss) as well as their history of being parented themselves. Being able to hold that history and the thoughts and feelings evoked in the moment-to-moment flow of life with self-compassion is important. Although more research is needed on compassion and trauma in parents, a brief online self-compassion resource was found to decrease birth-related trauma symptoms in mothers of infants in a prepost pilot study (Mitchell et al., 2018).

People with histories of developmental trauma have often learned to feel unsafe in connection; the repeated activation of the threat system following activation of the affiliative system has developed into a learned response through respondent conditioning. For these people, CFT is also a kind of exposure therapy. The use of compassionate imagery and exercises may initially seem to have no effect or even be anxiety provoking. Exercises that are not focused on people may be better tolerated at first; for example, soothing rhythm breathing or the imagery of a safe place.

Shame-based parenting

The theoretical framework underlying CFT serves as a warning for parents against using shame or social comparison to modify children's behavior. Such parenting strategies may work in the short term, in terms of immediate behavior change, but are likely to be associated with long-term challenges in mental health and well-being. In contrast, guilt, or the recognition of the effects of your behavior on others, with an intention to repair, is an adaptive part of our moral life.

Parenting to shape compassion in children

To date, parenting research has overwhelmingly focused on the reduction and management of antisocial behavior in children. There is comparatively little research on how interventions can support parents in building prosocial and compassionate repertoires in children (Kirby, 2016). Hopefully future research will consider this an equally important goal.

The parent–child relationship is our first experience of receiving compassion and is likely the first and perhaps the easiest context in which to learn compassion, both the giving and the receiving of it. How the parent responds to the child's suffering will underlie the development of the child's affiliative system, including capacities for self-compassion, compassion for others, and the ability to receive compassion from others. Through repeated experiences of soothing, the child learns that they can seek comfort socially, to soothe themselves, and may begin to experiment with soothing others. In addition, parenting informs the development of capacities related to compassion such as perspective taking and experiential acceptance (covered in previous chapters). Opportunities to encourage, scaffold, and reinforce compassion are readily available in everyday life within pretend play, fiction, and contact with other children or animals. Parents can deliberately provide exposure to opportunities to be compassionate; for example, exposure to babies and younger children (exposure to younger children brings out the caregiving side of even quite young children), to animals, to baby doll toys, and by introducing compassionate themes into joint play.

Yasmin and Amir

When Yasmin seeks help it is immediately clear to her therapist that she is in distress. She hands her 8-week-old baby, Amir, to her husband Ahmed in the waiting room, and follows the therapist through to the consultation room.
Yasmin tells her story, tears brimming in her eyes. She went into labor spontaneously a week before the due date. Amir was posterior and as a result the progress was slow and the back pain excruciating. Yasmin had intended to refuse pain medication but, given the agony she was experiencing and the advice of the

(*Continued*)

(Continued)

midwife, she felt that she had no choice but to have an epidural. The epidural brought reprieve from the pain but it also slowed down her progress and she was put on a syntocinon drip. This gave her painful contractions. By the time she had progressed to the pushing phase she had been in labor for 18 hours. After an hour and half of pushing the Amir's heart rate dropped and the obstetrician declared that the baby had to be removed immediately with an episiotomy and vacuum. Yasmin has a powerful memory of that awful declaration. She remembers that she was lying back on the bed, and the obstetrician was still between her legs as she talked, more to the midwife than to her. She remembers feeling absolutely powerless and terrified that her baby was dying. After Amir was birthed, he was placed on Yasmin's chest. Yasmin tried to feel relieved that Amir was alive, but she still felt frightened. Yasmin attempted to give Amir a breastfeed but she was aware of the whispering of the midwife and the obstetrician as they both attempted tugging on the umbilical cord. Yasmin's placenta did not come and the obstetrician had to perform a manual removal. Yasmin reported again feeling terrified, this time fearing for her own life. She was wheeled into theater for the manual removal, while Amir and Ahmed stayed in the birth room, waiting for the pediatrician. The separation was a shock. Yasmin feels intense shame that she was not able to birth without intervention.

Yasmin was intending to breastfeed, and was looking forward to the experience as part of early motherhood. But that too, proved difficult. Breastfeeding was painful and she soon had cracked and bleeding nipples. She sought help from a local child health nurse, but the nurse physically grabbed Yasmin's breast and forcefully attached Amir to her nipple without warning or explanation. Yasmin felt out of control and violated. She has not felt comfortable seeking any further support for breastfeeding and when Amir was 4 weeks old she accepted the advice of her doctor that, "some women just can't breastfeed and you are one of them." Unfortunately, ceasing breastfeeding triggered mastitis, an infection of the breast tissue, and Yasmin was extremely sick for a week. Yasmin still feels deep shame and regret around the difficulties she had breastfeeding and she grieves deeply for the breastfeeding experience that she wanted to have.

She ensures that you understand that she loves Amir with all her heart, but admits that she sees herself as "an absolute failure, as a woman, and a mother." She says that she still has nightmares about the birth and she thinks of her decision to stop breastfeeding regularly. The thoughts are often triggered by bottle feeding Amir. She also reports that she feels "stressed out" and "on edge." Her head hangs low, her eyes on the ground as she confesses that although she adores Amir she has fantasies of walking out of the house and just walking off into the distance, or perhaps getting on a random bus and going to the end of the line, far away.

Imagine you could, unseen and unheard, observe a typical, ordinary interaction between Yasmin and Amir. It might be something like this:

Parent–child interaction

Yasmin holds Amir as she stacks dishes into the dishwasher.

Amir is content and awake; he peeks around at the world from his mother's shoulder.

(Continued)

(Continued)

Yasmin puts the last of the dishes in and turns the dishwasher on.

"Well, that's all done now, little one," she says to Amir in her native tongue, "what shall we do now?"

Yasmin picks up a banana and walks into their living room, picking up a toy dog on the way. She sits down on her lounge and repositions Amir so he is lying on her legs and they can see each other. She puts the toy and the banana next to her on the couch.

"Hello bubby ..." Yasmin says to Amir.

Amir smiles back, his legs kicking.

"Oh I get smiles do I?" Yasmin says, "smiles for mummy?"

Amir kicks again.

"Who's this?" Yasmin says holding up the plastic dog toy, "is it Dog?"

Amir grins, his legs kicking as he cooes in reply, "ooo ... ah ..."

Yasmin listens to Amir's cooes and when his cooing reaches a natural end point she says, "oh it is Dog isn't it?"

Amir cooes again "ooo ... ah ..."

Yasmin nods at this, "does Amir like Dog?"

Amir cooes in reply, "ooo ... ah ..."

"Does Amir want to hold him?" Yasmin puts the toy into Amir's hand, "now Amir has Dog!"

Amir cooes, "ooo ... ah ..."

"Oh yes bub tell me all about it," Yasmin says.

Yasmin puts Amir down on the couch beside her, picking up the banana, peeling it and eating it while she continues to nod and smile to Amir's cooing.

Eventually, Amir's cooing turns grisly. Yasmin's eyes flick to the clock. "Ah, yes, you are hungry too, aren't you? Alright then. We'd better get that sorted."

Yasmin picks Amir back up, sitting him up on her shoulder, and takes him into the kitchen. He is still grizzling. She has some pre-sterilized bottles sitting on the kitchen bench and she begins to mix the formula. Amir's grizzling is beginning to escalate to a cry.

"Hang on, honey," Yasmin says, "I've just got to mix it."

A wave of self-criticism washes over Yasmin: if you were still breastfeeding you would be feeding him by now. With that thought, Yasmin finds herself back in the tangle of shame and self-blame that she's been struggling against since Amir was born. With a shudder, she recalls the nightmare she had last night: being once again a powerless body flooded with the terror that her baby might die. Tears well up in her eyes but Amir needs feeding so she keeps mixing the bottle up as best she can. In this mind-state, Amir's cries feel like accusations, like he too agrees that she is an absolute failure.

The bottle prepared, Yasmin walks back into the lounge room with Amir Both are crying. Yasmin sits herself on the couch and positions Amir in her arms ready for a feed. She offers him the bottle and he takes it enthusiastically. Yasmin does her best to calm, tears trickling down her face, "I'm so sorry little one," she whispers, "I'm so sorry."

(*Continued*)

(Continued)

As Amir feeds Yasmin's tears settle and she finds herself filled with the overwhelming urge to escape, to get out. She decides that after feeding Amir, she'll put him in the pram and go for a long walk.

What's happening for Yasmin and Amir?

Within this interaction, Yasmin demonstrates a sensitive and responsive pattern of care toward Amir, and Amir is responsive in return. That Yasmin and Amir have developed such an interactional pattern—even with the challenges to their early relationship—is a testament to the resilience of Yasmin and the resilience of parent–child relationships in general.

It is clear, however, that Yasmin is not doing well. Her reported nightmares and feeling "stressed out" and "on edge" are consistent with trauma symptoms in relation to a psychologically traumatic birth. The traumatic birth has been complicated still by early breastfeeding problems for which Yasmin did not receive appropriate clinical support or professional advice. Due to a lack of appropriate clinical support, Yasmin did not achieve her personal breastfeeding goals and it is understandable that she grieves this loss. From a CFT perspective, the evolved defensives of submissive display and flight were likely both activated during the birth but were either ineffective (in the case of the submissive display) or arrested (in the case of flight). The fact that these defenses have not resolved is clear in her continued fantasies of escape, sympathetic nervous system activation, and feelings of shame. Focusing on compassion may assist in activating the affiliative system and restoring parasympathetic balance and mental health. On her current trajectory, Yasmin is at risk for posttraumatic stress disorder in relation to her birth and postnatal depression.

It's clear from a clinical Relational Frame Theory perspective that for Yasmin, there is a dense network of derived relations among breastfeeding, competence, and good parenting; these are complicated by the derived relation to trauma cues that are no doubt evoked in feeding interactions with Amir. Yasmin's response in the presence of these equivalence relations is to engage in self-criticism—to punish herself—which in turn evokes depressed mood. Yasmin blames herself, rather than recognizing the contextual factors at play including a lack of appropriate clinical breastfeeding support. In engaging in compassion-focused work, gently and thoroughly exploring these relations and broadening the network to include self-kindness, gentleness, and self-care, through experiential work, will be very important. This type of work will likely involve an exposure component, and will unfold over time and multiple exercises.

Working with compassion clinically

Noticing compassion, shame, and criticism within the parent–child relationship

It is useful to pay attention to the degree to which parents are parenting with shame and criticism and/or parenting in a compassionate manner. High shame and criticism in parenting, and low-levels of parental compassion for the child, may indicate that targeting parental compassion for the child would be useful. Be alert for:

- A parent who is harshly critical of their child, either in their reports to you or directly to the child.
- Parents who use shame or social comparisons to modify their child's behavior.
- Parents who are disconnected from, dismissing of or lacking awareness of their child's emotions.
- Parents who seem insufficiently motivated to alleviate and prevent the suffering of their child. This may present as a parent who is overly focused on how parenting intervention can improve *their life*, and yet seems unconcerned by the long-term impacts of parenting behavior on *their child*. Note that this refers to workable long-term prevention and alleviation of suffering. For example, accommodation of child anxiety rather than an encouraging approach may seem like the compassionate response in the moment, but it is, in fact, increasing the child's suffering in the long term.
- Parents who have difficulty taking the perspective of their child.

Noticing parental evolved defenses and compassion capacities

It is also useful to pay attention to the evolved defenses activated in the parent, as well as the compassion capacities of the parent. These indicate that a focus on compassion, both self-compassion and, perhaps, receiving compassion would be beneficial for the parent. This could include:

- A parent that is unable to receive help from self or others may indicate a deficit in the ability to receive compassion. This parent may become uncomfortable or ashamed when receiving help, or have rigid ideas around the importance of independence and not asking for help.
- Themes of shame, self-hatred, self-criticism, social comparison, or self-blame could indicate arrested or ineffective submissive defenses.
- Themes of entrapment and wanting to escape could indicate arrested or ineffective flight defense.
- Unexpressed anger could indicate arrested or ineffective fight defense.

Reality check: not your fault

This exercise incorporates metaphor and psychoeducation to help clients to recognize that their current challenges are not simply their own fault. It also includes a focus on common humanity. This version draws upon aspects of CFT and also incorporates consideration of parenting in particular.

Reality check: not your fault script

So often when we look around for a cause of the challenges in our life we say, "ah it is me. It is my fault." We follow the casual chain back one step and stop there and blame ourselves. Have you ever done that? But in reality, it is far more complex than that. Let's think it through more carefully.

So, you were born a human being. Through no fault of your own, and not by choice, you were born a member of the species homo sapiens and you were, as a result, born with all the virtues, faults, and weaknesses of our species, characteristics that were shaped into your very DNA from millions of years of evolution. Events literally millions of years before you were born are with you today, influencing how you think, feel, and experience the world. Like other animals on Earth you feel fear, and you react instinctively to that feeling of fear by trying to escape or fighting or shutting down. You feel territorial. You form alliances. And not only do we feel fear but we've evolved to take the pessimistic point of view. Optimistic happy-go-lucky creatures who thought "nah, it won't be a lion, I'll be right" got eaten by the lion. We are the descendants of the scared and anxious creatures who were better safe than sorry.

And then we have our new human side, our capacity for language. Our new brain results in all of this: civilization. Yet it also interacts in a devastating way with the old brain. Because we don't just get scared of lions. We can get scared of thoughts about lions and we carry our thoughts around with us all the time. So an animal feels a burst of fear when confronted with a predator, acts on that, and then calms down. We continue to dwell on it. I nearly got eaten today. What if I get eaten tomorrow? Why do the lions always come for me? Is there something wrong with me? Sound familiar?

Evolution has given us very tricky brains. The pay off for all of this suffering is: culture, mathematics, science, novels, poetry, technology.... Which is cool right? But did anyone ask your permission? Maybe you'd have preferred to live as a cat or a bird, right?

And then there's your particular learning history. All of your experiences have shaped who you are, how you respond, what you have to draw upon. The you that's here today is just one potential you. What if you'd have been raised by different parents? Or in a different country? Or gone to a different school? Yet, you didn't choose any of that.

And then we add parenting into the mix. Congratulations, as a member of homo sapiens you have the most intensive, the most lengthy parenting job of any creature on the planet. Our children need lengthy childhoods to learn all of that language and culture. Not only that, did you know there are two kinds of parenting strategies in animals? There are the precocial animals. Think of horses. They have one baby at a time, and that baby walks the day they are born. The baby can follow the mom around from birth. Then there are the altricial animals. They give birth to litters and they nest. Think cats. Their babies are really immature but they can nest. The babies in the litter cuddle up to each other and the mother can leave the nest and hunt for food. The babies can go for longer in between feeds because they have high fat milk. Now guess which we are? We evolved from precocial

(*Continued*)

(Continued)

mammals, hence we have generally one baby at a time and our babies need to feed frequently. But our babies are born dependent like the altricials. And they are dependent for years. Parenting for humans is an intense and demanding job. So it is no wonder that's how you are experiencing it. And none of that is your fault.

Soothing rhythm breathing exercise

This exercise draws on mindfulness of breathing as practiced in Buddhism and combines it with a pattern of breathing—abdominal breathing—that activates the parasympathetic system. This version of the exercise is based on the mindfulness of breathing exercise included in Chapter nine Contact with the Present Moment including shared psychological presence.

Soothing rhythm breathing exercise

Get yourself into a comfortable position.
Your position should feel comfortable, as well as promoting wakefulness at the same time.
Let yourself have a relaxed, comfortable posture.
Settle into it.
You can leave your eyes open, resting on a point of focus.
Or closed.
Or hooded, whichever you prefer.
Let your hands rest gently on your knees or in your lap or in some other comfortable posture.
Allow your mind to settle into the here and now.
Now gently and as best you can, lengthen your breathing.
You might like to start by breathing all of the air out of your lungs.
Empty every last bit of air.
And let a natural in breath happen.
Noticing that it is longer and deeper than before.
Let your breathing find a slow and steady rhythm.
Count to 5 for each outbreathe and inbreathe.
Out 1, 2, 3, 4, 5.
Pause.
In 1, 2, 3, 4, 5.
Pause.
Out 1, 2, 3, 4, 5.
Pause.
If a count of 5 feels too much then start with three.
And as best you can, when you are ready, gently lengthen it to five.
You might like to put your hand on your heart as you breathe.

(Continued)

(Continued)

A gesture of compassion for yourself.
When you are ready to end the exercise, do so gently.
Bring your awareness with you back to the full present moment.

Compassionate figure

This exercise focuses on developing the ability to receive compassion from others. In people with the capacity to receive compassion from others it can also be a useful practice to stimulate the affiliative system.

Compassionate figure script

Imagine a person that you identify as a compassionate individual. It can be someone that you know personally or a public figure. It could be a religious figure or a fictional character. It could even be a matter of imagining someone new, creating a character in your own mind.
Imagine going to this person, this person of absolute compassion and kindness.
Imagine telling this person about your current struggles.
How would they respond?
Picture it clearly in your mind.
If you imagine they would say something to you, then try to really hear their words and take them on board.
If you imagine them hugging you, or putting a comforting hand on your shoulder pause and really imagine that
Feel the difference this makes.
If you feel a sense of wanting to push this away or dismiss it if you notice you have thoughts about what they are saying not being true then notice that and focus as best you can on simply absorbing their message.
If other emotions come up, if this feels uncomfortable or frightening in some way then notice that too, and focus on accepting all of it, including accepting the compassionate response of this perfectly compassionate person before you.

Accessing the compassionate self

There are a number of ways to support clients in accessing the compassionate aspects of themselves and bringing those qualities to bare in their overarching relationship with themselves. The first step, covered in depth in the next exercise, is to support the client in tuning in to the compassionate parts of themselves. For some clients this will be easily done, and simple prompts guiding them to pause and tune into the compassionate part of themselves will be sufficient. For other clients, simply tuning in to the compassionate part of themselves will be challenging. A guided exercise, such as the one that follows, may be particularly useful.

Tuning into the compassionate self

This is a guided exercise to facilitate accessing the compassionate self.

Tuning into the compassionate self

Pause and visualize yourself as your most compassionate self.
Bring to mind the aspects of you that are kind, gentle, nonjudgmental, open to yourself and to others.
Perhaps you see yourself as a child.
Or perhaps you see an older and wiser version of you.
Or perhaps it is helpful to imagine the you that connects with animals or nature.
Really picture yourself as best you can.
Does a particular image come to mind?
Perhaps you see yourself wearing specific clothes.
Standing or sitting with a particular posture.
Or perhaps you see yourself in a specific environment.
As best you can.
Tune into that aspect of yourself now.
Step into their shoes.
Become that compassionate self.
How does that compassionate self see the world?
How does that compassionate self think?
How does that compassionate self feel?
If other thoughts or feelings come up for you, that's fine.
Acknowledge them as best you can and return to focusing on yourself as your compassionate self.
When you are ready to end the exercise, do so gently.
Returning your focus to the here and now.

Once the client has tuned in to the compassionate self, then a dialogue between the compassionate self and other aspects of the self becomes possible. For example, you might facilitate the opening up of a dialogue between the compassionate self and the inner critic, or the vulnerable self, angry, fearful, or sad self as relevant. The first way you might do so is through letter writing.

Compassionate letter writing

If your client can successfully tune into their compassionate selves, they can write themselves a letter as their compassionate self. First, clients to ensure that they are fully in the role of the compassionate self, for example, by doing the *Tuning in to the Compassionate Self* exercise. When they are fully in the role of the compassionate self then they can begin to write themselves a letter. The letter could address some aspect of parenting, or their life in general where they feel shame or simply where they feel stuck. In writing the letter they could reflect:

- What does my compassionate self think about this?
- What does my compassionate self feel about this?
- What does my compassionate self wish for me in this situation?

Parents may also like to write a letter from the compassionate self to their child. They do not have to actually give the letter to their child (though with adolescent children, depending on the content of the letter that may be appropriate). However, thinking through a particular parenting challenge as how the compassionate self would like to address the child, may be helpful. In writing the letter they could reflect:

- What does my compassionate self have to say to my child?
- What does my compassionate self wish for my child in this situation?

Empty chair technique

The empty chair technique can be effectively used to facilitate a dialogue between the compassionate self and other aspects of the self. To use the empty chair technique, set up two chairs, facing each other. Your client will move between the two chairs. Designate one of the chairs as being the compassionate self chair and the other one as being for the other aspect of the self (as relevant). For example, the other aspect of the self might be the critical self. Begin with the client in the chair that does *not* represent the compassionate self. Let them speak as that aspect of themselves. When their speech comes to a natural stopping point, then direct them to move to the other chair, becoming the compassionate self. They may require prompts or a brief visualization to get fully into the role. Prompt your client to answer themselves, speaking this time as the compassionate self.

If your client slips back into an uncompassionate way of speaking while in the compassionate self chair, then have them change chairs accordingly, voice what that other aspect of themselves was wanting to say, and then move back to the compassionate self to respond as the compassionate self again. It is possible to access multiple aspects of the self, along with the compassionate self if that is needed.

It is important to keep the compassionate self chair for the compassionate self during the exercise. Swapping to the compassionate chair needs to be a salient prompt to switch to the compassionate self. However, it is possible for the other chair to swap between different other aspects of the self. For example, it may begin as a dialogue between the critical self and the compassionate self. But as the dialogue moves on, a vulnerable, hurt self may wish to speak. The dialogue may shift to a dialogue between the vulnerable self and the compassionate self.

It is often important to direct the client to pause and take a few mindful breaths when changing chairs and roles. You might also need to prompt them to remember the image of their compassionate self and to fully become that aspects of themselves before attempting to speak in that role.

Always end the exercise by giving the compassionate self the final word.

Safe place imagery

For some, any imagining of compassion is likely to evoke fear or simply feelings of numbness. Imagining, instead of a person, a safe and compassionate space, can be a good starting point to developing a compassionate repertoire. For example, imagining themselves on an island, or a beach, in a rainforest with a waterfall. This is a visualization exercise for a safe, compassionate space.

Safe place imagery script

Get yourself into a comfortable position.
Your position should feel comfortable, as well as promoting wakefulness at the same time.
Let yourself have a relaxed, comfortable posture.
Settle into it.
You can leave your eyes open, resting on a point of focus.
Or closed.
Or hooded, whichever you prefer.
Let your hands rest gently on your knees or in your lap or in some other comfortable posture.
Allow your mind to settle into the here and now.
Imagine yourself somewhere entirely safe.
In this safe place, you can be just you.
The very land you walk on.
The very air you breathe.
Supports and cherishes you.
Just as you are.
Perhaps you are imaging yourself on a beach.
The warm sand between your toes.
The gentle rhythmic thrum of the waves.
The sun shining down on you.
Warming you up.
Or perhaps you are imagining yourself in a rainforest.
Protected, sheltered by the strong green foliage.
The sounds of a waterfall in the background.
Or the gentle noises of frogs or birds singing.
Or perhaps you are imaging yourself somewhere else entirely.
This is your space and it can be however you need it to be.
When you are here you are safe.
You are supported.

(*Continued*)

(Continued)

You are at peace.
You feel grounded.
When you are ready to end the exercise, do so gently.
Bring your awareness with you back to the full present moment.

Self-compassion meditation

This is a mediation focusing on the cultivation of self-compassion.

Self-compassion meditation script

Get yourself into a comfortable position.
Your position should feel comfortable, as well as promoting wakefulness at the same time.
Let yourself have a relaxed, comfortable posture.
Settle into it.
You can leave your eyes open, resting on a point of focus.
Or closed.
Or hooded, whichever you prefer.
Let your hands rest gently on your knees or in your lap or in some other comfortable posture.
Allow your mind to settle into the here and now.
Visualize a ball of warm light in your heart.
This warm light is compassion.
First, imagine someone whom you naturally feel compassion toward.
It could be a friend, even an animal or a fictional character.
Allow yourself to feel compassion toward them.
Recall the ways in which they may suffer.
Allow your heart to open up to their suffering.
If it helps, you can imagine their suffering as a dark cloud over their heart.
Open yourself up to their suffering, taking it into you.
Perhaps even imagining breathing the dark cloud in.
As you take the suffering into yourself the warm, ball of light in your own heart glows brighter.
The dark cloud becomes fuel for the warm ball of compassion.
The cloud burns up and the ball of compassion in your heart grows brighter and stronger.
Allow the ball of warm light to grow and radiate out to the other.
See them bathed in the warm glow of your compassion.
When you are ready imagine yourself.
See yourself standing in front of you.
Yourself with all your faults, all your weaknesses, all of your history.
As best you can, allow yourself to feel compassion toward yourself.

(*Continued*)

(Continued)

Recall the ways in which you suffer.
Allow your heart to open up to your suffering.
If you feel stuck then try seeing yourself as a baby or a child.
If it helps, you can imagine your suffering as a dark cloud over your heart, the you that stands in front of you.
Open yourself up to your suffering, taking it into you.
Perhaps even imagining breathing the dark cloud in.
As you take the suffering into yourself the warm, ball of light in your own heart glows brighter.
The dark cloud becomes fuel for the warm ball of compassion.
The cloud burns up and the ball of compassion in your heart grows brighter and stronger.
Allow the ball of warm light to grow and radiate out to the you that stands in front of you.
See yourself bathed in the warm glow of your own compassion.
When you are ready to end the exercise, do so gently.
Bring your awareness with you back to the full present moment.

Compassion for your child

This meditation is focused on the parent cultivating compassion for their child.

Compassion for your child script

Get yourself into a comfortable position.
Your position should feel comfortable, as well as promoting wakefulness at the same time.
Let yourself have a relaxed, comfortable posture.
Settle into it.
You can leave your eyes open, resting on a point of focus.
Or closed.
Or hooded, whichever you prefer.
Let your hands rest gently on your knees or in your lap or in some other comfortable posture.
Allow your mind to settle into the here and now.
Visualize a ball of warm light in your heart.
This warm light is compassion.
First, imagine someone whom you naturally feel compassion toward.
It could be a friend, even an animal or a fictional character.
Allow yourself to feel compassion toward them.
Recall the ways in which they may suffer.
Allow your heart to open up to their suffering.
If it helps, you can imagine their suffering as a dark cloud over their heart.

(Continued)

(Continued)

Open yourself up to their suffering, taking it into you.
Perhaps even imagining breathing the dark cloud in.
As you take the suffering into yourself the warm, ball of light in your own heart glows brighter.
The dark cloud becomes fuel for the warm ball of compassion.
The cloud burns up and the ball of compassion in your heart grows brighter and stronger.
Allow the ball of warm light to grow and radiate out to the other.
See them bathed in the warm glow of your compassion.
When you are ready imagine your child.
See your child standing in front of you.
Yourself with all your child's faults and weaknesses.
With all of the history that's between you both.
As best you can, allow yourself to feel compassion toward your child.
Recall the ways in which your child may suffer.
Allow your heart to open up to your suffering.
If you feel stuck then it may help to remember your child as a baby.
If it helps, you can imagine your suffering as a dark cloud over your child's heart.
Open yourself up to your child's suffering, taking it into you.
Perhaps even imagining breathing the dark cloud in.
As you take the suffering into yourself the warm, ball of light in your own heart glows brighter.
The dark cloud becomes fuel for the warm ball of compassion.
The cloud burns up and the ball of compassion in your heart grows brighter and stronger.
Allow the ball of warm light to grow and radiate out to your child.
See your child bathed in the warm glow of your own compassion.
When you are ready to end the exercise, do so gently.
Bring your awareness with you back to the full present moment.

Supporting the development of compassion in children and adolescents

Children can be supported in developing compassionate repertoires by scaffolding and shaping compassionate behavior as opportunities arise in everyday life. In addition, parents can deliberately expose their children to opportunities to learn compassion. For example:

- Opportunities to play with and care for younger children and babies.
- Encouraging the practice of taking the perspective of others (see Chapter 11, Flexible Perspective Taking).
- Pretend play with baby dolls or animal toys.
- Interactions with animals.
- Introducing compassionate themes into pretend play.

- Introducing a compassionate perspective into discussions of books, media, or real life interactions such as peer-group interactions.
- Opportunities to engage with charitable organizations and activities.

Encouraging home practice

Home practice around compassion may include:

- Practicing compassion exercises, deliberately cultivating compassion for self or child.
- Deliberately taking compassionate actions toward self or child.
- Exploring compassion through writing a letter as the compassionate self to self or child.

Working with Yasmin and Amir

This interaction occurs several sessions in, after the therapist has already introduced a rationale for self-compassion and completed exercises such as reality check, soothing rhythm breathing, self-compassion meditations, and tuning into your compassionate self. Yasmin has a lingering feeling of shame and self-blame around the way her birth and breastfeeding experience unfolded. Yasmin and the therapist decide to explore this further through the empty chair technique.

Therapist:	We've been focusing on tuning in to your compassionate self. I'd like to now facilitate a dialogue between that blaming, self-critical part of you, and the compassionate part of you. Could we try that?
Yasmin:	Sure. If you think it will help.
Therapist:	Let's give it a try then. This might feel a bit strange. Go with it and I'll guide you through. You'll notice I've got an extra chair set up next to us.
Yasmin:	Yeah I was wondering who it was for.
Therapist:	Both of these chairs are for you. They are for different aspects of you. One is for your compassionate self and one is for your blaming, critical self. Do you have any preference for which is which?
Yasmin:	I'm in the blaming chair now I think.
Therapist:	Great. Your compassionate self is going to sit in that chair then. It is the blaming, critical part of you that we want to hear from first. So, giving voice to that blaming, self-critical aspect, tell me about your birth and breastfeeding experience.

(*Continued*)

(Continued)

Yasmin shakes her head angrily:	I shouldn't have had the epidural. I didn't want it. I knew I didn't want it. I was too weak. I shouldn't have stopped breastfeeding. Why didn't my body work properly? I failed Amir.
Yasmin pauses and begins to cry.	
Therapist nodding:	Give yourself a moment. When you are ready, I'm going to get you to swap to the compassionate self chair. Before you swap chairs, let's bring the compassionate self into the room. Let's start with a few steadying breaths ... in and out ... in and out ... good ... visualize yourself as your most compassionate self: kind, gentle, nonjudgmental, open to yourself. I remember you were picturing yourself as a wise old woman. See that wise old woman now. And step into her shoes. Become that compassionate self. And as you become her, swap chairs.
Yasmin takes several breaths, eyes closed, and hand on her heart. She gets up and swaps chairs.	
Therapist:	Good. Now respond to the blaming self, speaking as the compassionate self, speaking as that wise old woman.
Yasmin nodding and closing her eyes for a moment:	Yasmin, you did the best you could. You can't control everything. Sometimes, things just don't work out the way we wanted them to be. But you did your very best.
Yasmin shakes her head:	I didn't, though.
Therapist:	Okay, hold it there, we need to swap chairs, the blaming self is back.
Yasmin swaps chairs.	
Therapist:	Okay blaming self can answer now.
Yasmin:	I didn't do my best. Okay maybe with the birth. My body failed me but maybe I did the best I could. But with the breastfeeding? I shouldn't have listened to that doctor. I should have sought more help ...
Therapist:	Okay, let's bring that wise, old woman back, Yasmin's compassionate self. Bring her to mind: that wise, old woman. Step into her shoes.When you are ready, swap chairs again.
Yasmin breathes deeply, focusing on her compassionate self. Then, she swaps chairs, slipping back into the compassionate self role.	

(*Continued*)

(Continued)

Yasmin:	Alright then. Persisting a bit more and seeking more help would have been Yasmin's absolute best. You are right. But you weren't in a fit state to really give your best right then, were you? You were frightened of being manhandled again, of having your breast grabbed and Amir shoved on. You did seek help: from that child health nurse, from books, from your doctor. They failed you. It wasn't your fault.
Yasmin starts to cry.	
Therapist:	Swap chairs again when you are ready.
Yasmin swaps chairs.	
Yasmin, crying:	They failed me. I was terrified and exhausted. I just wanted some peace. I just wanted to be able to enjoy Amir. That's why I let breastfeeding go …
Therapist:	Does your compassionate self have a response to that?
Yasmin nods and swaps chairs.	
Yasmin, drying her tears:	You have the right to peace. You have the right to enjoy motherhood and to enjoy Amir. You made some difficult decisions. You did your best in the circumstances. And if it wasn't your absolute best, then I forgive you. You've been through a nightmare, Yasmin. And you got through in one piece, and you ensured that Amir got through too. I'm so sorry that this happened to you. I'm so sorry that you didn't get the help you asked for. I know it isn't what you wanted. And I'm so sorry.
Yasmin begins crying again.	
Therapist:	Swap chairs?
Yasmin nods and swaps. She keeps crying.	
Therapist:	Do you want to respond?
Yasmin shakes her head and dries her tears:	No, that's it. Thank you.

From initially CFT-focused intervention, working through Yasmin's shame and arrested defenses, Yasmin's therapist moved to more of an ACT-focus, supporting Yasmin in tuning into her values, introducing the concepts of mindfulness, experiential acceptance, flexible languaging, and flexible perspective taking and focusing on meaningful living.

Troubleshooting

Fear of compassion

Fear of compassion can develop with a learning history in which the activation of the soothing system was linked to the activation of the threat system. This may include a history of trauma. People with a fear of compassion may express beliefs around the importance of being independent. They may also see self-compassion or receiving compassion from others as weak or believe that taking a compassionate stance toward themselves would undermine their motivation. That is, they might believe that their self-criticism is necessary to maintaining motivation. When a compassion exercise is introduced, someone with a fear of compassion may report a paradoxical reaction of increased stress or anxiety, or they may simply report that it does nothing for them. They may be skilled at *giving* compassion to others, even to themselves, but exhibit a fearful or numbed reaction to *receiving* compassion (from others or themselves).

Where there is a fear of compassion, compassion work is itself a kind of exposure therapy, gradually increasing the person's capacity to give compassion to themselves and to receive compassion (from themselves and others). It is often helpful to shape compassion by degrees. For some, including people with histories of trauma, particularly developmental trauma, starting with compassion exercises that do not involve people such as the soothing rhythm breathing or the safe space meditation is beneficial. For parents with histories of developmental trauma in particular, people may be associated with danger and the learned activation of the threat system, rather than safety and genuine compassion. Compassionate imagery, that does not involve people, may be able to activate the soothing system without activating the threat system. When introducing compassion exercises involving people, clinicians might ask parents to envision a "kind coach," or "kind mentor" and imagine how that individual might speak to a struggling child attempting to learn a new skill. Sometimes, envisioning a fictional character is easiest. Similarly, one might have parents call to mind a younger version of themselves during a time when they were struggling, and imagine speaking to that child in the way the kind coach would. It is often difficult for parents to show compassion to themselves and to receive compassion from themselves. If they can generate in their imagination a person *outside* of themselves acting in a compassionate way, and receive compassion from them, then they may be better able to call upon self-compassion later.

Four key developmental periods and compassion

Infancy and compassion

Many women have experiences of being shamed by others in the perinatal period, including around birth experiences, infant feeding, and infant sleeping. Importantly, women with all different kinds of birth, feeding, and sleeping experiences report these experiences of shaming. So, for example, women who feed their babies formula commonly report being shamed for this, yet women who breastfeed commonly report being shamed for public breastfeeding or feeding for "too long" (Thomson, Ebisch-Burton, & Flacking, 2014). It is a period of time where a woman's behavior and choices in matters that are quite personal come under intense public scrutiny and social comparison. Women who also experience high degrees of internal shame will have no difficulty in identifying narratives by which they can criticize and shame themselves. Compassion may be an important way for women as individuals and society as a whole to live through and undo this pressure cooker of shame.

Birth trauma and breastfeeding challenges are not uncommon (Kendall-Tackett, 2014). Arrested defenses from birth trauma or feeding difficulties may be relevant to understanding a mother's psychological health in the postnatal period.

The capacity of parents to be compassionate toward themselves and to receive compassion from others may become apparent in these early months of parenthood. People who previously coped with a highly independent way of life may find themselves confronted with their fears around receiving compassion, from themselves and from others.

From the infant's perspective, the infant is receiving their first experiences of compassion from their parents. The way that parents and other caregivers respond to the child's suffering develops the child's later capacity to receive compassion both from themselves and from others. Thus, the parental ability to maintain compassion for their baby is crucial. Parents are more likely to be able to maintain a compassionate stance toward their baby if they are within a compassionate context.

Early childhood and compassion

Parents may experience contexts of social competition, judgment, criticism, and shame. Parents may compare themselves to others, and experience judgment and shame, around parenting choices and behavior such as the use and kind of childcare, bedsharing at night, continued breastfeeding, and the use of screens. They may also compare their child to other children in terms of milestones such as language development, toilet training, emerging independence, or emerging literacy or numeracy skills as well as in terms of behavior such as tantrums or noncompliance. Their child's seemingly being behind their peers may be experienced as a social threat, potentially triggering defensive reactions such as fight or flight or submissive behavior. With social media, social comparisons are easily made, and are often false has many people regulate their perception on social media. It is easy for parents to experience a context of social threat. Self-compassion is thus important to balance this mentality. It is also important, on a community level, to build compassionate contexts for parents, with affiliative rather than competitive social contact.

During this time, children may begin to show compassion, and their compassionate behavior may become increasingly elaborate as their own perspective taking abilities develop. The ways in which parents have responded to their children's suffering forms a model for how children begin to respond to the suffering of others and themselves.

Early childhood is a time when behavioral challenges such as noncompliance and temper tantrums are at their peak, and in which emotional dysregulation is common. Parental compassion for the distress of their children may be important in understanding the child's behavior as developmentally appropriate.

Middle childhood and compassion

Into middle childhood social competition may be particularly fierce around schooling. Parents may become preoccupied with their child's academic, social, athletic, or other forms of school success. Parents may feel that their child's success in various aspects of school life is a direct reflection of themselves as parents, and experience any "failure" of their child as a social threat. In the midst of defensive reactions, parents are less likely to respond with care and compassion, and are less likely to respond in a manner that promotes a growth mindset in their child.

During middle childhood, children may become aware, for the first time, of where they stand in relation to others. The child's evolved defensive reactions to social threat including fight or flight reactions or submissive behaviors may become dysfunctional patterns. Evolved defensive reactions may be part of externalising or internalising patterns of behavior. For some children, school may itself be an inescapable situation, associated with entrapment.

Adolescence and compassion

Adolescence is a developmental period characterized by preoccupation with identity, peers, and social standing. Social comparison and social competition are escalated during adolescence. This developmental focus may intensify defensive reactions and these defensive reactions may, in vulnerable adolescents, become dysfunctional patterns. At this time of life, adolescents may be accessing social media, with all its virtues and vices, including the ease of social comparison.

It is often difficult for parents to watch the risk-taking and experimentation of adolescence. A compassionate stance to their child's challenges, with genuine perspective-taking, and understanding of the developmental tasks of adolescence may be an important part of keeping the relationship strong during these times. Especially as adolescents push back against the parent.

Using compassion with specific populations

Parental mental health problems and compassion

Mental health problems may be associated with evolved defenses that are too easily aroused, prolonged, arrested, or ineffective (Gilbert, 2001). This may include arrested flight or entrapment, arrested fight, and shame or submissive display. Compassion, including self-compassion and improving capacity for receiving compassion, can provide parasympathetic balance and improve mental health and well-being.

Parental grief and compassion

Depending on the circumstances of the loss grief may be mixed in with shame or other arrested defenses. This may be particularly true, for example, in pregnancy and neonatal loss, the birth of a child with disabilities, or the injury of a child. In all of these cases, self-compassion and the ability to receive compassion provide a space in which the work of grieving can be done, while addressing self blame and shame.

Childhood externalizing problems and compassion

Compassion is relevant to parents of children with externalizing problems in two ways. First, social comparisons between their child and other children are likely to have created a psychological context of social threat. This context of social threat is not supportive of caring and effective parenting. Secondly, the evolved defenses of the parent—for example, a submissive or a flight reaction to aversive child behavior—may be undermining effective parenting. Focusing on self-compassion can thus be beneficial. It is also important for the parent to continue to find compassion for their child, even though their child may be genuinely difficult to live with.

For the child, the child's own defensive reactions; for example, fight reactions may be part of the pattern of externalizing behavior. A context of social safety *for the child* is thus likely to be beneficial.

Childhood internalizing problems and compassion

As with externalizing problems parents may engage in social comparisons with other children and experience a context of social threat. This is not likely to support caring and effective parenting. The evolved defenses of the parent—for example, a flight reaction—may be undermining effective parenting. Focusing on self-compassion can thus be beneficial. It is also important for the parent to continue to find compassion for their child. The compassion needs to include the capacity for sensitivity to suffering, including the ability to be accepting of their child's suffering, to not immediately need to push it away or "fix" it. It also includes the ability to take the child's perspective and to see the long-term ramifications of courses of action. That is, to compassionately parent in the child's long-term best interests.

For the child, the child's own defensive reactions—for example, flight or submissive display reactions—may be part of the pattern of internalizing behavior. A context of social safety *for the child* is thus likely to be beneficial.

Childhood neurodevelopmental disabilities and compassion

Parents of children with neurodevelopmental disabilities often blame themselves for their child's condition. Parents may also experience stigma as a result of their child's disability or make social comparisons between their child and typically developing children that may lead to experiences of social threat. In all of these circumstances, self-compassion and the ability to receive compassion from others is relevant.

Peer relations and bullying and compassion

The capacity to both give and receive compassion is important to social interaction including social interaction of children and adolescents. It is consistent with building long-lasting affiliative connections. In addition, self-compassion—the ability to both give compassion to yourself and to receive compassion from yourself—is an important buffer against the ill effects of peer challenges including bullying, but also social competition and loneliness.

Marital conflict and compassion

Finding compassion for your partner, including when there is marital conflict, may support resolving the conflict, or alternatively managing the conflict in a manner that is more consistent with the well-being of the children. Marital conflict may include patterns of mutually triggering social threat and evolved defenses. A stance of compassion, for self and partner, can provide balance to the more destructive elements of the evolved psyche.

Expressed emotion including critical and intrusive parenting and compassion

Critical, hostile, and intrusive parenting behavior may be part of the triggering of evolved defenses in the parent, with compassion being necessary to restore balance. One mechanism by which critical, hostile, and intrusive parenting behavior may be damaging to children is through shame. That is, the critical, hostile, and intrusive behavior of the parent may induce shame and submissive defense in the child. Over time, children internalize the harsh and critical voice of the parent.

Emotion dismissiveness and compassion

Parental compassion for their child, being sensitive to their child's suffering alongside a motivation to alleviate that suffering, stands in direct contrast to an emotionally dismissive parenting style. Emotionally dismissive parenting fails to be compassionate, whether it fails through the parental inability to recognize their child's emotions, parental inability to demonstrate experiential acceptance of their child's emotions, or parental inability to truly alleviate their child's suffering in the long term.

Inconsistent, or harsh and punitive parenting and compassion

Parenting that is overly harsh or punitive may be parenting in which the parent is failing to be fully compassionate to their child, either through a lack of sensitivity or a failure of motivation. In this case, building the parental capacity for compassion for their child may be useful. In addition, parental evolved defenses—vigilance to signals of threat or loss, mobilization behaviors of fight or flight, avoidance, hiding, immobilization shutdown behaviors, withdrawal and submissive displays vigilance to signals of threat or loss, mobilization behaviors of fight or flight, avoidance, hiding, immobilization shtudown behaviors, withdrawal and submissive displays—may be playing a role in the parenting behavioral pattern. If that is the case, self-compassion is an effective anecdote.

References

Carvalho, S., Pinto-Gouveia, J., Pimentel, P., Maia, D., Gilbert, P., & Mota-Pereira, J. (2013). Entrapment and defeat perceptions in depressive symptomatology: Through an evolutionary approach. *Psychiatry*, *76*(1), 53–67.

Cheung, M. S. P., Gilbert, P., & Irons, C. (2004). An exploration of shame, social rank and rumination in relation to depression. *Personality and Individual Differences*, *36*, 1143–1153.

Gilbert, P. (2000). The relationship of shame, social anxiety and depression: The role of the evaluation of social rank. *Clinical Psychology and Psychotherapy*, *7*, 174–189.

Gilbert, P. (2001). Evolutionary approaches to psychopathology: The role of natural defenses. *Australian and New Zealand Journal of Psychiatry*, *35*, 17–27.

Gilbert, P. (2009). *The compassionate mind*. London: Little, Brown Book Group.

Gilbert, P. (2014). The origins and nature of compassion focused therapy. *British Journal of Clinical Psychology*, *53*(1), 6–41.

Gilbert, P. (2015a). The evolution and social dynamics of compassion. *Social and Personality Psychology Compass*, *9*(6), 239–254.

Gilbert, P. (2015b). An evolutionary approach to emotion in mental health with a focus on affiliative emotions. *Emotion Review*, *7*(3), 230–237.

Gilbert, P., Allan, S., Brough, S., Melley, S., & Miles, J. N. V. (2002). Relationship of anhedonia and anxiety to social rank, defeat and entrapment. *Journal of Affective Disorders*, *71*, 141–151.

Gilbert, P., Gilbert, J., & Irons, C. (2004). Life events, entrapments and arrested anger in depression. *Journal of Affective Disorders*, *79*, 149–160.

Hayes, L. L., & Ciarrochi, J. (2015). *The thriving adolescent*. Oakland: New Harbinger Publications.

Irons, C., Gilbert, P., Baldwin, M. W., Baccus, J. R., & Palmer, M. (2006). Parental recall, attachment relating and self-attacking/self-reassurance: Their relationship with depression. *British Journal of Clinical Psychology*, *45*(3), 297–308.

Kendall-Tackett, K. (2014). Birth trauma: The causes and consequences of childbirth-related trauma and PTSD. In D. L. Barnes (Ed.), *Women's reproductive mental health across the lifespan*. Cham: Springer International Publishing.

Kirby, J. N. (2016). The role of mindfulness and compassion in enhancing nurturing family environments. *Clinical Psychology: Science and Practice*, *23*(2), 142–157.

Mitchell, A. E., Whittingham, K., Steindl, S., & Kirby, J. (2018). Feasibility and acceptability of a brief online self-compassion intervention for mothers of infants. *Archives of Women's Mental Health*, *21*(5), 553–561.

Neff, K. D., & Faso, D. J. (2015). Self-compassion and well-being in parents of children with autism. *Mindfulness*, *6*, 938–947.

Neff, K. D., Kirkpatrick, K. L., & Rude, S. S. (2007). Self-compassion and adaptive psychological functioning. *Journal of Research in Personality*, *41*(1), 139–154.

Porges, S. W. (1997). Evolution: An evolutionary by-product of the neural regulation of the autonomic nervous system. In C. S. Carter, I. Lederhendler, & B. Kirkpatrick (Eds.), *The integrative neurobiology of affliation* (pp. 62–77). New York: New York Academy of Sciences.

Psychogiou, L., Legge, K., Parry, E., Mann, J., Nath, S., Ford, T., & Kuyken, W. (2016). Self-compassion and parenting in mothers and fathers with depression. *Mindfulness (New York)*, *7*, 896–908.

Sloman, L., Gilbert, P., & Hasey, G. (2003). Evolved mechanisms in depression: The role and interaction of attachment and social rank in depression. *Journal of Affective Disorders*, *74*, 107–121.

Thomson, G., Ebisch-Burton, K., & Flacking, R. (2014). Shame if you do—Shame if you don't: Women's experiences of infant feeding. *Maternal and Child Nutrition*, *11*, 33–46.

Tirch, D., Schoendorff, B., & Silberstein, L. R. (2014). *The ACT Practitioner's Guide to the science of compassion*. Oakland: New Harbinger Publications.

Chapter 13

Committed action and exploration

Chapter Outline

What is committed action and exploration? 354
DNA-V model 356
How does committed action apply to parent–child interaction? 356
Parenting for a flexible, broad behavioral repertoire for the child 356
Parenting control agenda 357
Exploration and development 358
Working with committed action clinically 361
Setting goals and practice opportunities 361
Building resilience through debriefing 362
Working with willingness 363
Acting from the whole hexaflex 363
Getting off the hook 364
Metaphors 366
Parent supporting child exploration 366
Encouraging home practice 367
Troubleshooting 370
Refining parenting strategies in practice 370
It is tough work 370
Four key developmental periods and committed action and exploration 371
Infancy and committed action and exploration 371
Early childhood and committed action and exploration 371
Middle childhood and committed action and exploration 371
Adolescence and committed action and exploration 372
Using committed action with specific populations 372
Parental mental health problems and committed action and exploration 372
Parental grief and committed action and exploration 372
Childhood externalizing problems and committed action and exploration 372
Childhood internalizing problems and committed action and exploration 372
Childhood neurodevelopmental disabilities and committed action and exploration 373
Peer relations and bullying and committed action and exploration 373
Marital conflict and committed action and exploration 373
Expressed emotion including critical and intrusive parenting and committed action and exploration 374
Emotion dismissiveness and committed action and exploration 374
Inconsistent, or harsh and punitive parenting and committed action and exploration 374
References 374

Acceptance and Commitment Therapy. DOI: https://doi.org/10.1016/B978-0-12-814669-9.00013-8
© 2019 Elsevier Inc. All rights reserved.

Courage is not simply one of the virtues, but the form of every virtue at the testing point.

-C.S. Lewis

You can't stay in your corner of the Forest waiting for others to come to you. You have to go to them sometimes.

-A.A. Milne, *Winnie-the-Pooh*

It's a terrible thing, I think, in life to wait until you're ready. I have this feeling now that actually no one is ever ready to do anything. There's no such thing as ready. There is only now. And you may as well do it now. Generally speaking, now is as good a time as any.

-Hugh Laurie

What is committed action and exploration?

Committed action the component of Acceptance and Commitment Therapy (ACT) that focuses on actual behavioral change in the context of the person's life, guided by values. Simply put, it means making a promise to yourself to do something, and to follow through, no matter what. For children and adolescents, whose values are still forming at the proto-values stage, the equivalent is developmentally appropriate exploration. While all components of the ACT model may be relevant to committed action, committed action clearly rests on values and acceptance or willingness. Values define the actions taken—they are the basis for the goals made and give meaning and dignity to the challenges that are part of committed action.

Willingness is a necessary condition for committed action (Hayes, Strosahl, & Wilson, 2003). In moving toward valued directions, previously avoided thoughts, feelings, memories, and sensations are likely to surface. The client must be willing to experience what they experience in taking the steps that they have chosen. That is, to accept the thoughts, feelings, memories, and sensations that arise as part of taking committed action, to accept them as they are and not as they say they are. Willingness cannot be partially there. That is willingness cannot be conditional upon which private events show up, "I am willing but only if I don't start feeling anxious . . ." Willingness can only be safely limited by limiting the size of situation. That is, "I am willing to stick to my new parenting plan on a small shopping trip where I am only buying milk and bread."

It's important to remember that willingness is a *behavior that can be shaped.* This can be accomplished in a variety of ways. For example, a parent can consider the size of the situation, cutting big changes into smaller-sized bites. For parenting changes, this can often be achieved by specifically creating opportunities to practice the new way of parenting—artificial situations in which nothing is actually at stake. The size of the situation can be safely limited, and in fact, some people may choose to draw a permanent boundary in terms of size. If that doesn't interfere with valued living that is okay. We all have things we aren't willing to do! However, acting cannot be made conditional upon the thoughts, feelings, memories, and sensations that arise in that moment.

During committed action, verbal rules are likely to show up, with pliance to unworkable rules and inaccurate tracks being tested and abandoned. Defusion techniques are relevant to verbal rules as they surface. Also relevant is a flexible, experimental stance toward testing that sees verbal rules as hypotheses to be tested in practice and asks, again and again, does this work? This is about flexible languaging more broadly, where workable verbal rules may be used, with understanding of the limitations of language and verbal rules that are not workable can be discarded. Testing and discarding verbal rules and self-stories can itself be confronting. In order to "win" in terms of living a valued life, clients often have to surrender in terms of being "right." This may mean surrendering being "right" about their child, being "right" while their child is "wrong," or being "right" while their partner is "wrong."

Committed action involves setting goals and acting on goals (rather than moment-to-moment feelings). Goals should be grounded within values, specific, measurable, attainable, realistic, and time-bound. Within committed action, roleplays and observations of parent–child interactions are valuable. Never underestimate the value of bringing a behavior into the therapy room through a roleplay or a genuine parent and child interaction, rather than simply talking about a behavior. The rehearsal of new parenting behaviors and skills in the low-pressure context of the therapy room, with the therapist playing the role of the child, is invaluable for skill acquisition and for identifying verbal rules, emotions, and thoughts that may come up in the situation. Likewise, therapist feedback on parent–child interactions is also well-used in evidence-based parenting interventions.

Committed action and exploration can be likened to the concept of broaden and build, of broadening and building on the behavioral repertoire of the parent and the child (Hayes & Ciarrochi, 2015). For the parent, this means adopting a flexible, experimental approach to parenting, an approach of discovering what works. For the child, this means developmentally appropriate exploration (and for the parent, support for the child's developmentally appropriate exploration). Unlike the positive psychology concept of broaden and build, positive emotions are not seen as necessary to the process. A sense of safety, a compassionate context, makes broaden and build easier (Gilbert, 2009). If a sense of safety is absent it can be cultivated using compassion-focused techniques and through the therapeutic relationship, or for the child, the parenting relationship itself. However, more flexible responding cannot wait for the right emotional state. Instead, active experimentation with different behaviors (i.e., trial-and-error learning), broadening and building on the repertoire is the focus.

Committed action can also be understood from an evolutionary perspective of parenting (Hayes & Sanford, 2015; Hayes, Sanford, & Chin, 2017). Dysfunctional parenting can be understood as when parenting behavior persists through selection pressures other than its workability or effectiveness; for example, through parental experiential avoidance. Committed action is reintroducing variation into parenting. With variation, and selection based on workability in the context of parenting values, parenting that works is selected and retained.

DNA-V model

Committed action and exploration, as presented in this book, relates to all aspects of the DNA-V (Hayes & Ciarrochi, 2015). For children, exploratory behavior and flexible experimentation is important, with the gradual development of a flexible and broad behavioral repertoire. This exploratory aspect relates to the discoverer in DNA-V. For parents, a flexible and experimental approach to parenting is important, with an emphasis on workability. This also relates to the discoverer component of DNA-V. For example, clinicians might encourage parents to check in with their advisor regarding any "parenting rules" they might have about themselves, or their child; if they use their noticer to observe that those rules do not accurately reflect how their behavior is working, they might shift into discoverer mode to try a new strategy. In this way, flexible perspective taking across the advisor, noticer, and discoverer can help create flexibility, where needed, in the context of parenting values.

How does committed action apply to parent–child interaction?

Parenting for a flexible, broad behavioral repertoire for the child

To encourage the development of a flexible, broad behavioral repertoire in their child and to support developmentally appropriate exploration, it is important for the parent to understand and value developmentally appropriate exploration. For example, it is helpful for parents of adolescents to see the normality and value in their risk-taking behavior. It is also important for parents to adopt a sensitive and responsive parenting style, with minimal intrusiveness, in a way that is flexible to their child's changing developmental needs. A flexible, broad behavioral repertoire can also be supported through minimal use of punishment. Punishment narrows behavioral repertoires—what is learned is literally the avoidance of the punisher itself. Through parenting by positively reinforcing a broad range of behaviors, and simply refraining from reinforcing behaviors that are dysfunctional, flexibility promoted. Flexible, workable parenting in the parent is thus consistent with parent–child interaction that is likely to gradually shape a psychologically flexible child. It is also important for the parent to reinforce effort rather than merely reinforcing success.

Parenting control agenda

Committed action is also about parents shifting from a parenting control agenda to flexible, workable parenting. The parenting control agenda (discussed in Chapter 8: Experiential acceptance of self, child, and relationship) refers to when parents attempt to control their child's internal experiences. At times, parents may attempt to control the internal experiences of their child in order to control their own internal experiences, that is, their reactions to the child. Parents may also attempt to control their child's thoughts, feelings, and other internal experiences in order to control their child's behavior. There's a logic to this approach. After all, if tantrums seem to happen when a child is angry then it makes sense to fix the anger in order to decrease the tantrums. If your teenager says that they didn't try out for the school band because they aren't confident enough then it makes sense to try to build up their confidence in order to ensure that they don't miss out on opportunities. Yet, if attempting to control our own thoughts and feelings is often unworkable, then attempting to control the thoughts and feelings of others, too, is often unworkable. The parenting control agenda may lead to a variety of unworkable parenting behaviors including parenting that is lax, parenting that supports avoidance, and parenting that is coercive. The parenting control agenda suggests that the parent must *win* any given interaction: that the child must be forced, whether it be by aversion or cleverness, to immediately shift to feeling, thinking, and acting as the parent desires. Every challenging interaction may become a battleground.

In contrast, a flexible, workable parenting agenda is an agenda of shaping behavior through sensitivity to contingencies—or, simply put, how a behavior *works*—in contrast to how a parent *thinks* it may work. Any given interaction is not a battle to be won. Instead, the parent is looking beyond, across their child's development and asking: how can I influence my child, so that an adaptive behavior is more likely next time and the time after that? A parent with a flexible, workable parenting agenda doesn't seek to win an interaction. Rather, they seek to shape their child's behavior over time. Not by changing their child's internal experiences, but through the context, through shifting the contingencies. They can also recognize when they have miscalculated, and how to exit an interaction without escalation and without causing harm (i.e., without increasing the probability of aversive child behaviors in the future), to rethink and begin again tomorrow. To a parent with a shaping agenda, there is nothing lost in such a maneuvre, because the focus isn't on winning the interaction, or controlling their child's internal experiences, but on shaping behavior into the future. It is vital that parents be supported not just in adopting positive parenting strategies, but in shifting from a parenting control agenda to a flexible, workable parenting agenda grounded in shaping.

Exploration and development

Parental fostering of exploration and flexibility are important throughout childhood, but become particularly important during early childhood and adolescence (Gopnik, 2017). In early childhood, youngsters begin to emerge from the "nest" to explore their physical and social worlds, as their body experiences rapid physical, cognitive, and emotional development. At the same time, young children enter into the symbolic world—first in rudimentary joint-attention forged in the attachment relationship, then as they begin to understand words as symbols for things in the world, and then they derive meaning about their worlds.

In adolescence, shifts in the frontal cortex, responsible for reason, planning, inhibition, and judgment, are outmatched by the rate of growth in the amygdala, host of emotion regulation (Blakemore & Choudhury, 2006; Committee on the Science of Adolescence, 2011). As this happens, adolescents engage in more risk-taking behavior, driven by a more potent need for sensation-seeking—the same old enterprises and rewards that thrilled them in the past have become hum-drum. In the context of more intense and frequent risk taking, adolescents are more motivated by strong emotions, and less able to self-regulate. This process may continue until the brain matures at about age 25, as adolescents begin to develop more autonomy. The evolutionary purpose for the brain and related behavioral changes that occur in adolescence may be greater interest in exploring the world to find a mate. Thus, lower inhibition and more intense and labile emotional experience appears important to the development of effective and adaptive discovery, individuation, and increased autonomy. Although this process begins in the family, adolescents are also shaped by their social worlds—school, work, and more recently, the digital world. The more open adolescents are to mindful exploration and risk-taking in these domains, the more effectively they can track the consequences of their behavior, and thus, the better they will be able to navigate. The stronger and more open their relationship with their parents, the more willing they may be to engage parents in discussion and accept guidance, gently given, about their new discoveries.

An important aspect of of parenting, then, is for parents to support curiosity to explore the world including the ability to pay close attention to the effects of one's behavior, such that one can discriminate what works and what does not. Adolescents' strong emotions may play a role in this learning—since the more emotionally salient different experiences are, or the more potent one's lived experiences, the easier it is for an individual to derive relations among them. Children and adolescents take all kinds of risks, and to do this mindfully and well requires attention to the particular situational cues or context. What is important to have here is sensitivity to context—this is called *phenotypic plasticity*, or the ability to engage in different phenotypes (i.e., behavioral patterns, repertoires, or skills) contingent on different contexts (Fusco & Minelli, 2010). Committed action and exploration can be thought of as an engine that drives this: engagement in a variety of behaviors and trial-and-error learning, and experiencing how these behaviors work within particular contexts, can support the development—or evolution—of more effective, flexible child behaviors over time.

Scott, Harry, and Ava

Scott has joint custody of his two children, 8-year-old Harry and 5-year-old Ava, sharing custody with his first wife, Naomi. He works as an electrician. He is seeking help because he has become increasingly disconnected from his children and feels that he needs help to become the father he wants to be.

Scott explains that he has been in a slump since his first marriage unraveled 3 years ago. In the intervening time, he was briefly married again, an experience that he describes as a "short and crazy mistake." He says that his marriage to his first wife Naomi was based on a genuine connection and describes her as a "decent enough lady and a good mother." He says that they first began seeing each other at 15, explaining "what did we know about relationships? We were just kids." He says that they both made mistakes, and they went through a "rough patch," with Scott's dad dying unexpectedly when Naomi was pregnant with Ava, and Naomi experiencing birth trauma and postnatal depression. Scott has an amicable relationship with Naomi today.

When Scott's marriage with Naomi ended he initially felt devastated. On the days when he didn't have the children he would spend all his time working, binge watching television, or playing computer games. He drank alcohol most days. Scott feels that the divorce was hard on the children and that this is when they began to drift apart.

Scott describes his second marriage as whirlwind romance that quickly crashed. Harry and Ava disliked Scott's second wife, Hayley, and Scott's relationships with both of his children spiraled down at this time. Overall, Scott is relieved that his second marriage is over. But he feels that he has fallen back into "the slump" and he is concerned about how disconnected he now is from his children. He is determined to change.

Imagine you could, unseen and unheard, observe a typical, ordinary interaction between Scott, Harry, and Ava. It might be something like this:

Parent–child interaction

Scott opens the door, waving Harry and Ava into his town house.

Harry and Ava follow, both still sulking. They had wanted to stay at their mothers.

"Right, well," Scott says, "I've got some chocolate muffins for afternoon tea. Does that sound good?"

(*Continued*)

(Continued)

Ava nods and smiles slightly.
"Homemade or from the shops?" asks Harry, in a barbed tone.
"The shops," Scott answers, "you want one?"
Harry sighs and rolls his eyes, "Seriously? The shop muffins are gross."
"Well, that's what I've got, you want one?"
Harry sighs again, "Fine."
"Good," Scott sighs, "and I need to get the kettle on."
"I'll have a coffee too," Harry says.
"Oh no you won't Harry," Scott replies.
"Mum lets me have coffee," Harry answers back.
"She doesn't. We do talk, you know," Scott replies as they move into the kitchen and he gets the afternoon tea ready, "you can have juice, or milk or water."
"Milk then," Harry answers.
"Alright," Scott says, "One milk. And you, Ava?"
"Orange juice, please," Ava says.
"Easy, one milk and one orange juice," Scott says as he gets the drinks and the muffins.
A few minutes later they are all sitting at the table eating their afternoon tea.
"So, Harry, how has school been this week?"
Harry shrugs, "alright I guess."
"Who have you been playing with at lunchtime?"
"Lots of kids," Harry answers.
"Still into handball?" Scott asks.
"Nah," Harry replies.
"Lost interest, huh?"
Harry shrugs again.
"Daddy," Ava says, "can I watch Octonauts?"
"Sure, honey," Scott says, "when you've finished your muffin."
"I'm finished," Ava replies.
"Alright then," Scott takes Ava into the lounge room and puts Octonauts on the TV for her. He tries to initiate conversation about the show but Ava's answers are brief and she is quickly absorbed in watching.
When he returns to the kitchen Harry has left. He peaks in on Harry in his room and finds him engrossed in drawing. He thinks about asking Harry about what he is drawing but he knows Harry won't have much to say about it. He considers challenging him to a game of soccer but Harry will just refuse. It seems easier to just let the kids be.
Scott was looking forward to the kids coming over but now that they are here he feels even more disconnected from them. He goes to the computer and finds a simple game to occupy himself.

What's happening for Scott, Harry, and Ava?

Harry and Ava are somewhat withdrawn from Scott and unresponsive to his attempts to initiate interaction. There is some oppositional behavior from Harry, but it is minor. One wonders what the divorce and Scott's second marriage was

(*Continued*)

(Continued)

like from Harry and Ava's perspective. Did Scott maintain a sensitive and responsive parenting style throughout his brief second marriage? Or were Harry and Ava neglected somewhat? What did the divorce and Scott's second marriage mean to Harry and Ava and has that meaning ever been openly discussed with Scott? Overall, the interaction suggests relationships that are in need of repair, but relationships that can be repaired.

Scott has a narrowed pattern of behavior with patterns of avoidance. What Scott calls "the slump" is consistent with depression and his behavioral patterns of excessive working, watching television, playing computer games, and drinking are all likely functioning as avoidance. Importantly for Scott's relationships with his children, Scott appears to be stuck in a pattern of avoidance around doing the difficult work that needs to be done in order to reconnect with his children. For change to happen, Scott will need to persist in a consistent pattern of reconnecting with his children, and to be willing to experience negative thoughts, feelings and memories that this may trigger in him.

From a clinical RFT perspective, Scott appears to have derived relations with negative emotions as "intolerable" and "to be avoided." In a frame of opposition to his negative emotions are "being busy," "computer games," and "drinking." A clinician working with Scott on his engagement in his family might first explore, through experiential work, the process by which he becomes "disconnected" so that he might better track how it works. Very likely, his engagement in avoidance strategies doesn't protect him from negative emotions the way he wishes it might; however, his awareness of that is limited. Helping him walk through these types of relations and also broadening the frames of possible behaviors in which to engage—even when he is feeling down—will be helpful in supported small, committed actions in the service of reconnecting with his children.

Working with committed action clinically

Setting goals and practice opportunities

Goal setting and deliberate practice are key to creating behavior change. In setting goals and creating opportunities for practice consider:

- Ensuring that goals are grounded within values, specific measurable, attainable, realistic, and time-bound. In particular, it needs to be possible to know whether or not a particular goal was achieved.
- Finding opportunities for deliberate practice. That is, create artificial situations in which nothing is actually at stake so that the parent can focus on parenting. For example, a practice shopping trip to pick up a couple of items (that are not actually needed), a mock situation of needing to get 20 minutes of work done, or getting the children ready on the weekend as if they need to go to school. In the case of parenting an adolescent, when parenting shifts from the being more directive to a more

collaborative discussion of taking mindful risks, parents might practice stepping back and allowing their teen to explore, whether via an imaginal exercise or in small ways, such as allowing the teen to drive a short distance from home to the shop, by themselves.
- Considering practicing in session whether by roleplays, imaginal exposure, or in vivo is work observing a real parent and child interaction. By bringing the practice into the therapy room you have greater opportunity to observe and modify any relevant contingencies.
- Addressing any practical barriers and ensuring the parent's plans are realistic.
- Emphasizing the small. Often parents jump straight to grandiose plans and goals. Prompt parents to think of the little changes that they could make. For example, parents who are aware that they need to prioritize their couple relationship often leap straight to the goal of a date night. A date night may be nice, but for many families regular date nights might not be realistic. Instead, help the parent to focus on small but meaningful and sustainable changes that they could make. For example, regularly asking their partner how their day was and listening to the reply.
- Realizing it may be beneficial to have parents state their goals aloud, based on self-regulation literature on making public commitments.
- Ensuring the parent has the goals written down or a reminder of the goals in some form when they leave.

Building resilience through debriefing

Parents' attempts to achieve specific goals and their ongoing changes in behavioral patterns should always be discussed and debriefed in a way that attends to tracking (rules that specify the real-world consequences of behavior) and pliance (rules followed for social approval). In other words, the therapist should strive, in a collaborative way, to help parents observe in a defused way how their behavior worked—did it help? If not, what happened instead? In addition, this debriefing should be done in a way that promotes parental resilience and self-sufficiency. It is important to not position yourself as the expert or to make your approval something to be sought. Instead, encourage the development of a flexible and experimental approach to parenting with a focus on what works. This can be done by focusing debriefing on asking the parent's thoughts and scaffolding their capacity for accurate tracking and identification of contingencies (in FAP terms CRB3/DRB3s as discussed in Chapter 5: Case conceptualization) rather than telling them what to do as an "expert." This can be achieved through a habit of asking:

- What went well? That is, in terms of parenting behavior what worked? Ensure the parent does answer this as many parents will skip ahead to talking about what didn't work. It is just as important for parents to

recognize behavioral patterns that are working so that they can be retained and elaborated.
- What didn't go well? That is, in terms of parenting behavior what didn't work? Why didn't it work?
- Given this, what could you try differently next time?
- What showed up in terms of thoughts, feelings, memories, sensations, and behavioral impulses? Were you aware and willing to have them without getting stuck in them?
- Is there an ACT skill that is relevant to this situation, and if so, how can you use it in the moment?

Working with willingness

A number of things can get in the way of parents engaging in committed action. These may be logistical, or may come from deep-set beliefs about how parents *should* behave, rather than a clear-eyed assessment of how those strategies *actually* work, or experiencing uncomfortable private events in the context of engaging in particular parenting strategies. The use of selective attention (planned ignoring)—or the practice of attending to and verbally reinforcing desirable child behavior while ignoring disruptive child behavior—can elicit a host of reactions from parents. They may feel that disruptive behavior should merit a more punitive response, like scolding; or they may feel embarrassment or perhaps social censure when their child engages in public misbehavior. These triggers can lead to giving in, or inconsistent application of selective attention—or even escalation to engage in more punitive disciplinary strategies. Thus, as clinicians, it is important to debrief with parents and identify the antecedents of these for parents, and make a space to help parents lean in to those experiences and increase their *willingness* to engage in more effective parenting strategies, even in the presence of uncomfortable private events.

Acting from the whole hexaflex

Each aspect of the hexaflex is relevant to committed action. In the committed action phase of intervention every element is brought to bear on ensuring values consistent and effective patterns of behavior are cultivated in a sustainable manner. This may be done in tiny ways, so that the therapist and the client are jumping flexibly around the hexaflex in cultivating change. In particular:

- *Values and proto-values*: Values give dignity to the difficult work of behavior change. Framing goals and actions as part of values gives meaning and motivation. This can also create novel relational frames that aren't readily apparent. For example, linking the use of selective attention (or planned ignoring) to being kind or supporting your child's development. For example, "it can feel mean in that moment when you are ignoring your child's whining but really, it is the kindest thing to do. If your child learns to whine a lot then her life is going to be very difficult. People don't like whiners and she'll always be looking for what's going wrong in her life."

- *Experiential acceptance of parent, child, and relationship*: Experiential acceptance is especially relevant in terms of willingness: the willingness to experience the thoughts, feelings, memories, sensations, and behavioral impulses that arise as the parent takes effective action. This willingness is key to breaking down avoidance patterns. The metaphors of *the swamp* and *controlling the ocean* (discussed in Chapter 8: Experiential acceptance of self, child, and relationship) are particularly relevant.
- *Contact with the present moment including shared psychological presence*: It is important that the parent engages in effective action mindfully. This supports parental willingness and helps the parent to noticie what is working. The brief everyday life exercise *Wake up! A quick mindfulness meditation* as well as the lengthier *Parenting: a mindfulness meditation* (discussed in Chapter 9: Contact with the present moment including shared psychological presence) can be used.
- *Flexible languaging*: The therapist is likely to need to facilitate defusion to thoughts and rules that come up. In addition, promoting the cultivation of effective tracking of child behavior in context rather than inaccurate tracking (rules about real-world consequences that are inaccurate) or pliance (rules followed for social approval).
- *Flexible perspective taking*: Prompting taking the child's perspective in the challenging situation or afterward while debriefing the challenging situation can support the parent in developing effective tracking and discovering what works. This includes both other-as-process and other-as-context.
- *Compassionate context: self-compassion, compassion for others, receiving compassion from others:* Committed action by definition means taking effective action where it is psychologically difficult. In particular, it often means engaging in approach behavior where there's a history of avoidance behavior. The nature of the approach should be compassionate in quality. That is, it is not about forcing yourself but about compassionately, with full awareness, doing what's most effective.

Getting off the hook

One common obstacle to committed action is the belief that change, living a meaningful life, lets themselves, others or even the universe, "off the hook." It may seem as if, for example, a child's externalizing behavior is proof of an ex-partner's poor parenting and abandonment, or depression is proof of birth trauma, or anxiety is proof that parenting a child with complex disabilities is really tough. In other words, the dysfunctional patterns can be part of holding someone or simply the universe to account. Some key discrimination questions are relevant including:

- Do you want to be "right" or do you want to live the life you value?
- Do you want to memorialize your life as proof of someone else's or the universe itself's wrongdoing or do you want to live a valued life for yourself?
- Who, really, is "on the hook" if the current patterns continue and who is truly "off the hook" if they don't?

What is important is to unhook *yourself* from the anger and hurt that the actions caused you, not in the sense of changing how you feel, but in the sense of living a life of value to you instead of allowing the anger and hurt to determine your life. You can (and should if it is true) still believe that what someone else did was wrong and fully acknowledge the harm that they caused. Further, unhooking yourself means being realistic about future behavior, including choosing future actions based on avoiding harm from people who wronged you in the past. It also means freeing yourself from lingering and dysfunctional patterns, for yourself. For example, freeing yourself from an abusive ex-partner includes focusing on *living your own valued life*, rather than memorializing your life as proof of the ex-partner's abuse. For some, this may include a type of forgiveness. As in to "fore" "give", to give what came before.You can forgive an abusive ex-partner, genuinely wishing him well in life, and still remain realistic in understanding that he is likely to continue to behave in abusive ways if given the opportunity to do so, and hence you can ensure that he is not given opportunity. This kind of forgiveness is not about past wrongs being forgotten or even about relationships being repaired. Rather, it is about cultivating compassion and kindness for the wrong-doer. For some, even this concept of forgiveness may not be helpful. It may not be realistic to wish a past abuser well and it may not be the most clinically useful point of focus. Continued anger may part of an evolved defense mechanism that needs to be listened to and honored, before it can be "unhooked." Just as the words "acceptance," "willingness," and "mindfulness" may evoke different meanings in different people, not all of them consistent with ACT, so it is with the word "forgiveness." "Forgiveness" can used in coercive ways and often is in abusive relationships. It is also used in everyday life mean that a relationship is repaired which may, for good reason, not be possible. As always, find the words that work for each client. The key move is this: a shift towards psychological flexibility.

Metaphors

The metaphor of jumping can be used to support the parent in understanding that they can choose to limit the size of their goals, but they must be willing to experience everything that comes up when taking effective action.

Jump Metaphor

Changing our lives is like taking a leap. It is a jump. The size of the jump can be chosen. That bit you can choose. You can start with small jumps and build up from there if you like. You can also decide that some jumps you will never do. If you don't want to bungee jump from a cliff, and never doing so doesn't limit your ability to live a meaningful life then that's okay. However, whatever size jump you choose, you must jump. You must leave the ground completely. Be in midair.

Parent supporting child exploration

For the child this element of the hexaflex is about developmentally appropriate exploration. The parent can learn to support developmentally appropriate exploration by:

- Pausing for a moment, standing back and watching what the child does. Trying to cultivate a sense of curiosity about this. Pause and see: does the child really need me in this moment or can they handle it themselves?
- Being aware of tendencies toward intrusiveness. Is the child signaling that the parent is being intrusive?
- Cultivating flexible perspective taking including other-as-context—understanding the child as a perspective of their own—and other-as-process—tracking the child's unfolding moment-to-moment experience and taking these into account.
- Experimenting with scaffolding and shaping adaptive behaviors and skills rather than stepping in and taking over. For example, scaffolding the child's ability to find a solution to a problem rather than solving it.
- Cultivating the skill of being an available presence and waiting for the child's invitation to interact. Following the child's lead.
- Cultivating willingness to experience the thoughts, feelings, memories, sensations, and behavioral impulses that arise during child exploration and experimentation.
- Framing child exploration, experimentation and normal setbacks and suffering as valuable experiences that the child learns from. For example, my (Koa) husband says "the little falls prevent big falls." This doesn't mean that you can fully prevent big falls, of course, only that a child who

has had the opportunity to experience little falls—frustration, disappointment, setbacks—will develop the skills and the tracking to better navigate life preventing bigger falls and coping better with big falls when they happen.

- Evoke, scaffold, and reinforce approach behavior.
- Do not force a child into "approach" through coercion or shame. Approach cannot be forced. The child must be willing. If the child is forced fear may increase rather than decrease and the child's trust in the parent may be diminished.
- Patience and a long-term view is required with developmentally normal anxieties, preoccupations and tendencies; for example, separation anxiety in early childhood, fear of the dark or monsters in middle childhood, and social anxieties and preoccupation in adolescence. Parents need to persist in evoking, scaffolding, and reinforcing approach behavior and ensuring that they are not inadvertently reinforcing avoidance, while also being patient with development.

Encouraging home practice

Home practice is a focus of committed action because taking effective action *in context* is key. Home practice may include:

- monitoring behavior of parent or child;
- deliberate practicing;
- cultivating behavior change in everyday life.

Working with Scott, Harry, and Ava

The therapist and Scott have begun to focus on committed action, particularly around Scott's goal of reconnecting with his children. All other aspects of ACT have already been covered and the therapist draws upon this as needed.

Therapist:	So, it sounds like, if I've got you right, it is going to take a bit of persistence to reconnect with Harry and Ava, huh?
Scott nodding:	Yeah, definitely. Especially with Harry.
Therapist nodding:	Okay. So, my first thought is, what's getting in the way of persisting?
Scott laughs:	It is just so hard.
Therapist laughs:	I know. I know. Alright. Let's maybe explore this another way. Let's focus on Harry first of all. I'll be you and you show me how Harry's reacting, alright? So, you say, "Hey mate, let's go outside and kick the soccer ball around huh?" how does Harry respond?

(*Continued*)

(Continued)

Scott, as Harry, slumps in his chair and looks down	nah
Therapist still being Scott:	Alright, well how about we play a board game together?
Scott:	Nah
Therapist:	What would you like to do?
Scott:	Keep drawing.
Therapist:	Okay. You have really gotten into drawing, huh?
Scott:	Hmm.
Therapist:	What are you drawing there?
Scott:	Just stuff.
Therapist, pausing in being	Well, I see what you mean. That really felt like
Scott:	a big brick wall.
Scott:	Exactly. I can't break through.
Therapist:	That's real tough. What's that like for you when you are trying to break through and there's this big brick wall?
Scott:	It sucks. Feels awful.
Therapist:	Yeah it does.
Scott:	It is like he's rejecting me.
Therapist:	Like he's rejecting you. Ouch.
Scott with tears in his eyes	who can blame him I'm a loser.
Therapist:	Ah, and there's your mind with an explanation. Thanks, mind. Does your mind have anything else to say?
Scott:	That I've blown it. The kids are better off without me anyway. Who would want a loser dad hanging around. Better to just leave him to it.
Therapist:	"I'm a loser, so just give up and let him reject me," is that it?
Scott:	That's it.
Therapist:	Does your mind come up with that a lot when you've got that big brick wall in front of you?
Scott:	Oh yeah. All the time.
Therapist:	And do you get all stuck in it? It feels sticky.
Scott:	Yeah, totally.
Therapist:	And what happens to persisting then? What do you do?
Scott laughs:	I give up. Go distract myself with a game or a show or something.
Therapist:	Distract yourself from the feelings of rejection? From the "I'm a loser" story?

(*Continued*)

(Continued)

Scott:	That's right.
Therapist:	It's a familiar pattern, isn't it?
Scott:	Yeah, it's an avoidance pattern like we've been talking about, huh?
Therapist:	Sounds like it.
Scott:	But how do I get through the brick wall?
Therapist:	Well, we can experiment with that. In fact, over the next few weeks experimenting with exactly that will be our focus. Maybe we'll find you can jump over it, or maybe there's a little hole that we can make bigger with time or maybe you can build a ladder or something. I don't know, right? There's no guarantee that you even will get through because it depends on Harry. But there's two things we do know. The first is what happens if you give up. What's that?
Scott:	Nothing. The brick wall stays.
Therapist nodding:	Yep. The second is what's going to come up for you if you keep trying to break through the brick wall, as you experiment with jumping over it, or working away at little holes or building a ladder. What's going to come up for you as you do that?
Scott:	Rejection. I'm a loser.
Therapist:	Yeah that's it. Before we get to the experimenting, we need to know if you are willing to have all of that—the feelings of rejection, the thoughts about being a loser, your mind saying "just give up"—are you willing to have all of that and persist in experimenting to find a way around the wall?
Scott with tears in his eyes:	Yes. If there's a chance I can rebuild a connection with my kids then yes. Anything is worth that. I'd chop off my legs, honestly.
Therapist:	I don't think we'll have to go that far.
Scott laughing:	Well, that's something.

Scott finds willingness to push through the initial resistance and the painful feelings of rejection that it generates, as well as to experiment with different strategies to reconnect. The therapist uses in session roleplays to support Scott in some initial experimentation. With time, Scott finds that, although his children initially resist it, getting them out of the house and into the great outdoors together provides the right context for more open and playful interactions. Scott continues to ask his children about their lives and to make his affection for them

(*Continued*)

(Continued)

clear even though it feels like they keep rejecting him. In time, they have some difficult conversations. Harry and Ava express their hurt around Scott's relationship with Hayley, including the speed at which it proceeded and the fact that their dislike of her was dismissed, a dislike that they now feel is vindicated. Although it was difficult for Scott to hear how much his second marriage had hurt his children, he listened and validated their feelings. He agreed that he would take any future relationships slower, giving them all time to adjust. Open and honest communication around this issue, with Scott taking on Harry and Ava's feedback about the damage his whirlwind relationship had on them, was key to Scott fully regaining their trust. With time, Harry and Ava warm up to him again and they regain their former closeness.

Troubleshooting

Refining parenting strategies in practice

Often parents have already tried positive parenting strategies, and may report that they understand them, but they are not using them effectively in practice. There may be subtle errors in how they are implementing the strategies, or an individual strategy may be being implemented correctly but without the wider context that supports the strategy's use. For example, the parent by be ignoring a misbehavior and not experiencing success with that strategy because the parent is also not reinforcing alternative behaviors. Parents may also be implementing positive parenting strategies, but with a parenting control agenda or a punitive mindset. For example, a parent may be using time-out, but using it with a mindset of punishing the child, of giving the child "deserved" suffering following an inappropriate behavior. In this situation, time-out is not attachment-neutral, it is subtly different from time-out delivered in an attachment-neutral way with a mindset of shaping the child's behavior. These subtle distinctions are more easily seen and addressed by bringing parenting behavior into the room through behavioral rehearsal, or observations of parent–child interactions.

It is tough work

Committed action is tough work! It is important to acknowledge that and to give parents' permission to fit committed action in with other life commitments. For example, deliberately making changes in parenting around challenging work commitments. Parents should also be given permission to make other areas of life easier for several weeks so that they can focus on parenting.

Four key developmental periods and committed action and exploration

Infancy and committed action and exploration

Committed action during infancy is likely to be focused on establishing sensitive and responsive parenting patterns, and intervening with common parenting challenges of infancy: sleep and crying. In addition, postnatal care may include interventions targeting the mother or baby's health and lactation. The postnatal period is a high-risk time for the development of mental health problems, particularly for mothers, but also for fathers. Mental health interventions for depression or anxiety may be appropriate. The birth of an infant triggers seismic changes to the lifestyle of both parents, especially the primary caregiver. This makes the tasks of cultivating a reinforcement-rich life with baby essential. In addition, birth trauma or breastfeeding difficulties may be related to mental health problems in some mothers. It is important for parents to develop a flexible and experimental approach to parenting, discovering what works for them and their children.

Early childhood and committed action and exploration

During early childhood, it is important that parents expand their sensitive and responsive parenting pattern to include emotion coaching, labeling, and validating their children's emotional experiences, as well as supporting their children in problem-solving around emotions. This will support their children's continued emotional development. In addition, it is important that parents use mental state-rich language, with flexible perspective-taking part of the everyday life of the child, in order to foster perspective-taking capacities. Early childhood represents a normal developmental peak in challenging externalizing behaviors of noncompliance and temper tantrums. Parents need to find ways to manage these behaviors in positive ways. That is, to refrain from reinforcing them.

Middle childhood and committed action and exploration

In contemporary times, middle childhood is a time focused on the transition to school and academic and social pursuits within school. Previously established parenting patterns around sensitive and responsive parenting, emotion coaching, flexible perspective taking, and refraining from reinforcing problematic behaviors need to be maintained, while the parent also supports the child within the school. This includes maintaining a collegial relationship with the school, supporting the child's school-related activities from home, and supporting the child in working through peer-related social challenges. A growth mindset, or in ACT terms a flexible self-as-content, can be promoted through process-focused feedback, that is, feedback focused on effort and strategy.

Adolescence and committed action and exploration

During adolescence there is a shift in parenting toward supporting greater independence and autonomy. The parent is still emotionally available to the child, but the parent adapts to the child's increased autonomy. Adolescence is also a time of increased risk-taking and experimentation. Committed action might include allowing teens enough freedom to make mistakes and discover for themselves even though that may be anxiety-provoking or distressing.

Using committed action with specific populations

Parental mental health problems and committed action and exploration

For parents with mental health problems exposure therapy (for anxiety) and behavioral activation (for depression) are likely to be important. In both circumstances, it involves developing insight into avoidant patterns of behavior and deliberately changing those avoidant patterns, instead shifting in behavior in a manner consistent with values.

Parental grief and committed action and exploration

During grief, committed action is about finding meaningful ways to grieve. In a sense, the parent continues to express their parenting values towards the lost child, just in very different ways than what was expected. This may include ritual, artistic expression, or finding support in community. In addition, a degree of behavioral activation is important in preventing grief from becoming depression. That is, continuing to live a full, meaningful life with grief.

Childhood externalizing problems and committed action and exploration

For a parent of a child with externalizing problems, committed action is likely to be focused on changing parenting behavior in order to decrease the frequency of the externalizing behavior problems. For the child, exploration of alternative ways of behaving is important.

Childhood internalizing problems and committed action and exploration

For the parent of a child with internalizing problems, committed action is likely to involve the parent supporting the child in behavioral activation or exposure. For a younger child, the focus may be changes in parenting in order to bring about the changes for the child. For an older child or teenager, the child themselves may be in therapy and deciding for themselves on the steps to take in conjunction with therapist, with the parent taking on a supportive role. For the child themselves, exploration is a focus.

Childhood neurodevelopmental disabilities and committed action and exploration

For parents of children with neurodevelopmental disabilities, living values in domains other than parenting is often an issue. Behavioral activation may be needed, focused on experiences of pleasure and mastery in other domains of living and problem-solving about how to live these broader values while parenting. In addition, parents may be experiencing anxieties about their child's future or traumatic memories. If so, exposure might be helpful. Children with neurodevelopmental disabilities are at increased risk of externalizing behavior. Often, structured teaching is required—for example, for daily tasks, communication, or emotional regulation—where a typically developing child might only require encouragement and modeling.

Peer relations and bullying and committed action and exploration

For the child themselves, this might include developmentally normal exploration with peers. For the parent, it might include understanding the importance of exploration with peers and supporting their child in exploring the social world. At times, this might include deliberately standing back to let their child explore themselves and at other times it may include scaffolding of social experiences.

Marital conflict and committed action and exploration

It is important for committed action to be consistent between parents. The intervention itself, if both parents are involved, can give parents a common language to discuss parenting and find common ground. This consistency doesn't mean that both parents need to be parenting in exactly the same way. Rather, what is important is that parents are not undermining each other. In a long-term relationship, committed action is also about deliberately supporting your partner in small ways, such as asking them how their day was and listening to the reply, even when this is difficult. It also requires what Tony Biglan calls stepping over the aversives of others (Biglan, 2015). That is, allowing everyday aversive behavior to slide.

Expressed emotion including critical and intrusive parenting and committed action and exploration

Critical, hostile, and intrusive parenting is likely to be reactive parenting behavior, automatic reactions to thoughts and feelings triggered while parenting. Committed action is likely to involve bringing greater awareness to the thoughts and feelings triggered during parenting, to using mindfulness, acceptance, and flexible perspective-taking skills to pause and step back from them, and to choosing parenting behaviors based on parenting values and workability instead. Compassion may also be an important part of addressing such reactive patterns, both compassion for parent and for the child. Overlearning, through repeated practice in low-pressure situations, alternative ways of responding may be beneficial, increasing the chance the parent will be able to access the more positive parenting behavior when in the high-pressure everyday situations.

Emotion dismissiveness and committed action and exploration

Committed action around emotion dismissiveness is likely to involve building greater awareness of the child's ongoing psychological experiences, through mindfulness and flexible perspective taking, as well as greater acceptance of the child's emotional experiences and the emotions this triggers in the parent. Learning and rehearsing emotion-coaching skills, and applying emotion coaching with their child, is likely to be an important part of the intervention.

Inconsistent, or harsh and punitive parenting and committed action and exploration

Inconsistent, harsh, or punitive parenting may be partially the result of avoidant or otherwise dysfunctional patterns of parenting behavior or it may be partially the result of a skills deficit. Committed action is likely to involve bringing greater awareness to the inconsistent, harsh, or punitive parenting behavior, through mindfulness, acceptance and flexible perspective taking, and developing more accurate tracks of the parent's own behavior as well as the behavior of the child. From accurate tracks, alternative parenting strategies may be applied.

References

Biglan, A. (2015). *The nurture effect*. Oakland: New Harbinger Publications.

Blakemore, S. J., & Choudhury, S. (2006). Development of the adolescent brain: Implications for executive function and social cognition. *Journal of Child Psychology and Psychiatry*, *47* (3-4), 296–312.

Committee on the Science of Adolescence, Board on Children, Youth and Families, Institute of Medicine and National Research Council of the National Academies. (2011). *The science of adolescent risk-taking:Workshop report*. Washington, DC: National Academies Press.

Fusco, G., & Minelli, A. (2010). Phenotypic plasticity in development and evolution: Facts and concepts. *Philosophical Transctrips of the Royal Society of Biological Sciences*, *365*(1540), 547–556.

Gilbert, P. (2009). *The compassionate mind*. London: Little, Brown Book Group.

Gopnik, A. (2017). *The gardener and the carpenter*. London: Vintage publishing.

Hayes, L. L., & Ciarrochi, J. (2015). *The thriving adolescent*. Oakland: New Harbinger Publications.

Hayes, S. C., & Sanford, B. T. (2015). Modern psychotherapy as a multidimensional multilevel evolutionary process. *Current Opinion in Psychology*, *2*, 16–20.

Hayes, S. C., Sanford, B. T., & Chin, F. T. (2017). Carrying the baton: Evolution science and a contextual behavioral analysis of language and cognition. *Journal of Contextual Behavioral Science*, *6*(3), 314–328.

Hayes, S. C., Strosahl, K. D., & Wilson, K. G. (2003). *Acceptance and Commitment Therapy: An experiential approach to behavior change*. New York: Guilford Press.

Chapter 14

Integrating Acceptance and Commitment Therapy with other interventions

Chapter Outline

Parenting intervention	378
Behavioral activation	380
Exposure therapy	381
Postnatal care	383
Infant crying and sleep: a case illustration	384
Infant sleep	386
Working with Aurora, Chris, and Millie	22
Chapter summary	399
References	399

"Real isn't how you are made," said the Skin Horse. "It's a thing that happens to you. When a child loves you for a long, long time, not just to play with, but REALLY loves you, the you become Real. It doesn't happen all at once. You become. It takes a long time. Generally, by the time you are Real, most of your hair has been loved off, and your eyes drop out and you get loose in the joints and very shabby. But these things don't matter at all, because once you are Real you can't be ugly, except to people who don't understand."

Margery Williams, *The Velveteen Rabbit*

The best way to treat obstacles is to use them as stepping-stones. Laugh at them, tread on them, and let them lead you to something better.

Enid Blyton, *Mr. Galliano's Circus*

Acceptance and Commitment Therapy (ACT) may be used as a stand-alone treatment for parents: an intervention to address parental psychological well-being in the context of childrearing. In addition, however, it may be used as an augmentative strategy in concert with evidence-based interventions: parenting intervention, behavioral activation, exposure therapy, and postnatal care. Let's examine how ACT may be used in conjunction with other evidence-based interventions. We will spend some time discussing

Acceptance and Commitment Therapy. DOI: https://doi.org/10.1016/B978-0-12-814669-9.00014-X
© 2019 Elsevier Inc. All rights reserved.

postnatal care in particular, both because it is a controversial area and hence we are elucidating a new approach, and because it is useful to give a detailed case example.

Parenting intervention

ACT combines well with parenting interventions grounded in the relational-emotional and the behavioral traditions, covered in Chapter 3, Connect: the parent–child relationship and Chapter 4, Shape: building a flexible repertoire. ACT has been tested in conjunction with the parenting interventions Stepping Stones Triple P (Brown, Whittingham, Boyd, & McKinlay, 2015; Brown, Whittingham, Boyd, McKinlay, & Sofronoff, 2014; Brown, Whittingham, McKinlay, Boyd, & Sofronoff, 2013; Whittingham, Sanders, McKinlay, & Boyd, 2014, 2016)—a variant of Triple P for families of a child with a disability—and with Parent–Child Interaction Therapy (Coyne & Wilson, 2004; see Chapter 4: Shape: building a flexible repertoire, for a full discussion of the research to date).

ACT can be combined with parenting interventions to facilitate better engagement in those interventions, and perhaps, more robust treatment outcomes for children who are struggling. There is a robust literature on parenting interventions; however, not all parents respond well to these—some fail to engage at all, some drop out early, and more use evidence-based strategies inconsistently or ineffectively. In other words, we know with some certainty *what* to help parents do to support their children; however, it's easier said than done to help them do it sensitively, and consistently, across challenging situations, in a contextually contingent way. This is where we feel that ACT can help.

If you are already trained in a parenting intervention, you can combine ACT with that through considering the *function* you would hope to see. For example, you might incorporate elements of ACT to facilitate willingness to use, and persist in using behavioral techniques, or perhaps increase contextual sensitivity to inform *when* to use of those techniques, and to track what happens to their efficacy if they are used improperly or inconsistently. Another way to consider this is that ACT may *contextualize* evidence-based interventions: using values to guide and dignify difficult strategies such as planned ignoring, or exposure coaching, which can be emotionally demanding for parents. A third path—and perhaps the most important augmentation strategy—involves helping parents be better, more accurate observers of their behavior through using ACT to make them better *functional contextualists.*

Specifically, using ACT strategies of *mindfulness, defusion,* and *self-as-context* to begin to recognize when their behaviors are under the control of unworkable rules, and to begin to track the consequences of those behaviors. Using these concepts in concert with mindfulness can support the parent in building responsive patterns of parenting behavior. This "wiggle room" afforded by defused awareness of one's private events and actions in the context of those events allows for freedom and choice, and thus the possibility of more effective parenting behavior. Recent work across developmental stages has found that parent dispositional mindfulness was indirectly related to internalizing and externalizing symptoms through higher levels of mindful parenting and fewer negative parenting practices (Parent, McKee, Rough, & Forehand, 2016). To motivate consistent engagement in effective strategies over time and across difficult or challenging situations, parenting intervention should be grounded in the values of the parent. Finally, self-compassion can be very useful for parents when they apply behavioral parenting strategies imperfectly, as all parents certainly do. For example, recent work by Neff and Faso (2015) found in a sample of mothers raising children with autism that while child symptom severity was the strongest predictor of negative parent adjustment, self-compassion predicted parental well-being over and above the effects of child symptom severity. The easiest way to combine ACT with an existing parenting intervention is to introduce the ACT concepts first, and to move through the parenting intervention, drawing upon ACT concepts as relevant. You can also be flexible: drawing from the principles and strategies outlined in Chapter 3, Connect: the parent–child relationship, and Chapter 4, Shape: building a flexible repertoire as relevant to your case conceptualization.

In implementing a parenting intervention, it is crucial that parenting behavior is, in some way, "brought into the therapy room" in an experiential way rather than just discussed. This is important for two primary reasons—first, for the parent to experience the thoughts and feelings that are antecedents and consequences of engaging in a particular behavior in a particular situation, and second, for the clinician to observe this, and have access to that experience. It's also important to have access to the language parents use to describe their experiences in parenting—this allows clinicians to utilize RFT principles in understanding the particular meanings that parents derive about their own behavior, their children's behavior, etc.

In order to effectively help parents shape behavior, clinicians must have access to this wealth of data—otherwise, it may be difficult to understand and thus change maintaining contingencies. There are a number of ways of doing this including; behavioral rehearsal of parenting strategies, observing a parent–child interaction and then discussing that interaction, and giving live coaching during a parent–child interaction. By bringing the parenting behavior into the therapy room, clinicians also enhance their ability to detect and correct subtle errors in the implementation of parenting strategies, or subtle deviations from parental sensitivity. Furthermore, it is important for the parent to have the opportunity to work on changing their parenting behavior in a low-pressure and supportive context. One of the most challenging aspects of parenting, for all parents, is the fact that it is 24/7. Parents need to find parental sensitivity and effective parenting even in our worst moments. An effective strategy for stress-proofing positive patterns of parenting behavior is to overlearn the new parenting behavior through repeated practice in a low-pressure situation. This increases the chance that the parent will be able to use the new pattern of behavior in real high-stress situations.

Within any parenting invention it is important to promote a flexible, experimental stance, sensitive to the effect of one's actions on the environment, repeatedly emphasizing the workability of parenting. A parenting intervention should not involve clinicians presenting themselves as parenting experts, but rather, supporting the parent to engage in trial-and-error learning with parenting based on evidence-based parenting principles, an understanding of child's behavior, and examining the results for workability. One way to accomplish this is for clinicians to *model* such a stance in the therapy room, through being curious, acknowledging mistakes, expressing doubt and uncertainty, and making a space for parents to voice their fears and failings safely, in addition to their successes.

Behavioral activation

Behavioral activation as a stand-alone treatment for depression that arose out of a component analysis of cognitive behavioral therapy and is appropriate for depressed parents, children, and adolescents. The component analysis found the activation component was as effective as the complete CBT packages (Gorter, Gollan, Dobson, & Jacobson, 1998; Jacobson, Martell, & Dimidjian, 2001; Martell, 2018) and hence the activation component was developed and expanded upon. Depression is understood as a pattern of behavior in context, in fact, an understandable pattern of behavior given the context (Martell, 2018). Within traditional CBT packages the activation component is focused on remedying a deficit in positive reinforcement by structuring systematic, frequent activities that constitute pleasant events. In behavioral activation, depression is instead understood as a narrow repertoire of behavior that does not allow for the maximization of natural reinforcement. The intervention is highly individual. An individual functional analysis focuses on the behavioral changes likely to increase the availability of natural reinforcement to the client. A distinction is made between feelings of depression and the behavioral patterns characteristic of depression that are maintaining the depressed state, with emphasis placed on the importance of changing behavioral patterns rather than waiting for mood improvements. Consistent with ACT, there is a focus on identifying patterns of experiential avoidance that create long-term harm and workability.

Behavioral activation is highly consistent with ACT, most specifically with the *valuing* and *committed action* components. From an ACT perspective, engagement in *meaningful* activities, rather than merely *pleasant* activities, is important. From an ACT perspective, the *mindfulness and acceptance processes* can support a shift to examining and working through changing patterns of behavior that are maintaining a depressed state. Behavioral activation is often facilitated by using an activity chart. Clients can use the activity chart to both set goals and to monitor progress and patterns of activity. From a behavioral activation perspective, activities can be rated (e.g., on a 0–10 Likert scale) for both mastery and pleasure. It is important to consider both mastery and pleasure as sometimes there is a deficit in one of these components only. From an ACT perspective, clinicians might have clients rate behavior in terms of how *meaningful* it is, and how frequently they engage in that behavior. In terms of mindfulness and acceptance processes, it is also important to consider ruminative behavior and a loss of psychological contact with the here and now, as sometimes rich reinforcement may be available, but there may be a loss of psychological contact with that reinforcement. Importantly, behavioral activation is focused on the function not the form of a client's behavior.

Findings linking parental depression to impaired parenting and poorer childhood outcomes are robust across many different parenting situations (Thomas, O'Brien, Clarke, Liu, & Chronis-Tuscano, 2015) including raising children with chronic health or mental health issues, poverty, and other challenges. Hence, when parenting is of concern, it is often necessary to also address parental mental health and depressive symptoms (Chronis-Tuscano et al., 2013; Silk, Shaw, Forbes, Lane, & Kovacs, 2006; Silk, Shaw, Skuban, Oland, & Kovacs, 2006; Thomas et al., 2015). One specific domain in which the behavioral activation approach to depression is highly relevant is in the context of postnatal depression. The birth of a child creates a seismic shift in daily activity, especially for the primary caregiver. Behavioral patterns that are rich in reinforcement must be deliberately cultivated again, in the new life as a parent. Behavioral activation may also be an appropriate intervention for depressed children and adolescents (Pass, Lejuez, & Reynolds, 2018). In using behavioral activation with youth, parents will also be highly involved in implementation, as their role is key to overcoming barriers to change (Pass, Whitney, & Reynolds, 2016).

Exposure therapy

Exposure therapy is a core aspect of intervention for anxiety disorders. Exposure therapy may be relevant for parents, children, or adolescents. Generally speaking, exposure-based treatment involves both respondent and operant conditioning principles. Typically, anxiety disorders and obsessive-compulsive disorder (OCD) involve rigid patterns of avoidance of feared stimuli. Thus exposure involves motivating an individual to engage in behavioral approach rather than safety-seeking or rituals in the presence of fear cues. Engaging in this practice in a systematic, sustained way helps clients gain greater psychological flexibility when they are experiencing fear or discomfort. When clients no longer avoid fear cues and instead can engage in effective behavior, this is called *extinction*. Traditional exposure models focus on *habituation*, or the reduction in experienced anxiety postexposure. From an ACT perspective what is most important is not the reduction in anxiety per se but the regaining of psychological flexibility, even in the presence of fear cues or related anxiety (Hayes, Strosahl, & Wilson, 2003).

An exposure therapy approach may be relevant when using ACT with anxious parents, including for perinatal anxiety disorders (Marchesi et al., 2016). When working with anxious children or adolescents, parents too are highly involved in exposure therapy. Parents raising children with anxiety or OCD often engage in *accommodation* behavior in which they assist their children in avoidance-based behavior in order to maintain the equilibrium of the family as best they can, or know how. Unfortunately, this reinforces avoidance, thus maintaining, and inadvertently amplifying fear. In addition, parents of anxious children tend to be less likely to encourage autonomy and exploration in their children, and to be more dismissive and controlling of their children's emotions. Thus these are aspects of parenting that are treatment targets when working with children struggling with anxiety or OCD. This is accomplished by educating parents about how their behaviors work and engaging them as exposure coaches, when appropriate, for their children. In families with younger children, this is a more scaffolding and directive role for parents. In adolescents, it may shift into a more collaborative, encouraging role that includes limit-setting around avoidance-based behaviors.

ACT is an exposure-based treatment paradigm, in that it seeks to support experiential approach and *acceptance* of previously avoided private events to support engagement in flexible, effective behavior, especially in the context of pursuing one's values. Thus it extends traditional models of exposure to include *covert, or private* events as well as to overt stimuli. Mindfulness and acceptance processes can be used to facilitate more effective engagement in exposure. For example, individuals may "white-knuckle," or engage in subtle distraction strategies, to avoid fully experiencing their anxiety or discomfort. Shaping present moment awareness and openness to one's experiences, without defense, can enhance an individual's psychological contact with fear cues, and thus ensure their sensitivity to learning. Values and committed action can help motivate individuals to continue engagement in exposure across a greater variety of situations, thus supporting generalization.

It can be difficult for parents to support children in exposure-based treatment because for most parents, their typical behavior in the face of anxiety is to soothe, or protect. Experiencing their children feeling frightened is aversive—to ask parents to *deliberately* help their children feel anxious is antithetical to most notions of parenting. However, this is exactly what is required in exposure. ACT can help support parent engagement through facilitating parents' own psychological flexibility around the thoughts and feelings that supporting their children in exposure-based treatment can elicit. Values and committed action can sustain parents through difficult moments in which they are fearful themselves and uncertain about how to proceed.

Postnatal care

Postnatal care is an area rife with controversy. In particular, false conflict and misunderstandings between approaches grounded in the relational-emotional and the behavioral traditions. This makes postnatal care a challenging area for clinicians to navigate and the postnatal period a challenging time for parents. For this reason, we will examine postnatal care in some depth, pointing to a way through the controversy that fully integrates the relational-emotional and the behavioral literature with ACT. In particular, a novel approach to parent–infant sleep, delivered clinically in Australia since 2011, will be outlined in full.

Parental care during infancy can be understood as human ingenuity working to meet the needs of a secondarily altricial baby; either by "mimicking" the nesting of altricial mammals—encouraging early self-settling and lengthening the duration of time between parental signaling as well as using pacifiers (dummies), swing chairs, white noise makers, and other "nesting" aids—or mimicking the close physical proximity and rapid on-demand access to feeding and physical contact of a precocial infant—close physical contact to parent and on-demand feeding facilitated by baby wearing, cosleeper cots/cribs, or even bed-sharing. Variations in early parental care can be thought of as on a spectrum with an emphasis on "nesting" at one end ("structured" or "routine-based" parenting), to an emphasis on "close contact" at the other ("attachment" parenting), with many parents using some combination of "nesting" and "close contact" strategies. Individual parents may lean toward either end of the spectrum, particularly in terms of specific strategies, due to personal philosophy, cultural norms, practical considerations such as the length of maternity leave, or even the workability of various strategies with their individual baby.

Each approach has its costs and benefits (St James-Roberts, 2007; St James-Roberts et al., 2006). A "nesting" approach is more likely to result in a baby who sleeps for longer periods at night at an earlier age, but it is also more likely to result in increased crying and fussing in the first 3 months of life. The "close contact" approach is more likely to result in minimization of crying and fussing in the first 3 months of life and is related to sustained breastfeeding; however, it is also more likely to result in more frequent signaling during the night from 3 months.

Postnatal care needs to accommodate the full spectrum of early parental care, being mindful of individual preferences and cultural values, with the benefits and costs of each general approach openly discussed, and parents supported in discovering what is workable for them. Postnatal care may include professionals from a variety of professional backgrounds with the health of the mother and infant and lactation being prime sites of intervention, alongside early parenting. During early infancy there are two main challenges that prompt parents to seek *parenting* support: crying and sleeping.

Infant crying and sleep: a case illustration

Crying shows a natural developmental trajectory in infancy, typically peaking at 4–8 weeks and settling at 4–5 months of age (Runyan et al., 2009; Wake et al., 2006). Within the first 5 months of life crying behavior shows a diurnal pattern, peaking in the late afternoon and evenings. During this period infants are particularly prone to *unsoothable* crying, crying that persists no matter how parents respond. Although "close contact" parenting strategies are associated with decreased crying behavior in the first 3 months of life, parenting approaches are not associated with the frequency of *unsoothable* crying.

There is no scientific consensus on why infants show this developmental trajectory in crying. It is cross-cultural, has been found in other mammals, and the majority of infants who cry excessively show a similar developmental pattern to infants who cry less frequently (Runyan et al., 2009). It has been suggested that it may reflect a still immature regulatory capacity; for example, an immature ability to regulate attention resulting in under or over stimulation or an immature ability to downregulate the sympathetic nervous system (Douglas & Hill, 2011). It is possible that it serves an evolutionary purpose. For example, it is conceivable that, at lower levels, bouts of unsoothable crying in the early months activate parental nurturing capabilities and mobilize alloparenting support. However, this is speculative. The cause remains unknown.

Within babies who cry excessively, 5% have an underlying medical condition and some babies may be experiencing feeding difficulties, leading to a lack of satiety (Douglas & Hill, 2011). Medical conditions and feeding problems should always be ruled out by appropriately qualified professionals in an excessively crying baby. However, for the majority of babies crying excessively, no cause can be found and they can be best understood as at the extreme end of a normal developmental pattern.

Babies who continue to cry excessively beyond 5 months of age, particularly if excessive crying is combined with other regulatory difficulties, are at higher risk for behavioral difficulties and developmental challenges later in life (Smarius et al., 2017; Zeifman & St James-Roberts, 2017). Importantly, this does not necessarily mean that targeting crying behavior in early infancy can prevent later behavioral and developmental difficulties. It is more likely that these children have individual risk factors predisposing to both early regulatory difficulties and later behavioral and developmental difficulties. In other words, that this is simply the first sign of developmental challenges that later become fully apparent and diagnosable.

Crying in early infancy is best understood as a respondent behavior elicited by an aversive unconditioned stimulus or conditioned stimulus (Whittingham, 2014). Crying does not signal particular needs, that is, there isn't a "hunger" cry and a "sleepy" cry (Zeifman & St James-Roberts, 2017). Rather, crying is a graduated response, becoming more intense as the aversive stimulus intensifies or is not removed. To understand crying, and parental response to cries, it is important to remember that it is not the *only* respondent signaling behavior. Newborn infants show a range of respondent signaling behaviors; for example, in response to hunger a newborn may open their mouth, smack their lips, or engage in rooting (searching for the nipple) (Gill, White, & Anderson, 1984). Crying is often a *late cue*, occurring after other hunger cues have been missed.

This is likely why "close contact" parenting is associated with decreased crying in the first 3 months of life, as it increases the chance of parental response to earlier and more subtle cues, thus preventing crying. With time, infants develop a repertoire of *operant* signaling behaviors, the precursors to language, social interaction, and connection seeking (Goldstein, Schwade, & Bornstein, 2009). It is possible that the development of such a repertoire is one of the reasons for the reduction in crying behavior at 4–5 months of age. During early infancy it is important to distinguish between a parent who rapidly responds to crying alone and a parent who rapidly responds to a range of signaling behaviors (Whittingham, 2014). The first parent is ensuring crying becomes an operant signaling behavior. The second is ensuring their infant develops a broad and flexible operant signaling repertoire that includes crying but also many other behaviors.

Excessive infant crying is a risk factor for maternal postnatal depression (Petzoldt, 2018) and child abuse, including shaken baby syndrome (Runyan et al., 2009). As parental behavior doesn't change the frequency of unsoothable crying, it is appropriate to focus intervention on the parental ability to cope with infant crying in order to prevent these downstream effects (Powell et al., 2018).

In sum, for parents presenting with concerns about infant crying under 5 months:

- Medical conditions and feeding problems should be excluded.
- Parents can be reassured that bouts of unsoothable crying, particularly in the late afternoons and evenings are developmentally normal in the first 5 months of life, and are not associated with any particular parenting style. That is, it is not their fault. Excessive crying is usually resolved with development.
- Crying, especially unsoothable crying is stressful for parents, and a risk factor for postnatal depression and child abuse. Thus a focus on parental

mental health and self-care is appropriate. ACT is highly relevant to supporting parents through this challenging time. For example, grounding parenting behavior in parenting values, so that parenting behavior doesn't become rigid and inflexible trying to solve the unsolvable problem of an unsoothable baby; experiential acceptance of the thoughts and feelings that arise when with a crying baby; defusion of unhelpful thoughts that may arise trying to calm an unsoothable baby.

- Parental responding as best they can to all noncrying signaling attempts, will ensure that their infant develops a broad repertoire of signaling behavior and help to prevent crying by meeting infant needs before the baby has escalated to a cry. This will not eliminate crying in the first 5 months of life, but it will minimize it and ensure a rich repertoire of signaling behaviors is able to grow.

Infant sleep

One in four parents reports sleep problems in the first 6 months of their child's life (Armstrong, Quinn, & Dadds, 1994). For many mothers, the sleep challenges of infancy come after already experiencing sleeping difficulties during pregnancy (Kempler, Sharpe, Miller, & Bartlett, 2016). The longest expected sleep duration for a newborn baby is 4–5 hours, well short of the 8 hours of sleep their parent likely desires. However, there is wide variability in the amount of total sleeping time of healthy infants (Galland, Taylor, Elder, & Herbison, 2012) with no evidence base to support specific guidelines on sleep need of children (Matricciani, Blunden, Rigney, Williams, & Olds, 2013; Matricciani, Olds, Blunden, Rigmey, & Williams, 2012); instead, the wide variability within normal infant sleep must be emphasized. Furthermore, the adult pattern of sleeping for 8 hours in a single session at night is a modern phenomenon, a pattern that emerged with the invention of electricity and lighting (Ekirch, 2005). Preelectricity adult sleep usually involved taking sleep in two bouts of approximately 4 hours in length with a period of quiet activity in between. Hence, part of the conflict between adult and infant sleeping patterns is, in fact, conflict between our evolved tendencies as a species and modern life.

In the vast majority of cases, infant sleep problems are a self-limiting problem of infancy. In a longitudinal study of 1200 infants, 66% were found to sleep through the night five nights a week at 6 months (Weinraub et al., 2012). The majority of the other 34% were still waking every night at 6 months, and for this group too, sleeping difficulties were self-limiting with the majority of this group sleeping through the night by 18 months and the overwhelming majority by 24 months. Thus, infant sleep is a challenge of workability for the parents, rather than a developmental concern for the child.

There is a relationship between infant sleep and feeding method (Galbally, Lewis, McEgan, Scalzo, & Islam, 2013; Weinraub et al., 2012). Babies who are still waking every night at 6 months are more likely to be breastfeeding and more likely to maintain breastfeeding into the second year of life (Weinraub et al., 2012). Breastfeeding is related to more frequent nightwaking and greater difficulty sleeping alone but not more restless sleep or poorer sleep efficiency (Galbally et al., 2013). The physiology of breastfeeding is likely one reason for this relationship, especially in the early months, as the demand of infant feeding, particularly at night, is important to initiating and maintaining milk supply (Galbally et al., 2013). Another factor may be learned preferred sucking object. Infants who sleep for over 5 hours without signaling at 3 months of age were found to spend 8 times longer sucking their own fingers or hands than infants who did not (St James-Roberts, Roberts, Hovish, & Owen, 2015). It is possible that some breastfeeding infants learn to prefer suckling for downregulation at the breast (as opposed to on their own fingers or hands), and hence continue to wake their mothers for a feed during the night. Importantly, a baby who wakes during the night and suckles with the function of downregulation at the breast and a baby who wakes during the night and suckles with the function of downregulation on their fingers are developmentally on a par, although one may be "sleeping through the night." Both babies will need to learn, in the future, to downregulate *without suckling*. It is also important to note that although breastfed babies wake more frequently, breastfeeding mothers report more sleep themselves as well as more energy during the day (Kendall-Tackett, Cong, & Hale, 2011). The sleep of the mother is *not* determined by the frequency of night signaling alone, but also by how quickly and easily baby and mother fall back to sleep once woken.

All parents are advised to follow safe sleeping guidelines for the first 6–12 months of life in order to prevent sudden infant death syndrome (SIDS) and sleeping accidents (Mitchell, Freemantle, Young, & Byard, 2012). The guidelines include sleeping baby on their back, no exposure to cigarette smoke, no covering of baby's face, and sleeping baby within sensory distance of the parent or other caregiver. It is important to note that baby needs to sleep within sensory distance of the parent so that the baby can sense the parent (hearing the parent's movements and breathing helps the baby to regulate) *not* so the parent can sense the baby (SIDS and sleeping accidents are silent deaths). In some countries the recommendation is to avoid bed-sharing, but in other countries the recommendation is to avoid bed-sharing if other risk factors are present including excessive maternal fatigue and drug or alcohol use. Some parents choose to mitigate these risks with cosleeper cots or cribs. Importantly, cosleeping outside of the bed—for example, on a chair or couch—is dangerous and contributes to many of the infant deaths while "bed-sharing" (it is still counted in bed-sharing statistics even if mother and baby were sleeping on a chair). Bed-sharing—mother and baby sharing a bed—is very common and has been shown to facilitate breastfeeding (Ball, 2009). In American samples, a cultural context that does not support bed-sharing, up to 60% of mothers bed-share at least some of the time in the first year of life, and of course, bed-sharing is the norm in most cultures globally (Kendall-Tackett et al., 2011). Many babies begin the night in a separate sleeping space and end up in the parent's bed during the night. Worryingly, 25% of American mothers report falling asleep with their baby in an unsafe location such as a chair (Kendall-Tackett et al., 2011), highlighting the importance of recognizing when cosleeping is likely to occur due to maternal somnolence and doing so *in the safest manner possible* rather than persistently and rigidly implementing a "no bed-sharing" rule.

Traditional behavioral infant sleep interventions aim to reduce the frequency of *infant signaling* at night or to increase the *duration* of time between signaling, in order to then improve parental sleep. From birth, this involves using techniques such as delaying parental response, stretching the interval between feeds, encouraging settling without parental presence, and feed–play–sleep schedules. Beyond 6 months behavioral sleep interventions also include graduated extinction methods to fade parental presence during the initiation of sleep so that the baby falls asleep independently. These methods may include cry it out—baby is placed in cot/crib to fall asleep independently with no parental response—or controlled crying/controlled comforting—baby is placed in cot/crib to fall asleep independently with timed parental response at specific intervals—or camping out—baby is placed in cot/crib to fall asleep, initially with minimal parental response and parental response is gradually faded (Kempler et al., 2016; St James-Roberts, Roberts, Hovish, & Owen, 2017).

Traditional behavioral infant sleep interventions are therefore situated within a "nesting" approach to early parental care. A systematic literature review found that traditional behavior sleep interventions implemented in the first 6 months of life may increase the duration without signaling by 29 minutes but raised concerns about the effects of some techniques such as stretching the interval between feeds on breastfeeding (Douglas & Hill, 2013). A recent meta-analysis found that behavioral sleep interventions in the perinatal period increased parental report of total infant sleep duration but did not reduce the frequency of nightwaking (Kempler et al., 2016). In a 5-year follow-up of an RCT, traditional behavioral sleep intervention did not show long-lasting effects on child sleep difficulties, sleep habits, or child behavior, nor evidence of harm for the parent–child relationship (Price, Wake, Ukoumunne, & Hiscock, 2012). Given the longitudinal research showing that infant sleep difficulties are self-limiting (Weinraub et al., 2012) and the fact that babies who self-settle at 3 months of age are doing so by suckling their fingers or hands (St James-Roberts et al., 2015) this lack of long-term effect makes sense. The key message is this: infant sleep is a challenge of workability for the parents, not a developmental issue for the child.

I (Koa) and Pamela Douglas have published an alternative behavioral framework for intervening with parent–infant sleep, known as The Possums Sleep Intervention. This framework is consistent with either a "nesting" or a "close contact" approach to early infant care, and one that can be implemented in conjunction with traditional behavioral techniques aimed at decreasing the frequency of night signaling or without targeting signaling at all (Whittingham & Douglas, 2014). The Possums Sleep Intervention is delivered clinically and online as the sleep domain of the five-domain "Neuroprotective Developmental Care" or "Possums" approach to postnatal care, available for parent or health professional use (Douglas 2019; Douglas 2018; Douglas et al 2013; Douglas et al 2011). The Possums Sleep Intervention has also been adapted as "Sleep, Baby, and You" by a team in the United Kingdom, with the consent of the Possums charity, where it is currently undergoing further research (Ball, Douglas, Taylor, & Thomas, 2018)." Initial research suggests a positive response from parents (Ball, Douglas, Kulasinghe, Whittingham, & Hill, 2018). Instead of targeting the frequency of signaling, this alternative behavioral framework targets the *sleep efficiency* of parent and infant, that is, the aim is *to minimize the length of time it takes to fall asleep*. Importantly, this is the *same* target as behavioral sleep interventions for adults and, as such, the intervention is grounded within the behavioral sleep intervention literature more broadly.

The alternative behavioral framework also differs in how the stimulus control of infant sleep is understood. The traditional behavioral account focuses on whether or not parental presence is part of the stimuli controlling infant sleep, with the aim to minimize parental presence. This makes sense as infant signaling is the target. However, it also means that some stimuli are being understood and classified *by form*—whether or not a parental presence is required—rather than *by function* for the infant. For example, a baby who downregulates by suckling on their hand is said to be "self-soothing" or even "sleeping through the night" (although they may in fact be waking) but a baby who downregulates by suckling at the breast is seen as lacking the ability to "self-soothe" and "sleep through the night" even though both behaviors are *functionally* (downregulation) and *developmentally* (suckling) the same. Also, the fact that a baby who is suckling frequently at the breast during the night due to *hunger* is engaging in a *functionally different* pattern of behavior to both the baby suckling their hand *and* the baby suckling at the breast for downregulation is lost (such a baby likely has a feeding problem not a sleeping problem and should be referred to a lactation consultant).

From a behavior analytic perspective, is important that initiation of infant sleep comes under the stimulus control of *sleepiness,* the same as would be expected for adult sleep. If sleep is initiated *when sleepy* the biological regulation of sleep can proceed in a healthy way. Sleep associations—learning to associate sleep with a particular environmental stimulus through respondent conditioning—will likely develop. As long as the stimulus control of sleep *includes sleepiness,* all that matters is that the sleep associations are *workable for the parent.* That is, if the parent does not find feeding or rocking baby to sleep problematic, or even finds it pleasurable and easy as some parents do, then they should feel free to keep doing it.

There are two biological processes underlying the regulation of sleep. The first is the sleep–wake homeostat, a sleep pressure that builds the longer you go without sleeping, and the second is the circadian clock, an internal biological clock guiding patterns of arousal throughout a 24-hour day (Markov, Goldman, & Doghramji, 2012). Newborns are born with homeostatic regulation of sleep and circadian patterns that emerge within weeks of environmental exposure to circadian cues such as sunlight (Jenni & Carskadon, 2012).

This alternative behavioral paradigm for parent–infant sleep thus involves applying evidence-based behavioral strategies for supporting adult sleep efficiency *to the parent–infant dyad,* including sleep compression/sleep restriction, sleep hygiene, and supporting the circadian clock.

In sum, the Possums Sleep Intervention supports parents and babies in obtaining healthy sleep by:

- Adapted sleep compression/sleep restriction for parents and babies. Sleep compression/sleep restriction involves restricting the amount of time spend in bed trying to sleep to the amount of time that the person with sleeping difficulties is actually sleeping. In the absence of daytime naps, this allows the felt sleep pressure to build, and for sleep efficiency to be maximized, including settling back to sleep easily during the night. Once the person is falling asleep and staying asleep well, the time spent sleeping per night can be gradually increased. For babies, sleep compression need not be applied rigidly. Parents can experiment in a very gentle and gradual way. The core idea is this: if a baby consistently has poor sleep efficiency—is taking a long time to fall asleep—then the parents should consider that the baby has not built sufficient sleep pressure at bedtime. Parents might like to experiment with a later bedtime, an earlier start to the day or examine how their baby naps. As there is wide variation in infant sleep needs and needs vary across the first year of life, ongoing, flexible experimentation is key.
- Examining daytime naps. In adults, daytime naps longer than 20 minutes can interfere with nighttime sleep, as it interferes with the building of sufficient sleep pressure by nighttime. Babies need more sleep than adults in total, and hence, daytime naps are normal. However, babies can still oversleep during the day in accordance with their needs, which can interfere with the consolidation of nighttime sleep by interfering with the building of sleep pressure throughout the day. Parents can decrease the chances that their baby will oversleep during the day by letting their

baby take daytime naps in normal daylight and among normal noise and activity. Sometimes parents, especially primary caregivers, compensate for their own loss of sleep by napping during the day. If parents are able to do so without it affecting their own sleep then this is not problematic. However, if parents are reporting sleeping difficulties themselves, with poor sleep efficiency when they are free to fall asleep, reducing daytime napping for themselves may be helpful. For adults, napping for 20 minutes at a time can help with daytime drowsiness without interfering with nighttime sleep.

- Sleep when sleepy. Time naps and bedtime by sleepiness not by the clock. Importantly this should be flexible and experimental not a rigid application of "tired cues." Even yawning might happen due to reasons other than being sleepy enough to fall asleep; for example, feeling bored or lower arousal (but not sleepy enough to actually fall asleep).
- Supporting a healthy circadian rhythm. A healthy circadian rhythm involves ensuring that both parent and baby are living a lifestyle that supports the circadian clocks attunement to real time through environmental cues. This can be supported through a regular wake-up time, exposure to sunlight during the day, caution regarding blue-light exposure at night, and plenty of daytime activity and exercise. The regular wake-up time need not be early or rigid, simply regular enough. Parents may choose to actively wake their baby if they haven't woken naturally by a set time, or to simply treat further sleep like a daytime nap with normal daylight and noise. A key way our circadian clock keeps in tune with real time, with the actual revolution of the Earth over a 24-hour day, is light exposure, in particular blue spectrum light. It is thus important to receive plenty of exposure to blue spectrum light during daytime hours, especially sunlight if possible, and to minimize blue-light exposure at night. Parents of babies may particularly need to examine the use of night lights—light sources when they get up at night to feed or attend to baby and the use of devices during the night. Any light sources used during the night should be red-spectrum light sources (red-spectrum light night lights are available or you can purchase red-colored light bulbs). If parents look at devices during the night when they are up with their baby then they should set their devices to 24-hour light settings, so that the blue spectrum light is reduced during the nighttime hours. Daytime activity and exercise is also key to supporting the circadian rhythm. When sleep deprived it is easy to all into the trap of doing less during the day. While some adaptation for drowsiness is understandable, it is important for both parent and baby to receive plenty of stimulation, activity, and exercise during the day in order to sleep well at night.
- ACT strategies can be important in supporting the parent in coping with sleeping challenges, including defusion to not get hooked into anxious thoughts during the night ("I am going to be exhausted tomorrow, when will I get to sleep?"), mindfulness practices during nighttime responding,

and experiential acceptance so that parental stress is not escalated in a manner that then worsens parent sleep.

One common objection to this alternative way of viewing parent–infant sleep is the observation that babies have difficulty falling asleep when they are "overtired." This observation makes sense, however, the explanation—that they are having trouble sleeping because they feel too tired—contradicts our understanding of the sleep–wake homeostat. Instead, this observation has to do with the circadian clock. The circadian rhythm has peaks and troughs in arousal throughout a 24-hour day and the easiest times to fall asleep are when the circadian rhythm is dipping into a trough. If this "sleep window" is missed, it can be difficult to fall asleep during a peak in arousal even if sufficient sleep pressure has built. It is likely that when parents observe a baby or a child having difficulty sleeping despite being very sleepy, that this is what has occurred. If this has happened, then both parent and child need to wait it out, keeping the child as calm as possible until the next dip in arousal allows sleep to occur. If this is happening regularly then it indicates that the parent needs to focus on supporting the healthy operation of the circadian clock or experimenting with the timing of bedtime so that the child is initiating sleep during a dip in arousal.

Parents can combine this intervention with traditional behavioral sleep interventions to decrease the frequency of signaling behavior if they wish. There is no reason why sleep efficiency and the frequency of signaling cannot *both* be targeted. However, this is not necessary. This sleep intervention is entirely consistent with a "close contact" approach including breastfeeding and bed-sharing, thus overcoming cultural and individual obstacles to receiving support for infant sleeping challenges.

Aurora, Christopher, and Amelia

When Aurora, Christopher, and their 5-month-old baby Amelia come to see you, it is clear that they have reached a crisis point.

Aurora starts to cry as she explains their current difficulties. Christopher places a supportive hand on her shoulder as she talks, "She doesn't sleep. Getting her to sleep is such hard work and my sleep is so disturbed. When she finally does sleep or when Chris takes her for a bit then I can't sleep. I am exhausted. I can't do this anymore."

Millie sleeps in a separate cot/crib in Aurora and Christopher's bedroom. Her bedtime is 7 p.m. At 7 p.m. Aurora takes her into the bedroom, darkens the room, and puts on relaxation music. Aurora alternates between strategies to help Millie sleep from: walking with her, to feeding her, to lying her in the cot and patting her to sleep to lying her down in the cot and sitting in the room (this is the first step of the camping-out method). None of the methods reliably work. It

(*Continued*)

(Continued)

takes at least an hour for Millie to fall asleep and Aurora describes that hour as like "a pressure cooker."

Millie wakes from three to six times a night. When Aurora hears Millie she initially does nothing, hoping that Millie will self-settle. However, she rarely does. When Millie escalates to crying Aurora picks her up and offers her a feed. She feeds her in a feeding chair in the bedroom with a nightlight on. She says that she uses the feeding chair so that she doesn't fall asleep herself, however, she regularly does end up falling asleep while feeding in the chair.

Sometimes the feed is enough for Millie to fall back asleep. However, once or twice a night a feed is not enough. If the feed doesn't work then Aurora tries: lying her in her cot/crib and patting her on her back, walking with her and singing to her as well as simply putting her back into the cot/crib and hoping she'll self-settle. It usually takes 20–30 minutes of effort, after the feed, for Millie to fall back asleep if the feed alone hasn't been enough. After all of that effort, Aurora finds that she often has difficulty falling asleep.

Millie has three naps during the day. Aurora explains that she has to put in a lot of effort to get Millie to go to sleep during the day too. She naps in her cot/crib in the bedroom, with the blinds closed to darken the room. Aurora often has a nap then too to catch upon sleep.

Imagine you could, unseen and unheard, observe a typical, ordinary interaction between Aurora, Christopher, and Amelia. It might be something like this:

Parent–child interaction

It is 7 p.m., Millie's bedtime.

Aurora takes Millie into the bedroom, turning off the lights and turning on a nightlight and some relaxation music. She smiles at Millie in a tired way as she says, "it is bedtime little one. Let's go to sleep tonight, huh? Be good for mummy?"

Millie gurgles and coos.

Aurora shakes her head, "it is not time for that now it is time for sleep."

Aurora sits in their feeding chair and offers Millie the breast.

Millie gazes up at Aurora and smiles. She takes the breast enthusiastically. She feeds for 20 minutes, taking milk from both breasts. After she is finished she comes off, eyes closed, and mouth hanging open looking milk drunk.

Aurora sighs and whispers to herself, "Maybe we are going to have a good night tonight then."

But only a minute later Millie is opening her eyes.

Millie smiles up at Aurora, "ga ga ga!"

Aurora shakes her head, "No Millie. It is bedtime"

Millie smiles "Gah gah gah!"

Aurora puts Millie into the cot, "Shhh..."

She steps back and sits back in the feeding chair out of sight. She is visibly tense.

(Continued)

(Continued)

Millie continues to talk, "Gah gah gah! Bah bah bah!" This goes on for several minutes. She rolls over onto her stomach and looks around the room. Aurora is still just out of sight. "Gah? Gah?"

Millie's calls escalate and turn into cries.

Aurora grips at the chair tensely. *This is unbearable*, she thinks, *she has to go to sleep now. She just has to.* Finally the cries become too painful to ignore. Aurora goes to Millie and picks her up. Millie quickly calms.

Millie smiles at her mum, "gah gah"

Aurora shakes her head, "No gah gah, Millie. It is bedtime. Please Millie. I'll walk you okay?"

Aurora walks Millie back and forth for 10 minutes. Millie babbles all the time. Finally, Aurora tries putting her back in her cot. This time, as Aurora steps back Millie immediately begins to cry. She reaches up toward Aurora as she cries.

"Millie," Aurora groans, "Please, Mummy wants to have her dinner and go to sleep herself. I'm tried, Millie."

The door opens, Christopher pokes his head in as Aurora picks up Millie.

Christopher, "Everything okay in here?"

Aurora sighs, "Oh just the usual nonsense."

Millie says, "gah gah!" smiling at her daddy.

Christopher looks at Millie and smiles saying playfully, "You go to sleep you little rascal," he turns to Aurora, "Do you want me to take her?"

Aurora says, "No, that's okay. I'll give her another feed maybe and try putting her in the cot again. She has to learn to self-settle. I'll be more determined this time."

Chris nods, "Okay. Well, I'll get dinner organized then."

Aurora sighs, "Oh do you mind?"

"Of course not," Chris replies, "Good luck" he shuts the door.

Aurora gives Millie another feed. This one takes 20 minutes. Again, Millie comes off with eyes closed and mouth open, looking milk drunk.

Aurora settles her into the cot and this time it looks like she's going to stay asleep. But as Aurora creeps out of the room she calls out,"Gah gah!" *Oh, no,* Aurora thinks. *I just can't keep this up. I'm exhausted.*

Aurora slips just outside the door and waits, her body tense, hoping that Millie will self-settle. This time Millie quickly escalates to full-blown cries. Her screams echo throughout the house.

Aurora flinches and grips the wall. She holds herself back for 8 minutes but Millie just continues to scream. *This is ridiculous. It's just not working. Why can't I get this right?* Finally, she walks back in and picks up Millie. She wipes away Millie's tears and comforts her, "I'm sorry, honey. Mummy's here. I just want to have dinner and go to sleep, honey. You need to learn to go to sleep."

Aurora walks Millie back and forth for 10 minutes and Millie starts to drop off to sleep. She puts her back down in her cot and stays beside the cot for 5 more minutes, softly patting her bottom.

(*Continued*)

(Continued)

Millie is asleep. Aurora quietly tiptoes out of the room. She is exhausted. It is now well past 8 p.m. She knows it is only a couple of hours before Millie will wake and the whole process will start again. She already feels tense, dreading the long night. *I've failed again,* she thinks.

What's happening for Aurora, Chris, and Millie?

Millie has poor sleep efficiency. It is taking over an hour for her to fall asleep at night. From her behavior, it is clear that Millie has not yet built sufficient sleep pressure at 7 p.m. to fall asleep for the night. It is likely that Aurora also has poor sleep efficiency as she states that she has difficulty falling asleep during the night.

Aurora is regularly falling asleep with Millie in the feeding chair. This is understandable. It is not realistic to expect a sleep-deprived mother to be able consistently stay awake during nighttime feeds. However, this means that, in an attempt to avoid bed-sharing, she is regularly "bed-sharing"—sharing a sleeping space, the chair—in a dangerous manner. It would be better for Aurora to accept that she is falling asleep during nighttime feeds and to ensure that all nighttime feeds are done in such a way that if she does fall asleep, she is bed-sharing in the safest possible way. The best way to do this would be to give nighttime feeds in bed, set up for cosleeping safely. Aurora can still try, as best she can, to stay awake and return Millie to her cot/crib. But if she does fall asleep then at least the bed-sharing is as safe as possible.

Darkened rooms for daytime naps (for both Aurora and Millie) as well as a nightlight for nighttime feeds are undermining a healthy circadian rhythm.

The "pressure cooker" of attempting to control Millie's sleep, getting her to fall asleep "on time," is only making Millie's successful transition to sleep less likely and is a significant source of stress for Aurora.

From an RFT perspective, there may be derived meanings that are important to consider. Aurora and Chris appear to be following verbal rules around parenting, infant sleep, and bedtime, and they continue to follow those rules even when they aren't working. For example, Aurora is persisting in adhering to the rule "never bed-share" when the result is that she is regularly sharing a sleeping space with Millie in a dangerous manner (the chair). They are also persisting with a particular bedtime even though Millie is not falling asleep then. Furthermore, Aurora may also be feeling frustrated with Millie, as well as with her own tiredness and fatigue, and these may be framed in opposition with "good mothering." If this is the case, and Aurora becomes entangled in these thoughts, she may be less sensitive to Millie's behavioral cues indicating sleepiness. Helping Millie unpack these relations, and helping to shape new relations like "good mothers" and "not perfect" in equivalence; or "good mothers" and "Try things and learn as they go"; or "learning" is not equivalent to "failure," through experiential exercises, as well as simple discussion, may be helpful in supporting more defused and open tracking of Millie's signals.

Working with Aurora, Chris, and Millie

As part of gaining a full understanding of the challenge, the therapist explores Chris and Aurora's parenting values. The therapist suggests that they want to ensure that how Aurora and Chris approach Millie's sleep is not just focused on solving "the problem" but also on parenting according to their values. From there, the therapist begins to explore sleep with Chris and Aurora, drawing on the Possums Sleep Intervention and the experiment on sleep and control found in full in Chapter 8, Experiential acceptance of parent, child, and relationship.

Therapist:	So, we want to figure out what might work better for you all in terms of sleep. Let's do an experiment. I'm going to tell you to do things. You are going to do them. We'll see what we notice, okay? It is quite simple. Chris and Aurora both nod.
Therapist:	Stand up. Clap your hands. Stomp your feet. Chris and Aurora stand up, clap their hands, and stomp their feet, both smiling and looking a bit unsure.
Therapist:	Easy enough so far? Chris and Aurora both nod.
Therapist:	Great. Now, fall asleep. Chris and Aurora start laughing.
Therapist:	C'mon. Fall a sleep.
Chris:	I can't.
Therapist:	Ah. Interesting. Aurora? Aurora closes her eyes and tries.
Therapist:	Asleep yet?
Aurora laughs:	No
Therapist:	So, here's the first thing to notice. Although sleep is something that we do, we don't do sleep like we do moving our hands and feet. It isn't something we can choose to do the moment we want to. Let's try that again. But this time I want you to imagine that I'm not asking you. I'm commanding you. Somehow, your life is on the line here. If you can't do what I'm telling you to do there are going to be some big and nasty consequences. It is really, really important that you do as I ask. Let's see what we notice. Ready? Stand up. Clap your hands. Stomp your feet. Chris and Aurora stand up, clap their hands, and stomp their feet.
Therapist:	Easy enough so far, huh? Now, go to sleep and remember: it is incredibly important that you go to sleep right now. Your very life is on the line. Chris and Aurora laugh.
Chris:	Well, there's no way I'm going to sleep now.

(*Continued*)

(Continued)

Therapist:	Right. Not only can we not choose to fall asleep whenever we want to, we cannot force ourselves asleep. The more going to sleep right now matters, the more elusive sleep becomes. Your mind will tell you to try harder. But if you experiment, like we just did, we find that when it comes to sleep trying harder doesn't help, does it? In fact, it makes sleep less likely.
Aurora:	Because you're all stressed out about it
Therapist:	Exactly. And what if it was important to me for you to fall asleep right now? What if my life was on the line? What if I was really stressed out about ensuring that you fell asleep in the next five minutes? I could work really hard for that, maybe sing you lullabies or get you some warm milk. Would that make a difference do you think?
Aurora laughing	that sounds familiar...
Therapist:	It does doesn't it? Would all my trying make a difference? Can I choose for you to fall asleep when I want you to? Is there a little sleep switch on the back of your head?
Aurora:	Well, I know from firsthand experience that it doesn't work at all...Millie certainly doesn't have a sleep switch!
Therapist:	Right. So here's the question: if trying harder to fall asleep or to help Millie to fall asleep isn't the answer, what is?
Aurora:	I wish I knew!
Therapist:	Well, here it is: trying harder doesn't work. Sleep isn't under direct conscious control. But we can control our lifestyle. We can understand how sleep is regulated and live a life that promotes healthy sleep.
Chris:	Okay. So what does that mean?
Therapist:	Sleep is regulated by two biological patterns. The first is the sleep–wake homeostat. That's a need for sleep. The need to fall asleep builds the longer you've been without sleep. The longer you've been without sleep the sleepier you'll feel. The other pattern is the circadian clock. The circadian clock is a biological clock keeping track of time throughout a 24-hour day. It has peaks and troughs. Peaks, where you feel more alert, and troughs when it is easier to fall asleep if you've built up a need for sleep. The circadian clock keeps in sync with real time, with the actual rotation of the Earth through environmental cues, like sunlight and activity. Any questions so far? Chris and Aurora shake their heads.

(*Continued*)

(Continued)

Therapist: What we want to do is, firstly, to ensure that Millie has built up sufficient need for sleep at her bedtime so that she falls asleep without difficulty and has her longest sleep period at night, while you are both sleeping too. Secondly, we want to ensure that Millie's circadian clock, and yours as well Aurora and Chris, are in sync with real time and with each other. This will also help concentrate Millie's sleep during the night hours. There are a few things that you can do, including getting plenty of sunlight, limiting light exposure during the night, plenty of activity during the day, waking at a regular time and experimenting with the length of daytime naps and bedtime.

Aurora: So, maybe we should be taking her to bed later?

Therapist nods: Maybe. These are all things to experiment with. I can't emphasize that enough. It is about understanding the sleep homeostat and circadian clock and then experimenting to discover what works. A useful question to ask is this: how much sleep does Millie actually have at night now? Then adjust her bedtime and wake-up time to fit with that. You can also ask: when does Millie seem sleepy? That is also a good indication of bedtime. You'll probably find as you experiment that she then falls asleep more easily and sleeps better through the night.

From the psychoeducation on sleep Aurora and Chris decide to experiment with pushing Millie's bedtime back. She is currently falling asleep at 8 p.m. so they use that as a guide as well as watching for signs that she is sleepy. They also decide to experiment with Millie taking daytime naps among normal daylight and noise, including in her pram. Aurora and Millie start a routine of going for a walk every morning to get activity and sunlight. Aurora purchases a red light night light begins to use that for nighttime feeds. In addition, Aurora feeds Millie in bed during the night, setting the bed up in the safest possible way for cosleeping (with Millie lying at her chest, and adult pillow and blankets well out of Millie's way), so that if she does fall asleep she is bed-sharing in the safest way possible. The therapist also teaches Aurora a simple mindfulness exercise that she can practice during nighttime wake-ups. Aurora's tendency to get hooked on unworkable (though true) thoughts during the nighttime wake-ups such as "I am going to be exhausted in the morning" is targeted with defusion techniques.

After the intervention, Millie continues to wake 1–2 times a night. However, it is now usual for her to fall asleep easily after a breastfeed, both at bedtime initially going to sleep for the night and during nighttime wake-ups. If more settling is needed then it usually only takes about 10 minutes. Aurora reports that her own sleep has dramatically improved. Although Aurora's sleep continues to be broken by the need to feed Millie, Aurora does succeed in getting 8 hours of

(*Continued*)

(Continued)

sleep on most nights and no longer feels exhausted during the day. If Millie doesn't fall asleep with a feed during the night, Aurora still experiences a rush of anxious thoughts. She uses defusion techniques to hold the thoughts lightly, and focuses on turning the continued settling of Millie into a mindfulness exercise for herself. By doing so, she finds that when Millie has settled back to sleep 10 minutes later, she can fall asleep easily herself.

Chris and Aurora are very satisfied with their current sleeping arrangements. Before they ended the sessions with their therapist they clarified how to use the camping-out method. They are planning to use it when Millie is older. However, right now, their sleeping arrangements are working for them and they see no need for further immediate change.

Chapter summary

Other evidence-based therapies—exposure therapy, behavioral activation, attachment and behavioral parenting interventions, and postnatal care—can be integrated with ACT and applied in an ACT-consistent way.

References

Armstrong, K. L., Quinn, R. A., & Dadds, M. R. (1994). The sleep patterns of normal children. *The Medical Journal of Australia*, *161*(3), 202–206.

Ball, H. (2009). Bed-sharing and co-sleeping: Research overview. *NCT New Digest*, *48*, 22–27.

Ball, H., Douglas, P., Taylor C., Thomas V. (2018) Sleep, Baby & You: A new intervention for UK parents who are seeking support with infant sleep. Poster presentation at the UNICEF UK Baby Friendly Initiative Annual Conference, November 15–16, 2018, ACC Liverpool.

Ball, H. L., Douglas, P. S., Kulasinghe, K., Whittingham, K., & Hill, P. (2018). The Possums Infant Sleep Program: Parents' perspectives on a novel parent–infant sleep intervention in Australia. *Sleep Health*, *4*, 519–529.

Brown, F. L., Whittingham, K., Boyd, R. N., & McKinlay, L. (2015). Does Stepping Stones Triple P plus Acceptance and Commitment Therapy improve parent, couple and family adjustment following paediatric acquired brain injury? A randomised controlled trial. *Behaviour Research and Therapy*, *73*, 58–66.

Brown, F. L., Whittingham, K., Boyd, R. N., McKinlay, L., & Sofronoff, K. (2014). Improving child and parenting outcomes following paediatric acquired brain injury: A randomised controlled trial of Stepping Stones Triple P plus acceptance and commitment therapy. *Journal of Child Psychology and Psychiatry*, *55*(10), 1172–1183.

Brown, F. L., Whittingham, K., McKinlay, L., Boyd, R. N., & Sofronoff, K. (2013). Efficacy of Stepping Stones Triple P plus a stress management adjunct for parents of children with acquired brain injury: The protocol of a randomised controlled trial. *Brain Impairment*, *14*(2), 253–269.

Chronis-Tuscano, A., Clarke, T. L., O'Brien, K. A., Raggi, V. L., Diaz, Y., Mintz, A. D., ... Lewinsohn, P. (2013). Development and preliminary evalution of an integrated treatment targeting parneting and depressive symptoms in mothers of children with Attention Deficit/Hyperactivity Disorder. *Jounral of Consulting and Clinical Psychology, 81*(5), 918–925.

Coyne, L. W., & Wilson, K. G. (2004). The role of cognitive fusion in impaired parenting: An RFT analysis. *International Journal of Psychology and Psychological Therapy, 4*(3), 469–486.

Douglas, P. S. (2018). The Possums Sleep Program: supporting easy, healthy parent-infant sleep. *International Journal of Birth and Parent Education, 6*(1), 13–16, 9.

Douglas, P. S., Hill, P. S., & Brodribb, W. (2011). The unsettled baby: how complexity science helps. *Arch Dis Child, 96*, 793–797.

Douglas, P. S., & Hill, P. S. (2011). The crying baby: What approach? *Current Opinion in Pediatrics, 23*, 523–529.

Douglas, P. S., & Hill, P. S. (2013). Behavioral sleep interventions in the first six months of life do not improve outcomes for mothers or infants: A systematic review. *Journal of Developmental and Behavioral Pediatrics, 34*(7), 497–507.

Douglas, P., Miller, Y., Bucetti, A., Hill, P. S., & Creedy, D. (2013). Preliminary evaluation of a primary care intervention for cry-fuss behaviours in the first three to four months of life ("The Possums Approach"): effects on cry-fuss behaviours and maternal mood. *Australian Journal of Primary Health, 21*, 38–45.

Ekirch, A. R. (2005). *Atday's close night in times past*. New York: W.W. Norton and Company.

Galbally, M., Lewis, A. J., McEgan, K., Scalzo, K., & Islam, F. A. (2013). Breastfeeding and infant sleep patterns: An Australian population study. *Journal of Paediatric and Child Health, 49*(2), E147–E152.

Galland, B. C., Taylor, B. J., Elder, D. E., & Herbison, P. (2012). Normal sleep patterns in infants and children: A systematic review of observational studies. *Sleep Medicine Review, 16*(3), 213–222.

Gill, N. E., White, M. A., & Anderson, G. C. (1984). Transitional newborn infants in a hospital nursery: From first oral cue to first sustained cry. *Nursing Research, 33*(4), 213–217.

Goldstein, M. H., Schwade, J. A., & Bornstein, M. H. (2009). The value of vocalizing: Five month old infants associate their own noncry vocalizations with responses from caregivers. *Child Development, 80*(3), 636–644.

Gorter, E. T., Gollan, J. K., Dobson, K. S., & Jacobson, N. S. (1998). Cognitive-behavioral treatment for depression: Relapse prevention. *Journal of Consulting and Clinical Psychology, 66*(2), 377–384.

Hayes, S. C., Strosahl, K. D., & Wilson, K. G. (2003). *Acceptance and Commitment Therapy: An experiential approach to behavior change*. New York: Guilford Press.

Jacobson, N. S., Martell, C. R., & Dimidjian, S. (2001). Behavioural activation for depression: Returning to contextual roots. *Clinical Psychology: Science and Practice, 8*(3), 255–270.

Jenni, O. G., & Carskadon, M. A. (2012). Sleep behavior and sleep regulation from infancy through adolescence normative aspects. *Sleep and Medicine Clinics, 7*, 529–538.

Kempler, L., Sharpe, L., Miller, C. B., & Bartlett, D. J. (2016). Do psychosocial sleep interventions improve infant sleep or maternal mood in the postnatal period? A systematic review and meta-analysis of randomised controlled trials. *Sleep Medicine Reviews, 29*, 15–22.

Kendall-Tackett, K., Cong, Z., & Hale, T. W. (2011). The effect of feeding method on sleep duration, maternal well-being, and postpartum depression. *Clinical Lactation, 22*, 22–26.

Marchesi, C., Ossola, P., Amerio, A., Daniel, B. D., Tonna, M., & De Panfillis, C. (2016). Clinical management of perinatal anxiety disorders: A systematic review. *Journal of Affective Disorders, 190*. (543-500).

Markov, D., Goldman, M., & Doghramji, K. (2012). Normal sleep and circadian rythms. *Sleep and Medicine Clinics*, *7*, 417–426.

Martell, C. R. (2018). Behavioral activation. In S. C. Hayes, & S. G. Hofmann (Eds.), *Process-based CBT* (pp. 299–308). Oakland: Context Press.

Matricciani, L. A., Blunden, S., Rigney, G., Williams, M. T., & Olds, T. S. (2013). Children's sleep needs: Is there sufficient evidence to recommend optimal sleep for children? *Sleep*, *36* (4), 527–534.

Matricciani, L. A., Olds, T. R., Blunden, S., Rigmey, G., & Williams, M. T. (2012). Never enough sleep: A brief history of sleep recommendations for children. *Pediatrics*, *129*, 548–556.

Mitchell, E. A., Freemantle, J., Young, J., & Byard, R. W. (2012). Scientific consensus forum to review the evidence underpinning the recommendations of the Australian SIDS and Kids Safe Sleeping Health Promotion Programme–October 2010. *Journal of Paediatrics andChild Health*, *48*(8), 626–633.

Neff, K. D., & Faso, D. J. (2015). Self-compassion and well-being in parents of children with autism. *Mindfulness*, *6*, 938–947.

Parent, J., McKee, L. G., Rough, J. N., & Forehand, R. (2016). The Association of Parent Mindfulness with Parenting and Youth Psychopathology across three developmental stages. *Journal of Abnormal Child Psychology*, *44*(1), 191–202.

Pass, L., Lejuez, C. W., & Reynolds, S. (2018). Brief behavioural activation (Brief BA) for adolescent depression: A pilot study. *Behavioural and Cognitive Psychotherapy*, *46*(2), 182–194.

Pass, L., Whitney, H., & Reynolds, S. (2016). Brief behavioral activation for adolesent depression: Working with complexity and risk. *Clinical Case Studies*, *15*(5), 360–375.

Petzoldt, J. (2018). Systematic review on maternal depression versus anxiety in relation to excessive infant crying: It is all about the timing. *Archives of Women's Mental Health*, *21*, 15–309.

Powell, C., Bamber, D., Long, J., Garratt, R., Brown, J., Rudge, S., … St James-Roberts, I. (2018). Mental health and well-being in parents of excessively crying infants: Prospective evaluation of a support package. *Child: Care, Health and Development*, *44* (4), 607–615.

Price, A. M., Wake, M., Ukoumunne, O. C., & Hiscock, H. (2012). Five-year follow-up of harms and benefits of behavioral infant sleep intervention: Randomized trial. *Pediatrics*, *130*(4), 643–651.

Runyan, D. K., Hennink-Kaminski, H. J., Zolotor, A. J., Barr, R. G., Murphy, R. A., Barr, M., … Nocera, M. (2009). Designing and Testing a Shaken Baby Syndrome Prevention Program—The period of PURPLE crying: Keeping babies safe in North Carolina. *Social Marketing Quarterly*, *15*(4), 2–24.

Silk, J. S., Shaw, D. S., Forbes, E. E., Lane, T. L., & Kovacs, M. (2006). Maternal depression and child internalizaing: The moderating role of child emotion regulation. *Journal of Clinical and Child Adolescent Psychology*, *35*(1), 116–126.

Silk, J. S., Shaw, D. S., Skuban, E. M., Oland, A. A., & Kovacs, M. (2006). Emotion regulation strategies in offspring of childhood-onset depressed mothers. *Journal of Child Psychology and Psychiatry*, *47*(1), 69–78.

Smarius, L. J. C. A., Strieder, T. G. A., Loomans, E. M., Doreleijers, T. A. H., Vrijkotte, T. G. M., Gemke, R. J., & van Eijsden, M. (2017). Excessive infant crying doubles the risk of mood and behavioral problems at age 5: Evidence for mediation by maternal characteristics. *European Child and Adolescent Psychiatry*, *26*, 293–302.

St James-Roberts, I. (2007). Helping parents to manage infant crying and sleeping: A review of the evidence and its implications for services. *Child Abuse Review*, *16*(1), 47–69.

St James-Roberts, I., Alvarez, M., Csipke, E., Abramsky, T., Goodwin, J., & Sorfenfrel, E. (2006). Infant crying and sleeping in Londen, Copenhagen and when parents adopt a 'proximal' form of care. *Pediatrics*, *117*, 1146–1155.

St James-Roberts, I., Roberts, M., Hovish, K., & Owen, C. (2015). Video evidence that London infants can resettle themselves back to sleep after waking in the night, as well as sleep for long periods by 3 months of age. *Journal of Developmental and Behavioral Pediatrics*, *36*, 324–329.

St James-Roberts, I., Roberts, M., Hovish, K., & Owen, C. (2017). Video evidence that parenting methods predict which infants develop long night-time sleep periods by three months of age. *Primary Health Care Research and Development*, *18*(3), 212–226.

Thomas, S. R., O'Brien, K. A., Clarke, T. L., Liu, Y., & Chronis-Tuscano, A. (2015). Maternall depression history moderates parenting responses to compliant and noncompliant behaviors of children with ADHD. *Journal of Abnormal Child Psychology*, *43*(7), 1257–1269.

Wake, M., Morton-Allen, E., Poulakis, Z., Hiscock, H., Gallagher, S., & Oberklaid, F. (2006). Prevalence, stability and outcomes of cry-fuss and sleep problems in the first 2 years of life: Prospective community-based study. *Pediatrics*, *117*(3), 836–842.

Weinraub, M., Bender, R. H., Friedman, S. L., Susman, E. J., Knoke, B., Bradley, R., ... Williams, J. (2012). Patterns of developmental change in infants' nighttime sleep awakenings from 6 through 36 months of age. *Developmental Psychology*, *48*(6), 1511–1528.

Whittingham, K. (2014). Parenting in context. *Journal of Contextual Behavioral Science*, *3*(3), 212–215.

Whittingham, K., & Douglas, P. (2014). Optimizing parent–infant sleep from birth to 6 months: A new paradigm. *Infant Mental Health Journal*, *35*(6), 614–623.

Whittingham, K., Sanders, M., McKinlay, L., & Boyd, R. N. (2014). Interventions to reduce behavioral problems in children with cerebral palsy: An RCT. *Pediatrics*, *133*(5), e1249–e1257.

Whittingham, K., Sanders, M. R., McKinlay, L., & Boyd, R. N. (2016). Parenting intervention combined with acceptance and commitment therapy: A trial with families of children with cerebral palsy. *Journal of Pediatric Psychology*, *41*(5), 531–542.

Zeifman, D. M., & St James-Roberts, I. (2017). Parenting the crying infant. *Current Opinion in Psychology*, *15*, 149–154.

Chapter 15

Conclusion

Chapter Outline

References 405

Man and woman power devoted to the production of material goods counts a plus in all our economic indices. Man and woman power devoted to the production of happy, healthy and self-reliant children in their own homes does not count at all. We have created a topsy-turvy world.

John Bowlby, *A Secure Base*

We've all got both light and dark inside us. What matters is the part we choose to act on. That's who we really are.

J.K. Rowling, *Harry Potter and the Order of the Phoenix*

Because peace is milk,
Peace is milk
And the skinny, thirsty earth, its face covered with flies,
Screams like a baby.

Adrian Mitchell, *Peace is Milk*

This book has focused on clinical intervention—on using Acceptance and Commitment Therapy (ACT), Relational Frame Theory (RFT), and Compassion Focused Therapy (CFT)—to support flexible and workable parenting and the cultivation of psychological flexibility in children. But we can also look beyond clinical intervention. ACT, RFT, and CFT, the models of psychologically flexible parenting covered in this book, also have implications for societal change. Evolutionary and behavioral scientists are asking how we can harness the principles of evolution and behavioral change to create a more nurturing, prosocial society (Biglan, 2015). As our final thought, we'd like to speculate on what this might look like and how parents, parenting, professionals, and researchers might be part of it.

Parents, children, and parenting must be understood as crucial to any effort to reshape our society into a more nurturing one. Parents are a key agent of change in the shaping of the next generation and hence are crucial

Acceptance and Commitment Therapy. DOI: https://doi.org/10.1016/B978-0-12-814669-9.00015-1
© 2019 Elsevier Inc. All rights reserved.

to ensuring that the next generation is raised in a nurturing manner and raised to be nurturing. Further, a nurturing prosocial context *for parents* supports parents in being nurturing themselves. We must nurture parents, so that they can nurture children, and we must support parental capacity for nurturing. We must also build a society that is itself nurturing to children, and supports children in developing as psychologically flexible and compassionate individuals. At a societal level, what does that look like? It might include maternity leave, parental leave, universal prenatal and postnatal care, targeting poverty, early intervention, developmentally appropriate schooling, and questioning the private/public divide in contemporary life that forces parents into a juggling act.

At the same time as supporting the individual parents, children, and families that we see, we must also look to the ways that we can bring about societal level change. If we were to design a society in the best interests of parents and children, what would it look like?

The mother–child bond was the first relationship to evolve. The family—a flexible, caring group of parent/s and alloparents organizing around the needs of a child—is our species' most basic social group. Yet, all of that is currently relegated to the private sphere. What might it mean for children to be understood as the center of public community as well? How might public life need to shift and change to accommodate that? At this point in time such a proposition might seem daunting. But rapidly approaching changes such as increasing automation (Harari, 2015) offer opportunities to change and rebalance our understanding of family, work, and the private and public spheres. The nurturing, compassionate side of our nature first evolved to enable us to care for our children, and contact with children remains a potent stimulus for eliciting nurturing behavior (Hrdy, 2011). Perhaps, it is not only the case that a more nurturing society would better accommodate children, but perhaps a society that better accommodates children would also become more nurturing.

We are living in unique times. For the first time in the history of our species, children may grow almost entirely sheltered from the calamities of famine, natural disasters, war, and infectious disease (Harari, 2011, 2015). Not every community in the world experiences this sheltering but many of us no longer see these calamities as an inevitable part of life. Child mortality is now understood by many to be a solvable problem.

As a result, within sheltered communities we have fewer children, we expect all of our children to survive until adulthood, and we invest all the more into the success of each individual child. Seen within an historical context, considering reductions in child mortality and the number of children, increases in formal education, rapidly moving technological advancement, and supercharged behavioral and symbolic evolution, trends toward "hothouse" and "helicopter" parenting are understandable adaptations to the realities of contemporary life. But that doesn't mean we shouldn't be conscious of the potential costs.

We are also living in a time of unprecedented change (Harari, 2011, 2015). Across history, parents have prepared their children for the cultural context in which they found themselves. However, preparing your children for a cultural context that is itself unsustainable is an evolutionary dead-end. We know that our current way of life is unsustainable—the very children we support will have to face environmental crises on an unprecedented scale in their own lifetime—we know this, even as we hurtle toward still further change. Parents today cannot accurately predict the world they are raising their children for, only that it will be different to today that it *must* be.

What might it mean to parent our children for a future *beyond* our current social and ecological context, to parent our children for a *better* world, to parent our children to *create* a better world? What if we set ourselves the task of raising children who won't just succeed in our current cultural, historical, and environmental context but who will lead our species through current crises and shape a better society for the future? It is monumental aspiration. But surely, such children will need to be flexible, to collaborate and share resources equitably and sustainably, to be able to accept the suffering of life, to be aware and respectful of their own embodied feelings and impulses, to be able to language well and flexibly, to have strong self-knowledge, to be able to understand the perspectives of others, to be able to give and receive compassion, and to have a rich capacity act on their values even when it is difficult.

References

Biglan, A. (2015). *The nurture effect*. Oakland: New Harbinger Publications.
Harari, Y. N. (2011). *Sapiens: A brief history of humankind*. London: Vintage.
Harari, Y. N. (2015). *Homo Deus: A brief history of tomorrow*. London: Vintage.
Hrdy, S. B. (2011). *Mothers and others*. Cambridge: Harvard University Press.

Index

Note: Page numbers followed by "*f*" and "*t*" refer to figures and tables, respectively.

A

Acceptance, 4, 34, 45, 188–194, 380–382
  applying to parent–child interaction, 194–201
  behavioral account of acceptance and experiential control, 189–193
  DNA-V model, 193–194
  key developmental periods and acceptance
    adolescence and, 216
    early childhood and, 215
    infancy and, 214–215
    middle childhood and, 215–216
  mindfulness and, 225–226
  with specific populations
    childhood externalizing problems and acceptance, 217
    childhood internalizing problems and acceptance, 217
    childhood neurodevelopmental disabilities and acceptance, 217
    emotion dismissiveness and acceptance, 218
    expressed emotion and acceptance, 218
    inconsistent, or harsh and punitive parenting and acceptance, 218
    marital conflict and acceptance, 218
    parental grief and acceptance, 216
    parental mental health problems and acceptance, 216
    peer problems and bullying and acceptance, 217
  troubleshooting, 213–214
  work with acceptance clinically
    experiential exercises, 204–206
    getting rid of thoughts experiment, 206–207
    meditation, 207–208
    metaphors, 203–204
    noticing acceptance within parent–child interaction, 202–203
    simple questioning, 202–212
Accessing compassionate self, 336
Accommodation behavior, 382
Acquisition of language, 254–255
Activation component, 380
Adaptive behaviors, 142, 195
Adaptive primary emotions, 199–202
Adolescence/adolescents, 104–105, 129, 309–310, 315, 342–343
  and acceptance, 216
  and flexible languaging, 282
  mindfulness within daily life for, 242
  and psychological contact with present moment, 247–248
  and values, 183
Adulthood, 27
Affiliative system, 324
Ainsworth, 42
Alliances, 33
"Allowing" in experiential acceptance, 192
Antecedent control strategies, 79
Antecedent strategies, 79–81
Antenatal mindfulness meditation, 237–238
Anxiety disorders, 381–382
Anxious–ambivalent attachment style, 43
Appetitive control, 68
Approach-based behavior, 80
Arbitrarily relate stimuli, 17, 29
ASD. *See* Autism spectrum disorder (ASD)
Associative conditioning, 66
Associative learning development, 10–12
Attachment, 57, 228
  across cultures, 44–45
  and emotional connection, 54–57
  theory, 4, 28, 41–44
Attachment-neutral, 85
Attachment-rich, 85
Attachment–salient observations, 50–51
Attuned interactions, 16–17, 44, 57, 81–82, 291–292

Attunement, 16–17, 46–47
  empathic, 47, 56, 296, 309
Augmenting, 154–155
  interacts, 76
Autism spectrum disorder (ASD), 146–147, 230, 280, 293–294
Autonomic nervous system, 14
Availability, 46
Aversive control, 68
Avoidant attachment style, 43

B

Baby meditation, mindfulness of, 238–239
Bedsharing, 26, 387–388
Behavioral
  account of acceptance, 189–193
  activation, 373, 380–381
  change principles, 403
  development, 15
  evolution, 12–13
  impulses, 192–193
  models, 65–66
  parenting intervention, 86–89
  rehearsal of parenting strategies, 379–380
  repertoires, 191
  stream, 12–13
  theoretical framework, 28–29
  theory, 28
Body-to-body transmission, 12
Bond, 133–134
Breathing meditation, mindfulness of, 235–236
Bullying, 317, 373

C

Caregiving system, 140
Case conceptualization, 104
  assessment, 104–105
  clinical relational frame theory and ACT models, 119
  functional analysis, 112–118
  functional analytic psychotherapy and parent–child relationship, 125–127
  intake interview, 105–108
  monitoring, 109–111
  observation of parent–child interaction, 111–112
  questionnaires, 108–109
  sharing formulation with parent, 129
CBT. *See* Cognitive behavior therapy (CBT)
Cellular transmission, 12
CER. *See* Conditioned emotional responses (CER)
CFT. *See* Compassion-focused therapy (CFT)
Child behaviors, 89
Childhood externalizing problems
  and acceptance, 217
  and committed action and exploration, 372
  and compassion, 349
  and flexible languaging, 283
  and flexible perspective taking, 316
  and psychological contact with present moment, 248
  and values, 184
Childhood internalizing problems
  and acceptance, 217
  and committed action and exploration, 372–373
  and compassion, 349–350
  and flexible languaging, 283
  and flexible perspective taking, 316
  and psychological contact with present moment, 248
  and values, 184
Childhood neurodevelopmental disabilities
  and acceptance, 217
  and committed action and exploration, 373
  and compassion, 350
  and flexible languaging, 283
  and flexible perspective taking, 317
  and psychological contact with present moment, 249
  and values, 184–185
Circadian clock, 390
Classic emotionally dysregulated temper tantrum, 90–91
Classical conditioning, 66
Client resistance, 145–146
Clinical relational frame theory, 119
Clinically relevant behaviors (CRBs), 125–126, 141–143
"Close contact" approach, 383, 389, 392–399
Coercion theory, 77
Coercive cycles, 76–78
Cognitive behavior therapy (CBT), 89, 380
Cognitive defusion, 30
Cognitive development, 15
Cognitive fusion, 30, 258
Committed action, 354–356
  applying to parent–child interaction, 356–361
    exploration and development, 358–361
    parenting control agenda, 357–358

parenting for flexible, broad behavioral repertoire for child, 356–357
case examples, 367–370
component, 380–381
DNA-V model, 356
key developmental periods, 371–372
adolescence, 372
early childhood, 371
infancy and, 371
middle childhood, 371
with specific populations, 372–374
troubleshooting, 370
working with, 361–370
building resilience through debriefing, 362–363
forgiveness or getting off hook, 364–365
hexaflex, 363–364
home practice, 367–370
jump metaphor, 366
parent supporting child exploration, 366–367
setting goals and practice opportunities, 361–362
willingness, 363
Compassion, 4, 32, 197, 322–327, 374, 405
applying to parent–child interaction, 327–332
and history, 328
parental compassion for child, 328
and parenting, 327–328
parenting to grow compassionate children, 329–332
self-compassion and parental well-being, 327
shame-based parenting, 329
capacities, 333
for child, 341–342
in children and adolescents, 342–343
fear, 346
key developmental periods and
adolescence and compassion, 348–349
early childhood and, 347–348
infancy and, 346–347
middle childhood and compassion, 348
for others, 364
with specific populations
childhood externalizing problems and, 349
childhood internalizing problems and, 349–350
childhood neurodevelopmental disabilities and, 350
emotion dismissiveness and, 351
expressed emotion and, 350–351
inconsistent, or harsh and punitive parenting and, 351
marital conflict and, 350
parental grief and, 349
parental mental health problems and, 349
peer relations and bullying and, 350
working with compassion clinically, 332–345
Compassion-focused ACT, 33–34, 322
Compassion-focused therapy (CFT), 1, 26–27, 134, 322, 403
Compassionate context, 364
affiliative, incentive/resource, and threat systems, 323*f*
DNA-V model, 326–327
key developmental periods and compassion, 346–349
troubleshooting, 346
working with compassion clinically, 332–345
Compassionate letter writing, 337–338
Compassionate parenting, 197
Competing behavior, 82–83
Complimentary approach, 1
Conditioned emotional responses (CER), 66–67
Conditioned response (CR), 66
Conditioned stimulus (CS), 66, 112–113
Connect and shape, 90–95, 92*f*, 94*f*
Consequence strategies, 81–86
Constructive scientific conflict, 4
Contemporary parenting, 20–25
Contextual behavioral perspective, 64
Control psychological stimuli, 30
Cooperation, 46
cooperative behavior, 17
cooperative breeders, 16
Counterpliance, 75
CR. *See* Conditioned response (CR)
CRBs. *See* Clinically relevant behaviors (CRBs)
Criticism within parent–child relationship, 332–333
CS. *See* Conditioned stimulus (CS)
Cultural values, 45

D

Daytime activity and exercise, 391
Daytime naps, 390–391
Debriefing, building resilience through, 362–363

Defense of self-as-content, 312
Deficits in self-as-process, 313
Defusion, 258, 280, 302, 355, 378–379
Depression, 326, 380
Derived relational responding, 72–76, 254–257
Developmentally relevant behaviors (DRBs), 126
Direct conditioning, 65
  operant conditioning, 67–72
  respondent conditioning, 66–67
Discriminative stimuli, 112–113
Disorganized attachment, 43
DNA-V model
  and acceptance, 193–194
  and committed action and exploration, 356
  and compassion, 326–327
  and flexible languaging, 259
  and flexible perspective taking, 295
  in parenting, 31*f*, 34–35
  and psychological contact, 227
  and values, 160
DRBs. *See* Developmentally relevant behaviors (DRBs)
Drive system. *See* Incentive/resource-focused system
Dukkha, 225
Duration method, 110
Dyadic perspective, 48–51
Dysfunctional behavior, 33–34
Dysfunctional behavioral pattern, 109–110
Dysfunctional parenting, 77–78, 215, 356
  behavior, 195–196
  styles, 260

E

Early childhood, 51–52
  and acceptance, 215
  and compassion, 347–348
  and flexible languaging, 281
  and psychological contact with present moment, 247
  and values, 182
Early parental care, 14
Embryo, 12
Emotion dismissiveness
  and acceptance, 218
  and committed action and exploration, 374
  and flexible languaging, 284
  and flexible perspective taking, 318
  with present moment, 249
  and values, 185
Emotional availability, 57
  theory, 49–50, 53
Emotional connection, 39–40, 54–57
Emotional development, 15, 51–53
Emotional–relational approaches, 28
Emotions, 213
  coaching, 196
  emotion-focused parenting intervention, 53–54
  experiential acceptance and, 199–201
  mindfulness of, 207–208
Empathic attunement, 47, 56
Empty chair technique, 338–339
"Epigenetic landscape" metaphor, 12
Epigenetics, 12
  landscape, 12*f*
Evidence-based parenting rules, 261
Evoking behavior, 79
Excessive infant crying, 385
Exercise, 335–336
Existentialism, 154
Experiential acceptance, 30, 192, 213, 215, 217
  and compassionate parenting, 197
  and emotions, 199–201
  of parent, child, and relationship, 364
Experiential attachment, 30, 189
Experiential avoidance, 30, 189, 195–196
Experiential control, 30, 189–193, 203
Experiential exercises, 271–272, 304–306
Exploration, 354–356, 358–361
Exposure, 79
  coaching, 378
  therapy, 381–383
Expressed emotion, 374
Expressed emotion and flexible languaging, 284
Extensive early parental care, 14
Extinction, 69–70, 381–382
  burst, 70

F

FAP. *See* Functional analytic psychotherapy (FAP)
Fear of compassion, 346
Fiction, 255–256
Flexible cooperative breeding, 16–17
Flexible experimentation, 22
Flexible languaging, 254–259, 364
  applying to parent–child interaction, 260–268
  childhood externalizing problems and, 283

childhood internalizing problems and, 283
developmental periods and
adolescence, 282
early childhood, 281
infancy, 280–281
middle childhood, 281–282
DNA-V model, 259
games for parent and child, 274–275
parental grief and, 282–283
parental mental health problems and, 282
in rule-governed behavior, and fusion, 257–259
with specific populations
childhood neurodevelopmental disabilities, 283
emotion dismissiveness, 284
expressed emotion, 284
inconsistent, or harsh and punitive parenting, 284
marital conflict, 284
peer relations and bullying, 283–284
symbolic system development, 254–257
troubleshooting, 280
working with
encouraging home practice, 277–279
experiential exercises, 271–272
meditations, 272–273
metaphors, 268–269
signs of parental inflexible languaging, 268–279
taking children from pliance to tracking, 276–277
taking parents from pliance to tracking, 275
Flexible parenting, 1–4
Flexible perspective taking, 288–295, 364
adolescence and, 315
applying to parent–child interaction, 295–299
childhood externalizing problems and, 316
childhood internalizing problems and, 316
childhood neurodevelopmental disabilities and, 317
DNA–V model, 295
early childhood and, 314
emotion dismissiveness and, 318
expressed emotion and, 317–318
inconsistent, or harsh and punitive parenting and, 318
infancy and, 313–314
marital conflict and, 317
middle childhood and, 315
parental grief and, 316
parental mental health problems and, 315–316
peer problems and bullying and, 317
troubleshooting, 312–313
working with flexible perspective taking clinically, 299–312
Forgiveness or getting off the hook, 364–365
Formulation, 128
sharing formulation with parent, 129
"Freely chosen" behavior, 155–156
Frequency method, 110
Functional analysis, 111
of behavior, 76
of child and parent behavior, 112–118
Functional analytic psychotherapy (FAP), 5, 125–127, 141–143
Functional contextual perspective on attachment and emotional connection, 54–57
Functional emotional systems, 33
Functioning caregiving system, 136–137
Fusion, flexible languaging in, 257–259

G

Generalizing behavior, 72
Genetic dimension, 12
Genetic variation, 12
Genotype, 12
Good parenting, 25–29
theoretical frames, 12*f*, 27–29
"Goodness of fit", 48–49
Grandparent care, 137–138
Growth mindset, 297–299

H

Habituation, 381–382
"Helicopter" parenting, 22, 404–405
Hexaflex, 363–364
Home practice, 343–345, 367–370
"Hot house" parenting, 22, 404–405
Human
child, 16
history, 19
infants, 16
parental care, 16–20
parenting, 16, 25

I

Imagery, 146
Incentive/resource-focused system, 33, 324

Inconsistent, or harsh and punitive parenting, 374
Inconsistent parenting
and acceptance, 218
and values, 186
Indirect conditioning, 65, 72–76
Individual functional analysis, 380
Infancy
and acceptance, 214–215
and compassion, 346–347
and flexible languaging, 280–281
and flexible perspective taking, 313–314
and psychological contact with present moment, 246–247
and values, 181–182
Infant
crying and sleep, 384–386
irritability, 48
sleep, 386–399
Instrumental emotions, 52–53
Intake interview, 105–108
Internal working models, 47–48, 56
Interventions grounded within attachment theory, 53
Intrinsic reinforcement, 157, 160–161
Intrinsic reinforcers, 81–82

J
Jump metaphor, 366

K
Kinship-based forager society, 10

L
Living domains, values importance in, 164

M
Maladaptive primary emotions, 199–202
Mammalian component, 14
Mammalian species, 14
Mammalian threat system, 224
Marital conflict
and committed action and exploration, 373
and compassion, 350
and flexible languaging, 284
and flexible perspective taking, 317
and values, 185
Maternal insensitivity, 48
Maternal parenting-specific mindfulness, 222–223
Math-mediated language, 256
Meditations, 234
accepting space for parent and child, 208–212
script, 208–209
encouraging home practice, 211–212
encouraging home practice, 310–312
flexible perspective taking in child or adolescent, 309–310
mindfulness
awareness, parent, and child, 273–274
of emotions, 207–208
of thoughts meditation, 272–273
parenting, 307–308
pause and breathe, 209–210
seeing as-content and as-process from as-context, 308–309
Mental health
parental flexible perspective taking and, 296
psychological contact and, 229–232
Meta-emotion philosophy, 51
Meta-emotion theory, 53, 91
to parenting, 57
Metaphors, 146–147
battlefield, 303–304
epigenetic landscape, 12
of jumping, 366
passengers on the bus metaphor, 269
of the six animals, 233–234
Superhero's dilemma, 269–270
swamp metaphor, 203–204
and values, 170–171
West metaphor, 158, 170
Middle childhood
and acceptance, 215–216
and compassion, 348
and flexible languaging, 281–282
and flexible perspective taking, 315
and psychological contact with present moment, 247
and values, 182–183
Mind-mindedness, 292
Mindful parenting, 227–228
Mindful walking meditation, 237
Mindfulness, 147–148, 378–382. *See also* Psychological contact with present moment
of breathing meditation, 235–236
of emotions, 207–208
of thoughts meditation, 272–273
use of, 301–302
Monitoring process, 109–111

Mother–child relationship, 41–42, 404
Motivating operation, 71, 112–113

N

Neonatal intensive care unit (NICU), 265
"Nesting" approach, 383, 389
Neurogenesis, 12–13
Neutral stimulus (NS), 66
NICU. *See* Neonatal intensive care unit (NICU)
Noncompliance, 113–115
Nonverbal expressions, 112
Noticing compassion, 332–333
Noticing parental evolving defenses and compassion capacities, 333
NS. *See* Neutral stimulus (NS)
Nurturing psychological flexibility, 3*f*

O

Obsessive-compulsive disorder (OCD), 78, 381–382
Off-spring, 9–10
Operant conditioning
  models, 67–72
  strategies
    antecedent strategies, 79–81
    consequence strategies, 81–86
Optimal sensitivity, 50
Oral story-telling, 255–256
Other-as-content, 289
Other-as-context, 32, 291, 322–323
Other-as-process, 32, 290, 295
Overabundance of values, 179–180
Overlearning, 374

P

Paid caregivers, 137–138
Parent/parental/parenting, 39–40, 161–162, 176, 307–308, 347–348, 403–404
  ACT, 29–33
  behavior, 1–4, 89, 112–118
  care, 1
    evolution, 13–15
  CFT, 33–34
  compassion and, 327–328
  compassion for child, 328
  contemporary parenting, 20–25
  control agenda, 194–195
  DNA-V, 34–35
  evolution of parental care, 13–15
  in evolutionary context, 9–10
  experiential acceptance, 32, 196
  flexible, 162–163
  flexible perspective taking
    and mental health, 296
    and sensitivity, 295–296
  fostering of exploration and flexibility, 358
  four streams of evolution, 10–13, 11*f*
  good parenting, 25–29
  to grow compassionate children, 329–332
  human parental care, 16–20
  influence attachment, 45–48
  intervention, 378–380
    therapeutic relationship(s) complexities in, 136–141
  mindfulness meditation, 239–241
  from pliance to tracking, 275
  psychological well-being, 87–88
  rules, 260–262
  sharing formulation with, 129
  strategy, 82
  styles, 164
  supporting child exploration, 366–367
  theory, 28
  values, 396–399
Parental grief
  and committed action and exploration, 372
  and compassion, 349
  and flexible languaging, 282–283
  and flexible perspective taking, 316
  and psychological contact with present moment, 248
  and values, 183–184
Parental inflexible languaging, signs of, 268–279
Parental mental health problems
  and acceptance, 216
  and committed action and exploration, 372
  and compassion, 349
  and flexible perspective taking, 315–316
  mind-mindedness, 292
  mindfulness, 227–228
    practice, 273–274
  and psychological contact with present moment, 248
  psychological flexibility, 1–4
  self-compassion, 327
  sensitivity and attachment, 162
  and values, 183
  well-being, 327
Parent–child dance, 15
Parent–child hexaflex, 5, 28*f*, 30–31, 47

Parent–child interaction, 66, 393–395
acceptance applying to
acceptance and development, 197–198
experiential acceptance and compassionate parenting, 197
experiential acceptance and emotions, 199–201
experiential avoidance and dysfunctional parenting, 195–196
history, 198–199
parental experiential acceptance and child emotional development, 196
parenting control agenda, 194–195
committed action applying to, 356–361
compassion and history, 328
compassion and parenting, 327–328
flexible languaging applying to
flexible languaging and workable parenting, 260
parenting rules, 260–262
supporting development of helpful tracking and proto-values, 263–268
supporting flexible languaging, 263
flexible perspective taking
developing child's, 296–297
and growth mindset, 297–299
noticing acceptance within, 202–203
observation, 111–112
parental compassion for child, 328
parental flexible perspective taking
and mental health, 296
and sensitivity, 295–296
parenting to grow compassionate children, 329–332
psychological contact with present moment
mindful parenting, 227–228
psychological contact and mental health and well-being, 229–232
shared psychological contact and effective parenting, 228–229
shared psychological contact and relationship, 228
self-compassion and parental well-being, 327
shame-based parenting, 329
values applying to
dangers of pliance, 163–164
flexible parenting, 162–163
intrinsic reinforcement and persistence, 160–161
parental sensitivity and attachment, 162
supporting proto-values development, 165–168
values and history, 164–165
values importance in living domains, 164
Parent–child interaction therapy (PCIT), 88
Parent–child relationship, 1, 39–40
attachment, emotional availability, and meta-emotion theory to parenting, 57
attachment across cultures, 44–45
attachment theory, 41–44
dyadic perspective, 48–51
and emotion-focused parenting intervention, 53–54
emotional development and, 51–53
functional analytic psychotherapy and, 125–127
functional contextual perspective on attachment and emotional connection, 54–57
noticing compassion, shame, and criticism within, 332–333
parenting influence attachment, 45–48
Parent–infant sleep, 390, 392
Pause and breathe exercise, 209–210
Pavlovian conditioning, 66
PCIT. *See* Parent–child interaction therapy (PCIT)
Peer problems and bullying, 317
Peer relations and bullying, 283–284, 350, 373
Persistence, 160–161
Phenotypic plasticity, 358–361
Planned ignoring, 378
Pliance, 75, 257–258
dangers of, 163–164
taking children from pliance to tracking, 276–277
Positive parenting behaviors, 86
"Possums" programs, 389
Postnatal care, 383–384
Postnatal period, 371
Praise, 82
Precocial ancestors, 16
Pretend play, 255–256
Primary caregiver, 137–138
Primary emotion, 199–202
Problematic behavior patterns in families, 76–78
Process-focused criticism, 297–299
Process-focused parental praise, 297–299
Proto-values, 159–160, 363–364
supporting proto-values development, 165–168
Brooke and Kai case example, 166
Proto-values development, 263–268

Proximal development zone, 79
Psychological connection, 223
Psychological contact, 16–17
Psychological contact with present moment, 222–227, 364
 and acceptance, 225–226
 applying to parent–child interaction, 227–232
 benefits, 226–227
 developmental periods and
  adolescence, 247–248
  early childhood, 247
  infancy, 246–247
  middle childhood, 247
 DNA-V model, 227
 with specific populations
  childhood externalizing problems, 248
  childhood internalizing problems, 248
  childhood neurodevelopmental disabilities, 249
  emotion dismissiveness, 249
  expressed emotion, 249
  inconsistent, or harsh and punitive parenting, 250
  marital conflict, 249
  parental grief, 248
  parental mental health problems, 248
  peer relations and bullying, 249
 troubleshooting, 244–246
 work with mindfulness clinically
  antenatal mindfulness meditation, 237–238
  assessing parental mindfulness, 233
  encouraging home practice, 243–244
  meditation, 234
  metaphors, 233–234
  mindful walking meditation, 237
  mindfulness of baby meditation, 238–239
  mindfulness of breathing meditation, 235–236
  mindfulness within daily life, 241–242
  parenting, 239–241
  quick mindfulness meditation, 241
  simple questioning or prompts, 233
  taste of mindfulness meditation, 234–235
Psychological flexibility, 1–4, 26–27, 403
Psychological proximity, 17, 44, 57, 228
Psychologically flexible child, 1–4
Punishers, 67–68, 69*t*, 112–113
Punitive parenting
 and acceptance, 218
 and values, 186

Q

Questionnaires, 108–109
Quick mindfulness meditation, 241

R

Randomized controlled trials (RCTs), 88–89
Receiving compassion from others, 364
Reciprocal system, 45–46
Reinforcers, 67–68, 69*t*, 112–113
Reinforcing behavior, 79
Relational frame theory (RFT), 1, 17, 56, 72–73, 119, 154–155, 223, 254, 288, 403
Relational frame theory and parenting, 87
Relational framing, 72–73, 255
Relational learning processes, 73–74
Relational mindfulness, 227
Relational–emotional framework, 28–29
Relative reinforcement, 71–72
Resistance to specific techniques, 146–148
Respondent conditioning, 66–67, 79
Response cost, 83–84
Rewards, 82
RFT. *See* Relational frame theory (RFT)
Roleplays, 147
Rule-governed behavior, 72–76
 flexible languaging in, 257–259

S

Safe haven, 40–42, 162, 184, 214–216, 228, 328
Safe place imagery, 339–340
Scaffolding, 80
 exploration, 40–41
School, 25
School-aged children, 104–105
Science, 25
 and technology, 20–21
Secondary caregivers, 137–138
Secure attachment, 42–43
Secure base, 40–41
Selective attention, 83
Self-as-content, 289, 291, 308–309, 312
Self-as-context, 290–291, 296, 322–323, 378–379

Self-as-process, 32, 290–291, 295, 313, 315–316
awareness, 290–291, 298–299
from self-as-context, 308–309
Self-compassion, 327, 364, 378–379
meditation, 340–341
Self-criticism, 33–34
Self-designated "experts", 24
Sensitivity, 45, 295–296
Shame, 332–333
Shame-based parenting, 329
Shaping adaptive child behavior, 90
Shaping process, 64
acceptance and commitment therapy/ relational frame theory, 87
ACT
for augmentation for behavioral parenting interventions, 88–89
for parent psychological well-being, 87–88
for parenting/child behaviors, 89
behavioral parenting intervention, 86–87
connect and shape, 90–95
direct conditioning, 66–72
functional analysis of behavior, 76
indirect conditioning, 72–76
key behavior principles in shaping adaptive child behavior, 90
operant conditioning strategies, 79–86
parent–child interaction, 66
problematic behavior patterns in families, 76–78
supporting behavior change, 79
Shared psychological contact
and effective parenting, 228–229
and relationship, 228
Sleep
compression, 390
and control, 205–206
restriction, 390
sleep–wake homeostat, 390
"SMART" program, 256–257
Social
anxiety, 326
competence, 64
motivational systems, 33–34
reinforcers, 81–82
safety, 134
Sociodemographic variables, 45
Socioemotional signaling systems, 14
Soothing rhythm breathing exercise, 335–336
Stepping Stones Triple P, 88–89, 378
Still-face paradigm, 46–47
Stoicism, 154
Strengthen behavior, 67–68
Structured teaching, 373
Supporting behavior change, 79
Swamp metaphor, 203–204
Symbolic evolution, 13
Symbolic stream, 17
Symbolic system development, 254–257
Symbolic thinking, 255–256

T

Tanha, 225
Tantrums and control, 204–205
Task agreement, 133–134
Therapeutic alliance concept, 133–134
Therapeutic relationship
acceptance and commitment therapy and, 131–133
building and maintaining common understanding, 144–145
client resistance, 145–146
complexities of therapeutic relationship(s) in parenting intervention, 136–141
evoking, reinforcement, repeating, 143–144
functional analytic psychotherapy and, 141–143
resistance to specific techniques, 146–148
setting stage/dialogue, 133–134
supporting home practice, 148–149
therapist as a secure base, 134–136
Therapist as a secure base, 134–136
Time sampling method, 110
Time traveling, 306
Time-out, 84
Tracking, 75, 257–258
self-as-process, 295
Traditional behavioral infant sleep interventions, 388
Transactional process, 40
Transformation of function, 255
Transmission gap, 47–48
Trial-and-error parent behavior, 133–134
Troubleshooting
in acceptance
acceptance and trauma history, 214
acceptance or ignorance, 213–214
confusion with acceptance and compassion, 213
emotions, 213
compassionate context, 346

defense of self-as-content, 312
deficits in self-as-process, 313
in psychological contact with present moment, 244–246
refining parenting strategies in practice, 370
tough work, 370
in values, 179–181
children misbehavior, 181
client disconnected from values, 179
client goals instead of values, 179
getting values, 179
overabundance of values, 179–180
valued action, 180
Tuning into compassionate self, 337

U

Unconditioned responses (UR), 66
Unconditioned stimulus (US), 66, 112–113
Unsoothable crying, 384
Us-as-content, 289
Us-as-context, 32, 291
Us-as-process, 32

V

Vagus, 14
Values, 154–160, 354, 363–364
DNA-V model, 160
key developmental periods and values
adolescence and values, 183
early childhood and values, 182
infancy and values, 181–182
middle childhood and values, 182–183
meditation, 172–178
developing rich and flexible repertoire of valued acts, 176–177
encouraging home practice, 177–178
script, 172–175
tuning in to values, 175–176
proto-values, 159–160
with specific issues
childhood externalizing problems and values, 184
childhood internalizing problems and values, 184
childhood neurodevelopmental disabilities and values, 184–185
emotion dismissiveness and values, 185
expressed emotion and values, 185
inconsistent, harsh, or punitive parenting and values, 186
marital conflict and values, 185
parental grief and values, 183–184
parental mental health problems and values, 183
peer problems and bullying and values, 185
troubleshooting, 179–181
values applying to parent–child interaction, 160–168
working with values clinically, 168–172
experiential exercises, 171–172
metaphors, 170–171
prompts, 170
setting stage for values work, 168–169
values as side of pain, 170
Valuing component, 380–381
Verbal community, 288
Verbal processes, 289
Verbal rules, 30, 65, 355
Visualizations, 207–208

W

Willingness, 354
in experiential acceptance, 192
working with, 363
Workability of parenting, 380
Workable parenting
agenda, 357–358
flexible languaging and, 260
Working
with compassion
accessing compassionate self, 336
compassion for child, 341–342
compassionate figure, 336
compassionate letter writing, 337–338
development of compassion in children and adolescents, 342–343
empty chair technique, 338–339
encouraging home practice, 343–345
noticing compassion, shame, 332–333
noticing parental evolving defenses, 333
reality check, 333–335
safe place imagery, 339–340
self-compassion meditation, 340–341
soothing rhythm breathing exercise, 335–336
tuning into compassionate self, 337
with flexible perspective taking, 299–312
experiential exercises, 304–306
meditations, 307–312
metaphors, 303–304
simple questioning, 303
time traveling, 306
use of defusion, 302
use of mindfulness, 301–302

FSC
www.fsc.org
MIX
Papier | Fördert
gute Waldnutzung
FSC® C083411

Kolibri 360 GmbH
Ferdinand-Jühlke-Straße 7
99095 Erfurt, Deutschland
produktsicherheit@kolibri360.de